Serpentaire
e Sobieſki
le Scorpion

The Barchas Collection at Stanford University

The Barchas Collection at Stanford University

A Catalogue of the Samuel I. and Cecile M. Barchas Collection in the History of Science and Ideas

STANFORD UNIVERSITY LIBRARIES 1999

ISBN 0-911221-19-0

Dedicated to the determination, foresight,
perseverance, and taste of
Samuel I. & Cecile M. Barchas
in amassing and then making available
to the world of scholarship
their unparalleled Collection
on the History of Science and Ideas.

Contents

Illustrations

Guericke, *Experimenta nova*, 1672
Haller, *Icones anatomicæ*, 1743-1782
Herschel, *Results of Astronomical Observations ... at the Cape of Good Hope*, 1847
Hevelius, *Cometographia*, 1668
Hevelius, *Firmamentum Sobiescianum*, 1690
Hooke, *Micrographia*, 1665
Huygens, *The Celestial Worlds Discover'd*, 1698
Huygens, *Horologium*, 1673
Jenner, *An Inquiry into the Causes and Effects of the Variolae Vaccinae*, 1798
Kepler, *Mysterium cosmographicum*, 1596
Kepler, *Tabulae Rudolphinae*, 1627
Kircher, *Magnes*, 1643
Linné, *Philosophia botanica*, 1751
Lyell, *Principles of Geology*, 1832-1833
Maxwell, *A Treatise on Electricity and Magnetism*, 1873
Mersenne, *Harmonie universelle*, 1636-1637
Napier, *Rabdologiæ*, 1617
Newton, *Opticks*, 1704
Newton, *Principia*, 1687
Parkinson, *Organic Remains of a Former World*, 1804-1811
Pascal, *Traitez de l'équilibre des liqueurs, et de la pesanteur de la masse de l'air*, 1663
Perrault, *Mémoires pour servir à l'histoire naturelle des animaux*, 1676
Plato, *Platonis opera*, 1578
Ptolemy, *Almagest*, 1538
Rhäticus, *Opus palatinum de triangulis*, 1596
Regiomontanus, *Epitoma in Almagestum*, 1496
Sacro Bosco, *Sphaera mundi*, 1552
Salusbury, *Mathematical Collections and Translations*, 1661
Schott, *Cursus mathematicus*, 1661
Tartaglia, *Nova scientia*, 1537
Vesalius, *De humani corporis fabrica*, 1555
Wallis, *A Treatise of Algebra*, 1685

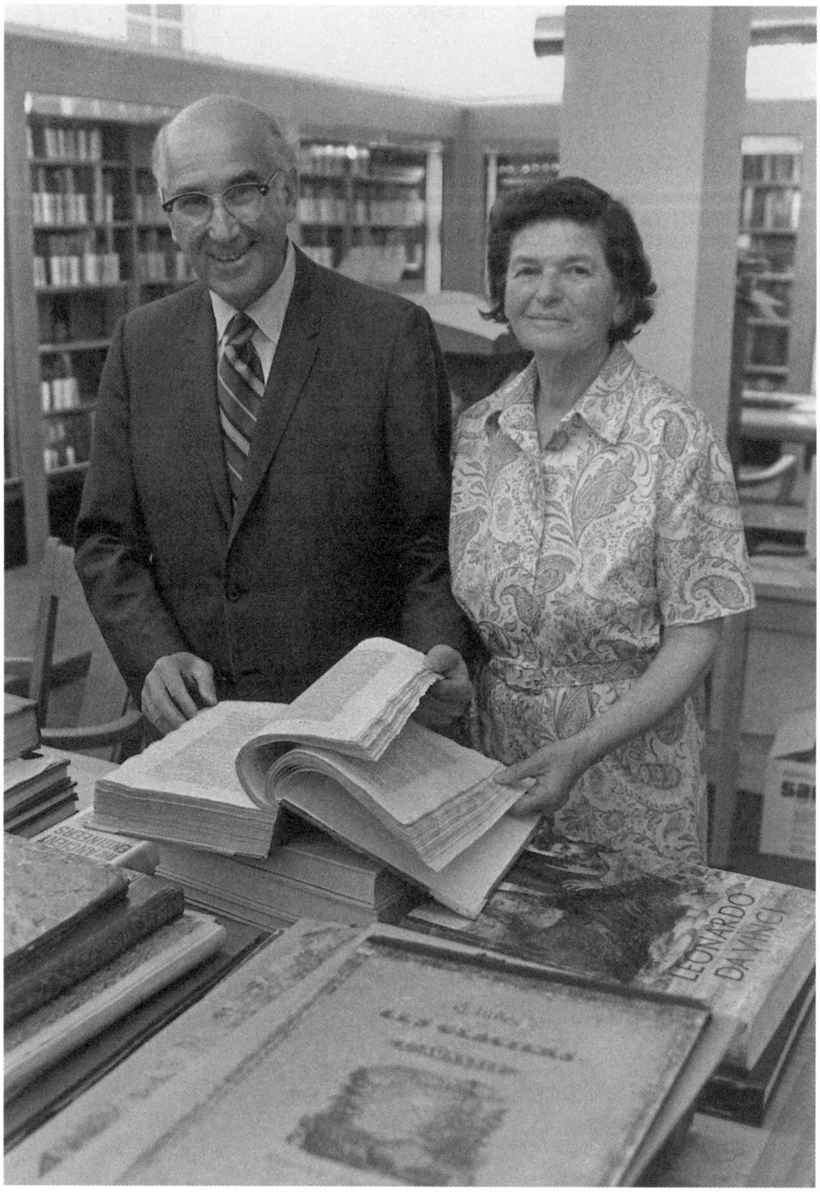

Samuel I. and Cecile M. Barchas, March 29, 1982 (Stanford News Service)

Foreword

It was in 1932, the year of our marriage, that Sam and I read a book on astronomy by Sir James Jeans entitled *The Universe Around Us* (1929). That was a fascinating book which we later realized helped shape the course of our lives. Sam was then a young law student attending law school at night while working full-time for the Los Angeles *Examiner* during the day. Reading the Jeans book on astronomy was like a revelation to Sam, and astronomy became a life-long interest to him.

The country was at that time in the throes of the Great Depression. Unemployment was very high and money was very scarce. However, as our limited funds allowed, we gradually accumulated a small, very modest collection of contemporary books on astronomy. I remember vividly the day when our collection took on a surprisingly new dimension.

It was at the beginning of 1940 on a Saturday in Los Angeles when we had been out shopping. On our way home we passed a bookstore. Sam parked our car outside the bookstore to see if there were any astronomy books that we would want to add to our little collection. I was with our then three children in the parked car in the parking lot and was holding Judy, a very young baby, in my arms, and taking care of children Jack and Sarah. After a few minutes, looking across the parking lot, I saw Sam running toward me, excitement shining in his eyes,

"Cecile!" he exclaimed. "I found a wonderful old book in the store, an astronomy book written by James Ferguson, printed in the 1700's." And then his voice fell in concern. "But it costs ten dollars. Do you think we should get it?"

Sharing his excitement, I made my voice as stern as I could under the circumstances. "You march right back into that store, Sammy, and you get that book!" And so he did, his face aglow as he emerged from the store. And that was our first significant book in astronomy.

Upon our arrival home, I watched as Sam sat at the table, carefully removing the wrapping, opening the book and reverently and tenderly turning the pages one by one. This was his first rare book, and he was completely enthralled at the idea of having such a book in his possession. It filled my heart with joy to see what it meant to him. And from such humble beginnings was born our rare book collection.

Astronomy became an absorbing interest to Sam, and from there it was a natural progression to his interest in the history of astronomy. As our collection of books increased, it evolved to an ever-increasing interest in the history of science – an interest which we shared.

The years passed in Los Angeles, and we were able to increase the scope of our library significantly. Through the serendipitous discovery by our thirteen-year old son, Jack, of a display in a rare book store, Sam made contact with Jake Zeitlin, a noted rare book dealer. Zeitlin had access to key items in an exceptional Herbert Evans collection in the history of science that was being dispersed. Professor Evans, associated with the University of California, was a great scientific researcher as well as rare book collector in the history of science. From this collection we were able to acquire a first edition of Copernicus' *De Revolutionibus...* (1543), and a first edition of Newton's *Principia*, (1687). We considered them to be the crown jewels of our collection,

In 1956, at the age of 44, my husband suffered a massive heart attack, which resulted in his retirement from law practice in Los Angeles. We moved with our large family to southeastern Arizona, where the night skies are clear and one can indulge one's interest in astronomical observations. Often the children would gather around Sam for a "star lesson," taking turns looking through our simple telescope as he pointed out the wonders of the heavens, inspiring us with a sense of awe. We bought a small family cattle ranch and learned a different way of life. We worked hard on the ranch during the day, with the help of many of our eight children. The outdoor work on the ranch helped Sam to regain his health. After the work was over, Sam would often enjoy reading some of the catalogues that we had been receiving from book dealers in this country and overseas in Europe. I can still see Sam sitting in the corner in his favorite chair, with his reference books spread out over a large table in the center of the room. It gave me infinite pleasure to see him thus engaged because I knew how much pleasure he derived from this.

A few years later, we learned from our book dealer friends Jake Zeitlin and Warren Howell, from whom we had bought many fine rare books, that a second outstanding Evans Collection had become available. Realizing that this was an opportunity of a lifetime, we bought it in its entirety. It stretched us, because it contained many significant books in the history of all the physical and biological sciences, including mathematics and medicine. Now we knew we had the nucleus of a great collection. It required many sacrifices on our part to accomplish this, and I can't remember when we weren't in financial debt to the bank, but it was well worth the cost, because a new world opened itself up before us. Our excitement and enthusiasm knew no bounds.

Sam was a true scholar who delved into the study of the history and philosophy of science. He had a tremendous passion for learning and was deeply absorbed in learning as much as he could about the great thinkers who contributed so much to our knowledge, each building on the accomplishments of those who had come before. It is as Isaac Newton recognized when he said, "If I have seen further than others, it is because I have stood on the shoulders of giants."

My beloved husband Sam was not only a practical person, but also a dreamer. What he was trying to do and what inspired him was the concept that the building of this collection was akin to the building of a cathedral. Each significant book was like a brick that helped to complete the cathedral. He looked for what he considered to be gaps in the collection and tried to fill them.

This collection contains many of the seminal works in the various sciences. Of course, no library is ever complete. What we are today, what we have and know today is based on the thinking and discovery of some of our greatest thinkers throughout history.

Sam passed away in 1988, at the age of 76, after having suffered a massive stroke. I am now 87 years old, and Sam is still the focus of my life. It's a comfort to me to remember how we shared everything together, and to feel that he is still a living part of me.

In closing, I would like to express my heartfelt love and gratitude to Jack, Sarah, Judy, Mark, Rudy, Rachel, David, and Rebecca – our eight children – who continue to sustain me in their circle of love, and whose devotion I cherish. It is indeed extraordinary that each of the children understood and appreciated our dream and vision for the collection and shared our pride in it.

We entrusted our collection to Stanford University, one of the leading academic and research institutions in the world, because of our confidence that they would care for it responsibly, help it to grow, and help it to be used by scholars effectively, responsibly, and with security. It is our hope that they will always continue to value it, care for it, and share our dreams.

CECILE M. BARCHAS
May, 1999

Cecile Barchas, who is my much loved, talented, and admired mother-in-law, asked me to write a few words as a *cadenza* to her eloquent statement. I do so with pride, both as a representative of the following generations of the large and closely-knit Barchas family, and as a Professor of History and Sociology of Science at the University of Pennsylvania.

The Barchas collection, like other collections large and small, carries more than one set of meanings. It is an extraordinary library of rare books in and about science, a collection that will make Stanford University an important international center for the history of science in the future. But this collection, built by two individuals out of their own love for learning, also celebrates the adventure, the possibilities, and indeed the passion of collecting. To the Barchas family the collection was a living enterprise. In family lore the collection is Sam and Cecile's "ninth child," to be nourished and appreciated, and capable of growth and change.

Rare book collections have invaluable scholarly significance as collections; that is, in one place one may find, study, compare and think about assembled books and documents in a systematic way in an intellectual treasure house. First editions of what were to become classical texts may be consulted, and subsequent editions may be examined as well for revealing changes in the texts and in their presentation. Historians ask what are at root simple questions though the answers may be contested and complex: for example, about what science is, how, why, when and where certain ideas (and not others) are created and by whom, and how (and how successfully) they are disseminated. The very existence of a major collection such as this – its character, richness and range of materials – may influence the type and amount of work done in a particular scholarly area. Thus historians of the future will be able to look back at the influence of the Barchas Collection on scholarship in the history of science.

Ideally this collection will also serve the history of science more generally, by introducing students to rare books and by stimulating the passion to collect, in one field or another, among many generations of students, faculty and visitors to Stanford. Both messages are implicit in the creation of the Barchas Collection. To hold in one's hand a leather-bound book centuries old is to enter the world of wonder. From finger tips touching the rich pleasure of an old binding to the visual delight, intellectual anticipation, and self-conscious care (both not to damage it and as instinctive gesture of ritual and respect) in opening the book and turning its pages, the reader experiences history at its most concrete. It is impossible not to wonder about this book's context as well as its content (why does it exist? what does it really say?); to imagine the author; to speculate who else and how many have read this very same volume; and to marvel at one's place in a long line of curious seekers. The fledgling collector becomes detective, seeking to define and master a field of learning. As the knowledge and passion grows, the collector becomes adventurer, seeking out those books, often over many years and in divers places, that will craft the collection so that it becomes an art form in itself. In turn, if we are lucky and the collection is not dispersed or held in seclusion, it may stimulate others. Thus the passion for knowledge continues.

Rosemary A. Stevens, Ph.D

Preface

The Samuel I. and Cecile M. Barchas Collection in The History of Science and Ideas was acquired by gift and purchase by the Stanford University Libraries in the winter of 1982. The collection of approximately 5,000 printed books, of which almost 2,000 volumes are first or early editions that focus on the "greatest books" since the invention of printing, established the University among this country's leading centers for scholarly research in the history of science: a field that bridges Stanford's established strengths in the sciences and engineering to its academic programs in the humanities.

The Barchas Collection is a resource of great value not only to scholars in the history of science but to faculty and students in each of the scientific disciplines it covers, and in several fields within the humanities. The Collection includes works that have never been translated from their original languages. Art historians will find a wealth of material in the illustrations; cultural historians, in the introductions and dedications to royal or aristocratic patrons; religious historians, in some authors' positions on religious, theological, or philosophical controversies of their day.

The Collection represented in this catalogue consists of over 2,000 of the most rare and valuable printed books and pamphlets dating from the 15th to the 20th centuries (but often of earlier authorship). The strengths of the Collection are on astronomy, mathematics, physics, biological sciences, and chemistry. The Collection is also strong in psychology, physiology, and anatomy. Within the Barchas Collection there are a great many works of great rarity that are listed in other important catalogues as well, among them: Harrison Horblit's *One Hundred Books Famous in Science,* John Carter's and Percy Muir's *Printing and the Mind of Man,* and I. Bernard Cohen's *A List of Books Famous and Important in the History of Science.* In terms of scope and its content, the Barchas Collection in the History of Science and Ideas is a significant achievement in book collecting and its creation of permanent value to scholars and students.

This catalogue consists of all Barchas Collection items represented in the Stanford University Libraries online catalogue. The full bibliographic description of each cataloged

Barchas item appears through the notes fields. The citations referred to throughout the notes in the catalogue entries correspond in form and style to those in Peter M. Van Wingen's *Standard Citation Forms for Published Bibliographies and Catalogs Used in Rare Book Cataloging.* 2nd ed. Washington, D.C., Library of Congress, 1996. Name and title indexes were produced based on the access points presented in the catalogue records. Title-page transcriptions are retained through the author statement as originally catalogued and appear in this volume in italics.

As in most university library catalogues where records are drawn from many database sources in a shared environment, there is some variety in the extent and style of bibliographic description within the records. All records and index entries do, of course, meet the accepted standards as articulated by the Library of Congress and national databases.

Cataloguing the Barchas Collection for Stanford's online catalogue, with subsequent loading to the RLIN and OCLC databases, was funded by the Pew Charitable Trusts. Contributors to both the cataloguing project and this printed catalogue have been many, including: Matthew Ahmed, Judit Brody (principal project cataloguer), Lucretia Cerny, Albert Cota, Mark Dimunation, Barry Hinman, Nancy Lennartsson, Henry Lowood, Rita Lunnon, Michael Lunnon, John McDonald, Kate McDowell, John Mustain, Philip Schreur, Viveca Seymour, Ryan Steinberg, Kate Thacher and many Stanford student assistants.

The publication of the catalogue marks a special gift to the Stanford University Libraries. In transferring this fine collection to Stanford, Samuel I. and Cecile M. Barchas sought to make it more accessible for teaching and research by placing it in the context of a major research library. The Library is particularly grateful for their thoughtfulness and generosity.

ROBERTO G. TRUJILLO
Frances & Charles Field Curator
of Special Collections and
Head, Department of Special Collections

DIANNE CHILMONCZYK
Editor

Publisher's Acknowledgments

The spirit, the energy, and the devotion of the Barchas family imbue these pages. Sam and Cecile Barchas have richly earned the gratitude of generations of scholars at Stanford and elsewhere. Their children have contributed to the growth of the collection after it came to Stanford and to the improvement of the bibliographic entries in this catalogue. This is an extraordinary family with deep devotion to the purposes and development of the Collection.

Numerous staff members of the Stanford University Libraries have applied their talents and persistence to the creation of this catalogue. Dianne M. Chilmonczyk was recruited from the Smithsonian Institution to head the unit that catalogued the collection in the 1980s and has applied herself intelligently and diligently to the heroic task of editing the catalogue records for this catalogue. Roberto Trujillo, Frances and Charles Field Curator and Head of the Department of Special Collections, and John Mustain, Rare Book Librarian and Classics Bibliographer, have engaged themselves ferreting out bibliographic details and checking the text of this catalogue. Assunta Pisani, Associate University Librarian for Library Collections and Services, shepherded the project along and contributed her special insight into the bibliographic arts and key points throughout. Henry Lowood, Curator for the History of Science and Technology, contributed his remarkable expertise throughout the project. Andrew C. Herkovic performed magnificently as managing editor of the project. All of these people and numerous others who provided their services cheerfully and effectively when asked deserve and have my gratitude for a job very well done.

MICHAEL A. KELLER
University Librarian
Director of Academic Information Resources
Publisher of HighWire Press
Stanford University

Introduction

The arrival in 1982 of the Samuel I. and Cecile M. Barchas Collection in the History of Science and Ideas at Stanford coincided fortuitously with the University's decision to establish an academic program in the history of science. Indeed, the subsequent success of this program would today be difficult to imagine without the crucial impetus – both real and symbolic – given to the history of science at Stanford by the momentous acquisition of the Barchas Collection. The presence of such a collection of landmark works in the history of science, the presentation and interpretation of these great books, and scholarly use of the Collection have all greatly stimulated the growth of the Program in the History and Philosophy of Science into a center of research and instruction at Stanford.

The dominant Bay Area program in the history of science through the early 1980s resided in the Office for the History of Science and Technology of the University of California, Berkeley. Like many other institutions founded during the 1950s and 1960s, the OHST benefited from what has been described as the "frantic creation" of new departments in the history of science during that period.[1] By 1980, roughly fifty or more American universities awarded graduate degrees in the field, compared to nearly none at the end of World War II. Several programs had grown substantially and had established successful Ph.D. programs, such as those at Harvard University, the University of Wisconsin, Indiana University, the Johns Hopkins University, and the University of Pennsylvania, in addition to the University of California. By then, it had become clear that Stanford lagged behind the explosive growth of this young discipline, despite strong traditions in the sciences and engineering, and that it was time to make a substantial institutional commitment to the history of science.

By the late 1970s, the School of Humanities and Sciences at Stanford decided to create a formal program in the history of science. The Program in the History of Science (renamed History and Philosophy of Science in 1993) began in earnest during the 1980-81 academic year, not long before the carefully packed moving vans arrived from Sonoita bearing magnificent books. The first description of the new program in the *Stanford*

University Bulletin called it "in part a consolidation of activities already in progress at Stanford and in part a new venture of considerable depth." The Committee in charge included distinguished faculty from the physical and exact sciences, history, philosophy, and mathematics, as well as the eminent engineer and historian of technology, Prof. Walter Vincenti. Its ambitious goal was nothing short of broad coverage of all the scientific and technical fields represented by the Committee, "reaching from antiquity through the twentieth century," with attention both to "the more general historical studies within the humanities and social sciences and to the more technical demands of the sciences." [2]

The substantial commitment of talent and energy to an aspiring new program provided a new context for evaluating the quality of Stanford's library collections in the history of science. The decision to establish a broadly represented center of teaching and research in the history of science and technology would have to be matched by the provision of resources, foremost among them strong library collections. In the history of science, so strongly focused on the beginnings of modern scientific thought in the sixteenth and seventeenth centuries, strong research collections implied the foundation of an exceptional rare book collection. Indeed, the creation of American programs in the history of science founded after World War II matched up consistently with the existence or timely acquisition of rare book collections: the Thordarson Library at the University of Wisconsin, the Edgar Fahs Smith Memorial Collection at the University of Pennsylvania, the library of J. K. Lilly, Jr., at the University of Indiana, and the Everette Lee DeGolyer collection at the University of Oklahoma furnish prominent examples.[3] In each case, the growth of a strong program in the history of science was founded to a significant degree on the availability of a library of seminal primary works from the Scientific Revolution and the emergence of modern scientific disciplines. In the words of Bern Dibner, the printed book "has preserved the record of the revolutionary innovations that have transformed our ideas of the world and universe in which we live," and it is to them that historians of early modern science must turn.[4]

As the School of Humanities and Sciences decided during the late 1970s to make a strong commitment to the history of science and create a solid research program, the Stanford University Libraries considered the state of the research collections in the field. Early surveys of local collections, notably Robert Multhauf's published evaluation of Bay Area libraries in the history of science, noted limited strengths in the history of physics and a few other scientific fields.[5] A series of collection studies carried out by Clay Ramsay in 1977 and 1978 extended Multhauf's earlier checklists and identified serious gaps and weaknesses in the collections, such as in the history of biology. He noted, for example, in his examination of Stanford's holdings in the history of chemistry that "both the unusual pieces and the areas of strength seem to have been collected no later than the 1930s." [6]

The exception to this judgment was the Newton Collection assembled by the bibliographer, librarian, and early promoter of the history of science in the United States, Frederick E. Brasch.[7] Brasch had joined the Libraries in 1948 as Honorary Consultant in Bibliography (later Curator of the Newton Collection) to assist in book selection for the Newton Collection, which he had given to Stanford after his retirement from the Library of Congress, and to complete research on Newton and on American colonial science. As early as 1936, he had modified his mentor George Sarton's proposal for a national library in the history of science, which Brasch hoped could be located at Stanford. But during the 1950s and 1960s, marked by limited funding for library collections, Brasch's efforts to build a research library in the history of science met significant obstacles. Still, the collection of primary works and research monographs focused on the work of Sir Isaac Newton and his influences represented one significant area of strength in Stanford's collections.

As the outstanding privately-held collection of rare books in the history of science in the United States, the depth and breadth of the Barchas Collection matched up well with the Libraries' needs in the history of science; with the creation of the Program in History of Science and the careful documentation of gaps in Stanford's holdings offered by the Ramsay study, negotiations aimed at bringing the Collection to Stanford intensified. The initial contact between Sam Barchas and David Weber, then Director of Libraries, had occurred in 1969, but subsequent discussions had languished in the absence of a strong academic program. In 1981, Stanford's Director of Collections, Paul Mosher, noted that "by acquiring the Barchas Collection, Stanford's capacity to support research in the History of Science would be improved several times. This collection, when added to our own presently inadequate holdings, would create the strongest research base for the field this side of the University of Oklahoma, whose DeGolyer Collection is among the best in the United States." [8] With approximately 2,000 primary works and a reference library approaching 3,000 volumes, the Barchas Collection offered resources that matched the aspirations of the new academic program; data collected by the Libraries in 1981 judged the caliber of the Barchas Collection as reaching the highest level in fields as diverse as the history of astronomy, geology, and medicine, for example, thus matching Stanford's explicit goal of wide coverage of scientific and technical fields. In short, both the Collection and the timing of its acquisition fit Stanford's needs perfectly.

The arrival of the Barchas Collection on campus on February 26, 1982, during Michael Ryan's tenure as head of Special Collections, immediately attracted attention both to the Libraries and to the Collection. The announcement of its accession appeared in the Stanford University *Campus Report*, including a special report by the Provost, Prof. Albert H. Hastorf, to the Faculty Senate, who noted that "this acquisition is a coup for Stanford – the equivalent of decades of normal collection development." [9] The first detailed survey of the many high-points from the collection then appeared in the *Annual Report* of the Stanford University Libraries for 1982-1983. This description of the Barchas Collection for the Libraries' many friends and supporters averred that the Collection's "landmark books can be counted, its distinguished provenances cited, its unusual copies singled out, its value as a scholarly research collection demonstrated, the breadth and depth of its holdings surveyed. The Barchas Collection passes all these tests with honors." [10]

The impact of the Barchas Collection on the academic program was immediate and substantial. First and foremost, the Collection provided for the general research and teaching needs of faculty concerned with the core historical periods in the history of science, such as the Scientific Revolution, nineteenth-century medicine, or early twentieth-century physics. The coverage and depth of the Collection in these areas can only be explained by an appreciation of Sam and Cecile Barchas as book collectors and their place in a tradition of book collecting in the history of science, particularly in the United States. Just as the history of science flourished only relatively recently as an academic discipline, it attracted the attention of bibliographers, book collectors, and libraries at first slowly, but then with increasing intensity, beginning with George Sarton's founding of the journal *Isis* in 1915 and his pioneering bibliographic and historical publications, so well represented in the Barchas Collection. Sam and Cecile were keenly aware of the significant collections and publications that documented the history of book collecting in the history of science, and the evidence of their engagement with that tradition are evident throughout the Collection, particularly in the excellent reference collection.

The collection of rare and antiquarian books benefited from the Sam and Cecile's keen awareness of the accomplishments of the first generation of bibliographers and collectors in the history of science. For example, they acquired a substantial lot of books from the library of the biochemist Herbert McLean Evans, generally acknowledged as the first significant American collector in the field. As a member of the faculty of the University of California in Berkeley, Evans actively encouraged the growth of the history of science in the Bay Area; the exhibit he prepared with a committee of the Berkeley History of Science Club for the 94th meeting of the American Association for the Advancement of Science in 1934 first defined a collecting specialization and a list of high points in the history of science with the publication of the exhibit catalogue, *Exhibition of First Editions of Epochal Achievements in the History of Science* (Berkeley, 1934).[11] Moreover, Evans joined with other leaders in the emerging History of Science Society and the bibliography of science, such as Sarton and Brasch, to promote the growth of the history of science as a field of bibliography and study. Traces of these important connections can be discovered in the Barchas Collection, such as the inscription by Sarton in a copy of *The Study of the History of Science* (Cambridge, Mass., 1936) presented to Evans.

Yet, the Barchases' relationship to the annals of book collecting in the history of science was not simply that they sought to document or illuminate the work of past collectors. Rather, they imposed on themselves the considerable challenge of equaling and perhaps surpassing the combined achievements of this tradition. Their initial guide and longstanding inspiration in this endeavor was The Grolier Club's remarkable exhibit of "One Hundred Books Famous in Science," held in 1958. As Sam was fond of pointing out, this exhibit did not represent the holdings of a single library; instead, it resulted from the combined efforts of 28 leading institutions and individuals, including such prominent collectors as Denis Duveen, Robert Honeyman, Jr., Dibner, and Evans, as well as a distinguished selection of elite university and scientific libraries. The subsequent publication of the exhibit catalogue, edited by Harrison Horblit, established the Grolier-Horblit list of 130 published works of science as definitive.[12] It is remarkable that 105 of these books were included in the Collection delivered to Stanford in 1982, and, with the continuing devotion of the Barchas Family to augmenting the Collection, the number now approaches 120. In other words, the Barchas Collection gathers together in one place the best selection of representative works in the history of science of any single collection in the history of science, nearly equaling by itself the combined efforts of more than two dozen libraries and private collections to present such a collection.

As the Program in the History of Science took shape in the early 1980s, the faculty took advantage of these riches. The late Wilbur Knorr was the first appointment in the new program, arriving in 1979 as professor in the history of science in the Departments of Classics and Philosophy. His research on the exact sciences in antiquity emphasized the definition, commentaries and transmission of Greek mathematics and mechanics in the ancient and medieval intellectual worlds, and his attention to the means by which scientific and mathematical ideas are interpreted and communicated focused his work sharply on manuscript and publishing traditions. These interests extended to the early publication of ancient mathematical works in the late fifteenth and sixteenth centuries, such as the remarkable editions of Aristotle, Euclid and Aristarchus in the Barchas Collection. His three-quarter survey course, the first in the new Program, introduced Stanford undergraduates to the history of cosmology and featured many visits to the Barchas Room for a closer look at Newton's *Principia*, Hevelius' magnificently illustrated books, and many other crucial works in the development of cosmological theory and astronomy.

The appointment of Peter Galison as professor of the history and philosophy of science in the Department of Philosophy in 1982 extended the Program to the history of twentieth-century physics. His research and courses both in the history and philosophy of recent and contemporary science combined an intense interest in post-war experimental traditions in physics with close attention to the work of Albert Einstein and other earlier physicists well-represented in the Barchas Collection. Like Knorr, Galison placed great value on providing opportunities for students, both graduate and undergraduate, to work with primary sources and original publications, and his commitment to this mode of learning led to many class visits to the Barchas Room. Moreover, his research and courses on the Scientific Revolution, with his particular interest in the Cartesian tradition in cosmology, led him to appreciate the availability of specific titles held in the Barchas Collection, such as the original edition of the *Discours sur la méthode* (1637).

Courses introduced during the 1980s and 1990s at Stanford have led hundreds of students to the riches of the Barchas Collection. These include Knorr's aforementioned "Introduction to Cosmology" series, first taught in 1980 and offered until his premature death in 1997, and his seminar on "Topics in the History of Mathematics from Antiquity to the Seventeenth Century," (1984-1997); "History of Modern Physics," taught by Peter Galison from 1983 to 1993 and today still among the core offerings in the Program, and Galison's popular "The Growth of Scientific Knowledge," which debuted in 1987; the core course on the "Scientific Revolution," introduced by John Beatty in 1985 and since then offered annually; my own "Science in the Enlightenment" (1986-present); "The Darwinian Revolution," introduced by Beatty in 1985 and since taught by a series of distinguished historians of biology, including Robert Proctor, Jane Maieinschein, Mott Greene, and Timothy Lenoir; Lenoir's "History of Biological Thought" (1990-present); and Paula Findlen's "When Worlds Collide: The Trial of Galileo" (1996-present). Other Stanford faculty have made substantial use of the Libraries' collections in the history of science and technology, such as Francis Everitt in his work on Maxwell and the history of nineteenth-century physics; Ian Hacking, Nancy Cartwright, Arnold Davidson, John Dupré, and Peter Godfrey-Smith, in the philosophy of science; Barton Bernstein in his research on the history of the atomic bomb; Michael Riordan in his work on the history of physics and the transistor; and Walter Vincenti, Robert McGinn, Joseph Corn, Stephen J. Kline, Gabrielle Hecht, and Paul Edwards in the history and philosophy of technology. The steady flow of visiting faculty, speakers in the ongoing Colloquium in History of Science (founded in 1983 by Peter Galison), and graduate and undergraduate students since the early 1980s has added to these rich course offerings and research programs to create a burgeoning program in the history of science at Stanford University.

Through the presentation and interpretation of original editions of seminal works in the history of science, the ultimate beneficiaries of the Barchas Collection are thus Stanford's students, for whom the experiences provided by these splendid books provide fresh, often exhilarating, insights into the nature and communication of scientific ideas. Few pedagogical techniques equal the immediate impact on students of showing manuscript notes in the hand of Sir Isaac Newton (in Newton's own copy of the 1668 edition of the

Chimia attributed to Geber); explaining the truncated dedication from Christiaan Huygens to Newton on the title-page of Huygens' *Horologium oscillatorium* (Paris, 1673); or simply encouraging them to study the magnificent illustrations in Leonhart Fuchs' *De historia stirpium commentarii* (1542), Robert Hooke's *Micrographia* (London, 1663), or Johannes Hevelius' *Firmamentum Sobiescianum* (Danzig, 1690), to name only a few prominent examples. The synergy between the academic program and the Barchas Collection also stimulated a series of activities at Stanford to commemorate the 300th anniversary of the publication of Isaac Newton's *Philosophiae naturalis principia mathematica* in 1987. In his proposal for a Stanford conference on this occasion, Prof. Knorr especially noted the significance of the arrival of the Barchas Collection on campus. Together with the Newton Collection, he reckoned that the Barchas Collection gave the Stanford University Libraries "one of the largest collections of Newton editions and Newton-related works anywhere." Events such as these would provide occasions to "exhibit the riches of this collection in the environment of a gathering of scholars ..." [13]

In light of the many benefits the Barchas Collection has provided to the academic program in the history of science at Stanford, the continuing efforts of the Libraries in concert with the Barchas Family to augment the Collection are especially significant. While the Libraries' program of exhibits and publications in the history of science directly benefits academic programs at Stanford, the weight of the curatorial program in the history of science and technology falls on the care, management, preservation and augmentation of the Barchas Collection. Particularly in the last area, the extension of the Collection through new acquisitions, Sam, Cecile, their children and even grandchildren have actively encouraged and substantially supported the Libraries' activities.

An especially important and symbolic example of this spirit of cooperation is provided by the acquisition over a period of more than a dozen years of a small group of especially rare and significant works from the early history of modern astronomy. This story first unfolded on the occasion of the dedication of the Barchas Room in the History of Science in January, 1985, when the Associates of the Stanford University Libraries presented Johannes Kepler's *Dissertatio cum sidereo nuncio* (Prague, 1610) to Sam and Cecile as a gift volume to the Barchas Collection. Just as Kepler's work had responded directly to Galileo's first observations with the telescope, the addition of the *Dissertatio* to the Collection followed upon the acquisition by Rudolf and Jean Barchas of Galileo's *Sidereus nuncius* (Venice, 1610), the published work to which Kepler had directly replied. The "Starry Messenger" contained the first announcement of Galileo's famous discoveries with the telescope, and it has become a classic work in the history of astronomy. Kepler's *Dissertatio* represented the closing link in a chain of events that joined the scientific work of these great astronomers. Thus, as I wrote in 1985, "one book, the *Sidereus nuncius,* has led to another, the *Dissertatio,* in two very different ways." [14] Fittingly, the binding of the catalogue of the 1985 exhibition of the Barchas Collection features an illustration from the *Sidereus nuncius.*[15] And yet, unlike the connection of Galileo and Kepler, the story did not end with the *Dissertatio.* In 1997, the Libraries acquired, again with the financial assistance of the Associates, and added to the Barchas Collection Galileo's *Difesa di Galileo Galilei contro alle Calunnie & imposture de Baldessar Capra Milanese* (1607), the original edition of Galileo's second publication. The *Difesa* is perhaps the rarest of all of Galileo's published works and as his first published work in astronomy, it set the stage for the "Starry Messenger." The rare opportunity of studying these three important works together, all so crucial for understanding the development of post-Copernican astronomy, demonstrates the vitality of the Barchas Collection. Through this recent acquisition and others – often with generous support from the Barchas Family [16] – the Libraries' program in the history of science and technology has sought to fulfill its responsibility to the academic program, to the Barchas Collection, and to the lasting achievement of Sam and Cecile Barchas.

Henry Lowood, Ph.D.
Curator for History of Science
& Technology Collections
Stanford University Libraries

1. Harrison Horblit, ed. *One Hundred Famous Books in Science* (New York: Grolier Club, 1964): 3.

2. Stanford University Bulletin: *Courses and Degrees 1980-81* (Stanford: Stanford University, 1980): 399.

3. John Neu, "The Acquisition of the Thordarson Collection," *University of Wisconsin Library News* 11 (1966): 1-6; University of Oklahoma. Library. *A Checklist of the E. DeGolyer Collections in the History of Science and Technology as of August 1, 1954*. 3d ed. Norman, Okla.: Univ. of Oklahoma Press, 1954; Eva V. Armstrong, *The Story of the Edgar Fahs Smith Memorial Collection in the History of Chemistry*. Philadelphia: Univ. of Pennsylvania, 1937.

4. Bern Dibner, "Preface 1955," in *Heralds of Science, as Represented by Two Hundred Epochal Books and Pamphlets in the Dibner Library, Smithsonian Institution* 25th anniversary edition (Norwalk, Ct.: Burndy Library; Washington, D.C.: Smithsonian Institution, 1980): 5.

5. Robert P. Multhauf. *History of Science Collections in the Library of the University of California, Berkeley, with Comparative Evaluations of Other Libraries in the San Francisco Bay Area* (Berkeley: Univ. of California, General Library, 1953). A comparison of this guide to Robin E. Rider and Henry E. Lowood, *Guide to Sources in Northern California for History of Science and Technology* (Berkeley: Office for History of Science and Technology, 1985) suggests the rapid buildup in the strength of Stanford's rare book and manuscript collections in the history of science by the mid-1980s, thanks in large part to the impetus gained from the acquisition of the Barchas Collection.

6. Clay Ramsay, "Multhauf Extended: Chemistry (Part I)," memorandum dated Dec. 13, 1977, p. 7.

7. Henry Lowood. *Frederick E. Brasch and the History of Science* (Stanford: Stanford Univ. Libraries, 1987)

8. "Samuel I. Barchas Collection," File memorandum, Dec. 18, 1981.

9. "Report of the Provost," *Stanford University Campus Report* (March 10, 1982)

10 "The Samuel I. and Cecile M. Barchas Collection in the History of Science and Ideas," Stanford University Libraries. *Annual Report 1982-1983*. (Stanford: Stanford University Libraries, 1983): 16-28. Quotation. p. 16.

11. Bern Dibner, for example, notes his debt to Evans and the 1934 exhibit in the 1955 preface to *Heralds of Science*. Bern Dibner, "Preface 1955," op. cit., p. 5.

12. Harrison Horblit, ed. *One Hundred Famous Books in Science* (New York: Grolier Club, 1964). There are 130 publications in the list, due to the practice of combining two or even three related books in single entries. In 1995, the Grolier Club issues *One Hundred Famous Books in Medicine,* edited by Hope Mayo and modeled after Horblit's project.

13 Wilbur Knorr, "Proposal for a Newton Tercentenary Conference at Stanford University in 1987," March 4, 1985.

14. Henry Lowood, "Kepler and Galileo: The Bond of Books," *Imprint* (Oct. 1985): 15.

15. Henry Lowood. *The Barchas Collection: The Making of Modern Science* (Stanford: Stanford Univ. Libraries, 1985)

16. Other examples of such joint ventures include the purchase of János Bolyai's exceedingly rare "Appendix scientiam spatii absolute veram exhibens" (Appendix explaining the true science of absolute space), published as an appendix to his father's *Tentamen* (1832); Simon Stevin's *De Beghinselen der Weeghconst* (1586); Marin Mersenne's *Harmonie universelle* (1636-1637), and the splendid 1469 edition of Pliny's *Historia naturalis,* to name only a few.

The Barchas Collection at Stanford University

[†]Dagger preceeding entries indicates that item was already held at Stanford and replaces an exact bibliographical duplicate in the Barchas Collection

Differentia.4.in qualitate scie ꝓprietatis figtionis ♀ ſm illud idē.

POstq̄ꝫ igiť p̄miſimus in dr̄a tercia ex ſignificationib⁹ martis ⁊ ꝙ appropriať ſoli deſignatiōe ſingulariť. Remēoreť igiť in hac dr̄a ſignificationes veneris ſm illud idē. Dicamus ergo ꝙ cū fuerint ei figtiones quas narrauim⁹ ⁊ fuerint ei appropriate ſm ſpēm humanā figť illud apparitionē moderationis ⁊ prouidentie ⁊ bonam intentionē in rebus fidei ⁊ mortē quorundā ſapientū ⁊ precipue de ciuib⁹ babylonie ⁊ ſuꝑ reuelationē ſublimationis ⁊ eleuationē regum ⁊ multum honorē ſibi adinuicē hoīes afferre ⁊ apparentiā gaudij ⁊ ꝓſperitatē eſſe cōiugij ⁊ multitudinē filioꝝ ⁊ fortaſſe abſoluent viri mulieres ſuas ⁊ patienť aborſum puelle ex fornicationibus ⁊ multiplicabiť inuidia ⁊ nocumentuꝫ corpoꝝ. Et ſi fuerit eius ſignificatio ſm ſpēm beſtialē qua homines vtunť figť illud multiplicationē earū ⁊ proficuū earum. Et ſi fuerit eius figtio ſm elementū terreum figť bonū eſſe ſeminū ⁊ arboꝝ ⁊ fructuū. Et ſi fuerit ſignificatio eius ſm elementū aquaticū figť illud habundantiā aquaꝝ ⁊ euaſionē nauiū in maribus.

ABU MA'SHAR, *Introductorium in astronomiam*, 1489

1. Abbot, C. G. (Charles Greeley), b. 1872. *The earth and the stars, by C. G. Abbot.*

New York: D. Van Nostrand Company, 1925. xi, 264 p. front, illus., plates, ports., maps, diagrs. 22 cm. Library of modern sciences. Includes index.

Fourth printing, 1928. Advertisements: [1] p. at end.

2. Abbott, Thomas Kingsmill, 1829-1913. *Elementary theory of the tides: the fundamental theorems demonstrated without mathematics, and the influence on the length of the day discussed, by T. K. Abbott....*

London: Longmans, Green, & Co., 1888. iv, 41 p.: ill.; 18 cm.

Provenance: Arnold K. Johnson (inscription).

3. Abel, Niels Henrik, 1802-1829. *Oeuvres complètes de N. H. Abel, mathématicien, avec des notes et développements, rédigées par ordre du roi, par B. Holmboe....*

Christiania: C. Gröndahl, 1839. 2 v. in 1. 29 x 22 cm. "Notices sur la vie de l'auteur (par l'éditeur)": p. [v]-xiv.

4. Abraham bar Hiyya Savasorda, ca. 1065 - ca. 1136. *La obra Forma de la tierra: de R. Abraham bar Hiyya ha-Bargeloni; traducción del hebreo, con prólogo y notas por José Ma. Millás Vallicrosa.*

Madrid: Consejo Superior de Investigaciones Científicas, Instituto Arias Montano, 1956. 126 p.: ill.; 26 cm. Serie D, Consejo Superior de Investigaciones Científicas. Instituto Arias Montano: núm. 5. Translation of: *Sefer tsurat ha'arets.* Advertisements on lower wrapper. Includes bibliographical references.

Wrappers are bound in.

5. Abraham bar Hiyya Savasorda, ca. 1065 - ca. 1136. *Sefer tsurat ha'arets: v'tavenit kadurei ha'ra'kia 'veseder mahalakh kokhveihem, hanikhtav al yedei r[av] Avraham b[ar] r[av] 'Hayya Ha'sefaradi; kitsur hamele'khet mispar asher 'hiber r[av] Eliyah Mizra'hi ... = Sphaera mundi, autore Rabbi Abrahamo Hispano filio R. Haijæ; Arithmetica secundum omnes species suas autore Rabbi Elija Orientali. Quos libros Oswaldus Schreckenfuchsius uertit in linguam latinam, Sebastianus uero Munsterus illustrauit annotationibus.*

[Basileæ: per Henrichum Petrum, 1546]. [12], 207, [2], 351, [8] p.: ill.; 20 cm. Title page romanized. Latin and Hebrew. Imprint taken from colophon of pt. 1. Pt. 2 has separate t. p. at the back.

Provenance: John Dee (inscription); Thomas Bryan Richards (inscription); British Museum (inkstamp).

6. Abu Ma'shar, 805 or 6-886. *Albumasar De magnis coniunctionibus; annorum reuolutionibus ac eorum profectionibus, octo continens tractatus.*

[Augsburg]: Erhardiq[ue] Ratdolt viri solertis ..., qua nup[er] Venetijs, unc Auguste Vindelico[rum] excellit no[m]I[n]atissim[us], pridie Kal[endus] Aprilis [31 Mar., 1489]. [236] p.: ill., diagrs. (woodcuts); 22 cm. Translation by Joannes Hispalensis of the author's Kitab a'hkam sinial-mawalid and other writings, based in great part on al-Kindi. cf. Sarton. *An introd. to the hist. of science.* Baltimore [1927] v. 1, p. 568; and Enzyk. d. Islam. Ed. by Johannes Angelus. Imprint from colophon. Signatures: A-N^8 O^6 P^8. BM *15th cent.*, II, p. 383 (IA.6689). Goff (rev.) A-360. *GW* 836. Hain-Copinger, 611*. *ISTC*, ia00360000. Stillwell, M. B. *Science*, 9.

Blank spaces for woodcut ill. on M8v and N4r. Binding: full calf, gilt spine. Binder's title: Albumasar. Provenance: Richard Biddulph Martin (book label). With: Abu Ma'shar. *Introductorium in astronomia[m] Albumasaris Abalachi octo continens libros partiales.* [Augsburg]: Erhardi Ratdolt ..., qua nuper Venetijs nunc Auguste Vindelico[rum] excellit no[m]i[n]atissimus, 7 Idus Februarij [7 Feb.] 1489.

7. Abu Ma'shar, 805 or 6-886. *Introductorium in astronomia[m] Albumasaris Abalachi octo continens libros partiales.*

[Augsburg]: Erhardi Ratdolt ... qua nuper Venetijs nunc Auguste Vindelico[rum] excellit no[m]i[n]atissimus, 7 Idus Februarij (7 Feb., 1489). (140) p.: ill., diagrs. (woodcuts); 22 cm. Translation of *Mudkhal al-kabir ila 'ilm a'hkam al-nujum* by Hermannus Dalmata. Imprint from colophon. Signatures: a-h^8 j^6. BM *15th cent.*, II, p. 382 (IA.6683). Goff (rev.) A-359. *GW* 840. Hain-Copinger, 612*. *ISTC*, ia00359000. Stillwell, M. B. *Science*, 9.

Binding: full calf, gilt spine. Binder's title: Albumasar. Provenance: Richard Biddulph Martin (booklabel). With: Abu Ma'shar. *Albumasar De magnis coniunctionibus.* [Augsburg]: Erhardiq[ue] Ratdolt viri solertis ..., qua nup[er] Venetijs, nunc Auguste Vindelico[rum] excellit no[m]i[n]atissim[us], pridie Kal[endis] Aprilis [31 Mar. 1489].

8. Académie royale des sciences (France). *Machines et inventions approuvées par*

l'Académie royale des sciences, depuis son établissement jusqu'à présent; avec leur description. Dessinées & publiées du consentement de l'Académie, par M. Gallon. t.1-7; 1666/1701-1734/54.

Paris, G. Martin [etc.] 1735-77. 7 v. plates. 27 cm. Rubricated t.-p. Title vignette. Vol. 7, which was published after the death of Gallon (imprint Paris, A. Boudet) has t.-p. amended as follows: in place of "depuis 1734 jusqu'en 1747" the latter date is amended to read 1754; in place of imprint date 1735 is the date 1777. "Table alphabétique": [35] p. at end of v. 6.

Provenance: Ladislao Reti (bookplate, v. 1-6)

9. *Acta eruditorum.*

Lipsiæ: [Apud J. Grossium & J. F. Gletitschium], 1682 – . v. ; 22cm. Title from caption. Founded by Otto Mencke and continued by his son, Johann Burkhard Mencke. Fabre du Faur, no. 1556.

Library has: 1684.

10. †ADAMS, GEORGE, 1720-1773. *A treatise describing the construction, and explaining the use, of new celestial and terrestrial globes: designed to illustrate in the most easy and natural manner, the phoenomena of the earth and heavens, and to shew the correspondence of the two spheres: with a great variety of astronomical and geographical problems, by George Adams ... The third edition, in which a comprehensive view of the solar system is given, and the use of the globes is farther shewn in the explanation of spherical triangles.*

London: Printed for and sold by the author, at Tycho Brahe's Head ..., 1772. xxviii, 345, [1] (blank), [18] p., 14 leaves of plates (some folded): ill.; 22 cm. Some plates signed: Goodnight sculp. "A catalogue of mathematical, philosophical, and optical instruments, made under the inspection and direction of George Adams ...": p. [1]-[17] at end. Publisher's advertisements: p. [18] at end.

11. ADAMS, GEORGE, 1750-1795. *Astronomical & geographical essays ... , by the late George Adams.... 4th ed. With the author's last improvements....*

Whitehall [Pa.]: Printed for William Young, bookseller and stationer N. 52 South 2d Street, Philadelphia, 1800 [i.e. 1808?]. xvi, 194, viii, ii, [9]-238, [9]-148 p., XVI folded leaves of plates: ill.; 23 cm. (From title page) I. A full and comprehensive view, on a new plan, of the general principles of astronomy – II. The use of the celestial and terrestrial globes ... – III. The description and use of the most improved planetarium, tellurian, and lunarium. – IV.An introduction to practical astronomy.

"This first American edition": p. viii (1st group). The "Essay on ... globes" has a special title page. It is fifth edition with imprint: Philadelphia: Published by William W. Woodward, 1808. Errors of pagination: p. 8-9 misnumbered as 24-25, p. 12 as 28. Variously illustrated by R. Scot, F. Shallus, I. Draper.

Provenance: Elizabeth Wanzer (inscription).

12. ADAMS, GEORGE, 1750-1795. *Essays on the microscope; containing a practical description of the most improved microscopes: a general history of insects ... an account of the ... Hydræ and Vorticellæ: a description of three hundred and seventy-nine animalcula, with a concise catalogue of interesting objects... .*

London: The Author [etc.], 1787. xxiii, 724 p.: front.; 28 cm. and atlas of 31 [i. e. 32] plates.; 29 x 42 cm. A catalogue of mathematical and philosophical instruments made and sold by George Adams ...: p. 720-724. Includes index. Plate numbering 26 repeated. Frontispiece signed: T. S. Duché pinxit, some plates signed: T. Milnedel., Jn. Lodge sc.

Plates are folded, both v. bound to 28 cm. Provenance: Herbert McLean Evans (bookplate).

13. ADAMS, JOHN COUCH, 1819-1892. *An explanation of the observed irregularities in the motion of Uranus: on the hypothesis of disturbances caused by a more distant planet, with a determination of the mass, orbit and position of the disturbing body. By J. C. Adams, Esq....*

London: Printed by W. Clowes & Sons ..., 1846. 31, [1] p.; 19 cm. On t. p.: "From the Appendix to the Nautical almanac for the year 1851." Adams' observations led to the discovery of the planet Neptune.

Provenance: Observatoire de Paris (inkstamp); Michael Chasles (bookplate); Robert B. & Marian S. Honeyman (bookplate); William Simms (presentation inscription from W. S. Stratford).

14. ADDISON, THOMAS, 1793-1860. *On the constitutional and local effects of disease of the supra-renal capsules, by Thomas Addison....*

London: Samuel Highley, 1855. viii, 43 p., XI leaves

AGASSIZ, *Études sur les glaciers*, 1840

of plates: ill.; 34 cm. Osler, W. *Bib. Osleriana*, 1744.

Provenance: Herbert McLean Evans (bookplate); Dr. Graham (author's presentation inscription); ms. notes ([3] l.) loosely inserted, with l. [3] recto being blank form of Dr. A. Gilpin [his notes?]; ms. pencil marginalia and underscoring throughout. In Mrs. Addison's presentation binding. In quarter red morocco slipcase. Illustrations are hand-colored.

15. AGASSIZ, LOUIS, 1807-1873. *Études sur les glaciers; par L. Agassiz. Ouvrage accompagné d'un atlas de 32 planches.*

Neuchâtel: Jent et Gassmann, 1840. 3 p. l., v, 346 p., 1 l. 26 cm. and atlas of 18 pl. 47 x 33 cm. Plates 1-14 each preceded by leaf with outline drawing of objects represented, lettered 1a - 14a. Atlas has cover title: Études sur les glaciers, par L. Agassiz. Dessinés d'après nature et lithographiés par Jph. Bettanier 1840. Neuchâtel, Lithographie de H. Nicolet.

Provenance: Alfred Wills (booklabel); L. Agassiz (signature). Imperfect: lacks 1 p. l. [half-title?]. Atlas lacks plates 4 & 14; includes 3 additional unnumbered plates; leaves 1a - 14a bound after each plate.

Atlas only, disbound. Plates 2, 3, 3a, 7 and 10 are mounted.

16. AGASSIZ, LOUIS, 1807-1873. *Untersuchungen über die Gletscher. Von Louis Agassiz. Nebst einem Atlas von 32 Steindrucktafeln....*

Solothurn: Jent & Gassmann, 1841. xii, 326 p., 1 l. 23 cm. and atlas of 18 pl. 48 x 33 cm. Plates 1-14 each preceded by leaf with outline drawing and explanation of objects represented, lettered 1a - 14a. Atlas has cover-title: Untersuchungen über die Gletscher, von L. Agassiz. Nach der Natur gezeichnet und lithographirt von Jph. Bettannier 1840. Neuchâtel, Litho-

Agricola, *De re metallica*, 1556

graphie von H. Nicolet. "Die deutsche Bearbeitung dieses gleichzeitig französisch erschienenen Werkes verdanke ich ... Dr. Carl Vogt." – Pref., p. xii.

Original printed wrappers bound in. Provenance: Dr. Einsele (signature); Herbert McLean Evans (bookplate).

17. Agricola, Georg, 1494-1555. *De ortu et causis subterraneorum Georgii Agricolæ. De ortu & causis subterraneorum: lib. V; De natura eorum quæ effluunt ex terra lib. IIII; De natura fossilium lib. X; De ueteribus & nouis metallis lib. II; Bermannus, siue De re metallica dialogus. Interpretatio Germanica, ocum rei metallicæ, addito indice fecundissimo.*

Basileae: Per Hieronymum Frobenium et Nic. Episcopium, MDXLVI [1546]. 487, [53] p.: ill.; 31 cm. Publisher from colophon; publisher also represented by device on title page and on last page. Decorated initials throughout text. Adams A345. Horblit, H. D. *Grolier 100 science books*, 2a. *Milestones of science* 3. *Yale Cushing Coll.* A57. Includes index.

Ms. notes.

18. †Agricola, Georg, 1494-1555. *Georgii Agricolæ De re metallica: libri XII; quibus officia, instrumenta, machinæ, ac omnia deniq[ue] ad metallicam spectantia, non modo luculentissimè describuntur, sed & per effigies, suis locis insertas, adiunctis latinis, germanicisq[ue] appellationibus ita ob oculos ponuntur, ut clariùs tradi non possint; eiusdem De animantibus subterraneis liber, ab autore recognitus; cum indicibus diuersis, quicquid in opere tractatum est pulchrè demonstrantibus.*

Basileae: Apud Hieron. Frobenium et Nicolaum Episcopium, 1556 mense Martio. [12], 538 [i.e. 502], [74] p., [2] folded leaves of plates: ill.; 34 cm. Publisher from colophon; printer's device on title page and on last page. Page 502 wrongly numbered 538; other errors in pagination. Decorated initials throughout text. Includes indexes. Dibner Lib. *Science*, 88. Horblit, H. D. *Grolier 100 science books*, 2b. *Milestones of science* 4.

Provenance: George F. K[reuz?] (signature). Imperfect: lacks 1 plate as called for by Horblit; 3 illustrated strips with instructions to place at fol. 97 bound in.

19. †Agricola, Georg, 1494-1555. *Georgius Agricola De re metallica, tr. from the 1st Latin ed. of 1556, with biographical introduction, annotations and appendices upon the development of mining methods, metallurgical processes, geology, mineralogy & mining law, from the earliest times to the 16th century, by Herbert Clark Hoover ... and Lou Henry Hoover....*

London: The Mining Magazine, 1912. 2 p. l., xxxi, [1], 640 p., 1 l. illus., fold. pl. 35 cm. With reproduction of original title page. "Bibliographical notes": p. 599-615. Includes indexes.

Binding: presentation binding of full red morocco, gilt foliage design, dated 1913. Provenance: Robert Honeyman (Honeyman sale). [Copy 1]

Provenance: signed presentation inscription from Herbert Hoover and Lou Henry Hoover to Ray Lyman Wilbur, Jr. [Copy 2]

20. Airy, George Biddell, Sir, 1801-1892. *Account of observations of the transit of Venus, 1874, December 8, made under the authority of the British government: and of the reduction of the observations. Edited by Sir George Biddell Airy.*

[London]: Printed for H. M. Stationery Off., under the authority of the Lords Commissioners of Her Majesty's Treasury, 1881. viii p., 1 l., 512 p., 1 l., 21, [1] p. XVII pl. (incl. maps, plans) 29 cm. I. Expedition to the Hawaiian (Sandwich) Islands, under Captain G. L. Tupman. II. Expedition to Egypt, under Captain C. Orde Browne. III. Expedition to the Island of Rodriguez, in the Indian Ocean, under Lieutenant Charles B. Neate. IV. Expedition to Keguelen Island, under the Reverend S. J. Perry. V. Expedition to New Zealand, under Major H. S. Palmer. Appendix.

21. Airy, George Biddell, Sir, 1801-1892. *Gravitation: an elementary explanation of the principal perturbations in the solar system. (Written for the Penny cyclopædia, and now previously published for the use of students in the University of Cambridge.) By G. B. Airy....*

London: C. Knight, 1834. 1 p. l., [v]-xxiii, 215, [1] p. 19 cm.

Provenance: Henry Collins (bookplate); Herbert McLean Evans (bookplate).

22. AKADEMIIA NAUK SSSR. *Commentarii Academiae scientiarvm imperialis petropolitanae. Commentarii Academiae scientiarum imperialis petropolitanae Ed. nova justa ed. petropolitanam.*

Bononiae: Ex typographia Laelii a Vulpe, 1740- . 14 v. plates, maps, diagrs. 26 cm. .t. 1-14; 1726-1744/46.

Library has: 1-6, 1726-33. v. I-VI: Provenance: C. Wildbore; Charles Atwood Kofoid.

23. AKERS, WALLACE A. *The generation of useful power from atomic energy, by Sir Wallace A. Akers.*

[London: Royal Institute of Chemistry, 1947?]. p. 247-248; 22 cm. Caption title. Detached from the *Journal and proceedings of the Royal Institute of Chemistry*, 1947?

24. ALBERTI, FRIEDRICH AUGUST VON, 1795-1878. *Beitrag zu einer Monographie des bunten Sandsteins, Muschelkalks und Keupers, und die Verbindung dieser Gebilde zu einer Formation. Von Friedrich von Alberti....*

Stuttgart und Tübingen: Verlag der J. G. Cotta'schen Buchhandlung, 1834. xx, 366, [2] p. II fold. pl. (1 col.) 21 cm. Cover title: Monographie des bunten Sandsteins, Muschelkalks und Keupers. "Beitrag zu einer Litteratur des Trias": p. [340]-366.

Original printed wrappers. Advertisements: [2] p. at end. Provenance: Herbert McLean Evans (bookplate).

25. †ALDROVANDI, ULISSE, 1522-1605? *De animalibus insectis libri septem ... autore Vlysse Aldrouando ...; cum indice copiosissimo.*

Bonon. [i.e. Bologna]: Apud Ioan. Bapt. Bellagambam ..., 1602. [12], 767, [45] p. (last page blank): ill., port; 36 cm. Engraved title page and portrait by Valesio. Errata: p. [42] (3rd group). "Catalogus authorum": p. [8-10] (first group). Nissen, C. *Zoologische Buchillustration*, 66. Sorbelli, A. "Contributo alla bib. di U. Aldrovandi." In *Intorno alla vita e alle opere di U. Aldrovandi*, 69-139, IV.1 (p. 99).

Bound as v.9 of a set of Aldrovandi's works on natural history.

26. ALDROVANDI, ULISSE, 1522-1605? *Vlyssis Aldrouandi patricii Bononiensis De quadrupedib[us] digitatis viuiparis libri tres: et De quadrupedib[us] digitatis ouiparis libri duo, Bartholomaeus Ambrosinus ... collegit ...; cum indice memorabilium ...copiosissimo.*

Bonon. [i.e. Bologna]: Apud Nicolaum Tebaldinum, sumptibus M. Antonij Berniæ ... 1645, [i.e. 1663]. [4], 718 [i.e. 716], [16] p.: ill.; 36 cm. Engraved title page., attributed to Coriolano. Cf. Sorbelli. "De quadrupedibus digitatis ouiparis libri II" (p. [587]-718) has special title page with imprint: Bononiæ: Typis Io. Baptistæ Ferronij ..., 1663. Colophon also dated 1663. Pagination: nos. 493-94 omitted. Signatures: pi^2 A-3B^6 3C^4 3D-3O^6 a-b^4. Includes index. Sorbelli, A. "Contributo alla bib. di U. Aldrovandi." In *Intorno alla vita e alle opere di U. Aldrovandi*, 69-139, IX.5 (p.118).

Imperfect? Sorbelli calls for 2 preliminary leaves, but Register specifies 4. Provenance: Earl of Aylesford (bookplate). Bound as v. 11 of a set of Aldrovandi's works on natural history.

27. ALDROVANDI, ULISSE, 1522-1605? *Vlyssis Aldrouandi patricii Bononiensis De quadrupedibus solidipedibus volumen integrum, Ioannes Cornelius Vteruerius ... collegit, & recensiut; Hieronymus Tamburinus in lucem edidit....*

Bononiae: Apud Victorium Benatium, 1616. [8], 495, [32] p.: ill.; 37 cm. Signatures: [cross]^4, A-2R^6, 2S^4, 2[cross]^4, 2T-2Y^4. Sig. [cross]1r is engraved title page, signed: Io. Bapta. Coriolanus... Colophon, sig. 2Y4r: Bononiæ: Typis Victorij Benatij ... M.DC.XVI. Sumptibus Hieronymi Tamburini. Includes index. Errata: p. [31] (3rd group). Nissen, C. *Zoologische Buchillustration*, 72.

Bound as v. 7 of a set of Aldrovandi's works on natural history.

28. ALDROVANDI, ULISSE, 1522-1605? *Vlyssis Aldrouandi patricii Bononiensis Dendrologiæ naturalis scilicet arborum historiæ libri duo sylua glandaria, acinosumq[ue] pomarium vbi eruditiones omnium generum vnà cum botanicis doctrinis ingenia quæcunque non parum iuuant, et oblectant. Ouidius Montalbanus ... summo labore collegit, digessit, concinnauit ...; Hieronymus Bernia propriis sumptibus in lucem editum dicauit.*

Bononiæ: Typis Io. Baptistæ Ferronii ..., 1668. [12], 660, [52] p.: ill.; 36 cm. Signatures: [cross]^6, A-3M^6, 3N^8 ([cross]6 bound as half title page before [cross]1) Colophon, sig. 3N8v: Bononiæ: Ex typographia Ferroniana, 1667 ... T. p. engraved, with illustrated border, sig. [cross]1r, signed: Laurent. Tinnis. sculp. Includes index. Sorbelli, A. "Contributo alla bib. di U. Aldrovandi." In *Intorno alla vita e alle opere di U. Aldrovandi,* 69-139, XIII.1 (p. 124).

Provenance: Earl of Aylesford (bookplate). Bound as v. 13 of a set of Aldrovandi's works on natural history.

29. ALDROVANDI, ULISSE, 1522-1605? *Vlyssis Aldrouandi patricii Bononiensis Monstrorum historia: cum Paralipomenis historiæ omnium animalium Bartholomæus Ambrosinus ... labore, et studio uolumen composuit; Marcus Antonius Bernia in lucem edidit proprijs sumptibus ... cum indice copiosissimo.*

Bononiæ: Typis Nicolai Tebaldini, 1642. 2 v. in 1: ill.; 36 cm. Engraved title page, with illustrated border, signed: Io. Bapta. Coriolanus F. Bonon. Separate t. p., pt. 2, sig. A1r: Paralipomena accuratissma [sic] historiæ omnium animalium ... Bononiæ: Typis Nicolai Tebaldini, 1642. Pt. 1: [8], 748, [28] p. (the last p. blank); pt. 2: 159, [9] p. (the last 2 blank). Signatures: pt. 1: [cross]^4, A-3P^6, 3Q^8, 3R^6, 3S^8; pt. 2: A-O^6 (O6 blank). Includes indexes. Errata: p. [27] (3rd group), pt. 1. Nissen, C. *Zoologische Buchillustration,* 74. Sorbelli, A. "Contributo alla bib. di U. Aldrovandi." In *Intorno alla vita e alle opere di U. Aldrovandi,* 69-139, XI. 1 (p.121).

Provenance: Earl of Aylesford (bookplate). Bound as v. 6 of a set of Aldrovandi's works on natural history.

30. ALDROVANDI, ULISSE, 1522-1605? *Vlyssis Aldrouandi patricii Bononiensis Musæum metallicum in libros IIII distributum, Bartholomæus Ambrosinus ... labore, et studio composuit; cum indice copiosissimo; Marcus Antonius Bernia proprijs impensis in lucem edidit.*

Bononiæ: Typis Io. Baptistæ Ferronij, 1648. [8], 979, [13] p.: ill.; 37 cm. Signatures: [par.]^4, A-4N^6, 4O^4 ([par.] 4 blank) Imprint supplied from colophon, sig. 4O4v. Sig. [par.]1r is engraved title page, signed: Coriolanus F. Includes index. Nissen, C. *Zoologische Buchillustration,* 75. Sorbelli, A. "Contributo alla bib. di U. Aldrovandi." In *Intorno alla vita e alle opere di U. Aldrovandi,* 69-139, XII.1 (p. 123).

Provenance: Earl of Aylesford (bookplate). Imperfect: lacks [par.]4 (p. [7-8], 1st group); p. [1]-12 [A6], 73-74[G1], 83-84 (G6), 567-68 (3B2), 573-74 (3B5), 725-28 (3P3-4), 913-924(4H^6) supplied in ms.; ms. note tipped in following p. [11] (3rd group). Bound as v. 8 of a set of Aldrovandi's works on natural history.

31. ALDROVANDI, ULISSE, 1522-1605? *Vlyssis Aldrouandi patricii Bononiensis Quadrupedum omniu[m] bisulcoru[m] historia, Ioannes Cornelius Vteruerius Belga colligere incæpit; Thomas Dempsterus ... perfectè absoluit; Hieronymus Tamburinus in lucem edidit ... cum indice copiosissimo... .*

Bononiae: Apud Sebastianum Bonhommium, 1621. [12], 1040, [12] p.: ill.; 36 cm. Signatures: [cross]^6, A-4R^6, 4S^4, a^6. Engraved t. p., with illustrated border, signed: Io. Bapta. Coriolanus. Colophon, sig. a6v: Bononiæ: Typis Sebastiani Bonomij, 1621 ...Impensis Hieronymi Tamburini. Includes index. Nissen, C. *Zoologische Buchillustration,* 76. Sorbelli, A. "Contributo alla bib. di U. Aldrovandi." In *Intorno alla vita e alle opere di U. Androvandi,* 69-139, VIII. 1 (p. 113).

Provenance: Earl of Aylesford (bookplate). Bound as v. 5 of a set of Aldrovandi's works on natural history.

32. ALDROVANDI, ULISSE, 1522-1605? *Vlyssis Aldrouandi patricii Bononiensis Serpentum, et draconu[m] historiæ libri duo, Bartholomæus Ambrosinus ... summo labore opus concinnauit ... cum indice....*

Bononiæ: Apud Clementem Ferronium, sumptibus M. Antonij Berni[a]e ... , 1640. [8], 427, [29] p.: ill.; 36 cm. Signatures: a^4, A-2M^6, 2N^4, 2O-2P^6, 2Q^2 (a4 a blank) Sig. a1r is engraved title page, signed Io. Bapta. Coriolanus F. Includes index. Sorbelli, A. "Contributo alla bib. di U. Aldrovandi." In *Intorno alla vita e alle opere di U. Aldrovandi,* 69-139, X.3 (p. 120).

Imperfect: lacks a4. Provenance: Earl of Aylesford (bookplate). Bound as v. 10 of a set of Aldrovandi's works on natural history.

33. ALDROVANDI, ULISSE, 1522-1605? *Vlyssis Aldrouandi philosophi ac medici Bononiensis ... Ornithologiæ: hoc est de auibus historiæ libri XII ...: cum indice septendecim linguarum copiosissimo.*

Bononiae: Apud Franciscum de Franciscis Senensem, 1599-1634. 3 v.: ill., port.; 36 cm. Title varies. Vols. 2-3 lack subtitle. Engraved title pages; woodcut initials. T. p. to v. 2 signed: Io. Bapta. Coriolanus. Portrait in v. 3 by Valesio. Vol. 2 has imprint: Bonon.: Apud Nicolaum Tebaldinum, 1634. Vol. 3 has imprint: Bononiæ: Apud Io: Bapt. Bellagambam, 1603. Colophon, v. 1: Bononiæ: Apud Io: Baptistam Bellagambam. 1599. Impensis magnifici domini Francisci de Franciscis Senensis. Briefer form for v.

3, preceded by Bellagamba's second device, a flaming brazier. The three volumes comprise 20 libri: v. 1, liber I-XII; v. 2, liber XIII-XVIII; v. 3, liber XIX-XX. Sorbelli, A. "Contributo alla bib. di U. Aldrovandi." In *Intorno alla vita e alle opere di U. Aldrovandi*, 69-139, I. 1, III. 1 (p. 85, 96).

Provenance: Earl of Aylesford (bookplate). Bound as v. 1-3 of a set of Aldrovandi's works on natural history.

34. Aldrovandi, Ulisse, 1522-1605? *Vlyssis Aldrouandi philosophi, et medici Bononiensis. De piscibus libri V et De cetis lib. vnus, Ioannes Cornelius Vteruerius ... collegit; Hieronymus Tamburinus in lucem edidit ...; cum indice copiosissimo....*

Bononiae: Apud Bellagambam, 1613. [8], 372 [i.e. 732], [28] p. (the last p. blank): ill.; 35 cm. Signatures: pi^4, A-3Q^6, 3R^8. Sig. [A]1r is engraved title page. Colophon, sig. 3R8r: Bononiæ: Apud Ioannem Baptistam Bellagambam, 1612... sumptibus ... Hieronymi Tamburini. Includes index. Errata: p. [26] (3rd group). Page 732 misnumbered 372; other errors in pagination. Nissen, C. *Zoologische Buchillustration*, 70. Sorbelli, A. "Contributo alla bib. di U. Aldrovandi." In *Intorno alla vita e alle opere di U. Aldrovandi*, 69-139, VI. 1 (p. 105).

Provenance: Earl of Aylesford (bookplate). Bound as v. 4 of a set of Aldrovandi's works on natural history.

35. Aldrovandi, Ulisse, 1522-1605? *Vlyssis Aldrouandi philosophi, et medici Bononiensis. De reliquis animalibus exanguibus libri quatuor, post mortem eius editi; nempè, De mollibus, crustaceis, testaceis, et zoophytis.*

Bononia[e]: Typis Io. Baptista[e] Ferronij, sumptibus Marci Antonij Bernia[e], 1642 i.e. 1654. [6], 593 [i.e. 595], [28] p.: ill.; 36 cm. Engraved title page. Colophon: Bononiæ M.DC.LIV. Typis Io. Baptistæ Ferronij ... Sumptibus Marci Antonij Berniæ. Includes index. Pagination: nos. 421-22, 431-32 repeated, 429-30 omitted. Dedication signed: Francisca Aldrouanda. Sorbelli, A. "Contributo alla bib. di U. Aldrovandi." In *Intorno alla vita e alle opere di U. Aldrovandi*, 69-139, V. 9 (p. 105).

Bound as v. 12 of a set of Aldrovandi's works on natural history.

36. Aldrovandi, Ulisse, 1522-1605? *[Works on natural history, by Ulisse Aldrovandi.]*

[1599-1668] 13 v.: ill.; 36 cm. Uniformly bound set from the library of the Earl of Aylesford of works by Aldrovandi published in Bologna, Italy. Those published after the author's death were edited from his manuscripts by Vterverius, Ambrosini, and others. Includes bibliographical references and indexes. v. 1-3. Vlyssis Aldrouandi philosophi ac medici Bononiensis. *Ornithologiæ: hoc est de auibus historiæ libri XII* (1599-1634). v. 4. Vlyssis Aldrouandi philosophi et medici Bononiensis. *De piscibus: libri V et De cetis lib. Vnus*, Ioannes Cornelius Vteruerius ... collegit ... (1613). v. 5. Vlyssis Aldrouandi patricii Bononiensis. *Quadrupedum omniu[m] bisulcoru[m] historia*, Ioannes Cornelius Vteruerius ... colligere incæpit; Thomas Dempsterus ... perfectè absoluit ... (1621). v. 6. Vlyssis Aldrouandi patricii Bononiensis. *Monstrorum historia ...*, Bartholomæus Ambrosinus ... labore ... (1642). v. 7. Vlyssis Aldrouandi patricii Bononiensis. *De quadrupedibus solidipedibus volumen integrum*, Ioannes Cornelius Vteruerius ... collegit ... (1616). v. 8. Vlyssis Aldrouandi patricii Bononiensis. *Musæum metallicum in libros IIII distributum*, Bartholomæus Ambrosinus ... labore ... (1648). v. 9. *De animalibus insectis libri septem ...* (1602). v. 10. Vlyssis Aldrouandi patricii Bononiensis. *Serpentum et draconu[m] historiæ libri duo*, Bartholomæus Amrbrosinus ... concinnauit ... (1640) v. 11. Vlyssis Aldrouandi patricii Bononiensis. *De quadrupedib[us] digitatis viuiparis libri tres: et De quadrupedib[us] digitatis ouiparis libri duo*, Bartholomæus Ambrosinus ... collegit ... (1663). v. 12. Vlyssis Aldrouandi philosophi et medici Bononiensis. *De reliquis animalibus exanguibus libri quatuor ...* (1654). v. 13. Vlyssis Aldrouandi patricii Bononiensis. *Dendrologiæ naturalis scilicet arborum historiæ libri duo ...*, Ouidius Montalbanus ... collegit ... (1668).

37. Alembert, Jean Le Rond d', 1717-1783. *Recherches sur la précession des equinoxes, et sur la nutation del'axe de la terre, dans le systême newtonien.*

Paris: David l'aîné, 1749. xxxviij, [2], 184 p. 4 fold. plates. 22cm. Fautes à corriger: on p. 184.

Provenance: École Sainte Geneviève (inkstamp).

38. Alembert, Jean Le Rond d', 1717-1783. *Traité de dynamique; dans lequel les loix de l'équilibre & du mouvement des corps sont réduites au plus petit nombre possible, & démontrées d'une maniére nouvelle, & où l'on donne un principe général pour trouver le mouvement de plusieurs corps qui agissent les uns sur les autres d'une manière quelconque. Par M. d'Alembert....*

Paris: Chez David l'aîné, 1743. 2 p.l., xvi, [2], 186, [2] p. 4 fold. plates. 22cm. Engraved title vignette; head and tail pieces.

39. ALFONSO X, KING OF CASTILE AND LEON, 1221-1284. *Libros del saber de astronomía del rey D. Alfonso X de Castilla, copilados, anotados y comentados por Don Manuel Rico y Sinobas ... Obra publicada de real orden....*

Madrid: Tip. de Don E. Aguado, 1863-67. 5 v.: ill., col. plates, facsims. in colors, tables, diagrs.; 47 cm. "Escritores ... que tomaron parte en la redaccion ... y que se citan": v. 1, p. xcii. For Contents, see Library of Congress. *Author catalog*, 1942, v. 3, p.29.

Provenance: Mr. Langier (inscription).

40. ALFONSO X, KING OF CASTILE AND LEON, 1221-1284. *Tabule astronomice Alfonsi Regis.*

Venetijs: Opera [et] arte mirifica viri solertis Ioha[n]nis Hamman de Landoia dictus Hertzog ..., 1492 currente: pridie Calen[das] Nouembr[is] [31 Oct.] [228] p. (last p. blank); 22 cm. Signatures: A-D^8, e^6, a-h^8, i-k^6 (missigned: e2 for e8 (true e2 unsigned, f2 for i2) Imprint from colophon. Woodcut initials and some spaces left for capitals. "Exhortatoria in impressione[m] tabularu[m] Astronomicaru[m] Alfonsi Regis, Augustinus Morauus Olomucensis Iohanni Lucilio Santritter Heilbronnensi": p. [3]-[4]. "Canones siue propositiones in tabulas Alfonsinas", by Santritter: p. [7]-[64] (A4r-D8v). Title from D8v. BM *15th cent.*, V, p. 424 (IA.23354). Goff (rev.) A-535. *GW* 1258. Hain 869*. *ISTC*, ia00535000. Klebs 50.2. Rhodes 66.

Binding: wooden boards, remains of tooled leather spine; remains of clasp on upper fore-edge; guards of vellum ms.fragments on 1st and last gatherings. Extensive ms. marginalia.

41. ALGAROTTI, FRANCESCO, CONTE, 1712-1764. *Il newtonianismo per le dame, ovvero, Dialoghi sopra la luce e i colori....*

In Milano, 1739. XII, 304 p. front. 19 cm. Dedication signed: Francesco Algarotti. Wallis & Wallis. *Newton*, 194.1

Frontispiece bound after p. XII.

42. ALGAROTTI, FRANCESCO, CONTE, 1712-1764. *Sir Isaac Newton's philosophy explain'd for the use of the ladies. In six dialogues on light and colours. [Translated by Elizabeth Carter] From the Italian of Sig. Algarotti....*

London: Printed for E. Cave, 1739. 2 v. 17 cm. Translation of *Il newtonianismo per le dame; ovvero, dialoghi sopra la luce, e i colori. Babson Newton Coll.* 147. Gray, G. J. *Newton*, 195.

Provenance: Elizabeth Harri[o?]t (signature); Fra Troysd[e?]n (signature); Middleton Park (armorial bookplate bearing motto, "Fidei coticula crux").

43. ALLEN, FRANK, 1874- *The universe; from crystal spheres to relativity, by Frank Allen....*

New York: Harcourt, Brace and Company [c. 1931]. xiv, 145 p. illus., pl., ports., diagrs. 20 cm. "This lecture was delivered as the first of the twenty-second series, 1928, of February popular lectures in the University of Manitoba." – Foreword.

44. ALLEN, JOHN STUART, 1907- *Astronomy: what everyone should know, by John Stuart Allen.*

Indianapolis, New York: The Bobbs-Merrill Company, 1945. 10 p., 2 l., 13-199 p. front., illus., plates, diagrs. 21 cm. "First edition." Includes index.

Provenance: Hokkaido Military Government District Library (inkstamp).

45. ALTER, DINSMORE, 1888-1968. *Introduction to practical astronomy, by Dinsmore Alter....*

New York: Thomas Y. Crowell Company [c. 1933]. viii, 80, [48] p.: diagrs.; 26 cm. Circular and rectangular coordinate paper: [48] p. at end.

46. AMERICAN ACADEMY OF ARTS AND SCIENCES. *Proceedings of the American Academy of Arts and Sciences.*

Boston : Metcalf and Co., 1848-[1958] 85 v. ; 24-26 cm. Irregular. Vol. 1 (from May 1846 to May 1848)-v. 85, no. 4 [May 1958]. Vols. for -1958 published by: American Academy of Arts and Sciences. Imprint varies. Vols. 84 and 85 published retrospectively. Indexed by: *GeoRef* ISSN:0197-7482 Notes: Vols. 9-31 called also new ser., v. 1-23. Cf. *Union list of serials*. Vol. 12 (from May 1876 to May 1877) includes: Researches in telephony / by A. Graham Bell. Vols. for -1958 include the Records of the Academy, ISSN 0065-6844. Issued with: American Academy of Arts and Sciences. *Records of the Academy* 0065-6844 (DLC) 61003014 (OCoLC)1926674. Continued by: *Daedalus* (Boston, Mass.) ISSN:0011-5266 (DLC) 12030299 (OCoLC)1565785.

Library has: v.12=n.s., v.4(1876/1877)

47. *The American almanac and repository of useful knowledge.*

Boston : Gray and Bowen, 1830-1861. 32 v. : ill. ; 18-20 cm. Volume/date range: Vol. 1-32. Vol. 31-32 also called 4th series, vol. 1-2. Vols. for 1834- published by Charles Bowen. Indexes: Vol. 1-10 (1830-1839) in v. 10; v. 11-20 (1840-1849) in v. 20; v. 21-30 (1850-1859) in v. 30.

Library has: 5, 1834.

48. AMERICAN INSTITUTE OF THE CITY OF NEW YORK. *Transactions of the American Institute of the City of New-York.*

[S.l. : s.n.], 1852- (Albany, N. Y. : Charles van Benthuysen). v. ; 24 cm. Volume/date range: 1851-1860/61. Continues: American Institute of the City of New York. *Annual report of the American Institute, on the subject of agriculture.* Continued by: American Institute of the City of New York. *Annual report of the American Institute, of the City of New York.*

Library has: 1852. Vol. for 1852: Provenance: John Hunt (presentation inscription from John M. Burney).

49. *American journal of hygiene.*

Baltimore, Published by School of Hygiene and Public Health, Johns Hopkins University through the Johns Hopkins Press. 80 v. Volume/date range: v. 1-80, no. 3; 1921-Nov. 1964. Indexed by: *CIS abstracts* ISSN:0302-7651. Issued 1928-64 by the School of Hygiene and Public Health of Johns Hopkins University. Indexes: Vols. 1-28, 1921-38. 1 v.; Vols. 29-60, 1939-54. 1 v. Continued by: *American journal of epidemiology* ISSN:0002-9262.

Library has: 54, 1951.

50. AMPÈRE, ANDRÉ-MARIE, 1775-1836. *Essai sur la philosophie des sciences: ou, Exposition analytique d'une classification naturelle de toutes les connaissances humaines.*

Paris: Bachelier, 1834. lxx, 272 p., [2] folded leaves of plates; 21 cm. Variant editions issued by Bachelier in 1834. In this ed., on verso of half-title: "De l'Imprimerie de Thibaud-Landriot, à Clermont-Ferrand." Part 1 only printed in 1834 eds.

51. AMPÈRE, ANDRÉ-MARIE, 1775-1836. *Mémoire prèsenté à l'Académie Royale des Sciences ... sur les effets des courans électriques, par M. Ampère.*

[À Paris: Chez Crochard ..., 1820]. p. 59-76, 170-218; 21 cm. Annales de chimie et de physique; t. 15. *De l'action mutuelle de deux courans électriques – Suite du mémoire sur l'action mutuelle entre deux courans électriques, entre un courant électrique et un aimant ou le globe terrèstre, et entre deux aimans.*

52. AMPÈRE, ANDRÉ-MARIE, 1775-1836. *Mémoire sur la théorie mathématique des phénomènes électro-dynamiques uniquement déduite de l'expérience: dans lequel se trouvent réunis les Mémoires que M. Ampère a communiqués à l'Académie Royale des Sciences, dans les séances des 4 et 26 décembre 1820, 10 juin 1822, 22 décembre 1823, 12 septembre et 21 novembre 1825.*

[Paris: Chez Firmin Didot ..., 1827]. p.175-387, [1], [2] fold. leaves of plates: ill.; 28 cm. Mémoires de l'Académie Royale des Sciences de l'Institut de France; t. 6. Caption title. Errata: p. [388].

53. AMPÈRE, ANDRÉ-MARIE, 1775-1836. *Recueil d'observations électro-dynamiques: contenant divers mémoires, notices, extraits de lettres ou d'ouvrages périodiques sur les sciences, relatifs a l'action mutuelle de deux courans électriques, à celle qui existe entre un courant électrique et un aimant ou le globe terrèstre, et à celle de deux aimans l'un sur l'autre; par M. Ampère...*

À Paris: Chez Crochard ... , 1822. [2], 383 [i.e. 385], [1] p., 10 folded leaves of plates: ill.; 21 cm. With half-title. Number 251 omitted in pagination, with unnumbered blank page between 258 and 259. Pages 382 to 385 incorrectly numbered 358, 359, 360, and 383. Illustrated by Girard and Adam.

Provenance: G. Lamaille (Prize binding and inscription).

54. AMPÈRE, ANDRÉ-MARIE, 1775-1836. *Théorie des phénomènes électro-dynamiques, uniquement déduite de l'expérience.*

Paris: Méquignon-Marvis [etc.] 1826. 226, [1] p. 2 fold. plates. 29 cm. On verso of title page: Imprimerie de Firmin Didot. Horblit, H. D. *Grolier 100 science books*, 3a.

Provenance: Robert Honeyman IV (Honeyman sale).

55. Ampère, André-Marie, 1775-1836. *Théorie mathématique des phénomènes électro-dynamiques, uniquement déduite de l'expérience. 2. éd. conforme a la première publiée en 1826.*

Paris : A. Hermann, 1883. 164 p. : illus. (part fold.) ; 27 cm.

56. Andrade, E. N. da C. (Edward Neville da Costa), 1887-1971. *More simple science; earth and man, by E. N. da C. Andrade ... and Julian Huxley ... with drawings by L. R. Brightwell and Comerford Watson.*

Oxford: B. Blackwell, 1935. x, 352 p. incl. front., illus., diagrs. 21 cm. "This volume is in a sense a continuation of the previous volume *Simple Science,* by Professor E. N. da C. Andrade and Dr. Julian Huxley, and the material in it will form part of a series of four separate books adapted for use in schools." – Pref. Includes index.

57. André, Charles Louis François, 1842-1912. *L'astronomie pratique et les observatoires: en Europe et en Amérique de puis le milieu du XVIIe siècle jusqu'à nos jours, par C. André, G. Rayet....*

Paris: Gauthier-Villars ..., 1874-1881. 5 v.: ill. (some col.), maps; 18 cm. Illustrated by: Perot, C. Laplante. Advertisements on lower wrappers. Includes bibliographical references. 1ère ptie: Angleterre. 1874 – 2e ptie: Écosse, Irlande et colonies anglaises. 1874 – 3e ptie: États-Unis d'Amérique, par C. André, A. Angot. 1877 – 4e ptie: Observatoires de l'Amérique de Sud, par C. André, A. Angot. 1881 – 5e ptie: Observatoires d'Italie, par G. Rayet. 1878.

Bound in 3 v. Some wrappers bound in. Provenance: F. Hugueny (inkstamp).

58. André, Charles Louis François, 1842-1912. *Traité d'astronomie stellaire, par Ch. André.*

Paris: Gauthier-Villars, 1899-1900. 2 v., [5] plates: ill.; 25 cm. Planned to be completed in three volumes; v. 3 never published. Includes bibliographical references. 1. ptie. Étoiles simples. – 2. ptie. Étoiles doubles et multiples. Amas stellaires.

Advertisements: p. [4] of original cover, v. 1 & 2.

59. *Annalen der Physik. Gilbert's annalen v. 1, 1799-v. 76, 1824. Poggendorff's annalen v. 1, 1824-v. 160, 1877. Annalen der Physik und der physikalischen Chemie. Erster-sechszehnter Band. Series [2-3]. Annalen der Physik und Chemie v. 61-76. Journal der Physik 1790-94. Neues Journal der Physik 1795-97. Annalen der Physik und der physikalischen Chemie 1819-24. Annalen der Physik und Chemie 1824-99.*

Leipzig, J. A. Barth; [etc.]. v. ill. (part col.) maps, diagrs. 20-24 cm. Bd. 1-76, 1790-1824; [2. F.] Bd. 1-160, 1824-77; n. F. [i.e. 3. F.] Bd. 1-69, 1877-99; 4. F. Bd. 1-87, 1900-28; 5. F. v. 1-43; 1929-44.; 6. F. v. 1-20, 1947-57; 7. F. v. 1-48, 1958-91; 8. F. v. 1- 1992- Suspended publication 1944-1946. Alternate numbering: v. 31-60 also called "Neue Folge, erster-dreissigster Band"; v. 61, "Neueste Folge, erster Band"; v. 62, "Neueste Folge, zwei und dreissigster Band"; [2d series], v. 31-60, "Zweite Reihe"; v. 61-90, "Dritte Reihe"; v. 91-120, "Vierte Reihe"; v. 120-150, "Fünfte Reihe"; v. 151-170, "Sechste Reihe"; v. 161- New series, v. 1- published with the cooperation of Deutsche Physikalische Gesellschaft.

Library has: ser. 3:31, 1887; ser. 4: 17-18, 1905, [49, 1916]. n. F. Bd. XXXI: Provenance: Bibl. Berchmanianum, Nijmegen (inkstamp); 4. F. Bd. 17-18: Provenance: Herbert McLean Evans (bookplate); 4. F. Bd. 49, Hft.7: Honeyman sale. References: Horblit, H. D. *Grolier 100 science books,* 26b.

60. *Annales de chimie et de physique. [Annales de chimie 1789-1815.]*

Paris, Masson, 1789-1913. 390 v. ill. 23 cm. t. 1-96, 1789-1815; [2. sér.] t. 1-75, 1816-40; 3. sér., t. 1-69, 1841-63; 4. sér., t. 1-30, 1864-73; 5. sér., t. 1-30, 1874-83; 6. sér., t. 1-30, 1884-93; 7. sér., t. 1-30, 1894-1903; 8. sér., t. 1-30, 1904-13. Publication suspended Oct. 1793-96. Indexes: v. 1-30, 1789-June 1799. 1 v.; v. 31-60, July 1799-1806, with index to v. 1-30; v. 61-96, 1807-15, with index to v. 1-30; ser. 2, v. 1-30, 1816-25, 1 v.; ser. 2, v. 31-60, 1826-35, with index to ser. 2, v. 1-30; ser. 2, v. 61-75, 1836-40, with index to ser. 2, v. 1-30; ser. 3, v. 1-30, 1841-50, 1 v.; ser. 3, v. 31-69, 1851-63, 1 v.; ser. 4-8, 1864-1913, 1 v. each. Editors: 1789-1815, Guyton-Morveau, Monge, BetholLet and others; 1816-50, Gay-Lussac, Arago and others; 1851-53, Arago, Chevreul, Dumas and others; 1854-Chevreul, Roussingault and others; 18 -19 Berthelot, Mascart and others; 19 -Apr. 1909, Mascart, Haller; May 1909-13, Haller, Lippmann, Bouty. Spine title: Annales de chimie. Absorbed: *Journal de pharmacie* Jan. 1800 Split into: *Annales de chimie. Annales de physique* ISSN:0003-4169.

Library has: ser.2: 15, 1820.

61. *The Annals of philosophy. [Annals of philosophy or, magazine of chemistry, mineralogy, mechanics, natural history, agriculture, and the arts, 1813-20.]*
London, Baldwin, Cradock, and Joy, 1815-26. 28 v. plates, maps, charts. 22 cm. v. 1-28, 1813-26. Vols. 17-28 called also new ser., v. 1-12. Absorbed by: *Philosophical magazine.*
Library has: 16, 1820.

62. *Annuli astronomici: instrumenti cum certissimi, tùm commodissimí, vsus / ex variis authoribus, Petro Beausardo, Gemma Frisio, Ioa[n]ne Dryandro, Boneto Hebræo, Burchardo Mythobio, Orontio Finæo, vna cum Meteoroscopio per Ioa[n]ne[m] Regiomontanum, & Annulo non vniuersali M. T. authore.*
Lutetiae: Apud Gulielmum Cauellat ..., 1557. 8, 159 leaves: ill.; 17 cm. Special title pages.

63. Apelt, Ernst Friedrich, 1812-1859. *Die Reformation der Sternkunde: ein Beitrag zur deutschen Culturgeschichte, von E. F. Apelt.*
Jena: Druck und Verlag von Friedrich Mauke, 1852. XVI, 440 p., V folded leaves of plates: ill.; 21 cm. Includes correspondence of Johannes Kepler and David Fabricius, p. 327-434. Includes bibliographical references.

64. Apian, Peter, 1495-1552. *Instrument Buch, durch Petrum Apianum erst von new beschriben....*
Ingolstat : [s.n.], am 22. Tag Augusti, 1533. [108] p. (the last page blank): ill.; 31 cm. Imprint taken from p. [4]. Probably printed by G.& P. Apian, as they were printing in Ingolstadt at this time. Signatures: [pi] A^4 [chi] B-N^4. Stillwell, M. B. *Science*, 812. *Wellcome catalogue of printed books*, 341.
Lacks the supplementary plates found in some copies. Provenance: Herbert McLean Evans (bookplate).

65. Apollonius, of Perga. *Apollonii Pergaei Conicorum libri quattuor. Vnà cvm Pappi Alexandrini lemmatibvs, et commentariis Eutocii Ascalonitæ. Sereni Antinsensis ... libri duo nunc primum in lucem ed. Quæ omnia nuper Federicus Commandinus Vrbinas mendis quam plurims expurgata è Græco conuertit, & commentariis illustrauit....*
Bononiae: Ex officina A. Benatii, 1566. 2 v. in 1. ([4], 114, [2], 36 leaves) diagrs. 29 cm. Vol. 2 has title: Sereni Antinsensis ... libri duo. Vnus de sectione cylindri, alter de sectione coni. À Federico Commandino ... è Græco conuersi ... Leaf 39 of v. 1 erroneously numbered 35; leaves 31, 32 of v. 2 erroneously numbered 28, 27. Horblit, H. D. *Grolier 100 science books*, 4.

66. Apollonius, of Perga. *Apollonii Pergæi Conicorum libri octo, et Sereni Antissensis De sectione cylindri & coni libri duo.*
Oxoniæ: E Theatro Sheldoniano, 1710. 3 pt. in 1 v. front., diagr. 41 cm. Engraved title page and frontispiece. Signed: delin. M. Burghers sculp. Univ. Oxon. Pts. I and III, Greek and Latin in parallel columns; pt. II, Latin, with "Pappi Lemmata" in Greek and Latin, in parallel columns. I. Conicorum libri IV. priores cum Pappi Alexandrini Lemmatis et Eutocii Ascalonitæ commentariis. Ex codd. mss. græcis edidit Edmundus Halleius. II. Conicorum libri tres posteriores (sc. V tus. VI tus. & VII mus.) ex arabico sermone in latinum conversi, cum Pappi Alexandrini Lemmatis. Subjicitur liber conicorum octavus restitutus. Opera & studio Edmundi Halleii. III. Sereni philosophi Antissensis. De sectione cylindriet coni libri duo. Ex codd. mss. græcis edidit Edmundus Halleius.

67. Arago, F. (François), 1786-1853. *Astronomie populaire, par François Arago. Publiée d'après son ordre sous la direction de M. J.-A. Barral. Œuvre posthume.*
Paris: Gide et J. Baudry; T. O. Weigel, 1854-1857. 4 v. illus., 24 plates (part fold., part double, incl. maps) tables, diagrs. 22 cm.
Provenance: R. M. Beverley (bookplate).

68. Arago, F. (François), 1786-1853. *Leçons d'astronomie professées à l'Observatoire royal, par M. Arago....*
Paris: Just Rouvier et E. Le Bouvier ..., 1835. 324 p., 5 folded leaves of plates: ill.; 17 cm. Houzeau & Lancaster. *Astronomie* (1964 ed.), 8195.

69. Arago, F. (François), 1786-1853. *Meteorological essays, by François Arago; with an introduction by Baron Alexander von Humboldt; translated under the superintendence of Colonel Sabine.*
London: Longmans, 1855. xxxvi, 504 p.; 23 cm. Includes index.

Provenance: prize presentation from James Clerk Maxwell to David Gill (slip with signed inscription pasted in); D. Wyllie & Son, Circulating Library (label); Universitas Aberdonensis (armorial tooling).

70. ARAGO, F. (FRANÇOIS), 1786-1853. *A popular treatise on comets: reprinted from "Popular Astronomy", by François Arago ... ; translated from the original and edited by Admiral W. H. Smyth ... and Robert Grant....*

London: Longman, Green, Longman, and Roberts 1861. x, 164 p., XV-XIX leaves of plates (1 folded): ill.; 23 cm. Half title: The comets. Translation of book 17 of *Popular astronomy* and of the 25th chapter of book 32. Illustrated by H. Adlard. Advertisements on pastedown endpapers.

Binder: Westleys & Co. (ticket).

71. ARAGO, F. (FRANÇOIS), 1786-1853. *Œuvres de François Arago. Deuxième édition, mise au courant des progrès de la science, par M. J.-A. Barral.*

Paris: Librairie des sciences naturelles, Theodore Morgand ..., 1865. 17 v.: ill.; 22 cm. Introduction by Alexandre de Humboldt. Vols. [13-16] have title: Astronomie populaire, par François Arago. Deuxième édition, mise au courant des progrès de la science, par M. J.-A. Barral. Œuvre posthume. Vol. [17] has title and imprint: Œuvres complêtes de François Arago...: tables, publiées d'après son ordre sous la direction de M. J.-A.Barral. Paris: Gide ...; Leipzig: T. O. Weigel ..., 1862. "Notice chronologique sur les œuvres d'Arago": v. [17], p.[VII]-CCLXIII. Includes indexes. Tables 1-3. Notices biographiques, tables 1-3. – tables 4-8. Notices scientifiques, tables 1-5 – table 9. Voyages scientifiques – tables 10-11. Mémoires scientifiques, tables 1-2 – table 12. Mélanges – tables [13-16]. Astronomie populaire, tables 1-4 – table [17] Tables.

Provenance: J. P. Armainvilliers (book label).

72. ARATUS, SOLENSIS. *Aratou Soleos Phainomena kai Diosemeia. Theonos scholia. Eratosthenous katasterismoi. Metron tes ges Peripherias. Tou kuboudiplasiasmos. Koskinon. Tou Neilou pegai. Tou kanonos tome Dionysiouhumnoi. Accesserunt annotationes in Eratosthenem et hymnos Dionysii.*

Oxonii: E Theatro Sheldoniano, 1672. [10], 147, [13], 69 p.: ill., 2 fold. plates; 19 cm. Title page romanized. Added engraved title page, signed "D.L." Edited by John Fell, bp. of Oxford. Erastothenes, etc. preceded by half title. Hymns of Dionysius edited by Edmund Chilmead with his essay De musica antiqua Græca. Wing A3596.

73. ARATUS, SOLENSIS. *Hvg. Grotii Batavi Syntagma Arateorvm: opvs poeticæ et astronomiæ stvdiosis vtilissimvm.*

Lvgdvni Batavorvm: Ex Officinâ Plantinianâ, apvd C. Raphelengivm, Academiæ Lugduno-Batauæ typographum, 1600. 1 v. (various pagings) illus. 24 cm. Arati Phænomena & Diosemeia Græce. – Ciceronis interpretatio, H. Grotij versibus interpolata. – Phænomena Aratea Germanico Cæsare interprete. – Eiusdem fragmenta Prognosticorum. –Notæ H. Grotij adAratum. –Notæ eiusdem ad Germanici Phænomena. – Notæ eiusdem ad Germanici Prognostica. – Notæ ad fragmenta Ciceronis. – Festi Avieni Paraphrasis.

74. ARCHIMEDES. *Ta mechri nun sozomena, hapanta ... Opera, quæ quidem extant, omnia, multis iam seculis desiderata ... nuncq[ue] primùm & graecè & latinè in lucem edita ... Adiecta quoq[ue] sunt Evtocii Ascalonitae in eosdem Archimedis libros commentaria, item Græcè & Latinè, nunquam antea excusa....*

Basileae, Ioannes Heruagius excudi fecit, 1544. 4 p. l., 139 p., [4] l., 163 p., [2] l., 65, 68 p., [2] l. illus. 32 cm. Editio princeps, edited by Thomas Venatorius. Printer's device on verso of last leaf. "Archimedis ... opera, quae quidem extant omnia latinitate iam olin donata" ([4] l., 163 p.) and "Eutocii Ascalonitae in Archimedis libros de sphaera et cylindro, atq[ue] alios quosdam, commentaria" ([2] l., 65, 68 p.) have special title pages and separate paginations. Contents: Archimedis opera: De sphæra & cylindro libri II. Circuli dimensio. De conoidibus & sphæroidibus. De lineis spiralibus. Planorum æqueponderantium inuenta, uel centra grauitatis planoru[m]. II. De harenæ numero [aka 'Arenarius']. Quadratura parbolæ. – Evtocii Ascalonitæ Commentarius: In primum & secundum Archimedis de sphæra & cylindro. In circuli dimensionem. In primu[m] & secudu[m] æquepo[n]derantiu[m]. Horblit, H. D. *Grolier 100 science books*, 5.

75. ARCHIMEDES. *Archimedis Opera: Apollonii Pergæi Conicorum, libri IIII. Theodosii Sphærica: methodo nova illustrata & succinctè demonstrata. Per Is. Barrow....*

Londini: Excudebat G. Godbid, vneunt apud R. Scott, in vico Little Britain, 1675. 4 p. l., 285 [i.e. 185] p., 1 l., [2], 104 p., 1 l., [2], 38 p. diagrs.on fold. plates. 21 cm. Each work has special title page. Errors in paging: p. 125, 145-150, 152-158, 160, 165-185 numbered 225, 245-250, 252-258, 260, 265-285 respectively. Wing A-3621. Wing A-3536. Wing T-857A.

Errata leaf to pt. 2 inserted after p. 104 (2nd group).

76. ARCHIMEDES. *Archimedis Opera non nulla a Federico Commandino Urbinate nuper in Latinum conuersa, et commentariis illustrata.*

Venetiis: Apud Paulum Manutium, Aldi f., 1558. 2 v. in 1: ([4], 55, [3], 63 leaves) diagrs. 29 cm. Vol. 2 has special title page: Commentarii in opera non nulla Archimedis. Adams A1532. Adams C2468.

77. ARCHIMEDES. *Archimedous tou Syrakousiou Psammites, kai kyklou metresis. Eutokiou Askalonitou eis auten hypomnema = Archimedis Syracusani Arenarius, et Dimensio circuli. Eutocii Ascalonitæ, in hanc commentarius. Cum versione & notis. Joh. Wallis.*

Oxonii: E Theatro Sheldoniano, 1676. 3 p. l., 159, [50] p., 4 fold. diagr. 15 cm. Greek and Latin on alternate leaves.

Provenance: Ædes Christi in Academià Oxonieusi (armorial bookplate); Radcliffe Observatory, Oxford (inkstamp); Harrison D. Horblit (bookplate); ms. notes and marginalia.

78. Erratum. Original citation duplicates citation 74.

79. ARGELANDER, FR. (FRIEDRICH), 1799-1875. *De fide Uranometriæ Bayeri: dissertatio academica, scripsit D. Fridericus Guilelmus Augustus Argelander....*

Bonnae: Typis Caroli Georgii, 1842. [2], 23 p.; 26 cm. bound to 31 cm. Includes bibliographical references.

With: Ioannis Bayeri ... *Vranometria.* Vlmæ: Sumptibus Iohannis Görlini, 1639. Provenance: Herman S. Davis (bookplate)

80. ARGELANDER, FR. (FRIEDRICH), 1799-1875. *Uranometria nova. Stellæ per mediam Europam solis oculis conspicuæ secundum veras lucis magnitudines e coelo ipso discriptæ d. Fr. Argelandro ... Neue Uranometrie. Darstellung der im mittlern Europa mit blossen Augen sichtbaren Sterne nach ihren wahren, unmittelbar vom Himmelentnommenen Grössen....*

Berlin: S. Schropp u. comp, 1843. 1 p. l., XVII pl. 18 x 41 cm.

81. ARGOLI, ANDREA, 1570-1657. *Andreæ Argoli Ephemeridum iuxta Tychonis hypotheses et cœlo deductas obseruationes.*

Patauii: Ex typographia Pauli Frambotti, MDCXXXVIII [1638]. 2 v.: ill. (woodcuts); 23 cm. Caption title of each year: Noua ephemeris Andreæ Argoli. Vol. 1: [2], 763, [1] p.; v. 2: [2], 751, [1] p. Title vignettes. Riccardi, P. *Bib. matematica*, I, columns 49-50; Houzeau & Lancaster. *Astronomie* (1964 ed.), 15115; Grässe, I, p. 194; Lalande, J. J. Le F. de. *Bib. astronomique*, p. 208. (From t. p.s.) v. 1. Ab anno 1631. ad 1655. – v. 2. Ab anno 1656. Ad 1680.

Provenance: Michaelis Amargos (inscription).

82. ARISTARCHUS, OF SAMOS. *Aristarchi De magnitudinibus, et distantiis solis, et lunæ, liber; cum Pappi Alexandrini explicationibus quibusdam. À Federico Commandino Vrbanitate in latinum conuersus, ac commentarijs illustratus. Cumpriuilegio Pont. Max. in annos X.*

Pisauri: apud Camillum Francischinum, 1572. 3 p.l., [1] (blank), 38 numb. l. diagrs. 20 cm. Title vignette; publisher's device. Initials. English title: *On the size and distances of the sun and moon.*

Printed on blue paper.

83. ARISTOTLE. *Aristotelis Stagiritæ Moralia Nichomachia: cum Eustratii, Aspasii, Michaelis Ephesii, nonnulorumque aliorum Græcorum explanationibus, nuper a Ioanne Bernardo Feliciano Latinitate donata, et cum antiquo codice collatione, suæ integritati restituta.*

Parisiis: Apud Ioannem Roigny ..., 1543. [12], 253, [9] leaves: ill.; 32 cm. Latin text with Greek side notes. English title: *Nicomachean ethics.* Errors in foliation: leaf 22 misnumbered 19, 116-118 as 126-128, 245 as 244. Includes index. Errata: leaf [9] at end.

84. ARISTOTLE. *Aristotelous hapanta = Aristoteli's summi semper philosophi ... opera quæ-*

cunq[ue] hactenus extiterunt omnia ... per Des. Eras.

Roterdamum. Basileæ: Per Io. Beb. et Mich. Ising., 1550. 2 v.: ill.; 35 cm. Some errors in pagination. Vol. 1: [10], 572 p.; v. 2: [2], 425, [1] p. Title partly romanized. Adams A1732.

3 prelim. leaves missing.

85. ARISTOTLE. *Aristotelous tou Stageiritou ta Sozomena = Operum Aristotelis Stagiritæ, philosophorum omnium longe principis, nova editio, Græcè & Latinè: Græcus contextus quàm emendatissimè præter omnes omnium editiones est editus, adscriptis ad oram libri & interpretum veterum recentiorúmque & aliorum doctorum virorum emendationibus, in quibus plurimæ nunc primùm in lucem prodeunt, ex bibliotheca Isaaci Casauboni: Latinæ interpretationes adiectæ sunt quæ Græco contextui meliùs respondent, unà cum iis quæ antehac in hoc opere desiderabantur, partim recentiorum, partim veterum interpretum, in quibus & ipsis multa nunc emendata atque illustrata eduntur: accesserunt huic editioni Kyriaci Strozæ libri duo politicorum græcolatini, in quibus ea quæ ab Aristotele in 8. libris explicata non fuerunt persequitur, insuper addita sunt ex libris Aristotelis qui hodie non supersunt Fragmenta quædam: adiecti suntetiam indices duo perutiles, quorum alter nomina auctorum qui in Aristotelem scripserunt continet, alter quid sit à quoque in singulas librorum eius partes scriptum indicat necnon alius index rerum omnium locupletissimus.*

Aureliae Allobrogum [Geneva]: Apud Petrum de la Rouiere, 1605. 2 v.; 39 cm. Titles in red and black, with printer's devices. Latin and Greek in double columns, with marginal notes. Vol. 2 has title: Operum Aristotelis tomus II librorum Aristotelis quinon extant, fragmenta quædam: item, indices duo, quorum prior nomina eorum continet qui in Aristotelem scripserunt, alter quid sit à quoque eorum in singulos Aristotelis libros scriptum indicat, alius index rerum omnium locupletissimus. Vol. 2 has colophon: Execudebat Petrus de la Roviere, 8. Iunii anno MDVI [i.e. 1606]. *Wellcome cat. of printed books,* I, 424. Includes index.

Provenance: "Ad Bibliothecam Seminarii Episcopalis Brixensis" (bookplate); "Ex libris Ioa. Aut. Cibbini Theol. D. Consil. Eccles. ep. Seminarii Reg. Brixinæ" (inscription).

86. ARISTOTLE. *Ton en tede te biblo periechomenon onomata kai taxis = Eorum quæ hoc uolumine continentur nomina & ordo.*

Excriptum Venetiis: Manu stamnea i[n] domo Aldi Manutii Romani, & græcorum studiosi, mense Februario M.III D. [Feb. 1497]. [32], 268 leaves; 31 cm. Forms the second volume of Manuzio's edition of Aristotle's complete works in Greek. Text in Greek; title page and colophon in Greek and Latin. Dedication, "Aldus Manutius Bassianàs Romanus Alberto Pio principi Carpensi S.P.D." (*1v-*2v) in Latin. Imprint from colophon. Signatures: $*^{8}$ [tilted cross]^{8} [cross]^{8} [os]^{8} a[alpha]-z[psi]^{8} & [omega]^{8} A_B^{8} C[Gamma]^{6} D[Delta]-H[Theta]^{8} I^{8} K^{6}. Woodcut initials and headpieces. BM *15th cent.*, V, p. 556 (IB.24431). Goff (rev.), A-959. GW 2334. *ISTC*, ia00959000. (From title page) Aristotelous bios ek ton Laertiou – Tou autou bios kata Philoponon – Theophrastou bios ek ton Laertiou – Galenou periphilosophou historias – Aristotelous physikes akroaseos biblia okto – Peri ouranou biblia tessara – Peri geneseos kai phthoras biblia duo – Meteorologikon biblia tessara – Peri kosmou pros Alexandron biblion hen – Philonos Ioudaiou peri kosmou biblion hen – Theophrastou peri pyrosbiblion hen – Tou autou peri anemon biblion hen – Peri semeionhydaton [kai] pneumaton anonymou – Theophrastou peri lithon biblionhen.

Imperfect: lacks leaves 265-66 [K3.4]. Binding: half calf, brown marbled boards; edges red & yellow. Binder's title: Aristotelis et Theophrastes opera. Aldus, Venice, 1497.

87. ARRHENIUS, SVANTE, 1859-1927. *The destinies of the stars, by Svante Arrhenius. Authorized translation from the Swedish by J. E. Fries.*

New York, London: G. P. Putnam's Sons, 1918. xvii, 256 p. plates, fold. maps. 19 cm. Origin of star-worship. The mystery of the Milky Way. The climatic importance of water vapour. Atmosphere and physics of the stellar bodies. The chemistry of the atmosphere. The planet Mars. Mercury, the Moon, and Venus.

Advertisements: publisher's catalog: [6] p. at end.

88. *ARS journal. Bulletin June 1930-Apr. 1932. Astronautics May 1932-Dec. 1944. Journal*

Mar. 1945-Nov./Dec. 1953. Jet propulsion Feb. 1954-Dec. 1958.

Easton, Pa., American Rocket Society. Began publication with the June 1930 issue; ceased with v. 32, Dec. 1962. No. 1-85 (June 1930-June 1951) have no volume numbering but constitute v. 1-21, no. 4. Issued June 1930-May 1934 by the society under its earlier name: American Interplanetary Society. No. 1-50, June 1930-Oct. 1941, with no. 1-25. Merged with the *Journal of the aerospace sciences* (Institute of the Aerospace Sciences) to form the *AIAA journal* (American Institute of Aeronautics and Astronautics).

Reprint: *Jet propulsion, journal of the American Rocket Society* : (*Bulletin of the American Interplanetary Society*) : (*Astronautics*) : Volumes 1-2 (Nos. 1-25) : 1930-1932. New York : Kraus Reprint Corp., 1958.

89. ARTEDI, PETER, 1705-1735. *Petri Artedi sueci, medici Ichthyologia, sive Opera omnia de piscibus ... : omnia in hoc genere perfectiora, quam antea ulla, posthuma vindicauit, recognouit, coaptauit & edidit Carolus Linnæus....*

Lugduni Batavorum: Apud Conradum Wishoff, 1738. 5 pts. in 1 v.; 21 cm. Each part has special title page. Vignette on several of the added title pages: decorated borders and initials throughout text. Full extent: [24], 66, [6], 92 [i.e. 102], [2] (blank), [8], 84, [8], 102 [i.e. 112], [2], 118, [24] p.; numbers 71-80 repeated in the pagination of 4th group; p. 112 misnumbered 102 in 8th group. "Vita Petri Artedi descripta a Carolo Linnæo": p. [3]-[13] of 1st group. Includes indexes. Errata on p. [24] of last group. Waller E. *Bibliotheca Walleriana*, 11771. Soulsby. *Linnæus*, 3563. Wood, C. *Vertebrate zoology*, p. 204. (From title page) Bibliotheca ichthyologica. Philosophia ichthyologica. Genera piscium. Synonymia specierum. Descriptiones specierum.

"Privilegie" (in Dutch): [3] p. at end.

90. ASCHOFF, L. (LUDWIG), 1866-1942. *Ehrlich's Seitenkettentheorie und ihre Anwendung auf die künstlichen Immunisierungsprozesse, zusammenfassende Darstellung von Ludwig Aschoff.*

Jena: G. Fischer, 1902. [185] p., [1] folded leaf of plates: ill. (1 col.); 24 cm. "Abdruck aus: Zeitschrift für allgemeine Physiologie ... I. Band, III. Heft, 1902." Pagination: iv, [69]-100, 113-176, 165-248, [1] p. Includes bibliographies. Errata: final page.

91. ASPIN, JEHOSHAPHAT. *A familiar treatise on astronomy: explaining the general phenomena of celestial bodies ..., by Jehoshaphat Aspin; written expressly to accompany Urania's Mirror, or, A View of the Heavens, consisting of thirty-two cards, on which are represented all the constellations visible in Great Britain, on a plan perfectly original, designed by a lady. Fourth edition, with considerable augmentations and improvements.*

London: Printed for M. A. Leigh ..., 1834. xii, 199, [1] p., [4] folded leaves of plates: ill.; 24 cm. "Errata", p. [200].

92. ASTON, FRANCIS WILLIAM, 1877-1945. *Isotopes, by F. W. Aston....*

London: E. Arnold & Co., 1922. viii, 152 p. iv pl., diagrs. 22 cm.

93. *Astronomie / bearb. von L. Ambronn ... [et al.] ; unter Redaktion von J. Hartmann.*

Leipzig : B. G. Teubner, 1921. vii, 639 p., [4] leaves of plates : ill. ; 26 cm. Die Kultur der Gegenwart ; T. 3, Abt. 3, Bd. 3 Includes bibliographies and index.

Provenance: Eidgnössische Zentralbibliothek (inkstamp).

94. *Astronomy for amateurs. Prepared by the editorial staff of Popular Science monthly.*

New York: Grosset & Dunlap 1934. 192 p.: ill.; 21 cm. "Do-it-yourself" Books. Includes index.

95. *Astronomy for everyman. Contributors: M. B. B. Heath [and others].*

London: Dent; New York: Dutton 1953. 494 p. illus., maps, 23 cm. Ed. by Martin Davidson. Includes index.

96. *The atomic age opens. Prepared by the editors of Pocket Books.*

New York: Pocket Books, Inc., [1945]. 252 p., 1 l. illus. (incl. ports.) diagrs. 16 cm. Pocket Book, 340; "1st printing, August, 1945."

97. AUENBRUGGER, LEOPOLD, 1722-1809. *Leopoldi Auenbrugger ... Inventum novum: ex percussione thoracis humani ut signo abstrusos interni pectoris morbos detegendi.*

Vindobonæ: Typis Joannis Thomæ Trattner ..., 1761. 95 p.; 21 cm. Errors in pagination: p. 54 misnumbered as 45. In slipcase.

Provenance: Herbert McLean Evans (bookplate).

98. Babbage, Charles, 1791-1871. *Reflections on the decline of science in England: and on some of its causes , by Charles Babbage, esq.*
London: Printed for B. Fellowes ... and J. Booth ..., 1830. xii, 120 p.; 33 cm.
"Notes on a letter addressed by the Secretary of the Royal Society to the President" pasted in. Provenance: Mercantile Library Association, New York (inkstamp).

99. Babson Institute. Library. *A Supplement to the Catalogue of the Grace K. Babson Collection of the works of Sir Isaac Newton and related material in the Babson Institute Library, Babson Park, Massachusetts, compiled by Henry P. Macomber.*
Babson Park: Babson Institute, 1955. viii, 91 p.; 26 cm. "450 copies printed ... by the Anthoensen Press, Portland, Maine" – Colophon. "Errata in original catalogue": p. viii. Includes index.

100. Bacon, Francis, *1561-1626. Fr. Baconis de Verulam. Angliæ cancellarii De augmentis scientiarum lib. IX.*
Amstelædami: Sumptibus J. Ravesteinij, 1662. 10 p. l., 607, [67] p., [1] fold. table. 14 x 7 cm. Engraved title page.
Provenance: G[eo?] Cooke (signature).

101. Bacon, Francis, 1561-1626. *Francisci de Verulamio summi Angliæ cancelsarii Instauratio magna: multi pertransibunt & augebitur scientia.*
Londini: Apud Joannem Billium ... , 1620. [12], 172, 181-360, 36, [1] p.; 30 cm. Signatures: [a]^2, [paragraph sign]^4, A-C^6, D-S^4, 2T^6, a-e^4 ([a]1 and C4 blanks) "Distributio operis. Eius constituuntur partes sex. 1. Partitiones scientiarum. 2. Nouum organum. 3. Phænomena vniuersi. 4. Scala intellectus. 5. Prodromi. 6. Philosophia seunda." – p. 15. Of the six parts, this edition contains only the second part, the *Nouum organum*, followed by a sketch of the third, which the author calls "Parasceve, ad historiam naturalem, et experimentalem," and a "Catalogus historiarum particularium, secundùm capita". Works which represent the first and third parts were published later; of the fourth and fifth parts only prefaces were written. *STC* 1163. Engraved title page signed: Sim. Pass. sculp. Errata: on last page. Gibson, R. W. Bacon, 103b. Horblit, H. D. *Grolier 100 science books,* 8b.
Provenance: William Stirling Maxwell (armorial bookplate); Herbert McLean Evans (bookplate). Ms. notes pasted in.

102. Bacon, Francis, 1561-1626. *Of the proficience and advancement of learning, by Francis Lord Verulam; edited by B. Montagu....*
London: William Pickering, 1840. [2], xvi, 350 p.; 17 cm. Added title page dated 1838. Colophon: C. Whittingham, Tooks Court, Chancery Lane. Previously published in 1605, with title: The advancement of learning. cf. preface. Includes index.
Provenance: Estcourt Library (bookplate). Binder: H. Bull (ticket).

103. Bacon, Francis, 1561-1626. *The philosophical works of Francis Bacon, Baron of Verulam, Viscount St. Albans, and Lord High-Chancellor of England; Methodized, and made English from the Originals, with occasional notes, To explain what is obscure; and show how far the several PLANS of the AUTHOR, for the Advancement of all the Parts of Knowledge, have been executed to the Present Time. In Three Volumes. By Peter Shaw, M.D. Moniti Meliora.*
London: Printed for J. J. and P. Knapton; D. Midwinter and A. Ward; A. Bettesworth and C. Hitch; J. Pemberton; J. Osborn and T. Longman; C. Rivington; F. Clay; J. Batley; R. Hett; and T. Hatchett. M.DCC.XXXIII [1733]. 3 v. 26 cm. Includes index.
Provenance: James F. Torr, John B. Torr, Albert Lane (inscriptions).

104. Bacon, Francis, 1561-1626. *The tvvoo bookes of Francis Bacon, of the proficience and aduancement of learning, diuine and humane.*
At London: Printed for Henrie Tomes ..., 1605. [1], 45, 118 [i.e. 121], [1] leaves (last leaf blank); 20 cm. "To the King." Better known under title: *Advancement of learning.* An expanded translation was published in 1623 under title: *De dignitate et augmentis scientiarum,* becoming afterward better known as *De augmentis scientiarum* and forming the first part of the author's *Instauratio magna.* Signatures: A-L^4 M^2 2A-3G^4 3H^2. Many errors of foliation. Without the two leaves of errata sometimes found after leaf 3H2. STC 1164. Pforzheimer 36. Horblit, H. D. *Grolier 100 science books,* 8a. Gibson 81.

Last (blank) leaf missing. Provenance: William Reynell Anson (armorial bookplate).

105. Bacon, Roger, 1214?-1294. *Opus majus. Fratris Rogeri Bacon, ordinis minorum, Opus majus ..., Ex MS. Codice Dubliniense, cum aliis quibusdam collato, nunc primum edidit S. Jebb....*

Londini: Typis Gulielmi Bowyer, MDCCXXXIII [1733]. [30], 477, [5] p., [3] folded leaves of plates: ill.; 39 cm. Yale. *Cushing*, B20. Includes index. Plates signed: Clark sc.

Provenance: Tho. Llewelyn (armorial giftplate); Library, Baptist College, Bristol (bookplate).

106. Baden-Powell, B. F. S. (Baden Fletcher Smyth), 1860- . *Recent aeronautical progress, and deductions to be drawn therefrom, regarding the future of aerial navigation, by B. F. S. Baden-Powell.*

p. 121-131; 23 cm. Caption title. "Presidential address before the Aeronautical Society of Great Britain, London, December 4, 1902. Reprinted ... from the *Aeronautical Journal*, No. 25, Vol. VII, January, 1903", p. 121. In: Smithsonian Institution. Board of Regents. *Annual report of the Board of Regents of the Smithsonian Institution.* 1902.

107. Baer, Karl Ernst von, 1792-1876. *De ovi mammalium et hominis genesi; epistolam ad Academiam Imperialem Scientiarum Petropolitanam dedit Carolus Ernestus a Baer. Cum tabulaæ nea.*

Lipsiae: L. Vossii, 1827. 40, [1] p. col. pl. 30 x 24 cm. Illustrated by the author. Horblit, H. D. *Grolier 100 science books*, 9b.

Provenance: Herbert McLean Evans (bookplate); Harrison D. Horblit (bookplate).

108. Baer, Karl Ernst von, 1792-1876. *Entwickelt sich die Larve der einfachen Ascidien in der ersten Zeit nach dem Typus der Wirbelthiere? / von Dr. K. E. v. Baer....*

St.-Pétersbourg: Commissionnaires de l'Académie Impériale des Sciences; MM. Eggers et Cie [and 3 others]; M. N. Kymmel; M. A. E. Kechribardchi; M. Léopold Voss, [1873]. [2], 35, [1] p., [1] leaf of plates: ill.; 31 cm. Mémoires de l'Académie Impériale des Sciences de St.-Pétersbourg. VIIe série; t. 19, no. 8. "Lu le 28 août 1873." Includes bibliographical references.

Original printed wrapper bound in. Provenance: Herbert McLean Evans (bookplate); author's presentation inscription to Professor Waldeyer.

109. Baer, Karl Ernst von, 1792-1876. *Reden gehalten in wissenschaftlichen Versammlungen und kleinere Aufsätze vermischten Inhalts.*

St. Petersburg: H. Schmitzdorff, 1864-76. 3 v. ill., ports. 21 cm. Bibliographical footnotes. Th. 1. Reden. Th. 2. Studien aus dem Gebiete der Naturwissenschaften. Th. 3. Historische Fragen mit Hülfe der Naturwissenschaften beantwortet. 1873.

2.T., 1. Hälfte imprint date: 1873. Provenance: Ernst Mach (inkstamp); Herbert McLean Evans (bookplate).

110. Baer, Karl Ernst von, 1792-1876. *Über Entwickelungs-geschichte der Thiere: Beobachtung und Reflexion, von Dr. Karl Ernst v. Baer. Erster[-zweiter Theil ...].*

Königsberg: Bei den Gebrüdern Bornträger, 1828-1888. 2 v. in 3: ill. (some col.); 25 cm. Consists of Erster Theil [1828], Zweiter Theil [1837], and Zweiter Theil, Schlussheft, edited by Ludwig Stieda [1888]. Imprint varies: 2. Theil, Schlussheft published by Wilh. Koch. Full extent: Vol. 1: xxii, [2], 271, [1] p., III folded leaves of plates, 1 folded table; v. 2: [4], 315, [1] p., plates IV-VII; v. 2, pt. 2:V, [1], 84 p. Zweiter Theil, Schlussheft has double numbering: separately as p. 1-84, and continuous from first part of Zweiter Theil as p. [317]-400. Includes bibliographical references. 1. Th. Entwickelungsgeschichte des Hühnchen's im Eie. Scholien und Corollarien zu der Entwickelungsgeschichte des Hühnchens im Eie. 2. Th.Vorlesungen über Zeugung und Entwickelung der organischen Körper ...3. Th., Schlusshft. Studien aus der Entwickelungs-geschichte des Menschen. Horblit, H. D. *Grolier 100 science books*, 9a. Wood, C. *Vertebrate zoology*, p. 215.

Provenance: Herbert McLean Evans (bookplate).

111. Bailly, Jean Sylvain, 1736-1793. *Histoire de l'astronomie ancienne, depuis son origine jusqu'à l'établissement de l'école d'Alexandrie, par M. Bailly.*

Paris: Frères De Bure, 1775. 1 p. l., xxii, 526 p. 3 fold. pl. 27 cm. Illustrated by Fossier and Y. le Gouaz. Includes bibliographical references.

Provenance: James Banks Stanhope (armorial bookplate).

112. Bailly, Jean Sylvain, 1736-1793. *Histoire de l'astronomie moderne depuis la fondation de*

l'école d'Alexandrie, jusqu'à l'époque de M.D.CC.XXX.....
À Paris: Chez les Frères De Bure, 1779-82. 3 v. 18 plates. 27 cm. On title page of v. 3: Jusqu'à l'époque de M.D.CC.LXXXII.

113. BAILLY, JEAN SYLVAIN, 1736-1793. *Lettres sur l'origine des sciences, et sur celle des peuples de l'Asie, adressées à M. de Voltaire, par M. Bailly, & précédées de quelques lettres de M. de Voltaire à l'auteur....*
À Londres: Chez M. Elmesly; Chez les frères De Bure, 1777. [4], 348 p.: 21 cm. Faute á corriger: on p. 348.

114. BAILLY, JEAN SYLVAIN, 1736-1793. *Traité de l'astronomie indienne et orientale, ouvrage qui peut servir de suite à l'histoire de l'astronomie ancienne. Par M. Bailly....*
À Paris: Chez De Bure l'aîné, 1787. 2 p. l., clxxx, 427 p. 26 cm. Head- and tail vignettes.
Provenance: James Banks Stanhope (armorial bookplate).

115. BAILY, FRANCIS, 1774-1844. *Astronomical tables and formulæ together with a variety of problems explanatory of their use and application. To which are prefixed the Elements of the solar system. By Francis Baily....*
London: Printed by R. Taylor, 1827. xvi, 304 p. 22 cm. Problems: p. [217]-264.
Provenance: Thomas Aiskew Larcom (armorial bookplate).

116. BAILY, FRANCIS, 1774-1844. *On the new method of determining the longitude by the culmination of the moon and stars: being a paper read before the Astronomical Society of London. To which are now added an appendix and a list of stars, applicable to the purpose, for the year 1825. By Francis Baily....*
London: Printed by R. Taylor, 1824. 1 p. l., 48 p. tables. 28 x 22 cm.

117. BAKER, ROBERT HORACE, 1883- *Introducing the constellations, Robert H. Baker.*
New York: Viking Press, 1942, c1937. 205 p., [30] p. of plates: ill.; 21 cm. Includes index.

118. BAKER, ROBERT HORACE, 1883- *The universe unfolding; the story of man's increasing comprehension of the universe around him, by Robert H. Baker.*
Baltimore: The Williams & Wilkins Company and Associates in cooperation with the Century of Progress Exposition, 1932. x, 140 p. illus., 8 pl., diagrs. 20 cm. Century of Progress series.

119. BAKER, ROBERT HORACE, 1883- *When the stars come out.*
New York: The Viking Press, 1934. ix, 188 p. illus., plates. 22 cm. Illustrated lining-papers. At head of title: Robert H. Baker. Includes index.
Provenance: Frederic H. Maude (signature).

120. BALL, ROBERT S. (ROBERT STAWELL), SIR, 1840-1913. *Astronomy, by R. S. Ball. Specially revised for America by Simon Newcomb.*
New York: H. Holt and Company, 1878. 1 p. l., [v]-xiii, 154 p. illus., diagrs. 17 cm. Handbooks for students and general readers. Includes index.

121. BALL, ROBERT S. (ROBERT STAWELL), SIR, 1840-1913. *An atlas of astronomy; a series of seventy-two plates, with introduction and index. By Sir Robert Stawell Ball.*
London: 1892. xi, 57, 17 p. 72 pl. (part col.) 22 x 19 cm. Plates 12 and 27-38 accompanied by key maps.

122. BALL, ROBERT S. (ROBERT STAWELL), SIR, 1840-1913. *The earth's beginning, by Sir Robert Stawell Ball, with four colored plates and numerous illustrations.*
New York: D. Appleton and Company, 1902. xii, 384 p. col. front., illus. (incl. port) 2 col. pl., map. 20 cm. Royal Institution of Great Britain Christmas lectures, 1900. Includes index. "Earthquakes and volcanoes," p. [158]-190, includes illustrated account of the Krakatoa eruption, 1883.

123. BALL, ROBERT S. (ROBERT STAWELL), SIR, 1840-1913. *Great astronomers, by Sir Robert S. Ball. Cheap ed.*
London; New York: I. Pitman, 1920. xii, 372 p.: ill, ports.; 21 cm. Advertisements: title page verso.

124. BALL, ROBERT S. (ROBERT STAWELL), SIR, 1840-1913. *Great astronomers, by Sir Robert S. Ball ... With numerous illustrations.*

London: Isbister and Company ..., 1895. xii, 372 p. front., illus., ports., diagrs. 21 cm. Advertisements: verso half-title. Ptolemy. Copernicus. Tycho Brahe. Galileo. Kepler. Isaac Newton. Flamsteed. Halley. Bradley. William Herschel. Laplace. Brinkley. John Herschel. The Earl of Rosse. Airy. Hamilton. Le Verrier. Adams.

125. BALL, ROBERT S. (ROBERT STAWELL), SIR, 1840-1913. *In starry realms, by Sir Robert S. Ball.*

London: Isbister and Co., 1893. x, 371 p.: ill., maps; 21 cm. "Sixth thousand." Includes index.

Provenance: Delia A. Montgomery (inscription).

126. BALL, ROBERT S. (ROBERT STAWELL), SIR, 1840-1913. *In the high heavens, by Sir Robert S. Ball. Cheap edition.*

London; New York: I. Pitman & Sons, 1908. 383 p.: ill., maps; 21 cm. Includes index.

Provenance: University Club of Chicago (bookplate).

127. BALL, ROBERT S. (ROBERT STAWELL), SIR, 1840-1913. *A popular guide to the heavens: a series of eighty-three plates, with explanatory text & index, by Sir Robert Stawell Ball. 3rd edition.*

New York: D. Van Nostrand, 1913. xii, 96 p., 83 leaves of plates: ill., maps; 22 cm. Cover title: Ball's popular guide to the heavens. "Third edition, 1910. Re-issued in cheaper form in 1913". Title page verso. Includes index.

128. BALL, ROBERT S. (ROBERT STAWELL), SIR, 1840-1913. *Star-land. Being talks with young people about the wonders of the heavens. By Sir Robert Stawell Ball ... Illustrated. 5th thousand.*

London, New York [etc.]: Cassell & Company, Limited, 1890. xii, 376 p. incl. front., illus. 19 cm. Includes index.

Provenance: Frank S. Simons (signature).

129. BALL, ROBERT S. (ROBERT STAWELL), SIR, 1840-1913. *Star-land; being talks with young people about the wonders of the heavens, by Sir Robert Stawell Ball ... New and revised edition.*

Boston, London: Ginn & Company, [c1899]. viii, 402 p. front., illus. 19 cm. Includes index. I. The sun. II. The moon. III. The inner planets. IV. The giant planets. V. Comets and shooting stars. VI. Stars. How to name the stars.

Provenance: L. A. Thompson (signature).

130. BALL, ROBERT S. (ROBERT STAWELL), SIR, 1840-1913. *The story of the heavens, by Sir Robert Stawell Ball ... Second edition.*

London, Paris, New York & Melbourne: Cassell & Company, Limited, 1886. xix, [1], 551 p., XVI leaves of plates: ill. (some col.); 24 cm. Includes index.

131. BALL, ROBERT S. (ROBERT STAWELL), SIR, 1840-1913. *The story of the heavens, by Sir Robert Stawell Ball....*

London, Paris, New York, Melbourne: Cassell and Company, 1885. xix, 551 p. XVI plates (part col.). 22 cm. Includes index.

Binder: Robertson, Edin[burgh] (stamp). Provenance: Society of Writers to the Signet (stamp on binding).

132. BALL, ROBERT S. (ROBERT STAWELL), SIR, 1840-1913. *The story of the heavens, by Sir Robert S. Ball.*

New York: Funk and Wagnalls, [1886?] xix, 568 p. ill. (some col.), maps; 24 cm. Includes index. "Preface to original edition": p. [5], dated 1886.

133. BALL, ROBERT S. (ROBERT STAWELL), SIR, 1840-1913. *The story of the sun, by Sir Robert S. Ball.*

London; New York: Cassell, 1910. viii, 376 p., XI leaves of plates: ill. (some col.), maps; 23 cm. Includes index.

134. BALL, ROBERT S. (ROBERT STAWELL), SIR, 1840-1913. *Time and tide, a romance of the moon. By Sir Robert S. Ball ... 4th edition, revised.*

E. & J. B. Young & Co., 1899. 4 p. l., [9]-192 p. incl. front., illus. 18 cm. Romance of science. Based on lectures on the theory of tidal evolution, delivered before the London Institution. Includes index.

Advertisements: 8 p. at end. Provenance: Dr. R. N. Bell (signature); ms. marginalia.

135. BALL, ROBERT S. (ROBERT STAWELL), SIR, 1840-1913. *A treatise on spherical astronomy, by Sir Robert Ball.*

Cambridge: University Press, 1908. xii, 506 p. diagrs. 23 cm. Includes index.
Provenance: Harold S. Jones (signature).

136. Bardeen, John, 1908- . *The transistor, a semi-conductor triode, J. Bardeen and W. H. Brattain.*
Lancaster: Published for the Physical Society by the American Institute of Physics, 1948. p. 230-231: ill.; 27 cm. Physical review; 2nd ser., v. 74 no. 2. Caption title. Includes bibliographical references.

137. Barlow, C. W. C. (Crossley William Crosby), b. 1863. *Elementary mathematical astronomy, by C. W. C. Barlow and G. H. Bryan. 7th impression [2nd edition].*
London: W. B. Clive, University Tutorial Press, Ltd., 1919. [8], vi, 442 p.: ill.; 18 cm.
Provenance: Dr. W. Harvey Callander (signature).

138. Barnard, Edward Emerson, 1857-1923. *Photographs of the Milky Way and of comets, made with the six-inch Willard lens and Crocker telescope during the years 1892 to 1895, by E. E. Barnard....*
Sacramento: F. W. Richardson, Superintendent of State Printing, 1913). 46 p. front., CXXIX pl. 30 x 25 cm. University of California Publications. Publications of the Lick Observatory; v. 11. Each plate accompanied by guard sheet with descriptive letterpress. Bibliography: p. 43-44.

139. Barozzi, Francesco, 1537-1604. *Cosmografia in quattro libri diuisa: la quale con sommo ordine, e marauigliosa facilità, e breuità introduce alla grande Mathematicaco [n]struttione di Tolomeo, & à tutta l'astrologia, composta da Francesco Barozzi gentil'huomo Venetiano; con la prefatione di esso autore.*
In Venetia: Presso Gratioso Perchacino, 1607. [8], 230 [i.e. 228], [16] leaves, [3] folded leaves of plates: ill.; 19 cm. Includes index. Translated from the Latin. Leaf 77 misnumbered 66, 79 as 69, 184 as 172, 200 as 220, 223 as 225, 225-226 as 227-228, 227 as 129, 228 as 230. Riccardi, P. *Bib. matematica*, v. 1, column 85.

140. Bartholin, Thomas, 1616-1680. *Thomae Bartholini D. & Prof. Reg. De Lacteis thoracicis in homine brutisque nuperrimè observatis, historia anatomica: publicè proposita respondente M. Michaele Lysero.*
Londini: Impensis Octaviani Pulleyn, typis Johannis Grismond, 1652. [4], 103 p., [1] folded leaf of plates: ill.; 15 cm. Error in pagination: p. 92 misnumbered 100. Wing (2nd edition) B978.
Provenance: T. Canonge (inscription), Herbert McLean Evans (bookplate).

141. Battani, Mu'hammad ibn Jabir, d. 929. *De numeris stellarum et motibus, Albategnius.*
Bononiæ: Typis hæredis Victorij Benatij, 1645. [16], 228, [4] p.: ill.; 24 cm. Additional engraved title page: Mahometis Albatenii De scientia stellarum liber cum aliquot additionibus Ioannis Regiomontani ex Bibliotheca Vaticana transcriptus. Signed: Coriolanus F. Statement of responsibility transposed. Imprint from colophon. Errata: p. [1]-[2] following text.
Provenance: J. Willmet (inscription), Radcliffe Observatory, Oxford (inkstamp).

142. Bauhin, Caspar, 1560-1624. *Catalogus plantarum circa Basileam sponte nascentium cum earundem synonymiis & locis in quibus reperiuntur....*
Basileae: Typis Johan. Jacobi Genathii, 1622. 113, [15] p.; 18 cm. At head of title: Caspari Bauhini Basil. Archiatri.
Provenance: Franz Bernoulli. Bernoulli & Daniel Bernoulli-Glitsch (bookplate); Prof. G. Senn-Bernoulli (inscription). Extensive ms. marginalia throughout.

143. Bauhin, Caspar, 1560-1624. *Pinax theatri botanici, Caspari Bauhini ... siue Index in Theophrasti Dioscoridis, Plinii et botanicorum qui à seculo scripserunt opera: plantarum circiter sex millium ab ipsis exhibitarum nomina cum earundem synonymiis & differentiis methodicè secundùm earum & genera & species proponens. Opus XL. annorum hactenus non editum summoperæ expetitum & ad auctores intelligendos plurimùm faciens....*
Basileæ Helvet: Sumptibus & typis Ludovici Regis., MDCXXIII, 1623. [24], 522, [24] p.; 25 cm. First word of title romanized. Title vignette; decorated borders and initials. "Nomina authorum quorum operà usi summus": p. [11]-[17] of 1st group. Errata on p. [23] of last group; appendix of addenda and emendanda on p. 516-522. Pritzel 509. Yale. *Cushing Coll.* B174. *PMM* 121. Includes index.

144. Bavink, Bernhard, 1879-1947. *Grundriss der neueren Atomistik. Mit einem Anhang: Elementare Ableitung einiger wichtiger mathematischer Formulierungen, von Bernhard Bavink. Mit 41 Abbildungen.*
Leipzig: S. Hirzel, 1922. vi, 130 p. illus., diagrs. 24 cm. Bibliography: p. iv, 129-130, and in footnotes. Advertisements on lower wrapper. Includes index.

145. Bayer, Johann, fl. 1600. *Ioannis Bayeri Rhainani I. C. Vranometria: omnium asterismorum continens schemata....*
Vlmæ: Sumptibus Iohannis Görlini, 1639. [1], [51] folded leaves: all ill.; 31 cm.
Provenance: Herman S. Davis (bookplate). Ms. notes. Typed note attached. With: *De fide Uranometriæ Bayeri*, scripsit D. Fridericus Guilelmus Augustus Argelander. Bonnæ: Typis Caroli Georgii, 1842.

146. Beaumont, William, 1785-1853. *Experiments and observations on the gastric juice, and the physiology of digestion. By William Beaumont....*
Plattsburgh: Printed by F. P. Allen., 1833. 280 p.: ill.; 24 cm. Based upon observations of the digestive processes of Alexis St. Martin. Errata on p. 279. Horblit, H. D. *Grolier 100 science books*, 10.
Newspaper cutting (New York Times, Sept. 9, 1901) pasted in.

147. Becher, Johann Joachim, 1635-1682. *Actorum laboratorii chymici monacensis, seu Physicæ subterraneæ libri duo, quorum prior profundam subterraneorum genesin, nec non admirandam globi terr-aque-aerei super & subterranei fabricam, posterior specialem subterraneorum naturam, resolutionem in partes partium[que]; proprietates exponit, accesserunt sub finem mille hypotheses seu mixtiones chymicæ ante hac nunquam visæ, omnia, plusquam mille experimentis stabilita, sumptibus & permissu serenissimi electoris. Bavariæ & c. domini sui clementissimi elaboravit & publicavit Joannes Joachimus Becherus.*
Francofurti: imp. J. D. Zunneri, 1669. 19 p. l., 653 [i.e. 631], [7] p. front. 17 cm. 1st edition. Errata: [7] p. Errors in pagination: p. 113-114 omitted from numbering. Duveen, D. I. *Alchemica et chemica*, p. 56. Ferguson, J. *Bib. chemica* I, p. 88.
Provenance: Bibliothec. Monast. Lambacens. (book stamp); Robert Honeyman IV (bookplate).

148. Becquerel, Henri, 1852-1908. *Betrachtungen über eine moderne Theorie der Materie / von Henri Becquerel.*
Leipzig : S. Hirzel, 1908. p. [361]-369 ; 25 cm. In: Jahrbuch der Radioaktivität und Elektronik, 4. Bd. 1907. Caption title. At head of title: Originalabhandlungen.

149. Becquerel, Henri, 1852-1908. *Recherches sur une propriété nouvelle de la matière: activité radiante spontanée ou radioactivité de la matière, par M. Henri Becquerel.*
[Paris]: Firmin-Didot, 1903. p. 1-360, [4] p., xiii leaves of plates: ill.; 29 cm. Mémoires de l'Académie des Sciences de l'Institut de France; t. 46. Caption title. Errata: p. [361]. Bibliography: p. [337]-355.

150. Becquerel, Ed., 1820-1891. *Mémoire sur l'analyse de la lumière émise par les composés d'uranium phosphorescents, par M. Edmond Becquerel; lu dans la séance du 5 août 1872.*
Paris: Typographie de Firmin Didot frères, fils et cie ..., 1872. [2], 40 p.: ill.; 29 cm. At head of title: Institut de France. "Extrait du tome XL des Mémoires de l'Académie des Sciences." Includes bibliographical references.

151. Bede, the Venerable, Saint, 673-735. *Opera Bedæ Venerabilis ... omnia in octo tomos distincta, prout statim post præfationem suo elencho enumerantur. Addito rerum & verborum indice copiosissimo....*
Basileae: per Ioannem Hervagium, 1563. 8 v. in 4. illus. (incl. maps, music) tables, diagrs. 39 cm. Title within architectural border, with device of Johann Herwagen the younger; another form of this device on leaf at end of v. 8; initials. Vols. 2-8 have special title page only; v. 4-6, undated. Printed in double columns. Includes index.
Provenance: Rev. Mgr. McMahon (bookplate).

152. Beer, Wilhelm, 1797-1850. *Mappa selenographica : totam lunae hemisphaeram visibilem complectens observationibus*

propriis ... / quatuor sectionibus constructa et delineata ; suae Majestati Friderico Sexto, regi daniae illustrissimo summa veneratione dedicata ; auctoribus Guilelmo Beer et Joanne Henrico Maedler ; ex autographo in lapidem incidit Carolus Vogel. Editio genuina. Scale not given.

Berolini : Apud Simon Schropp & Soc., [1836] 1 map in 4 sections : mounted on linen ; 94 cm. in diam., on sheets 76 x 60 cm., folded to 38 x 30 cm. "Geogr. Milliaria, 15=1^{0} Aequatoris terrestris, 4,088=1^{0} Aequatoris lunaris." "Secundum projectionem orthographicam." Relief shown by hachures and shading. Ancillary maps: Mittlere Gegend der Mondoberfläche – Ringgebirg Petavius : gezeichnet in Dorpat in vier ausgezeichnet heitern Nächten, 1832 Januar 9.10. März 4.6.

Provenance: Herbert McLean Evans (bookplate).

153. Beer, Wilhelm, 1797-1850. *Der Mond nach seinen kosmischen und individuellen Verhältnissen; oder, Allgemeine vergleichende Selenographie. Mit besondrer Beziehung auf die von den Verfassern herausgegebene Mappa selenographica. Von Wilhelm Beerund dr. Johann Heinrich Mädler.*

Berlin: S. Schropp & Comp., 1837. xviii p., 1 l., 412 p. 5 pl. 31 cm. Includes index. "Historische übersicht der selenographie": p. [169]-188. Errata: p. xviii. 1. Th. Mathematische und physische Selenographie. 2. Th. Topographieder sichtbaren Mondsoberfläche.

Provenance: Herbert McLean Evans (bookplate).

154. Beet, E. A. (Ernest Agar). *A text book of elementary astronomy, by Ernest Agar Beet. Reprinted with corrections.*

Cambridge: University Press, 1953. x, 110 p., [13] leaves of plates: ill.; 19 cm. Bibliography: p. 106. Includes index.

155. Behring, Emil von, 1854-1917. *Die Geschichte der Diphtherie: mit besonderer Berücksichtigung der Immunitätslehre, von Stabsarzt Prof. Dr. Behring.*

Leipzig: Verlag von Georg Thieme, 1893. VI, [2], 208 p.; 23 cm. Includes bibliographical references and index.

Provenance: Prof. Löffler (inscription).

156. Beima, Elto Martens, 1807-1873. *Verhandeling over den ring van Saturnus: van zijne eerste ontdekking af tot op den tegenwoordigen tijd: een leesboek voor alle standen, door E. M. Beima....*

Te Leiden: Bij S. en J. Luchtmans, 1843. VIII, 237, [2] p., IV folded leaves of plates: ill.; 24 cm. "Verbeteringen": p. [239]. Includes bibliographical references.

157. *Beiträge zur Biologie der Pflanzen.*

Breslau : J. U. Kern's Verlag (Max Müller), 1870- v. : ill. (some col.); 26 cm. 1. Bd.- Title from cover. Indexed by: *Life sciences collection, Excerpta medica, Biological abstracts* ISSN:0006-3169, *Bibliography of agriculture* ISSN:0006-1530, *Energy research abstracts* ISSN:0160-3604. Publication suspended 1945-1949. Vols. for 1932- : text in German, English, or French; Summaries in German or English. Editors: 1. Bd-7. Bd., F. Cohn; 8. Bd., O. Brefeld; 9. Bd.-14 Bd., pt. 2, F. Rosen.

Library has: 1-2, 1870-77. vol. I-II: Provenance: Herbert McLean Evans (bookplate); Senn Collection, Newberry Library (bookplates, perforation stamp); D. V. Dean (signature).

158. Belon, Pierre, 1517?-1564. *L'histoire de la nature des oyseaux: avec leurs descriptions, & naïfs portraicts retirez du naturel: escrite en sept livres, par Pierre Belon du Mans.*

À Paris: Chez Guillaume Cauellat ..., 1555. [28], 381, [1] p.: ill., port.; 35 cm. Running title: De la nature des oyseaux. Colophon contains statement: Imprime a Paris par Benoist Preuost ... 1555. Each part except the first has a separate title page. Includes index. Wood, C. *Vertebrate zoology*, p. 230. Nissen. *Vogelbücher*, 86. Zimmer, J. T. *Ayer Lib.*, pt. 1, p. 52.

159. Belon, Pierre, 1517?-1564. *Les observations de plvsievrs singvlaritez et choses memorables, trouuées en Grece, Asie, Iudée, Egypte, Arabie, & autres pays estranges, redigées en trois liures, par Pierre Belon du Mans....*

Paris: En la boutique de Gilles Corrozet, 1553. 12 p. l., 210 numb. l., [4] p. illus. 25 cm. Colophon: Imprimé à Paris par Benoist Preuost ... Pour Gilles Corrozet. & Guillaume Cauellat libraires, 1553. Books 2 and 3 have special title pages. Brunet, v.1, column 762. Grässe, v.1, p. 331.

Leaves 206 & 207 bound in reverse order. Provenance: Oetting Wallerstein (inkstamp); Herbert McLean Evans (bookplate).

DES OYSEAVX, PAR P. BELON. 41

La comparaison du susdit portraict des os humains monstre combien cestuy cy qui est d'vn oyseau, en est prochain.

Portraict des os de l'oyseau.

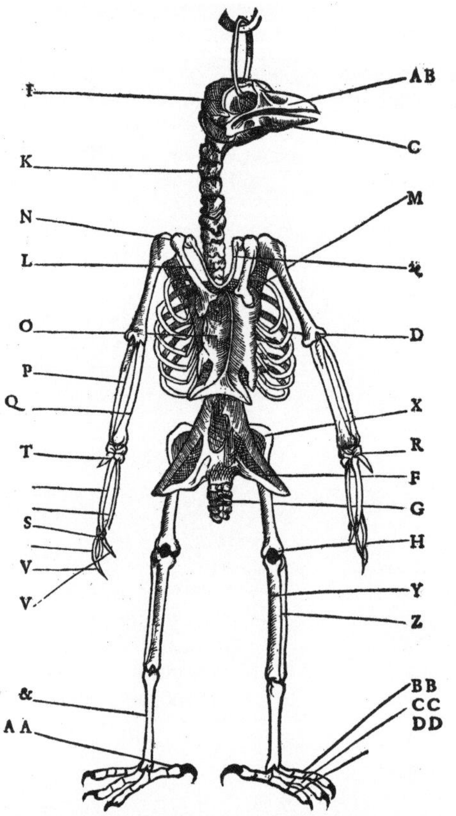

A B Les Oyseaux n'ont dents ne leures, mais ont le bec tranchant fort ou foible, plus ou moins selon l'affaire qu'ils ont eu à mettre en pieces ce dont ils viuent.

M Deux pallerons longs & estroicts, vn en chascun costé.

ꝛ L'os qu'on nommé la Lunette ou Fourchette n'est trouué en aucun autre animal, hors mis en l'oyseau.

D Six costes, attachees au coffre de l'estomach par deuāt, & aux six vertebres du dos par derriere.

F Les deux os des hanches sont longs, car il n'y a aucunes vertebres au desoubs des costes.

G Six osselets au cropion.

H La rouelle du genoil.

I Les sutures du test n'apparoissent gueres sinon qu'il soit boully.

k Douze vertebres au col, & six au dos.

d iii

Belon, *L'histoire de la nature des oyseaux*, 1555

160. BELOT, EMILE, b. 1857. *L'origine dualiste des mondes: essai de cosmogonie tourbillonnaire, par E. Belot....*

Paris: Gauthier-Villars ..., 1911. XI, [1] (blank), 280 p., [3] leaves of plates: ill.; 25 cm. Includes bibliographical references.

Advertisements: 2 p., loosely inserted; [1] p. lower wrapper.

161. BENEDEN, ÉDOUARD VAN, 1846-1910. *Recherches sur la composition et la signification de l'oeuf: basées sur l'étude de son mode de formation et des premiers phénomènes embryonnaires (mammifères, oiseaux, crustacés, vers), par Édouard van Beneden....*

Bruxelles: F. Hayez ..., 1870. [2], 283 p., XII leaves of plates: ill.; 29 cm. "Mémoire présenté le 1er août 1868 et couronné par l'Académie Royale de Belgique dans la séance publique de la classe des sciences du 16 décembre 1868." "Extrait du tome XXXIV des *Mémoires couronnés et Mémoires des savants étrangers*, publiés par l'Académie Royale de Belgique." Includes bibliographical references.

Provenance: Herbert McLean Evans (bookplate); author's signed presentation inscription to Alex Brandt. Original printed buff wrapper used as endsheet.

162. BENTLEY, RICHARD, 1662-1742. *The folly and unreasonableness of atheism: demonstrated from the advantage and pleasure of a religious life, the faculties of human souls, the structure of animate bodies, & the origin and frame of the world: in eight sermons preached at the lecture founded by the Honourable Robert Boyle, esquire; in the first year MDCXCII, by Richard Bentley....*

London: Printed by J. H. for H. Mortlock ..., 1693. [6], 40, 39, [1], 33, [1], 36, 36, [2], 34, 40, 42 p.; 21 cm. Each pt. has separate title page dated 1692.

Provenance: J. Coke Sutton (inscription); Herbert McLean Evans (bookplate).

163. BENZI, UGO, 1376-1439. *Excellentissimi viri Vgonis senensis in prima[m] fen primi canonis Auicene expositio feliciter incipit.*

Impressum Ferrarie: opera Andree Galli ..., 1491, die v[er]o xiii me[n]sis Augusti [13 Aug., 1491]. [320] p.; 33 cm. Title from incipit, p. [3]. Imprint from colophon, p. [307] (N8r). Described in Goff as: *Expositio in primam et secundam fen primi canonis Avicennæ.* Signatures: a-g^8 h^4 A-D^8 E^6 F-G^8 H-I^6 K^8. Two columns, 55 lines. Initial spaces with printed guide letters. BM *15th cent.*, VI, p. 604 (IB.25711). Goff (rev.), H-544. Hain-Copinger-Reichling, 9016. *ISTC*, ih00544000. Klebs, 998.1. Stillwell, M. B. *Science*, 303. "Eiusde[m] magistri Antonij Fauentini q[uaesti]o de febre nup[er] editain felici studio Ferrariensi": p. [308]-[318].

Rubrication: paragraph marks and initial-strokes added in red or brown. Binding: modern vellum, in red half-morocco case. Binder: James MacDonald Co., New York City (stamp on case). Spine title: Hugo Senensis expositio. Ferrara. Case title: Expositio Avicene. Provenance: Robert Honeyman IV (bookplate); ms. marginalia & underscoring.

164. BERG, OTTO. *Das Relativitätsprinzip der Elektrodynamik.*

Göttingen: Vandenhoeck & Ruprecht, 1910. 50 p. 24 cm. Double paging. "Sonderdruck aus den 'Abhandlungen der Fries'schen Schule', III. Bd.,2. Heft." Advertisements on lower wrapper. Bibliographical footnotes.

165. BERGH, GEORGE VAN DEN, 1890-1966. *Astronomy for the millions, by Prof. G. van den Bergh; translated from the Dutch by Joan C. H. Marshall & Th. de Vrijer; with 18 halftone and 34 line illustrations.*

New York: E. P. Dutton and Company, Inc. c1937. xi, [1] p., 1 l., 370 p. illus., diagrs. 23 cm. "First (American) edition." "Published in England as "The universe in space and time". Translation of *Aarde en wereld in ruimte en tijd.* Includes index.

166. BERKELEY, GEORGE, 1685-1753. *Alciphron, or, The minute philosopher: in seven dialogues, containing an apology for the Christian religion, against those who are called free-thinkers.*

Dublin: Printed for G. Risk, G. Ewing, and W. Smith ..., 1732. 2 v. in 1: ill.; 21 cm. "An essay towards a new theory of vision. First published in the year MDCCIX" [with a special title page]: v. 2, p. [143]-245.

167. BERKELEY, GEORGE, 1685-1753. *The analyst; or, a discourse addressed to an infidel mathematician: wherein it is examined whether the object, principles, and inferences of the modern analysis are more distinctly con-*

ceived, or more evidently deduced, than religious mysteries and points of faith, by the author of The minute philosopher.
London: Printed for J. Tonson ... , 1734. [8], 94, [2] p.: ill.; 20 cm. Errata: p. [96]. Keynes, G. Berkeley, 32.
On p. 85 the printed word: "Science" is scored out by hand and "evidence" written on the margin.

168. Berkeley, George, 1685-1753. *An essay towards a new theory of vision. By George Berkeley,....*
Dublin: Printed by Aaron Rhames ... for Jeremy Pepyat ..., MDCCIX [1709]. xiv, [10], 187, [1] p. (last page blank): ill.; 23 cm. Jessop, T. E. (2nd edition) Berkeley 25a. Errata: p. [10]. Keynes, G. Berkeley, 1.
Large, thick paper copy. Provenance: Herbert McLean Evans (bookplate); W. Palliser (presentation copy from the author).

169. Berkeley, George, 1685-1753. *A treatise concerning the principles of human knowledge. Part I.: wherein the chief causes of error and difficulty in the sciences, with the grounds of scepticism, atheism, and irreligion, are inquir'd into, by George Berkeley ...*
Dublin: Printed by Aaron Rhames, for Jeremy Pepyat ... , 1710. [2], iii, [3], 214 p.; 21 cm. Errata: p [3]. No more published. Jessop, T. E. *Berkeley* (2nd ed.), 35a. Keynes, G. *Berkeley*, 5.
Provenance: Herbert McLean Evans.

170. Bernard, Claude, 1813-1878. *Introduction à l'étude de la médecine expérimentale, par M. Claude Bernard....*
Paris: J. B. Baillière et fils ...; Hippolyte Baillière; C.Bailly-Baillière; Baillière-Brothers; E. Jung-Treuttel ..., 1865. 400 p.; 23 cm. "Ce travail doit servir d'introduction aux *Principes de médecine expérimentale* du même auteur, actuellemente sous presse." Title conforms to second illustration in Horblitt 11b, with fuller imprint. Advertisements: p. [2]. Includes bibliographical references. Horblit, H. D. *Grolier 100 science books*, 11b.

171. Bernard, Claude, 1813-1878. *Leçons de physiologie expérimentale appliquée à la médecine, faites au Collège de France, par m. Claude Bernard....*
Paris: J. B. Baillière et fils; [etc., etc.] 1855-56. 2 v. ill. 22 cm. I. Cours du semestre d'hiver, 1854-1855. II. Cours du semestre d'été, 1855.
Provenance: Bibliothèque de Sichel (inkstamp).

172. Bernard, Claude, 1813-1878. *Leçons sur la physiologie et la pathologie du système nerveux, par M. Claude Bernard....*
Paris: J.-B. Baillière et fils ...; Hippolyte Baillière; C. Bailly-Baillière; Baillière Brothers, 1858 ... 2 v.: ill.; 23 cm. Cours de médecine du Collège de France. Publisher's advertisements: [1] p. preceeding each title page and [1] p. on each lower wrapper, v. 1-2; 12 p. at end of v. 2, dated 15 janv. 1875 (conjugate). Includes bibliographical references.

173. Bernard, Claude, 1813-1878. *Leçons sur les effets des substances toxiques et médicamenteuses.*
Paris: J. B. Baillière, H. Baillière, 1857. vii, 488 p. 32 illus. 23 cm. Cours de médecine du Collège de France. Advertisements: p. [2]. "De la nicotine": p. [397]-412. "Errata": p. 488. "List des publications de Magendie": p. 31-36.
Provenance: Bibliothèque de Sichel (bookstamp). Publisher's catalogue: 48 p. at end.

174. Bernard, Claude, 1813-1878. *Sur une nouvelle fonction du foie chez l'homme et les animaux, par M. Claude Bernard (extrait par l'auteur).*
[Paris]: Bachelier, Imprimeur-Libraire ..., 1850. p.571-574; 28 cm. Comptes rendus hebdomadaires des séances de l'Académie des Sciences; t. 31. Caption title. Horblit, H. D. *Grolier 100 science books*, 11a (variant).

175. Bernoulli, Daniel, 1700-1782. *Danielis Bernoulli Joh. fil. med. prof. Basil. ... Hydrodynamica, sive De viribus et motibus fluidorum commentarii. Opus academicum ab auctore, dum Petropoli ageret, congestum.*
Argentorati: Sumptibus J. R. Dulseckeri, 1738. 4 p.l., 304 p. XII fold. pl. 26 x 21cm. Illustrated by I. M. Weis.
Provenance: George Sarton (inscription and bookplate).

176. Bernoulli, Jakob, 1654-1705. *Ars conjectandi. Jacobi Bernoulli... Ars conjectandi:*

opus posthumum: accedit Tractatus de seriebus infinitis, et Epistola Gallicè scripta de ludo pilae reticularis.

Basileae: Impensis Thurnisiorum, fratrum, 1713. [4], 24, [1] folded leaf, 25-172, [1] folded leaf, 173-306, [2], 35, (1) p., (1) folded leaf of plates; 21 cm. The letter in French has caption title: Lettre à un amy, sur les parties du jeu de paume. Signatures: pi[2] A-2P[4] [2Q4 blank] a-d[4] e[2]. Errata: e2 verso. Horblit, H. D. *Grolier 100 science books*, 12.

"Lettre à un amy" (35 p.) misbound after pi2. Provenance: Herbert McLean Evans (bookplate).

177. BERQUIN, M. (ARNAUD), 1747-1791. *Astronomie pour la jeunesse, ou, Le système du monde expliqué aux enfants, Berquin.*

Paris: Victor Lecou ..., 1852. [4], IV, 141, [2] p.: ill., ports.; 20 cm. Author's name appears at head of title. "Berquin, dans son introduction à la Science de la nature, a enseigné l'astronomie avec cette clarté qui lui est naturelle, et qui saisit si vivement l'esprit de la jeunesse. Nous avons détaché de l'ouvrage ces chapitres si intéressants, nous y avons ajouté quelques notions que les découvertes modernes rendaient indispensables, et nous en avons fait cette petite astronomie que nous publions aujourd'hui. Les enfants la pourront comprendre, et bien des grandes personnes ne la liront pas sans intérêt". Introd., signed: J. C. D. Colophon: Arras: Typ. de Mme. veuve J. Degeorge.

Provenance: Paul Gavault (bookplate).

178. BERTHELOT, M. (MARCELLIN), 1827-1907. *Chimie organique fondée sur la synthèse, par Marcellin Berthelot....*

Paris: Mallet-Bachelier, 1860. 2 v.; 24 cm. Includes bibliographical references. 1. Introduction. Synthèse des carbures d'hydrogène. Synthèse des alcools et des corps qui en dérivent. 2. Des principes sucrès. Des méthodes.

Provenance: Organic Chemical Laboratory, Oxford (ink-stamp).

179. BERTHELOT, M. (MARCELLIN), 1827-1907. *Essai de mécanique chimique: fondée sur la thermochimie, par M. Berthelot....*

Paris: Dunod, 1879. 2 v. front. (port.) diagrs. 25 cm. "Mémoires et Notes que j'ai publies sur les actions électrochimiques": Footnote, v. 2, p. 325-326. "Bibliographie – mémoires dont les résultats numériques ont été employés dans le calcul des tableaux": v. 1. p. 326-328. 1. Calorimétrie. t. 2. Mécanique.

Provenance: Kir. Magyar Pázmány Péter Tudományegyetem Szervetlen és Analitikai Kámiai Intezetének Könyvtára (inkstamp).

180. BERTHELOT, M. (MARCELLIN), 1827-1907. *Les origines de l'alchimie, par M. Berthelot....*

Paris: G. Steinheil, 1885. xx, 445, [1] p. front. (port.) II pl. 25 cm.

181. BERTHOLLET, CLAUDE-LOUIS, 1748-1822. *Essai de statique chimique, par C. L. Berthollet.*

Paris: Chez Firmin Didot, Libraire ... , an XI [1803]. 2 v. [543, 555 p.] 21 cm. On title-page: De l'imprimerie de Demonville et soeurs.

Provenance: Herbert McLean Evans (bookplate).

182. BERZELIUS, JÖNS JAKOB, FRIHERRE, 1779-1848. *Die Anwendung des Löthrohrs in der Chemie und Mineralogie, von J. Jacob Berzelius. Zweite Auflage.*

Nürnberg: bei Joh. Leonhard Schrag, 1828. XVI, [2], 282 p., IV folded leaves of plates: ill.; 21 cm. Translation of *Om blåsrörets användande i kemien och mineralogien*. Includes bibliographical references and index.

Provenance: "Apotheke, 1837" (inscription).

183. BERZELIUS, JÖNS JAKOB, FRIHERRE, 1779-1848. *Essai sur la théorie des proportions chimiques et sur l'influence chimique de l'électricité, par J. J. Berzelius ...; traduit du suèdois sous les yeux de l'auteur, et publié par lui-même.*

À Paris: Chez Méquignon-Marvis ..., 1819. XVI, 190, [2], 120, [2] p.; 21 cm. Original Swedish version comprises part of the author's *Lärbok ikemien*, v. 3 (1818). On last unnumbered page: De l'Imprimerie de Cellot ... Signatures: pi[8] 1-12[8] A-P[4] Q1. Reference: Holmberg, A. Berzelius, ptie. 1, 1819: 20. "Tables alphabétiques, qui montrent le poids de l'atome de la plu part des substances inorganiques, ainsi que leur composition en centièmes," 2nd paging.

184. BERZELIUS, JÖNS JAKOB, FRIHERRE, 1779-1848. *Lehrbuch der Chemie. Nach des Verfassers schwedischer Bearbeitung der Blöde-Palmstedt'schen Aufl. übers. von F. Wöhler.*

Dresden: Arnold, 1825-31. 4 v. in 8. illus. 21 cm. Vols. 3-4: Aus dem Schwedischen übersetzt von F. Wöhler. Vol. 4, pt. 1 has added t. p.: Lehrbuch der Thier-Chemie. pt. 2: Chemische Operationen und Geräthschaften, nebst Erklärung chemischer Kunstwörter in alphabetischer Ordnung.

Provenance: W. Teschke (label, v. 4, pt. 1).

185. Bessel, F. W. (Friedrich Wilhelm), 1784-1846. *Fundamenta astronomiæ pro anno MDCCLV: deducta ex observationibus viri incomparabilis James Bradley, in specula astronomica Grenovicensi per annos 1750-1762 institutis, auctore Friderico Wilhelmo Bessel.*

Regiomonti [i.e. Königsberg]: In Commissis apud Frid. Nicolovium, 1818. [12], 325, [1] p.; 33 cm. First edition, Gillispie, II, p. 99. Signatures: [*]^2, b-c^2, A-Z^2, Aa-Zz^2, Aaa-Zzz^2, Aaaa-Mmmm^2, Nnnn1. Errata: p. [1] following text. Houzeau & Lancaster. *Astronomie.* (1964 ed.), 10, 117.

Provenance: Robert Honeyman IV (Honeyman sale).

186. Bessel, F. W. (Friedrich Wilhelm), 1784-1846. *Tabulæ Regiomontanæ reductionum observationum astronomicarum ab anno 1750 usque ad annum 1850 computatæ. Auctore Friderico Wilhelmo Bessel.*

Regiomonti Prussorum: Sumtibus fratrum Borntraeger; etc. etc. 1830. 2 p. l., lxiii, 542 p., 1 l. 25 cm. Errata: p. [543].

Provenance: Charles N. Haskins (bookplate), ms. note pasted in.

187. Bessel, F. W. (Friedrich Wilhelm), 1784-1846. *Untersuchungen über die Länge des einfachen Secundendpendels, von F. W. Bessel.*

Berlin: Kgl. Akademie der Wissenschaften, 1828. 254, [1] p., II leaves of plates: ill.; 28 cm. Caption title. First published in *Abhandlungen der mathematischen Klasse der Kgl. Akademie der Wissenschaften zu Berlin,* 1826. Publisher and date of reissue supplied from colophon.

188. Besson, Jacques, Dauphinois. *Theatrvm instrvmentorvm et machinarum. Cum Franc. Beroaldi figurarum declaratione demonstratiua.*

Lvgdvni: Apud B. Vincentium, 1578. [22] p., 60 plates. 40 cm. Plates engr. by Jacques Androuet du Cerceau and René Byvin.

189. Bethe, Hans Albrecht, 1906- . *Reaction of radiation on electron scattering and Heitler's theory of radiation damping / H. A. Bethe and J. Robert Oppenheimer.*

New York: Macmillan, 1946. p. 451-458; 27 cm. Caption title. "Reprinted from *The physical review,* vol. 70, nos. 7 and 8, 451-458, October 1 and 15, 1946." Includes bibliographical references.

190. Bevis, John, 1693-1771. *Atlas céleste; or, the Celestial atlas: being the most correct, copious, and superb work of the kind, that has ever been offered to the public.*

London: John Neale, 1786?. [2] leaves, [1], LI leaves of plates: ill.; 42 x 54 cm. Some copies have cover title: Uranographia Britannica. Includes index.

Unbound in box. Imperfect: lower half of t. p., plate I, V, VI, XI, XXI, XXIV, XXV, XXXVII-XXXIL, XLII, XLVI, XLVII missing. 2 copies of plate III. Hand colored. [Copy 1]

Plates only. Imperfect: plates XXVIII and LI missing. Bound to 35 x 43 cm. and shelved "f". [Copy 2]

191. Beyda, Heinrich Friedrich Theodor. *Die imaginären Grössen: und ihre Auflösung (aus dem Jahre 1863), von Heinrich Friedrich Theodor Beyda.*

Stuttgart: J. B. Metzler'sche Buchhandlung, 1881. 60 p.; 23 cm.

No. 4 in a v. of 11 items with binder's title: Geometrie. Provenance: Ernst Mach (inkstamp).

192. Bible. *O.T. Genesis. Hebrew 1556. Bereshit = Liber Genesis.*

Parisiis: Ex officina Caroli Stephani ..., 1556. 143 p.; 23 cm. Pagination in Hebrew characters. Signatures: A-S^4. Imprint follows title in Hebrew: Sher nidfas, al yedei 'Ka'rolus Sötefanìus ...[5] 316 ... po Pariàs....

Provenance: Ludovic Vander Eycken (inscription); Stephan Vai (inscription).

193. Bickerton, A. W. (Alexander William), 1842-1929. *The birth of worlds and systems, by Professor A. W. Bickerton ... with a preface by Professor Ernest Rutherford, F.R.S.*

London; New York: Harper & Brothers, 1911. xix, 161, [1] p. front., plates, diagrs. 18 cm. Harper's Library of

Living Thought. Added t.-p., illus. Includes index. "List of former papers": p. xix.

Advertisements: [2] p. at end.

194. Bidloo, Govard, 1649-1713. *Godefridi Bidloo ... Anatomia humani corporis, centum & quinque tabulis, per artificiosiss. G. de Lairesse ad vivum delineatis, demonstrata....*

Amstelodami: Sumptibus viduæ Joannis à Someren (etc.) 1685. [136] p. 105 pl., port. 53 cm. Descriptive letterpress facing each plate. Added t.-p., engr. Choulant, L. *Anatomic illustration*, p. 250-253.

Imperfect: added engraved t. p., port; plates 1-3, 20, 31, 41, 44, 47-48, 50-51, 53-54, 56 missing.

195. Bigelow, Henry Jacob, 1818-1890. *Insensibility during surgical operations produced by inhalation: read before the Boston Society of Medical Improvement, Nov. 9th, 1846, an abstract having been previously read before the American Academy of Arts and Sciences, Nov. 3d, 1846, by Henry Jacob Bigelow....*

Boston: s.n., 1846. p. [309]-316; 25 cm. Caption title. "Reprinted from the Boston medical and surgical journal. Vol. XXV, Wednesday, November 18, 1846. No. 16." Garrison-Morton (4th ed.), 5651.

Provenance: Herbert McLean Evans (bookplate).

196. Bigourdan, G. (Guillaume), 1851-1932. *L'astronomie: évolution des idées et des méthodes; 50 illustrations.*

Paris: E. Flammarion, 1924. vii, 399 p. diagrs. 19 cm. Bibliothèque de philosophie scientifique. Includes index. Advertisements on wrappers.

197. Biot, Jean-Baptiste, 1774-1862. *Études sur l'astronomie indienne et sur l'astronomie chinoise, par J. B. Biot....*

Paris: Michel Lévy Frères ..., 1862. lii, 398 p., [3] folded leaves of plates: ill.; 22 cm. Printer's device on title page. Includes bibliographical references.

Original printed wrappers bound in; advertisements on p. [4] of wrapper. Provenance: Charles Atwood Kofoid (bookplate).

198. Biot, Jean-Baptiste, 1774-1862. *Traité élémentaire d'astronomie physique, par J. B. Biot, avec des additions relatives à l'astronomie nautique par m. de Rossel. 2. éd., destinée à l'enseignement dans les lycées imprériaux et les écoles secondaires.*

Paris: J. Klostermann fils; [etc., etc.] 1810-11. 3 v. tables (part fold.) diagrs. on plates (part fold.) 21 cm. t. 1. Phénomènes généraux et moyens d'observations. – t. 2. Théorie du soleil. Théorie de la lune. – t. 3. Théorie des planètes, des comètes, et des satellites. Additions: I. De la mesure des hauteurs parles observations du baromètre. II. Gnomonique: ou, Théorie des cadrans solaires, par m. Berroyer. III. Sur le mouvement de translation du système planètaire. IV. Sur la rectification de la lunette méridienne par le calcul des azimuths. V. Sur la longueur du pendule à secondes à différentes latitudes. VI. Méthode générale pour déterminer les orbites des comètes, par m. Laplace. Traité des calculs de l'astronomie nautique, avec des tables, par m. de Rossel.

Provenance: Bibl. Coll. S. F. Xaverii Venetensis (bookplate); P. Y. A. (inkstamp).

199. Birkenmajer, Aleksander, 1890-1967. *Mikolaj Kopernik.*

Warszawa: "Sztuka", 1953. 7 p. 45 plates (incl. ports., part. col., facsims.) 36 cm. In portfolio.

200. Birkhoff, George David. *Relativity and modern physics, by George David Birkhoff ... with the coöperation of Rudolph Ernest Langer....*

Cambridge, Harvard University Press; [etc., etc.] 1923. xi, 283 p. diagrs. 23 cm. Includes index. Bibliography: p. 273-276.

Provenance: Captain E. C. Goldsworthy (signature).

201. Birmingham, J. (John), 1829-1884. *The red stars: observations and catalogue, by J. Birmingham. New edition, by Rev. T. E. Espin....*

Dublin: Published by the Academy ..., 1890. [2], 201, [1] p.: ill.; 33 cm. Cunningham Memoirs, Royal Irish Academy; no. 5. Title from cover. Errata: p. [202]. Includes bibliographical references.

Imperfect, lacks cover.

202. Bischoff, Th. Ludw. Wilh. (Theodor Ludwig Wilhelm), 1807-1882. *Entwicklungsgeschichte des Hunde-Eies. Von Th. Ludw. Wilh. Bischoff ... Mit fünfzehn Steintafeln.*

Braunschweig: F. Vieweg und Sohn, 1845. 3 p. l., 134 p., 1 l. XV pl. ill.; 28 cm. Verbesserungen: p. [135]. Plates signed: A. Schütter lith.

Bound in 2 v. Provenance: Herbert McLean Evans (bookplate).

203. BISCHOFF, TH. LUDW. WILH. (THEODOR LUDWIG WILHELM), 1807-1882. *Lepidosiren paradoxa, anatomisch untersucht und beschrieben durch D.Th. Ludw. Wilh. Bischoff....*

Leipzig: Verlag von Leopold Voss, 1840. VI, 34 p., VII leaves of plates (1 folded): ill.; 35 cm. Includes bibliographical references.

Provenance: Herbert McLean Evans (bookplate); Dr. Alexander Goette (book stamp).

204. BITRUJI, 12th cent. *De motibus celorum; critical edition of the Latin translation of Michael Scot. Edited by Francis J. Carmody.*

Berkeley: University of California Press, 1952. 180 p. diagrs. 26 cm. Translation of: *Kitab fi al-hay'ah*. Bibliographical footnotes.

205. BLACK, DAVIDSON, 1884-1934. *[Collection of articles on Peking man, 1925-1933, by Davidson Black et al.]*

[1925-1933]. 18 pieces: ill.; 22-31 cm. (1) Asia and the dispersal of primates (1925) – (2) The human skeletal remains from the Sha Kuo T'un cave deposit in comparison with those fromYang Shao Tsun and with recent north China skeletal material (1925) – (3)Tertiary man in Asia: the Chou Kou Tien discovery (1926) – (4) Further hominid remains of lower Quaternary age from the Chou Kou Tien deposit(1927) – (5) On a presumably Pleostocene human tooth from Sjaro-Osso-Gol (South-Eastern Ordos) deposits, E. Licent, Teilhard de Chardin and D.Black (1927) – (6) The lower molar hominid tooth from the Chou Kou Tien deposit (1927) – (7) Discovery of further hominid remains of lower Quaternary age from the Chou Kou Tien deposit (1928) – (8) A study of Kansu and Honan Aeneolithic skulls and specimens from later Kansu prehistoric sites in comparison with North China and other recent crania. Part I. (1928). (9) Sinanthropus Pekinensis: the recovery of further fossil remains of this early hominid from the Chou Kou Tien deposit (1929) – (10) Preliminary note on additional Sinanthropis material discovered in Chou Kou Tien during 1923 (1929) – (11) Preliminary notice of the discovery of adult Sinanthropus skull at Chou Kou Tien (1929) – (12) An account of the discovery of an adult Sinanthropus skull in the Chou Kou Tien deposit, by W. C. Pei (1929) – (13) Interim report on the skull of Sinanthropus (1930) – (14) Notice of the recovery of a second adult Sinanthropus skull specimen (1930). (15) On an adolescent skull of Sinanthropus Pekinensis in comparison with an adult skull of the same species and with other hominid skulls, recent and fossil (1931) – (16) Evidences of the use of fire by Sinanthropis (1931) – (17) Skeletal remains of Sinanthropus other than skull parts (1932) – (18) Fossil man in China: the Chou Kou Tien cave deposits with a synopsis of our present knowledge of the late Cenozoic in China (1933).

Provenance: [no.1] bears Herbert McLean Evans' bookplate and [no.3] bears Black's marginalia and presentation inscription to Evans.

206. BLACK, F. A. (FREDERICK ALEXANDER), b. 1862. *Problems in time and space; a collection of essays relating to the earth, physically and astronomically, and cognate matters, by F. A. Black....*

London [etc.]: Gall & Inglis 1910. xx, 362 p. front., plates, ports., diagrs. 21 cm. Preface dated: 11th Dec. 1909. Includes index. How the distance and size of the sun were measured. – A simple means of ascertaining the day of the week of any given date in the Christian era. – Measuring the earth. – Solar and sidereal time. – The reform of the calendar. – The magnetism of the earth. – The movements of the sun and of the earth in space. – Logarithms and their inventor. – Gravitation the chief cause of the general oceanic circulation. – Twilight and dawn. – Appendix.

207. BLACK, JOSEPH, 1728-1799. *Lectures on the elements of chemistry, delivered in the University of Edinburgh; by the late Joseph Black ... Now published from his manuscripts, by John Robison....*

Printed by Mundell and Son for Longman and Rees, London, and W. Creech, Edinburgh, 1803. 2 v. front. (port.) III pl. 29 cm. Plates signed: "D. Lizars, sculps."

Provenance: Herbert M. Evans (mailing label loosely inserted); ms. note card loosely inserted. Index at end of v. 2 has pages misbound.

208. BLACKSTONE, WILLIAM, SIR, 1723-1780. *The Great charter and Charter of the forest,*

with other authentic instruments: to which is prefixed an introductory discourse, containing the history of the charters.
Oxford: Clarendon Press, 1759. [4], lxxvi, [4], 86 p. illus. 37 cm. Includes bibliographical references.
Provenance: Charles Carroll (bookplate); Herbert McLean Evans (bookplate); presentation inscription from Evans to Sam Barchas.

209. Blake, John Frederick, 1839-1906. *Astronomical myths, based on Flammarion's "History of the heavens." By John F. Blake.*
London: Macmillan and Co., 1877. xvi, 431 p. incl. front., illus., diagrs. 4 pl., fold. chart 21 cm. "Not exactly a translation, but rather a book founded on the French author's work." – Pref.

210. Blumenbach, Johann Friedrich, 1752-1840. *Über den Bildungstrieb, Joh. Fr. Blumenbach....*
Göttingen: bey Johann Christian Dieterich, 1791. 116 p.: ill.; 17 cm. Author's name transposed from head of title. Previously published under title: *Über den Bildungstrieb und das Zeugungsgeschäfte*. Göttingen: bey Johann Christian Dieterich, 1781. Includes bibliographical references.
Provenance: Herbert McLean Evans (bookplate); Dr. Max Bartels (bookplate).

211. Boerhaave, Herman, 1668-1738. *Elementa chemiæ, quae anniversario labore docuit, in publicis, privatisque, scholis, Hermannus Boerhaave....*
Lugduni Batavorum: Apud I. Severinum, 1732. 2 v. 17 plates. 26 cm. Half-title: Hermanni Boerhaave Chemia. II. vol. Engraved title vignettes (printer's device); initials; head pieces. Includes indexes.

212. Bohr, Niels Henrik David, 1885-1962. *Abhandlungen über Atombau aus den Jahren 1913-1916. Autorisierte deutsche Übersetzung, mit einem Geleitwort von N. Bohr, von Dr. Hugo Stintzing.*
Braunschweig: F. Vieweg, 1921. xix, 155 p. 24 cm. Includes bibliographical references and index.
Provenance: Karl Horovitz (signature).

213. Bohr, Niels Henrik David, 1885-1962. *Biology and atomic physics, relazione del Niels Bohr.*
Bologna: Luigi Parma, 1938-16. 15 p.; 25 cm. At head of title: Celebrazione del secondo centenario della nascita di Luigi Galvani, Bologna - ottobre 1937-XV. Congressi scientifici, seduta plenaria. Istituto di fisica - 19 ottobre.

214. Bohr, Niels Henrik David, 1885-1962. *[Collection of offprint articles, by Niels Bohr].*
[1926-1958] 6 pieces: ill.; 21-26 cm. Includes bibliographic references. (1) Atomic theory and mechanics (1926) – (2) Atomic stability and conservation laws (1932) – (3) Light and life (1932) – (4) Dansk Kultur (1941) – (5) Discussion with Einstein on epistemological problems in atomic physics (1949) – (6) Quantum physics and philosophy: causality and complementarity (1958).

215. Bohr, Niels Henrik David, 1885-1962. *Drei Aufsätze über Spektren und Atombau / von N. Bohr.*
Braunschweig : F. Vieweg, 1922. vi, 148 p. : ill. ; 23 cm. (Sammlung Vieweg : Tagesfragen aus den Gebieten der Naturwissenschaften und der Technik ; Heft. 56).

216. Bohr, Niels Henrik David, 1885-1962. *On the application of the quantum theory to atomic structure. Part I. The fundamental postulates.*
Cambridge: The University Press, 1924. 42 p., 1 l. 22 cm. Proceedings of the Cambridge Philosophical Society. Supplement. Cover title. No more published. "From the Zeitschrift für physik, 13, p. 117, 1923 ... Translated by L. F. Curtiss." – p. [1].

217. Bohr, Niels Henrik David, 1885-1962. *On the quantum theory of line-spectra, by N. Bohr.*
København: A. F. Høst & Søn, 1918-[22]. 118 p.; 28 cm. D. Kgl. danske vidensk. selsk. skrifter. Naturvidensk. og mathem. afd. 8. ræakke, IV, 1. Issued in 3 parts. 1. General principles – 2. On the hydrogen spectrum – 3. On the spectra of elements of higher atomic number. Includes bibliographical references.
Provenance: Herbert McLean Evans (bookplate).

218. Bohr, Niels Henrik David, 1885-1962. *Open letter to the United Nations, June 9th, 1950.*
Copenhagen: J. H. Schultz 1950. 12 p. 23 cm.

219. BOHR, NIELS HENRIK DAVID, 1885-1962. *The seventh Guthrie lecture on "The effect of electric and magnetic fields on spectral lines", by Niels Bohr.*

London: Fleetway Press, 1923. p. 275-302; 26 cm. At head of title: The Physical Society of London. "In substance this report represents the contents of the seventh Guthrie lecture delivered before the Physical Society, March 24, 1922. Due to unavoidable circumstances the publication of this report has unfortunately been delayed until now. N.B. July, 1923." – p. 275 footnote. Includes bibliographical references.

Ms. corrections throughout text.

220. BOHR, NIELS HENRIK DAVID, 1885-1962. *Les spectres et la structure de l'atome: trois conférences, par Niels Bohr; traduit sur le manuscrit de l'auteur par A. Corvisy.*

Paris: J. Hermann, 1923. 152 p.: ill.; 23 cm.

"Note additionnelle" ends on p. 150.

221. BOHR, NIELS HENRIK DAVID, 1885-1962. *The theory of spectra and atomic constitution; three essays, by Niels Bohr.*

Cambridge [Eng]: The University Press, 1922. x, 126 p. diagrs. 23 cm. On the spectrum of hydrogen. – On the series spectra of the elements. – The structure of the atom and the physical and chemical properties of the elements.

222. BOHR, NIELS HENRIK DAVID, 1885-1962. *The theory of spectra and atomic constitution: three essays, by Niels Bohr. 2d ed.*

Cambridge: University Press, 1924. x, 138 p.; 22 cm. I. On the spectrum of hydrogen – II. On the series spectra of the elements – III. The structure of the atom and the physical and chemical properties of the elements.

Provenance: Herbert McLean Evans (bookplate).

223. BOHR, NIELS HENRIK DAVID, 1885-1962. *Über die Quantentheorie der Linienspektren. Übersetzt von P. Hertz.*

Braunschweig: F. Vieweg, 1923. iv, 168 p. 24 cm. Includes bibliographical references. English title: *On the quantum theory of line-spectra.*

Upper wrapper with advertisements bound in. Provenance: Horovitz (inscription).

224. BOHR, NIELS HENRIK DAVID, 1885-1962. *Zur Frage der Messbarkeit der elektromagne-tischen Feldgrössen, von N. Bohr und L. Rosenfeld.*

København: Levin & Munksgaard, 1933. 65 p. 25 cm. Kgl. danske videnskabernes selskab. Mathematisk-fysiske meddelelser. XII, 8.

Provenance: presentation inscription to R. Oppenheimer.

225. BÖLSCHE, WILHELM, 1861-1939. *Haekel; his life and work.*

Philadelphia: Jacobs [1906]. 336 p. ill., ports. Translation of: *Ernst Haeckel; ein Lebensbild.*

Provenance: Reginald B. Weiler (inscription and label).

226. BOLTZMANN, LUDWIG, 1844-1906. *Populäre Schriften, von Ludwig Boltzmann.*

Leipzig: J. A. Barth, 1905. vi, 440 p.; 22 cm. Advertisements: [4] p. following text. Includes bibliographical references and index.

227. BOLTZMANN, LUDWIG, 1844-1906. *Vorlesungen über die Principe der Mechanik, von Ludwig Boltzmann... .*

Leipzig: J. A. Barth, 1897-1904. 2 v. diagrs. 23 cm. I.th. Die Principe, bei denen nicht Ausdrücke nach der Zeit integriert werden, welche Variationen der Coordinaten oder ihrer Ableitungen nach der Zeit enthalten. – II.th. Die Wirkungsprinzipe, die Lagrangeschen Gleichungen und deren Anwendungen.

Provenance: Edmund Neusser (bookplate).

228. BOLTZMANN, LUDWIG, 1844-1906. *Vorlesungen über Gastheorie, von Ludwig Boltzmann. 2., unverënderter Abdr.*

Leipzig: J. A. Barth, 1910-1912. 2 v.; 22 cm. Advertisements: v. 2, p. [266]. Includes bibliographical references.

229. BOLYAI, FARKAS, 1775-1856. *Tentamen: juventutem studiosam in elementa matheseos puræ, elementaris ac sublimioris, methodo intuitiva, evidentiaque huic propria, introducendi: cum appendice triplici, auctore professore matheseos et physices chemiaeque publ. ordinario.*

Maros Vásárhelyini: Typis Collegii Reformatorum per Josephum, et Simeonem Kali de felsö Vist., 1832-1833. 2 v.: ill.; 21 cm. Vol. 1: [4], LXXIII [i.e. C], 502, [2], 26, [2], XVI p., [1], 3, [1] folded leaves of plates; v. 2: [6], XVI, 402 p., 10 folded leaves of plates. Appendix: scientiam spatii absolute veram exhibens, auctore Johanne Bolyai: [2], 26 p. at end of v. 1. Errata: v. 1: p. XXXIII-XXXVII, LIII-LXXIII [i.e. C], p. [27-28]; v. 2: p. 373-383, 385-402. Horblit, H. D. *Grolier 100 science books*, 69b.

Imperfect: plate 6 pasted on; slip is missing.

230. Bólyai, János, 1802-1860. *La science absolue de l'espace: indépendante de la vérité ou de la fausseté de l'axiôme XI d'Euclide (que l'on ne pourra jamais établir a priori) précédé ... d'une notice sur la vie et les travaux de W. et de J. Bolyai, par M. Fr. Schmidt.*

Paris: 1868. 64 p. diagrs. 22 cm. Includes bibliographical references.

No. 18 in a v. with binder's title: Geometrie, I.

231. Bond, George Phillips, 1825-1865. *Account of the great comet of 1858. By G. P. Bond....*

Cambridge: Welch, Bigelow and Company, printers to the University, 1862. xx, 372 p. illus., 41 pl. (partly col., 5 fold.) 30 x 25 cm. *Annals of the Astronomical Observatory of Harvard College.* vol. III. Subscribers' list: p. [v]. "List of authorities for observations, drawings, &c used in this work": p. xvii-xix.

Provenance: author's presentation inscription to Prof. Cherryman.

232. Bonnycastle, John, 1750?-1821. *An introduction to astronomy: in a series of letters, from a preceptor to his pupil, in which the most useful and interesting parts of the science are clearly and familiarly explained, illustrated with copper-plates by John Bonnycastle ... The second edition, corrected and improved.*

London: Printed for J. Johnson, No. 72, St. Paul's Church-Yard, [1787]. vi, [2], 437, [3] p., XIX [i.e. 20] leaves of plates (19 folded): 20 ill.; 21 cm. Advertisements: Last [2] p. Signatures: A^4B-$2F^8$.

Dealer information suggests allegorical frontispiece is by W. Blake; not in Keynes.

233. Boole, George, 1815-1864. *An investigation of the laws of thought, on which are founded the mathematical theories of logic and probabilities. By George Boole.*

London: Walton and Maberly; Macmillan and Co., 1854. [14], 424, [2] p. 20 cm. Errata: p. [1]) (1st group). Includes bibliographical references.

Provenance: Herbert McLean Evans (bookplate); Ralph P. Hardy (signature); Robert Honeyman (Honeyman sale). Imperfect? lacks 2 prelim. p. (half-title?).

234. Borelli, Giovanni Alfonso, 1608-1679. *De motu animalium Jo. Alphonsi Borelli Neapolitani matheseos professoris. Opus posthumum.*

Romae: Ex typographia Angeli Bernabò, 1680-81. 2 v. 18 fold. pl. 22 cm. Pars altera dated 1681. Horblit, H. D. *Grolier 100 science books*, 13. Osler, W. *Bib. Osleriana*, 2087.

235. Borelli, Giovanni Alfonso, 1608-1679. *De vi percussionis liber, Io. Alphonsi Borelli....*

BononiæEx typographia Iacobi Montij, 1667. [14], 300, 30, [2] p., 5 leaves of plates: ill.; 23 cm. Errata: p. [1] at the end. Includes indexes. Riccardi, P. Bib. matematica, v. 1, column 159.Provenance: Horatij Xanexij Pacificij (signature).

236. Born, Max, 1882-1970. *Atomic physics, by Max Born; authorized translation from the German edition by John Dougall.*

New York: G. E. Stechert & Co., 1936. xii, 352 p., viii leaves of plates: ill.; 23 cm. "The German edition of this book, which appeared in 1933 under the title *Moderne Physik*, had its origin in a course of lectures which I gave at the Technical College, Berlin-Charlottenburg, at the instance of the Society of Electrical Engineers, and which were reported by Dr. F. Sauter." – Pref. p. vii. Bibliography: p. 343-344. Includes index.

Provenance: Claude C. Van Nuys (booklabel).

237. Born, Max, 1882-1970. *Der Aufbau der Materie; drei Aufsätze über moderne Atomistik und Elektronentheorie, von Max Born. Mit 36 Textabbildungen.*

Berlin: J. Springer, 1920. 3 p. l., 81 p.: illus., diagrs.; 23 cm. Includes bibliographies. Contents. – Das Atom. – Vom mechanischen Äther zur elektrischen Materie. – Die Brücke zwischen Chemie und Physik. Advertisements on lower wrapper.

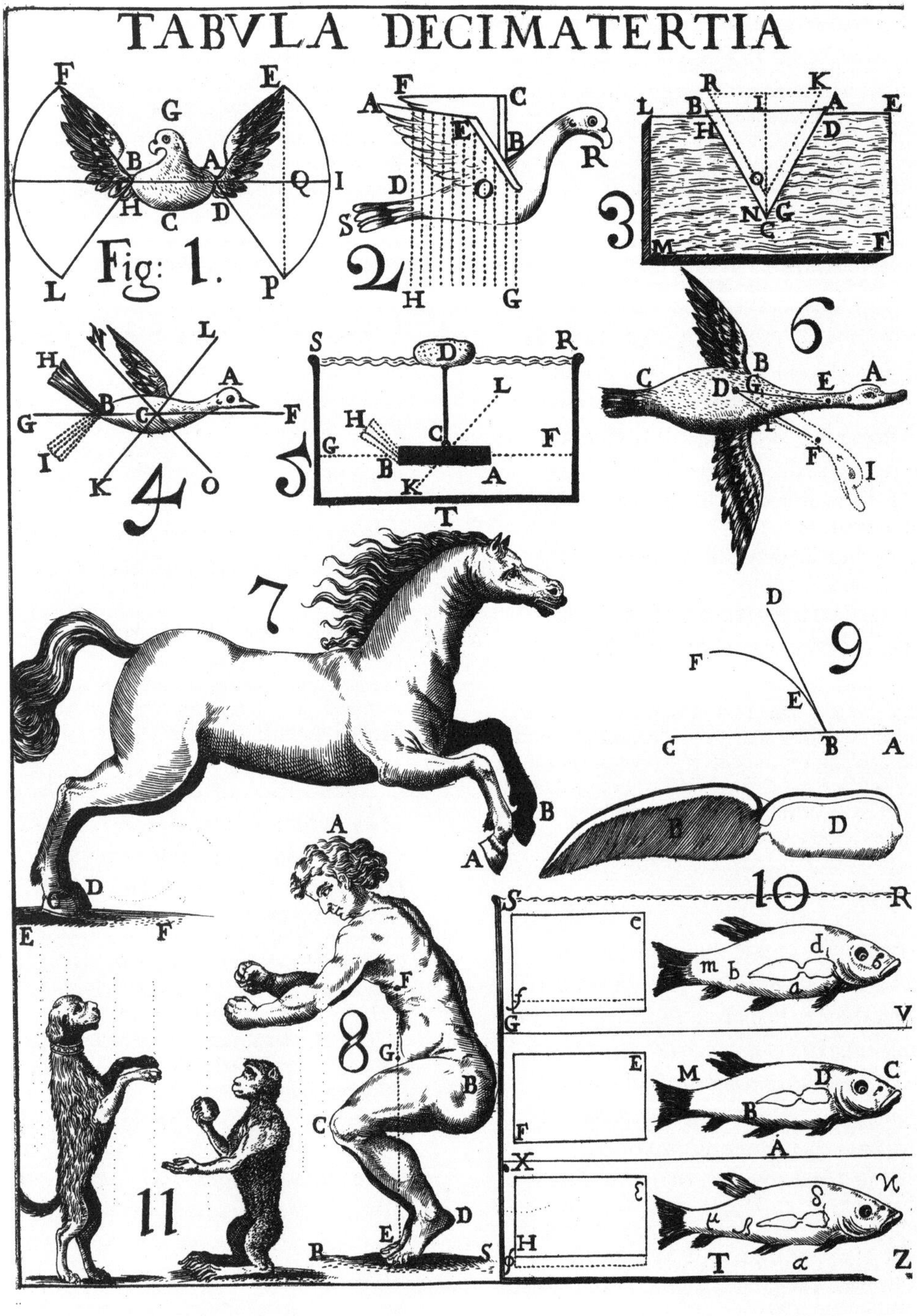

Borelli, *De motu animalium*, 1680-1681

238. Born, Max, 1882-1970. *The constitution of matter, modern atomic and electron theories, by Max Born ... translated from the 2d revised German edition by E. W. Blair and T. S. Wheeler...with thirty-seven diagrams.*
London: Methuen 1923. vii, 80 p. illus., diagrs. 23 cm. Original title: *Aufbau der Materie.* Printed in Great Britain. Contains bibliographies.

239. Born, Max, 1882-1970. *Experiment and theory in physics, by Max Born....*
Cambridge [Eng]: The University Press, 1943. 2 p. l., 43, [1] p.; 19 cm. "Represents in a slightly expanded form an address given to the Durham Philosophical Society, and the Pure Science Society, King's College, at Newcastle-upon-Tyne on 21 May, 1943."

240. Born, Max, 1882-1970. *The mechanics of the atom, by Max Born, translated by J. W. Fisher and revised by D. R. Hartree.*
London: G. Bell and Sons, Ltd., 1927. xvi, 317 p. fold. tab., diagrs. 23 cm. International Text-books of Exact Science. Translation of *Vorlesungen über Atommechanik*, v. 1. Includes bibliographical references and index.
Advertisements: [2] p. at end.

241. Born, Max, 1882-1970. *Moderne Physik; sieben Vorträge über Materie und Strahlung, von dr. Max Born. Veranstaltet durch den Elektrotechnishen Verein, e.V., zu Berlin in Gemeinschaft mit dem Ausseninstitut der Technischen Hochschule zu Berlin, ausgearb. von dr. Fritz Sauter. Mit 95 Textabbildungen.*
Berlin: J. Springer, 1933. vii, 272 p. illus., diagrs. 25 cm. Advertisements: p. [273-276]. "Literaturverzeichnis": p. [271]-272. Kinetische gastheorie. – Elektrische Elementarteilchen; Protonen, Elektronen. – Wellen-Korpuskeln. – Atombau und Linienspektren. – Elektronenspin und Paulisches Prinzip. – Quantenstatistik. – Molekülbau. – Anhang.

242. Born, Max, 1882-1970. *Physics in my generation; a selection of papers.*
London: Pergamon Press 1956. viii, 232 p. illus. 23 cm. Includes bibliographies.

243. Bornemann, Christian Ernst. *Versuch einer systematischen Abhandlung von den Kohlen. Christian Ernst Bornemann's Versuch einer systematischen Abhandlung von den Kohlen.*
Göttingen: Bey Johann Christian Dieterich, 1776. 40 p., [1] leaf of plates: ill.; 17 cm. Illustrated by the author.
Provenance: Josephus Andreas Freyherr von Beretzko (armorial bookplate). With: Carl Wilhelm Scheele's ... *Chemische Abhandlung von der Luft und dem Feuer.* Upsala und Leipzig: Verlegt von Magn. Swederus ... zu finden bey S. L. Crusius, 1777.

244. Borrhaus, Martin, 1499-1564. *Elementale cosmographicum: quo totius & astronomiæ & geographiæ rudimenta, certissimis breuissimisáque docentur apodixibus : Recens castigatum & emendatum, figurísque & annotationibus opportuniss. illustratum. Adiunximus huic libro Cosmographiæ introductio: cum quibusdam geometriæ ac astronomiæ principiis ad eam rem necessariis.*
Parisiis: Apud Gulielmum Cauellat, in pinqui gallina, ex aduerso collegij Cameracensis., 1551. 35, [1], 38, [1] leaves: ill.; 18 cm. First published: Strassburg: Cratones Mylius, 1539. By Martin Borrhaus. Signatures: A-D⁸ E⁴ A-D⁸ E⁸ [-E8; E7 verso blank] Leaf 10, 1st count, misnumbered 01. Cosmographiæ introductio by Peter Apianus has special t. p. and separate paging. *JCB Lib. cat., pre-1675*, 1:162. Alden, J. E. *European Americana*, 551/12.

245. Borro, Girolamo, 1512-1592. *Del flusso, e reflusso del mare, & dell'inondatione del Nilo, Girolamo Borro Aretino. La terza volta ricorretto dal proprio autore.*
In Fiorenza: Nella Stamperia di Giorgio Marescotti, 1583. [32], 220, [1] p.; 19 cm. Author at head of title. Includes index. Brunet v. 1, 1120.
Provenance: Luigi Gattinara (signature).

246. Bortkiewicz, Ladislaus von, 1868-1931. *Die radioaktive Strahlung als Gegenstand wahrscheinlichkeitstheoretischer Untersuchungen.*
Berlin: J. Springer, 1913. 84, [4] p. diagrs. 24 cm. Colophon: Druck der Spamerschen Buchdruckerei in Leipzig. Advertisements: p. [85-88] and on lower wrapper. Includes bibliographical references.

247. BOSCOVICH, RUGGERO GIUSEPPE, 1711-1787. *Abhandlung von den verbesserten dioptrischen Fernröhren: aus den Sammlungen des Instituts zu Bologna, Roger Joseph Boscovich; sammt einem Anhange des Übersetzers, C.S.S.J.*

Wein: Gedruckt bey Johann Thomas Edlen von Trattnern, 1765. 183, [1] p., II folded leaves of plates: ill.; 21 cm. Druckfehler: p. [1]. Statement of responsibility transposed from head of title.

With: *Preissschrift über die 1768 von der Oekonomischen Gesellschaft in Bern aufgegebene Frage: welches ist die bests Theorie der Küchenherde ...*, von Hrn. Ritter. Bern: In Verlag der neuen Buchhandlung, 1771. Provenance: Knigl. Medicin. Chirurg. Friedrich Wilhelms Institut (inkstamp).

248. BOSCOVICH, RUGGERO GIUSEPPE, 1711-1787. *De inæqualitatibus quas Saturnus et Jupiter sibi mutuo videntur inducere præsertim circa tempus conjunctionis, opusculum ad Parisiensem Academiam transmissum et nunc primum editum authore P. Rogerio Josepho Boscovich, Societatis Jesu.*

Romae: Ex Typographia Generosi Salomoni, 1756. XXIV, 187 p., IV folded leaves of plates: ill.; 20 cm.

Provenance: Stockholms högskola (inkstamp).

249. BOSCOVICH, RUGGERO GIUSEPPE, 1711-1787. *Dissertatio de lunæ atmosphæra, auctore P. Rogerio Josepho Boscovich....*

Vindobonæ: Typis Joannis Thomæ nob. de Trattnern ..., 1766. [2], 111 p., [1] leaf of plates: ill.; 25 cm. First published in 1753 with title: *De lunæ atmosphæra dissertatio.*

250. BOSCOVICH, RUGGERO GIUSEPPE, 1711-1787. *Philosophiæ naturalis theoria: redacta ad unicam legem virium in natura existentium, auctore P. Rogerio Josepho.*

Prostat Viennæ Austriæ: In Officina Libraria Kaliwodiana, 1758. [28], 322, [2], 16, [4] p., IV folded leaves of plates: ill.; 23 cm. Epistola P. Rogerii Jos. Boscovich Societatis Jesu ad P. Carolum Scherffer ejusdem Societatis: p. 1-16 (2nd numbered sequence). Adnotanda, et corrigenda: p. [3-4] at the end. Includes index.

Provenance: Bibliothek des k.k. Bombardier Corps (inkstamp).

251. BOSCOVICH, RUGGERO GIUSEPPE, 1711-1787. *A theory of natural philosophy, put forward and explained by Roger Joseph Boscovich, S. J. Latin-English edition from the text of the first Venetian edition published under the personal superintendence of the author in 1763, with a short life of Boscovich.*

Chicago, London: Open Court Publishing Company, 1922. xix, 463 p., 3 l. diagrs. 39cm. Printed in Great Britain. Includes reproduction of original t.-p.: Theoria philosophiæ naturalis ... Venetiis, ex typographia Remondiniana, 1763. Translated by J. M. Child. "Catalogus operum P. Rogerii Josephi Boscovich": p. [465]-[468].

252. BOUCHER DE PERTHES, M. (JACQUES), 1788-1868. *Antiquités celtiques et antédiluviennes. Mémoire sur l'industrie primitive et les arts à leur origine. Par M. Boucher de Perthes....*

Paris: Treuttel et Wurtz [etc.], 1847-64. 3 v. plates. 25 cm. Label mounted on verso of half-title of v. 1: Cet ouvrage imprimé en 1847, n'a pu, en raison des circonstances, être publié qu'en 1849. "Extraits des Comptes-rendus de l'Institut de France, des sociétés géologique et archéologique d'Angleterre, et de divers journaux": v. 3, p. 544-598.

Vol. 3 in original printed wrappers. Provenance: Herbert McLean Evans (bookplate); presentation inscription to Alfred Langevin; Alfred John Dunkin (signature); ms. notes tipped in, v. 1; Robert Honeyman (Honeyman sale).

253. BOUGUER, M. (PIERRE), 1698-1758. *Essai d'optique sur la gradation de la lumière, par M. Bouguer....*

À Paris: Chez Claude Jombert ..., 1729. [24], 164, [4] p. (the first leaf blank), 3 folded leaves of plates: diagrams; 18 cm. Signatures: ã^{8} e^{4} A-O^{8} [diacritic alone]^{4}. Errata: p. [165-166]. Advertisements: p. [166-167].

Binder: James Macdonald Co. (stamp). Provenance: Robert Honeyman IV (Honeyman sale); Maraldi (signature).

254. BOUGUER, M. (PIERRE), 1698-1758. *La figure de la terre, déterminée par les observations de Messieurs Bouguer & de la Condamine, de l'Académie Royale des Sciences,*

envoyés par ordre du roy au Pérou, pour observer aux environs de l'équateur. Avec une relation abrégée de ce voyage qui contient la description du pays....
Paris: C. A. Jombert, 1749. 12 p.l., cx, 394, [2] p. fold. plates. 26 cm.

255. BOUGUER, M. (PIERRE), 1698-1758. *Traité d'optique sur la gradation de la lumière: Ouvrage posthume de M. Bouguer et publié par M. l'abbé de La Caille. Pour servir de suite aux Mémoires de l'Académie Royale des Sciences.*
Paris: De l'Imprimerie de H. L. Guerin & L. F. Delatour, 1760. xviii, [2], 368 p. 7 fold. pl. 26 cm.
Provenance: Bibliothèque de Varagnes (bookplate).

256. BOULLIAU, ISMAEL, 1605-1694. *Ismaelis Bullialdi astronomia philolaica. Opus nouum, in quo motus planetarum per nouam ac veram hypothesim demonstrantur ... Superque illa hypothesi tabulæ constructæ omnium, quotquot hactenus editæ sunt, facillimæ. Addita est noua methodus cuius ope eclipse solares ... expeditissime computantur. Historia ortus et progressus astronomiæ in prolegomenis describitur, & breuiter recensentur ea, quae in hoc opere nunc primum prodeunt.*
Parisiis: S. Piget, 1645. 469, [2], 232 p. illus. 36cm. Title vignette, initials, head and tail pieces.
Imperfect: half t. p. between pts. 1 & 2 missing.

257. BOWDITCH, N. I. (NATHANIEL INGERSOLL), 1805-1861. *The ether controversy. Vindication of the hospital report of 1848. By N. I. Bowditch.*
Boston: Printed by J. Wilson, 1848. 32 p. 24 cm. Written in reply to "A defence of Dr. [Charles T.] Jackson's claims to the discovery of etherization," which appeared shortly after the publication of the *Report of the Trustees of the Massachusetts General Hospital*, Jan. 26, 1848.
Provenance: Presented to the Boston Daily Advertiser by the author (inscription).

258. BOWDITCH, NATHANIEL, 1773-1838. *The new American practical navigator: being an epitome of navigation; containing all the tables necessary to be used with the nautical almanac... with an appendix ..., by Nathaniel Bowditch....*
Washington: Government Printing Office, 1868. [2], 8, [iii]-xix, [1], 289, [1] (blank), 460 p., XIV leaves of plates (1 folded): ill., maps; 25 cm. "Now printed from the original stereotype plates as used in the last edition (1867) with exception of a few corrections on the plates of discovered errors in the tables." "Corrections and additions": [8] p.
Binder: Homecrafters, Tucson, Ariz. (ticket). Provenance: A. J. O'Reilly (book stamp); B. A. Hill (book stamp).

259. BOYER, CARL B. (CARL BENJAMIN), 1906- *The rainbow from myth to mathematics.*
New York: T. Yoseloff [1959]. 376 p. illus., plates. 26 cm. Bibliography: p. 355-366. Includes index.

260. BOYLE, ROBERT, 1627-1691. *Certain physiological essays, written at distant times, and on several occasions: by the Honourable Robert Boyle.*
London: Printed for H. Herringman ..., 1661. [4], 36, [2], 37-105, [13], 107-249 p. 20 cm. Errors in pagination: p. 100-101 misnumbered 102-103. Two essays, concerning the unsuccessfulness of experiments. – Some specimens of an attempt to make chymical experiments. – A physico-chymical essay. – The history of fluidity and firmnesse. Wing B3929. Fulton, J. F. *Boyle* (2nd ed.), 25.
Provenance: Robert Honeyman IV (Honeyman sale).

261. BOYLE, ROBERT, 1627-1691. *A continuation of new experiments physico-mechanical, touching the spring and vveight of the air, and their effects. The I. part : Written by way of letter, to the Right Honourable the Lord Clifford and Dungarvan : VVereto is annext a short discourse of the atmosphere of consistent bodies. By the Honourable Robert Boyle....*
Oxford: Printed by Henry Hall printer to the University, for Richard Davis, 1669. [2], 198, [10] p., VIII folded leaves of plates: ill.; 21 cm. Half title: Mr. Boyle's Continuation of experiments of the air. Wing (2nd ed.), B3934. Fulton, J. F. *Boyle* (2nd ed.), 16. Yale. *Cushing*, B552. "Errata": p. [19] of 1st group.
Plate IV bound between p. 154-155. Provenance: Sir John Martin Harvey (armorial bookplate).

262. BOYLE, ROBERT, 1627-1691. *Essays of the strange subtilty, great efficacy, determinate nature of effluviums. To which are annext New experiments to make fire and flame ponderable: together with A discovery of the perviousness of glass. By the Honorable Robert Boyle....*

London: Printed by W. G. for M. Pitt, 1673. 4 p l., 69 p., 1 l., 47, 74 p., 5 l., 85, [6] p. 18 cm. Each of the three essays is separately paged. The two annexed treatises are paged continuously. "Of the strange subtility of effluviums," "New Experiments ..." and "A discovery of the perviousness of glass" have special title-pages. Fulton, J. F. *Boyle*, 105. Wing B-3951.

263. BOYLE, ROBERT, 1627-1691. *Experiments and considerations touching colours. First occasionally written, among some other essays, to a friend; and now suffer'd to come abroad as the beginning of an experimental history of colours. By the Honourable Robert Boyle....*

London: H. Herringman, 1664. 20 p. l., 423 p. fold. pl. 17 cm. "A short account of some observations made by Mr. Boyle about a diamond that shines in the dark" (p. [389]-423) has special t.-p. Errata: p. [40] (1st group). Wing B-3967. Fulton, J. F. *Boyle.* (2nd ed.) 57.

Ms. marginalia throughout and 2 l. of ms. notes at end.

264. BOYLE, ROBERT, 1627-1691. *New experiments physico-mechanical, touching the spring of the air, and its effects, (made, for the most part, in a new pneumatical engine) written by way of letter to the Right Honorable Charles Lord Vicount of Dungarvan, eldest son to the Earl of Corke. By the Honorable Robert Boyle Esq. The second edition.*

Oxford: Printed by H. Hall, printer to the University, for Tho: Robinson., 1662. [16], 207, [13], 122, [10], 86, [2] (blank), 85-98 p., [2] leaves of plates (1 folded): ill.; 20 cm. Half-title: New experiments physico-mechanical, touching the air. The second edition. Where unto is added A defence of the authors explication of the experiments, against the obiections of Franciscus Linus, and, Thomas Hobbes. Title p. vignette. Special t. p.: A defence of the doctrine touching the spring and weight of the air, propos'd by Mr. R. Boyle in his New physico-mechanical experiments ..., by the author of those experiments. London: Printed by J. G. for Thomas Robinson ..., 1662. – An examen of Mr. T. Hobbes his *Dialogus physicus de naturæ aëris.* As far as it concerns Mr. R. Boyle's book of New experiments ..., by the author of those experiments. London: Printed by J. G. for Thomas Robinson ..., 1662. Issued together. Includes index. Edition statement taken from half t. p. Edited by Robert Sharrock. Errata: pt. 2, p. 122 and pt. 3, p. 98. Horblit, H. D. *Grolier 100 science books,* 15. Fulton, J. F. *Boyle* (2nd ed.), 14. Wing (2nd ed.) B999.

2nd plate bound after preface of pt. 2. Provenance: G. Lindsey (signature) Albert Parsons Sachs (bookplate).

265. BOYLE, ROBERT, 1627-1691. *New experiments physico-mechanicall, touching the spring of the air, and its effects: (made, for the most part, in a new pneumatical engine), written by way of letter to ... Charles, Lord Vicount of Dungarvan ... By the Honorable Robert Boyle....*

Oxford: Printed by H. Hall ... for Tho. Robinson, 1660. [32], 399 [i.e. 389], [3] (last 2 blank) p., [1] folded leaf of plates: ill.; 17 cm. Half-title: New experiments physico-mechanicall touching the air. Errors in pagination: p. nos. 90-99 omitted. *ESTC (RLIN),* R019421. Wing (2nd ed., 1994), B3998. Fulton, J. *Boyle,* 13. Errata: [1] p. at end.

Provenance: Knowsley Library (inscription); David P. Wheatland (booklabel). With: Hooke, Robert. *An attempt for the explication of the phænomena observable in an experiment published by the Honourable Robert Boyle.* London: Printed by J. H. for Sam. Thomson ..., 1661.

266. BOYLE, ROBERT, 1627-1691. *The origine of formes and qualities: (according to the corpuscular philosophy,) illustrated by considerations and experiments, (written formerly by way of notes upon an essay about nitre). By the Honourable Robert Boyle....*

Oxford: Printed by H. Hall printer to the university, for Ric: Davis., An. Dom. MDCLXVI. 1666. [50], 269, [5], 271-433, [1] p.; 14 cm. Wing (2nd ed.) B4014. Fulton, J. F. *Boyle* (2nd ed), 77. Yale. *Cushing,* B592. Waller, E. *Bib. Walleriana,* 10757. "Errata": p. [434].

Provenance: Ed. Wheeler (signature); Herbert McLean Evans (bookplate). Endpapers printed fragments.

267. Boyle, Robert, 1627-1691. *The sceptical chymist; or, Chymico-physical doubts & paradoxes, touching the experiments whereby vulgar spagirists are wont to endeavour to evince their salt, sulphur and mercury, to be the true principles of things. To which in this edition are subjoyn'd divers experiments and notes about the producibleness of chymical principles.*
Oxford: Printed by H. Hall for R. Davis and B. Took, 1680. 10 p.l., 440, [27], 268 p. 18 cm. "Experiments and notes about the prodvcibleness of chymicall principles" with special t.-p. and separate pagination: [27], 268 p. at end. Fulton, J. F. *Boyle.* (2nd ed.) 34. Wing B-4022.
Provenance: George Tennyson (armorial bookplate).

268. Boyle, Robert, 1627-1691. *The sceptical chymist: or Chymico-physical doubts & paradoxes, touching the spagyrist's principles commonly call'd hypostatical, as they are wont to be propos'd and defended by the generality of alchymists : Whereunto is præmis'd part of another discourse relating to the same subject. By the Honourable Robert Boyle, Esq.*
London: Printed by J. Cadwell for J. Crooke, ... , MDCLXI. [1661]. [18], 34, [2], 35-442, [2] p. (the last 2 pages blank); 17 cm. Added t. p. following p. 34: The sceptical chymist: or Chymico-physical doubts & paradoxes, touching the experiments whereby vulgar spagyrists are wont to endeavour to evince their salt, sulphur and mercury, to be the true principles of things. London,: Printed for J. Crooke, ... , 1661. T. p.s in black and red. Wing (2nd ed.) B4021. Fulton, J. F. *Boyle* (2nd ed.), 33. *Milestones of science,* 27. Waller, E. *Bib. Walleriana,* 11092. Burndy. *Science,* 39. Horblit, H. D. *Grolier 100 science books,* 14. Carter & Muir. PMM, 141. Yale. *Cushing,* B594. "Errata": p. 441-442.
R2 not a cancel, p. 437-442 and last (blank) leaf not present.

269. Boyle, Robert, 1627-1691. *Some considerations touching the vsefvlnesse of experimental natural philosophy. Propos'd in a familiar discourse to a friend, by way of invitation to the study of it. By the Honourable Robert Boyle ... A 2d ed. (since the first published June 1663.)*
Oxford: Printed by H. Hall for R. Davis, 1664-71. 2 pt. in 3 v. bd. in 1. 21 x 16 cm. Vol. 1 only is of the 2d edition. Includes indexes. The first part. Of its usefulnesse in reference to the mind of man. 1664. – The second part; the first section (with half-title only) Of its vsefulnesse to physick (1664) – The second tome, later section of the second part. Of its vsefulnesse to the empire of man over inferior creatures. 1671. The six essays composing the "second tome" are separately paged; the last one has caption "Essay X". One leaf, between p. 28 and 29 of the fourth essay (p. 29-31 being an "Appendix") is the table of "Contents" of the six essays. Fulton, J. F. *Boyle.* (2nd ed.) 52 (Oxford issue: B), 53.
Imperfect: ddd4 missing, catchword on last p. cut off.

270. Boyle, Robert, 1627-1691. *Some observations and directions about the barometer / communicated by the same hand [i.e. Robert Boyle] to the author of this tract.*
In the Savoy [London] : Printed by T. N. for John Martyn ... and James Allestry ..., 1667. p. 181-185 ; 23 cm. In: *Philosophical transactions* / Royal Society of London, v. 1 (1665-1666). Caption title. Date of publication from colophon. "These shall be set down, as they came to hand in another Letter; videl."

271. Boyle, Robert, 1627-1691. *The works of the Honourable Robert Boyle. In five volumes; to which is prefixed the life of the author (by Thomas Birch).*
London: Printed for A. Millar, 1744. 5 v. illus., port., fold. plates. 38 cm. Title in red and black; title vignettes (author's port.); tail pieces. Portrait of R. Boyle (front.) engraved by B. Baron.
Provenance: Duke of Buccleugh (armorial bookplate), Herbert McLean Evans (bookplate).

272. Boyle, Robert, 1627-1691. *The works of the Honourable Robert Boyle. In six volumes. To which is prefixed the life of the author ... New ed.*
London: Printed for J. and F. Rivington [and 17 others], 1772. 6 v.: front. (port.), 16 pl. [14 fold.], diagrs.; 30 cm. Vols. 2-6: Printed for W. Johnston [etc.]. Includes index. Title vignette: portrait of the author. Edited by Thomas Birch. "The life of the Honourable Robert Boyle. By Thomas Birch ...": v. 1, p. [v]-ccxviii. "List of the titles of the mss. ... not inserted": v. 1, p. ccxxxvi-ccxxxviii. Port. signed: J. Kersseboom pinxit, B. Baron sculp. Fulton, J. F. *Boyle.* (2nd ed.), 241.
Provenance: Manchester Grammar School Library (inscription).

Brahe, *Astronomiæ instauratæ mechanica*, 1602

273. Bradley, James, 1693?-1762. *A letter from the Reverend Mr. James Bradlely, Savilian Professor of Astronomy at Oxford, and F.R.S., to Dr. Edmond Halley, Astronom. Reg. &c., giving an account of a new discovered motion of the fix'd stars.*

London: Printed for W. Innys ..., 1729. p. 637-661 ; 23 cm. In: *Philosophical transactions* / Royal Society of London, v. 35 (Jul.-Dec. 1727, 1728). Caption title.

274. Bragg, William Henry, Sir, 1862-1942. *X rays and crystal structure, by W. H. Bragg and W. L. Bragg.*

Bell and Sons, Ltd., 1915. vii, 228 p., 1 l. IV pl., diagrs. 23 cm. Includes index. Advertisements: [2] p. at end.

Provenance: Herbert McLean Evans (bookplate); Robert Honeyman IV (Honeyman sale).

275. Brahe, Tycho, 1546-1601. *Historia coelestis [ex libris commentariis manu-scriptis observationum vicennalium ...].*

[Augustae Vindelicorum: Apud Simonem Utzschneiderum, 1666]. 2 v. front., illus. 34cm. Paged continuously. Edited by Lucius Barrettus (anagram of Albertus Curtius). Contains Brahe's observations for the years 1582-1592 and 1594-1601. Observations for the year 1593 are supplied from those of the observatory of Hesse. Engraved frontispiece and port. by Philip Kilian. Calligraphic title pages.

Bound in 1 v. Imperfect: Brahe's full length port. missing.

276. Brahe, Tycho, 1546-1601. *Tycho Brahe's description of his instruments and scientific work, as given in Astronomiæ instauratæ mechanica (Wandesburgi, 1598). Tr. and ed. by Hans Ræder, Elis Strömgren and Bengt Strömgren.*

København I Kommission hos E. Munksgaard, 1946. 144 p. illus., port. 27 cm. At head of title: Det Kongelige danske Videnskabernes selskab.

277. Brahe, Tycho, 1546-1601. *Tychonis Brahe Astronomiæ instauratæ mechanica.*

Noribergae: Apud Leuinum Hulsium., M.DCII [1602]. [108] p. (last p. blank): ill., maps, plans.; 32 cm. Engraved port. on t. p. First published at Wandsbek in 1598. A description of instruments used at Uraniborg and Stjerneborg, on the island of Hven or Ven, with an "Appendix" (p. [95]-[107]) in which the construction of those observatories is shown. Houzeau & Lancaster. *Astronomie* (1964 ed.), 2703. Waller, E. *Bib. Walleriana*, 11999.

With: *Theodori Marcilii ... Ad Q. Horatii Flacci opera omnia ... lectiones.* Parisiis: Apud Bartholomæum Macæum, 1604.

278. Brahe, Tycho, 1546-1601. *Tychonis Brahe Astronomiæ instauratæ progymnasmata: quorum hæc prima pars de restitutione motuum solis et lunæ stellarumque inerrantium tractat: et prætereá de admirandâ nova stella anno 1572 exortâ luculenter agit.*

Typis inchoata Vraniburgi Daniae, absoluta Pragae Bohemiae [s.n.], 1602. [16], 9-112, 01-028, [1], 113-822 [i.e. 864], [12] p.: ill.; 23 cm. Running title: De nova stella anni 1572. First published Copenhagen 1589 – cf. Brunet, *Manuel*, p. 1199. Irregularities in paging: p. 021 omitted, p. 116 misnumbered as 117, 312 as 311, 351 as 331, 367 as 376, 393 as 389, p. 257-272 numbered on one side only; numbers 497-498 omitted, p. 581 misnumbered as 185. Includes index. Errata: last [2] p. Houzeau & Lancaster. *Astronomie* (1964 ed.), 2700.

On spine: Tychonis volum. 1. Provenance: Iohn Marques of Tueedale, Earle of Gifford ... (armorial bookplate); Charles W. Williams (bookplate).

279. Brahe, Tycho, 1546-1601. *Tychonis Brahe, Dani. De noua et nullius æui memoria prius visa stella, iam pridem anno à nato Christo 1572. mense Nouembrj primùm conspecta, contemplatio mathematica. Cui, præter exactam eclipsis lunaris, huius anni, pragmatian, et elegantem in Vraniam elegiam, Epistola quo[que] dedicatoria accessit: in qua, noua & erudita conscribendi diaria metheorologica methodus, vtrius[que] astrologiæ studiosis, eodem autore, proponitur: cuius, ad hunc labentem annum, exemplar, singulari industriæ laboratum conscripsit, quod tamem, multiplicium schematum exprimendorum, quo totum fermè constat, difficultate, edi, hac vice, temporis angustia non patiebatur.*

Hafniæ: Impressit Laurentius Benedictj., 1573. [108] p. (p. [15]-[16] and last page blank): ill.; 21 cm. "Tycho Brahe's earliest work. By his discovery and proof of the existence of a new star in outer space, the assumptions of the infallibility of the ancients and of the immutability of the heavens were upset" – Horblit. Detailed account of the work in: *Tycho Brahe: a picture of scientific life and work in the sixteenth century*, by J. L. E. Dreyer. New York: Dover, 1963, p. 44-57. "The central parts were later reprinted in Tycho's larger work, 'Astronomiæ Instauratæ Progymnasmata' [1602]". Signatures: (:)-(::)4A-K4L6. Horblit, H. D. *Grolier 100 science books*, 16. "Errata": p. [107].

Imperfect: L6 missing and supplied in facsim. (::)4 (blank) is missing. T. p. damaged. Provenance: Robert Honeyman IV (Honeyman sale). Binder: G. Hedberg (label); James Macdonald Co. (stamp on slipcase.)

280. BRAHE, TYCHO, 1546-1601. *Tychonis Brahe Dani, die XXIV Octobris A.D. MDCI defuncti, Operum primitias De nova stella, summi civis memor denuo edidit Regia Societas Scientiarum Danica. Insunt effigies et manus specimen Tychonis.*

Hauniae: 1901. xvi, facsim ([103] p. illus.), 1 l., 30 p. port. 26cm. The facsimile is of the 1573 edition of *De nova et nullius.*

Provenance: Bibliotheca Lindesiana (armorial bookplate).

281. BRAHE, TYCHO, 1546-1601. *Tychonis Brahe De mundi aetherei recentioribus phænomenis liber secundus.*

Typis inchoatus Vraniburgi Daniæ, absolutus Pragæ Bohemiæ: Absolvebatur typis Schumanianis, 1603. [16], 465, [3] p.: ill.; 24 cm. The 2nd volume of a projected work on recent astronomical phenomena. The 1st volume was published in 1602 under title: *Astronomiæ instauratæ progymnasmata.* The 3rd and final volume was never written. Cf. *Tycho Brahe*, by J. L. E. Dreyer. 1890. p. 162-163. Running title: De cometa anni 1577. A reissue of the 1588 ed. with a new t. p. and added preliminary matter. Cf. Dreyer, p. 369. Pages 465-[466] are reset and the colophon is new. Dedication signed: Franciscus Gansneb Tengnagel. Signatures: *-2*4 A-3M4 3N2. Printer statement in imprint is from colophon. Zinner, E. *Astronomische Lit. in Deutschland*, 3952. Houzeau & Lancaster. *Astronomie* (1964 ed.) 2699.

On spine: Tychonis vol. 2 cum aliis. With: *Dialexis de nouæ et prius incognitæ stellæ*, per Thaddæum Hagecium ab Hayck. Francofurti ad Moenum, 1574 – *Alæ seu scalæ mathematicæ*, Thoma Diggeseo. Londini, 1573 – *Parallaticæ commentationis*, authore Joanne Dee. Londini, 1573. Provenance: Iohn, Marques of Tueeddale, Earle of Gifford (armorial bookplate); Charles W. Williams (bookplate).

282. BRAHE, TYCHO, 1546-1601. *Tychonis Brahe mathim eminent Dani Opera omnia, sive Astronomiæ instauratæ progymnasmata, in duas partes distributa, quorum prima de restitutione motuum solis & lunæ, stellarumq[ue] inerrantium tractat. Secunda autem de mundi ætherei recentioribus phænomensis agit. Editio ultima nunc cum indicibus & figuris prodit.*

Francofvrti: Impensis I. G. Schönvvetteri, 1648. 2 p.l., 3-470, [7], 217, [1] p. illus, tables, diagrs. 23x19cm. Part I has running title: De nova stella anni 1572; pt. II: De cometa anni 1577. Part 2 has special t. p.: Operum Tychonis Brahe De mvndi ætherei recentioribus et phænomenis pars secunda.

Schönwetter's 2-leaf dedicatory letter bound in pt. 2 between p. 8 and 10.

283. BRANLEY, FRANKLYN MANSFIELD, 1915- . *The sun: star number one, by Franklyn M. Branley; illustrated by Helmut K. Wimmer.*

New York: Crowell, c1964. 139 p.: ill.; 23 cm. Exploring our universe. Includes index. Bibliography: p. 133.

284. BRAUNMÜHL, ANTON, EDLER VON, 1853-1908. *Christoph Scheiner als Mathematiker, Physiker und Astronom.*

Bamberg: Buchner, 1891. 92 p. illus., facsim., ports., 19 cm. Bayerische Bibliothek, 24. Bd. Verzeichnis der Werke Scheiners: p. 90.

Lower wrapper missing.

285. BRAVAIS, A. (AUGUSTE), 1811-1863. *Études cristallographiques, par M. A. Bravais....*

Paris: Bachelier ..., 1851. IV, 176 p.; 28 cm. Title from cover. "Présentées à l'Académie des Sciences: la première partie, le 26 février 1849; la deuxième partie, le 6 août 1849. La troisième partie, communiquée à la Société Philomathique, le 8 juin 1850." "Extrait du Journal de l' École Polytechnique, XXXIVe cahier." Includes bibliographical references. 1ère ptie. Du cristal considéré comme un simple assemblage de points – 2me ptie. Du cristal considéré comme un assemblage de molécules polyatomiques – Des macles et des hémitropies.

Imperfect: lacks 2 prelim. p. [t. p.?] and all after p. 172. Provenance: author's presentation inscription to Commandant Duprey.

286. Brennan, Martin S. (Martin Stanislaus), 1845-1927. *Familiar astronomy, by Rev. Martin S. Brennan. Rev. and enl. ed.*
St. Louis, Mo.: B. Herder, 1921. vii, 260 p., [8] leaves of plates: ill.; 20 cm. Edition statement from p. vii. Includes index.

287. Brennand, W. *Hindu astronomy, by W. Brennand ...*
London: Published by Chas. Straker & Sons ..., 1896. xiv, [2], 329 [i.e. 309] p., XII leaves of plates: ill.; 25 cm. "Apparent omission of 20 pages is a printer's error. Page 277 reads on from 256." – slip mounted on p. 277. Includes bibliographical references.
Provenance: Herbert Thompson from R. E. B. (inscription).

288. Brester, Albert, 1843-1919. *A summary of my theory of the sun, by A. Brester.*
The Hague: W. P. Van Stockum and Son, 1919. 62, [2] p.: ill.; 24 cm. Bibliography: p. 54-62.

289. Breuer, Josef, 1842-1925. *Über den psychischen Mechanismus hysterischer Phänomene: (Vorläufige Mittheilung), von Dr. Josef Breur und Dr. Sigm. Freud in Wien.*
Leipzig: Veit & Co., 1893. p. 4-10, 43-47; 24 cm. Neurologisches Centralblatt; Jahrg. 12. Caption title. Includes bibliographical references.

290. Brewster, David, Sir, 1781-1868. *The life of Sir Isaac Newton. By David Brewster....*
London: J. Murray, 1831. xv, 366 p. front. (port.) illus., diagrs. 16 cm. Family library; no. 41. Title vignette. Port. by Sir G. Kneller. *Babson Newton Coll.* 600. Gray, G. J. *Newton*, 368.
Provenance: Samuel Hoare (bookplate); Herbert McLean Evans (bookplate).

291. Brewster, David, Sir, 1781-1868. *The life of Sir Isaac Newton, the great philosopher... Revised and edited by W. T. Lynn ... of the Royal Observatory, Greenwich.*
London and Edinburgh: Gall and Inglis [188-?]. 3 p. l., 346 p. illus., port., diagrs. 21 cm.

292. Brewster, David, Sir, 1781-1868. *The martyrs of science, or, The lives of Galileo, Tycho Brahe, and Kepler, by Sir David Brewster ... Sixth edition.*
London: John Murray ..., 1867. ix, [3], 220 p.; 17 cm. Includes bibliographical references.

293. Brewster, David, Sir, 1781-1868. *Memoirs of the life, writings, and discoveries of Sir Isaac Newton. By Sir David Brewster....*
Edinburgh: T. Constable and Co.; [etc., etc.] 1855. 2 v. fronts. (ports.) illus., diagrs. 24 cm. Includes index. Port. by Sir Godfrey Kneller. *Babson Newton Coll.* 258. Gray, G. J. *Newton*, 370.

294. Brewster, David, Sir, 1781-1868. *More worlds than one: the creed of the philosopher and the hope of the Christian, by Sir David Brewster....*
London: John Murray, 1854. vii, [1] (blank), 259 p.; 19 cm.
Provenance: Lees-Museum Bibliotheek (inkstamp); Charles Atwood Kofoid (bookplate). Advertisements: 32 p. following text.

295. Brewster, David, Sir, 1781-1868. *A treatise on the microscope, forming the article under that head in the seventh edition of the Encyclopædia britannica. By Sir David Brewster....*
Edinburgh: A. and C. Black, 1837. viii, 193 p., 1 l. XIV pl. (incl. front.) diagrs. 21 cm. "Erratum": p. [195].
Publisher's flyer pasted inside upper cover. Provenance: Charles Atwood Kofoid (bookplate).

296. Bright, Richard, 1789-1858. *Reports of medical cases: selected with a view of illustrating the symptoms and cure of diseases by a reference to morbid anatomy, by Richard Bright.*
London: Printed by Richard Taylor ... Published by Longman, Rees, Orme, Brown, and Green, 1827-1831. 2 v.; 32 cm. + portfolio (atlas, 62 leaves of plates): ill.; 49cm. Includes index. Atlas contains 41 leaves of explanatory letterpress to accompany the plates of v. 2. Vol. 2, pt. 4, 8 were never engraved. Vol. 2, pts. 1 and 2 paged continuously. Plates signed: Drawn by F. R. Say, engraved by W. Say.
Provenance: Presented to Mr Yarde by the author (inscription); Herbert McLean Evans (bookplate).

297. BRINKLEY, JOHN, BISHOP OF CLOYNE, 1763-1835. *Brinkley's Astronomy, revised and partly re-written, with additional chapters, by John William Stubbs ... and Francis Brünnow ... Third edition, enlarged and improved.*

London: Longmans, Green, and Co., 1886. xx, 335 p.: ill.; 20 cm. Includes index. Includes "Questions for examination": p. 319-330.

Advertisements: 16 p. at end dated August, 1889. Binder's ticket: W. B. Clive & Co. Provenance: M.S. (monogram stamp).

298. BRINKLEY, JOHN, BISHOP OF CLOYNE, 1763-1835. *Elements of astronomy. By John Brinkley ... 2d. ed.*

Dublin: R. E. Mercier; [etc., etc.] 1819. xxiii, 328 p. diagrs. on 6 fold. pl. 21 cm. Includes bibliographical references and index.

Provenance: Saunder, Edith (inscription).

299. BRINKLEY, JOHN, BISHOP OF CLOYNE, 1763-1835. *Elements of plane astronomy, by John Brinkley ...; edited by the Rev. Thomas Luby ... Sixth edition.*

Dublin: Hodges and Smith ..., 1845. xxiii, [1] (blank), 287 p., [1], VI folded leaves of plates: ill.; 22cm. Includes bibliographical references. First ed. published in 1808 as: *Elements of astronomy.*

Binder: J. Edmond (ticket). Provenance: Jacob Strachan (presentation leaf signed John Cruickshank, Math. Prof.; Academia Mariscallana Aberdonensis, (prize binding). Spine title: Brinkley's astronomy.

300. BRIOT, M. (CHARLES), 1817-1882. *Cours de cosmographie ou éléments d'astronomie, par Charles Briot... Deuxième édition.*

Paris: Victor Dalmont ..., 1856. [4], 291 p., III folded leaves of plates: ill.; 22 cm. Ill. signed by Himely and by Lemaitre.

Provenance: J. Rostafiúski (inscription).

301. BRIOT, M. (CHARLES), 1817-1882. *Cours de cosmographie ou éléments d'astronomie: comprenant les matières du programme officiel pour l'enseignement des lycées, par Charles Briot ... Quatrième édition revue et augmentée.*

Paris: Dunod, éditeur ..., 1867. [4], 319 p., [1] folded leaf of plates: ill.; 22 cm. Ill. signed by Dulos and by Lemaitre.

302. BROCKLESBY, JOHN, 1811-1889. *Elements of astronomy: for schools and academies, with explanatory notes, and questions for examination, by John Brocklesby ... A new edition, revised.*

New York: Sheldon and Company ..., 1866. [1], xii, [13]-336 p.: ill.; 20 cm.

Binder: Verrico (ticket).

303. BROGLIE, LOUIS DE, 1892- . *Matter and light; the new physics, tr. by W. H. Johnston.*

New York: Dover Publications 1946. 300 p. illus. 20 cm. Translation of: *Matière et lumière.* "First edition published in English in 1939 ... Reprint edition." "The undulatory aspects of the electron; (address delivered at Stockholm on receiving the Nobel prize, December 12, 1929): p. [165]-179. Includes index.

304. †BROGLIE, LOUIS DE, 1892- . *Ondes et mouvements.*

Paris: Gauthier-Villars, 1926. vi, 133 p. diagrs. 25 cm. Collection de physique mathématique, fasc. 1. Includes bibliographical references. *PMM* 417. La dynamique des quanta. – L'optique des quanta. – Statistique des quanta.

Advertisements: [4] p. following text, [2] p. laid in.

305. BROMME, TRAUGOTT, 1802-1866. *Atlas zu Alex. v. Humboldt's Kosmos: in zweiundvierzig Tafeln mit erläuternden Texte, herausgegeben von Traugott Bromme.*

Stuttgart: Verlag von Krais & Hoffmann, [1854?]. [4], 136 p., 42 leaves of plates: ill., maps (some col.); 30 x 35 cm. Originally issued in 8 parts, 1851-1854. Cf. *NUC pre-1956,* v. 260, p. 104. Printed in triple columns. Illustrated by Bromme, E. Winckelmann, and others. "Chronologische Reihenfolge der vorzüglichsten geographischen Entdeckungen und Reisen, vom Jahre 812 bis 1850": p. 128-134. Includes bibliographical references and index.

Provenance: Min. d. Innern (ink-stamp).

306. BRONGNIART, ADOLPHE, 1801-1876. *Prodrome d'une histoire des végétaux fossiles. Par M. Adolphe Brongniart....*

Paris [etc.]: F. G. Levrault, 1828. viii, 223 p. 21 cm. Includes bibliographical references and index.

Original green printed wrappers bound in. Advertisements: [1] p., lower wrapper.

307. Brooke, Henry. *A guide to the stars, being an easy method of knowing the relative positions of all the fixed stars from the first to the third magnitude in either hemisphere, particularly those that are useful for finding the longitude and latitude at sea. With twelve planispheres, on a new construction, in which the stars are exhibited as they actually appear in the heavens with relation to each other. By Henry Brooke....*

London: Printed for Taylor and Hessey, 1820. xi, 101 p. XII pl. (incl. front.) tables 31 cm.

Provenance: E. B. Robinson (signature).

308. Brown, John Young, 1858-1921. *To the moon and back in ninety days; a thrilling narrative of blended science and adventure, by John Young Brown....*

Providence, Ky.: Lunar Publishing Company, 1922. 9 p. l., 214 p. front., plates, maps, ports. 19 cm.

309. Bruce, E. *An introduction to geography and astronomy: with the use of the globes, by E. and J. Bruce. Ninth edition, with considerable additions and improvements, by the Rev. J. C. Bruce....*

London: Printed for Baldwin and Cradock ..., 1836. viii, 352 p., [360] pages of plates; 24 cm. Colophon reads: G. Woodfall, Printer, Angel Court, Skinner Street, London. Includes index.

Pages of 9th ed., 12mo, interleaved with quarto sheets on which manuscript corrections and additions have been made, probably by the editor of the 9th ed., J. C. Bruce, presumably in preparation for the 10th ed. Spine title: Bruce's Geography and astronomy.

310. Brunfels, Otto, 1488-1534. *Onomasikon [sic], seu, Lexicon medicinæ simplicis, Othonis Brunfelsii primum ingenio, tum amicorum post se recognitione & studio, justiore lima repurgatum, auctum[que]: addita uocum quarundam Germanica expositione, juxta veriorem Dioscoridis historiam.*

Argentorati: Ioannes Schottus ære perennius dedit, 1543, i.e. 1544. [401] p.; 26 cm. First published with title: *Onomastikon medicinæ.* Argentorati: Apud Ioannem Schottum, [14 Apr.] 1534. cf. Adams. Colophon reads: Argentorati: Apud Io. Schottum. 21. Martÿ, 1544. Signatures: a⁶ a-2h⁶ 2i⁴ 2k⁵[2k6blank]. Adams B2929.

Provenance: Ezechiel Bautschner (signature); Edwin S. Clarke (signature) With: Iani Damasceni... Therapeutice methodi. Basilæam: per Henrichum Petrum, (1543). Blank 2k6 missing. Some p. cropped.

311. Brünnow, F. (Franz), 1821-1891. *Lehrbuch der sphärischen Astronomie, von Dr. F. Brünnow. Mit einem Vorwort von J. F. Encke....*

Berlin: F. Dümmler, 1851. xxiv, 591, [1] p. diagrs. on fold. pl. 23 cm.

312. Bruno, Giordano, 1548-1600. *Le ciel reformé: essai de traduction de partie du livre italien, Spaccio della bestia trionfante.*

[S.l. : s.n.]; 1000 700 50 [i.e. 1750]. [4], 92 p.; 15 cm. Translation attributed to Louis De Vougny. Cf. *NUC pre-56*, v. 81, p. 33. Contains the 1st pt. of the 1st dialogue of the 1584 ed. Salvestri, V. *Bruno*, 114.

With: *La vie de mâistre Jean Baptiste Morin.* Paris: Chez Jean Henault, 1660.

313. Bruno, Giordano, 1548-1600. *Opere di Giordano Bruno Nolano, ora per la prima volta raccolte e pubblicate da Adolfo Wagner.*

Lipsia: Weidmann, 1830. 2 v. front. (port.) diagrs. 22 cm. Port. by C. Mayer. Includes reproductions of original title-pages.

Bound in 1 v. Provenance: F. H. Bowring (inscription).

314. Bruno, Giordano, 1548-1600. *Spaccio della bestia trionfante, or, The expulsion of the triumphant beast, translated from the Italian of Jordano Bruno; by J. Toland.*

Paris: [s.n.], 1707. [2], 280 p.; 20 cm. Fictitious t. p.? Cf. Bruno, G. *The expulsion of the triumphant beast.* Translated by A.D. Imerti. New Brunswick, N.J.: Rutgers, U.P., 1964. p. 28, note 4. Translation attributed to William Morehead, cf. *NUC pre-1956*, v. 81, p. 35. Signatures: [pi] B-S⁸ T⁴.

With: *A letter from an Arabian physician to a famous professor in the University of Hall in Saxony.* Paris: [s.n.], 1706.

315. BRYAN, MARGARET, fl. 1815. *A compendious system of astronomy: in a course of familiar lectures, in which the principles of that science are clearly elucidated, so as to be intelligible to those who have not studied the mathematics; also trigonometrical and celestial problems, with a key to the ephemeris, and a vocabulary of the terms of science used in the lectures, which latter are explained agreeably to their application in them, by Margaret Bryan. Second edition.*
London: Printed by H. L. Galabin ... for J. Wallis ..., 1799. xxxviii, 415 p., XVI leaves of plates (3 folded): ill.; 23 cm. Illustrations drawn by author and engraved by T. Condor; frontispiece portrait of author and her daughters painted by Samuel Shelley and engraved by W. Nutter. Subscribers: p. xv-xxix.
Provenance: John Wood (armorial bookplate); John Smith (inscription); A. Le Maire (inscription); P. E. Willem (inkstamp).

316. BRYAN, MARGARET, fl. 1815. *Lectures on natural philosophy: the result of many years' practical experience of the facts elucidated: with an appendix containing a great number and variety of astronomical and geographical problems: also some useful tables and a comprehensive vocabulary, by Margaret Bryan.*
London: Printed by Thomas Davison ...: and sold for the authoress by George Kearsley ... and James Carpenter ..., 1806. [36], 388, [1] p., XXXVI, [1] leaves of plates: ill., port.; 28 cm. At head of title: Dedicated, by permission, to her Royal Highness, the Princess Charlotte of Wales. "Subscribers": p. [21-34] (1st group). Errata: p. [36] (1st group) and [1] p. at end.
Binder: Lubbock, Newcastle (ticket). Provenance: H. E. Relton (booklabel and monogrammed binding).

317. BUCH, LEOPOLD VON, FREIHERR, 1774-1853. *Physicalische Beschreibung der Canarischen Inseln, von Leopold von Buch.*
Berlin: Gedruckt in der Druckerei der K. Akademie der Wissenschaften, 1825. 2 p. l., [2] p., 1 l., 407 p. illus. 30 cm. and atlas of [2] p., XIIIpl. (partly fold., incl. maps) 56 cm. Erratum: verso of p. 407. Includes bibliographical references.
Provenance: Herbert McLean Evans (bookplate); Physikalisch-ökonomische Gesellschaft zu Königsberg (book stamp). From Honeyman sale, pt. 1, no. 537. Extra-illustration: [1] folded leaf with title: Coupes de l'Isle de Teneriffa, engraved by A. Stounder. Set incomplete: atlas wanting.

318. BUCH, LEOPOLD VON, FREIHERR, 1774-1853. *Reise durch Norwegen und Lappland, von Leopold von Buch....*
Berlin: bei G. C. Nauck, 1810. 2 v., [3] folded leaves of plates: ill., maps; 19 cm. Plates signed: F. Guimpel. Includes bibliographical references.
Provenance: B. Westermann & Co. (stationer's label); Mercantile Library, New York (stamp); Errata: [2] p. at end of v. 2.

319. BÜCHNER, LUDWIG, 1824-1899. *Kraft und Stoff: empirisch-naturphilosophische Studien: In allgemein-verständlicher Darstellung, von Louis Büchner.*
Frankfurt a. M.: Meidinger, 1855. xvi, 269 p.; 18 cm. "Berichtigung": p. [vi].
Advertisements, [2] p. following text. Provenance: Herzogl. Karls-Gymnasium, Lehrer-Bibliothek, Bernburg (bookstamp); "Geprüft 19.Jan.47" (book stamp); "Thiele" (inscription); ms. marginalia and underscoring throughout.

320. BUCHWALD, EBERHARD, 1886- . *Das Korrespondenzprinzip, von Eberhard Buchwald.*
Braunschweig: F. Vieweg, 1923. VI, 127 p.: ill.; 23 cm. Sammlung Vieweg: Tagesfragen aus den Gebeiten der Naturwissenschaften und der Technik; Heft 67. Includes bibliographical references and index.
Provenance: E. C. Goldworth (signature). Advertisements on wrappers.

321. BUCKLAND, WILLIAM, 1784-1856. *Reliquiæ diluvianæ, or, Observations on the organic remains contained in caves, fissures, and diluvial gravel, and on other geological phenomena, attesting the action of an universal deluge, by the Rev. William Buckland....*
London: John Murray ..., 1823. vii, [1], 303 p., [28] leaves of plates (some folded): ill. (some col.), maps; 28 cm. On verso of t. p.: London: Printed by Thomas Davison, Whitefriars. Plates signed: Js. Basire, sc.; J. Cross, sc.; W. Buckland [et al.], del.; G. Scharf, lithog. Includes bibliographical references and index.
Provenance: Charles Singer (signature); J. W. (armorial bookplate with motto "Patientia vinces").

Engraved by W. Nutter from a Miniature of the same size painted by Sam. Shelley
Mrs. BRYAN and CHILDREN.

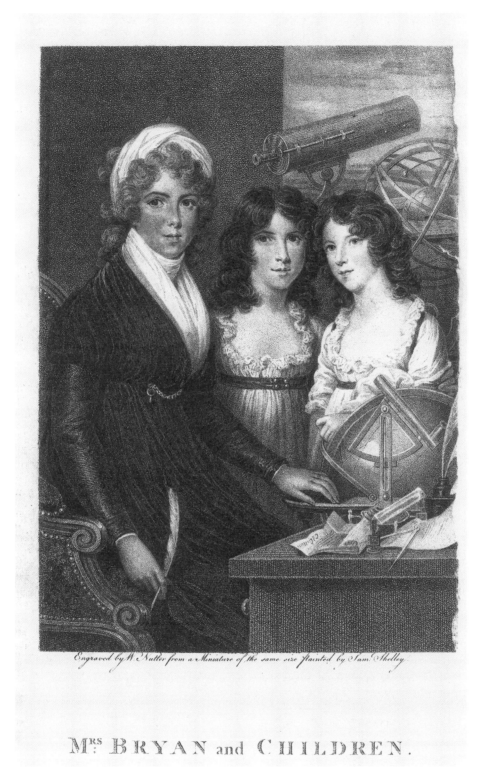

Bryan, *A Compendious System of Astronomy*, 1799

322. BUCKLEY, ARABELLA B. (ARABELLA BURTON), 1840-1929. *A short history of natural science and of the progress of discovery from the time of the Greeks to the present day. For the use of schools and young persons. By Arabella B. Buckley....*

London: J. Murray, 1876. xxv, 467 p. illus., diagrs. 18 cm. "Chronological tables of the rise and progress of the various branches of science": p. [439]-[451]. Includes index.

Provenance: presentation inscription from H. G. Madan to E. J. Mills.

323. BUCKLEY, ARABELLA B. (ARABELLA BURTON), 1840-1929. *A short history of natural science and of the progress of discovery from the time of the Greeks to the present day: for the use of schools and young persons, by Arabella B. Buckley....*

New York: D. Appleton and Company ... , 1884. xxiii, [1] (blank), 467 p., 1 leaf of plates: ill. (1 col.); 20 cm. "Chronological tables of the rise and progress of the various branches of science"; p. [439]-[451]. Includes bibliographical references and index.

Advertisements: [12] p. at end.

324. BÜDELER, WERNER, 1928- *Teleskope, Raketen, Gestirne; die Erforschung des Universums.*

Munich: P. Müller, 1953. 249 p. illus. 23 cm. Welt von Heute; 4. Bd. Bibliography: p. [250].

325. BUFFON, GEORGES LOUIS LECLERC, COMTE DE, 1707-1788. *1781. Epochen der Natur, übersetzt aus dem Französischen des Herrn Grafen von Buffon....*

St. Petersburg: Verlegts Johann Zacharias Logan, 1781. 2 v.: ill., maps; 20 cm. Maps signed: Berndt sculp.; Kellner sc. French original: *Époques de la nature.*

Bound in 1 v.

326. *Builders of the Universe; from the Bible to the Theory of Relativity.*

Westwood Village, Los Angeles, Calif.: The U. S. Library Association, Inc., c1932. 96 p. incl. front., ports. 19 cm. Introduction by Albert Einstein, whose name appears at head of title. Extracts from the Book of Genesis, Copernicus, Brahe, Kepler, Galileo, Newton and Einstein. "Address to the students of the University of California at Los Angeles [February, 1932]" by Albert Einstein (in English and German): p. 91-96.

327. BULLINGER, E. W. (ETHELBERT WILLIAM), 1837-1913. *The witness of the stars, by the Rev. Ethelbert W. Bullinger....*

London: The author, 1893. viii, 204 p. illus., plates (part fold.) 24 cm.

Binder: A. W. Bain & Co. (ticket). Provenance: E. Coley (inscription); Charles Atwood Kofoid (bookplate).

328. BÜRGEL, BRUNO HANS, 1875- . *Astronomy for all, by Bruno H. Bürgel, tr. from the German by Stella Bloch, with over 300 illustrations.*

London, New York [etc.]: Cassell and Company, Ltd. Funk & Wagnalls, 1911. xvi, 352 p. illus., plates, ports. 24 cm. Translation of *Aus fernen Welten.* Includes index. Flap of New York publisher pasted over imprint.

329. BÜRJA, ABEL, 1752-1816. *Lehrbuch der Astronomie, von Abel Bürja.*

Berlin: Bei Schöne, 1794-1806. 5 v., [1] leaf of plates: ill., map; 21 cm."Verbesserungen": v. 5, p. [318-322]. "Verzeichniss": p. [245-6] Bd. 4.

Advertisements: [1] p. at end of Bd. 4.

330. BURNET, THOMAS, 1635?-1715. *Telluris theoria sacra: orbis nostri originem & mutationes generales, quas aut jam subiit, aut olim subiturus est, complectens....*

Londini: Typis R. N., impensis Gualt. Kettilby ..., 1681-1689. 2 v.: ill., maps; 21 cm. Dedication signed: T. Burnetius. Liber II has special t. p. with title: Telluris theoria sacra ... : liber secundus, De tellure primigeniâ & de paradiso. Liber IV has special t. p., dated 1688, with title: Telluris theoria sacra: liber ultimus, De novis cœlis & nova terra, ac de beato seculo, sive, De mundo renovato et rerum omnium consummatione. Advertisements: [1] p. at end of v. 1 and v. 2. Wing B-5948. Wing B-5949. [v. 1] Libri duo priores, De diluvio & paradiso – [v. 2] Libri duo posteriores, De conflagratione mundi, et de futuro rerum statu.

Bound in 1 v.; v. 2 precedes v. 1.

331. Burnet, Thomas, 1635?-1715. *The theory of the earth: containing an account of the original of the earth, and of all the general changes which it hath already undergone, or is to undergo, till the consummation of all things....*

London: Printed by R. Norton, for Walter Kettilby, 1684-1690. 2 v. illus., plates, 2 double maps, diagrs. 34 cm. Engraved half-titles: The sacred theory of the earth. Dedication signed: Thomas Burnet. In four books; second and fourth book each have special t.-p. Published first in Latin with title: *Telluris theoria sacra*, 1681-89. Wing (2nd ed.) B-5950. Wing (2nd ed.) B-5954. Wing (2nd ed.) B-5945. "A review of the Theory of the earth", with special title-page and separate paging ([2], 52 p.) bound at end of v. 2. Advertisements on last p. of v. 2. v. 1. The first two books, Concerning the Deluge, and Concerning Paradise. – v. 2. The last two books, Concerning the burning of the world, and Concerning the new heavens and the new earth.

Bound in 1 v. Provenance: Colonel Cooper (bookplate).

332. Burr, E. F. (Enoch Fitch), 1818-1907. *Ecce clum, or, Parish astronomy: in six lectures, by Enoch Fitch Burr ... Twenty-first edition, revised.*

New York: American Tract Society ..., [after 1878, c1867]. 198 p.; 19 cm. Eighteenth ed.: Boston, 1878, cf. Houzeau & Lancaster. *Astronomie* (1964 ed.), 8458. Publisher's advertisements: p. [2].

Pencil scoring throughout.

333. Burritt, Elijah H. (Elijah Hinsdale), 1794-1838. *Atlas: designed to illustrate Burritt's Geography of the heavens ... A new edition, revised and corrected by Hiram Mattison....*

New York: American Book Company, [1856?]. [10] leaves: all. ill. (some col.); 45 cm. Title from cover. Engraved by W. G. Evans. Some leaves are irregularly numbered.

334. Burritt, Elijah H. (Elijah Hinsdale), 1794-1838. *Atlas, designed to illustrate The geography of the heavens: comprising the following maps ..., by Elijah H. Burritt, A. M. New edition.*

New York: Published by F. J. Huntington and Co ..., [1835?]. VIII leaves of plates (2 folded): all ill. (some col.); 40 cm. Cover title. "Entered according to Act of Congress, in the year 1835, by F. J. Huntington in the Clerk's office of the District Court of Connecticut." Advertisements: lower wrapper. Engraved by W. G. Evans.

Provenance: Abby G. Perry (inscription).Sequence of plates as bound: I, III, II, V, IV, VII, VI, VIII.

335. Burritt, Elijah H. (Elijah Hinsdale), 1794-1838. *The geography of the heavens, and class-book of astronomy: accompanied by a celestial atlas. By Elijah H. Burritt. Greatly enl., rev., and illustrated by H. Mattison. New and rev. ed., cor.*

New York: Sheldon, c1873. 348 p. illus., diagrs. 19 cm. "Explanations and problems adapted to Whitall's planisphere": p. [344]-348. Advertisements on end papers.

Provenance: Mrs. L. C. Francis (inkstamp); Mabel Rice (inscription).

336. Burritt, Elijah H. (Elijah Hinsdale), 1794-1838. *The geography of the heavens, and class-book of astronomy: accompanied by a celestial atlas, by Elijah H. Burritt ... A new edition, revised and illustrated by Hiram Mattison....*

New York: F. J. Huntington and Mason Brothers ..., 1854. xxiv, [25]-324, [27] p.: ill.; 17 cm. At head of title: Revised edition. The atlas (issued separately) has title: *Atlas designed to illustrate Burritt's Geography of the heavens* (varies slightly). Advertisements: p.[4] of cover. Includes bibliographical references.

Provenance: Dr. John R. Leffler (inkstamp); L. C. Springer (signature).

337. Burritt, Elijah H. (Elijah Hinsdale), 1794-1838. *The geography of the heavens, and class-book of astronomy: accompanied by a celestial atlas, by Elijah H. Burritt ... Fifth edition, with an introduction by Thomas Dick....*

New York: Published by F. J. Huntington and Co., 1841. xxiv, [25]-305, [27] p.: ill.; 17 cm. Advertisements on p. [4] of cover. Includes bibliographical references. The atlas (issued separately) has title: *Atlas designed to illustrate Burritt's Geography of the heavens* (varies slightly).

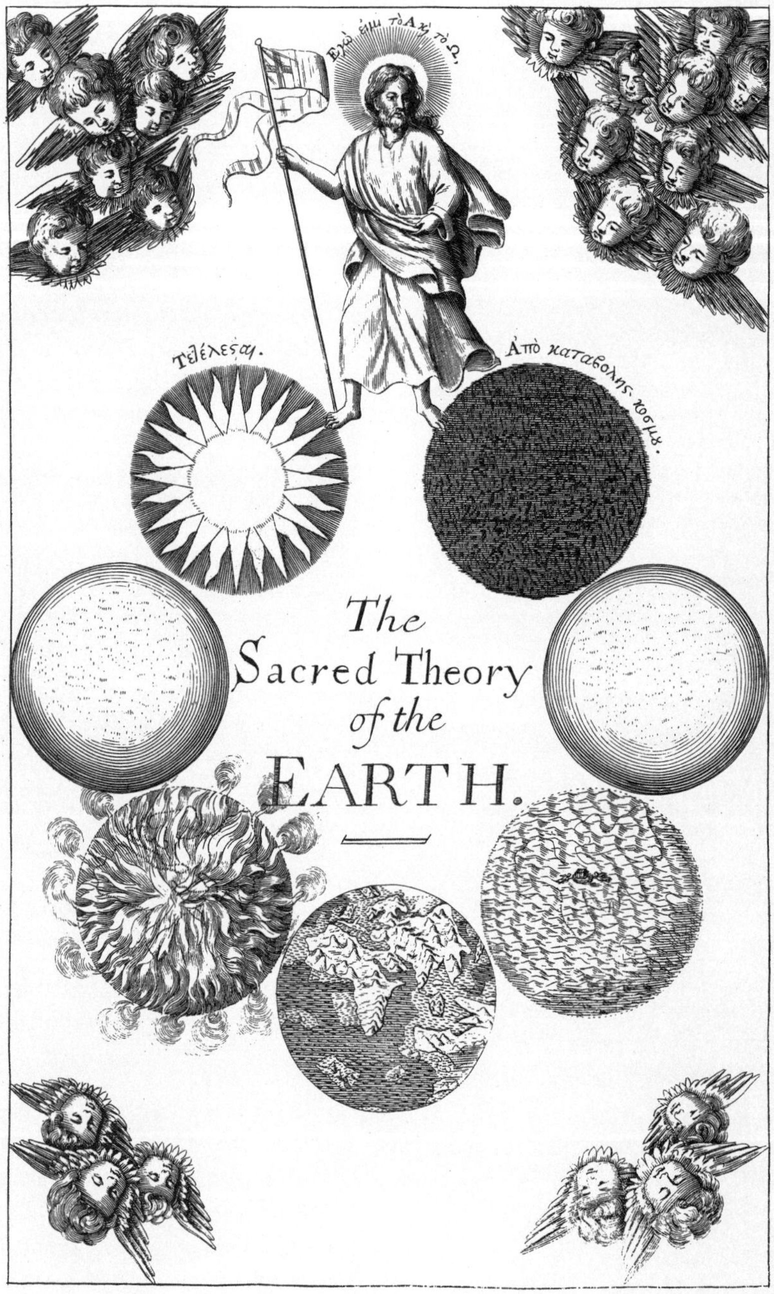

Burnet, *The Theory of the Earth*, 1684-1690

338. BUSCH, AUGUST LUDWIG, 1804-1855. *Reduction of the observations made by Bradley at Kew and Wansted, to determine the quantities of aberration and nutation. By Dr. Busch.*
Oxford: At the University Press, 1838. 1 p. l., 25, 56 p. tables. 28 x 22 cm.
Provenance: translator's presentation copy to Thomas Galloway (inscription).

339. BUTTERFIELD, ARTHUR D. (ARTHUR DEXTER), b. 1870. *A history of the determination of the figure of the earth from arc measurements. By Arthur D. Butterfield....*
Worcester, Mass.: The Davis Press, 1906. 4 p. l., 168 p. 23 cm. Bibliography: p. 162-168. Includes index.
Provenance: author's signed presentation inscription to C. B. Breed; Herbert McLean Evans (bookplate).

340. BUTTERFIELD, HERBERT, SIR, 1900- *The origins of modern science, 1300-1800, by H. Butterfield.*
London: G. Bell, 1949. x, 217 p.; 22 cm. Bibliography: p. 211-213. Includes index.

341. *By starlight and moonlight: with the Warner & Swasey prism terrestrial telescope. Some easy astronomical observations.*
Cleveland, Ohio: Warner & Swasey, c1909. 41 p.: ill.; 23 cm.

342. C. G. S. (C. G. SCHWARTZ), d. 1824. *Le zodiaque expliqué, ou, Recherches sur l'origine et la signification des constellations de la sphère grecque ..., traduit du suédois de C. G. S. Seconde édition.*
Paris: Chez Migneret ... , Desenne ... 1809. [4], 151 p.; 21 cm. First ed. published under the title: *Recherches sur l'origine ... des constellations.* Cf. *BLC*, v. 286, p. 276. Includes bibliographical references. Advertisements: 4 p. inserted following text.
Imperfect: plates and map missing. Provenance: Libraria Barzilay (inscription).

343. CAJORI, FLORIAN, 1859-1930. *A history of mathematics, by Florian Cajori. 2d ed., rev. and enl.*
New York: The Macmillan company; London: Macmillan & Co., Ltd., 1929. viii p., 1 l., 516 p. diagrs. 22 cm.
Provenance: Herbert McLean Evans (signature and bookplate); Marjorie Mayo (signature).

344. CALIFORNIA INSTITUTE OF TECHNOLOGY. *Dedication of the Palomar Observatory and the Hale Telescope, June 3, 1948.*
[Pasadena]: California Institute of Technology, 1948. 33 p. 33 cm. Colophon reads: Printed at the Grabhorn Press, San Francisco.

345. CAMPDOMERCUS, JOHANNES JACOBUS, fl. 1693-1696. *Epistola anatomica, problematica quarta, ad ... Fredericum Ruyschium... de glandulis, fibris, cellulisque lienalibus....*
Amstelaedami: Apud Joannem Wolters, 1696. 16 p. illus. 22 cm. "Frederici Ruyschii responsio ...": p. 6-12.
With: *Frederici Ruyschii ... Observatio anatomico-chirurgicarum centuria.* Amstelodami: Apud Henricum & Viduam Theodori Boom, 1691.

346. CANTOR, GEORG, 1845-1918. *Ein Beitrag zur Mannigfaltigkeitslehre. Von G. Cantor.*
Berlin: G. Reimer 1877. [1], [242]-258 p. 23 cm. "Abdruck aus dem 'Journal für die reine und angewandte Mathematik', Bd. 84."

347. CANTOR, GEORG, 1845-1918. *Grundlagen einer allgemeinen Mannichfaltigkeitslehre; ein mathematisch-philosophischer Versuch in der Lehre des Unendlichen.*
Leipzig: B. G. Teubner, 1883. 47 p. 24 cm.
No. 10 in a v. of 11 items with binder's title: Geometrie.

348. CARDANO, GIROLAMO, 1501-1576. *Hieronymi Cardani medici Mediolanensis De subtilitate libri XXI.*
Lugduni: Apud Gulielmum Rouillium, 1551. [64], 621, [1] p.: ill.; 17 cm. Includes index. Colophon reads: Lugduni, excudebat Philibertus Rolletius.

349. CARL ZEISS (FIRM: 1846). *Astronomical instruments, observatory domes, observation stages and rising floors.*
Jena: Carl Zeiss, [1933]. 87 p.: ill.; 26 cm. "Astro 516e." "Printed in Germany" – p. [4] of cover. Date of publication from *GV, 1911-1965*, v. 63, p. 359.

350. Carl Zeiss (Firm: 1846). Astro Dept. *Astronomical instruments, optical equipment, observatory domes, observation ladders, rising floors.*

[New York?]: Carl Zeiss Jena, Astro Department, [1923]. 142 p.: ill.; 27 cm. Probable place and date of publication from *NUC pre-56*, v. 682, p. 384.

351. Carlyle, Thomas, 1795-1881. *The French revolution; a history ... By Thomas Carlyle....*

London: J. Fraser, 1837. 3 v. 20 cm. First edition. v. 1. The Bastille – v. 2. The constitution – v. 3. The guillotine.

Provenance: J. B. Paton (signature); some ms.notes.

352. Carnot, Lazare, 1753-1823. *Géométrie de position, par L. N. M. Carnot....*

Paris: Chez J. B. M. Duprat, 1803. [4], xxxviij, [2], 489 p., XV folded leaves of plates: ill.; 27 cm.

Provenance: Herbert McLean Evans (bookplate).

353. Carnot, Sadi, 1796-1832. *Réflexions sur la puissance motrice du feu et sur les machines propresa développer cette puissance, par S. Carnot....*

À Paris: Chez Bachelièr ..., 1824. [4], 118 p., [1] folded leaf of plates: ill.; 22 cm. Includes bibliographical references.

Provenance: Herbert McLean Evans (bookplate).

354. Carpenter, William Benjamin, 1813-1885. *Mechanical philosophy, horology, and astronomy. By William B. Carpenter... New ed.*

London: H. G. Bohn, 1857. vii, 579 p. ill., diagrs. 19 cm. Bohn's Scientific Library. Advertisements on endpapers and 4 p. both preceding and following text. Includes bibliographical references and index.

355. Carus, Carl Gustav, 1789-1869. *Von den Ur-Theilen des Knochen- und Schalengerüstes ..., Carl Gustav Carus....*

Leipzig: Bei Gerhard Fleischer, 1828. XVI, 186 p., [1], XII leaves of plates: ill.; 43 cm. Author's name transposed from position at head of title. Plates signed: Carus, del.; Hüllmann, sc. Includes bibliographical references.

Provenance: Herbert McLean Evans (bookplate).

356. Casati, Giuseppe. *Elementi di astronomia, del Dott. Giuseppe Casati ...*

[Turin]: Stamperia Reale di Torino: di G. B. Paravia e Comp., 1880. 179 p.: ill.; 21 cm. Collezione di libri d'istruzione e d'educazione; 188. Advertisements on lower wrapper.

Binder: Homecrafters. Wrappers bound in.

357. Casati, Paolo, 1617-1707. *Fabrica et vso del compasso di proportione : doue insegna à gli artefici il modo di fare in esso le necessarie diuisioni, e con varij problemi vsuali mostra l'vtilità di questo stromento / del molto rev. P. Paolo Casati della Compagnia di Giesù ; dando le ragioni, & apportando le dimostrationi di tutte le operationi nella fabrica, e nel-l'vso ; opera vtile non solo à geometri, agrimensori ... ma anche a bombardieri, sergenti di battaglia, mercanti, & altri, per molte operationi aritmetiche, fatte con grandissima facilità.*

In Bologna : Presso Gio. Battista Ferroni, 1664. [8], 172, [12] (last p. blank) p., [4] leaves of folded plates : ill., 22cm. Errata: p. [9]-[11] (last sequence).

Label with 'Il' mounted over 'del' of statement of responsibility on title.

358. Caspar, Max, 1880-1956. *Bibliographia Kepleriana. Ein Führer durch das gedruckte Schrifttum von Johannes Kepler. Im Auftrag der Bayerischen Akademie der Wissenschaften unter Mitarbeit von Ludwig Rothenfelder hrsg. von Max Caspar. (Mit 86 Faksimiles.) 2. Aufl. Besorgt von Martha List.*

München: Beck, 1968. xiv, 181, [84] p.: facsims.; 31 cm.

359. Casseri, Giulio Cesare, ca. 1552-1616. *Iulii Casserii Placentini philosophi atq[ue] medici Patauii ... De vocis auditusq[ue] organis historia anatomica: singulari fide methodo ac industria concinnata tractatibus duobus explicata ac variis iconibus œre excusis illustrata.*

Ferrariæ: Excudebat Victorius Baldinus ..., 1601. [60], 191, [1], 126, [1] p.: ill., 2 ports.; 41 cm. Colophon (p. [127] at end): Ferrariæ, Excudebat Victorius Baldinus ...sumptibus Unitorum Patavii, 1600. Imprint

from colophon on p. [192] dated 1601. This is probably the correct date for both parts. Errata: p. [60]. Engraved title page. Includes indexes. 34 full-page engravings by Josias Murer. Cf. Choulant. *Hist. and bibl. of anatomic illus.* Chicago [1920], p. 223.
Provenance: Kimbolton Castle (bookplate).

360. CASSINI, GIOVANNI DOMENICO, 1625-1712. *Novæ observationes circa systema Saturni, habitæ in Observatorio Regio Parisiis a Dn. Joh. Dom. Cassino, lentibus Dn. Joannis Campani.*
[Leipzig]: J. Grossium & J. F. Gletitschium, 1686. p. 469-470, [1] folded leaf of plates: ill.; 20 cm. Caption title. Detached from: *Acta eruditorum*, mensis septembris, a. 1686.

361. CASSINI, JACQUES, 1677-1756. *Éléments d'astronomie. Par Mr. Cassini.*
A Paris: De l'Imprimerie Royale, 1740. xvj, [12], 643 p. 88 diagr. on [21] fold. pl. 26 cm. Title vignette. To accompany volume for 1740 of "Académie des Sciences, Paris. *Histoire.*" cf. Lasteyrie. Illustrated by Simonneau.

362. CASSINI, JACQUES, 1677-1756. *Tables astronomiques du soleil, de la lune, des planètes, des étoiles fixes, et des satellites de Jupiter et de Saturne: avec l'explication & l'usage de ces mêmes tables, par Mr. Cassini....*
À Paris: De l'Imprimerie Royale, 1740. xiv, [6], 120, 222, [2] p.: diagr.; 26 cm. First edition. Title vignette. Pictorial head pieces; initial. To accompany volume for 1740 of Académie des Sciences, Paris. *Histoire.* cf. Lasteyrie. Illustrated by Simonneau and Thomassin.
Spine title: Table astro tom 2.

363. CASTELLI, BENEDETTO, 1577 or 8-1643. *Risposta alle opposizioni del s. Lodovico delle Colombe e del s. Vincenzio di Grazia, contro al trattato del sig. Galileo Galilei. Delle cose che stanno sù l'acqua, ò che in quella si muouono. All illvstriss. sig. Enéa Piccolomini Aragona, signore de Sticciano, &c. Nella quale si contengono molte considerazioni filosofiche remote dalle vulgate opinioni....*
In Firenze: Appresso Cosimo Giunti, MDCXV [1615]. 2 p. l., 319 [i.e. 335], [5]; 22 cm. Numerous errors in pagination. Preface signed: Benedetto Castelli. Marginalia.

364. CASWELL, JOHN, 1654 or 5-1712. *A brief (but full) account of the doctrine of trigonometry, both plain and spherical, by John Caswell....*
London: Printed by John Playford for Richard Davis, bookseller in the University of Oxford, 1685. (2), 17 p. diagrs. 31 cm. Wing C1252. Bound, as issued, with Wallis, John. *A treatise of algebra* ... London, 1685.
Provenance: Lord Gerard (bookseller's label); Robert Honeyman (Honeyman sale).

365. *Catalogue des livres composant la Bibliothèque de feu M. Joseph-Jêrome Le François de la Lalande ... : dont la vente aura lieu dans le courant du mois de mars 1808, au Collège de France, place Cambrai.*
À Paris: Chez MM. Leblanc ...; Mérault ... 1808. xij, 218 p.; 22 cm.
Provenance: Mr. Ja[net?] Palais de Justice (inscription).

366. CATHOLIC CHURCH. COMMISSIO AD KALENDARII EMENDATIONEM. *Kalendarium perpetuum: secundum vsum Sanctæ Romanæ Ecclesiæ. Seruata forma breuiarii nuperrimè restituti, ac ad nouum kalendarii Gregoriani ordinem accomodatum.*
Venetiis: Apud Iuntas, 1584. [480] p.; 17 cm. Date on colophon: 1582. Signatures: $+^8$ $++^8$ $+++^4$ A-2D^8 2E^4.

367. CAUCHY, AUGUSTIN LOUIS, BARON, 1789-1857. *Mémoire sur la dispersion de la lumière, par M. A. L. Cauchy ... Pub. par la Société Royale des Sciences de Prague.*
Prague: J. G. Calve, 1836. iv, 236 p. tables. 26 x 21 cm. Errata: p. 235-236. On p. 234: Extrait des mémoires publiés par la Société royale des sciences de Prague.
Provenance: J. Horner (signature).

368. CAUCHY, AUGUSTIN LOUIS, BARON, 1789-1857. *Mémoire sur la théorie de la lumière, par M. Augustin-Louis Cauchy....*
À Paris: Chez de Bure Frères ..., 1830. [2], 24 p.,; 23 cm.

369. Cavallo, Tiberius, 1749-1809. *The elements of natural or experimental philosophy, by Tiberius Cavallo ... Fourth American edition, with additional notes, selected from various authors, by F. X. Brosius.*
Philadelphia: Towar & Hogan ..., 1829. xii, [13]-783 p., 21 folded leaves of plates: ill.; 23 cm. Includes bibliographical references and index. "Two volumes in one." Paged continuously.

370. Cavendish, Henry, 1731-1810. *The electrical researches, of the honourable Henry Cavendish, F.R.S., written between 1771 and 1781, ed. from the original manuscripts, by J. Clerk Maxwell.*
Cambridge [Eng.]: University Press, 1879. lxvi, 454 p. illus., facisms. 24 cm. Includes index.
Provenance: George E. Hale (inscription).

371. Cavendish, Henry, 1731-1810. *Experiments on air / by Henry Cavendish, Esq.....*
London : Sold by Lockyer Davis and Peter Elmsly ..., 1784. p. 119-153 ; 23 cm. In: *Philosophical transactions* / Royal Society of London, v. 74. Caption title. "Read Jan. 15, 1784". Followed by: Remarks on Mr. Cavendish's Experiments on air : in a letter from Richard Kirwan, Esq., F.R.S., to Sir Joseph Banks, Bart., P.R.S. (p. 154-169); Answer to Mr. Kirwan's Remarks upon the Experiments on air / by Henry Cavendish, Esq. ... (p. 170-177); and Reply to Mr. Cavendish's Answer / by Richard Kirwan, Esq ... (p. 178-180). Cavendish contributed another paper, with the same title to v. 75 of the *Philosophical transactions*: Experiments on air / by Henry Cavendish, Esq. ... : read June 2, 1785 (p. 372-384, [1] leaf of plates). Burndy. *Science*, 42.

372. Cavendish, Henry, 1731-1810. *Experiments to determine the density of the earth, by Henry Cavendish...; from the Philosophical transactions.*
[London]: Royal Society, 1798. [2], 58 p., [2] folded leaves of plates: ill.; 28 cm. Title from half-title page. "Read before the Royal Society, June 21, 1798" – p. [1].

373. Cellarius, Andreas. *Harmonia macrocosmica, seu atlas universalis et novus: totius universi creati cosmographiam generalem, et novam exhibens ..., studio, et labore Andreæ Cellarii Palatini....*
Amstelodami: Apud Petrum Schenk & Gerardum Valk, 1708. [6] p., 29 folded leaves of plates: chiefly ill., maps; 50 cm. Added engraved t. p. signed: F. H. v. Hoven fec. With title: *Atlas coelestis seu Harmonia macrocosmica...* Some plates signed: J. van Loon f. Hand coloured.

374. Cellarius, Andreas. *Harmonia macrocosmica, seu atlas universalis et novus: totius universi creati cosmographiam generalem, et novam exhibens ..., studio, et labore Andreæ Cellarii Palatini....*
Amstelodami: Apud Joannem Janssonium, 1661. [16], 125, [1] (blank), 219 p., [29] folded leaves of plates: ill., maps; 52 cm. Added engraved t. p. signed F. H. v. Hoven fec., with title: *Atlas coelestis seu Harmonia macrocosmica* ... Some plates signed: J. van Loon f.

375. Cesalpino, Andrea, 1524 or 5-1603. *De plantis libri XVI. Andreæ Cæsalpini....*
Florentize: Apud G. Marescottum, 1583. 20 p. l., 621, [10] p. 22 cm. Erratorum grauiorum correctio: p. [7-9] at end. Colophon reads: Excudebat Georgius Marescottus, 1583. Includes indexes. Adams C20. Pritzel 1640*.
Provenance: Thomas Aloysius Olivieri (inscription), Herbert McLean Evans (bookplate).

376. Chadwick, James, Sir, 1891- *[Collection of journal articles, by James Chadwick].*
[1932-1934] 3 pieces: ill.; 26-27 cm. Includes bibliographical references. (1) Possible existence of a neutron (1932) – (2) The neutron (1933) – (3) Some experiments on the production of positive electrons (1934).

377. Chalmers, Thomas, 1780-1847. *A series of discourses on the Christian revelation, viewed in connection with the modern astronomy. By Thomas Chalmers....*
New York: American Tract Society [185-?]. 263 p. 20 cm.
[1] p. of advertisements at end. Provenance: Don Maxfield (signature).

378. Chamber, John, 1546-1604. *Astronomiae encomium. A Ioanne Chambero ante annos 27. peroratum, quo tempore Ptolemæi Almagestum, in alma Vniuersitate Oxonien. Publice enarrauit.*

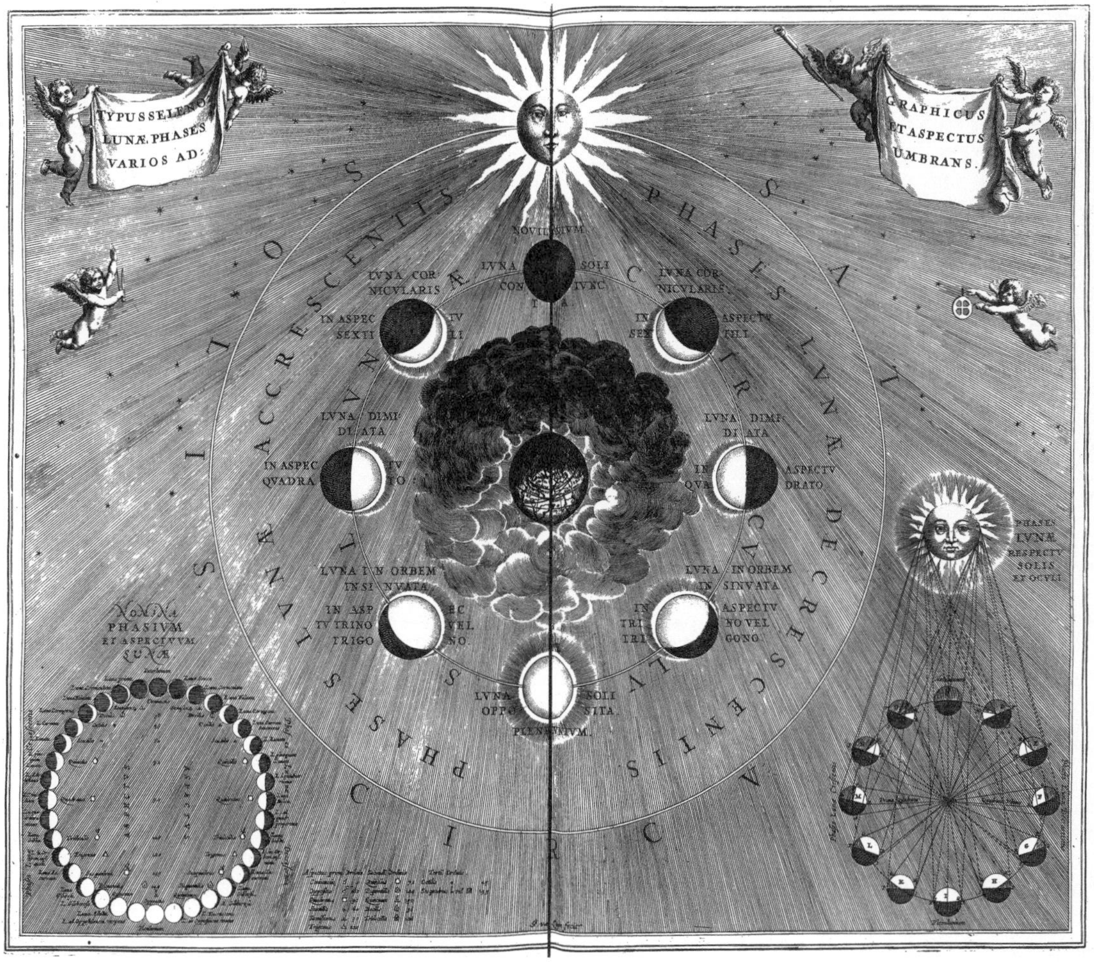

CELLARIUS, *Harmonia macrocosmica*, 1661

Londini: Excudebat Ioannes Harisonus, 1601. [2], 41 p.; 18 cm. Errata: p. 41. English translation by the author: p. 21-41, with running title The praise of astronomie.

Binder: Lloyd (ink-stamp); binder's blank leaves bound at end.

379. CHAMBER, JOHN, 1546-1604. *A treatise against iudicial astrologie. written by Iohn Chamber....*

Printed at London: by John Harison ..., 1601. [16], 132 [i.e. 142], [1] p.: ill.; 19 cm. Errors in pagination: p. 53-54 repeated, p. 97-98 omitted, between p.114 and 115 are p. 117-125 with the first 5 lines onp. 117 duplicated on p. 115; p. 131 misnumbered 133 and 134 as 132. Errata: last p. *STC* 4941. Houzeau & Lancaster. *Astronomie* (1964 ed.), 5012.

Binder: Riviere (stamp). Provenance: Johannes Sothernns (inscription); some manuscript notes; (MAW)? (monogram on binding).

380. CHAMBERS, GEORGE F. (GEORGE FREDERICK), 1841-1915. *Astronomy by George F. Chambers.*

New York: D. Van Nostrand, [1912?]. xxiii, 335 p., 135 p. of plates: ill. (some col.), maps; 16 cm. Advertisements: [2] p. following text. Includes index.

381. Chambers, George F. (George Frederick), 1841-1915. *A handbook of descriptive and practical astronomy, by George F. Chambers....*

London: John Murray ..., 1861. xlvi, 514 p., LII leaves of plates: ill. (some col.); 20 cm. Includes bibliographies and indexes.

Advertisements: [2] p. following text. Binder: Edmonds & Remnants (ticket). Provenance: Henry M. E. Crofton (inscription). Errata slip tipped in following p. xlvi.

382. Chambers, George F. (George Frederick), 1841-1915. *A handbook of descriptive and practical astronomy. By George F. Chambers. 4th ed.*

Oxford: Clarendon Press, 1889-1890. 3 v. fronts., illus., plates (part col., part fold.) tab., diagrs. (part fold.) 23 cm. Clarendon Press Series. Plates XXVII and XXVIII of v. 2 (observatory plans) in pocket.. Title vignettes. First edition, 1861; 2d., 1867; 3d., 1876. "Catalogue of ... comets": v. 1, p. 511-588. "Tables of the planets": v. 1, p. [651]-671. "Sketch of the history of astronomy ... a chronological summary": v. 2, p. [468]-486. "Vocabulary of definitions": v. 2, p. [541]-554. Catalogues of stars: v. 3, p. 119-334. Includes indexes. Astronomical bibliography: List of published star catalogues and celestial charts: v. 2, p. [487]-505; list of books relating to, or bearing on, astronomy: v. 2, p. 506-515. v. 1. The sun, planets, and comets. – v. 2. Instruments and practical astronomy. – v. 3. The starry heavens.

Advertisements: publisher's catalogs, 8 p. at end, v. 1; [2], 8 p. at end, v. 2; 72 p. at end, v. 3. Provenance: J. Jay Pierrepont (ink-stamp). Vol. 1 lacks series statement.

383. Chambers, George F. (George Frederick), 1841-1915. *Pictorial astronomy: for general readers, by George F. Chambers....*

London: Whittaker & Co. ..., 1891. xv, [1], 268, [4] p.: ill.; 18 cm. Library of Popular Science. On cover: Whittakers Library of Popular Science. Advertisements: [4] p. at end. Includes index.

Newspaper cuttings and ms. notes pasted in.

384. Chambers, George F. (George Frederick), 1841-1915. *The stars, by George F. Chambers. 2nd ed.*

London: Hodder and Stoughton, 1912. 192 p.: ill; 18 cm. Also published as: *The story of the stars.* Date of publication taken from preface. Includes index.

Provenance: J. M. Kukman (inscription).

385. Chambers, George F. (George Frederick), 1841-1915. *The story of eclipses, by George F. Chambers.*

New York: University Society, Inc., 1909. 208 p.: ill.; 19 cm. Library of Valuable Knowledge. Series title stamped on spine. Includes bibliographical references and index.

386. Chambers, George F. (George Frederick), 1841-1915. *The story of the comets simply told for general readers, by George F. Chambers.*

Oxford: The Clarendon Press, 1909. xiii p., 1 l., 256 p. incl. diagrs., tables. xxvii pl. (incl. front.) 23 cm. Appendixes: I. A catalogue of recent comets, 1888-1908. – II. A supplementary catalogue of comets recorded, but not with sufficient precision to enable their orbits to be calculated. – III. The literature of comets. – IV. Ephemeris of Halley's comet, September, 1909-July, 1910. Includes index.

387. Chambers, George F. (George Frederick), 1841-1915. *The story of the stars, by George F. Chambers.*

New York: D. Appleton, 1902, c. 1895. x, 160 p.: ill; 20 cm. Library of Valuable Information.

388. Chambers, George F. (George Frederick), 1841-1915. *The story of the stars: simply told for general readers, by George F. Chambers.*

New York: D. Appleton, 1900. 160 p. : ill; 16 cm. *Library of Useful Stories* (New York, N.Y.). Includes index. Originally published: 1895.

389. Chambers, Robert, 1802-1871. *Explanations: a sequel to "Vestiges of the natural history of creation", by the author of that work.*

New York: Wiley & Putnam ..., 1846. vii, [1] (blank), 142 p.; 21 cm. Includes bibliographical references.

Advertisements: [4], xxvii-[xxxiv], vi p. following text. Provenance: Herbert McLean Evans (bookplate); T. B. Lawson (inscription).

390. CHAMBERS, ROBERT, 1802-1871. *Vestiges of the natural history of creation.*
London: J. Churchill, 1844. vi, 390 p. incl. diagr. 20 cm.
Binder: Remnant & Edmonds (ticket).

391. CHAMISSO, ADALBERT VON, 1781-1838. *De animalibus quibusdam e classe vermium Linnæana in circumnavigatione terræ auspicante Comite N. Romanzoff duce Ottone de Kotzebue annis 1815. 1816. 1817. 1818. peracta observatis, Adelbertus de Chamisso.*
Berolini: apud Ferd. Dümmlerum, 1819. IV, 24 p., [1] folded leaves of plates: col. ill.; 29 cm. Plate signed by the author and by F. Guimpel. Includes bibliographical references. (From t. p.) Fasciculus primus. De salpa. (No more published cf. *BLC* v. 58, p. 178).
Provenance: Herbert McLean Evans (bookplate).

392. CHANDRASEKHAR, S. (SUBRAHMANYAN), 1910- *Principles of stellar dynamics, by S. Chandrasekhar....*
Chicago, Ill.: University of Chicago Press, 1942. x, 251 p. incl. illus., tables, diagrs., front., vi plates. 24 cm. Astrophysical monographs, sponsored by the *Astrophysical Journal;* ed. by P. W. Merrill, J. H. Moore, Harlow Shapley [and] Otto Struve. "Bibliographical notes" at end of each chapter. Includes index.
Provenance: Arthur A. Finch, M.D. (book label).

393. CHANT, CLARENCE AUGUSTUS, 1865- *Our wonderful universe; an easy introduction to the study of the heavens, by Clarence Augustus Chant....*
London [etc.]: G. G. Harrap & Company Ltd. 1928. 191 p. incl. front., illus., charts, tables. 20 cm. Includes index.

394. CHARPENTIER, JOHANN VON, 1786-1855. *Essai sur les glaciers et sur le terrain erratique du bassin du Rhône, par Jean de Charpentier ... Avec des vignettes, des planches, et une carte du terrain erratique du bassin du Rhône.*
Lausanne: M. Ducloux, 1841. 2 p. l., x, 363 [i.e. 362] p., 1 l. illus., 9 pl. (1 fold.), fold. map, diagrs. 22 cm. Final p. misnumbered 363 for 362.
Errata leaf bound after p. 358.

395. CHASLES, M. (MICHEL), 1793-1880. *Catalogue de la bibliothèque scientifique, historique et littéraire de feu Michel Chasles (de l'Institut): dont la vente aux enchères publiques aura lieu du 27 juin au 18 juillet 1881 ... par le ministère de Me Georges Boulland assisté de M. A. Claudin....*
Paris: A. Claudin ..., 1881. vii, [1] (blank), 390, [1] p.; 23 cm.
Provenance: Scipion du Roure (inscription).

396. CHAUCER, GEOFFREY, d. 1400. *The works of Geoffrey Chaucer and others; being a reproduction in facsimile of the first collected edition 1532, from the copy in the British Museum; with an introduction by Walter W. Skeat....*
London: A. Moring, Ltd., H. Frowde 1905. xliv, facsim.: 793 p. ill. 38 x 29 cm. Original title (within ornamental border): *The workes of Geffray Chaucer newly printed with dyuers workes whiche were neuer in print before: As in the table more playnly dothe appere.* Cum priuilegio (Colophon: Thus endeth the workes of Geffray Chaucer. Printed at Lodon byThomas Godfray. The yere of our lorde. M.D.XXXII ...). Original collation: 22 p.l. (incl. all but last leaf of the Knyghtestale) xiii-ccclxxxiii [i.e. ccclxxxvii] numb. l. (3 unnumb. l. being inserted, and number ccc repeated). Half-titles preceding longer works have same border as t.-p. Original edition published by William Thynne. "Exclusive of The Romaunt of the rose, part of which is by Chaucer, and Surigon's Latin epitaph, the folio includes 40 pieces. Of these, 18 are by Chaucer; 8 [apparently] by Lydgate; 2 by Hoccleve; 1 apiece by Henryson, Ros, Usk, Gower, Clanvowe, and Scogan (6 in all); and 6 are anonymous. To these we may add 1 more piece by Chaucer, viz. his Balade on gentilesse, introduced into the midst of the piece by Scogan ... If we reckon by pages, the genuine works occupy less than three-fourths of the volume." – Introd. "One thousand copies of this facsimile have been printed." "List of subscribers": p. [v]-vii.
No. 255. Binding: full reverse calf with self-ties.

397. CHAULNES, MICHEL-FERDINAND D'ALBERT D'AILLY, DUC DE, 1714-1769. *Nouvelle méthode pour diviser les instruments de mathématique et d'astronomie / par M. le duc de Chaulnes.*

[Paris] : De l'imprimerie de L. F. Delatour, 1768. [2], 44 p., XV leaves of plates : ill. ; 42 cm. Corrections et additions: verso of t.p.

398. CHIEVITZ, JOHAN HENRIK, 1850-1901. *Anatomiens historie, I. H. Chievitz; en række foredrag samlede og udgivne af E. Hauch.*
Kjøbenhavn: Gyldendalske Boghandel; Nordisk Forlag, 1904. [4], 289, [2] p.: ill., ports.; 26 cm. Author's name appears at head of title. Includes bibliographical references and index.
Provenance: Lund Universitets Biblioteket (book stamp).

399. CHLADNI, ERNST FLORENS FRIEDRICH, 1756-1827. *Die Akustik, bearb. von Ernst Florens Friedrich Chladni ... Mit 12 Kupfertafeln.*
Leipzig: Breitkopf und Härtel, 1802. 2 p.l., [iii]-xxxii, 304 p., 1 l., 305-310 p. XII pl. 25 cm. Title vignette: portrait of author, signed: F. W. Bollinger. Errata: p. 310. Engelmann, W. *Bibliotheca mech.-tech.* Leipzig 1844 (Repr. 1970), p. 66.
In slipcase. Binder: B. Vera (stamp). Imperfect copy?: XI numbered plates only.

400. CHLADNI, ERNST FLORENS FRIEDRICH, 1756-1827.*Entdeckungen über die Theorie des Klanges, von Ernst Florens Friedrich Chladni ... Mit eilf Kupfertafeln.*
Leipzig: Bey Weidmanns Erben und Reich, 1787. [4], 77, [1] p.: xi pl.; 21 cm.
Ms. note: [1] leaf following text.

401. CHOULANT, LUDWIG, 1791-1861. *History and bibliography of anatomic illustration, by Ludwig Choulant, translated and annotated by Mortimer Frank. Further essays by Fielding H. Garrison, Mortimer Frank [and] Edward C. Streeter, with a new historical essay by Charles Singer, and a bibliography of Mortimer Frank, by J. Christian Bay....*
New York: Schuman's, 1945. xxvii, 435 [i.e. 453] p. illus., plates, 2 port (incl. front.) facsims., diagrs. 26 cm. Translation of: *Geschichte und Bibliographie der anatomischen Abbildung.* Includes extra numbered pages, 21-A-21-R. "Revised edition, October 1945." Includes facsimile of original t.-p. Includes bibliographies.

402. CLAIRAUT, M., 1713-1765. *Théorie de la figure de la terre, tirée des principes de l'hydrostatique. Par m. Clairaut....*
Paris: Durand, 1743. xl, 305, [5] p. diagrs. 21 cm. Title vignette.

403. CLARK, LATIMER, 1822-1898. *The star-guide: a list of the most remarkable celestial objects visible with small telescopes with their positions for every tenth day in the year and other astronomical information, by Latimer Clark ... and Herbert Sadler....*
London: Macmillan and Co., 1886. xvi, 48, 6 p.: ill.; 26 cm. Advertisements: 6 p. at end.
Provenance: Radcliffe Library, Oxford (inkstamp); Alexander Bernstein (inscription).

404. CLARKE, ARTHUR CHARLES, 1917- . *The exploration of space, Arthur C. Clarke.*
New York: Harper, [c1951]. xiii, 199 p., [15] p. of plates: ill. (some col.); 21 cm. Includes index.

405. CLARKE, ELIOT C. (ELIOT CHANNING), 1845-1921. *Astronomy from a dipper, Eliot C. Clarke.*
Boston ; New York: Houghton Mifflin Company, [1910, c1909]. x, 66 p.: ill.; 12 x 21 cm. With charts by the author.

406. CLARKE, ELIOT C. (ELIOT CHANNING), 1845-1921. *Astronomy from a dipper, by Eliot Clarke.*
Boston: Houghton Mifflin, 1909. x, 66 p.: ill.; 12 x 21 cm.
Provenance: L. H. Thompson (signature).

407. CLAUSIUS, R. (RUDOLF), 1822-1888. *Abhandlungen über die mechanische Wärmetheorie. Von R. Clausius....*
Braunschweig: F. Vieweg und Sohn, 1864-67. 2 v. tables, diagrs. 22 cm. 1. Abt. Abhandlungen, welche die Begründung der mechanischen Wärmetheorie, nebst ihrer Anwendung auf die in die Wärmelehre gehörigen Eigenschaften der Körper und auf die Dampfmaschinentheorie enthalten; vervollständigt durch eine mathematische Einleitung und durch erläuternde Anmerkungen und Zusätze. – 2. Abt. Abhandlungen über die Anwendung der mechanischen Wärmetheorie auf die elektrischen Erschei-

nungen, nebst einer Einleitung in die mathematische Behandlung der Electricität; Abhandlungen über die zur Erklärung der Wärme angenommenen Molecularbewegung und eine auf die allgemeine Theorie bezügliche Abhandlung; vervollständigt durch erläuternde Anmerkungen und Zusätze.

Bound in 1 v. Provenance: Ernst Mach (inkstamp and signature).

408. CLAVIUS, CHRISTOPH, 1538-1612. *Christophori Clauii Bambergensis ex Societate Iesu in Sphæram Ioannis de Sacro Bosco commentarius. Nunc tertio ab ipso auctore recognitus, & plerisque in locis locupletatus. Maiori item cura correctus.*

Venetiis: Apud Bernardum Basam ... , 1596. [32], 483, [1] p.: ill.; 22 cm. Originally published: Rome, 1570. Signatures: [cross]-2[cross]^8 A-2F^8 2G^{10} (2[cross]8 blank). P. [31-32] blank. Alden, J. E. *European Americana*, 596/28. Contains scattered references to the New World. Includes index.

Provenance: Simonelli, Fabritius (inscription).

409. CLAVIUS, CHRISTOPH, 1538-1612. *Christophori Clavii Bambergensis e Societate Iesu Astrolabium.*

Romae: Impensis Bartholomæi Grassi, ex typographia Gabiana, 1593. [48], 759 [i.e. 749], [6] (last 2 blank) p.: ill.; 22 cm. Signatures: *^{4} a-e^4 A-5A^4 5B^6. Errata: p. [1]-[3] (3rd sequence). Many errors in paging, notably p. 185-192 numbered 189-196 and p. 440-749 numbered 450-759. Title vignette (astrolabe) with the motto: Sic luditur astris. Page [4] (3rd sequence) is dated "die Assumptionis Gloriosæ Beatiss. Virginis 1593"; the dedication III. non. Septemb. MDXCIII; the præfatio" die 26. Augusti 1593." Adams, C-2093. Backer-Sommervogel, II: 1217

410. CLEOMEDES. *Cleomedis Meteora Græce et Latine, a Roberto Balforeo ex Ms codice bibliothecæ illustrissimi Cardinalis Ioyosii multis mendis repurgata, latinè versa, & perpetuo commentario illustrata.*

Burdigalæ: Apud Simonem Milangium ..., 1605. [20], 285, [9] p.: ill.; 23 cm. Admonitio: last p. Includes bibliographical references and index. *Roberti Balforei commentarius in libros duos Cleomedis De contemplatione orbium cælestium* has separate t. p. Greek and Latin text in parallel columns.

P. 127-128 (blank) missing.

411. CLERKE, AGNES M. (AGNES MARY), 1842-1907. *Geschichte der Astronomie während des neunzehnten Jahrhunderts, gemeinfasslich dargestellt von A. M. Clerke; autorisierte deutsche Ausgabe von H. Maser.*

Berlin: Verlag von Julius Springer, 1889. XV, [1] (blank), 540 p., [1] leaf of plates: ill.; 24 cm. Translation of: *A popular history of astronomy during the nineteenth century*. Includes bibliographical references and indexes.

412. CLERKE, AGNES M. (AGNES MARY), 1842-1907. *A popular history of astronomy during the nineteenth century....*

Edinburgh: A. & C. Black, 1885. xiv, 468 p. 22 cm. Bibliographical footnotes. Includes index.

413. CLERKE, AGNES M. (AGNES MARY), 1842-1907. *A popular history of astronomy during the nineteenth century, by Agnes M. Clerke.*

London: A. and C. Black, 1908. xv, 489 p., vi, [1] leaves of plates: ill.; 22 cm. "Chronology, 1774-1893": p. [445]-461. Includes bibliographical references and index. Frontispiece and title vignette are mounted photographs.

Advertisements: verso half-title; [2] p. at end. Provenance: William Andrews Clark, Jr. (bookplate); W. A. Clark Observatory (inscription).

414. CLERKE, AGNES M. (AGNES MARY), 1842-1907. *A popular history of astronomy during the nineteenth century, by Agnes M. Clerke. 3d ed.*

London: A. and C. Black, 1893. xv, [3], 573 p., [6] leaves of plates: ill.; 23 cm. Includes bibliographical references and index.

Provenance: ecclesiastical binding with motto: Honi soit qui mal y pense; Charles Atwood Kofoid (bookplate); presentation bookplate to George Herbert L. Mallory.

415. CLERKE, AGNES M. (AGNES MARY), 1842-1907. *The system of the stars, by Agnes M. Clerke.*

London: Longmans, Green, and Co., 1890. xix, [1], 424 p. front. (fold. chart) illus., 5 pl., tables. 23 cm. Appendix. Tables of stellar data: p. [399]-409. Includes bibliographical references and index.

416. Coley, Henry, 1633-1695? *Clavis astrologiæ elimata; or, A key to the whole art of astrology, newfiled and polished. In three parts. Containing, 1. An introduction ... 2. Select aphorismes ... 3. The genethliacal part, wherein is shewed how to rectifie and calculate nativities ...To which are added, the Rudolphine tables; whereby the places of the planets may be calculated for any time past, present, or to come. By Henry Coley ...The second ed. Much enlarged and amended.*

London: Printed for B. Tooke, and T. Sawbridge, 1676. 17 p. l., 16 numb. l., 759, [1], 103 [i. e. 93] p. incl. plates, tables. port. 18 cm. Error in pagination: (5th group) nos. 70-80 omitted in numeration. Johannes Kepler's *Rudolphine tables* have special t.-p. dated 1675, and separate pagination. Errata: p. [760]. Wing C5099. *Justin Wright collection*, no. 60.

T. p. repaired and mounted; pt. 1, p. 18 top of volvelle supplied in ms.; pt. 2, p. 45 repaired and some figures added by hand.

417. [Collection of reprints from the *Smithsonian report* on radioactivity and radium].

[1902-1904]. 1 v. (various pagings) : ill. ; 22 cm. Includes bibliographical references. Radium / by E. [sic] Curie (1904) – Radium / by J. J. Thompson (1903) – Experiments in radio-activity and the production of helium from radium / by Sir William Ramsay and Frederick Soddy (1903) – On the radioactivity of matter / by Henri Becquerel (1902).

418. Collins, A. Frederick (Archie Frederick), 1869- . *The book of stars; being a simple explanation of the stars and their uses to boy life, written to conform to the tests of the Boy Scouts, by A. Frederick Collins.*

New York: D. Appleton and Company, 1915. xv, 230 p. illus., diagrs. 19 cm. Includes index.

419. Collins, A. Frederick (Archie Frederick), 1869- . *The greatest eye in the world; astronomical telescopes and their stories, by A. Frederick Collins....*

New York: D. Appleton-Century, 1942. xviii p., 1 l., 266 p. front., illus., plates, diagrs. 21 cm. Includes index.

420. Collins, Anthony, 1676-1729. *A letter from an Arabian physician to a famous professor in the University of Hall in Saxony: concerning Mahomet's taking up arms, his marrying of many wives, his keeping of concubines, and his paradise.*

Paris: [s.n.], June 14, 1706. 15, [1] p.; 20 cm. Imprint taken from p. 15. French version published with: *Discours sur la liberté de penser Anthony Collins*. London: [s.n.], 1714. Cf. *NUC pre-1956*, v. 115, p. 605, and v. 329, p. 239. *ESTC* T110395.

With: *Spaccio della bestia trionfante, or, The expulsion of the triumphant beast*, translated from the Italian of Jordano Bruno. Paris: [s.n.], 1707.

421. Collins, Matthew. *A tract on the possible and impossible cases of quadratic duplicate equalities in the diophantine analysis: to which is added a short, but comprehensive appendix, in which most of the useful and important propositions in the theory of numbers are very concisely demonstrated. By Matthew Collins,....*

Dublin: This tract and Mr. Collins' other works, can be procured direct from the author, 13 Anglesea-street, Dublin. They are sold by Messrs. Ponsonby, Cornish, Kelly, Rooney, and Morris of Dublin: Mulcahy, Cork: O'Gorman, Limerick: Douglas and Nicholson, Kilkenny., 1858. [4], [1], 2-60 p.; 22 cm. Includes list of subscribers on p. 56-60. Errata on p. 60.

422. *Comptes rendus des séances de l'Académie des sciences. Vie académique. Tables des Comptes rendus des séances de l'Académie des sciences. Vie académique.*

Paris: Gauthier-Villars, 1966-1973. v. 27 cm. Semiannual t. 262-277; 1966-1973. On cover of some issues: Supplément aux Comptes rendus de l'Académie des sciences. Indexed by: *Chemical abstracts* ISSN:0009-2258. Some volumes accompanied by supplements. Continued by: *Comptes rendus hebdomadaires des séances de l'Académie des sciences. Vie académique.*

Library has: 262-263, 1966; 275-27,1973.

423. *Comptes rendus hebdomadaires des séances de l'Académie des sciences.*

Paris: publiés avec le concours du Centre national de la recherche scientifique par MM. les secrétaires perpétuels : Gauthier-Villars, 1835-1965. 261 v. : ill., maps. ; 27-29 cm. T. 1, [no 1] (3 août 1835)-t. 261, no 25 (20 déc. 1965). Publisher varies. The proceedings for the period prior to 1835 are contained in: Académie des sciences (France). *Procès-verbaux des séances de l'Académie tenues depuis la fondation de l'Institut jusqu'au mois d'août 1835.* Split into: *Comptes rendus hebdomadaires des séances de l'Académie des sciences. A, Sciences mathématiques. B, Sciences physiques (1966); Comptes rendus hebdomadaires des séances de l'Académie des sciences. Série C, Sciences chimiques;* and: *Comptes rendus hebdomadaires des séances de l'Académie des sciences. Série D, Sciences naturelles.*

Library has: 1-261, 1835-1965.

424. *Comptes rendus hebdomadaires des séances de l'Académie des sciences / publiés conformément à une décision de l'Académie en date du 13 juillet 1835 par MM. les secrétaires perpétuels. T. 122.*

Paris : Gauthier-Villars et fils, 1896. 1633 p. : ill. ; 27 cm. "Janvier-juin 1896". Includes the earliest communications by Henri Becquerel concerning radioactivity, notably: "Sur les radiations invisibles émises par les corps phosphorescents" (p. 501-503); "Sur quelques propriétés nouvelles des radiations invisibles émises par divers corps phosphorescents" (p. 559-564); "Sur les radiations invisibles émises par les sels d'uranium" (p. [689]-694); and "Emission de radiations nouvelles par l'uranium métallique" (p. 1086-1088). Includes indexes. *PMM,* 393.

425. *Comptes rendus hebdomadaires des séances de l'Académie des sciences. A, Sciences mathématiques. B, Sciences physiques.*

Paris: Gauthier-Villars. 24 v. ill. 27 cm. t. 262-277, 1966-73. Continues, in part, the academy's *Comptes rendus hebdomadaires des séances* and assumes its numbering. Summaries and table of contents in English. Pagination is continuous within each series, with separate series title pages and tables of contents issued at the end of each volume. Split into: *Comptes rendus des seances de l'Académie des sciences. Série A, Sciences mathematiques. Comptes rendus hebdomadaires des séances de l'Académie des sciences. Série B, Sciences physiques.*

Library has vols. 262-263, 1966: Series A and B bound separately.

426. *Comptes rendus hebdomadaires des séances de l'Académie des sciences. Série C, Sciences chimiques.*

Paris : publiés avec le concours du Centre national de la recherche scientifique par MM. les secrétaires perpétuels : Gauthier-Villars, 1966-1978. 26 v. : ill. ; 27 cm. T. 262, no 1 (3 janv. 1966)- t. 287, no 16 (11 et 18 déc. 1978). Indexed by: *Bibliography of agriculture* ISSN:0006-1530. *Computer & control abstracts* ISSN:0036-8113 Jan. 1970-Dec. 1978. *Electrical & electronics abstracts* ISSN:0036-8105 Jan. 1970-Dec. 1978. *GeoRef* ISSN:0197-7482. *Physics abstracts. Science abstracts.* Series A ISSN:0036-8091 Jan. 1970-Dec. 1978. Indexes: T. 270-274. 1 v. Continued in 1979 by: *Comptes rendus des séances de l'Académie des sciences. Série C, Sciences chimiques.* Continues in part: *Comptes rendus hebdomadaires des séances de l'Académie des sciences* ISSN:0001-4036.

Library has: 262-263, 1966; 266, 1968; [267, 1968]

427. *Comptes rendus hebdomadaires des séances de l'Académie des sciences. Série D, Sciences naturelles.*

Paris: publiés avec le concours du Centre national de la recherche scientifique par MM. les secrétaires perpétuels : Gauthier-Villars, 1966-1978. 26 v. : ill. ; 26-27 cm. T. 262, no 1 (3 janv. 1966)-t. 287, no 16 (11 et 18 déc. 1978). Indexed by: *Mathematical reviews* ISSN:0025-5629. *GeoRef* ISSN:0197-7482. *Bibliography of agriculture* ISSN:0006-1530. Continued in 1979 by: *Comptes rendus des séances de l'Académie des sciences. Série D, Sciences naturelles.* Continues in part: *Comptes rendus hebdomadaires des séances de l'Académie des sciences.*

Library has: 262-263.

428. *Comptes rendus hebdomadaires des séances de l'Académie des sciences. T. 9.*

Paris: Bachelier, 1839. [4], 903, [1] p. ; 27 cm. : "Juillet-décembre 1839." "Publiés conformément à une décision de l'Académie en date du 13 juillet 1835." "Le Daguerréotype" by F. Arago: p. 250-267. The separately published *Rapport ... sur le daguerréotype* (Paris : Bachelier, 1839) is cited, as no. 21b, in H. D. Horblit, *Grolier 100 science books.* "Des procédés photogéniques considérés comme moyens de gravure" by L. J. M. Daguerre: p. 423-429. Also includes reports on photographic processes by F. Arago, J. Donné, Niépce, and others on p. 227, 289, 376-379, 411-412, 429-430, 455, 485, 487, 512-514, 539, 554, 560, 595, 714, 772, 801-802, 824. Errata: p. [904]. Includes bibliographical references and index.

429. COMTE, AUGUSTE, 1798-1857. *Cours de philosophie positive, par M. Auguste Comte....*

Paris: Bachelier, 1830-42. 6 v. fold. tab. 21 cm. t. 1. Les préliminaires généraux et la philosophie mathématique. – t. 2. La philosophie astronomique et la philosophie de la physique. – t. 3. La philosophie chimique et la philosophie biologique. – t.4. La partie dogmatique de la philosophie sociale. – t. 5. La partie historique de la philosophie sociale. – t. 6 Le complément de la philosophie sociale, et les conclusions générales.

v. 1 has imprint: Paris, Rouen Frères ...; Bruxelles, Au dépôt de la Librairie medicale française, 1830.

430. COMTE, AUGUSTE, 1798-1857. *Traité philosophique d'astronomie populaire, ou Exposition systématique de toutes les notions de philosophie astronomique, soit scientifiques, soit logiques, qui doivent devenir universellement familières; par M. Auguste Comte....*

Paris: Carilian-Goeury et Vor. Dalmont, 1844. x, 486 p. 1 fold. pl. 22 cm. "Discours préliminaire, sur l'esprit positif": p. 1-108.

Imperfect? lacks 2 prelim. p. (half-title?).

431. CONGRÈS INTERNATIONAL DE PHYSIQUE (1900: PARIS). *Rapports présentés au Congrès international de physique réuni à Paris en 1900 sous les auspices de la Société française de physique, rassemblés et publiés par Ch.-Éd. Guillaume et L. Poincaré.*

Paris: Gauthier-Villars, (1900-01). 4 v. ill. 26 cm. Vol. 4 has title: Travaux du Congrès international de physique ... Includes bibliographical references. t. I. Questions générales. Métrologie. Physique mécanique. Physique moléculaire. – t. II. Optique. Électricité. Magnétisme. – t. III. Électro-optique et ionisation. Applications. Physique cosmique. Physique biologique. – t. IV. Procès-verbaux. Annexes. Liste des membres.

432. *Connaissance des temps, ou des mouvements célestes, pour le méridien de Paris à l'usage des astronomes et des navigateurs pour l'an 17 – .*

Paris : Gauthier-Villars [etc.], 1797- v. : fold. plates, fold. maps, fold. tables, diagrs. (part fold.) ; 19-24 cm. Began in 1797? Subtitle varies slightly. Publishers: L'imprimerie de la République, floréal an v, mai 1797-nivôse an XII (1804) – L'imprimerie impériale, frimaire an XIII (1804)-juillet 1811 – Mme. Ve Courcier, avril 1812-1821. – Bachelier, 1822-1829, 1833-décembre 1852. – Bachelier père et fils, 1830-1832. – Mallet-Bachelier, décembre 1853-septembre 1863. – Gauthier-Villars, août 1864- . Continues: *Connoissance des temps, ou connoissance des mouvements célestes pour l'année bissextile* ... 1799-1800, 1802-1818, 1821-1878 include "Additions et tables nouvelles pour la Connaissance des temps"; afterward published in "Annales du Bureau des longitudes". 1806, 1822 and 1867 include "Table alphabétique des matières et des tables contenues dans les volumes de la *Connaissance des temps*" 1760-1805, 1806-1822 and 1823-1867 respectively.

Library has: vol. for 1849: Provenance: Bibliothèque de la Science française (bookplate); Univ. of California (inkstamp).

433. CONNECTICUT ACADEMY OF ARTS AND SCIENCES. *Transactions of the Connecticut Academy of Arts and Sciences.*

New Haven, Connecticut Academy of Arts and Sciences; distributed by Archon Books, Hamden, Conn. [etc.] 1866 – . v. ill., plates (part col.) ports., maps, facsim., diagrs. 24 cm. v. 1 – . Title varies slightly. Horblit, H. D. *Grolier 100 science books,* 40. Indexed by: *Bibliography of agriculture* ISSN:0006-1530. *Biological abstracts* ISSN:0006-3169. *Chemical abstracts* ISSN:0009-2258. Notes: Vols. 1-11 each in 2 parts (v. 4, pt. 3, announced as in preparation, was never published); v. 12 in 1 vol.; v. 13- issued in the form of monographs. Vol. 11, "Centennial volume." Vol. 15, "To the University of Leipzig on the occasion of the five hundredth anniversary of its foundation, from Yale University and the Connecticut Academy of Arts and Sciences, 1909." Vols. 1-11 published by the Academy; v. 12- by Yale University; v. by the Academy.

Library has: [2-3, 1873-78]. Vol. II, pt. 2 and v. III, pt. 1 and 2: Provenance: Yale Medical Library. Historical Library (bookplate); John Farquhar Fulton (bookplate); Herbert McLean Evans (bookplate). Binder: case stamped, Maltby, Oxford.

434. *Connoissance des temps, ou connoissance des mouvements célestes pour l'année bissextile....*

Paris, De l'Imprimerie royale. v. plates (part fold.) 18 cm. Publiée par l'ordre de l'Academie royale des sciences. Variant title: *Connaissance des temps, ou connaissainee des mouvements célestes pour l'année bissextile* ... Former title: *Connoissance des mouvements célestes* 1762-67. Continued by: *Connaissance des temps, ou des mouvements célestes, pour le méridien de Paris, à l'usage des astronomes et des navigateurs pour l'an 17 –* .

Library has: 1784. Vol. for 1784: Provenance: E. Mareuse (bookplate); Herbert McLean Evans (bookplate).

435. Conybeare, William Daniel, 1787-1857. *Outlines of the geology of England and Wales, with an introductory compendium of the general principles of that science, and comparative views of the structure of foreign countries ... By the Rev. W. D. Conybeare ... and William Phillips ... Part I.*

London: W. Phillips, 1822. 4 p. l., lxi p., 1 l., 470 p., front. (fold. map) fold. col. pl., fold.tab., diagrs. 20 cm. Folded table printed on both sides. "This was originally intended to form the second edition of 'A selection of facts ... arranged ... to form an outline of the geology of England and Wales.' By W. Phillips." No more published.

Provenance: M. Smythe (signature); Herbert McLean Evans (bookplate).

436. Copernicus, Nicolaus, 1473-1543. *De revolutionibus orbium cœlestium libri VI.*

Amsterdam: Roskam, 1943. [9], 196 l. port. 33 cm. Facsim. of ed. Norimbergæ, Apud Ioh. Petreium, 1543. 300 copies printed by Vincenzo Bona, Turin: 200 numbered 1-200 for Chiantore, Torino; 100 numbered I-C for Roskam, Amsterdam.

No. IC.

437. Copernicus, Nicolaus, 1473-1543. *De revolvtionibvs orbium cœlestium, libri VI....*

Norimbergæ: Apud Ioh. Petreium, 1543. [6], 196 l. diagrs. 27 cm. Horblit, H. D. *Grolier 100 science books,* 18b.

Repeated t. p. with errata on its verso is bound following text. Provenance: Herbert McLean Evans (bookplate). With: C. *Iulii Hygini ... Poeticon astronomicon.* Salingiaci: Opera et impensa Ioannis Soteris, 1539; and *Cl. Ptolomæi ... Phænomena stellarum.* Excusum Coloniæ Agrippinæ, 1537.

438. Copernicus, Nicolaus, 1473-1543. *Nicolai Copernici Thorunensis De revolutionibus orbium cœlestium libri VI. Ex auctoris autographo recudi curavit Societas Copernicana Thorunensis. Accedit Georgii Ioachimi Rhetici De libris revolutionum narratio prima.*

Thoruni: Sumptibus Societas Copernicanæ, 1873. xxx p., 1 l., 494 p. tables, diagrs. 36 x 28 cm. Prolegomena signed: C. Boethke; R. Brohm; M. Curtze; Herford; Dr. Hirsch. Includes index.

439. Copernicus, Nicolaus, 1473-1543. *Nicolai Copernici Torinensis Astronomia instaurata: libris sex comprehensa, qui De revolutionibus orbium cœlestium inscribuntur: Nunc demum post 75 ab obitu authoris annum integritati suæ restituta, notisque illustrata, opera & studio D. Nicolai Mulerii....*

Amstelrodami: Excudebat VVilhelmus Iansonius, sub Solari aureo, cAn[n]o M.DC.XVII, [1617]. [22], 487, [1] (blank) p.: ill.; 24 cm. Previous eds. were published under title: *De revolutionibus orbium cœlestium libri VI.* Title vignette (publisher's device). Grässe, v. 2, p. 260. Houzeau & Lancaster. *Astronomie* (1964 ed.), 2503. Errata: p. [22] of 1st group.

440. Copernicus, Nicolaus, 1473-1543. *Nicolaus Coppernicus aus Thorn Über die Kreisbewegungen der Weltkörper. Übersetzt und mit Anmerkungen von C. L. Menzzer. Durchgesehen und mit einem Vorwort von Moritz Cantor. Hrsg. von dem Coppernicus-Verein für Wissenschaft und Kunst zu Thorn.*

Thorn: E. Lambeck, 1879. xxii, 363, 66 p. tables, diagrs. 26 cm. Originally published: *De revolutionibus orbium cœlestium.*

Provenance: Niels Nielsen (inscription).

441. Copernicus, Nicolaus, 1473-1543. *Nicolai Copernici Torinensis De revolvtionibus orbium coelestium, libri VI : in qvibvs stellarvm et fixarvm et erraticarvm motvs, ex veteribus atq[ue] recentibus obseruationibus, restituit hic autor : praeterea tabulas expeditas luculentasq[ue] addidit, ex quibus eosdem motus ad quoduis tempus mathematum studiosus facillime calculare poterit. / Item, De libris revolvtionvm Nicolai Copernici narratio prima, per M. Georgium Ioachimum Rheticum ad D. Ioan. Schonerum scripta.*

Basileae : Ex Officina Henricpetrina, [1566]. [5], 213, [1] leaves : ill. ; 31 cm. "Cum gratia & priuilegio caes. maiest." Imprint date from colophon, which reads: Basileae ex Officina Henricpetria anno M.D.LXVI, mense Septembri. Printer's device on last leaf (cf. Bigmore & Wyman, p. 324). Includes tables from Erasmus Reinhold's *Prutenicae.*

net, in quo terram cum orbe lunari tanquam epicyclo contineri diximus. Quinto loco Venus nono mense reducitur. Sextum denicp locum Mercurius tenet, octuaginta dierum ſpacio circũ currens. In medio uero omnium reſidet Sol. Quis enim in hoc

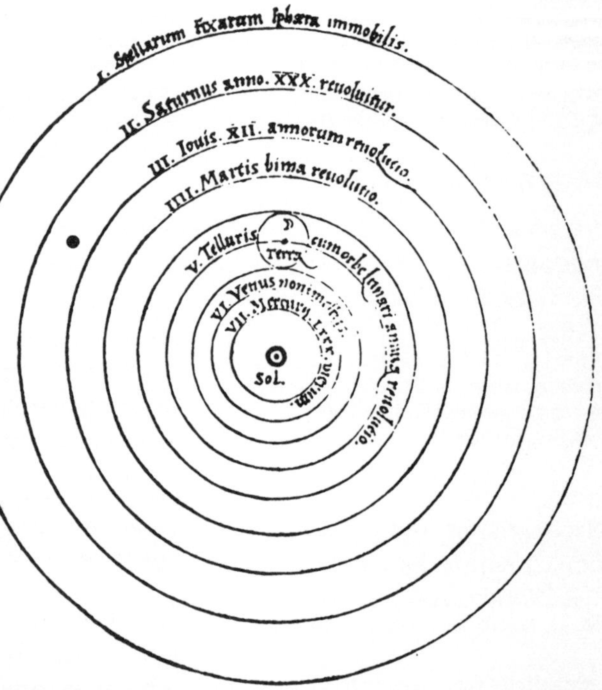

pulcherrimo templo lampadem hanc in alio uel meliori loco poneret, quàm unde totum ſimul poſsit illuminare? Siquidem non inepte quidam lucernam mundi, alij mentem, alij rectorem uocant. Trimegiſtus uiſibilem Deum, Sophoclis Electra intuentẽ omnia. Ita profecto tanquam in ſolio regali Sol reſidens circum agentem gubernat Aſtrorum familiam. Tellus quocp minime fraudatur lunari miniſterio, ſed ut Ariſtoteles de animalibus ait, maximã Luna cũ terra cognationẽ habet. Concipit interea à Sole terra, & impregnatur annuo partu. Inuenimus igitur ſub hac

Copernicus, *De revolutionibus*, 1543

Binding: full vellum; mss. on vellum pieces used in binding (some rubricated in red and blue).

442. Copernicus, Nicolaus, 1473-1543. *Nikolaus Kopernikus Gesamtausgabe, im Auftrage der Deutschen Forschungsgemeinschaft hrsg. von Fritz Kubach.*
München: R. Oldenbourg, 1944-1949. 2 v. port., diagrs. 29 cm. Vol. 2: Hrsg. von der Kopernikus-Kommission. Bd. 1. Opus de revolutionibus cælestibus manu propria. Faksimile-Wiedergabe. – Bd. 2. De revolutionibus orbium cælestium. Textkritische Ausgabe.

443. Costard, George, 1710-1782. *The history of astronomy, with its application to geography, history, and chronology; occasionally exemplified by the globes ... By George Costard.*
London: Printed by J. Lister, and sold by J. Newberry, 1767. xvi, 308 p., 1 l. diagrs. 28x22 cm. Errata: p. [309].
Imperfect: half-title and errata leaf missing. Provenance: E. Roberts (inscription).

444. Costard, George, 1710-1782. *A letter to Martin Folkes, esq., president of the Royal Society: concerning the rise and progress of astronomy amongst the antients.*
London: Printed by Jacob Ilive, for T. Osborne ... and J. Hildyard, at York, 1746. [2], 158, [1] p.: ill.; 21 cm. Letter signed (on. p. 158): G. Costard. Includes bibliographical references. Errata: p. [159].
Imperfect: lacks errata leaf. Ms. marginalia throughout.

445. Cottam, Arthur. *Charts of the constellations: from the North Pole to between 30 & 40 degrees of south declination, by Arthur Cottam ... Popular edition, on a reduced scale, with three additional key maps, and an introduction and notes.*
London: Edward Stanford ..., 1891. vii, 32 p.: ill.; 40 cm. + 36 charts, 3 plates (2 folded).
Charts of various sizes mounted on board, in portfolio.

446. Cotte, L. (Louis), 1740-1815. *Leçons élémentaires de physique, d'hydrostatique, d'astronomie & de météorologie: avec un traité de la sphère, par demandes et résponses, à l'usage des enfans ..., par L. Cotte ... Seconde édition corrigée & augmentée.*
À Paris: Chez H. Barbou ..., L'an VI. de la Rép. [1798 ere vulg.]. [2], x, 240 p., [1], 6 folded leaves of plates: ill.; 18 cm. "Pour servir de suite aux 'Leçons élémentaires d'histoire naturelle, par demandes & résponses, à l'usage des enfans', publiées en 1785, & réimprimées en 1792." "Fautes à corriger": p. 234. Advertisements: p. [238]-240.

447. Couderc, Paul. *The wider universe. [Translated by Martin Davidson].*
New York: Harper [c 1960]. 128 p., [4] p. of plates illus. 19 cm. Science Today Series (ST4). Translation of *L'univers.*

448. Coulomb, C. A. (Charles Augustin), 1736-1806. *Premier [-troisième] mémoire sur l'électricité et le magnétisme par M. Coulomb.*
[Paris]: Académie Royale des Sciences, 1785. p. 569-638, [2] folded leaves, [3] folded leaves of plates: ill.; 26 cm. Caption title. Includes 3 of the 7 memoirs by Coulomb on electricity and magnetism published by Bachelier, 1795-1798. Cf. Horblit. Detached from: *Mémoires de l'Académie Royale des Sciences,* an. 1785. Tables on 2 folded leaves. Plates numbered XIII-XV. Horblit, H. D. *Grolier 100 science books,* 31b (variant). Construction & usage d'une balance électrique, fondée sur la propriété qu'ont les fils de métal, d'avoir une force de réaction de torsion proportionnelle à l'angle de torsion – Second mémoire ... où l'on détermine, suivant quelles loix le fluide magnétique, ainsi que le fluide électrique, agissent, soit par répulsion, soit par attraction – De la quantité d'électricité qu'un corps isolé perd dans un temps donné, soit par le contact de l'air plus où moins humide, soit le long des soutiens plus où moins idio-électriques.
Provenance: Herbert McLean Evans (bookplate).

449. Courant, Richard, 1888-1972. *Methoden der mathematischen Physik, von R. Courant und D. Hilbert.*
Berlin: J. Springer, 1924-26. 2 v. 25 cm. Die Grundlehren der mathematischen Wissenschaften in Einzeldarstellungen mit besonderer Berücksichtigung der Anwendungsgebiete, v. 12, 48. Includes index. Advertisements: [4] p. at the end of v. 1.
Provenance: William Howell Williams (bookplate).

450. COWLEY, JOHN. *A view of the British trade to the Mediterranean: shewing its importance to us, it precarious situation at present, and that a total loss of it must ensue, unless the views of France and Spain are vigorously opposed ..., by J. Cowley....*
London: Printed for M. Cooper ... , 1744. iv, 5-27, [1] p., [1] folded leaf of plates: map; 26 cm. Advertisement: [1] p.
With: *Experiments and observations on electricity*, by Mr. Benjamin Franklin. London: printed and sold by E. Cave ..., 1751-1753. Provenance: L'Ab. Boyer (bookplate); Domus Massiliensis (bookplate).

451. CRANZ, KARL JULIUS, 1858-1945. *Gemeinverständliches über die sogenannte vierte Dimension; Vortrag, gehalten bei dem Stiftungsfest des Mathem.-naturw. Vereins der Technischen Hochschule im Stuttgart am 8. Dezember 1888.*
Hamburg: Verlaganstalt A.-G. (vormals J. R. Richter), 1890. 70 p. diagrs. 22 cm. Sammlung gemeinverständlicher wissenschaftlicher Vorträge ... n. f., 5. ser., Hft. 112/113.
No. 2 in v. with binder's title: Geometrie, I.

452. CREDÉ, CARL SIEGMUND FRANZ, 1819-1892. *Die Verhütung der Augenentzündung der Neugeborenen [ophthalmoblennorrhoæ neonatorum]: der häufigsten und wichtigsten Ursache der Blindheit, von Carl S. F. Credé....*
Berlin: Verlag von August Hirschwald ... , 1884. iv, [2], 63, [3] p.; 23 cm. Advertisements: last [2] p. Summary and continuation of paper published in *Archiv für Gynäkologie*, Bd. 17, p. 50, 1881, Bd. 18, p. 367, 1881 and Bd. 21, p. 179, 1883.
Provenance: Herbert McLean Evans (bookplate).

453. CROOKES, WILLIAM, SIR, 1832-1919. *The mechanical action of light, by William Crookes.*
[London]: Offices of the Quarterly Journal of Science ..., 1875-1876. 2 v. (p. 337-352; p. 228-256): ill.; 23 cm. *Quarterly Journal of Science, and Annals of mining, metallurgy, engineering, industrial arts, manufacturing, and technology;* v. 12 and 13. Caption titles. Includes bibliographical references.

454. CROWTHER, J. G. (JAMES GERALD), 1899- *An outline of the universe, by J. G. Crowther.*
London: K. Paul, Trench, Trubner, & Co., Ltd., 1931. xvii, 376 p. front., illus., plates, diagrs. 23 cm. Includes index. Bibliography: p. xvii.

455. CUNNINGHAM, EBENEZER. *The principle of relativity, by E. Cunningham.*
Cambridge: University Press, 1914. xiv, 221 [1] p. diagrs. 23 cm. Includes index. Advertisements: [2] p. following text.
Imperfect: p. 114-115, 118-119, 122-123, 126-127 blank.

456. CURIE, MARIE, 1867-1934. *Recherches sur les substances radioactives ..., par Mme Sklodowska Curie.*
Paris: Gauthier-Villars, 1903. [2], 142, [1] p.: ill., diagrs.; 25 cm. "Propositions données par la Faculté": p. [143]. Thesis (doctoral) – Paris, 1903. Includes bibliographical references. Horblit, H. D. *Grolier 100 science books*, 19. *PMM*, 394a.

457. CURIE, MARIE, 1867-1934. *Traité de radioactivité, par Madame P. Curie.*
Paris: Gauthier-Villars, 1910. 2 v.: ill., port.; 26 cm. Includes bibliographical references. Advertisements on p. [4] of cover, v. 1-2.

458. CURIE, PIERRE, 1859-1906. *Sur une substance nouvelle radio-active, contenue dans la pechblende, note de M. P. Curie, de Mme. S. Curie, présentée par M. Becquerel.*
[Paris]: Gauthier-Villars ..., 1898. p. 175-178; 29 cm. *Comptes rendus hebdomadaires des séances de l'Académie des Sciences;* t. 127. Caption title. Comptes rendus t. 127 also contains further work by the Curies, G. Bemont and E. Demarcay on radium (Cf. t. 127, p. 1215-18).

459. CURIE, PIERRE, 1859-1906. *Œuvres de Pierre Curie, publiées par les soins de la Société française de physique.*
Paris: Gauthier-Villars, 1908. 22, 621 p. front. (port.) illus., 2 pl., diagrs. 25 cm.

460. CUSHING, HARVEY, 1869-1939. *The pituitary body and its disorders, clinical states produced by disorders of the hypophysis cerebri, by Harvey Cushing ... an amplification of the Harvey lecture for December, 1910.*
Philadelphia, London: J. B. Lippincott Company, [c 1912]. x, 341 p. col. front., illus., fold. pl. 26 cm. Bibliography: p. 323-333.
Provenance: Ernest S. du Bray (inscription).

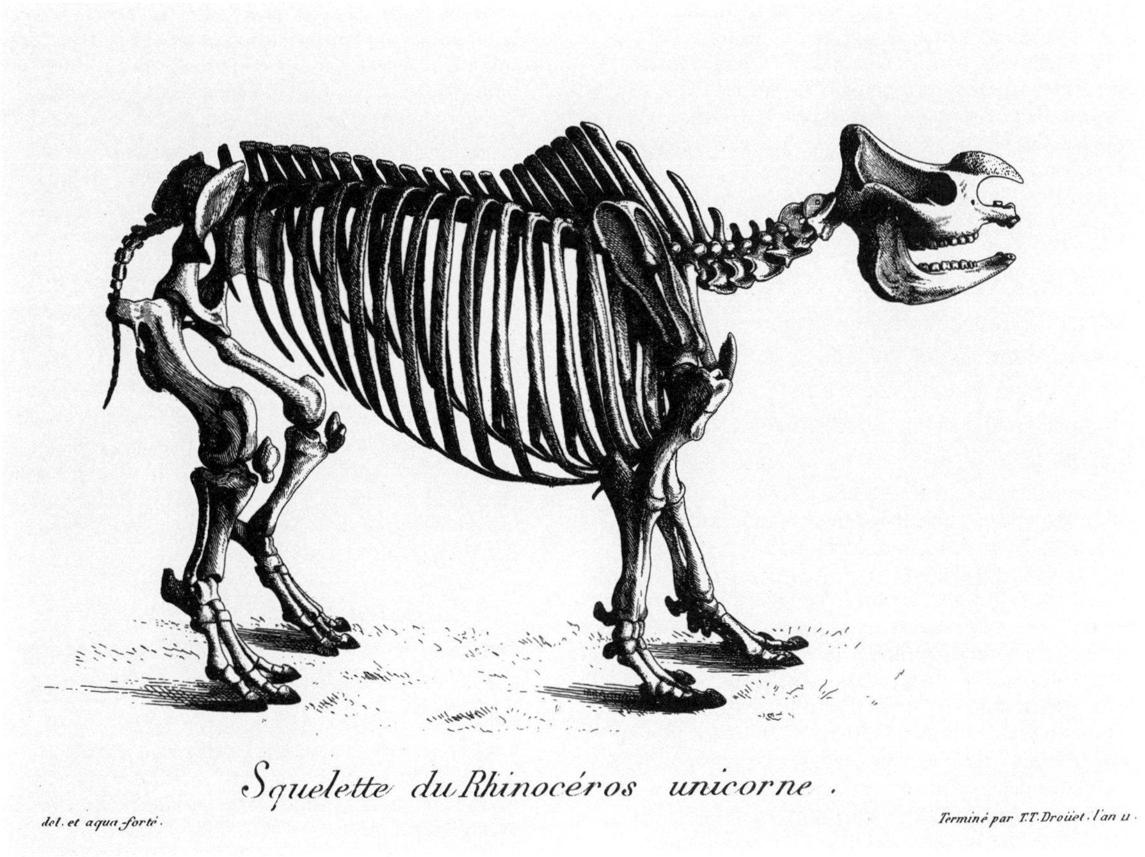
Squelette du Rhinocéros unicorne.
Terminé par T.T. Droüet. l'an 11.

CUVIER, *Recherches sur les ossemens fossiles de quadrupèdes*, 1812

461. CUVIER, GEORGES, BARON, 1769-1832. *Essay on the theory of the earth By Baron G. Cuvier ... With geological illustrations, by Professor Jameson. 5th ed., tr. from the last French ed., with numerous additions by the author and translator.*

Edinburgh: W. Blackwood; [etc., etc.], 1827. xxiv, 550 p. front., IX [i.e. 10] pl. 22 cm. Translation of: *Discours sur les révolutions de la surface du globe.* Plates engraved by W. H. and D. Lizars. Includes bibliographical references.

Provenance: Cecil St. Quintin (signature); K. Ricerdo [?] (signature).

462. CUVIER, GEORGES, BARON, 1769-1832. *Histoire des progrès des sciences naturelles, depuis 1789 jusqu'à ce jour, par M. le baron G. Cuvier....*

À Paris: Chez Baudouin Frères ... et chez N. Delangle ... , 1826. 2 v.; 21 cm. At the foot of the page: Buffon. Complém. t. 1. Includes bibliographical references.

Provenance: Alfred Still (bookplate).

463. †CUVIER, GEORGES, BARON, 1769-1832. *Leçons d'anatomie comparée, de G. Cuvier ...; recueillies et publiées sous ses yeux par C. Duméril....*

Paris: Crochard, libraire ..., Fantin, libraire ..., Baudouin, imprimeur ..., (an 14, 1805). 5 v.: ill.; 21 cm. Vol. 3-5 edited by G. L. Duvernoy. Plates engraved by Miger and N. Ransonnette. Full extent: v. 1: [4], xxxi, [1] (blank), 521, [1] p., [7] folded leaves (tables); v. 2: [4], xvi, 697, [3] p.; v. 3: [4], xxviii, 558, [2] p.; v. 4: [4], xii, 539, [3] p.; v. 5: [4], vii, [1] (blank), 368 p., LII leaves of plates. Advertisements on last page of v. 2. Errata: v. 1: final p.;v. 2: p. [1-2] (last group); v. 3: final [2] p.; v. 4: final [3] p.; v. 5: p. 297. t. I. Les organes du mouvement – t. II. Les organes des sensations – t. III. La première partie des organes de la digestion – t. IV. La suite des organes de la digestion et ceux de la circulation, de la respiration et de la voix – t. V. Les organes de la génération et ceux des sécrétions excrémentitielles ou des excrétions. Horblit, H. D. *Grolier 100 science books,* 20a (variant).

Provenance: Steevens's Hospital Library (inkstamp); James W. Cusack (signature).

464. CUVIER, GEORGES, BARON, 1769-1832. *Recherches sur les ossemens fossiles de quadrupèdes: où l'on rétablit les caractères de plusiers espèces d'animaux que les révolutions du globe paroissent avoir détruites; par M. Cuvier....*

À Paris: Chez Deterville, libraire ..., 1812. 4 v.: ill., 1 col. map; 27 cm. "Inauguration of vertebrate paleontology" – *Grolier 100 science books,* 20b. Vol. 1: [8], vj, 120, 20, viij, 278, [2?], 23, [1] p., [6] leaves ofplates (3 folded); v. 2: 370 p. in various pagings, [43] leaves of plates; v. 3: 404 p. in various pagings, [67?] leaves of plates (17 folded); v. 4: 606 p. in various pagings, [38] leaves of plates (3 folded). Variously illustrated by: Mlle. Balzac, Lecerf, Cloquet, Laurillard, Couet, Canu, de Wailly, Cuvier. Horblit, H. D. *Grolier 100 science books,* 20b. v. 1. Contenant le discours préliminaire et la géographie minéralogique des environs de Paris – v. 2 Contenant les pachydermes des couches-meubles et des terrains d'alluvion – v. 3. Contenant les osfossiles des environs des Paris – v. 4. Contenant les ruminans, les onguiculés et les reptiles fossilles.

Provenance: Herbert McLean Evans (bookplate); Charles L. Camp (gift inscription from H. M. Evans)

465. CUVIER, GEORGES, BARON, 1769-1832. *Le règne animal distribué d'après son organisation, pour servir de base a l'histoire naturelle des animaux et d'introduction à l'anatomie comparée, par M. le Cher. Cuvier....*

Paris: Deterville, 1817. 4 v. XV plates. 21 cm. Plates drawn by Laurillard; engraved by Pierron and Louvet. "De l'imprimerie de A. Belin." "Table alphabétique des auteurs cités dans cet ouvrage": v. 4, p. [95]-170. Includes index. Wood, C. *Vertebrate zoology,* p. 307. t. 1. L'introduction, les mammifères et les oiseaux. – t. 2. Les reptiles, les poissons, les mollusques et les annélides. – t. 3. Les crustacés, les arachnides et les insectes, par M. Latreille. – t. 4. Les zoophytes, les tables, et les planches.

Provenance: Bibliothèque du Chapitre, Viviers, Ardèche (inkstamp). Bound with v. 4: *Manuel pour servir a l'histoire naturelle des oiseaux, des poissons, des insectes, et des plantes* ..., traduit du Latin de J. Reinhold Forster ... par J. B. F. Léveillé ... A Paris: Chez Villier ..., an 7 [1799?].

466. S. J. (DIRK SANTVOORT JR.) *De oorsaak van de beweeging en de beginsselen der vaste lichamen, door D. S. J.*

Tot Utrecht: By Herman Hardenberg ... , 1703. [16], 561, [20] p., 6 folded leaves of plates: ill., maps, 20 cm. Plates signed: Henderine Drogenhams, G. Drogenham. Includes index. Kempenaer, A. de. *Vermomde Nederlandsche en Vlaamsche schrijvers,* column 122.

With: *De oorsaak van het door-wateren, en het inbreken der zee-dyken.* Tot Utrecht: By Herman Hardenberg, 1702, and: *Vervolg van het boek genaamt De oorsaak van de beweeging en de beginsselender vaste lichamen.* Tot Utrecht: By Herman Hardenberg ... , 1707.

467. S. J. (DIRK SANTVOORT JR.) *Vervolg van het boek genaamt. De oorsaak van de beweeging en debeginsselen der vaste lichamen ..., door D. S. J.*

Tot Utrecht: By Herman Hardenberg ... , 1707. [2], 562-627, [10] p.; 20 cm. Errata: p. [10]. Kempenaer, A. de. *Vermomde Nederlandsche en Vlaamsche schrijvers,* column 122.

With: *De oorsaak van de Beweeging en debeginsselen der vaste lichamen.* Tot Utrecht: By Herman Hardenberg, 1703.

468. DAGUERRE, LOUIS JACQUES MANDÉ, 1787-1851. *Historique et description des procédés du daguerréotype et du diorama, par Daguerre....*

Paris: Susse Frères, éditeurs ...; Delloye, libraire ..., 1839. [4], 79 p., VI leaves of plates: ill.; 22 cm. Includes act of June 15, 1839, granting pensions to Daguerre and J. I. Niepce; report relative to the pensions, presented to the Chambre des députés by Arago, July 3, 1839; report presented to the Chambre des députés by Gay-Lussac, July 30, 1839. "Notice sur l'héliographie, par J. N. Niepce": p. [39]-46. Cf. Horblit, H. D. *Grolier 100 science books,* 21a.

In original yellow printed wrappers, in slipcase. Advertisements: [3] p. following text.

469. DALTON, JOHN, 1766-1844. *Dalton's memoirs.*

[1798-1824] 1 v. (various pagings): ill., col. map; 22

cm. Binder's title. Extracted from: *Memoirs of the Literary and Philosophical Society of Manchester*, v. 5, pt. 1 (1798), pt. 2 (1802); Second series, v. 1 (1805), v. 2 (1813), v. 3 (1819), v. 4 1824. Includes bibliographical references. Extraordinary facts relating to the vision of colours, with observations – Experiments and observations to determine whether the quantity of rain and dew is equal to the quantity of water carried off by the rivers and raised by evaporation: with an enquiry into the origin of springs – Experiments and observations on the power of fluids to conduct heat: with reference to Count Rumford's seventh essay on the same subject – Experiments on the velocity of air issuing out of a vessel in different circumstances: with the description of an instrument to measure the force of the blast in bellows, &c., by Mr. Banks ...; communicatd by Mr. Dalton – Experiments and observations on the heat and cold produced by the mechanical condensation and rarefaction of air – Experimental essays: On the constitution of mixed gases; On the force of steam or vapour from water and other liquids in different temperatures, both in a Torricellian vacuum and in air; On evaporation; and On the expansion of gases by heat – Meteorological observations – Experimental enquiry into the proportion of the several gases or elastic fluids constituting the atmosphere – On the tendency of elastic fluids to diffusion through each other – On the absorption of gases by water and other liquids – Remarks on Mr. Gough's two essays on the doctrine of mixed gases: and on Professor Schmidt's experiments on the expansion of dry and moist air by heat. On respiration and animal heat. Appendix – Experiments and observations on phosphoric acid, and on the salts denominated phosphates – Experiments and observations on the combinations of carbonic acid and ammonia – Remarks tending to facilitate the analysis of spring and mineral waters – Account of the floating island in Derwent Lake, Keswick, by Mr. Jonathan Otley, in a letter to Mr. Dalton. Note by Mr. Dalton – Memoir on sulphuric ether – Observations on the barometer, thermometer and rain: at Manchester, from 1794 to 1818 inclusive – On oil and the gases obtained from it by heat – Observations in meteorology, particularly with regard to the dew-point, or quantity of vapor in the atmosphere: made on the mountains in the north of England from 1803 to 1820 – On the saline impregnation of the rain which fell during the late storm, December 5th, 1822 – Appendix to the essay on salt rain ...: with additional observations on the succeeding storms of wind and rain – On the nature and properties of indigo: with directions for the valuation of different samples.

Provenance: Thomas Hoyle, Jr. (signature and bookplate).

470. DALTON, JOHN, 1766-1844. *A new system of chemical philosophy. By John Dalton.*

Manchester [England]: Printed by S. Russell, ... for R. Bickerstaff, Strand, London., 1808-1827. 2 v.: ill.; 22 cm. No more published. Cf: *NUC pre-1956*, v. 131, p. 662. Imprint varies: v. [1] pt. 2: Manchester: Printed by Russell & Allen,... for R. Bickerstaff, Strand, London., 1810; v. 2, pt. 1: Manchester [England]: Printed by the executors of S. Russell, for George Wilson, ... London., 1827. Vol. [1] pt. 1: vi, [2], 220 p., 4 leaves of plates; v. [1] pt. 2: [8], 221-560 p., 5-8 leaves of plates; v. 2, pt. 1: xii, 357, [3] p. "Books, essays, &c., published by the same author": v. 2, pt. 1, p. [358]-[360]. Smyth, A. L. *John Dalton*, 9. Horblit, H. D. *Grolier 100 science books*, 22.

Bound in 1 v. Provenance: Tho. Clark (signature), Vaughan Cornish (inscription), Herbert McLean Evans (bookplate).

471. DALTON, JOHN CALL, 1825-1889. *The origin and propagation of disease. An anniversary discourse, delivered before the New York Academy of Medicine, November 20, 1873. By John C. Dalton....*

New York: D. Appleton and Company, 1874. 30 p., 24 cm. Includes bibliographical references.

Provenance: Jared Linsly (embossing).

472. DANA, JAMES DWIGHT, 1813-1895. *A system of mineralogy; including an extended treatise on crystallography: with an appendix, containing the application of mathematics to crystallographic investigation, and a mineralogical bibliography. With two hundred and fifty wood cuts, and four copperplates, containing one hundred and fifty additional figures. By James Dwight Dana....*

New Haven: Durrie & Peck and Herrick & Noyes, 1837. xiv, 144, *145-*152, [145]-452, 119, [1] p. pl. (partly fold.) diagr. 24 cm. Errata: [1] p. at end. "Catalogue of works on mineralogy": Appendix, p. [89]-106. Includes index.

Provenance: F. W. Hunton (signature); Sereno Watson (signature).

473. DANA, JAMES FREEMAN, 1793-1827. *Outlines of the mineralogy and geology of Boston and its vicinity, with a geological map. By J. Freeman Dana, M.D. and Samuel L. Dana, M.D.....*

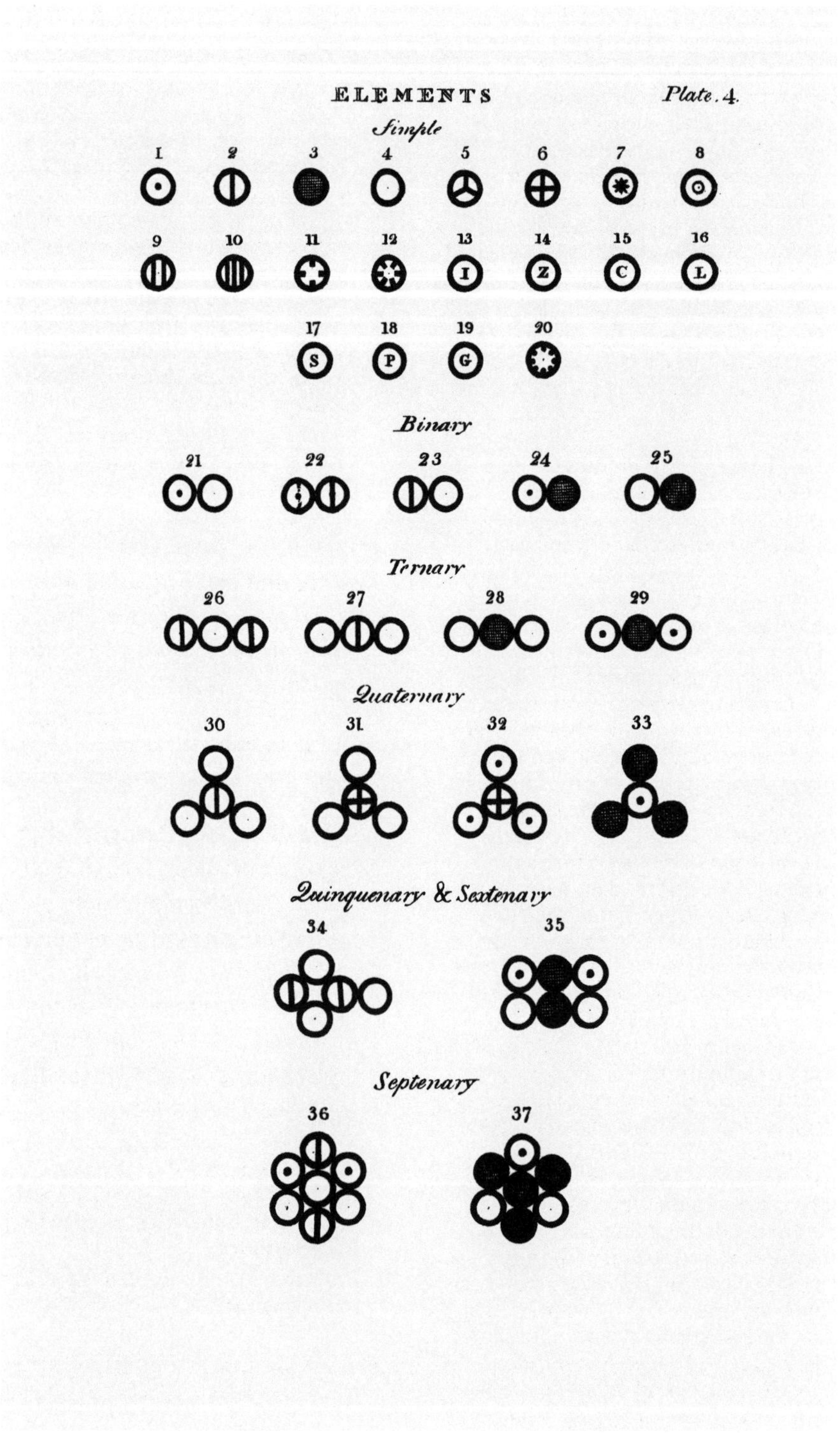

DALTON, *New System of Chemical Philosophy*, 1808-1827

Boston: Published by Cummings and Hilliard, no. 1 Cornhill. University Press... Hilliard and Metcalf, 1818. 108 p. front. (fold. map) 26 cm. "List of the authors and editions of the works consulted": p. [7].
Provenance: Essex Institute, Library of Francis Peabody (book label). Map is hand-colored.

474. DANTE ALIGHIERI, 1265-1321. *Dante Alighieri's Göttliche Comödie. Metrisch übertragen und mit kritischen und historischen Erläuterungen versehen von Philalethes.*
Leipzig: Druck and Verlag von B. G. Teubner, 1877. 3 v.: ill., port., maps; 21 cm. Translation of: *Divina commedia.* Portrait engraved by Weger after Giotto. Philalethes is pseud. for Johann, King of Saxony. Dritter und veränderter Abdruck der berichtigten Ausgabe von 1865-66, besorgt von J. Petzholdt. Includes bibliographical references. 1.T. Die Hölle – 2.T. Das Fegfeuer – 3.T. Das Paradies.

475. DANTE ALIGHIERI, 1265-1321. *Dante con l'espositioni di Christoforo Landino, et d'Alessandro Vellvtello. Sopra la sua Comedia dell'Inferno, del Purgatorio, & del Paradiso. Con tauole, argomenti, & allegorie, & riformato, riueduto, & ridotto alla sua vera lettura, per Francesco Sansovino Fiorentino.*
Venetia: Appresso Giouambattista, Marchió Sessa, et fratelli, 1578. 28 p.l., 163 numb. l., 4 l., 164-392 numb. l. illus. 32 cm. Translation of: *Divina commedia.* Colophon: In Venetia, Appresso gli Heredi di Francesco Rampazetto. Adinstantia di Giouambattista, Marchiò Sessa, et fratelli, M D LXXVIII. Woodcut title vignette (large portrait of Dante); headpieces; initials. Sessa's device at end. Reprint of the edition of 1564.

476. DARWIN, CHARLES, 1809-1882. *The descent of man, and selection in relation to sex. By Charles Darwin....*
London: J. Murray, 1871. 2 v. illus. 20 cm. First edition, first issue. Errata: verso t. p., v. 2. Includes bibliographical references and index.
Advertisements: verso t. p., 16 p. at end, v. 1; 16 p. at end, v. 2.

477. DARWIN, CHARLES, 1809-1882. *The expression of the emotions in man and animals. By Charles Darwin...; with photographic and other illustrations.*
London: John Murray ..., 1872. vi, 374, 4 p., VII leaves of plates (3 folded): ill.; 20 cm. First edition, second issue. Caption title: On the expression of the emotions in man and animals. On verso of t. p.: London: Printed by William Clowes and Sons ... Freeman, R. B. *Darwin* (2nd ed.) 1142. Includes bibliographical references and index. Publisher's advertisements: p. [1]-4 at end.
Provenance: Charles Atwood Kofoid (bookplate).

478. DARWIN, CHARLES, 1809-1882. *Journal of researches into the geology and natural history of the various countries visited by* H.M.S. Beagle, *under the command of Captain Fitz Roy, R.N., from 1832 to 1836.*
London: H. Colburn, 1839. [5], viii-xiv, 615 p. fold. maps. 25 cm. Cover title: Researches in geology and natural history. Advertisements: 16 p. following text. Includes index. Freeman, R. B. *Darwin,* 11.

479. DARWIN, CHARLES, 1809-1882. *Journal of researches into the natural history and geology of the countries visited during the voyage of the* H.M.S. Beagle *round the world: under the command of Capt. Fitz Roy, R.N., by Charles Darwin ... [2nd ed.], tenth thousand.*
London: John Murray ..., 1860. xv, [1] (blank), 519 p.: ill.; 21 cm. Spine title: Naturalist's voyage round the world. Includes bibliographical references and index.
Advertisements, printed by Bradbury, Evans, and Co., Whitefriars, 32 p. following text. Provenance: Charles Atwood Kofoid (bookplate); Geo. E. Blood (bookplate).

480. DARWIN, CHARLES, 1809-1882. *On the movements and habits of climbing plants, by Charles Darwin....*
London: Sold at the Society's apartments ... ; and by Longman, Green, Longman, Roberts & Green and Williams and Norgate, 1865. [2], 118 p.: ill.; 21 cm. "From the Journal of the Linnean Society." Includes bibliographical references.
Provenance: Herbert McLean Evans (bookplate). Original printed wrapper bound in.

481. DARWIN, CHARLES, 1809-1882. *On the origin of species by means of natural selection, or, The preservation of favoured races in the struggle for life, by Charles Darwin.*

London: John Murray, 1859. ix, [1], 502 p., [1] folded leaf of plates: 1 ill.; 21 cm. Freeman, R. B. *Darwin* (2nd ed.), 373, binding variant b. Horblit, H. D. *Grolier 100 science books*, 23b.

32 p. of advertisements inserted following text. Provenance: Sir Philip Rose, of Rayners (armorial bookplate); Herbert McLean Evans (bookplate). Binder: Edmonds & Remnants (ticket).

482. Darwin, Charles, 1809-1882. *On the origin of species by means of natural selection, or The preservation of favoured races in the struggle for life. By Charles Darwin....*

New York: D. Appleton and Company, 1860. 432 p. fold. diagr. 20 cm. 1st edition, London, 1859. Includes index. Freeman, R. B. *Darwin*, 377.

Provenance: Herbert McLean Evans (bookplate).

483. Darwin, Charles, 1809-1882. *On the origin of species by means of natural selection, or The preservation of favoured races in the struggle for life. By Charles Darwin... 3rd ed., with additions and corrections. (7th thousand)*

London: J. Murray, 1861. xix, 538 p. fold. diagr. 20 cm. First edition, 1859. Advertisements: [2] p. following text. Includes index. Freeman, R. B. *Darwin* (2nd ed.), 381, binding variant a.

Provenance: William Tomline (armorial bookplate).

484. Darwin, Charles, 1809-1882. *On the origin of the species by means of natural selection, or, The preservation of the favoured races in the struggle for life, by CharlesDarwin ... Fourth edition, with additions and corrections. (8th thousand.)*

London: John Murray ..., 1866. xxi, (1) blank, 593 p., [1] folded leaf of plates: ill.; 21 cm. First published: London: J. Murray, 1859. Advertisements: p. [iv]. Includes bibliographical references and index.

Binder: Edmonds & Remnants (ticket). Provenance: Walter W. Maires (book stamp); E. H. Shaw (inscription); pencil marginalia on first pages.

485. Darwin, Charles, 1809-1882. *On the origin of species by means of natural selection, or, The preservation of favoured races in the struggle for life. By Charles Darwin ... 5th thousand.*

London: J. Murray, 1860. ix, [1], 502, 32 p. fold. diagr. 21 cm. Second ed., second issue; Freeman, R. B. *Darwin*, no. 376. Includes index. Advertisements: 32 p. at end.

Provenance: Charles Atwood Kofoid (bookplate).

486. Darwin, Charles, 1809-1882. *On the origin of species. The origin of species: by means of natural selection, or the preservation of favoured races in the struggle for life / by Charles Darwin ... Sixth edition, with additions and corrections (twelfth thousand).*

London: John Murray ... , 1872. xxi, [1] (blank), 458 p., [1] folded leaves of plates: ill.; 19 cm. Includes index. Glossary: p. 430-441, by W. S. Dallas. Freeman, R. B. *Darwin* (2nd ed.), 392.

487. Darwin, Charles, 1809-1882. *On the tendency of species to form varieties: and on the perpetuation of varieties and species by natural means of selection / by Charles Darwin ... and Alfred R. Wallace ...; communicated by Sir Charles Lyell ... and J. D. Hooker....*

London: Longman [and 4 others] and Williams and Norgate, 1858. p. 45-62; 23 cm. Journal of the proceedings of the Linnean Society. Zoology, v. 3, no. 9. Caption title. Horblit, H. D. *Grolier 100 science books*, 23a.

488. Darwin, Charles, 1809-1882. *The power of movement in plants / by Charles Darwin ...; assisted by Francis Darwin ... Second thousand.*

London: John Murray ..., 1880. x, 592 p.: ill.; 20 cm. Caption title: The movements of plants. Second issue, without the errata on p. x. Cf. Freeman, p. 161. Includes bibliographical references and index. Freeman, R. B. *Darwin* (2nd ed.), 1326.

Advertisements: verso half-title; 32 p. catalogue dated January 1879 at end.

489. Darwin, Charles, 1809-1882. *The variation of animals and plants under domestication. By Charles Darwin....*

London: J. Murray, 1868. 2 v. illus. 23 cm. First edition, 2nd issue. Cf. Freeman. Erratum: p. vi, v. 1. Includes bibliographical references and index. Freeman, R. B. *Darwin* (2nd ed.), 878.

Advertisements: 32 p. dated April 1867 at end, v. 1; [2] p. dated February 1868 at end, v. 2. Binding: original green cloth; in slipcase. Provenance: Herbert McLean Evans (bookplate).

490. DARWIN, ERASMUS, 1731-1802. *Zoonomia, or, The laws of organic life / by Erasmus Darwin....*

London: Printed for J. Johnson, in St. Paul's Churchyard, 1794-1796. 2 v.: ill. (some col.); 28 cm. Includes bibliographical references and indexes. v. I. Part 1. Sect. XL. On the ocular spectra of light and colours /by Dr. R. W. Darwin (p. 534-566). v. II. Part II. A catalogue of diseases distributed into natural classes according to their proximate causes, with their subsequent orders, genera, and species, and with their methods of cure. part III. The articles of the materia medica, with an account of the operation of medicines. Garrison-Morton (4th ed.), 105. Wood, C. *Vertebrate zoology*, p. 311.

Provenance: Charles Atwood Kofoid (bookplate); Dr. Charles Rooke (bookplate).

491. DARWIN, GEORGE HOWARD, SIR, 1845-1912. *The tides: and kindred phenomena in the solar system: the substance of lectures delivered in 1897 at the Lowell Institute, Boston, Massachusetts / by George Howard Darwin. 2nd ed.*

London: John Murray, 1901. 20, 346 p., [3] leaves of plates: ill.; 20 cm. Includes bibliographical references and index.

Provenance: New University Club Library (embossing).

492. DAUB, J. H. *De sterrenhemel: christelijke bespiegelingen tot verheffing des harten/ naar het hoogduitsch van J. H. Daub. Tweede druk.*

Amsterdam: J. D. Sijbrandi, 1841. VII, [1], 118 p.; 23 cm.

Advertisements: [2] p. following text.

493. DAVIDSON, MARTIN. *An easy outline of astronomy / by M. Davidson. 2nd ed.*

London: Watts & Co., 1946. iv, 112 p., [2] p. of plates: ill.; 17 cm. Thinker's Library; no. 95. Includes index.

494. DAVIDSON, MARTIN. *The stars and the mind: a study of the impact of astronomical development of human thought / by Martin Davidson.*

London: Scientific Book Club, [1947]. x, 210 p., [8] p. of plates: ill., ports.; 20 cm. Date of publication from verso of t. p. Includes index.

495. DAVY, HUMPHRY, SIR, 1778-1829. *The Bakerian lecture on some new phenomena of chemical changes produced by electricity: particularly the decomposition of the fixed alkalies, and the exhibition of the new substances which constitute their bases: and onthe general nature of alkaline bodies / by Humphry Davy ...; read November 19, 1807.*

[London]: Royal Society, 1808. 44 p.; 27 cm. Caption title. Detached from: *Philosophical transactions of the Royal Society*, v. 98 1808. Includes bibliographical references.

Provenance: Herbert McLean Evans (bookplate).

496. DAVY, HUMPHRY, SIR, 1778-1829. *Electro-chemical researches on the decomposition of the earths: with observations on the metals obtained from the alkaline earths and on the amalgam procured from ammonia / by Humphry Davy ...; read June 30th, 1808.*

[London]: Royal Society, 1808. p. 333-368; 27 cm. Caption title. Detached from: *Philosophical transactions of the Royal Society*, v. 98 1808. Includes bibliographical references.

497. DAVY, HUMPHRY, SIR, 1778-1829. *Elements of agricultural chemistry: in a course of lectures for the Board of Agriculture, delivered between 1802 and 1812 / by Sir HumphryDavy ... The third edition.*

London: Printed for Longman, Hurst, Rees, Orme, and Brown ...: and A. Constable and Co., Edinburgh, 1821. x, 415 p., [10] folded leaves of plates: ill.; 24 cm. "Appendix. An account of the results of experiments on the produce and nutritive qualities of different grasses, and other plants, used as the food of animals. Instituted by John Drake of Bedford", by Davy and George Sinclair: p. [343]-400. "Notes, by T. A. Knight": p. 401-407. Bibliography: p. 346. Includes indexes. Plates engraved by W. Lowry and Milton.

Imperfect: lacks half-title. Provenance: Hugh Reveley (signature).

498. DAVY, HUMPHRY, SIR, 1778-1829. *On the safety lamp for coal miners; with some researches on flame. By Sir Humphry Davy.*

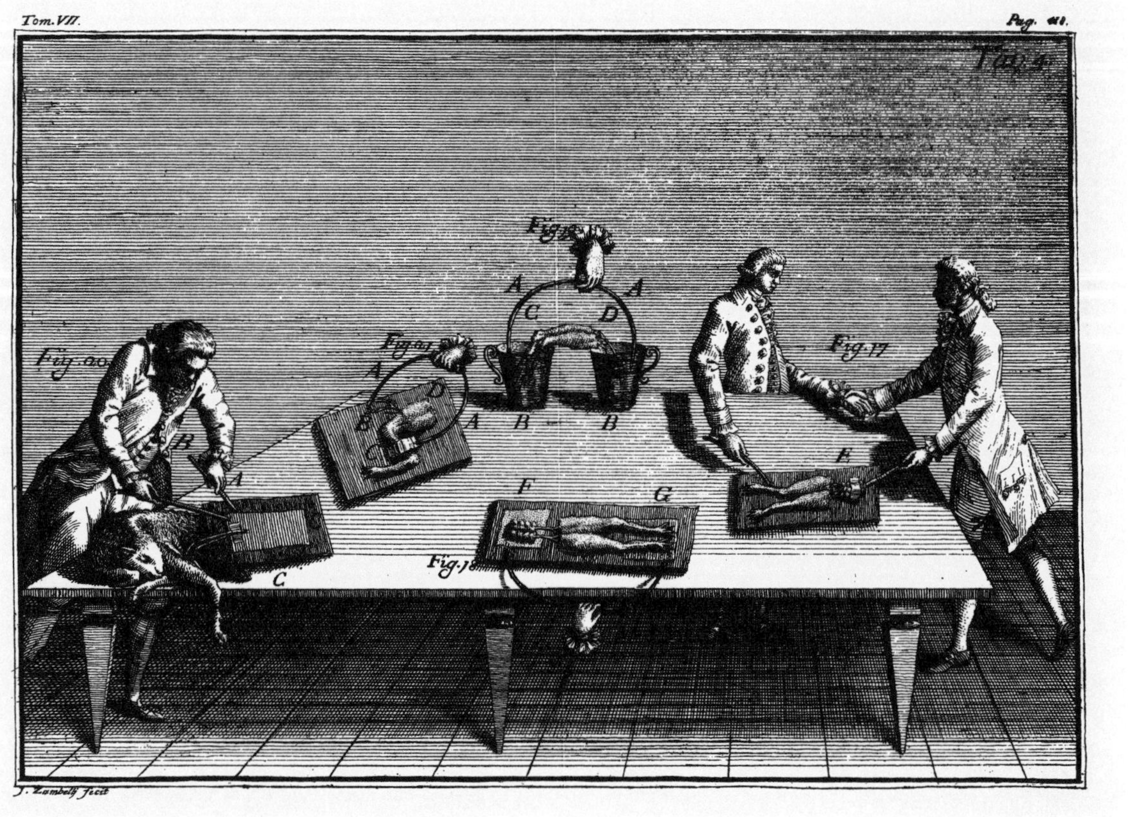

De Bononiensi scientiarum et artium instituto atque academia commentarii, 7 (1791)

London: Printed for R. Hunter, 1818. viii, 148 p. fold. front. 23 cm. Plate engraved by Lowry.

Provenance: Smith (inkstamp).

499. *De Bononiensi scientiarum et artium instituto atque academia commentarii.*

Bononiæ: Ex typographia Lælii A Vulpe, 1748-1791. 7 v. : ill., maps. ; 30 cm. Includes bibliographical references. Issued by: Accademia delle scienze dell' Instituto di Bologna.

Library has: 1-7.

500. *De la méthode dans les sciences, 2. série, par MM. B. Baillaud, Léon Bertrand, L. Blaringhem [et al.].*

Paris: F. Alcan, 1911. ii, [1], 367 p. 19 cm. Nouvelle collection scientifique.

Advertisements: [1], 36 p. at end; on p. [4] of wrapper.

501. DE MORGAN, AUGUSTUS, 1806-1871. *Arithmetical books from the invention of printing to the present time : being brief notices of a large number of works drawn up from actual inspection / by Augustus De Morgan.*

London: Taylor and Walton, 1847 (Printed by Robson, Levey, and Franklyn) [4], xxviii, 124 p. ; 22 cm. Includes index.

Bound to 20 cm. Provenance: [?] John Falk.

502. DE MORGAN, AUGUSTUS, 1806-1871. *The book of almanacs, with an index of reference, by which the almanac may be found for every year, whether in old style or new, from any epoch, ancient or modern, up to A.D. 2000. With means for finding the day of any new or full moon from B.C. 2000 to A.D. 2000. Comp. by Augustus De Morgan....*

London: Taylor, Walton, and Maberly, 1851. xix, 89 p. 14 x 22 cm. Advertisements: [2] p. following text.

Errata slip inserted between half title and t. p. Provenance: Radcliffe Observatory, Oxford (inkstamp).

503. DE MORGAN, AUGUSTUS, 1806-1871. *An explanation of the gnomic projection of the sphere; and of such points of astronomy as are most necessary in the use of astronomical maps; being a description of the construction and use of the larger and smaller maps of the stars; as also of the six maps of the earth. By Augustus De Morgan....*

London: Baldwin and Craddock, 1836. 2 p. l., 126 p. tables, diagrs. 23 cm. At head of title: Published under the superintendence of the Society for the Diffusion of Useful Knowledge. List of memoirs on double stars and nebulæ: p. 118-121.

Advertisements: 2 p. at end.

504. DEBYE, PETER J. W. (PETER JOSEF WILLIAM), 1884- . *Polare Molekeln.*

Leipzig: S. Hirzel, 1929. viii, 200 p. illus. 23 cm. Includes bibliographical references and index. Translation of: *Polar molecules.*

Provenance: Herbert McLean Evans (bookplate).

505. DECHALES, CLAUDE-FRANÇOIS MILLIET, 1621-1678. *R. P. Claudii Francisci Milliet Dechales Camberiensis e Societate Iesu Cursus seu mundus mathematicus, tomus primus [-tertius]....*

Lugduni: Ex Officina Anissoniana, 1674. 3 v.: ill.; 36 cm. Printed in double columns. Includes indexes.

506. DEE, JOHN, 1527-1608. *Parallaticæ commentationis praxeosq[ue]: nucleus quidam / authore Joanne Dee, Londinensi.*

Londini: Apud Johannem Dayum typographum, 1573. [30] p.; 20 cm. Signatures: A-D⁴. Issued with: *Alæ sev scalæ mathematicæ ... / Thoma Diggeseo* ...Londini, 1573. Cf. *NUC pre-1956,* v. 136, p. 416. *STC* 6462.

With: *Tychonis Brahe De mundi ætherei recentioribus phænomenis liber secundus.* Vraniburgi Daniæ, 1603. D4 (blank) missing. Bound to 23 cm.

507. DELAMBRE, J. B. J. (JEAN BAPTISTE JOSEPH), 1749-1822. *Abrégé d'astronomie, ou, Leçons élémentaires d'astronomie théorique et pratique / par M. Delambre....*

Paris: Mme. Ve Courcier ..., 1813. xvj, 652, [2] p., XIV leaves of folded plates: ill.; 21 cm. "Cet Abrégé est extrait des leçons que j'ai données au Collége Impérial de France, et dont le recueil formera un traité complet en trois volumes in-4ê. Les deux premiers sont terminés, et le troisième est sous presse" – Préf.

Addenda: "Table alphabetique des matières contenues dans l'Abrégé de l'astronomie de Delambre," 5 ms. pages on [2] folded leaves, loosely inserted. Marginalia throughout. Errata: [2] p. following text.

508. DELAMBRE, J. B. J. (JEAN BAPTISTE JOSEPH), 1749-1822. *Astronomie théorique et pratique; par M. Delambre....*

Paris: Ve. Courcier, 1814. 3 v. 29 fold. pl., tables. 27 x 21 cm.

Advertisements: publisher's catalogue dated May 1817 (10 p.) following text, v. 3. Provenance: Samuel Smith (signature); Dr. W. P. Gibbons (signature).

509. DELAMBRE, J. B. J. (JEAN BAPTISTE JOSEPH), 1749-1822. *Histoire de l'astronomie ancienne; par m. Delambre....*

Paris: Ve Courcier, 1817. 2 v. diagrs. on 17 folded pl. 27 x 21 cm. Illustrated by Ambroise Tardieu.

Provenance: James Stokley (bookplate).

510. DELAMBRE, J. B. J. (JEAN BAPTISTE JOSEPH), 1749-1822. *Histoire de l'astronomie au dix-huitième siècle; par m. Delambre ...pub. par M. Mathieu....*

Paris: Bachelier, 1827. lii, 796 p. front. (port.) diagrs. on 3 fold. pl. 26 x 21 cm. Port. by E. Desmoulins.

Provenance: Herbert McLean Evans (bookplate).

511. DELAMBRE, J. B. J. (JEAN BAPTISTE JOSEPH), 1749-1822. *Histoire de l'astronomie du moyen âge / par M. Delambre.*

Paris: Ve. Courcier, 1819. lxxxiv, 640 p.: diagrs. on 17 plates; 26 x 20 cm.

Provenance: Herbert McLean Evans (bookplate).

512. DELAMBRE, J. B. J. (JEAN BAPTISTE JOSEPH), 1749-1822. *Histoire de l'astronomie moderne; par m. Delambre....*

Paris: Ve Courcier, 1821. 2 v. diagrs. on 17 fold. pl. 27 x 22 cm. Illustrated by Ambroise Tardieu.

Provenance: Herbert McLean Evans (bookplate).

513. DELAMBRE, J. B. J. (JEAN BAPTISTE JOSEPH), 1749-1822. *Méthodes analytiques*

pour la détermination d'un arc du méridien; par J. B. J. Delambre. Précédées d'un mémoire sur le même sujet, par A. M. Legendre.

Paris: Impr. de Crapelet, an VII 1799. xv, [1], 176, [16], 6 p. 2 fold. pl., tables, diagrs. 26 cm. Plates signed: Duruisseau sculp.

Provenance: Perrier (inscription).

514. DELAUNAY, CHARLES, 1816-1872. *Cours élémentaire d'astronomie / par M. Ch. Delaunay ... Septième édition / revue et complété par M. Albert-Lévy.*

Paris: Garnier frères ... G. Masson ..., 1885. VIII, 676 p., 3 folded leaves of plates: ill., maps, 18 cm. "Notice sur M. Delaunay": p. V-VIII. Plates engraved by E. Wormser.

515. DELAUNAY, CHARLES, 1816-1872. *Essay on the velocity of light. By M. Delaunay ... Translated for the Smithsonian Institution by Alfred M. Mayer....*

[Washington: 1864]. p. [135]-165. 23 cm. From the *Smithsonian Institution Report*, 1864.

516. DENNING, WILLIAM F. (WILLIAM FREDERICK), b. 1848. *Telescopic work for starlight evenings. By William F. Denning....*

London: Taylor and Francis, 1891. xi, 361, [1] p. front., illus., pl., tab., diagr. 23 cm. Includes index. A series of articles on "Telecopes and telescopic work," written for the "Journal of the Liverpool astronomical society" in 1887-88, together with contributions on "Large and small telescopes," "Planetary observations," and kindred subjects written for "The Observatory" and other scientific serials; the articles appear here in revised and extended form. cf. Pref.

Provenance: T. R. Hake (inscription).

517. DERHAM, W. (WILLIAM), 1657-1735. *Astro-theology, or, A demonstration of the being and attributes of God: from a survey of the heavens ... / by W. Derham ... The fifth edition.*

London: Printed by William and John Innys ..., 1726. [16], lvi, [8], 246, [10] p., [3] folded leaves of plates: ill.; 21cm. Plates signed: I. Senex. Includes bibliographical references and index.

Provenance: Edward S. Sullivan (bookplate); R. Belasyse (signature); John M. Pryse (bookseller's ticket).

518. DERHAM, W. (WILLIAM), 1657-1735. *Astro-theology: or, A demonstration of the being and attributes of God, from a survey of the heavens. Illustrated with copper-plates. By W.Derham.*

London: Printed for W. Innys, 1715. lviii, [6], 228, [12] p. 3 fold. pl. 20 cm. Title vignette (printer's mark?) Plates signed: I. Senex.

Provenance: Fulke Southwell Greville (armorial bookplate).

519. DESCARTES, RENÉ, 1596-1650. *Discours de la methode: pour bien conduire sa raison, & chercher la verité dans les sciences. Plus La dioptrique. Les meteores. Et La geometrie. Qui sont des essais de cete methode.*

À Leyde: De l'Impimerie de Ian Maire, MDCXXXVII. [1637]. 78, [2], 413, [35] p.: ill.; 22 cm. Errata on p. [32] of last group. Title vignette. Guibert, A. J. *Descartes*, p. 14, no. 1. Dibner Lib. *Science* 81. Horblit, H. D. *Grolier 100 science books*, 24. *Yale Cushing Coll.* D119.

Provenance: James Erskine of Alva (armorial bookplate); Herbert McLean Evans (bookplate).

520. DESCARTES, RENÉ, 1596-1650. *Discours de la methode: pour bien conduire sa raison, et chercher la verité dans les sciences. Plus La Dioptrique et Les Meteores, qui sont essais de cette methode / par René Descartes. Reueuë, & corrigée en cette dernière ed.*

Paris: Chez Theodore Girard ..., 1668. [4], 413, [31] p.: ill.; 23 cm. Errors in pagination: p. 121 misnumbered as 221, p. 128 as 228 and p. 334 as 314. Advertisements: p. [4] first group. Guibert, A. J. Descartes, p. 20, no. 5.

521. DESCARTES, RENÉ, 1596-1650. *Geometria / à Renato Des Cartes anno 1637 Gallicè edita; postea autem unà cum notis Florimondi de Beaune ... Gallicè conscriptis in Latinam linguam versa, & commentariis illustrata, opera at que studio Francisci à Schooten....*

Amstelædami: Apud Ludovicum & Danielem Elzevirios, M DC LIX.-M DC LXI. 1659-1661. 2 v.: ill., 1 port.; 21 cm. Title vignette: Elsevier device (Minerva, Rahir 19). Vol. 1: [16], 520 p.; v. 2: [18], 420, [4] p. Half title reads: Renati Des-Cartes Geometria. Editio secunda, multis accessionibus exornata, & plus alterâ sui parte ad aucta. [Pars I] Geometria, à Renato Des Cartes. Florimondi de Beaune In Geometriam

Renati Des Cartes notæ breves. Francisci à Schooten In Geometriam Renati Des Cartes commentarii. Appendix, de cubicarum æquationum resolutione. Additamentum. Johannis Huddenii Epistola prima dereductione æquationum. Johannis Huddenii Epistola secunda, de maximis et minimis. Henrici van Heuraet Epistola de transmutatione curvarum linearumin rectas. Pars II. Principia matheseos universalis, seu Introductio ad geometriæ methodum Renati Des Cartes, / conscripta ab Er. Bartholino ... (1661). De æquationum natura, constitutione, & limitibus opuscula duo. / Incepta à Florimondo de Beaune ...; absoluta verò, & post mortem ejus edita ab Erasmio Bartholino ... (1659). Johannis de Witt Elementa curvarum linearum. / Edita operâ Francisci à Schooten ... (1659). Francisci à Schooten ... Tractatus de concinnandis demonstrationibus geometricis excalculo algebraëico. / In lucem editus à Petro à Schooten ... (1661). T. p. of pt. 2: Principia matheosos vniuersalis, seu introducto ad geometriæ methodum / Renati Des Cartes; conscripta ab Er. Bartholino ... Editio secunda. - Amstelædami: Apud Ludovicum & Danielem Elzevirios,1661. Port signed by Franciscus á Schooten. Signatures: v. 1: *-2*4 A-3T4; v.2: [pi]2 (-[pi]1?) :-2:4 A-3G4. Brunet, II, column 610; Guibert, A. J. *Descartes,* p. 29, no. 3. Willems, A. *Les Elzevier,* 1244. Errata: v. 2, p. [421-422].

Provenance: Liechtensteinianis (armorial bookplate).

522. DESCARTES, RENÉ, 1596-1650. *Passiones animæ, per Renatum Descartes: Gallicè ab ipso conscriptæ, nunc autem in exterorum gratiam Latina civitate donatæ, ab H. D. M.*

Amstelodami: D. Elsevir, 1677. [21], 92 p. 20 cm. Translation of: *Passions de l'âme.* Title vignette. With: *Renati Descartes Principia philosophiæ.* Amstelodami: Apud Danielem Elsevirium, 1677. Guibert, A. J. *Descartes,* p. 167, no. 18.

Provenance: James Plunkett, Earl of Fingall (armorial bookplate).

523. DESCARTES, RENÉ, 1596-1650. *Philosophische Werke, übers. und hrsg. von A. Buchenau.*

Leipzig: F. Meiner, 1922. 2 v. port. 20 cm. Philosophische Bibliothek; Bd. 26-29. Reissue of v. 26-29 of Philosophische Bibliothek published 1911-1922, each with special t. p. Advertisements: last 2 p., v. 2. Includes bibliographical references and indexes. Bd. 1. Abhandlung über die Methode. – Regeln zur Leitung des Geistes. – Die Erforschung der Wahrheit durch das natürliche Licht. – Meditationen über die Grundlagen der Philosophie. – Bd. 2. Die Prinzipien der Philosophie. – Über die Leidenschaften der Seele.

524. DESCARTES, RENÉ, 1596-1650. *Renati Des-Cartes Opera philosophica. Editio secunda, ab auctore recognita.*

[Amstelodami: Apud Ludovicum Elzevirium, 1650]. 4 v.: ill.; 21 cm. Each part has special t. p. and separate paging. Imprint from t. p. of *Principia philosophiæ.* Willems, A.C.J. *Les Elzevier* 1105-1107. Copinger, H. B. *Elzevier Press* 1368, 1355.

Bound in one v. in different order. Meditationes: Editio ultima. 1654. (From t. p. verso): Meditationes de prima philosophia; BC. ... – Principia philosophiæ – Dissertatio de methodo. Dioptrice. Meteora. Tractatus de Passionibus animæ.

525. DESCARTES, RENÉ, 1596-1650. *Renati Des-Cartes Principia philosophiæ.*

Amstelodami: Apud Ludovicum Elzevirium, 1644. 12 p.l., 310 p. illus., diagrs. 21 cm. Title vignette: device of Louis Elzevir. Errata: on p. 310.

With (as issued): the author's *Specimina philosophiæ.* Amstelodami: Apud Ludovicum Elzevirium, 1644.

526. DESCARTES, RENÉ, 1596-1650. *Renati Descartes Principia philosophiæ. Vltima editio cum optima collata, diligenter recognita, & mendis expurgata.*

Amstelodami: Apud Danielem Elsevirium, 1677. [40], 222 p.: ill., port.; 21 cm. Half title: Renati Des-Cartes Opera philosophica. Includes indexes. Port. signed: Franciscus à Schooten. With: *Renati Descartes Specimina philosophiæ, seu Dissertatio de methodo ... Dioptrice, et Meteora.* Amstelodami: Apud Danielem Elsevirium, 1677; and: *Passiones animæ* / Per Renatum Descartes. Amstelodami: Apud Danielem Elsevirium, 1677. Guibert, A. J. Descartes, p. 131, no. 15.

Provenance: James Plunkett, Earl of Fingall (armorial bookplate).

527. DESCARTES, RENÉ, 1596-1650. *Renati Des Cartes Specimina philosophiæ seu Dissertatio de methodo: rectè regendæ rationis, & veritatis in scientiis investigandæ: Dioptrice, et Meteora. / Ex gallico translata, & ab auctore perlecta, variisque in locis emendata.*

Amstelodami: Apud Ludovicum Elzevirium., MDCXLIV. 1644. [16], 331, [1] p. (the last page blank): ill.; 21 cm. Translation by Étienne de Courcelles of: *Discours de la méthode.* Title vignette: device of Louis Elzevir; decorated initials at the beginning of each chapter. Errata: p. 331. Guibert, A. J. *Descartes,* p.104, no. 1. Yale. *Cushing* D124.

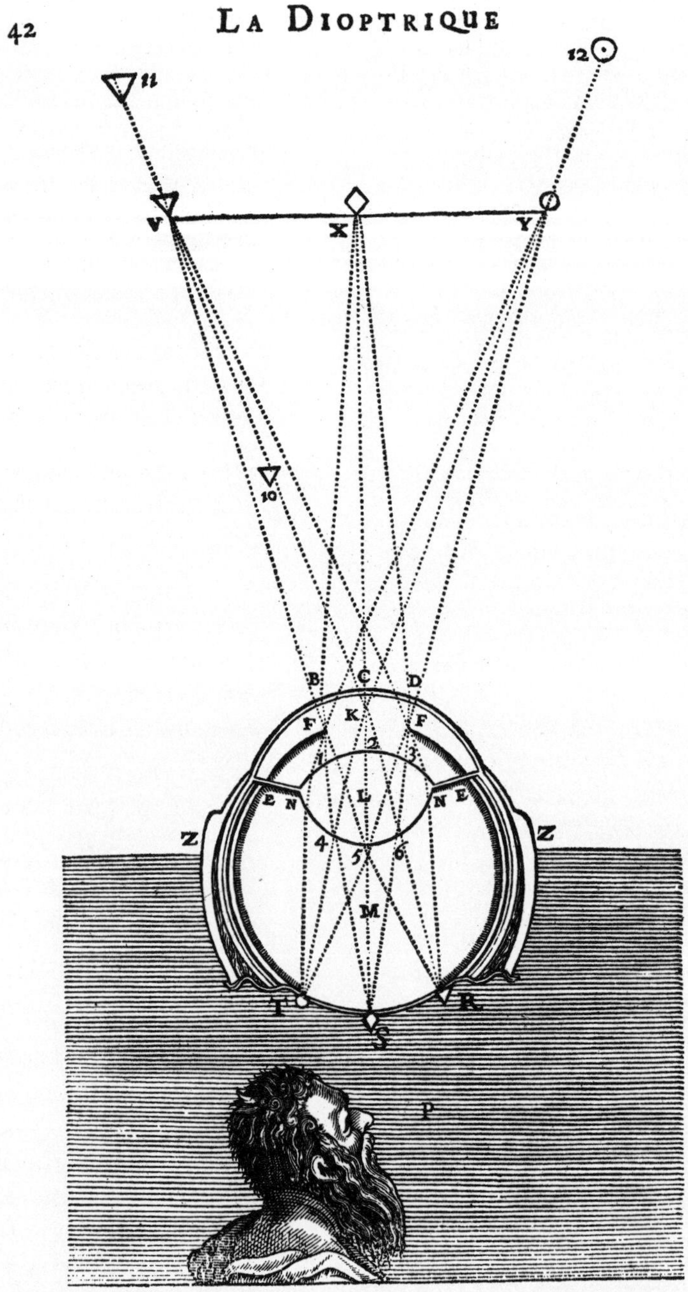

DESCARTES, *Discours de la méthode*, 1637

With (as issued): the author's *Principia philosophiæ.* Amstelodami: Apud Ludovicum Elzevirium, 1644.

528. DESCARTES, RENÉ, 1596-1650. *Renati Descartes Specimina philosophiæ: seu Dissertatio de methodo ... Dioptrice et Meteora / ex Gallico translata, & ab auctore perlecta, varisque in locis emendata. Ultima editio cum optima collata, diligenter recognita, & mendis expurgata.*
Amstelodami: Apud Danielem Elsevirium, 1677. [16], 248 p.: ill.; 21 cm. With: *Renati Descartes Principia philosophiæ.* Amstelodami: Apud Danielem Elsevirium, 1677. Guibert, A. J. *Descartes,* p. 109, no. 7.

529. DESCARTES, RENÉ, 1596-1650. *Renatus Des Cartes De homine, figuris, et latinitate donatus a Florentio Schuyl.*
Lugduni Batauorum: Apud Franciscum Moyardum & Petrum Leffen, 1662. [36], 121 [i.e. 123], [1] p., [10] leaves of plates (some folded): ill.; 21 cm. Translation of: *Traités de l'homme et de la formation de foetus.* A variant with the publishers reversed was also issued. Device on t. p.: angel under laurel tree. Errors in pagination: p. 12 misnumbered as 14, p. 54-55 as 56-57, p.111-112 repeated. Guibert, A. J. *Descartes,* p. 197, no. 2. BN v. 38, p. 1203, R. 3533.
Provenance: Charles Leeson Prince (signature); Frederic Wood Jones (bookplate).

530. DESHAYES, G. P. (GÉRARD PAUL), 1795-1875. *Description de coquilles caractéristiques des terrains, par M. G. P. Deshayes....*
Paris: F. G. Levrault; [etc., etc.] 1831. vii, 264 p. 14 pl. 22 cm. Intended as a supplement to the *Traité élémentaire de géologie,* by C. A. Rozet. Paris, 1830. Illustrated by P. Oudart.
Provenance: Sociéte de lectures de Genève (inkstamp); Herbert McLean Evans (bookplate).

531. DESLANDRES, HENRI ALEXANDRE, b. 1853. *Histoire des idées et des recherches sur le soleil: révélation récente de l'atmosphère entière de l'astre / par H. Deslandres.*
Paris: Gauthier-Villars, 1906. vii, 147 p.: ill.; 23 cm. "Extrait de l'*Annuaire* du Bureau des longitudes pour 1907."
Provenance: Author's presentation copy (inkstamp); E. A. Milne (inscription).

532. DICK, THOMAS, 1774-1857. *The atmosphere and atmospherical phenomena / by Thomas Dick....*
Philadelphia: E. C. & J. Biddle ..., 1850. 112 p.: ill.; 20 cm.
With the author's: *The practical astronomer.* Philadelphia: E. C. & J. Biddle, 1850.

533. DICK, THOMAS, 1774-1857. *Celestial scenery: or, the wonders of the planetary system displayed: illustrating the perfections of the deity and a plurality of worlds / by Thomas Dick....*
London: Ward and Co., [1852?]. xvi, 428 p.: ill., port.; 19 cm. Portrait engraved by H. Cook. "Tenth thousand."
Provenance: Henry Poulter (inscription).

534. DICK, THOMAS, 1774-1857. *The practical astronomer: comprising illustrations of light and colours; practical descriptions of all kinds of telescopes ... / by Thomas Dick ... Uniform edition.*
Philadelphia: E. C. & J. Biddle ... stereotyped by L. Johnson and Co., 1850. 396 p.: ill.; 20 cm. Preface dated: 1845.
With: the author's *Solar system.* Philadelphia: E. C. & J. Biddle, 1850; and the author's *The atmosphere and atmospherical phenomena.* Philadelphia: E. C. & J. Biddle, 1850. Advertisements: [24] p. bound behind the last work.

535. DICK, THOMAS, 1774-1857. *The practical astronomer: comprising illustrations of light and colours - practical description of all kinds of telescopes ... / by Thomas Dick....*
London: Seeley, Burnside, and Seeley, 1845. xx, 567, [1] p.: ill.; 20 cm.
Provenance: Eva Williams (inscription).

536. DICK, THOMAS, 1774-1857. *The sidereal heavens: and other subjects connected with astronomy, as illustrative of the character of the deity, and of an infinity of worlds / by Thomas Dick. Uniform edition.*
Philadelphia: Published by Edward C. Biddle ..., 1842. viii, [9]-394, V folded leaves of plates: ill.; 19 cm. Includes index.

537. DICK, THOMAS, 1774-1857. *The solar system: with moral and religious reflections in reference to the wonders therein displayed / by Thomas Dick ... Uniform edition.*
Philadelphia: E. C. & J. Biddle ... stereotyped by L. Johnson and Co., 1850. 235 p.: ill., maps; 20 cm.
With the author's: *The practical astronomer*. Philadelphia: E. C. & J. Biddle, 1850.

538. DICQUEMARE, ABBÉ (JACQUES FRANÇOIS), 1733-1789. *Idée générale de l'astronomie: ouvrage à la portée de tout lemonde / par M. L'Abbé Dicquemare.*
Paris: [C]hez Herissant, fils ..., 1769. xij, 114, [5] p., XXIV leaves of plates (part fold.): ill.; 21 cm. Faute a corriger: p. [5]

539. DIESEL, RUDOLF, 1858-1913. *Theorie und Konstruktion eines rationellen Wärmemotors: zum Ersatz der Dampfmaschinen ... / von Rudolf Diesel.*
Berlin: J. Springer, 1893. vi, 96 p., [3] folded leaves of plates: ill.; 24 cm. Two folded plates in pocket.
Provenance: United States Patent Office. Scientific Library (bookplate); Library of Congress (inkstamp). Imperfect: Wanting two folded plates in pocket and pocket.

540. DIESTERWEG, FRIEDRICH ADOLPH WILHELM, 1790-1866. *Diesterwegs Populäre Himmelskunde und mathematische Geographie: nach der Bearbeitung von Dr. M. Wilhelm Meyer ... und Professor Dr. B. Schwalbe... neu herausgegeben und vermehrt von Professor Dr. Arnold Schwassman ... 24., verb. und verm. Auf., mit 2 Sternkarten, 3 Pausekarten, 36 zum Teil mehrfarbigen Tafeln, 3 Doppeltafeln, über 100 Textbildern und den Bildnissen / von A. Diesterweg und M. Wilhelm Meyer in Kunstdruck.*
Hamburg: Henri Grand, 1921. xix, 530, [6] p., xxiv, [1] leaf of plates (some fold.): ill. (some col.), charts, maps., port.; 25 cm. Advertisements: [6] p. at end. Includes index.

541. DIGGES, LEONARD, D. 1571? *A geometrical practical treatize named pantometria: diuided into three bookes, longimetra, planimetra, and stereometria ... / first published by Thomas Digges esquire ...; lately reviewed by the author himselfe, and augmented with sundrie additions, diffinitions, problemes and rare theoremes....*
At London: Printed by Abell Jeffes, 1591. [6], 195 [i.e. 197], [2] p.: ill., coats of arms; 29 cm. Authorship assigned *STC* 6859. Errors in pagination: p. 151-152 repeated. Catchword does not match. "Faultes escaped": p. [2] at end. *STC* 6859.
Provenance: John Galard (signature); Macmillan A. Bowes (label); ms. notes on endpapers.

542. DIGGES, THOMAS, D. 1595. *Alæ sev scalæ mathematicæ, quibus visibilium remotissima cœlorum theatra conscendi, & planetarum omnium itinera nouis & inauditis methodis explorari: tùm huius portentosi syderis in mundi boreali plaga insolito fulgore coruscantis, distantia, & magnitudo immensa, situs[ue] protinùs tremendus indagari, dei[que] stupendum ostentum, terricolis expositum, cognosci liquidissimè possit. Thoma Diggeseo, Cantiensi ... authore.*
Londini: [Apud Thomam Marsh] 1573. [95] p. illus., diagrs. 19 cm. Signatures: A^4 $2A^4$ B-L^4. Errata: p. [94]. Printer's name taken from colophon. *STC*, 6871.
With: *Tychonis Brahe De mundi æthere irecentioribus phænomenis liber secundus*. Vraniburgi Daniæ, 1603. Bound to 23 cm.

543. DINGLE, HERBERT, 1890- . *Modern astrophysics, by Herbert Dingle.*
London: W. Collins Sons & Co. Ltd. c1924. xxviii, 420 p. front., illus., plates, diagrs. 23 cm. Includes index.

544. DIOPHANTUS, OF ALEXANDRIA. *Diophanti Alexandrini Arithmeticorum libri sex, et De numeris multangulis liber unus / nunc primùm græcè & latinè editi, at que absolutissimis commentariis illustrati auctore Claudio Gaspare Bacheto, Meziriaco Sebusiano, v.c.*

Lutetiae Parisiorum: Sumptibus Sebastiani Cramoisy ..., 1621. [12], 32, 451, [1], 58, [2] p.: ill.; 35 cm. Greek and Latin in parallel columns. P. 10: "Latinum damus tibi Diophantum ex Xilandri versione accuratissimæ castigata". Errors in pagination: p. 68 misnumbered as 60, 124 as 120. Errata: [2] p. at the end.

545. DIOPHANTUS, OF ALEXANDRIA. *Diophanti Alexandrini Arithmeticorvm libri sex, et De nvmeris mvltangvlis liber vnvs. Cvm commentariis C. G. Bacheti ... & obseruationibus D. P. de Fermat ... Accessit Doctrinæ analyticæ inuentum nouum, collectum ex varijs eiusdem D. de Fermat epistolis.*

Tolosae: Excudebat Bernardvs Bosc, 1670. 6 p.l., 64, 341, 48 p. 37 cm. Greek text of Diophantus and Latin translation by Xylander in parallel columns. Dedication signed: S. Fermat. Title vignette; head- and tail-pieces; initials.

Provenance: Herbert McLean Evans.

546. DIOSCORIDES PEDANIUS, OF ANAZARBOS. *The Greek herbal of Dioscorides; illustrated by a Byzantine, A.D. 512; Englished by John Goodyer, A.D. 1655; edited and first printed, A.D. 1933, by Robert T. Gunther ... with three hundred and ninety-six illustrations.*

Oxford: Printed by J. Johnson for the author, at the University Press, 1934. ix p., 1 l., 701 p. incl. front. (facsim.), illus. 26 cm. Translation of: *De materia medica.*

Provenance: (Richardson Wright?) (signature).

547. DIOSCORIDES PEDANIUS, OF ANAZARBOS. *Pedacii Dioscoridis Anazarbei De medicinali materia libri quinque: de virulentis animalibus, & venenis, cane rabioso, eorum notis, ac remedijs libri quatuor / Ioanne Ruellio Suessionensi interprete; insuper additæ sunt Stirpium differentiæ ex Dioscoride secundum locos communes ...authore Benedicto Textorio Segusiano....*

Venetiis: Per Ioan. Ant. de Nicolinis de Sabio, 1538. mense Septembris. [12], 212, 59, [24] leaves; 17 cm. Imprint partially from colophon. Includes index. Errors in foliation: 72 misnumbered 71 and 208 as 200. Adams, D662.

Ms. note pasted in.

548. DIRAC, P. A. M. (PAUL ADRIEN MAURICE), 1902- . *The principles of quantum mechanics / by P. A. M. Dirac.*

Oxford [Oxfordshire]: Clarendon Press, 1930. x, 257 p.; 25 cm. International series of monographs on physics.

549. DOLBEAR, A. E. (AMOS EMERSON), 1837-1910. *The machinery of the universe; mechanical conceptions of physical phenomena, by A. E. Dolbear....*

London [etc.]: Society for Promoting Christian Knowledge; 1897. vi, 7-122 p. illus. 18 cm. Romance of science. Enlarged from the author's lecture on "Mechanical conceptions of electrical phenomena," which appeared in the *Journal of the Franklin Institute* and in *Nature*. cf. Pref. Advertisements: 6 p. following text.

550. DOLMAGE, CECIL GOODRICH JULIUS. *Astronomy of to-day; a popular introduction in nontechnical language, by Cecil G. Dolmage ... with a frontispiece in colour and 45 illustrations & diagrams.*

Philadelphia: J. B. Lippincott Company; [etc., etc.] 1909. xvi, 17-362 p., 1 l. 25 pl. (incl. col. front.) diagrs. 21 cm. Printed in Great Britain. Includes index. Frontispiece after André Moch.

Provenance: L. A. Thompson (inscription).

551. DONALD, ARCHIBALD, 1860-1937. *An introduction to midwifery; a handbook for medical students and midwives.*

London: Griffin, 1894. xii, 188 p. ill. 21 cm. Includes index. Advertisements: 24 p. following text.

552. DOPPELMAYR, JOHANN GABRIEL, 1671-1750. *Atlas cœlestis: in quo mundus spectabilis et in eodem stellarum omnium phœnomena notabilia ... / e celeberrimorum astronomorum obseruationibus graphice descripta exhibentur a Ioh. Gabriele Doppelmaiero....*

Norimbergae: Sumptibus heredum Homannianorum, 1742. [6] p., 30 folded leaves of plates: chiefly ill., charts, maps; 53 cm. Additional engraved t. p. signed: J. J. Preisler del., J. C. Reisensperger sc. GV1700-1900 v. 440, p. 195.

Hand col. ill., hand col. folded leaves. With: *Kalendarium Juliano Romanum perpetuum* / Matth. Seutter. Augustæ Vindel – *Tabula anemographica* / â Matthæo Seuttero – *Schematismus geographiæ mathematicæ / Da Schazio in elementis geographiæ.* Norimbergæ: Cura Homann. heredum, 1753 – *Planisphærium cœleste* / Opera G. C. Eimmarti. (Nuremberg): Prostat Officina Homanniana – *Sterre kaert of hemels pleyn* / Gemaeckt door Remmet Jeunisse Backer. Tot Amsterdam: Uytgegeven door Reinier & Josua Ottens; *Die verfinsterte Erdkugel ...25ten Iulii Ao. 1748* / verzeichnet von Georg Moriz Lowiz. Norimb.: Prostat in Officina Homanniana, 1747. (2 leaves) – *Vorstellung der in der Nacht zwischen den 8. u. 9. Aug. 1748 vorfallenden partialen Mond-Finsternis* / von Tobias Mayer. [Nuremberg]: zu finden in der Homännischen Officin., 1748; and broadsheets: *Vertoning van de merkwaardige zons-verduistering of te groote son-eclips* / Symon Panser. Gedrukt 't Amsterdam: By Reinier & Iosua Ottens, 1733 – *Verklaringe overden loop van Mercurius* / Symon Panser. [Amsterdam: 1736?]; and col. ms. chart: *Vertooning van de notabele sons.*

553. Doppler, Christian, 1803-1853. *Über das farbige Licht der Doppelsterne und einiger anderer Gestirne des Himmels: Versuch einer das Bradley'sche Aberrations-Theorem als integrirenden Theil in sich schliessenden allgemeineren Theorie / von Christian Doppler....*
Prag: In Commission bei Borrosch & André, 1842. 18 p., [1] leaf of plates: ill.; 27 cm. "Aus den Abhandlungen der k. böhm. Gesellschaft der Wissenschaften (V Folge, Bd. 2) besonders abgedruckt."

554. Douglas, Janet Mary, "Mrs. Stair Douglas." *The life and selections from the correspondence of William Whewell ... by Mrs. Stair Douglas; with portrait after a painting by Samuel Laurence.*
London: C. K. Paul & Co., 1881. xv, 591 p. front. (port.) 23 cm. Includes index.
Advertisements: 32 p. at end. Provenance: Raymond Pearl (bookplate); presentation inscription from Maggie to A.B.

555. Downes, John, 1799-1882. *The United States' almanac; or complete ephemeris, for the year 1843: wherein the sun's rising, setting, &c. are given ... a complete census of the United States ... / by John Downes....*
Philadelphia: Published by E. H. Butler, 1842. 4, iii-vi, 5-324, 9, 13-14 p.; 20 cm. Advertisements on lower wrapper. Includes index. Sabin B.20769.

556. Downey, John F. (John Florin), 1846- . *The new revelation through the spectroscope and the telescope, by John F. Downey.*
New York, Cincinnati: The Abingdon press [c1914]. 87 p. 20 cm.
Provenance: Leslie B. Briggs (inkstamp).

557. Drayson, Alfred W. (Alfred Wilks), 1827-1901. *The cause of the supposed proper motion of the fixed stars and an explanation of the apparent acceleration of the moon's mean motion; with other geometrical problems in astronomy hitherto unsolved. A sequel to The glacial epoch. By Lieut.-Col. Drayson.*
London: Chapman and Hall, 1874. xxiv, 311 p. diagrs. 23 cm. Errata slip inserted after p. xxiv. Binder's lettering: On the motion of the fixed stars.

558. Dubois, Edmond, 1822-1891. *Cours d'astronomie / par Edmond Dubois. Troisième édition corrigée et considérablement augmentée.*
Paris: Arthus Bertrand ..., 1876. [8], XLIV, 806 p., [4] folded leaves of plates: ill., map; 26 cm. Imprint date from preface. Advertisements: on verso of half title.
Provenance: H. B. Bone (signature).

559. Dudley Observatory. *Annals of the Dudley Observatory.*
Albany: The Observatory, 1866-1871. 2 v. : ill. (some col.) ; 23 cm. Vol. 1-2. Includes annual reports of the director, 1862-1870.
Library has 2v. Vol. II: Provenance: Columbia College Astronomical Observatory, New York (inkstamp).

560. Dufrénoy, A. (Armand), 1792-1857. *Carte géologique de la France. Exécutée sous la direction de Mr. Brochant de Villiers, Inspecteur général des mines, par Mm. Dufrénoy et Elie de Beaumont, ingénieurs des mines. Le dessin du relief a été exécutée par A. Desmadryl. La topographie gravée par C. E. Collin, la lettre par J. M. Hacq.*
[Paris?] 1840. col. map 216 x 213 cm. on 6 sheets 75 x 114 cm. fold. to 25 x 19 cm. Scale ca. 1:500,000.

Hand colored. Relief shown by hachures. Sheets segmented and mounted on cloth backing. Each sheet has book plate of J. Andriveau Goujon, géographe-éditeur, on verso.

561. DUMAS, J.-B. (JEAN-BAPTISTE), 1800-1884. *Mémoires de chimie, par M. J. Dumas....*
Paris: Béchet jeune [etc.], 1843. x, 412 p. 7 fold. pl. 24 cm.
Plates missing. Signed presentation copy to M. Johnston from the author.

562. DUNKIN, EDWIN, 1821-1898. *The midnight sky: familiar notes on the stars and planets / by Edwin Dunkin....*
London: The Religious Tract Society, 1869. [8], 325, [3] p.: ill.; 29 cm. Date of imprint from preface. Advertisements: [2] p. at end.
Binder: Westleys & Co. (ticket).

563. DUNKIN, EDWIN, 1821-1898. *Obituary notices of astronomers, fellows and associates of the Royal Astronomical Society written chiefly for the annual reports of the council. By Edwin Dunkin....*
London, Edinburgh: Williams & Norgate, 1879. viii, 257 p. 20 cm.
Obituaries of William Ellis from the Q. J. R. Meteor. Soc. and J. Instn. El. Eng. pasted in. Bound by Spottiswoode & Co. (ticket).

564. DUNNE, J. W. (JOHN WILLIAM), 1875-1949. *The serial universe, by J. W. Dunne.*
London: Faber & Faber, Limited, 1934. 241, [1] p., 1 l. incl. front., illus., diagrs. 23 cm. "Some of the chapters, greatly condensed, have been delivered in lecture form to the Royal College of Science (Mathematical Society and Physical Society)" – Pref. Includes index.

565. DUNTHORNE, RICHARD, 1711-1775. *The practical astronomy of the moon: or, New tables of the moon's motions, exactly constructed from Sir Isaac Newton's theory, as published by Dr. Gregory in his Astronomy. With precepts for computing the place of the moon, and eclipses of the luminaries.*
Cambridge [Eng.]: Printed for the author, and sold by J. Senex, 1739. 4 p.l., 88 p. folded plate, tables. 21 cm.
Provenance: W. C. E. Napier (bookplate).

566. *Eclectic repertory and analytical review, medical and philosophical.*
Philadelphia, A. Finley, T. Dobson. 10 v. 22 cm. v. 1-10; 1810-1820. Continued by: *Journal of foreign medical science and literature* ; new ser. vol. 1, 1821.
Library has: 7, 1817

567. EDDINGTON, ARTHUR STANLEY, SIR, 1882-1944. *The expanding universe.*
Cambridge [Eng.]: University Press, 1952. vii, 127 p. 2 plates. 19 cm. "This book is an expanded version of a public lecture delivered at the meeting of the International Astronomical Union at Cambridge [Massachusetts] in September 1932." Includes bibliographical references and index.

568. EDDINGTON, ARTHUR STANLEY, SIR, 1882-1944. *Fundamental theory, by Sir A. S. Eddington.*
Cambridge [Eng.]: The University Press, 1949. viii, 292 p. diagrs. 27 cm. "Editor's preface" signed: Edmund T. Whittaker. First edition 1948. Reprinted 1949. Includes bibliographical references and index.

569. EDDINGTON, ARTHUR STANLEY, SIR, 1882-1944. *The mathematical theory of relativity / by A. S. Eddington....*
Cambridge [Eng.]: The University Press, 1923. ix, 247, [1] p.; 28 cm. "A first draft of this book was published in 1921 as a mathematical supplement to the French edition of *Space, time and gravitation.*" – Pref. Includes index. Bibliography: p. [241]-243.
Provenance: G. B. Jeffery (signature).

570. EDDINGTON, ARTHUR STANLEY, SIR, 1882-1944. *Matter in interstellar space / by A. S. Eddington....*
London: British Broadcasting Corp., 1929. 27 p.; 19 cm. Broadcast national lectures; 2nd Lecture delivered on April 15th 1929.

571. EDDINGTON, ARTHUR STANLEY, SIR, 1882-1944. *The nature of the physical world / by A. S. Eddington.*
Cambridge: At the University Press, 1930. xix, 361 p.: ill.; 22 cm. Gifford lectures; 1927. Includes index.

572. EDDINGTON, ARTHUR STANLEY, SIR, 1882-1944. *The philosophy of physical science, by Sir Arthur Eddington.*

Cambridge [Eng.]: The University Press, 1949. ix, 230 p. 23 cm. Tarner Lectures; 1938.

573. EDDINGTON, ARTHUR STANLEY, SIR, 1882-1944. *Relativity theory of protons and electrons, by Sir Arthur Eddington.*
New York: The Macmillan Company; Cambridge, Eng.: The University Press, 1936. vi p., 1 l., 336 p. 27 cm. Printed in Great Britain. Includes index.

574. EDDINGTON, ARTHUR STANLEY, SIR, 1882-1944. *Report on the relativity theory of gravitation.*
London: Fleetway Press, 1918. vii, 91 p. diagrs. 23 cm. At head of title: The Physical Society of London. Bibliography: p. vi-vii.

575. EDDINGTON, ARTHUR STANLEY, SIR, 1882-1944. *Science and the unseen world, by Arthur Stanley Eddington....*
New York: Macmillan, 1929. 91 p. 19 cm. Swarthmore lecture; 1929.

576. EDDINGTON, ARTHUR STANLEY, SIR, 1882-1944. *Space, time and gravitation; an outline of the general relativity theory, by A. S. Eddington.*
Cambridge: The University Press, 1921. vi p., 1 l., 218 p., 1 l., front., diagrs. 23 cm.

577. EDDINGTON, ARTHUR STANLEY, SIR, 1882-1944. *Stellar movements and the structure of the universe, by A. S. Eddington....*
London: Macmillan and Co., Limited, 1914. xii, 266 p. front., plates, tables, diagrs. 23 cm. Macmillan's Science Monographs. "References" and "Bibliography" at end of most chapters. Includes index.
Advertisements: 2 p. at end. Provenance: William Howell Williams (bookplate).

578. EDWARDS, JOHN, fl. 1781-1803. *Directions for making the best composition for the metals of reflecting telescopes: and the method for casting, grinding, polishing, and giving them the true parabolic figure / by the Rev'd John Edwards....*
[London]: Published by order of the Commissioners of Longitude, 1790? 60, [4] p.; 24 cm. Published as a supplement to the *Nautical Almanac for 1787*. Advertisements ([4] p. at end) list works published between 1767 and 1790. "An account of the cause and cure of the tremors particularly affecting reflecting telescopes more than refracting ones," by the Rev'd John Edwards, p. [50]-60.
Provenance: W. McCree (signature and ms. Slip detailing bibliographic information).

579. EDWARDS, LAWRENCE. *The spangled heavens: an introduction to astronomy / by Lawrence Edwards; with foreword by the Astronomer Royal; & introduction by Cecil Grant.*
Philadelphia: J. B. Lippincott, 1932. xii, 115 p., [8] p. of plates: ill.; 20 cm. Date of publication supplied by *NUC pre-1956*, v. 156, p. 195. Printed in Great Britain. Preface signed: F. W. Dyson. Includes index. Errata slip mounted on p. 68.

580. *The Edwin Smith surgical papyrus, published in facsimile and hieroglyphic transliteration with translation and commentary in two volumes, by James Henry Breasted....*
Chicago, Ill.: The University of Chicago Press, 1930. 2 v. 54 pl. (part fold., incl. facsims.) 31 x 24 cm. (v. 2: 41 x 30 cm.) University of Chicago Oriental Institute Publications; v. 3-4. Includes index. "Printed in Great Britain." The papyrus is named after Edwin Smith, who purchased the document in January 1862 during his stay at Thebes. After his death in 1906 it was presented to the New York Historical Society. cf. General introduction. Errata slip inserted between p. 596 and plate I of v. 1. "List of abbreviated book titles": v. 1, p. [592]. v. 1. Hieroglyphic transliterations, translation and commentary. – v. 2. Facsimile plates and line for line hieroglyphic transliteration.
Provenance: L. M. Boyers (embossing).

581. *The Effects of atomic weapons. Prepared for and in cooperation with the U. S. Department of Defense and the U. S. Atomic Energy Commission; under the direction of the Los Alamos Scientific Laboratory, Los Alamos, New Mexico; board of editors J. O. Hirschfelder ... [et al.]*
Washington: Atomic Energy Commission, 1950. x, 456 p. ill. 23 cm. 4 p. errata and revision laid in. Includes bibliographical references and index.

582. EHINGER, ELIAS, 1573-1653. *Von dem newen Cometa welcher den 1. Decemb. 1618*

am Morgen vor vnd nach 6 Uhren zu Augspurg von vilen Personen gesehen worden / gestelt von M. Elia Ehingero....

Gedruckt zu Augspurg : Bey Johann Schultes, ca. 1621? [12] (last p. blank) p. ; 19 cm. Cover title: Von dem neuen cometen. At head of title: Iudicium astrologicum. Reference to anno 1622 on p. [10].

583. EHRENBERG, CHRISTIAN GOTTFRIED, 1795-1876. *Die Infusionsthierchen als vollkommene Organismen. Ein Blick in das tiefere organische Leben der Natur. Von d. Christian Gottfried Ehrenberg. Nebst einem Atlas von vierundsechszig colorirten Kupfertafeln, gezeichnet vom Verfasser.*

Leipzeg: L. Voss, 1838. xviii, [4], 547, [1] p. illus., LXIV col. pl. 47 cm. + atlas. Includes index. Engraved variously by: C. E. Weber, C. Haas, Wienker, Guinand.

Bound in 1. Provenance: Herbert McLean Evans (bookplate).

584. EHRLICH, PAUL, 1854-1915. *Die experimentelle Chemotherapie der Spirillosen (Syphilis, Rückfallfieber, Hühnerspirillose, Frambösie) von Paul Ehrlich und S. Hata; mit Beiträgen von H. J. Nichols, J. Iversen, Bitter, und Dreyer, mit 27 Textfiguren und 5 Tafeln.*

Berlin: J. Springer, 1910. viii, 164 p. plates, tables (part fold.) diagrs. 25 cm. Advertisements: [4] p. at the end. Includes bibliographies. Osler, W. *Bib. Osleriana*, 1697.

585. †EINSTEIN, ALBERT, 1879-1955. *Äther und Relativitätstheorie. Rede gehalten am 5. Mai 1920 an der Reichs-Universität zu Leiden, von Albert Einstein.*

Berlin: J. Springer, 1920. 15, [1] p. 23 cm.

Advertisements: on p. [4] of wrapper. Provenance: G. Robinow[?] (signature).

586. EINSTEIN, ALBERT, 1879-1955. [Collection of offprints and journal articles published post-1920 / by Albert Einstein].

[1922-1955] 55 pieces: ill.; 20-29 cm. Includes bibliographical references. (1) Zur Theorie der Lichtfortpflanzung in dispergierenden Medien (1922) – (2) Zur allgemeinen Relativitätstheorie (1923) – (3) Zur affinen Feldtheorie (1923) – (4) Bietet die Feldtheorie Möglichkeiten für die Lösung des Quantenproblems? (1923) – (5 & 6) Quantentheorie des einatomigen idealen Gases (Pts I & II) (1924-1925) – (7) Einheitliche Feldtheorie von Gravitation und Elektrizität (1925) – (8) Zur Quantentheorie des idealen Gases (1925) – (9) Über die formale Beziehung des Riemannschen Krümmungstensors zu den Feldgleichungen der Gravitation (1926) – (10) Über die interferenzeigenschaften des durch Kanalstrahlen emittierten Lichtes (1926) – (11) Vorschlag zu einem die Natur des elementaren Strahlungs-Emissionsprozesses betreffenden Experiment (1926) – (12) Isaac Newton (1927) – (13 & 14) Allgemeine Relativitätstheorie und Bewegungsgesetz (1. & 2. Mit.) (1927) – (15) Zu Kaluzas Theorie des Zusammenhanges von Gravitation und Elektrizität (1927) – (16) Riemann-Geometrie mit Aufrechterhaltung des Begriffes des Fernparallelismus (1928) – (17) Neue Möglichkeit für eine einheitliche Feldtheorie von Gravitation und Elektrizität (1928) – (18) Einheitliche Feldtheorie und Hamiltonsches Prinzip (1929) – (19) Zur einheitlichen Feldtheorie (1929). (20) Über den gegenwärtigen Stand der Feld-theorie (1928) – (21) Zwei strenge statische Lösungen der Feldgleichungen der einheitlichen Feldtheorie (1930) – (22) Auf die Riemann-Metrik und den Fern-Parallelismus gegründete einheitliche Feldtheorie (1930) – (23) Raum, Äther und Feld in der Physik (1930) – (24) Die Kompatabilität der Feldgleichungen in der einheitlichen Feldtheorie (1930) – (25) Thëorie unitaire du champ physique (1930) – (26 & 27) Einheitliche Theorie von Gravitation und Elektrizität (1931) – (28) Zum kosmologischen Problem der allgemeinen Relativitätstheorie (1931) – (29) Systematische Untersuchung über kompatible Feldgleichungen welche in einem Riemannschen Raume mit Fernparallelismus gesetzt werden können (1931) – (30) Semi-Vektoren und Spinoren (1932) – (31) Zu Dr. Berliners siebzigstem Geburtstag ((1932)) – (32) Einheitliche Theorie von Gravitation und Elektrizität: 2. Abhandlung (1932) – (33) Die Dirachgleichungen fuer Semivektoren (1933) – (34) Spaltung der natuerlichsten Feldgleichungen fuer Semi-Vektoren in Spinor-Gleichungen vom DIRAC'shen Typus (1933) – (35) Darstellung der Semi-Vektoren als gewöhnliche Vektoren von besonderem Differentations Charakter (1934) – (36) On the method of theoretical physics (1934) – (37) Elementary derivation of the equivalence of mass and energy (1935). (38) On gravitational waves (1937) – (39) Demonstration of the non-existence of gravitational fields with a non-vanishing total mass free of singularities (1941) – (40) Demonstración de la no existencia de campos gravitacionales sin singularidades de masa total no nula (1941) – (41) Considerations concerning the fundaments of theoretical physics (1942) – (42) The work and personality of Walther Nernst (1942) – (43) Bivector fields (1944) – (44) Bivector fields II (1944) – (45) A generalization of the relativistic theory of gravitation (1945) – (46) Atomic energy (1945) – (47) The influence of the expansion of space on the gravitational fields surrounding the individual stars (1945) – (48) A generalization of the relativistic theory of gravitation, II (1946) – (49) Quanten-Mechanik und Wirklichkeit (1948) – (50) A generalized theory of gravitation (1948) – (51) On the motion of particles in general relativity theory (1949) – (52) The Bianchi identities in the generalized theory of gravitation (1950) – (53) Generalization of gravitation theory (1953) – (54) Algebraic properties of the field in the relativistic theory of the asymmetric field (1954) – (55) A new form of the general relativistic field equations (1955).

587. Einstein, Albert, 1879-1955. [Collection of offprints and journal articles published through 1920 / by Albert Einstein].

[1901-1920] 45 pieces: ill.; 20-29 cm. Includes bibliographical references. (1) Folgerungen aus den Capillaritätserscheinungen (1901) – (2) Über die thermodynamische Theorie der Potentialdifferenz zwischen Metallen und vollständig dissociirten Lösungen ihrer Salze, und über ein elektrische Methode zur Erforschung der Molecularkräfte (1902) – (3)Kinetische Theorie des Wärmegleichgewichtes und des zweiten Hauptsatzes der Thermodynamik (1902) – (4) Eine Theorie der Grundlagen der Thermodynamik (1903) – (5) Zur allgemeinen molekularen Theorie der Wärme(1904) – (6) Eine neue Bestimmung der Moleküldimensionen (1906) – (7) Zur Theorie der Brownschen Bewegung (1906) – (8) Zur Theorie der Lichterzeugung und Lichtabsorption (1906) – (9) Das Prinzip von der Erhaltung der Schwerpunktsbewegung und die Trägheit der Energie (1906) – (10) Über eine Methode zur Bestimmung des Verhältnisses der transversalen und longitudinalen Masse des Elektrons (1906) – (11) Die Plancksche Theorie der Strahlung und die Theorie der spezifischen Wärme (1907) – (11A) Berichtung zu meiner Arbeit: "Die Plancksche Theorie der Strahlung etc." (1907) – (12) Über die Gültigkeitsgrenze des Satzes vom thermodynamischen Gleichgewicht und über die Möglichkeit einer neuen Bestimmung der Elementarquanta (1907) – (13) Über die Möglichkeit einer neuen Prüfung des Relativitätsprinzips (1907) – (14) Bemerkungen zu Notiz des Herrn P. Ehrenfest: Translation deformierbarer Elektronen und der Flachensatz (1907) – (15) Über die vom Relativitätsprinzip gefordete Trägheit der Energie (1907) – (16) Über die electromagnetischen Grundgleichungen für bewegte Körper (1908) – (16A) Berichtigung zur Abhandlung: "Über die elektromagnetischen ... (1908) – (17) Über die im elektromagnetischen Felde auf ruhende Körper ausgeübten ponderomotorischen Kräfte (1908) – (18) Eine neue elektrostatische Methode zur Messung kleiner Elektrizitätsmengen (1908) – (19) Bemerkungen zu unserer Arbeit: "Über die elektromagnetischen Grundgleichungen für bewegte Körper (1909) – (20) Bemerkung zu der Arbeit von D. Mirimanoff: "Über die Grundleichungen..." (1909) – (21) Über einen Satz der Wahrscheinlichkeitsrechnung und seine Anwendung in der Strahlungstheorie (1910) – (22) Theorie der Opaleszenz von homogenen Flüssigkeiten und Flüssigkeitsgemischen in der Nähe des kritischen Zustandes (1910) – (23) Bemerkung zu dem Gesetz von Eötvös (1911) – (23A) Bemerkung zu meiner Arbeit: "Eine Beziehung zwischen dem elastischen Verhalten ..." (1911) – (24) Bemerkungen zu den P. Hertzschen Arbeiten: "Über die mechanischen Grundlagen der Thermodynamik (1911) – (25) Berichtigung zu meiner Arbeit: "Eine neue Bestimmung der Moleküldimensionen" (1911) – (26) Über den Einfluss der Schwerkraft auf die Ausbreitung des Lichtes (1911). (27) Elementare Betrachtungen über die thermische Molekularbewegung in festen Körpen (1911) – (28) Bemerkung zu Abrahams vorangehender Auseinandersetzung "Nochmals Relativität und Gravitation" (1912) – (29) Thermodynamische Begründung des photochemischen Äquivalentgesetzes(1912) – (30) Nachtrag zu meiner Arbeit: "Thermodynamische Begründungdes photochemischen Aquivalentgesetzes" (1912) – (31)Lichtgeschwindigkeit und Statik des Gravitationsfeldes (1912) – (32) Zur Theorie des statischen Gravitationsfeldes (1912) – (33) Antwort auf eine Bemerkung von J. Stark: "Über eine Anwendung des Planckschen Elementargesetzes (1912) – (34) Relativität und Gravitation: Erwiderung auf eine Bemerkung von M. Abraham (1912) – (35) Zum gegenwärtigen Stande des Gravitationsproblems (1913) – (36) Physikalische Grundlagen einer Gravitationstheorie (1913) – (37) Einige Argumente für die Annahme einer molekularen Agitation beim absoluten Nullpunkt (1913) – (38) Die Nordstëromische Gravitationstheorie vom Standpunkt des absoluten Differentialkalküls (1914) – (39) Theoretische Atomistik (1915) – (40) Die Relativitätstheorie (1915) – (41) Spielen Gravitationsfelder im Aufbau der materiellen Elementarteilchen eine wesentliche Rolle? (1919) – (42) Schallausbreitung in teilweise dissoziierten Gasen (1920).

588. Einstein, Albert, 1879-1955. *Einstein on peace / edited by Otto Nathan and Heinz Norden; pref. By Bertrand Russell.*

New York: Simon and Schuster, 1960. xvi, 704 p.: facsims., port.; 22 cm. Bibliographical references included in "Notes" (p. [648]-683). Includes index.

589. EINSTEIN, ALBERT, 1879-1955. *Entwurf einer verallgemeinerten Relativitätstheorie und einer Theorie der Gravitation. I. Physikalischer Teil von Albert Einstein. II. Mathematischer Teil von Marcel Grossmann.*

Leipzig: B. G. Teubner, 1913. 38 p. 26 cm. "Separatabdruck aus *Zeitschrift für Mathematik und Physik* Band 62."

Original printed wrappers. Advertisements on p. [4] of cover. Provenance: Karl Horovitz (signature).

590. EINSTEIN, ALBERT, 1879-1955. *Essays in science.*

New York: Philosophical Library, [1955? c1934]. xi, 114 p. 17 cm. Selected essays from *Mein Weltbild*, translated by Alan Harris.

591. EINSTEIN, ALBERT, 1879-1955. *Essays in science / by Albert Einstein.*

New York: Philosophical Library, [1959?, c1934]. xi, 114 p.; 20 cm. Selected scientific essays, translated from *Mein Weltbild.*

592. EINSTEIN, ALBERT, 1879-1955. *L'éther et la théorie de la relativité, par Albert Einstein; traduction française par Maurice Solovine.*

Paris: Gauthier Villars, 1921. 15, [1] p. 22 cm. Translation of: *Äther und Relativitäts-Theorie.* Advertisements on lower wrapper.

593. EINSTEIN, ALBERT, 1879-1955. *The evolution of physics: the growth of ideas from early concepts to relativity and quanta / by Albert Einstein and Leopold Infeld.*

New York: Simon and Schuster, 1951. 316 p., [3] p. of plates: ill.; 21 cm. Includes index.

594. EINSTEIN, ALBERT, 1879-1955. *Les fondements de la théorie de la relativité générale. Théorie unitaire de la gravitation et de l'électricité. Sur la structure cosmologique de l'espace. Traduit de l'allemand par Maurice Solovine.*

Paris: Hermann et cie, 1933. 109 p., 1 l. front. (port.) diagr. 25 cm. Half title: Théorie de la relativité. Advertisements: p. [4] and wrapper. The first paper appeared in *Annalen der physik*, 1916. v. 49, p. [769]-822 under title: Die Grundlage der allgemeinen Relativitätstheorie. The second paper, by A. Einstein and W. Mayer, appeared in *Sitzungsberichte der Preussischen Akademie der Wissenschaften, Phys.-math.klasse*, 1931, p. 541-557, under title: Einheitliche Theorie von Gravitation und Elektrizität. The third paper was translated from manuscript. cf. Footnotes, p. [7], [73] and [99].

595. EINSTEIN, ALBERT, 1879-1955. *Geometrie und Erfahrung; erweiterte Fassung des Festvortrages gehalten an der Preussischen Akademie der Wissenschaften zu Berlin am 27. Januar 1921 von Albert Einstein, mit 2 Textabbildungen.*

Berlin: J. Springer, 1921. 20 p. diagrs. 22 cm.

Provenance: Herbert McLean Evans (bookplate). With: *Über die spezielle und die allgemeine Relativitätstheorie,* von A. Einstein. Braunschweig, F. Vieweg, 1917.

596. EINSTEIN, ALBERT, 1879-1955. *Die Grundlage der allgemeinen Relativitätstheorie, von A. Einstein.*

Leipzig: J. A. Barth, 1916. 64 p. 24 cm. "Sonderdruck aus den *Annalen der Physik* Band 49, 1916."

Binding: original printed wrappers. Advertisements on p. [4] of wrapper. Provenance: Herbert McLean Evans (bookplate).

597. EINSTEIN, ALBERT, 1879-1955. *Die Grundlage der allgemeinen Relativitätstheorie / von A. Einstein.*

[Leipzig]: J. A. Barth, 1916. p. [769]-822; 23 cm. In: *Annalen der Physik,* 4. F., Bd. 49, Heft 7. Horblit, H. D. *Grolier 100 science books,* 26c.

598. EINSTEIN, ALBERT, 1879-1955. *Ideas and opinions / by Albert Einstein; based on Mein Weltbild, edited by Carl Seelig, and other sources; new translations and revisions by Sonja Bargmann.*

New York: Crown, 1954. 377 p.: ill.; 22 cm. Includes items from The *world as I see it, Out of my later years, Mein Weltbild,* a few selections from other publications, and articles not previously published in book form. Cf. "Publisher's note."

599. EINSTEIN, ALBERT, 1879-1955. *Ist das Trägheit eines Körpers von seinem Energieinhalt abhängig ? / von A. Einstein.*
[Leipzig: J. A. Barth, 1905]. p. 639-641; 22 cm. In: *Annalen der Physik,* 4. F., Bd. 18, no. 13. Includes bibliographical references.

600. EINSTEIN, ALBERT, 1879-1955. *Lettres à Maurice Solovine: reproduites en facsimilé / Albert Einstein; traduites en français avec une introduction [par Maurice Solovine].*
Paris: Gauthier-Villars, 1956. xiii, 139 p., [3] p. of plates: facsims., 3 ports.; 29 cm. Facsims. of letters in German with French translations. On dust cover: Briefe an Maurice Solovine: Faksimile-Wiedergabe von Briefen aus den Jahren 1906 bis 1955 ... / Albert Einstein; französischer Übersetzung ... [und] Einführung ... [von] Maurice Solovine. Paris: Gauthier-Villars; Düsseldorf: Alleinrertrieb für die Deutschsprachigen Länder, Progress-Verlag J. Faldung.
Provenance: Herbert McLean Evans (bookplate).

601. EINSTEIN, ALBERT, 1879-1955. *The meaning of relativity. 4th ed., including the Generalization of gravitation theory.*
Princeton: Princeton University Press, 1953. 165 p. diagrs. 21 cm. "Translated by Edwin Plimpton Adams ... Ernst G. Straus ... [and] Bruria Kaufman." Includes index.

602. EINSTEIN, ALBERT, 1879-1955. *Mein Weltbild.*
Amsterdam: Querido Verlag, 1934. 269 p. diagrs. 21 cm. "Vorwort" signed: J. H. Wie ich die Welt sehe. – Von Politik und Pazifismus. – Deutschland 1933. – Judentum. – Wissenschaft.

603. EINSTEIN, ALBERT, 1879-1955. *Out of my later years / Albert Einstein.*
New York: Philosophical Library, [1960?, c1950]. 282 p., [1] leaf of plates: port.; 21 cm. Essays. Includes index.

604. EINSTEIN, ALBERT, 1879-1955. *Relativity: the special and general theory / by Albert Einstein; translated by Robert W. Lawson.*
New York: H. Holt, 1921, c1920. xiii, 168 p., [1] leaf of plates: ill., port.; 22 cm. Translation of: *Über die spezielle und allgemeine Relativitätstheorie.* Bibliography: p. 161-162. Includes index.

605. EINSTEIN, ALBERT, 1879-1955. *Sidelights on relativity, by Albert Einstein ... I. Ether and relativity. II. Geometry and experience, tr. by G. B. Jeffery, D. SC., and W. Perrett, Ph. D.*
London: Methuen & Co. Ltd. 1922. 3 p. l., 3-56 p., 1 l. illus. 20 cm.
Advertisements: 8 p. at end. Provenance: G. Freebeville (signature).

606. EINSTEIN, ALBERT, 1879-1955. *Statistische Untersuchung der Bewegung eines Resonators in einem Strahlungsfeld / von A. Einstein und L. Hopf.*
Leipzig : Verlag von Johann Ambrosius Barth, 1910. p. 1105-1115 ; 22 cm. In: *Annalen der Physik,* 4. Folge, Bd. 33. Caption title.

607. EINSTEIN, ALBERT, 1879-1955. *Über das Relativitätsprinzip und die aus demselben gezogenen Folgerungen / von A. Einstein.*
[Leipzig: S. Hirzel, 1908]. p. 411-462; 25 cm. In: *Jahrbuch der Radioaktivität und Elektronik;* 4. Bd. Caption title. Includes bibliographical references.

608. EINSTEIN, ALBERT, 1879-1955. *Über die spezielle und die allgemeine Relativitätstheorie: (gemeinverständlich) / von A. Einstein.*
Braunschweig: F. Vieweg, 1917. iv, 70 p.: ill.; 22 cm. Includes bibliographical references.
Provenance: A. Einstein (inscription); Herbert McLean Evans (bookplate). With: *Geometrie und Erfahrung* / von Albert Einstein. Berlin: J. Springer, 1921.

609. EINSTEIN, ALBERT, 1879-1955. *Über einen die Erzeugung und Verwandlung des Lichtes betreffenden heuristischen Gesichtspunkt; Über die von molekularkinetischen Theorie der Wärme geforderte Bewegung von in ruhenden Flüssigkeiten suspendierten Teilchen; Zur Elektrodynamik bewegter Körper / von A. Einstein.*
[Leipzig: J. A. Barth, 1905]. p. 132-148; 549-560; 891-921; 22 cm. In: *Annalen der Physik;* 4. F., Bd. 17, No. 6, 8, 10. Caption titles. Includes bibliographical references. Horblit, H. D. *Grolier 100 science books,* 26b.

610. EINSTEIN, ALBERT, 1879-1955. *Vier Vorlesungen über Relativitätstheorie gehalten im Mai 1921 an der Universität Princeton ... Mit vier Abbildungen.*

Braunschweig: F. Vieweg, 1922. 2 p. l., 70 p. diagrs. 24 cm. Advertisements: 2 p. following text and lower wrapper.

Provenance: Horovitz (signature).

611. EINSTEIN, ALBERT, 1879-1955. *The world as I see it / by Albert Einstein; translated by Alan Harris.*

London: Watts, 1940. xv, 112 p.; 17 cm. Thinker's Library; no. 79. Translation of: *Mein Weltbild,* pts. 1-4 only. Cf. "Note," p. (viii). The world as I see it – Politics and pacifism – Germany 1933 – The Jews.

Provenance: Frank O'Donnell Finigan (armorial bookplate).

612. ELSON, HENRY WILLIAM, 1857- . *Comets, their origin, nature and history, by Henry W. Elson....*

New York: Sturgis & Walton Company, 1910. 3 p. l., 3-54 p. front., plates, diagrs. (1 double) 17 cm.

613. EMELÉUS, H. J. (HARRY JULIUS). *Chemical aspects of recent work on atomic fission / by H. J. Emeléus.*

[London: , 1946?]. p. 42-43; 22 cm. Caption title. Detached from: *Journal and Proceedings, Royal Institute of Chemistry.*

614. EMELÉUS, H. J. (HARRY JULIUS). *Some aspects of nuclear chemistry.*

London: Royal Institute of Chemistry of Great Britain and Ireland, 1947. 19 p. diagr. 22 cm. "Lecture ... delivered before the Royal Institute of Chemistry ... on 18 April, 1946."

615. EMERSON, EDWIN, 1869- . *Comet lore: Halley's comet in history and astronomy, by Edwin Emerson.*

New York: Printed by the Schilling Press, c1910. 144 p. incl. front., plates, port. 21 cm. Cover title: The ominous peril in our sky: full story of Halley's comet.

616. EMERSON, WILLIAM, 1701-1782. *The elements of geometry, in which the principal propositions of Euclid, Archimedes, and others are demonstrated after the most easy manner. To which is added a collection of useful geometrical problems, also the Doctrine of proportion, arithmetical and geometrical, together with a general method of arguing by proportional quantities. By William Emerson. New ed.*

London: Printed for F. Wingrave, 1794. viii, 216 p. 298 diagr. on 14 pl. 22 cm.

Provenance: Signet Library.

617. ENCKE, JOHANN FRANZ, 1791-1865. *Betrachtungen über die Anordnung des Sternsystems. Ein vortrag im Wissenschaftlichen Vereine zu Berlin am 3. Februar 1844 gehalten, von J. F. Encke....*

Berlin: Bei W. Besser, 1844. 35, [1] p. 22 cm.

Provenance: Herbert McLean Evans (bookplate).

618. *Encyclopædia britannica, or, A dictionary of arts, sciences, and miscellaneous literature: constructed on a plan, by which the different sciences and arts are digested into the form of distinct treatises or systems ... The third edition, in eighteen volumes, greatly improved.*

Edinburgh: Printed for A. Bell and C. Macfarquhar, MDCCXCVII, [1797]. 18 v.: ill.; 28 cm. "Illustrated with five hundred and forty-two copperplates." Directions for placing the plates at end of each v.; some vols. have errata at end; v. 18 includes errata from several vols. Volumes 1-12 edited by C. Macfarquhar; v. 13-18 by G. Gleig. Text in double columns. Shoulder-notes and catch words. Plates numbered continuously, excluding frontispieces. *ESTC* (RLIN), N006642.

Library has: v. 1-18, as well as plates bound as v. 19-20. Provenance: Eardley (armorial bookplate).

619. *Encyclopædia britannica. Supplement to the third edition of the Encyclopædia brittanica, or, A dictionary of arts, sciences, and miscellaneous literature ... / by George Gleig....*

Edinburgh: Printed for Thomson Bonar ... by John Brown ..., 1801. 2 v.: ill.; 28 cm. Colophon (v. 1.) reads: Edinburgh printed by John Brown, Anchor Close, 1799. "Directions for placing the plates" at end of each v. Errata at end of v. 1. Includes bibliographical references.

Provenance: Eardley (armorial bookplate).

620. *The Encyclopædia britannica : a dictionary of arts, sciences, and general literature, with new maps and original American articles by eminent writers. [9th ed.] / with American revisions and additions by W. H. DePuy.*

Chicago : Werner, 1895, c1893. 25 v. : ill., maps ; 28 cm. Vol. 25 is an index.

Library has: v.1-25.

621. ENFIELD, WILLIAM, 1741-1797. *Institutes of natural philosophy, theoretical and practical. By William Enfield, LL. D. With some corrections; change in the order of the branches; and the addition of an appendix to the astronomical part, selected from Mr. Ewing's Practical Astronomy. By Samuel Webber ... 4th American ed., with improvements ....*

Boston: Cummings Hilliard & Co., 1824. xxvii, 297 p. incl. tables. xvi fold. pl. (incl. diagrs.) 27 cm. "Appendix to the astronomy. Containing solar and lunar tables, with their explanation and use, and the projection of eclipses, selected from "Ewing's Practical Astronomy": p. [233]-297.

Provenance: Charles Atwood Kofoid (bookplate).

622. ENGLEFIELD, HENRY, SIR, 1752-1822. *On the determination of the orbits of the comets: according to the methods of Father Boscovich and Mr. De la Place; with new and complete tables and examples of the calculation by both methods / by Sir Henry Englefield, bart.....*

London: Printed by Ritchie and Sammells for Peter Elmsly ..., 1793. xi, [1] blank, iv, 200, [4], 201-204, [52], 4 p., [1], IV leaves of plates (some folded): ill., port.; 28 cm. "The method of Father Boscovich ... he first published ... in the 7th v. of the 'Mémoires des scavans etrangers' ... and in a ... treatise which makes a part of a work ... intitled [sic] 'Opuscula,' printed at Bassano in 1785 ... The ... method of Mr. De la Place is given by him in... the 'Mémoires de l'Académie des Sciences,' for the year 1780" – Pref.,p. viii-ix. "Tables": [4] p. following p. 200 and [52] p. following p. 204.

Provenance: John Thomas Stanley (bookplate and Englefield's presentation inscription).

623. ESCHUID, JOANNES, fl. 1350. *Summa astrologiæ judicialis. Summa astrologiæ iudicialis de accidentibus mundi quæ anglicana uulgo nuncupatur Ioannis Eshcuidi [sic] niri [i.e. uiri] anglici peritissimi scie[n]tiæ astrologiæ foelici sidere inchoat.*

Impressione completum est Venetiis: Iohannis Lucilii Sanctiter, ... impensis ... Fra[n]cisci Bolani ..., 1489 nonis Iulii, [7th July]. [2], 306 [i.e. 218], [1] leaves: ill., map; 31 cm. Title from incipit (leaf a1); imprint from colophon (D7v). Signatures: pi^{2} a-i^{8} k^{4} l^{6} m^{8} n^{9} o-z^{8} &^{8} A-D^{8}. Many errors in foliation. Printed in double columns. Woodcut initials, and some spaces with guide letters. BM *15th cent.*, V, p. 462 (IB.23335). Goff (rev.) E-109. *GW* 9392. Hain 6685*. *ISTC* ie00109000.

Binding: quarter white cloth, brown boards. Binder's title: Eschcudii J Summa astrologiæ. Provenance: Heinrich Tränker (inkstamp).

624. *Essays and observations, physical and literary: read before a society in Edinburgh, and published by them.*

Edinburgh : Printed by G. Hamilton and J. Balfour, Printers to the University, 1754-1771. 3 v. : ill. ; 22 cm. v. 1 (1754)-v.3 (1771) Spine title: Physical essays. "This is the second series of essays published by the society. In the first series the name of the society does not occur." - British Mus. *Cat,* v.59, col.358.

Library has: v.2 (1756). Provenance (v.2): Benjamin Travers (armorial bookplate with motto: "Studio minuente laborem"); Library of the Charing Cross Hospital Medical School (bookplate); Frank Sondheimer (bookplate). Inscription: "Presented to the Medical Library of Charing Cross Hospital by Benjamin Travers Esq., President of the College of Surgeons, July 1856."

625. ESTÈVE, PIERRE, b. ca. 1720. *Origine de l'univers: expliquée par un principe de la matière.*

À Berlin: [s.n.], 1748. x, 246, [7] p., [1] folded leaf of plates: ill.; 16 cm. Errors in pagination: p. 227 misnumbered as 272. Errata: p. [7]. Includes bibliographical references. BN v. 48, col. 406. Lalande, J. de. *Bibliographie astronomique,* p. 436. Place of publication fictitious? Cf. Lalande, op. cit.

626. ETTMÜLLER, MICHAEL ERNST, 1673-1732. *Epistola anatomica, problematica, duodecima ... ad ... Fredericum Ruyschium ... De cerebri corticali substantia, &c.*

Amstelædami: Apud Joannem Wolters, 1699. 29, [3] p., plates. 22 cm. "Frederici Ruyschii responsio ...": p. [7]-29. Plates numbered: 14, 15, 13.

With: *Frederici Ruyschii ... Observationum anatomico-chirurgicarum centuria.* Amstelodami: Apud Henricum & Viduam Theodori Boom, 1691.

627. †EUCLID *Elementa geometria.*

[Venice] : Erhardus Ratdolt Augustensis impressor

solertissimus Venetiijs impressit, anno salutis M.cccc.lxxxij octauis calen[darum] Iun[ii] [25 May 1482]. [276] p. (1st and last 2 blank) : woodcuts ; 30 cm. Title from Goff (rev.), E-113. Translated by Adelardus of Bath; edited, with notes, by Campano da Novara. Book XIV is a 2nd century B.C. work by Hypsicles; Book XV of uncertain attribution. Cf. *Dictionary of scientific biography*. Imprint from colophon. Signatures: a^{10} b-r^{8}. Headlines, beginning with page [20]. BM *15th cent.*, V, p. 285 (IB.20513). Goff (rev.), E-113. *GW* 9428. Hain-Copinger 6693. Horblit, H. D. *Grolier 100 science books*, 27. *ISTC (RLIN)*, ie00113000.

Rubrication: untouched. Binding: full dark blue morocco, gilt panels; upper and lower covers have blind-stamped panels bordered in gilt with arabesques and devices at corners; marbled endpapers; all edges gilt. Binder: Riviere & Son (stamp). Binder's title: Euclid. Venetus 1482; in case, with title: Elementa geometrica. Provenance: Wm. Crocker deposit (inscription); Bequest of Mr. and Mrs. William H. Crocker (bookplate); scant ms. marginalia on p. [2]-[3].

628. EUCLID. *Contenta. Euclidis Megarensis geometricorum eleme[n]torum libri XV. Campani Galli tra[m]salpini in eosdem co[m]mentariorum libri XV. Theonis Alexandrini Bartholamæo Zamberto Veneto interprete, in tredecim priores, commentariorum libri XIII. Hypsiclis Alexa[n]drini in duos posteriores, eode[m] Bartholamæo Zamberto Veneto interprete, comme[n]tariorum libri II. Vtcunque noster valuit labor conciliata sunt hæc omnia, ad studiosorum non paruam (quam optamus) vtilitatem: id magnifico D. Francisco Briconneto postula[n]te. Si hæc beneuole suscipia[n]tur, & tructum adfera[n]t que[m]cupimus: alia eiusde[m[authoris opera prodibu[n]t in luce[m], successum præsta[n]te deo, & adiutoribus (vbivbi ge[n]tiu[m] sint) ad bonaru[m] literaru[m] inititutione[m] probe affectis Gallis, Italia, Germanis, Hispanis, Anglis. quibus omnibus prospera imprecamur: & puram prodignitate veramq[ue] cognitionis lucem.*

Parisiis: In officina Henri Stephani e regione scholæ decretorum, 1516. 261 leaves: ill.; 29 cm. Signatures: a-y^{8} z $\&^{6}$ A-H^{8} I^{10} (I10 blank) . Cribled initials. Numerous errors in foliation. Dedication by Iacobvs Faber, dated: Anno M. D. XVI postridie Epiphaniæ Domini. Schreiber, F. *The Estiennes*, 26. Renouard, A.A. *Annales de l'imprimerie des Estienne*, p. 18, no. 8. Steck, M. *Euclid*, III. 13.

Imperfect: I10 (blank) missing.

629. EUCLID. *Andreæ Tacquet Societatis Jesu Elementa Euclidea geometriæ planæ, ac solidæ: et selecta ex Archimede theoremata: ejusdemque trigonometria plana / Plurimis corollariis, notis, ac schematibus quadraginta illustrata a Guilielmo Whiston; quibus nunc primum accedunt Trigonometria sphærica Rogerii Josephi Boscovich S.J. & Sectiones conicæ Guidonis Grandi, annotationibus satis amplis Octaviani Cameti explicatæ....*

Romæ: Sumtibus Venantii Monaldini ... typis Hieronymi Mainardi ..., 1745. 2 v.: ill.; 20 cm. Selecta ex Archimede Theoremata has special t. p. Vol. 1: XXXV, [1], 326, [2] (blanks) p., 6 folded leaves of plates; v. 2: 226, [21] p., XI, [3] folded leaves of plates. First published in 1683. Steck, M. *Euclid*, V. 18.

Bound in 1 v.

630. EUCLID. *Elementi piani, e solidi d' Euclide....*

Firenze: Nella stamperìa di G. B. Stecchi, per il Carlieri, 1746. 2 v. diagrs. 15 cm. Preface signed by Jacopo Carlieri. Title of v. 2: Quinto libro degli elementi d'Euclide ... / pubblicata da Vincenzio Viviani ... Binder's title: Viviani Euclide. First edition published in 1690. Riccardi, P. *Bib. matematica*, v. 1, column 628.

631. EUCLID. *The elements of Euclid, with dissertations ... / by James Williamson....*

Oxford: Clarendon Press, 1781-1788. 2 v. in 1: ill.; 27 cm. Contains the 13 books of the Elements and 8 dissertations by Williamson. Vol. 2 has imprint: London: Printed by T. Spilsbury, 1788. Full extent: v. 1: [2], iii, [1] (blank), 96, 145, [1] (blank), 68 p.; v. 2: [2], xxiii, [1] (blank), 323 p.

Provenance: University College London (binding); prize bookplate from College to Robert B. Clifton.

632. EUCLID. *The Elements of geometrie of the most auncient philosopher Euclide of Megara / faithfully (now first) translated into the Eng-*

lishe toung by H. Billingsley ...; whereunto are annexed certaine scholies, annotations, and inuentions of the best mathematiciens ...; with a very fruitfull praeface made by M. I. Dee....
Imprinted at London: By Iohn Daye, 1570. [28], 464 leaves, 1 folded leaf: ill., port.; 32 cm. First edition of the first complete English translation. Dee's preface dated Feb. 9, 1570. Many errors in foliation. Illustrated t. p. Some of the illustrations are movable overslips, forming three-dimensional models. Date from colophon. Portrait of the printer, J. Daye, above the imprint on the last page. "The sixteenth booke of the Elementes of geometrie, added by Flussas," leaves 445-464. *STC* 10560. Thomas-Stanford, C. *Euclid.* 41. Errata: leaves 463b-464a.
Provenance: Hugh Cecil Earl of Lonsdale (armorial bookplate); Herbert McLean Evans (bookplate).

633. Euclid. *Euclide Megarense acutissimo philosopho solo introduttore delle scientie mathematice / Diligentemente rassettato, et alla integrità ridotto, per il degno professore di tal scientie Nicolò Tartale a Brisciano; Secondo le due tradottioni; Con vna ampla espositione dello istesso tradottore di nuouo aggionta, ... Di nuouo con ogni diligenza ben corretto, e ristampato.*
In Venetia: Appresso gli Heredi di Troian Nauo, alla libraria dal Lione., M DLXXXV. [1585]. 120, 125-315, [1] leaves: ill. (woodcuts); 21 cm. Signatures: A-2Q^8; confirmed by '"Registro" (leaf [216] verso). Title vignette. Errors in foliation: leaf 23 misnumbered as 32, 66 as 96, 121-124 omitted, 126 misnumbered as 124, 136 as 137, 208 as 218, 209 as 920, 221 as 262, 224 as 214, 237 as 244, 242 as 239, 247 as 248, 253 as 254, 264 as 265 and 266 as 26. Steck, M. *Euclid,* III.97. Grässe, II, p. 513. Thomas-Stanford, C. *Euclid,* 44. BM *STC Italian,* 1465-1600, p. 239. Marshall, R.G. *STC Italian,* I, p. 568. Riccardi, P. *Bib. matematica,* II, column 498.
Leaves 17-24 are bound behind leaf 32. T. p. hand-coloured.

634. Euclid. *Euclidis Elementorium libri priores sex: item undecimus & duodecimus / ex versione latina Federici Commandiní; quibus accedunt trigonometriæ planæ & sphæricæ elementa....*
Oxoniæ, e Theatro Sheldoniano: Impensis Ric. Clements ..., prostat apud J. Knapton & C. Rivington ..., 1731. [8], 230, [2], 76, [3] p., [2] folded leaves of plates: ill.; 21 cm. Advertisements: p. [231] and [3] p. following text. Errors in pagination: p. 130 misnumbered as 125, p. 214 as 114. Trigonometriæ planæ & sphæricæ elementa has separate t. p.
Provenance: George Rice (armorial bookplate).On p. 39 (2nd sequence) ill. pasted in, with movable flap.

635. Euclid. *Euclidis Elementorum lib. XV: accessit XVI. De solidoru[m] regularium cuiuslibet intra quodlibet comparatione. Omnes perspicuis demonstrationibus, accuratisq[ue] scholijs illustrati. Nunc iterum editi, ac multar[um] rerum accessione locupletati / Auctore Christophoro Clauio Bambergensi è Societate Iesu.*
Pisauri: Apud Bartholomæum Grassium; MDLXXXIX. [1589]. 2 v.: ill.; 18 cm. Sixteenth book of the elements added by Flussas [i.e. François de Foix, comte de Candale]. Colophon reads: Romæ, Apud Sanctium, & soc. M. D. LXXXIX. [1589]. Engraved titles within architectural borders; decorated initials throughout prefatory matter and at beginning of each book; type page enclosed withing rule throughout text; some decorated borders. Translation of Euclid's Elementa. Errata on p. [12]-[13] of 1st group of v. 1. Includes indexes. Thomas-Stanford, C. *Euclid,* 22. Steck, M. *Euclid,* III.100.
Provenance: Franciscus Bulgarinus (signature).

636. Euclid. *Euclidis Elementorum libri XIII / succinctis & perspicuis demonstrationibus comprehensi à D. Ambrosio Rhodio, Kembergensi ... Editio novissima, priore correctior & emendatior.*
Wittebergæ: Typis & impensis Jobi Wilh. Fincelij, 1661. [16], 594 [i.e. 604] p.: ill.; 16 cm. First published in 1609. cf. *Bibliographia Euclideana* / Max Steck. Hildesheim: Gerstenberg, 1981. p. 89. Corrigenda præcipua: p. 594. Errors in pagination: p. 57 misnumbered as 75, 190 as 192, 233 as 321, 356 as 354, 380 as 30, 416 as 146, 433-442 omitted, 478 misnumbered as 748, 558-559 as 358-359.
Provenance: Duque de Medinaceli y Santisteban (bookplate).

637. Euclid. *Euclidis Elementorum libri XV. Unà cum scholijs antiquis, à Federico Commandino Vrbinate nuper in Latinum conuersi, commentarijsque quibusdam illustrati.*
Pisauri: Apud C. Francischinum, 1572. [12], 255 l. illus., diagrs. 32 cm. Imprint from colophon. Thomas-Stanford, C. *Euclid,* 18. Steck, M. *Euclid,* III.83.

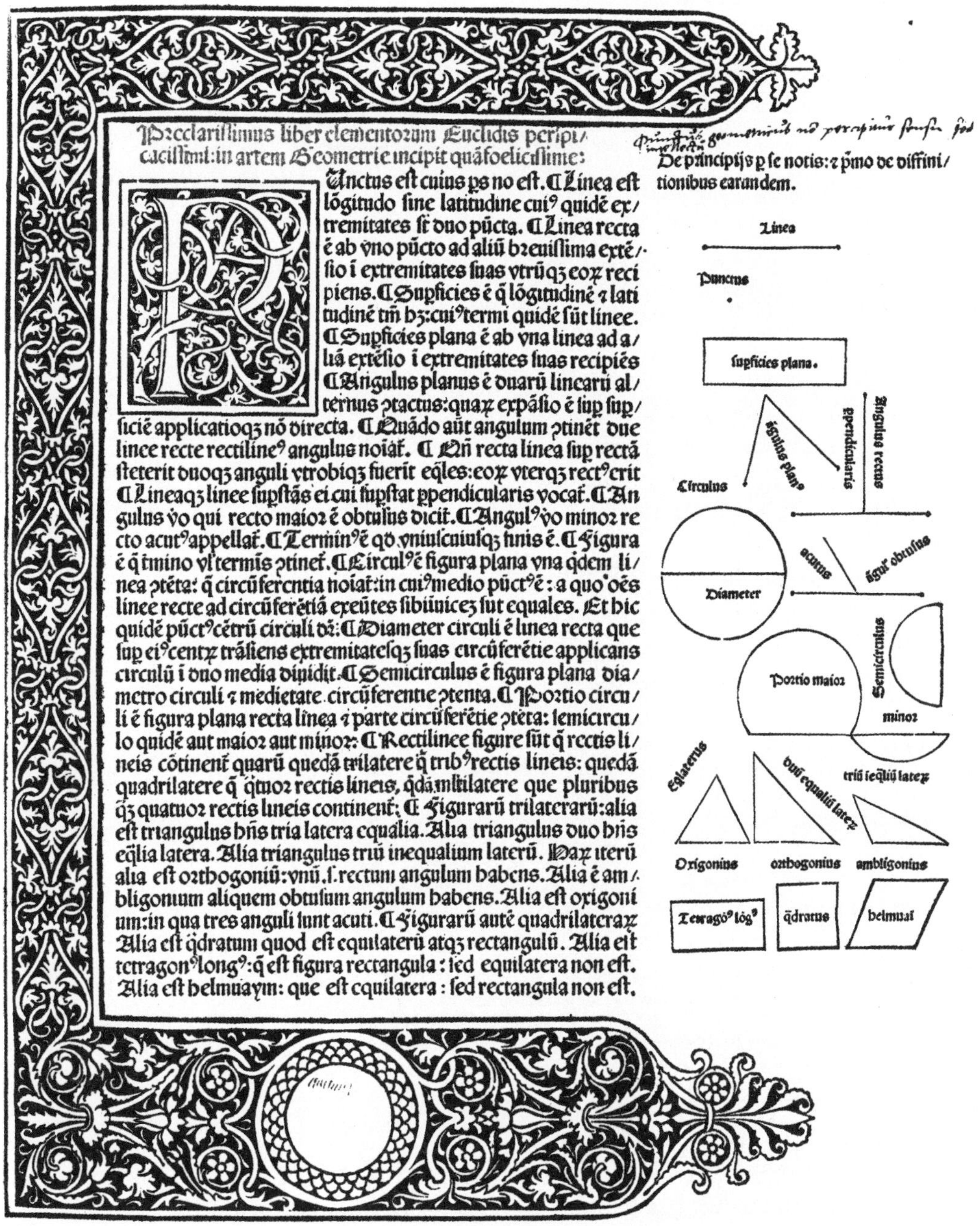

Preclarissimus liber elementorum Euclidis perspi/
cacissimi: in artem Geometrie incipit quã foelicissime:
Punctus est cuius ps no est. ⁋ Linea est
lõgitudo sine latitudine cui⁹ quidẽ ex/
tremitates sũt duo pũcta. ⁋ Linea recta
ẽ ab vno pũcto ad aliũ breuissima extẽ/
sio i extremitates suas vtrũq3 eoꝝ reci
piens. ⁋ Supficies ẽ q̃ lõgitudinẽ ⁊ lati
tudinẽ tm̃ h3: cui⁹ termi quidẽ sũt linee.
⁋ Supficies plana ẽ ab vna linea ad a/
liã extẽsio i extremitates suas recipiẽs
⁋ Angulus planus ẽ duarũ linearũ al/
ternus ɔtactus: quaꝝ expãsio ẽ sup sup/
ficiẽ applicatioq3 nõ directa. ⁋ Quãdo aũt angulum ɔtinẽt due
linee recte rectiline⁹ angulus noiat. ⁋ Qñ recta linea sup rectã
steterit duoq3 anguli vtrobiq3 fuerit eq̃les: eoꝝ vterq3 rect⁹ erit
⁋ Lineaq3 linee supstãs ei cui supstat ppendicularis vocat. ⁋ An
gulus vo qui recto maior ẽ obtusus dicit. ⁋ Angul⁹ vo minor re
cto acut⁹ appellat. ⁋ Termin⁹ ẽ qd vniuscuiusq3 finis ẽ. ⁋ Figura
ẽ q̃ tmino vl termis ɔtinet. ⁋ Circul⁹ ẽ figura plana vna q̃dem li
nea ɔtẽta: q̃ circũferentia noiat: in cui⁹ medio pũct⁹ ẽ: a quo oẽs
linee recte ad circũferẽtiã exeũtes sibiinuicẽ sũt equales. Et hic
quidẽ pũct⁹ cẽtrũ circuli dr. ⁋ Diameter circuli ẽ linea recta que
sup ei⁹ centꝝ trãsiens extremitatesq3 suas circũferẽtie applicans
circulũ i duo media diuidit. ⁋ Semicirculus ẽ figura plana dia/
metro circuli ⁊ medietate circũferentie ɔtenta. ⁋ Portio circu/
li ẽ figura plana recta linea ⁊ parte circũferẽtie ɔtẽta: semicircu/
lo quidẽ aut maior aut minor. ⁋ Rectilinee figure sũt q̃ rectis li/
neis cõtinent quarũ quedã trilatere q̃ trib⁹ rectis lineis: quedã
quadrilatere q̃ q̃tuor rectis lineis, q̃dã multilatere que pluribus
q̃3 quatuor rectis lineis continent. ⁋ Figurarũ trilaterarũ: alia
est triangulus hñs tria latera equalia. Alia triangulus duo hñs
eq̃lia latera. Alia triangulus triũ inequalium laterũ. Haꝝ iterũ
alia est orthogoniũ: vnũ .s. rectum angulum habens. Alia ẽ am/
bligonium aliquem obtusum angulum habens. Alia est oxigoni
um: in qua tres anguli sunt acuti. ⁋ Figurarũ autẽ quadrilateraꝝ
Alia est q̃dratum quod est equilaterũ atq3 rectangulũ. Alia est
tetragon⁹ long⁹: q̃ est figura rectangula: sed equilatera non est.
Alia est helmuaym: que est equilatera: sed rectangula non est.

De principijs p se notis: ⁊ pmo de diffini/
tionibus earundem.

Euclid, *Elementa geometria*, 1482

638. EUCLID. *Euclidis Elementorum libri XV. breviter demonstrati, opera Is. Barrow....*
Cantabrigiae: Excudebat R. Daniel, impensis G. Nealand, 1659. 8 p. l., 399 p. diagrs. 15 cm. "Euclidis Dat succincte demonstrata" (with special t.-p.): p. [353]-399.
Provenance: J. Hutton (signature). Wing E-3393.

639. EUCLID. *Euclidis Elementorum libri XV, Græcè & Latinè....*
Lutetiae: Apud Gulielmum Cauellat ..., 1558. [16], 130 [i.e. 160] leaves: ill.; 18 cm. Errors in foliation: 59-80 repeated. Errata on leaf 130 recto. Ad candidum lectorem, præfatio by St. Gracilis. Adams, E998. Steck, M. *Euclid,* III.58.

640. EUCLID. *Euclidis Megarensis ... Elementorum geomericorum libri XV: cum expositione Theonis in priores XIII à Bartholomæo Zamberto Veneto latinitate donata, Campini in omnes, & Hypsiclis Alexandrini in duos postremos: his adiecta sunt Phænomena, Catoptrica & Optica, deine Protheoria marini, & data: postremùm uerò, opusculum de leui & ponderoso, hactenus non uisum, eiusdem autoris.*
Basiliæ: Per Ioannem Hervagium, & Bernhardum Brand, 1558. [8], 587, [1] p. (the last blank); 33 cm. Cuts: initials, head pieces, diagrams. Adams, E976. Steck, M. *Euclid,* III.57.

641. EUCLID. *Euclid's Elements of geometry: in XV books: with a supplement of divers propositions and corollaries. To which is added a treatise of regular solids / by Campane and Flussas; likewise Euclid's Data; and Marinus his preface thereunto annexed; also a treatise of the divisions of superfices, ascribed to Machomet Bagdedine, but published by Commandine, at the request of John Dee of London; whose preface ... declares it to be the worke of Euclide ...; published by the care and industry of John Leeke and George Serle....*
London: Printed by R. & W. Leybourn for Richard Tomlins ..., 1661. [51], 650, [1] p., [1] folded leaves of plates: ill., port.; 30 cm. A book of the divisions of superficies has special t. p. with imprint: London: Printed by R. & W. Leybourn, 1660. Preface dated: 1570 Febr. 9. Errata: last p.
Provenance: Agnew, Bart. of Lochnaw (armorial bookplate).

642. EUCLID. *Eukleidou Dedomena. Kai Marinou philosophou Eis Dedomena Eukleidou hypomnema. = Euclidis data. Opus ad veterum geometriæ autorum Archimedis, Apollonij, Pappi, Eutocij, cæterorúmque non modo lectionem, sed ad geometricæ quoque analyseos instaurationem planè necessarium, & à multisdiu desíderatum. Claudius Hardy Sebast. fil. in supremâ parisiensi curiâ aduocatus, à regis christianissimi bibliothecâ græcè nunc primum edidit, latinè vertit, scholijsq; illustrauit. Adiectus est ex eadem bibliothecâ Marini philosophi commentarius græcè & latinè, quo datinatura, datorúmque euclideorum vtilitates explicantur.*
Lutetiæ Parisiorum: Impensis M. Mondiere, 1625. 8, 181, [1] p., 1 l. diagrs. 23 cm. Steck, M. *Euclid,* VIII. 10.
Short errata, last leaf is a second privilege. Binder's blanks at end. Ms. notes and diagrams pasted in.
Provenance: Grossherzogliche Bibliothek Neustrelitz.

643. EUCLID. *Kitab Ta'hrir u'sul / li-uqlidis min ta'lif Khawjah Na'siral-Din al-'Tusi.*
[Rome: Typographia Medicea, 1594?]. [24], 25-453, [1] p.: ill.; 36 cm. Translation of: *Elements.* Paginated also in Arabic. Romanized t. p. Thomas-Stanford, C. *Euclid,* 46a.
p. 395-396 are bound between p. 398 and 399.

644. EULER, LEONHARD, 1707-1783. *Institutiones calculi differentialis cum eius vsu in analysi finitorum ac doctrina serierum.*
Petropolitanae: pensis Academiæ Imperialis Scientiarum, 1755. 2 v. in 1. (xxiv, 880 p.) 26 cm. Colophon reads: Berolini: Ex Officina Michaelis.
Provenance: J. F. W. Herschel (inscription).

645. EULER, LEONHARD, 1707-1783. *Introductio in analysin infinitorum.*
Lausannæ: M. Bousquet, 1748. 2 v. plates, port., folded table. 23 cm. Title vignettes; v. 1 has engraved half-title in French engraved by Soubeyran after De La Monce. Port. engraved by Ficquet after L. Toquet.

646. Euler, Leonhard, 1707-1783. *L. Euleri Opuscula varii argumenti....*

Berolini: sumtibus A. Haude & J. C. Speneri, 1746-51. 3 v. tables, diagrs. on 12 fold. pl. 23 x 18 cm. Vols. 1-2 not numbered; signatures: Euleri Opuscula tom. II-III. Vol. 2 has title: Conjectura physica circa propagationem soni ac luminis, una cum aliis dissertationibus analyticis ... Vol. 3 has title: L. Euleri opusculorum tomus III. Continens novam theoriam magnetis ab illustr. Academia regia scient: parisina præmio condecoratum a. 1744. Una cum nonnullis aliis dissertationibus analytico-mechanicis. [v. 1] I. Solutio problematis mechanici de motu corporum tubis mobilibus inclusorum. II. Nova tabulæ astronomicæ motuum solis ac lunæ. III. Nova theoria lucis et colorum. IV. De perturbatione motus planetarum a resistentia ætheris orta. V. Enodatio quæstionis: An materiæ facultas cogitandi tribui possit? VI. Recherches sur la nature des moindres particules des corps. – [v. 2] Conjectura physica de propagatione soni ac luminis. De numeris amicabilibus. Demonstratio gemina theorematis Neutoniani quo traditur relatio inter coëfficientes cujusvis æquationis algebraicæ & summas potestatum radicum ejusdem. Animadversiones in rectificationem ellipsis. – v. 3. Dissertatio de magnete. Nova methodus inveniendi trajectorias reciprocas algebraicas. De motu corporum flexibilium.

Provenance [v.1]: Carolus [Fort?]aurner[?] (inscription); loose ms. notes and ephemera throughout.

647. Euler, Leonhard, 1707-1783. *Letters of Euler on different subjects in natural philosophy. Addressed to a German princess. Tr. from the French by Henry Hunter, D.D. With original notes, and a glossary of foreign and scientific terms. 2d. ed.....*

London: Printed for Murray and Highley [etc.], 1802. 2 v. 20 pl. 22 cm. "Elogium of Euler" by Condorcet: v. 1, p. xxxiii-lxvii.

Provenance: Society of Writers to the Signet (gilt stamped on cover).

648. Euler, Leonhard, 1707-1783. *Methodus inveniendi lineas curvas maximi minimive proprietate gaudentes, sive Solutio problematis isoperimetrici latissimo sensu accepti. Auctore Leonhardo Eulero.*

Apud M. M. Bousquet, 1744. 1 p. l., 322 p. 5 fold. tables. 25 cm. Title page in red and black; engraved title vignette, initial, and headpiece. Horblit, H. D. *Grolier 100 science books*, 28.

Provenance: R. Hendle (bookplate). Additional leaf: Monitum ad bibliopegam, at the end.

649. Euler, Leonhard, 1707-1783. *Theoria motuum planetarum et cometarum. Continens methodum facilem ex aliquot observationibus orbitas cum planetarum tum cometarum determinandi. Una cum calculo, quo cometæ, qui annis 1680. et 1681. itemque eius, quin uper est visus, motus verus investigatur....*

Berolini: Sumtibus A. Haude 1744. 187 p. [i.e. 186] p. front., diagrs. on 4 fold. plates, tables. 23 x 19 cm. Date from colophon. Title vignette. Illustrated by F. H. Frisch. Errors in paging: 7-8 omitted; 187 repeated.

Provenance: G. M. Lowiz (inscription), ms. notes.

650. Euler, Leonhard, 1707-1783. *Vollständige Anleitung zur Algebra / von Hrn. Leonhard Euler.*

St. Petersburg: Gedruckt bey der Kays. Acad. der Wissenschaften, 1770. 2 v.; 19 cm. Vol. 1: [16], 356 p.; v. 2: [2], 532 p. (From title pages) 1.T.: Von den verschiedenen Rechnungs-Arten,Verhältnissen und Proportionen – 2.T.: Von Auflösung algebraischer Gleichungen und der unbestimmten Analytic.

Bound in 1 v. V. 2 last leaf damaged with some loss of text.

651. Eustachi, Bartolomeo, d. 1574. *Tabulæ anatomicæ / clarissimi viri Bartholomæi Eustachii quas è tenebris tandem vindicatas ...; præfatione, notisque illustravit, ac ipso suæ bibliothecæ dedicationis die publici juris fecit Jo. Maria Lancisius....*

Romæ: Ex officina typographica Francisci Gonzagæ ..., MDCCXIV 1714. xliv, 115, [14] p., XXXXVII leaves of plates: ill.; 38 cm. Illustrated by the author. Engraved vignette on t. p. by Petrus Leo Gherrius. Osler, W. *Bib. Osleriana*, 2543. Yale. *Cushing Coll.*, E115. Emendanda, et addenda: p. [14]. Includes index.

Provenance: Herbert McLean Evans (bookplate).

652. *Evening amusements; or, the beauty of the heavens displayed ... Frend's evening amusements.*

London, Printed for J. Mawman. v. 20 cm. "...In which several striking appearences, to be observed on various evenings in the heavens, during the year are described..." Edited by William Frend.

Library has: 1812-13.

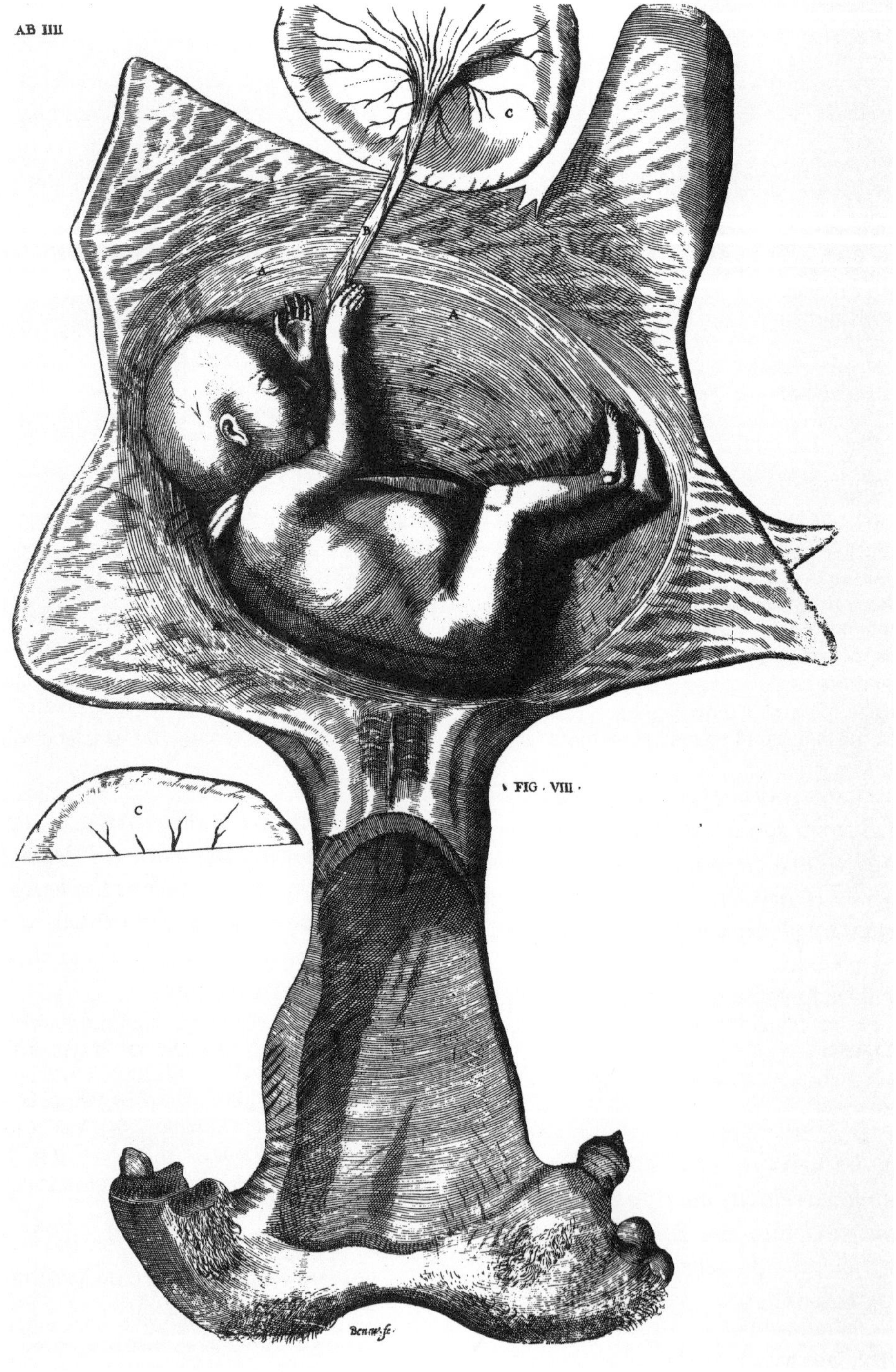

FABRICIUS, *De formato foetv*, 1600

653. Fabre, Jean-Henri, 1823-1915. *The heavens, by J. H. Fabre, translated by Dr. E. E. Fournier d'Albe.*
Philadelphia, J. B. Lippincott Company, 1925. xvi, 336 p. front., illus., plates, diagrs. 23 cm.

654. Fabricius, ab Aquapendente, ca. 1533-1619. *Hieronymi Fabricii ab Aquapendente De formato foetu.*
Venetiis: Per Franciscum Bolzettam, 1600. [10], 151, [1] (blank), [2] p.: ill.; 39 cm. Errores: [2] p. following text. Colophon reads: Patauii: Ex typographia Laurentij Pasquati ... T. p. signed: Iacobus Valegius sculp., some ill. signed: Ben.W. fe. Includes index.
Provenance: Herbert McLean Evans (bookplate).

655. Fabricius, ab Aquapendente, ca. 1533-1619. *Hieronymi Fabricii ab Aquapendente De visione, voce, auditu.*
Venetiis: Per Franciscum Bolzeltam, 1600. [12], 133, [15], 83, [9], 38 p.: ill.; 37 cm. T. p. signed: Iacobus Valegius sculp. Includes index. Colophon on p. [134] reads: Patauii: Ex officina Laurentij Pasquati ... Blank leaf between pt. 1 and pt. 2. Osler, W. *Bib. Osleriana*, 2558.

656. Fahie, J. J. (John Joseph), 1846-1934. *Memorials of Galileo Galilei, 1564-1642. Portraits and paintings, medals and medallions, busts and statues, monuments and mural inscriptions.*
Leamington [England]: Printed for the author, The Courier Press, 1929. xxiv, 172 p. front., plates, port. 25 cm. "Two hundred copies only printed." Bibliographical foot-notes.

657. Fahrenheit, Daniel Gabriel, 1686-1736. [Collection of articles published in *Philosophical transactions*, vol. 33, on measuring temperature / by Daniel Fahrenheit].
[1724] 5 pieces: ill.; 23 cm. *Philosophical transactions*; no. 381-385. Caption title. Experimenta circa gradum caloris liquorum non-nullorum ebullientium instituta – Experimenta & observationes de congelatione aquæ in vacuofactæ – Materiarum quarundam gravitates specificæ, diversis temporibus advarios scopos exploratæ – Aræometri novi descriptio & usus – Barometrinovi descriptio.

658. Fale, Thomas, fl. 1604. *Horologiographia. The art of dialling: teaching, an easie and perfect way to make all kinds of dials ... / by Thomas Fale.*
London: Printed by Felix Kingstone, 1652. [4], 90 [i.e. 60], [16] leaves: ill.; 18 cm. Many errors of foliation.

659. Faraday, Michael, 1791-1867. *Experimental researches in chemistry and physics. By Michael Faraday. Reprinted from the* Philosophical transactions *of 1821-1857; the* Journal of the Royal Institution*; the* Philosophical Magazine, *and other publications.*
London: R. Taylor and W. Francis, 1859. viii, 496 p. illus., 3 pl. (1 fold.) diagrs. 22 cm. Includes index. Illustrated by J. Basire.

660. Faraday, Michael, 1791-1867. *Experimental researches in electricity / by Michael Faraday....*
London: Bernard Quaritch ... 1839-55 [i.e. 1878?-1882?] 3 v.: ill.; 23 cm. Vol. 1: Reprinted from the *Philosophical transactions* of 1831-1838. Vol. 2: Reprinted from the *Philosophical transactions* of 1838-1843, with other electrical papers from the *Quarterly Journal of Science* and *Philosophical Magazine*. Vol. 3: Reprinted from the *Philosophical transactions* of 1846-1852, with other electrical papers from the *Proceedings of the Royal Institution* and *Philosophical Magazine*. Facsimile reprint, probably published 1878-1882. Cf. *Michael Faraday* /Alan E. Jeffreys. New York, 1960, p. 39. Illustrated by J. Basire.
Provenance: Henry A. Rowland (bookplate and signature).

661. †Faraday, Michael, 1791-1867. *Experimental researches in electricity. / By Michael Faraday....*
London: Richard and John Edward Taylor, printers and publishers to the University of London, ..., 1839-1855. 3 v.: ill.; 24 cm. Vol. 3 has imprint: London: Richard Taylor and William Francis...,1855. Vol. 1: "Reprinted from the *Philosophical transactions* of 1831-1838"; v. 2: "Reprinted from the *Philosophical transactions* of 1838-1843. With other electrical papers from the *Quarterly Journal of Science* and *Philosophical Magazine*"; v. 3: "Reprinted from the *Philosophical transactions* of 1846-1852. With other electrical papers from the *Proceedings of the Royal Institution* and *Philosophical Magazine*." The *Philosophical transactions* are those of the Royal Society of London. Vol. 1: viii, 574, [2] p., VIII folded leaves of plates; v. 2: viii, 302 p., V leaves of plates (2 folded); v. 3: viii, 588 p., IV leaves of plates (3 folded). Illustrated by J. Basire. Includes bibliographical references and

indexes. Advertisements: v. 1, [2] p. at end. Jeffreys, A.E. *Michael Faraday*, 297. Horblit, H. D. *Grolier 100 science books*, 29. v. 1. Series I-XIV – v. 2. Series XV-XVIII – v. 3. Series XIX-XXIX.

Binder: James Macdonald Co. (stamped on slipcase). Provenance: author's presentation copy to the Countess of Lovelace (inscription); Robert Honeyman (Honeyman sale); Henry A. Rowland (booklabel, v. 3).

662. FAREY, JOHN, 1766-1826. *General view of the agriculture and minerals of Derbyshire: with observations on the means of their improvement. Drawn up for the consideration of the Board of Agrigulture [sic] and Internal Improvement... / by John Farey, Sen.....*

London: Printed by B. McMillan ... sold by G. and W. Nicol ... [and 4 others], 1811-1817. 3 v.: ill., maps; 22 cm. Imprint varies. Illustrated by J. Farey. Includes bibliographical references and indexes.

v.2: 1815. Provenance: S. Peyton (bookplate).

663. FAUJAS-DE-ST.-FOND, CIT. (BARTHÉLEMY), 1741-1819. *Description des expériences de la machine aérostatique de Mm. De Montgolfier, et de celles auxquelles cette découverte a donné lieu. Suivie de recherches sur la hauteur à laquelle est parvenu le ballon du Champ-de-Mars....*

Paris: Cuchet, 1783-84. 2 v. illus., plates. 21 cm. Vol. 2 has title: Première suite de la Description des expériences aérostatiques. Illustrated by Sellier, le chevalier de Lorimier, and N. DeLaunay. Errata: [1] p. at end, v. 2. Dibner Lib. *Science*, 179.

Provenance: Esther Acklom (armorial bookplate, v. 1); Harvard College Library (bookplate, v. 2).

664. FAUTH, PH. (PHILIPP), 1867-1941. *Der Mond und Hörbigers Welteislehre / von Philipp Fauth.*

Leipzig: Koehler & Amelang, 1925. vi, 231 p., 5 leaves of plates: ill.; 21 cm. "Die erste Ausgabe dieses Werkes erschien unter dem Titel *Mondesschicksal: wie er ward und untergeht.*" – t. p. verso. Includes index.

665. FAUTH, PH. (PHILIPP), 1867-1941. *The moon in modern astronomy: summary of twenty years selenographic work, and a study of recent problems, by Philip Fauth ... Tr. by Joseph McCabe, with an introduction by J. Ellard Gore.*

New York: D. van Nostrand Co., 1909. 160 p. front., illus. 22 cm. Translation of *Was wir vom Monde wissen.*

Provenance: John Jay and Elise Pierrepont (armorial bookplate).

666. FECHNER, GUSTAV THEODOR, 1801-1887. *Über die Frage des Weber'schen Gesetzes und Periodicitaetsgesetzes im Gebiete des Zeitsinnes / von G.Th. Fechner....*

Leipzig: Bei S. Hirzel, 1884. [2], 107, [1] p.; 28 cm. "Des XIII. Bandes der *Abhandlungen der mathematisch-physischen Class der Königl. Sächsischen Gesellschaft der Wissenschaften*, no. 1." Includes bibliographical references.

Provenance: Edmund Neusser (bookplate); F. E. Roter (signature).

667. FERGUSON, JAMES, 1710-1776. *Astronomy, explained upon Sir Isaac Newton's Principles / by James Ferguson ...; with notes, and supplementary chapters by David Brewster... Third edition.*

Edinburgh: Printed for Stirling and Slade, Edinburgh, and for G. and W. B. Whittakers, London, 1841. 2 v.: ill., maps; 23 cm. Includes indexes. Illustrated by D. Lizars.

Provenance: George Pope (inscription). Binder: Bone & Son (ticket).

668. FERGUSON, JAMES, 1710-1776. *Astronomy explained upon Sir Isaac Newton's Principles; and made easy to those who have not studied mathematics. To which are added, a plain method of finding the distances of all the planets from the sun, by the transit of Venus over the sun's disc, in the year 1761. An account of Mr. Horrox's observation of the transit of Venus in the year 1639: and, of the distances of all the planets from the sun, as deduced from observations of the transit in the year 1761. By James Ferguson ... 5th ed., corr.*

London: W. Strahan [etc.], 1772. 4 p. l., 489, [14] p. incl. tables. fold. front., 17 fold. Plates (incl. map) 21 cm. Gray, G. J. *Newton*, 75.

Imperfect: lacks plates.

669. FERGUSON, JAMES, 1710-1776. *Astronomy explained upon Sir Isaac Newton's Principles, and made easy to those who have not studied mathematics. To which are added, a plain method of finding the distances of all the planets from the sun, by the transit of Venus over the sun's disc, in the year 1761. An account of Mr. Horrox's observation of the transit of Venus in the year 1639: and, of the distances of all the planets from the sun, as deduced from observations of the transit in the year 1761 ... 3d ed.*
London: Printed for A. Millar, 1764. 4 p.l., 354, [10] p. incl. tables., fold. front., 17 fold. Plates (incl. map) 28 x 22 cm. Includes index. *Babson Newton Coll.*, 58.

670. FERGUSON, JAMES, 1710-1776. *Astronomy explained upon Sir Isaac Newton's principles, and made easy to those who have not studied mathematics ... The 2d ed.*
London: Printed for, and sold by the author, at the Globe, 1757. 4 p.l., 283, [9] p., incl. tables. fold. front., 13 fold. plates. 27 cm. Includes index. Illustrated by the author, G. Child and J. Mynde. Gray, G. J. *Newton*, 75.

671. FERGUSON, JAMES, 1710-1776. *Astronomy explained upon Sir Isaac Newton's principles, and made easy to those who have not studied mathematics.*
London: Printed for and sold by the author, 1756. 4 p. l., 267, [9] p. fold. plates, tables. 27 cm. Includes index. Errata: on p. [8] 1st count. Illustrated by the author, G. Child and J. Mynde.
25 cm. A 4 p. description of the Newtonian globes invented by Abbé Vinson; card-dial with [1] p. instructions; hand-made volvelle in front pocket; [1] p. description of The perpetual almanack in back pocket. With: *The theory of comets ...* / by Benjamin Martin. London: Printed for the author, 1757; and: *A treatise on the various lengths of the days, nights, and twilights ...* / by Richard Mihill. London: Printed by D. Henry and R. Cave, for the author, 1755.

672. FERGUSON, JAMES, 1710-1776. *Astronomy explained upon Sir Isaac Newton's Principles, and made easy to those who have not studied mathematics : To which are added, a plain method of finding the distances of all the planets from the sun, by the transit of Venus over the sun's disc, in the year 1761. An account of Mr. Horrox's observation of the transit of Venus in the year 1639: and, of the distances of all the planets from the sun, as deduced from observations of the transit in the year 1761. / By James Ferguson ... The tenth edition, with some additional notes.*
London: Printed for J. Johnson [etc.], 1799. [8], 503, [17] p., [18] folded leaves of plates: ill., map; 23 cm. Advertisements: p. [4] (first group). Illustrated by the author, G. Child and J. Mynde. Includes bibliographical references and index.
Provenance: Elijah Towns (inkstamp).

673. FERGUSON, JAMES, 1710-1776. *A dissertation upon the phænomena of the harvest moon. Also, The description and use of a new four-wheel'd orrery, and an essay upon the moon's turning round her own axis / By James Ferguson.*
London: Printed for the author and sold by J. Nourse ... and by S. Paterson..., 1747. vi, 7-72 p.: 3 fold. pl.; 20 cm. Errata: p. 72. Illustrated by J. Ferguson and G. Child.

674. FERGUSON, JAMES, 1710-1776. *An easy introduction to astronomy for young gentlemen and ladies ... By James Ferguson, F.R.S. 2d American, from the 7th London ed. Illustrated with copperplates.*
Philadelphia: Published by Johnson and Warner, no. 147, High-street. Ann Cochran, printer, 1812. 178 p., 1 l. VII fold. pl. 18 cm. In ten dialogues. Illustrated by the author.

675. FERGUSON, JAMES, 1710-1776. *Ferguson's Astronomy explained upon Sir Isaac Newton's Principles. With notes and supplementary chapters. By David Brewster....*
Edinburgh: Printed for J. Ballantyne and Co.; [etc., etc.], 1811. 2 v. tables. 22 cm. + atlas of 25 pl. (part double, part fold.) 26 x 22 cm. Atlas has title: Plates illustrative of Ferguson's Astronomy and of the twelve supplementary chapters, by David Brewster. Includes indexes. Errata: [1] p. at end, v. 2.
Provenance: Wm. C. Bowly (signature); John Westacott (signature). Imperfect: lacks plates.

676. Ferguson, James, 1710-1776. *An idea of the material universe, deduced from a survey of the solar system. By James Ferguson.*
London: Printed for the author, 1754. 31 p. 2 plates. 19 cm.

677. Ferguson, James, 1710-1776. *Lectures on select subjects in mechanics, hydrostatics, pneumatics, optics and astronomy. By James Ferguson, F.R.S. A new and improved edition adapted to the present state of science, by C. F. Partington....*
London: Printed for T. Tegg and Son; [etc., etc.], 1837. xlvii, 463 p. front. (port.) illus., x pl., tables, diagrs. 23 cm. Publisher's lettering: Ferguson's lectures on experimental philosophy, astronomy, &c., &c. New edition by C. F. Partington. "A short account of the life of the author. Written by himself, and continued by the editor," with a "List of Mr. Ferguson's published works": p. [xvii]-xlvii. Includes index.
Provenance: Theosophical University Library, Point Loma, Calif. (bookplate and inkstamp); Samuel James Neill (signature).

678. Ferguson, James, 1710-1776. *A plain method of determining the parallax of Venus, by her transit over the sun; and from thence, by analogy, the parallax and distance of the sun, and of all the rest of the planets. By James Ferguson.*
London: Printed for, and sold by the author [etc.], 1761. 1 p. l., 54 p. 4 fold. plates, maps, 28 cm. "Dr. Halley's Dissertation on the method of finding the sun's parallax and distance from the earth, by the transit of Venus over the sun's disc on the 6th of June 1761. Translated from the Latin copy thereof in Motte's abridgment of the *Philosophical transactions,* vol. I. pag. 243; with additional notes.": p. 15-26. Plates signed: J. Ferguson delin., J. Mynde sc. Errata pasted onto p. 54.

679. Ferguson, James, 1710-1776. *Select mechanical exercises: shewing how to construct different clocks, orreries, and sun-dials, on plain and easy principles: with several miscellaneous articles, and new tables. I. For expeditiously computing the time of any new or full moon within the limits of 6000 years before and after the 18th century. II. For graduating and examining the usual lines on the sector, plain scale, and gunter: illustrated with copper-plates: to which is prefixed a short account of the life of the author / by James Ferguson....*
London: Printed for W. Strahan, and T. Cadell ..., 1773. [12], xliii, [1], 272 p., IX folded leaves of plates: ill.; 22 cm. Errata: p. [1] (3rd count).

680. Ferguson, James, 1710-1776. *Tables and tracts relative to several arts and sciences / by James Ferguson.*
London: A. Millar and T. Cadell, 1767. xiii, [2], 328 p.: 3 fold. pl.; 21 cm. Illustrated by J. Ferguson and J. Mynde.
Provenance: J. P. Wm. Ellis (signature).

681. Ferguson, James, 1710-1776. *Tables and tracts, relative to several arts and sciences / by James Ferguson. 2d ed., with additions.*
London: Printed for W. Strahan, J. and F. Rivington, W. Johnston, T. Longman, and T. Cadell, 1771. xv, 334, [1] p., [3] fold. leaves of plates: ill.; 22 cm. Signatures: pi^{4}a^{4}B-Z^{4}Aa-Uu^4. Advertisements: p. [335].

682. Fermat, Pierre de, 1601-1665. *Varia opera mathematica / D. Petri de Fermat ...; accesserunt selectæ quædam ejusdem epistolæ, vel ad ipsum à plerisque doctissimis viris Gallicè, Latinè, vel Italicè, de rebus ad mathematicas disciplinas, aut physicam pertinentibus scriptæ.*
Tolosæ: Apud Joannem Pech ..., M.DC.LXXIX., [1679]. [12], 210, [4] p., [5] leaves of plates: ill.; 37 cm. Edited by Samuel de Fermat. Signatures: ã^2 e^2 i^2 A-2C^4 2D^1 2E^2. Title vignette; decorated initials throughout text. Some copies contain an engraved portrait of Fermat (not included in extent statement). "Apollonii Pergæi Libri duo de locis planis restituti": p. 12-43. Horblit, H. D. *Grolier 100 science books,* 30; Burndy, *Science,* 108; BM *STC French,* 1601-1700, F170.
Lacks portrait. Leaves ã1 and ã2 are second state; l. ã2 is first state as described by Horblit. Provenance: Robert Honeyman IV (bookplate); Jacobi Manzoni (book label).

683. Fernel, Jean, 1497-1558. *Ioannis Fernelii ... Universa medicina: a doctissimo et experientissimo medico diligenter recognita, & ab innumeris mendis & erroribus, quibus priores scatebant editiones repurgata, collatis inuicem*

vetustissimis & optimis exemplaribus. Editio emendatissima. Addita sunt eiusdem Fernelij Consilia: & Guliel. Plantii scholia in pharmacopoœm seu librum Therapeutices septimum.

Genevae: Apud Iacobum Chouët, 1644. [16], 631 [i. e. 611], [53], 484, 397, [63] p.; 18 cm. Includes indexes. Physiologiæ libri VII. – Pathologiæ libri VII. – Therapeutices universalis, seu Medendi rationis, libri septem. – Febrium curandarum methodus generalis. – De luis venereæ curatione perfectissima liber. – Consilium epileptico præscriptum. – De abditis rerum causis libriduo. – Consiliorum medicinalium liber.

Provenance: Joannis Géorgÿ Küffner (inscription).

684. Fichte, Johann Gottlieb, 1762-1814. *Grundlage der gesammten Wissenschaftslehre: als Handschrift für seine Zuhörer / von Iohann Gottlieb Fichte.*

Leipzig: bei Christian Ernst Gabler, 1794. xii, [3]-48, [3], 50-339, [1] p.; 21 cm. Errors in pagination: p. 299 misnumbered as 283, 302 and 303 as 393 & 302. Folgende Fehler bittet man zu berichtigen: last p.

With the author's: *Über den Begriff der Wissenschaftslehre.* Weimar: im Verlage des Industrie-Comptoirs, 1794.

685. Fichte, Johann Gottlieb, 1762-1814. *Grundriss des Eigentümlichen der Wissenschaftslehre: in Rücksicht auf das theoretische Vermögen: als Handschrift für seine Zuhörer / von Iohann Gottlieb Fichte.*

Jena; Leipzig: bei Christian Ernst Gabler, 1795. [2], 108, [1] p.; 21 cm. Errors in pagination: p. 65 misnumbered as 63. Druckfehler: last p.

With the author's *Über den Begriff der Wissenschaftslehre.* Weimar: im Verlage des Industrie-Comptoirs, 1794.

686. Fichte, Johann Gottlieb, 1762-1814. *Über den Begriff der Wissenschaftslehre: oder der sogenannten Philosophie, als Einladungsschrift zu seinen Vorlesungen über diese Wissenschaft / von Johann Gottlieb Fichte....*

Weimar: Im Verlage des Industrie-Comptoirs, 1794. viii, [9]-68 p.; 21 cm. Einige Druckfehler: p. 68. Signatures: A-D^8 E^2.

With the author's: *Grundlage der gesammten Wissenschaftslehre.* Leipzig: bei Christian Ernst Gabler, 1794; and *Grundriss des Eigentümlichen der Wissenschaftslehre.* Jena: bei Christian Ernst Gabler, 1795.

687. Ficino, Marsilio, 1433-1499. *Epistolæ Marsilii Ficini Florentini.*

[Nuremberg]: Per Antonium Koberger impraesse, [1497, 24 Februarii]. [10], CCXLIII, [1] (blank) leaves; 21 cm. Printer and date from colophon. Signatures: pi^{10} (2-6 numbered; 3 signed i3) A-Z^8 a-g^8 h^4 (blank: h4; missigned: C2 for D2, X4 for X3). Spaces left for initials. BM *15th cent.*, II, p. 443 (IA.7529). Goff (rev.) F-155. *GW* 9874. Hain 7062*. *ISTC*, if00155000. Rhodes 775.

Binding: half white pigskin, marbled boards; morocco title label on spine. Binder's title: Marsilii Ficini Epistolæ M.CCCC.XCVII. Imperfect: lacks leaves XCI-XCIV (M3-6). Provenance: Jo.Bapt. Galanti J. C. (inscription); underscoring and ms. marginalia.

688. Finch, Henry, Sir, d. 1625. *Law, or A discourse thereof, in four books. Written in French by Sir Hen. Finch, kt. ... And done into English by the same author.*

London: Printed by the assignes of Richard and Edward Atkins; for H. Twyford [etc.], 1678. 3 p. l., 506 [i.e. 504], [13] p. 16 cm. Signatures: title not signed, A$^{3-4}$, B-Z^8, Aa-Kk^8, Ll^4 (last verso blank). Pages 497-498 omitted in numbering. Originally issued with title: *Nomotechnia* (Romanized); *cestascavoir, Vn description dei common leys Dangleterre solonqve les rules del art* ... London, 1613. “A catalogue of some lawbooks, printed for the booksellers in Fleetstreet and Holbourne”: [2] p. at end. Includes bibliographical references and index. Wing (2nd ed.) 932.

Provenance: Charles Dilburn (armorial bookplate).

689. Fine, Oronce, 1494-1555. *Orontii Finei Delphinatis, liberalium disciplinarum professoris regii, Protomathesis: opus uarium, ac scitu non minus utile quàm iucundum, nunc primùm in lucem fœliciter emissum. Cuius index uniuersalis, in uersa pagina continetur.*

Parisiis: impensis Gerardi Morrhij & Ioannis Petri, 1532. 8, 207 [i.e. 209], [1] leaves: ill.; 39 cm. Errors in foliation: leaf 188 misnumbered as 189, 193 as 194, 209 as 207. Title within architectural border; initials; head-pieces. Illustrated by the author. Errata: last p. Publisher statement taken from colophon. In 4 pts.; pts. 2-4 have each special t.-p., with imprint: Lutetiæ Parisiorvm, M.D.XXX [-M.D.XXXI]. De arithmetica practica libri IIII. – De geometria libri II. – De cosmographia, sive mvndi sphæra libri V. – De solaribvs horologis et qvadrantibvs libri IIII. Adams F477. Smith, D. E. *Rara arithmetica* (4th ed.), p. 160.

Imperfect: leaves 100 (blank), 101 missing. 5 newspaper extracts inserted. T. p. repaired and partially hand-drawn.

690. Fine, Oronce, 1494-1555. *Orontij Finei Delphinatis, regii mathematicarum professoris, In sex priores libros geometricorum elementorum Euclidis Megarensis demonstrationes.: Quibus ipsius Euclidis textus græcus, suis locis insertus est: vnà cum interpretatione latina Bartolomæi Zamberti ..., ad fidem geometricã per eundem Orontium recognita.*

Parisiis: Apud Simonem Colinæum, 1536. [8], 174, [2] p. (last leaf blank): ill. (woodcuts); 29 cm. In Greek and Latin. Commentary in Latin. Thomas-Stanford, C. *Euclid*, 8. Steck, M. *Euclid*, III.31. Errata: p. 174. Bibliography of Fine: p. [7].

691. Fine, Oronce, 1494-1555. *Opere di Orontio Fineo del delfinato: diuise in cinque parti; arimetica, geometria, cosmografia, e oriuoli, / tradotte da Cosimo Bartoli ... et gli specchi, tradotti dal caualier Ercole Bottrigaro ... Nuouamente poste in luce.*

In Venetia: Presso Francesco Franceschi Senese, 1587. [8], 81, [1], 84, 126, 88, 18, [2] leaves (leaf [1], 3rd count, blank): ill.; 22 cm. Translated from the Latin. BM *STC Italian*, 352.

Blank leaf missing, binder's blanks between sections.

692. Firmicus Maternus, Julius. *Iulii Firmici Materni Siculi v.c. ad Mauortium Lollianum, Astronomicon libri VIII / per Nicolaum Prucknerum astrologum nuper ab innumeris mendis uindicati....*

Basileae: Per Ioannem Heruagium, (1551, mense Aprili). [12], 244, 227, [1] p.: ill.; 33 cm. Several errors in pagination. Errata: on p. 227. (From t. p.): Claudii Ptolemæi ... Quadripartitum lib. IIII – De inerrantium stellarum significationibus lib. I – Centiloquium ... – Hermetis ... Centum Aphoris. lib. I – Bethem Centiloquium – Eiusdem De horis planetarum liber alius – Almanzoris ... Propositiones ad Saracenorum regem – Zahelis Arabis De electionibus lib. I – Messahalah De ratione circuli & stellarum ... – Omar De Natiuitatibus lib. III – Marci Manilii ... Astronomicon lib. V – ... Othonis Brunfelsii De diffinitionibus & terminus astrologiæ libellus isagogicus.

With: *Albohazen Haly filii Aben ragel Libri deiudiciis astrorum.* Basileæ: Ex Officina Henrichi Petri, 1551.

693. Firsoff, V. A. (Valdemar Axel), 1912- *Moon atlas.*

New York: Viking Press, 1962, c1961. 32 p. illus. col. maps (2 fold.) 36 cm. A Studio book. Bibliography: p. 32.

694. Firsoff, V. A. (Valdemar Axel), 1912- *Strange world of the moon; an inquiry into its physical features and the possibility of life.*

New York: Basic Books, 1960, c1959. x, 226 p. illus., plates. 24 cm. Includes bibliographies and index.

695. Fischer, Emil, 1852-1919. *Die Chemie der Kohlenhydrate und ihre Bedeutung für die Physiologie: Rede, gehalten zur Feier des Stiftungstages der militär-ärztlicher Bildungsanstaltfn [sic] am 2. August 1894 / von Professor Dr. Emil Fischer. ...*

Berlin: Verlag von August Hirschwald ..., 1894. 36 p.; 21 cm.

696. Fisher, Clyde, 1878-1949. *The story of the moon, by Clyde Fisher. 1st ed.*

Doubleday, Doran, 1943. xiv, 301 p. front., illus. (charts), plates, ports., diagrs. 24 cm. The American Museum of Natural History. Science Series, vol. IV. Includes index. Bibliography: p. 293-295.

697. Fiske, John, 1842-1901. *A century of science, and other essays, by John Fiske....*

Boston and New York: Houghton Mifflin and Company, 1900. vii p., 1 l., 477, [1] p. 21 cm. Century of science. – Doctrine of evolution; its scope and purport. – Edward Livingston Youmans. – Part played by infancy in the evolution of man. – Origins of liberal thought in America. – Sir Harry Vane. – Arbitration treaty. – Francis Parkman. – Edward Augustus Freeman. – Cambridge as village and city. – Harvest of Irish folk-lore. – Guessing at half and multiplying by two. – Forty years of Bacon-Shakespeare folly. – Some cranks and their crochets.

[2] p. of advertisements at end.

698. Fison, Alfred Henry, 1857-1923. *Recent advances in astronomy, by Alfred H. Fison, D. Sc.*

London [etc.]: Blackie & Son, Limited, 1900. vi p., 1 l., 242 p. diagrs. 20 cm. Victorian Era Series. Includes index.

Advertisements: [2] p. at end. Provenance: Harrogate Ladies College Library (inscription).

699. Fizeau, H. (Hippolyte), 1819-1896. *Recherches sur les modifications que subit la vitesse de la lumière dans le verre et plusieurs autres corps solides sous l'influence de la chaleur / par M. H. Fizeau....*
Paris: Mallet-Bachelier, Imprimeur-Libraire ..., 1862. 56 p.; 25 cm. "Extrait des *Annales de chimie et de physique,* 3e série, t. LXVI."

700. Flammarion, Camille, 1842-1925. *Astronomie des dames / Camille Flammarion.*
New York: E. Flammarion, [1903?]. 380 p., [1] folded leaf of plates: ill., map; 19 cm. Dedication dated: novembre, 1903. Verso of half title reads: "il a été tiré, de cet ouvrage, dix exemplaires sur papier du Japon, tous numérotés et parafés par l'Éditeur."

701. Flammarion, Camille, 1842-1925. *Astronomie populaire. Description générale du ciel, illustrée de 360 figures, planches en chromolithographie, cartes célestes, etc.*
Paris: C. Marpon et E. Flammarion, 1880. 4 p.l., 839 p. col. front., illus., plates (partly col.) diagrs. 28 cm.
Binder: Jarrolds, Norwich (ticket). Imperfect: lacks 1 p.l. (half-title?) Frontispiece is portrait of Flammarion, rather than col. plate.

702. Flammarion, Camille, 1842-1925. *Astronomy, by Camille Flammarion....*
Garden City, N.Y: Doubleday, Page & Co., 1914. xi, 191, [1] p. illus. (incl. maps, diagrs.) 19 cm. Thresholds of Science. Includes index. Printed in Great Britain.

703. Flammarion, Camille, 1842-1925. *Astronomy for amateurs / by Camille Flammarion; authorized translation by Frances A. Welby.*
New York: D. Appleton, 1908. xii, 345 p., [1] leaf of plates: ill.; 20 cm. Translation of: *Astronomie des dames.* Includes index.

704. Flammarion, Camille, 1842-1925. *The atmosphere. Tr. from the French of Camille Flammarion. Ed. By James Glaisher....*
New York: Harper & Brothers, 1873. 453 p. illus., 10 col. pl., diagrs. 26 cm.
Advertisements: 7 p. at end.

705. Flammarion, Camille, 1842-1925. *Contemplations scientifiques / par Camille Flammarion.*
Paris: E. Flammarion, 1909. x, 372 p.; 19 cm. Advertisements: half title verso and lower wrapper. Date from colophon. Engraving on wrapper signed by Lemoine and Fonseca.

706. Flammarion, Camille, 1842-1925. *Dreams of an astronomer / by Camille Flammarion; translated from the French by E. E. Fournier d'Albe.*
New York: Appleton, 1923. 223 p.; 23 cm. Translation of: *Rêves étoilés.* Includes index.

707. Flammarion, Camille, 1842-1925. *Les étoiles et les curiosités du ciel; description complète du ciel visible à l'il nu et de tous les objets célestes faciles à observer; supplément de l'Astronomie populaire. Illustré de 400 figures, cartes celestes, planches et chromolithographies.*
Paris: C. Marpon et E. Flammarion, 1882. viii p., 1 l., 792 p. front. (port) illus., 3 col. pl., diagrs. 28 cm.
Imperfect? lacks 1 leaf following p. viii. Binder: Jarrolds, Norwich (ticket).

708. Flammarion, Camille, 1842-1925. *Études et lectures sur l'astronomie, par Camille Flammarion....*
Paris: Gauthier-Villars, 1867-1880. 9 v. ill. 17 cm. Advertisements on wrappers. Includes bibliographical references.
Bound in 3 v.

709. Flammarion, Camille, 1842-1925. *L'inconnu. The unknown. By Camille Flammarion.*
New York London: Harper & Brothers, c1900. xii, [1], 487, [1] p. pl., diagrs. 21 cm.

710. Flammarion, Camille, 1842-1925. *Komet und Erde: eine astronomische Erzählung / von Camille Flammarion; autorisierte Übersetzung aus dem Französischen von J. Cassirer.*
Leipzig: Philipp Reclam jun., 1910. 93 p.; 16 cm. Reclams universal Bibliothek; Nr. 5183. For date of imprint Cf. GV (1700-1910), v. 149, p. 116.

711. FLAMMARION, CAMILLE, 1842-1925. *Lumen: experiences in the infinite / by Camille Flammarion; translated by Mary J. Serrano....*
New York: The Mershon Company ..., c1892. v, [1] (blank), 275 p., [1] leaf of plates: port.; 19 cm. Translation of: *Lumen.*
Advertisements: [4] p. at end.

712. FLAMMARION, CAMILLE, 1842-1925. *Les merveilles célestes: lectures du soir / par Camille Flammarion. 12me éd.*
Paris: Hachette, 1909. viii, 320 p.: ill.; 27 cm. Bibliothèque des écoles et des familles.
Provenance: Alfred Mayner (signature).

713. FLAMMARION, CAMILLE, 1842-1925. *Les mondes imaginaires et les mondes réels: voyage pittoresque dans le ciel ... / par Camille Flammarion. Quatrième édition.*
Paris: Librairie académique Didier et cie ...: Gauthier-Villars ..., 1866. [4], vii, 577 p.: ill.; 18 cm.

714. FLAMMARION, CAMILLE, 1842-1925. *La planète Vénus, discussion générale des observations; étude accompagnée de 94 dessins, par Camille Flammarion.*
Paris: Gauthier-Villars et fils, 1897. 1 p. l., 32 p. illus. 25 cm. Advertisements on lower wrapper. Includes bibliographical references.
Provenance: author's signed presentation inscription.

715. FLAMMARION, CAMILLE, 1842-1925. *La pluralité des mondes habités: étude où l'on expose les conditions d'habitabilité des terres célestes ... / par Camille Flammarion. Trente-huitième mille.*
Paris: Ernest Flammarion, éditeur ..., [188-?]. [4], VI, 479, [1] p., VI, [1] leaves of plates (2 folded): ill., col. maps; 19 cm. Advertisements on verso of half title and lower wrapper. Includes index.

716. FLAMMARION, CAMILLE, 1842-1925. *Popular astronomy: a general description of the heavens / by Camille Flammarion; translated from the French with the author's sanction by J. Ellard Gore. New impression, rev., with an appendix.*
New York: D. Appleton, [1907?]. xix, 696 p., iii folded leaves of plates: ill.; 25 cm. Translation of: *Astronomie populaire.* Preface dated 1907. Includes bibliographical references and index.
Provenance: L. A. Thompson (signature).

717. FLAMMARION, CAMILLE, 1842-1925. *Promenades dans les étoiles ... / par Camille Flammarion.*
Paris: Armand Colin, 1910. 153 p.: ill., ports.; 21 cm. Petite bibliothèque. Série C, Science Récréative. Advertisements on half title verso and lower wrapper.

718. FLAMMARION, CAMILLE, 1842-1925. *Les terres du ciel: description astronomique, physique, climatologique, géographique des planètes qui gravitent avec la terre au tour du soleil et de l'état probable de la vie a leur surface / par Camille Flammarion ... Deuxième édition.*
Paris: Librairie Académique Didier et cie ..., 1877. [8], 600 p., IX col. leaves of plates: ill., maps; 26 cm. Advertisements: p. [2]. Ill. signed by: E. Morieu, C. Laplante, Sellier, T. Smeeton, L. Sonnet & C. Flammarion.

719. FLAMMARION, CAMILLE, 1842-1925. *Les terres du ciel: voyage astronomique sur les autres mondes et description des conditions actuelles de la vie sur les diverses planètes du système solaire; ouvrage illustré de photographies célestes, vues télescopiques, cartes et nombreuses figures....*
Paris: C. Marpon et E. Flammarion, 1884. [6], 773, [2] p.: ill., plates, maps, diagrs.; 27 cm.
Original printed wrappers bound in.

720. FLAMMARION, CAMILLE, 1842-1925. *Thunder and lightning / by Camille Flammarion; translated by Walter Mostyn.*
London: Chatto & Windus, 1905. 281 p., [4] leaves of plates: ill.; 20 cm. Translation of: *Les caprices de la foudre.*
Advertisements: 32 p. at end; [1] p. preceding half-title.

721. FLAMMARION, CAMILLE, 1842-1925. *The wonders of the heavens, by Camille Flammarion;*

from the French by Mrs. Norman Lockyer.
New York: C. Scribner & Co., 1871. iv, 289 p. col. front., illus. 18 cm. Translation of *Les merveilles célestes.*
26 p. advertisements following text.

722. FLAMSTEED, JOHN, 1646-1719. *An accompt of such of the more notable celestial appearances of the year 1670, as will be conspicuous in the English horizon / written by the learned and industrious Mr. John Flamstead Nov. 4, 1669, and by him addressed and recommended for encouragement, to the Right Honorable, the Lord Viscount Brouncker, as president of the Royal Society.*
London: Royal Society of London, [1670?]. p.1099-1112; 21 cm. Caption title. Detached from the *Philosophical transactions* of the Royal Society, 1670, no. 55.

723. FLAMSTEED, JOHN, 1646-1719. *Atlas céleste de Flamstéed, approuvé par l'Académie Royale des Sciences, et publié sous le privilege de cette compagnie. Seconde édition. Par M. J. Fortin....*
À Paris: Chez F. G. Deschamps, ... l'Auteur ..., 1776. viij, 40 p., 30 double maps. 23 cm.

724. FLAMSTEED, JOHN, 1646-1719. *Atlas cœlestis / by the late Reverend Mr. John Flamsteed....*
London: Printed for C. Nourse ..., 1781. [5] (last blank), 9, [1] p., 14, [1], 15-27 folded leaves of plates: ill., port; 56 cm. Edited by Margaret Flamsteed and James Hodgson. Portrait signed: T. Gibson pinx., Geo. Vertue sculp.; illustrated by I. B. Catenaro Jn, L. du Guernier, I. Mynde. Originally published: 1729. Cf. *DSB*, v. 5, p. 26.
Provenance: Dollond (signature).

725. FLAMSTEED, JOHN, 1646-1719. *Lunæ ad fixas Saturnumque, anno 1671: appulsus observabiles, prædicti, & ad meridianum latitudinemque Londini accurate supputati / à Joh. Flamsteadio....*
London: Royal Society of London, [1670?]. p. 2029-2034; 21 cm. Caption title. Detached from the *Philosophical transactions* of the Royal Society of 1670, no. 66.

726. †FLINDERS, MATTHEW, 1774-1814. *A voyage to Terra Australis; undertaken for the purpose of completing the discovery of that vast country, and prosecuted in the years 1801, 1802 and 1803....*
London: Printed by W. Bulmer and Co. ... and published by G. and W. Nicol ..., 1814. 2 v. 9 pl. 32 cm. + atlas of 12 pl., 16 maps. 70 cm. "General remarks, geographical and systematical, on the botany of Terra Australis. By Robert Brown": p. 533-613, v. 2. Illustrations by W. Westall; botanical illustrations by F. Bauer. Ferguson, J. A. *Australia*, 573, 576.
Ten botanical plates to accompany Brown's work bound in v. 2, rather than in atlas.

727. FLOURENS, P. (PIERRE), 1794-1867. *Analyse de la philosophie anatomique, où l'on considère plus particulièrement l'influence qu'aura cet ouvrage sur l'état actuel de la physiologie et de l'anatomie.*
Paris: Béchet, 1819. 28 p.

728. †FLUDD, ROBERT, 1574-1637. *Utriusque cosmi maioris scilicet et minoris metaphysica, physica atqve technica historia, in duo volumina secundum cosmi differentiam diuisa. Avthore Roberto Flud aliàs de Fluctibus....*
Oppenhemii: Ære Johan-Theodori de Bry, typis Hieronymi Galleri, 1617-21. 2 v. in 1. illus. (incl. maps, diagrs., music) fold. plates. 32 cm. Engraved title-pages; only the first treatise of v. 1 has general t.-p.; the other parts have special title-pages: Tractatus secundus De natvræ simia seu technica macrocosmi historia. Oppenheimio, ære Iohan-Theodori de Bry, typis Hieronymi Galleri, 1618 (788 p., 5 l.); Tomvs secvndvs De svpernatvrali, naturali, præternaturali et contranaturali microcosmi historia, in tractatus tres distributa. Oppenhemij, impensis Iohannis Theodori de Bry, typis Hieronymi Galleri, 1619 (277 p.); Tomi secvndi, tractatus primi, sectio secunda, De technica microcosmi historia [n.p., n.d.] (191, [1] p., 5 l.); Tomi secundi, tractatus secundus, De præternaturali utriusque mundi historia. Francofurti, typis Erasmi Kempfferi, sumptibus Joan. Theodori de Bry, 1621 (6 p.l., 199 p.). The second volume ends with the first section of the second treatise. It was to have contained three treatises, but was never completed. Includes several folded leaves. Houzeau & Lancaster, *Astronomie* (1964 ed.), 2965-2966.
Binder: [R?] Petit (stamp). Binding: full rebacked calf, gilt stamped. Provenance: Grimaux (inkstamp);

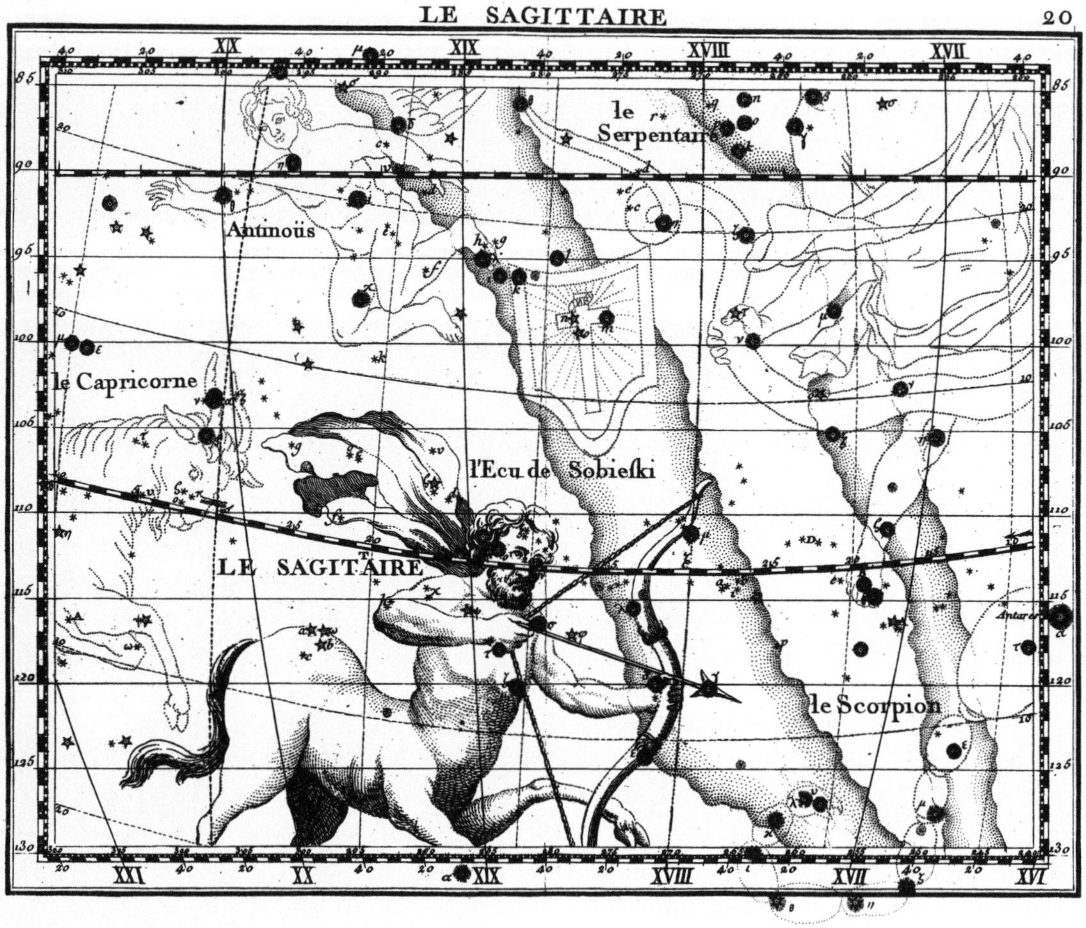

Flamsteed, *Atlas céleste*, 1776

Bibliothèque de Sorbonne (inkstamp). Imperfect: lacks second treatise of v. 2.

729. Fontenelle, M. de (Bernard Le Bovier), 1657-1757. *A plurality of worlds / written in French by the author of the Dialogues of the dead; translated into English by Mr. Glanvill.*
London: Printed for R. W. and sold by Tho. Osbourne ..., 1702. [14], 156, [4] p., [1] folded leaf of plates: ill.; 17 cm. Advertisements: [4] p.
Provenance: J. Savill (signature).

730. Fontenelle, M. de (Bernard Le Bovier), 1657-1757. *Conversations on the plurality of worlds. By Monsieur Fontenelle. Translated from the last Paris ed. Wherein are many improvements throughout; and some new observations on several late discoveries which have been made in the heavens. By William Gardiner, esq.*
London: Printed for A. Bettesworth [etc.] 1715. 6 p. l., 192 p. front. 16 cm.
Provenance: J. Tuppy (signature), Catherine Wheel (inscription).

731. Fontenelle, M. de (Bernard Le Bovier), 1657-1757. *Conversations on the plurality of worlds / by M. de Fontenelle; a new transla-*

View in Sir Edward Pellew's Group; — Gulph of Carpentaria

Flinders, *A Voyage to Terra Australis*, 1814

tion from the last edition of the French, with great addtions, ... by a Gentleman of the Inner Temple. The second edition.
London: Printed for Thomas Caslon ..., 1767. liv, 401, [1] p., [4] folded leaves of plates: ill.; 20 cm. Translation of: *Entretiens sur la pluralité des mondes.* Advertisement: [1] p. Errors in pagination: p. xxxv, xlvii, 34, 289-304, 346 are misnumbered xvii, xlvi, 20, 293-308, 303 respectively.

732. Fonvielle, W. de (Wilfrid), 1824-1914. *L'astronomie moderne / par W. De Fonvielle.*
Paris; New York: Germer Baillière ..., 1868. xxxvi, 153, [2] p.; 19 cm. p. xxix misnumbered as xxv, 107 as 197.

733. Fonvielle, W. de (Wilfrid), 1824-1914. *Les merveilles du monde invisible / par Wilfrid de Fonvielle ...Deuxième édition.*
Paris: Librairie de L. Hachette ..., 1867. [4], 360 p.: ill.; 19 cm. Bibliothèque des merveilles.

734. Forbes, George, 1849-1936. *The earth, the sun and the moon / by George Forbes.*

FLUDD, *Utriusque cosmi maioris scilicet et minoris metaphysica*, 1617-1621

Garden City, N. Y.: Doubleday, Doran & Company, 1928. 78 p.; 17 cm. Little Books of Modern Knowledge.

735. FORBES, GEORGE, 1849-1936. *The stars, by George Forbes....*

New York: J. Cape & H. Smith 1929. 126 p. illus. 18 cm. New Library. Bibliography: p. 125-126.

736. FORBES, GEORGE, 1849-1936. *The wonder & the glory of the stars, by George Forbes....*

New York: Dodd, Mead and Company, 1926. 221 p. illus., plates. 23 cm. "This volume of ... sketches is the outcome of nearly two hundred ...lectures delivered ... under the David Elder Foundation, at the Royal Technical College ... A ... selection from these lectures was published in Chambors's journal; and these, with some additions to the text, and illustrations, are now brought together ..." – Pref.

737. FORSTER, JOHANN REINHOLD, 1729-1798. *Manuel pour servir a l'histoire naturelle des oiseaux, des poissons, des insectes et des plantes; oú sont expliqués les termes employés dans leurs descriptions, et suivant la méthode de Linné; traduit du latin de J. Reinhold Forster. Augmenté d'un mémoire de Murray sur la Conchyliologie, traduit de la même langue, et de plusieurs additions considérables extraites des ouvrages des Cit. Lacépède, Jussieu, Lamarck, Cuvier, etc. Par J. B. F. Léveillé....*

Paris: Villier, an VII, [1799?]. xxiv, 436 p., 1 l. 20 cm. Translation of: *Enchiridion historiæ naturali inserviens.* Half-title: Manuel d'histoire naturelle.

Final page misnumbered 456; corrected in ms. to 436. With: *Le règne animal distribué d'après on organisation...,* par M. le Cher. Cuvier...Paris, Deterville, 1817. Bound with v. 4.

738. FOUCAULT, LÉON, 1819-1868. *Démonstration physique du mouvement de rotation de la terre au moyen du pendule / par M. L. Foucault.*

Paris : Bachelier, 1851. p. 135-138 ; 27 cm. In: *Comptes rendus hebdomadaires des séances de l'Académie des sciences,* t. 32. Caption title. Foucault published, the following year, in t. 35 of the *Comptes rendus:* "Sur les phénomènes d'orientation des corps tournants entraînés par un axe fixe à la surface de la terre : nouveaux signes sensibles du mouvement diurne" (p. 424-427). Reports published separately as: *Sur divers signes sensibles du mouvement diurne de la terre,* cited in Burndy. *Science,* no. 17.

739. FOURIER, JEAN BAPTISTE JOSEPH, BARON, 1768-1830. *The analytical theory of heat, by Joseph Fourier. Translated, with notes, by Alexander Freeman. Edited for the Syndics of the University Press.*

Cambridge: 1878. xxiii, 466 p. diagrs. 23 cm. Translation of: *Théorie analytique de la chaleur.*

Provenance: L.F.G. Simmons (inscription). [1] p. of advertisements follow text.

740. FOURIER, JEAN BAPTISTE JOSEPH, BARON, 1768-1830. *Théorie analytique de la chaleur / par M. Fourier.*

À Paris: Chez Firmin Didot, père et fils ..., 1822. [4], xxij, 639 p., II leaves of plates: ill.; 27 cm. Half title: Théorie de la chaleur. Errata: p. [638]-639. Burndy. *Science* 154.

741. FOWLER, A. (ALFRED), 1868-1940. *Report on series in line spectra. By A. Fowler.*

London: Fleetway Press, Ltd., 1922. 4 p.l ., 182 p. 1 l. 5 pl., diagrs. 27 cm. At head of title: The Physical Society of London. "Sources of data": p. 6.

Provenance: Herbert McLean Evans (bookplate).

742. FOWLER, RICHARD ANDREWS. *Definitions and explanations of navigation and nautical astronomy. For the use of naval cadets on board H.M.S.* Britannia.

Portsmouth: Griffin & Co.; London: Simpkin, Marshall & Co., 1876. 2 p. l., 57, [1] p. illus., diagrs. 21 cm. Includes "blank pages ... for auxiliary definitions, and for amendments on those which are given." Compiled by R. A. Fowler. cf. Pref.

Advertisements: 8 p. following text.

743. FRACASTORO, GIROLAMO, 1478-1553. *Hieronymi Fracastorii Veronensis. De sympathia et antipathia rerum liber unus. De contagione et contagiosis morbis et curatione libri III.*

Venetiis: Apud Heredes Lucaeantonij Iuntæ Florentini, 1546. [4], 76, [3] leaves; 19 cm. Errata: leaves [2]-[3]

DISCOURSE OF THE PLURALITY OF WORLDS

FONTENELLE, *A Plurality of Worlds*, 1702

at end. Printer's name from colophon. Includes index. Errors in foliation: 24 as 42, 26 as 29, 68 as 98. Adams F821. Stillwell, M. B. *Science*, 368. Osler, W. *Bib. Osleriana*, 2652.

Ms. notes. Provenance: Herbert McLean Evans (bookplate).

744. Fracastoro, Girolamo, 1478-1553. *Hieronymi Fracastorii Veronensis opera omnia ... Ex tertia editione.*

Venetiis: Apud Iuntas, 1584. [22], 213 leaves: ill., port.; 23 cm. Hieronymi Fracastorii vita: p. [3-11]. Includes index. Signatures and foliation of leaf 186 and 192 are interchanged. Adams F819.

Some p. shaved.

745. Fracastoro, Girolamo, 1478-1553. *The sinister shepherd: a translation of Girolamo Fracastoro's Syphilidis; sive, De morbo gallico libri tres, by William Van Wyck.*

Los Angeles: The Primavera Press, 1934. xxii, [2], 85, [3] p. illus., ports. 25 cm. Author's portrait on t. p. "One thousand copies printed by Ward Ritchie." Printer's device in red on last page. Original black cloth with printed label on spine; with dust jacket.

746. France. Service de la carte géologique de la France. *Explication de la carte géologique de la France.*

Paris: Imprimerie Royale, 1841-1879. 4 v. in 5. illus. 28 cm. and atlas to v. 4, of 176 plates. 38 cm. Vol. 3, pt. 2, and text of v. 4, pt. 1 never pub. "Pub. par ordre de M. le ministre des travaux publics." Tome 2-4 printed by the Imprimerie Nationale. Tome 1-2, Par A. Dufrénoy et Élie de Beaumont, 1841-48. Tome 3, pt. 1, Par A. Dufrénoy, 1873. Tome 4, pt. 1: Fossiles principaux des terrains, par E. Bayle; 1878. (Atlas only; text never published.) Tome 4, pt. 2: Végétaux fossiles du terrain houiller, par R. Zeiller. 1878-79. Includes bibliographical references.

Provenance: Herbert McLean Evans (bookplate).

747. Francoeur, L. B. (Louis Benjamin), 1773-1849. *Uranographie; ou, Traité élémentaire d'astronomie, à l'usage des personnes peu versées dans les mathématiques, des géographes, desmarins, des ingénieurs, etc., accompagné de planisphères; par L.-B.Francoeur ... 4. éd., rev. et considérablement augm.*

Paris: Bacheliér, 1828. xvi, 575, [1] p. incl. tables. 8 fold. pl. 21 cm. Errata: last p. Plates engraved by Adam. Includes index.

Provenance: Briot (signature).

748. Francoeur, L. B. (Louis Benjamin), 1773-1849. *Uranographie, ou, Traité élémentaire d'astronomie: à l'usage des personnes peu versées dans les mathématiques: accompagné de planisphères ... / par L.-B. Francoeur ... Cinquième édition.*

Paris: Bacheliér ..., 1837. xiv, [2], 512 p., [8] folded leaves of plates: ill.; 21 cm. Errata: [2] p. (2nd group). Advertisements: half-title verso.

Binder: Rivage (stamp). Provenance: Collége Royal de Henri IV, Université de France (gilt stamp on binding).

749. Franklin, Benjamin, 1706-1790. *Experiments and observations on electricity, made at Philadelphia in America, by Mr. Benjamin Franklin, and communicated in several letters to Mr. P. Collinson, of London, F. R. S. pt. [I]-II.*

London: Printed and sold by E. Cave, 1751-53. 2 v. fold. pl. 22 x 17 cm. (pt. II: 23 x 18 cm.) Paged continuously. Title of pt. II reads: Supplemental experiments and observations on electircity [!], part II. Made at Philadelphia in America, by Benjamin Franklin, esq; and communicated in several letters to P. Collinson, esq; of London, F.R.S. Cf. Ford, *Franklin bibliography*, no. 77 and 93. Errors in pagination: p. 79 misnumbered as 76, p. 109 as 107. "Books printed and sold by Edward Cave, at St. John's Gate." (part 1: p. [1-2] at end). Plate signed: T. Jeffreys sculp. Errata: p. 85-86 and last p. Horblit, H. D. *Grolier 100 science books*, 31a.

Bound in 1 v. With: *Some thoughts on the reasonableness of a general naturalization.* London: printed for H. Shute..., 1753 – *A view of the British trade to the Mediterranean* / by J. Cowley. London: printed for M. Cooper ..., 1744 – *Nature: a poem; being an attempt towards a vindication of providence.* London: printed for M. Cooper ... and sold by J. Fletcher ..., 1748 – *A letter to a friend in the country.* London: printed for T. Cooper ..., 1740 – *London, or the progress of commerce* / by Mr. Glover. London: printed for T. Cooper ..., 1739 – *An essay on the invention of engraving and printing in chiaroscuro* / by Mr. Jackson. London: printed for A. Millar ... [and 4 others], 1754. Provenance: L'Ab. Boyer (bookplate); Domus Massiliensis (bookplate); Congrég. Missiona. Oblat. M. J. Domus Stud. Leodiensis (inkstamp).

750. Franklin, Benjamin, 1706-1790. *A letter from Mr. Franklin to Mr. Peter Collinson, F.R.S. concerning the effect of lightning; A letter of Benjamin Franklin, Esq. to Mr. Peter Collinson, F.R.S. concerning an electrical kite.*

[London: Printed for C. Davis ..., 1753]. p.289-291; 565-567; 25 cm. *Philosophical transactions, giving some account of the present undertakings, studies, and labours, of the ingenious in many considerable parts of the world;* v. 47. Caption titles.

751. Franklin, Benjamin, 1706-1790. *New experiments and observations on electricity: made at Philadelphia in America / by Benjamin Franklin, esq; and communicated in several letters to P. Collinson ... The second edition.*

London: Printed and sold by D. Henry and R. Cave ..., 1754. 3 v.: ill. 23 cm. Full extent: [4], 86, [4], 89-107, [10], 111-154 p. Part III has title: New experiments ... By Benjamin Franklin, esq; communicated to P. Collinson, esq; of London, F.R.S. and read at the Royal Society June 27, and July 4, 1754. To which are added a paper on the same subject, by J. Canton ... and read at the Royal Society Dec. 6, 1753; and another in defence of Mr. Franklin against the Abbe Nollet, by Mr. D. Colden, of New York. Part III. "Remarks on the Abbe Nollet's Letters on electricity ... by Mr. David Colden, of New York": p. [130]-142. "Electrical experiments, with an attempt to account for their several phænomena; together with some observations on thunder-clouds, by John Canton ... from the *Philosophical transactions*": p. [143]-152. Errata: on last p. of pt. 2. The 1st ed.: *Experiments and observations on electricity* was published in 2 pts. only. For pt. 3: Horblitt, H. D. *Grolier 100 science books* 31a.

With: *A series of experiments relating to phosphori* / by B. Wilson. London: printed for J. Dodsley (and 4 others), 1775 – *Oratio de re medica cognoscenda et promovenda* / auctore Nathanaële Hulme ... Londini: prostant apud G. Robinson ... et P. Elmsly ... 1777 – *Philosophical collections, numb. 1.* London: printed for John Martyn ..., 1679 – *An attempt to prove the motion of the earth from observations* / made by Robert Hooke. London: printed by T. R. for John Martyn ..., 1674. Provenance: Darwin family (signatures). Boxed, spine title: The motion of earth / Hooke.

752. Fraunhofer, Joseph von, 1787-1826. *Bestimmung des Brechungs- und Farbenzerstreuungs- Vermögens verschiedener Glasarten in Bezug auf die Vervollkommnung achromatischer Fernröhre / von Joseph Fraunhofer ...*

[München: s.n., 1817]. p. 193-226, III leaves of plates (2 folded): ill.; 27 cm. Caption title. Half-title: Denkschriften der Königlichen Akademie der Wissenschaften zu München für die Jahre 1814 und 1815. Classe der Mathematik und Naturwissenschaften.

753. Frentz, Gerardus, fl. 1695-1696. *Epistola anatomica, problematica quinta / authore Gerardo Frentz ... ad... Fredericum Ruyschium ... de vasis sanguiferis periostii tibiæ, ut & viis, per quas vesicula fellea sarcinam acquirit.*

Amstelaedami: Apud Joannem Wolters, 1696. 10, [2] (blank), [2] p., [2] leaves of plates (1 folded) :ill.; 22 cm. "Frederici Ruyschii responsio ...": p. 5-10. Plates are numbered: 5 and 6.

Plate 1 belonging to Johannis Gaubii Epistola problematica bound in here. With: *Observationum anatomico-chirurgicarum centuria* / Frederici Ruyschii. Amstelodami: Apud Henricum & Viduam Theodori Boom, 1691.

754. Fresa, Alfonso. *La luna: movimenti, configurazioni, influenze e culto / Alfonso Fresa; prefazione di Giorgio Abetti. 3a. ed. migliorata.*

Milano: U. Hoepli, 1952. xxiv, 566 p., [8] folded leaves: ill., maps; 20 cm. Tables and maps on folded leaves, numbered A-H. Includes bibliographies and indexes.

755. Fresnel, Augustin Jean, 1788-1827. *Mémoire sur la diffraction de la lumière / par M. A. Fresnel.*

[Paris: Imprimé par autorisation du roi, a l'Imprimerié Royale, 1826]. p. 339-475: ill.; 27 cm. *Mémoires de l'Académie des Sciences de l'Institut de France;* t. 5. Caption title. Includes bibliographical references.

756. Fresnel, Augustin Jean, 1788-1827. *Mémoire sur la double refraction / par M. A. Fresnel.*

[Paris: Chez Firmin Didot, Père et Fils, Libraires ..., 1827]. p. 45-176, [1] fold. leaf of plates: ill.; 27 cm. *Mémoires de l'Académie des Sciences de l'Institut de France;* t. 7. Caption title. Includes bibliographical references.

757. Fresnel, Augustin Jean, 1788-1827. *Mémoire sur la loi des modifications que la*

réflexion imprime a la lumière polarisée / par M. A. Fresnel.

[Paris: De l'Imprimerie de Firmin Didot Frères ..., 1832]. p. 393-434; 29 cm. *Mémoires de l'Académie Royale des Sciences de l'Institut de France;* t.. 11. Caption title.

758. FREUD, SIGMUND, 1856-1939. *Das Ich und das Es / von Sigm. Freud.*

Wien: Internationaler Psychoanalytischer Verlag, 1923. 77 p.; 23 cm.

Advertisements: [2] p. at end; on lower wrapper. Ms. marginalia throughout.

759. FREUD, SIGMUND, 1856-1939. *Introductory lectures on psycho-analysis; a course of twenty-eight lectures delivered at the University of Vienna, by Prof. Sigm. Freud ...Authorized English translation by Joan Riviere, with a preface by Ernest Jones ...*

London: Allen & Unwin, 1922. 395 p. ill. 23 cm. Translation of *Vorlesungen zur Einführung in die Psychoanalyse.* American ed. has title: *A general introduction to psychoanalysis.* Includes index.

Advertisements: [4] p. at end.

760. FREUD, SIGMUND, 1856-1939. *Die Traumdeutung / von Sigm. Freud.*

Leipzig: F. Deuticke, 1900 [i.e. 1899]. [4], 371, [5] p.: 3 diagrs.; 23 cm. Published in 1899. Cf. *The standard edition of the complete psychological works of Sigmund Freud,* v. 4, 1953, p. xii. Bibliography: p. [372-374]. Horblit, H. D. *Grolier 100 science books,* 32.

761. FROST, EDWIN BRANT, 1866-1935. *Let's look at the stars / Edwin Brant Frost.*

Boston: Houghton Mifflin, [c1935]. 118 p., [2] leaves of plates: ill. (1 col.); 21 cm. Includes index. Errata slip tipped in.

762. FROST, GEORGE EDWIN. *Planets, stars, and atoms / by George Edwin Frost.*

Caldwell, Idaho: Caxton Printers, 1941, [c1939]. 295 p., [16] leaves of plates: ill.; 24 cm. Includes index.

763. FUCHS, LEONHART, 1501-1566. *De historia stirpium commentarii insignes, maximis impensis et vigiliis laborati, adiectis earundem vivis plusquam quingentis imaginibus, nunquam antea ad naturæ imitationem artificiosius effictis & expressis, Leonharto Fuchsio medico hac nostra ætate longè clarissimo, autore ... Accessit ijs succincta admodum uocum difficilium & obscurarum passim in hoc opere occurrentium explicatio. Unà cum quadruplici Indice, quorum primus quidem stirpium nomenclaturas græcas, alter latinas, tertius officinis seplasiariorum & herbarijs usitatas quartus germanicas continebit....*

Basileæ: in officina Isingriniana, 1542. [28], 896, [4] p., ill., ports. 37 cm. Names of plants in Latin, Greek and German. Printer's mark on t. p. and final p. 509 full page woodcuts paged in. Ports. of author and illustrators. Illustrated by H. Füllmaurer, A. Meyer and V. R. Speckle. Horblit, H. D. *Grolier 100 science books,* 33b.

Six woodcuts are hand-colored. Provenance: C. L. Guerin (inscription); Herbert McLean Evans (bookplate).

764. FUCHS, LEONHART, 1501-1566. *Paradoxorum medicinæ libri tres: in quibus sanè multa à nemine hactenus prodita, Arabum aetatisâq[ue] nostrae medicorum errata non tantum indicantur, sed & probatissimorum autorum scriptis, firmissimisâq[ue] rationibus ac argumentis confutantur / D. Leonardo Fuchsio ... autore; obiter denique hic Sebastiano Montuo ... respondetur, eiusâq[ue] Annotatiunculae velut omnium frigidissimae prorsus exploduntur.*

Venetiis: Apud Hæredes Petri Rauani & Socios, 1547. [16], 191, [1] leaves; 16 cm. A considerably revised and enlarged version of the author's *Errata recentiorum medicorum,* Hagenoæ, 1530. As in the original work, the three books concern questions of medical botany, therapeutics, and anatomy. Cf. Stübler, p. 198-200. Publisher from colophon. Last leaf bears printer's device only. Monteux's *Annotatiunculæ in Errata recentiorum medicorum* was published in Lyons in 1533. He replied to the first two books of the Paradoxa in his *Dialexeon medicinalium libri duo,* Lyons, 1537. Includes index.

765. FUNK, CASIMIR, 1884-1967. *The vitamines. Authorized translation from 2d German ed. by Harry E. Dubin.*

Baltimore: Williams & Wilkins, 1922. 502 p. ill. Includes indexes. Bibliography: p. 395-475.

Provenance: Herbert McLean Evans (inscription).

DE HISTORIA STIRPIVM COMMENTARII INSIGNES, MAXIMIS IMPENSIS ET VIGILIIS ELABORATI, ADIECTIS EARVNDEM VIVIS PLVSQVAM quingentis imaginibus, nunquam antea ad naturæ imitationem artificiosius effictis & expreſsis, LEONHARTO FVCHSIO medico hac nostra ætate longè clariſsimo, autore.

Regiones peregrinas pleriq;, alij alias, sumptu ingenti, studio indefesso, nec sine discrimine uitæ nonnunquam, adierunt, ut simplicium materiæ cognoscendæ facultatem compararent sibi: eam tibi materiam uniuersam summo & impensarum & temporis compendio, procul discrimine omni, tanquam in uiuo iucundiſsimoq; uiridario, magna cum uoluptate, hinc cognoscere licebit.

Acceſsit ijs succincta admodum uocum difficilium & obscurarum paſsim in hoc opere occurrentium explicatio.

Vnà cum quadruplici Indice, quorum primus quidem stirpium nomenclaturas græcas, alter latinas, tertius officinis seplasiariorum & herbarijs usitatas, quartus germanicas continebit.

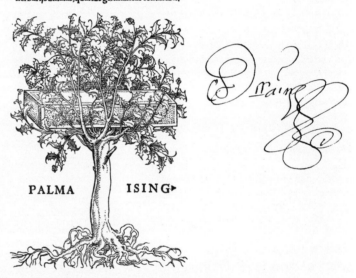

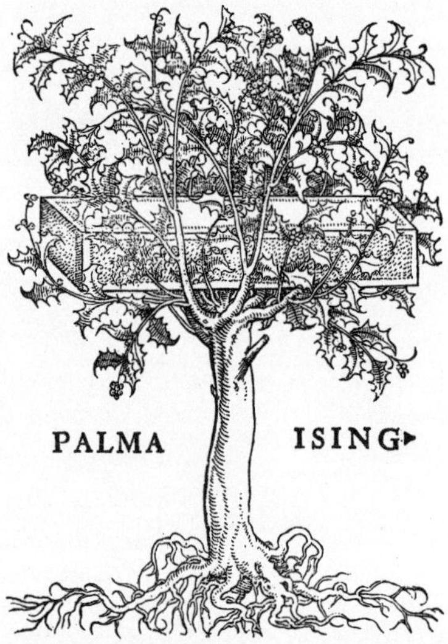

Cautum præterea est inuictiſsimi CAROLI *Imperatoris decreto, ne quis alius impunè usquam locorum hos de stirpium historia commentarios excudat, iuxta tenorem priuilegij antè à nobis euulgati.*

BASILEAE, IN OFFICINA ISINGRINIANA, ANNO CHRISTI M. D. XLII.

Cl. Guerin doctor medicus Parisiensis

FUCHS, *De historia stirpium*, 1542

766. Gadroys, Claude, 1642-1678. *Le systême du monde, selon les trois hypotheses, où conformement aux loix de la mechanique l'on explique dans la supposition du mouvement de la terre: les apparences des astres, la fabrique du monde, la formation des planètes, la lumière, la pesanteur, &c. Et cela par de nouvelles demonstrations.*
Paris: G. Desprez, 1675. 18 p.l., 457 p. diagrs. 16 cm. "Epistre" signed: C. Gadroys.

767. Galilei, Galileo, 1564-1642. *Dialogo / di Galileo Galilei Linceo ... Doue ne i congressi di quattro giornate si discorre sopra i due massimi sistemi del mondo tolemaico, e copernicano; proponendo indeterminatamente le ragioni filosofiche, e naturali tanto per l'vna, quanto per l'altra parte.*
In Fiorenza: Per Gio. Batista Landini, 1632. [10], 458, [32] p.: illus.; 24 cm. Known as: *Dialogo dei massimi sistemi.* Added engraved title page, signed: Stefan Della Bella f. Suppressed by the Inquisition in 1633. Errata: p. [1-2] (third group). Signatures: $[pi]^4$, A-Ee^8, Ff^6, Gg-Kk^4. Shoulder note on p. 92 pasted on. Includes index. Yale. *Cushing Coll.* G67. Horblit, H. D. *Grolier 100 science books* 18c. Carli & Favaro. *Galileo,* 128.
Provenance: Albert Edgar Lownes (bookplate), Herbert McLean Evans (bookplate).

768. Galilei, Galileo, 1564-1642. *Dialogo di Galileo Galilei linceo matematico supremo dello studio di Padova, e Pisa. E filosofo, e matematico primario del serenissimo granduca di Toscana: Dove ne i congressi di quattro giornate si discorre sopra i due massimi sistemi del mondo tolemaico, e copernicano; proponendo indeterminatamente le ragioni filosofiche, e naturali tanto per l'una, quanto per l'altra parte. In questa seconda impressione / accresciuto di una Lettera dello stesso, non più stampata, e di varj trattati di più autori, i quali si veggono nel fine del libro.*
In Fiorenza [i.e. Naples? : s.n.], MDCCX. [1710]. [12], 458, [32], 83 [i.e. 81], [1] p.: ill.; 24 cm. Known as: *Dialogo dei massimi sistemi.* Text mostly in Italian, partly in Latin. Galileo's "Lettera" has special t. p.: Lettera del signor Galileo Galilei accademico linceo escritta alla granduchessa di Toscana. In Fiorenza, [i.e. Naples: s.n.], MDCCX. [1710]. Dedication signed by the editor: Cellenio Zacclori [i.e. Lorenzo Ciccarelli]. Originally published: In Fiorenza,: Per Gio: Batista Landini, MDCXXXII. [1632]. Title in red and black, with engraved vignette. Carli, A. *Bib. Galileiana,* 413. Yale. *Cushing,* G68. Waller, E. *Bib. Walleriana,* 12044. Rocco di Torrepadula, G. *Bibl. Galileiana,* 168. Includes index. "Lettera del r.p.m. Paolo-Antonio Foscarini, carmelitano, sopra l'opinione de Pittagorici, e del Copernico ...": p. 36-68 of 4th group. "Perioche ex introductione in Martem Joannis Kepleri, mathematici Cæsarei": p. 69-74 of 4th group. "Excerptum ex Didaci à Stunica Salmanticensis Commentariis in Job, editionis Tolotanæ, ap. Joannem Rodricum, anno 1584. in 4. pag. 205. & seq. in hæc verba cap. 9. vers. 6. Qui commovet terram de loco suo, & columna ejus concutiuntur": p. 74-76 of the 4th group. "Sententia cardinalium in Galilæum et Abjuratio ejusdem, excerptæ ex J. B. Riccioli Almagesto novo": p. 76-83 [i.e. 81] of 4th group.

769. Galilei, Galileo, 1564-1642. *Dialogo di Galileo Galilei, Dove nei congressi di quattro giornate si discorre sopra i due massimi sistemi del mondo Tolemaico, e Copernicano... In questa impressione migliorato ed accresciuto sopra l'esemplare dell'autore stesso.*
In Padova: Appresso Gio: Manfrè, 1744. [9], 342, [1] p. ill., port. 25 cm. Known as: *Dialogo dei massimi sistemi.* Port signed: Fus. Zucchi sculp. Includes bibliographical references and index. Carli & Favaro, *Galilei,* 479.
Provenance: Stillman Drake (bookplate).

770. Galilei, Galileo, 1564-1642. *Dialog über die beiden hauptsächlichsten Weltsysteme: das Ptolemäische und das Kopernikanische / von Galileo Galilei; aus dem italienischen übersetzt und erläutert von Emil Strauss....*
Leipzig: Druck und Verlag von B. G. Teubner, 1891. LXXIX, [5], 586, [2] p.: ill.; 25 cm. Translation of: *Dialogo dei massimi sistemi.* Advertisements: last [2] p. Berichtigung: p. 573. Includes bibliographical references and index.
Provenance: Stillman Drake (bookplate).

771. Galilei, Galileo, 1564-1642. *Difesa di Galileo Galilei nobile fiorentino ... : contro alle calunnie & imposture di Baldessar Capra : usategli si nella considerazione astronomica*

Galilei, *Dialogo*, 1632

sopra la nuoua stella del MDCIIII. come (& assai piu) nel publicare nuouamente come sua inuenzione la fabrica, & gli usi del compasso geometrico, & militare, sotto il titolo di vsus & fabrica circini cuiusdam proportionis, &c.

In Venetia : Presso Tomaso Baglioni, 1607. 41, [2] leaves : ill. ; 22 cm. Title vignette; tail-piece, initials.

772. GALILEI, GALILEO, 1564-1642. *Discorsi e dimostrazioni matematiche: intorno à due nuoue scienze attenenti alla mecanica & i movimenti locali / del Signor Galileo Galilei Linceo ... ; con una appendice del centro di grauità d'alcuni solidi.*

In Leida: Appresso gli Elsevirii, 1638. [8], 306 [i.e. 314], [6] p.: ill; 21 cm. Tauola de gli errori della stampa: p. [5-6] at the end. Running title: Dialogo primo...quarto, followed by Appendix. Includes index. Pages [265-272, 282-283, 305, 308-309, 312-314] misnumbered as 285-292, 382-383, 297, 300-301, 304-306 respectively. Horblit, H. D. *Grolier 100 science books*, 36. Carli & Favaro. *Galilei*, 162.

Provenance: Herbert McLean Evans (bookplate).

773. GALILEI, GALILEO, 1564-1642. *Istoria e dimostrazioni intorno alle macchie solari e loro accidenti: comprese in tre lettere / scritte all'illustrissimo signor Marco Velseri ... dal signor Galileo Galilei....*

In Roma: Appresso Giacomo Mascardi., MDCXIII, [1613]. 4, 164 p.: ill., 1 port.; 22 cm. Title vignette: device of the Accademia dei Lincei; decorated initials throughout text. Includes four letters from Welser to Galilei. Edited by Angelo de Filiis. Signatures: A^6 B-S^4 T^6 V^4; confirmed by "Registro" (p. 164). Waller, E. *Bib. Walleriana*, 12046; Grässe, III, p. 16; Riccardi, p. Bib. matematica, I, columns 509-510; Michel & Michel, IV, p. 16; Gamba, B. Testi di lingua, 473; Carli, A. *Bib. Galileiana*, 60 note; Yale. *Cushing collection*, G71; Lalande, J. J. Le F. de. *Bib. astronomique*, p. 161. Errata on p. 164.

774. GALILEI, GALILEO, 1564-1642. *Opere di Galileo Galilei ... In questa nuoua editione insieme raccolte, e di varij trattati dell'I stesso autore non più stampati accresciute....*

Bologna: Per gli HH del Dozza, [MDCLV]-LVI. 19 pt. in 2 v.: fronts., ill. (incl. tables, diagrs.), fold. pl.; 23 cm. Title vignettes. Initials. Head and tail pieces. The dedication, signed Carlo Manolessi, is dated Bologna li 17. Febraio 1656. The 19 parts have each special t. p. and for the most part separate paging; a half-title is prefixed to each volume, that of "volume primo" having Galilei's portrait (by F. Villamoena) on verso facing the first special t. p. The general title as above with a general half-title, and allegorical frontispiece (by Stefano della Bella), table of contents (Ordine dell'opere contenute ne'due presenti volumi), and other preliminary matter – 10 prelim. l. in all – are prefixed to the half-title of the 1st volume. Vol. I.: 1. Dedica. Lettera di Maffeo Barberini seguita dalla Advlatio perniciosa. Epigrafe. Le operationi del compasso geometrico e militare di Galileo Galilei. 1656. [24], 48 p. – 2. Annotationi di Mattia Bernaggeri [!] sopra 'l Trattato dell'instrumento delle proportioni del Sig. Galileo Galilei. 1655. 48 p. – 3. Usus et fabrica circini cuiusdam proportionis, per quem omnia ... problemata facili negotio resoluuntur, opera et studio Balthasaris Capræ ... explicata. 1655. [8], 80 p. – 4. Difesa di Galileo Galilei ... contro alle calunie & imposture di Baldessar Capra ... 1655. p. [81]-160. – 5. Discorso ... intorno alle cose, che stanno sù l'acqua, à che in quella si muouono. Di Galileo Galilei ... 2 éditione. 1655. [4], 68 p. – 6. Discorso apologetico di Lodovico delle Colombe, d'intorno al Discorso del S. Galileo Galilei, circa le cose, che stanno sù l'acqua ... 1655. 58 p. – 7. Considerationi di M. Vincentio di Gratia sopra il discorso del Sig. Galileo Galilei intorno alle cose che stanno sù l'acqua ... 1655. p.[59]-127. – 8. Risposta alle oppositione del Sig. Lodovico delle Colombe e del Sig. Vincenzo di Gratia, contro al Trattato del Sig. Galileo Galilei, delle cose che stano sù l'acqua ...[di Benedetto Castelli] 1655. [4], 264 p. – 9. Della scienza mecanica ...opera del Signor Galileo Galilei ... La bilancetta del Signore Galileo Galilei ... 1655. 43 p. This pt. bound in v. 2. Vol II.: 1. Sydereus nuncius ... a Galileo Galilei ... 1655. 41p. – 2-3. Continuatione del nuntio sidereo ... Lettera di Galileo Galilei attenente alla titubation lunare, da esso nuovamente auuertita, scritta a richiesta del Sig. Alfonso Antonini ... Risposta del Sig. Alfonso Antonini. 1655. p. [43]-60. – 4. Istoria e dimostrationi intorno alle macchie solari ... in tre lettere scritte all'illustriss. Sig. Marco Velseri dal Signor Galileo Galilei ... [con tre lettere di Marco Velseri]. Si aggiungono nel fine le Lettere e disquisitioni del finto Apelle [Galileo Galilei] 1655. 7, [1], 156, p. – 5. De tribus cometis anni M.D.C.XVIII. disputatio astronomica ... [P. Horatio Grassi, S. J. auctore] 1655. 12 p. – 6. Discorso delle comete di Mario Guiducci ... 1655. p. [13]-48. – 7. Il saggiatore. 1655. [8], 179, [1] p. – 8. Lettera al ...Tarquinio Galluzzi ... di Mario Guiducci. Nella quale si giustifica dell'imputationi da tegli da Lottario Sarsi ... (Cap. L) ex libro inscripto Liteosphoros ... Fortunii Liceti ... (con) Lettera del *maggior chiarezza ce lo figureremo essere vna cordicella: non è dubbio, che premendo gagliardamente i due Cilindri l'uno contro all' altro, la corda* F E *tirata dall' estremità* F *resisterà à non piccola violenza prima che scorrere trà i due solidi comprimentila: mà se rimuoueremo l'uno di loro, la corda benche continui di toccar l'altro, non però da tal toccamento sarà ritenuta, che liberamente non scorra. Mà se ritenendola benche debolmente attaccata verso la sommità del Cilindro* A *l'auuolgeremo intorno à quello à foggia di spira* A F L O T R, *e dal capo* R *la tireremo: è manifesto, che ella comincerà à strignere il Cilindro, e se le spire, e volute saranno molte, sempre più nel validamente tirare si comprimerà la corda addosso al Cilindro: e facendosi con la multiplicazione delle spire più lungo il toccamento, & in consequenza men superabile, difficile si farà sempre più lo scorrer della corda, e l'acconsentir alla traente forza. Hor chi non vede, che tale è la resistenza delle filamenta, che con mille, e mille simili auuolgimenti il grosso canapo contessono? Anzi lo strignimento di simili tortuosità collega tanto tenacemente, che di non molti giunchi, nè anco molto lunghi, si che poche son le spire, con le quali trà di loro s'intrecciano, si compongono robustissime funi, che mi par che domandino, suste.*

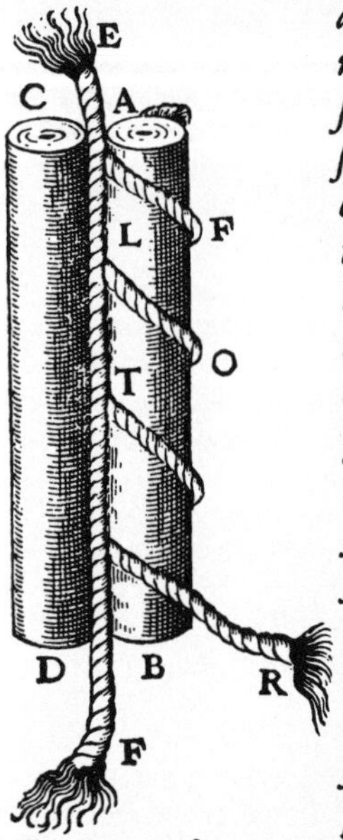

Sagr. *Cessa per il vostro discorso nella mia mente la marauiglia di due effetti, de i quali le ragioni non bene erano comprese da me. Vno era il vedere, come due, ò al più tre riuolte del canapo intorno al fuso dell' Argano poteuano non solamente ritenerlo, che tirato dall' immensa forza del peso, che ei sostiene, scorrendo non gli cedesse, mà che di più girando l'Argano il medesimo fuso col solo toccamento del canapo, che lo strigne, potesse con li succedenti rauuolgimenti*

gimenti

GALILEI, *Discorsi*, 1638

Galilei [a] Leopoldo di Toscana. De lunarium montium altitudine [con tre lettere di]: Gioseffo Biancano al p. Christoforo Grembergero, Christophorusm Griembergerus Galilaeo Galileao, Galileo Galilei a Benedetto Castelli. – 9. Lettera del Galilei al padre Christoforo Grienberger ... in materia della montuosità della luna. 1655. p. [103]-126. – 10. Discorsi e dimostrationi matematiche ... del Signor Galileo Galilei. 1655. [8], 238, [6] p. Carli & Favaro. *Galilei*, 251.

Provenance: Luigi Fortunato Pieri (bookplate).

775. GALILEI, GALILEO, 1564-1642. *Le opere di Galileo Galilei. Prima edizione completa, condotta sugli autentici manoscritti palatini.*

Firenze: Società Editrice Fiorentina, 1842-1856. 15 v. illus. 26 cm. Suppl. (4 pl. l., ix, 376, [3] p., 2 l. diagrs. on II fold. pl. 26 cm.) Edited by Eugenio Albèri, assisted by Celestino Bianchi. "Epoche principali della vita di Galileo Galilei": v. 6, p. [xiii]-xvi. "Racconto istorico della vita di Galileo Galilei ... da Vincenzo Viviani": v. 15, p. [321]-415. "Bibliografia galileiana: I. Opere pubblicate in vita dell'autore. – II. Scritti postumi e successive collezioni delle opere. – III. Nostra edizione (1842-1856) – IV. Cronologia degli scritti galileiani": v. 15, p. [I]-L following p. 415. v. 1-5. Opere astronomiche. 1842-1853. – v. 6-10. Commercio epistolare. 1847-1853. – v. 11-14. Opere fisico-matematiche. 1854-1855. – v. 15. Opere letterarie. 1856. – Supplemento. 1856.

Provenance: Bib. Maj. Collegii Stonyhurst (inkstamp). Bound in 8 v.

776. GALILEI, GALILEO, 1564-1642. *Il saggiatore: nel quale con bilancia esquisita e giusta si ponderano le cose contenute nella Libra astronomica e filosofica di Lotario Sarsi Sigensano / scritto in forma di lettera all'illmo ... Virginio Cesari ni... dal Sig. Galileo Galilei....*

In Roma ... : Appresso Giacomo Mascardi, M.D.C.XXIII. [1623]. [4], 236 p., [1] leaf of plates: ill., port.; 22 cm. Engraved title within architectural border, the arms of Urban VIII in the upper panel, the Lincei device in the lower; engraved illustrations and diagrams; some decorated borders and initials. Title and portrait of Galileo engraved by Francesco Villamena. Errata on p. 236. 16 items. Cf. *The controversy on the comets of 1618* / Galileo Galilei [et al.]. Philadelphia: Univ. of Pennsylvania Press, 1960. p. xix, and p. 360, note 25. Carli & Favaro. *Galilei*, 95.

Provenance: Samuel V. Hoffman; New York Historical Society Library (bookplate). Prelim. leaves with poems not present.

777. GALILEI, GALILEO, 1564-1642. *Sidereus nuncius: magna longeque admirabilia spectacula pandens ... / quæ à Galileo Galileo, patritio Florentino ... perspicilli nuper à se reperti beneficio sunt observata in lunæ facie, fixis innumeris, lacteocirculo, stellis nebulosis, apprimè verò in quatuor planetis circa Jovis stellam ... circumvolutis ... Medicea sidera nuncupandos decrevit.*

Londini: Typis Jacobi Flesher: Prostant apud Cornelium Bee ..., 1653 [i.e.1675?]. 173 p., 4 leaves of plates: ill.; 19 cm. Detached from: *Petri Gassendi Institutio Astronomica*. Secunda editio... For imprint cf. *NUC pre-1956*, v. 192, p. 249-250, and *BLC*, v. 119, p. 20; *BLC* v. 120, p. 378. Possibly issued in 1675? *Joannis Kepleri ... Dioptrice: seu demonstratio eorum quæ visui & & visilibus [sic] propter conspicilla non ita pridem inventa accidunt* ... Londini: Typis Jacobi Flesher, 1653: p. [51]-173, with separate t. p.

Ms. notes.

778. GALILEI, GALILEO, 1564-1642. *Sidereus nuncius: magna, longeque admirabilia spectacula pandens, suspicienda âque proponens vnicuique, præsertim verò philosophis, at[âque] astronomis, / quæ à Galileo Galileo ... perspicilli nuper à se reperti beneficio sunt obseruata in lunæ facie, fixis innumeris, lacteo circulo, stellis nebulosis, apprime verò in quatuor planetis circa Iouis stellam disparibus interuallis, atque periodis, celeritate mirabili circumuolutis; quos, nemini in hanc vsque diem cognitos, nouissimè author depræhendit primus; atque Medicea Sidera nuncupandos decreuit.*

Venetiis: Apud Thomam Baglionum., MDCX. [1610]. 16, [2], 17-28 leaves: ill.; 22 cm. Title vignette; decorated initials. Horblit, H. D. *Grolier 100 science books*, 35. Dibner Lib. *Science*, 7. *Milestones of science* 78.

779. GALLUCCI, GIOVANNI PAOLO, 1538-1621? *Della fabrica et vso di diversi stromenti di astronomia et cosmografia, oue si uede la somma della teorica et practica di queste due nobilissime scienze.*

Venetia: R. Meietti, 1597. 8, 228 leaves, [1] folded leaf of plates, [3] volvelles: ill.; 24 cm. Several errors in foliation. Includes index. Adams, G 166.

IL SAGGIATORE
Nel quale
Con bilancia esquisita e giusta
si ponderano le cose contenute
nella
LIBRA ASTRONOMICA E FILOSOFICA
DI LOTARIO SARSI SIGENSANO
Scritto in forma di lettera
All'Ill.mo et Reuer.mo Mons.re D.
VIRGINIO CESARINI
Acc.o Linceo M.o di Camera di N.S.
Dal Sig.re
GALILEO GALILEI
Acc.o Linceo Nobile Fiorentino
Filosofo e Matematico Primario
del
Ser.mo Gran Duca di Toscana.
FILOSOFIA NATVRALE
MATEMATICA
IN ROMA MDCXXIII
Appresso Giacomo Mascardi
F. Villamoena Fecit.

Galilei, *Il saggiatore*, 1623

780. GALOIS, EVARISTE, 1811-1832. *Manuscrits de Évariste Galois. Publiés par Jules Tannery.*
Paris: Gauthier-Villars, 1908. [4], 67, [3] p. 25 cm. "Extrait du *Bulletin des Sciences Mathématiques,* 2e série, t. XXX et XXXI; 1906-1907." Advertisements on p. [4] of wrapper.
Provenance: H. v. d. Kamp (inkstamp).

781. GALTON, FRANCIS, SIR, 1822-1911. *Finger prints, by Francis Galton....*
London and New York: Macmillan and Co., 1892. xvi, 216 p. 23 illus. on 15 pl. (1 col. double pl.) 23 cm. Includes index.

782. GALTON, FRANCIS, SIR, 1822-1911. *Hereditary genius: an inquiry into its laws and consequences. By Francis Galton.*
London: Macmillan, 1869. vi, [2], 390 p. [2] folded leaves of plates: ill.; 23 cm. Errata: on p. [2]. Advertisements: [2] p. following text. Includes index.
Provenance: Herbert McLean Evans (bookplate). Binder: Burn & Co.

783. GALVANI, LUIGI, 1737-1798. *Aloysii Galvani De viribus electricitatis in motu musculari commentarius.*
Bononiae: Ex Typographia Instituti Scientiarum, 1791. p. 363-418, [4] folded leaves of plates : ill. ; 30 cm. In: *De Bononiensi scientiarum et artium instituto atque academia commentarii,* tomus septimus. First publication of Galvani's theory of animal magnetism; also published separately. The plates signed: J. Zambelli fecit. Horblit, H. D. *Grolier 100 science books,* 37a.

784. GARCET, H. (HENRI), 1815-1871. *Leçons nouvelles de cosmographie / rédigées conformément au nouveau plan d'études par H. Garcet ... Sixième édition, revue et corrigée.*
Paris: Ancienne Maison Dezobry, E. Magdeleine et Cie: Charles Delagrave et Cie ..., 1869. [4], [VII]-VIII, 440 p., III leaves of plates (2 folded): ill., charts; 23 cm. "Description du cosmographe inventé et construit par M. Ouvière": p. [433]-434.
Provenance: publisher's presentation copy (inkstamp).

785. GÄRTNER, CARL FRIEDRICH VON, 1772-1850. *Versuche und Beobachtungen über die Befruchtungs-organe der vollkommeneren Gewächse und über die natürliche und künstliche Befruchtung durch den eigenen Pollen, von Carl Friedrich Gärtner.*
Stuttgart: E. Schweizerbart, 1844. x, [2], 644 p. 23 cm. His *Beiträge zur Kenntniss der Befruchtung der vollkommeneren Gewächse,* von Carl Friedrich Gärtner ... Theil. Includes indexes. Bibliography: p. 601-620.
Provenance: Emil Schüz (bookplate); Herbert McLean Evans (bookplate).

786. GASSENDI, PIERRE, 1592-1655. *Abregé de la philosophie de Mr Gassendi: seconde partie ... / par F. Bernier....*
À Paris: Chez Estienne Michallet ... , 1675. [6], 280 p.: ill.; 23 cm. Running title: Des choses celestes. (From t. p.): L'institution astronomique – Les systêmes de Ptolomée, de Copernic, & de Tycho-Brahé – Plusieurs questions qui regardent la nature, & les proprietez des cieux & des astres – Et la refutation del'astrologie judiciaire.
Provenance: H. Simon (inscription).

787. GASSENDI, PIERRE, 1592-1655. *Institutio astronomica: iuxta hypotheseis tam veterum, quam Copernici, et Tychonis / dictata à Petro Gassendo ... ; eiusdem Oratio inauguralis iteratò edita.*
Parisiis: Apud Ludouicum de Heuqueuille ..., 1647. [14], 222, 3-32 p.: ill.; 23 cm. Errata: on p. [13]. Index calls for p. 223 instead of p. 3 as the beginning of the "Oratio inauguralis." Houzeau & Lancaster. *Astronomie.* (1964 ed.), 9222.

788. GASSENDI, PIERRE, 1592-1655. *Tychonis Brahei, equitis Dani., astronomorum coryphæi, vita. Authore Petro Gassendo ... Accessit Nicolai Copernici, Georgii Peurbachii, & Joannis Regiomontani, astronomorum celebrium, vita. Editie secunda auctior & correctior.*
Hagæ Comitvm: ex typographia Adriani Vlacq, 1655. lx, 373, [11] p. ports., diagrs. 21 cm. Prefixed: frontispiece (portrait of Brahe) by I. v. Meurs cf. Rahir, *Les Elzevier,* no. 2077. "De vita, et morte dn. Tychonis Brahei ... oratio d. Johan. Jessenii"; p. 224-235. Includes indexes.
With additional t. p. of 1654 ed.

789. GATLAND, KENNETH WILLIAM, 1924- . *The inhabited universe; an inquiry staged on*

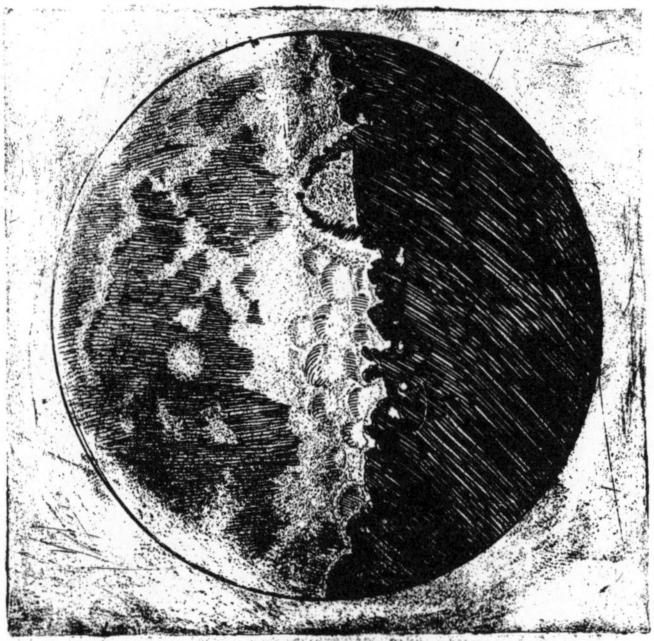

Galilei, *Sidereus nuncius*, 1610

the frontiers of knowledge by Kenneth W. Gatland, and Derek D. Dempster. Illustrated with photographs and drawings by John W. Wood.
London: A. Wingate, 1957. 182 p. illus. 23 cm. Bibliography: p. [173]-178. Includes index.

790. GAUBIUS, JOHANNES, fl. 1696-ca. 1720. *Johannis Gaubii Epistola problematica prima [-tertia]: ad virum clarissimum Fredericum Ruyschium....*
Amstelædami: Apud Johannem Walters, 1696. 31 [i.e. 32] p., 3 leaves of plates (1 folded): ill.; 24 cm. Error in pagination: p. 32 misnumbered as 31.
Plate 1 misbound in Epistola anatomica, problematica quinta / authore Gerardo Frentz. Amstelædami: Apud JohannemWalters, 1696. With: *Observationum anatomico-chirurgicarum centuria / Frederici Ruyschii.* Amstelædami: Apud Henricum & Viduam Theodori Boom, 1691.

791. GAUSS, CARL FRIEDRICH, 1777-1855. *Disquisitiones arithmeticæ / auctore D. Carolo Friderico Gauss.*
Lipsiae: Apud Gerh. Fleischer, 1801. xviii, 668, [10] p.: tables; 20 cm. Errata: p. [7-10]. Horblit, H. D. *Grolier 100 science books,* 38.
K3, 2F7, 2T6 are cancels. Provenance: Valpergadi Masino e di Caluso (bookplate), Herbert McLean Evans (bookplate).

792. GAUSS, CARL FRIEDRICH, 1777-1855. *Theoria motus corporum cœlestium in sectionibus conicis solem ambientium. Auctore Carolo Friderico Gauss.*
Hamburgi: Sumtibus F. Perthes et I. H. Besser, 1809. xi, [1], 20 p., 1 l, 227, [1] p. 1 ill. 30 cm. Errata: p. [228].
Tables (20 p.) and plate bound after text.

793. GAY-LUSSAC, JOSEPH LOUIS, 1778-1850. *Recherches physico-chimiques, faites sur la pile; sur la préparation chimique et les propriétés du potassium et du sodium; sur la décomposition de l'acide boracique; sur les acides fluorique, muriatique et muriatique oxigéné; sur l'action chimique de la lumière; sur l'analyse végétale et animale, etc., par mm. Gay-Lussac et Thénard ... Avec six planches en taille-douce....*
Paris: Deterville, 1811. 2 v. 6 fold. pl., tables. 21 cm. Advertisements on lower wrappers. Provenance: Herbert McLean Evans (bookplate).

794. GEBER, 13th cent. *Gebri Arabis Chimia; sive, Traditio summæ perfectionis et investigatio magisterii innumeris locis emendata, à Caspare Hornio ... Accessit ejusdem Medulla alchimiæ Gebricæ. Omnia edita à Georgio Hornio.*
[Lugduni Batavorum: Apud A. Doude, 1668]. 10 p.l., 179 [i.e. 279] p. 14 cm. Added t. p., engr. has imprint. Pages 241-279 incorrectly numbered. Ferguson, J. *Bib. chemica.* p. 299. Duveen, D. I. *Alchemica et chemica,* p. 239.
Provenance: [2] leaves of ms. notes detailing contents, said to be in the hand of Isaac Newton; "Philosophemur" (armorial bookplate); Carol[u]s Huggins (armorial bookplate).

795. GEIKIE, JAMES, 1839-1915. *Address to the Geological Section of the British Association / by James Geikie....*
London: Printed by Spottiswoode and Co., ..., [1889?]. 14 p.; 22 cm. "An outline ... of the results obtained ... by continental workers in the domain of glacial geology." – p. [1]. Caption title. At head of title: Newcastle-upon-Tyne, 1889. Includes bibliographical references.

796. GEMMA, FRISIUS, 1508-1555. *De principijs astronomiæ & cosmographie: de(que) vsu globi ab eodem editi. Item de orbis diuisione & insulis, rebus[que] nuper inuentis / Gemma Phrysius.*
Antuerpiæ: Excudebat Ioannes Richard, 1544. [184] p.: ill.; 14 cm. Colophon: Antuerpiæ: typis excudebat Ioannes Grauius, 1544. Statement of responsibility transposed. Signatures: A-L^{8}M^4.
Bound in ms. fragment.

797. GEOFFROY SAINT-HILAIRE, ETIENNE, 1772-1844. *Principes de philosophie zoologiques: discutés en mars 1830, au sein de l'Académie Royale des Sciences / par M. Geoffroy Saint-Hilaire.*
Paris: Pichon et Didier, libraires ... ; Rousseau, libraire ..., 1830. [4], 226, [1] p.; 22 cm. Errata on last p. Includes bibliographical references.
Provenance: Herbert McLean Evans (bookplate).

Specchio Settentrionale con l'Horizonte alla latitudine di Venetia.

Gallucci, *Della fabrica et vso di diversi stromenti di astronomia et cosmografia*, 1597

Dell'vſo dell'Aſtrolabio
Faccia del Planisferio .

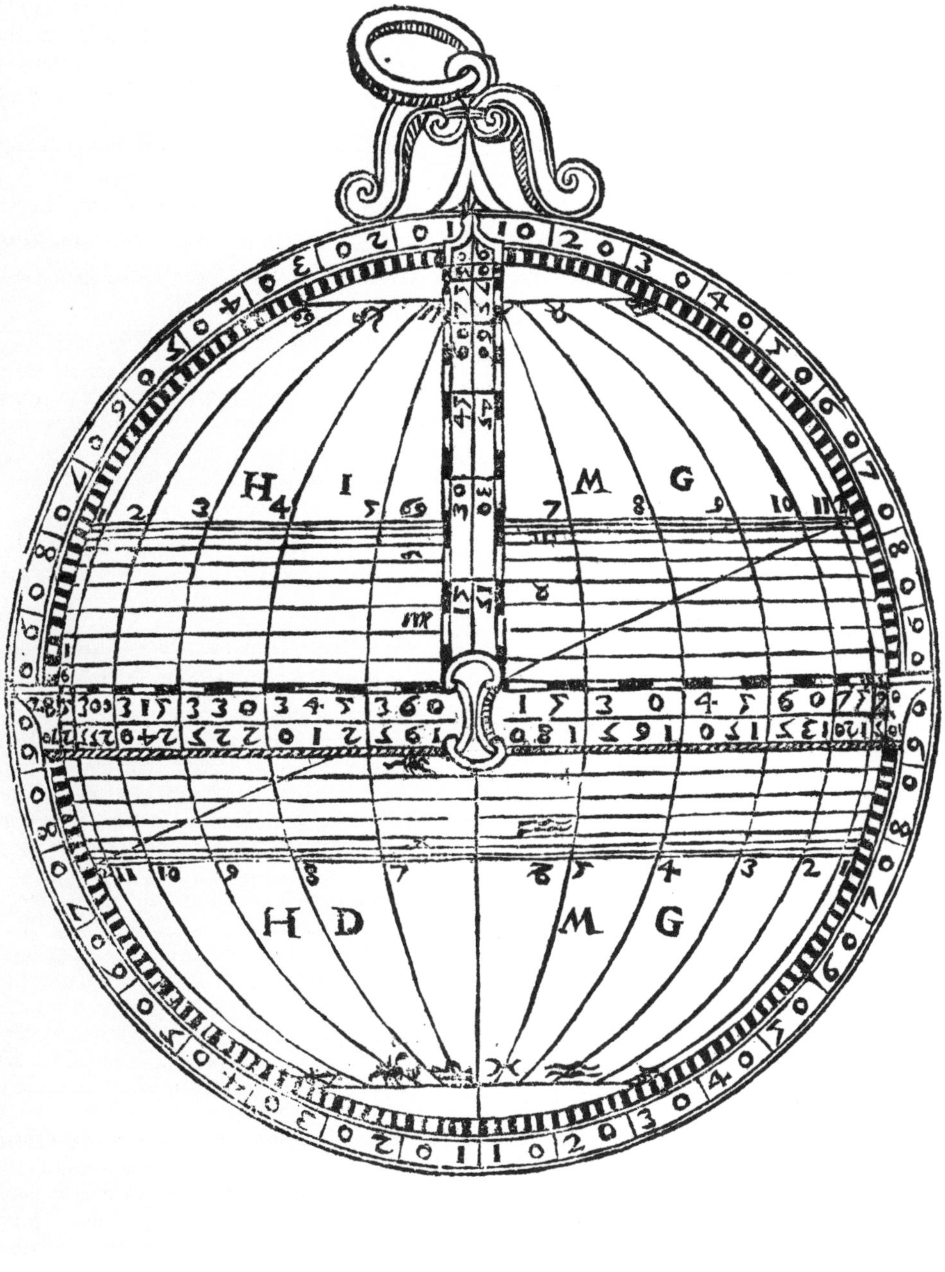

Gallucci, *Della fabrica et vso di diversi stromenti di astronomia et cosmografia*, 1597

798. GERARD, JOHN, 1545-1612. *The Herball Or Generall Historie of Plantes. Gathered by John Gerarde.*

Imprinted at London: By Iohn Norton, 1597. 10 p.l., 1392, [71] p. illus., port. 34 cm. Colophon: Imprinted at London by Edm. Bollifant, for Bonham and Iohn Norton, M.D.XCVII. Title, within elaborate engraved border, coat of arms of Lord Burghley on verso. Full page portrait of author facing p. 1, dated 1598. Includes indexes. *STC* 111750. Osler, W. *Bib. Osleriana*, 2722.

Provenance: Dalyell[?] (signature). T. p. repaired.

799. GERARD, JOHN, 1545-1612. *The herball, or General historie of plantes. Gathered by John Gerarde. Very much enlarged and amended by Thomas Johnson.*

London: Printed by A. Islip, J. Norton and R. Whitakers, 1636. 19 p. l., 1630, [46] p. illus. 36 cm. Engr. t.-p. "2nd edition of revised Gerard," first pub. 1633. "A catalogue of the British [i. e. Welsh] names of plants, sent me by Master Robert Dauyes of Guissaney in Flintshire": p. [31]-[32] at end. Includes indexes.

Imperfect: p. [35-38] at the end missing.

800. GERDY, DR. (PIERRE NICOLAS), 1797-1856. *Traité des bandages et appareils de pansement / par P. N. Gerdy.*

Paris : Chez Crevot, 1826. xvi, 646 p. : ill. ; 21 cm. + 1 atlas (xx leaves of plates ; 28 cm.) "Avec un atlas de XX planches, in-4°" – upper cover. Errata: p. [645]-646. Includes index.

801. GERHARDT, CH., 1816-1856. *Introduction a l'étude de la chimie: par le systême unitaire / par M. Charles Gerhardt ...*

Paris: Chamerot ... , 1848. XIX, [1], 338 p., [1] folded leaf of plates: ill.; 18 cm. Errata: on p. XIX.

Binder: P. Bonvoisin.

802. GERMANY. REICHSGESUNDHEITSAMT. *Mittheilungen aus dem Kaiserlichen Gesundheitsamte. Herausgegeben von Dr. Struck....*

Berlin: Norddeutschen Buchdruckerei und Verlagsanstalt, 1881-1884. 2 v. ill., plates (part col.), tables. 32 cm. Vol. 2 published by August Hirschwald. Includes bibliographical references. Advertisements on p. [4] of cover, v. 2. 1. Bd. Zur Untersuchung von pathogenen Organismen, von Regierungsrath Dr. Robert Koch. Zur Aetiologie des Milzbrandes, von demselben ... Über Desinfection, von ... Dr. Robert Koch ... Untersuchungen über die Desinfection mit heisser Luft, von Dr. Robert Koch und Dr. Gustav Wolffhügel. Versuche über die Verwerthbarkeit heisser Wasserdämpfe zu Desinfectionszwecken, von Dr. Robert Koch, Dr. Gaffky und Dr. Löffler ... – 2. Bd. Die Aetiologie der Tuberkulose, von Dr. R. Koch ... Experimentelle Studien über die künstliche Abschwächung der Milzbrandbacillen und Milzbrandinfection durch Fütterung, von Dr. R.Koch, Dr. Gaffky und Dr. Löffler ... Horblit, H. D. *Grolier 100 science books*, 60.

Provenance: Herbert McLean Evans (bookplate).

803. GESELLSCHAFT DEUTSCHER NATURFORSCHER UND ÄRZTE. *Verhandlungen der Gesellschaft Deutscher Naturforscher und Ärzte.*

Berlin [etc.] v. ill. 21-31 cm. Title varies. Beginning with 1890 the proceedings of each meeting are in two parts; 1893-1913, the 2d part is in two sections (hälfte). Continued in *Die Naturwissenschaften.*

Library has: [1908]. Vol. for 1908: Provenance: Biblioth. Amstelaed. (inkstamp).

804. GESNER, KONRAD, 1516-1565. *De omni rerum fossilium genere, gemmis, lapidibus, metallis, et huiusmodi, libri aliquot, plerique nunc primum editi. Operâ Conradi Gesneri: quorum catalogum sequens folium continet.*

Tiguri: Excudebat Iacobus Gesnerus, 1565. 8 v. in 1. illus. 18 cm. Vols. 2-7 have special t.-p. Kentmann, Johann. Nomenclaturæ rerum fossilium quæ in Misnia præcipue, & in aliis quoque regionibus inueniuntur. – Kentmann, Johannes. Calculorum qui in corpore ac membris hominum innascuntur genera XII. – Fabricius, Georgius. De metallicis rebus ac nominibus observationes variæ... ex schedis Georgii Fabricii: quæ Georgius Agricola præterijt. – Goebel, Severin. De succino, libri duo. – Cordus, Valerius. Valerii Cordi ... De halosantho seu spermate ceti vulgo dicto, liber, nunc primum lucem æditus. – Epiphanus, Saint, bp. of Constantia in Cyprus. Sancti patris Epiphanii episcopi Cypri ad Diodorum Tyri episcopum, de XII. gemmis quæ erant in veste Aaronis, liber græcus, & e regione latinus, Iola Hierotarantiano interprete: cum corallario Conradi Gesneri. – La Rue, François. De gemmis aliquot, lis praesertim quarum Diuus Ioannes apostolus in sua Apocalypsi meminit. – Gesner, Konrad. De rerum fossilium, lapidum et gemmarum ... figuris ... liber. Osler, W. *Bib. Osleriana* 646.

Provenance: Herbert McLean Evans (bookplate).

805. GIBBON, EDWARD, 1737-1794. *The history of the decline and fall of the Roman Empire / by Edward Gibbon, esq. A new edition.*

London: Printed for T. Cadell and W. Davis [and 34 others], 1813. 12 v.: ill., maps, port.; 22 cm. "Some account of the life and writings of Edward Gibbon, esq.": v. 1, p. iii-xxxviii. Port. engraved by W. Evans after Sir Joshua Reynolds. Includes bibliographical references and index.

Provenance: Muriel Pringle (bookplate).

806. GIBBS, J. WILLARD (JOSIAH WILLARD), 1839-1903. [Collection of articles on thermodynamics and equilibrium from the *Transactions of the Connecticut Academy of Arts and Sciences* / by J. Willard Gibbs.]

[1873-1878] 3 pieces: ill.; 24 cm. In case. Caption titles. Horblit, H. D. *Grolier 100 science books*, 40. Includes bibliographical references. (1) Graphical methods in the thermodynamics of fluids (1873) – (2) A method of geometrical representation of the thermodynamic properties of substances by means of surfaces (1873) – (3) On the equilibrium of heterogenous substances (1876 & 1878).

In maroon leather case. Provenance: (evidence on case) Yale Medical Library. Historical Library (bookplate); John Farquhar Fulton (book label); Herbert McLean Evans (bookplate).

807. GIBBS, J. WILLARD (JOSIAH WILLARD), 1839-1903. *The early work of Willard Gibbs in applied mechanics, comprising the text of his hitherto unpublished Ph. D. thesis and accounts of his mechanical inventions; assembled by Lynde Phelps Wheeler, Everett Oyler Waters & Samuel William Dudley.*

New York, H. Schuman [c1947]. [3] l., v-vii, 78 p. illus., port., diagrs., facsim. 25 cm. *Publication* (Yale Medical Library. Historical Library) ; no. 17. "Issued in connection with the centennial anniversary of the Sheffield Scientific School, Yale University, 1847-1947" – leaf [2]. Introduction, by L. P. Wheeler. – On the form of the teeth of wheels in spur gearing, by Willard Gibbs. – Commentary upon the Gibbs monograph "On the form of the teeth of wheels in spur gearing," by E. O. Waters. – An improved railway car brake, by S. W. Dudley. – The Gibbs governor for steam engines, by L. P. Wheeler.

808. GIBBS, J. WILLARD (JOSIAH WILLARD), 1839-1903. *Elementary principles in statistical mechanics, developed with especial reference to the rational foundation of thermodynamics, by J. Willard Gibbs.*

New York: C. Scribner's Sons, 1902. xviii, 207 p. 23 cm. Yale Bicentennial Publications.

Provenance: presentation copy from the author to W. F. Magie (inscription).

809. GIBBS, J. WILLARD (JOSIAH WILLARD), 1839-1903. *The scientific papers of J. Willard Gibbs.*

London, New York, Bombay: Longmans, Green and Co., 1906. 2 v. front. (port.) diagrs. 26 cm. Edited by H. A. Bumstead and R. G. Van Name. Reprint of papers previously published in scientific journals and transactions with a small amount of hitherto unpublished matter. cf. Pref. "Josiah Willard Gibbs": v. 1, p. [xiii]-xxvii. 1948 edition published under title: *The collected works of J. Willard Gibbs*. Bibliography: v. 1, p. xxvii-xxviii. Thermodynamics. – Dynamics. Vector analysis and multiple algebra. Electromagnetic theory of light, etc.

Provenance: John Barter (signature).

810. GIBBS, J. WILLARD (JOSIAH WILLARD), 1839-1903. *Thermodynamische Studien von J. Willard Gibbs unter Mitwirkung des Verfassers aus dem englischen übersetzt von W. Ostwald.*

Leipzig: W. Engelmann, 1892. xiv, [2], 409 p. 24 cm. Druckfehler: p. [xv].

Provenance: Herbert McLean Evans (bookplate).

811. GIBBS, J. WILLARD (JOSIAH WILLARD), 1839-1903. *Vector analysis; a text-book for the use of students of mathematics and physics, founded upon the lectures of J. Willard Gibbs ... by Edwin Bidwell Wilson....*

New York: C. Scribner's Sons; [etc., etc.], 1901. xviii p., 1 l., 436 p. 23 cm. Yale Bicentennial Publications.

Provenance: William Howell Williams (bookplate).

812. GIBERNE, AGNES, 1845-1939. *Among the stars or wonderful things in the sky / by Agnes Giberne....*

New York: American Tract Society, 1884. x, 311 p., [5] leaves of plates: ill.; 19 cm. Preface dated 1884.

813. GIBERNE, AGNES, 1845-1939. *The starry skies: or, First lessons on the sun, moon and stars. By Agnes Giberne....*

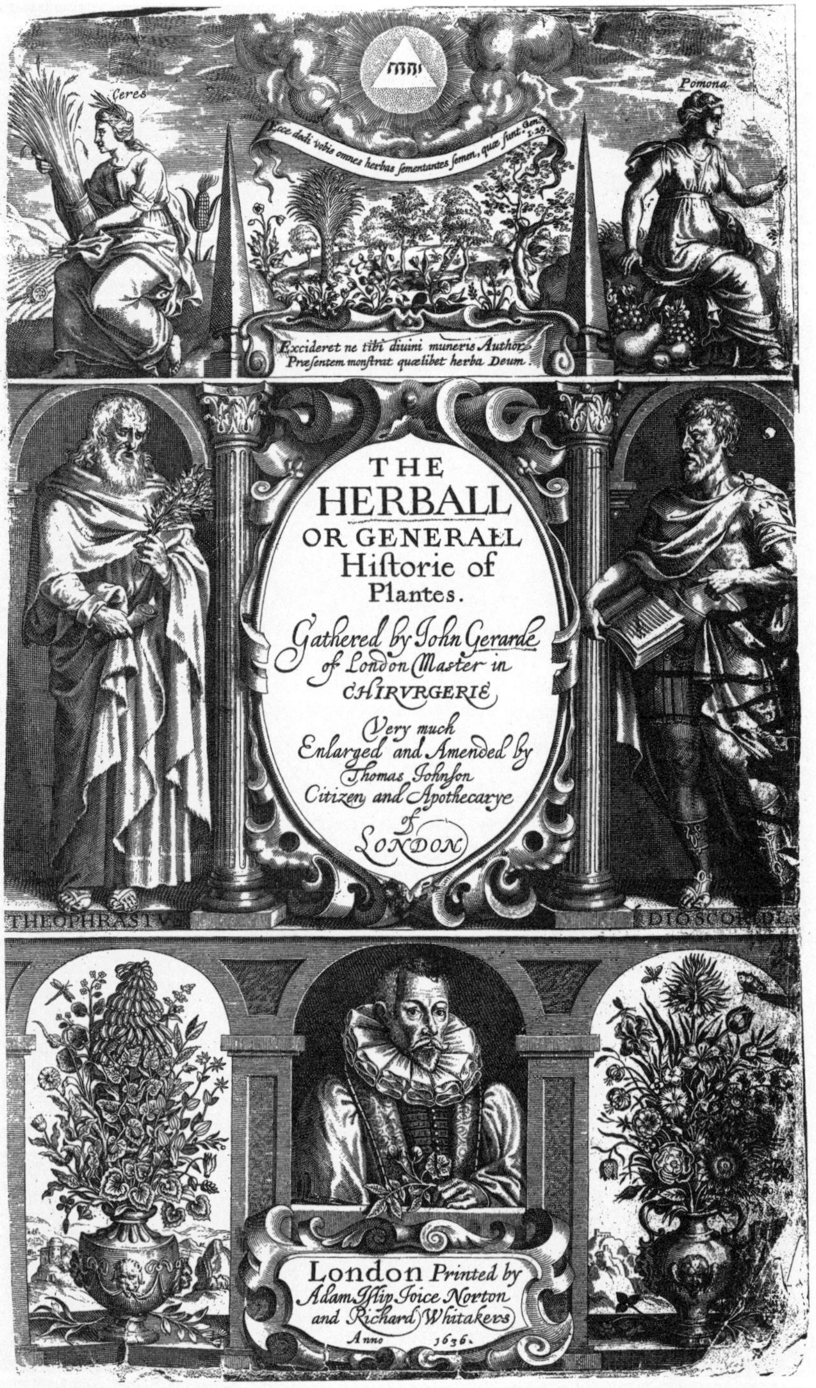

Gerard, *Herball*, 1636

New York: American Tract Society, [c. 1894]. 234 p. front., plates. 19 cm.

Advertisements: [5] p. at end.

814. GIBERNE, AGNES, 1845-1939. *Sun, moon, and stars. Astronomy for beginners. By Agnes Giberne ... With a preface by the Rev. C. Pritchard ... New and rev. ed.*

New York: American Tract Society, [c. 1893]. 334 p. front., plates. 20 cm.

Provenance: Kathryn Cavell (bookplate); Jane DeVore (signature).

815. GIBERNE, AGNES, 1845-1939. *Sun, moon, and stars: astronomy for beginners / by Agnes Giberne; with a preface by C. Pritchard. Twenty-sixth thousand, with additions.*

London: Seeley, 1903. [2], xvi, 329 p., [16] leaves of plates: ill. (some col.); 20 cm. "New and enlarged edition" – P. [v]. Includes index.

Advertisements: verso half-title, [2] p. at end. Provenance: Kathleen N. Scott (inscription).

816. GIBSON, CHARLES R. (CHARLES ROBERT), 1870-1931. *The stars and their mysteries; an interestingly written account of the wonders of astronomy, told in simple language, by Charles R. Gibson, with 19 illustrations & diagrams.*

Philadelphia: J. B. Lippincott Company; Seeley, Service & Co. Ltd., 1916. 247, [1] p. col. front., plates, diagrs. 20 cm. Science for children. Includes index.

817. GIBSON, FRANK M. (FRANK MARKEY), b. 1857. *The amateur telescopist's handbook, by Frank M. Gibson....*

New York: Longmans, Green, and Co., 1894. xi p., 1 l., 163 p. fold. front., diagrs. 19 cm.

Advertisements: [5] p. at end.

818. GILBERT, WILLIAM, 1540-1603. *Guilielmi Gilberti Colcestrensis, medici Londinensis, De magnete, magneticisque corporibus, et de magno magnete tellure: physiologia noua, plurimis & argumentis, & experimentis demonstrata.*

Londini: Excudebat Petrus Short ..., MDC. [1600]. [16], 240 p., [1] folded leaf of plates: ill.; 30 cm. Title vignette; coat of arms of William Gilbert on verso of t. p.; decorated borders and initials throughout text. "Ad grauissimum doctissimumque virum D. Guilielmum Gilbertum ... de magneticis hisce libris, Edwardi VVrighti Parainesis enkomiasike": p. [6]-[10] of 1st group. Errata on p. 240. STC, 11883. Horblit, H. D. *Grolier 100 science books*, 41. Osler, W. *Bib. Osleriana*, 675.

Ms. notes on endpapers. Provenance: Herbert McLean Evans (bookplate).

819. GILLET, J. A. (JOSEPH ANTHONY), 1837-1908. *Astronomy for the use of schools and academies / by J. A. Gillet ... and W. J. Rolfe....*

New York and Chicago: Potter, Ainsworth, & Co., 1884. ix, [1], 405 p., [1], V leaves of plates: ill. (some col.); 20 cm. Issued also under title: *The heavens above*. On cover: New works on physics. Includes index.

Provenance: W. L. Miller (booklabel).

820. GILLET, J. A. (JOSEPH ANTHONY), 1837-1908. *First book in astronomy: for the use of schools and academies / by, J. A. Gillet ... and W. J. Rolfe....*

New York; Cincinnati; Chicago: American Book Company, [c. 1882]. vi, 214 p.: ill., maps; 20 cm. Stamped on cover: New works on physics. Includes index.

821. GLAUBER, JOHANN RUDOLF, 1604-1670. *De auri tinctura sive auri potabili vero. Quid sit & quommodo [sic] differat ab auro potabili falso & sophistico quomodo spaygrice Præperandum & quomodo in medicinà usurpandum. Per Joannem Rudolphum Glauberum.*

Amsterodami: Prostant apud J. Janssonium, 1651. 22 p. 16 cm. First published in German, cf. Poggendorff, J. C. *Biographisch literarisches Handwörterbuch.* Leipzig: Barth, 1863, 1. Bd. column 910.

With the author's *Operis mineralis pars prima[-tertia].* Amsterodami: prostant apud Joannem Janssonium, 1651-1652. Provenance: Bibliothèque de Cisteaux (lettering); Herbert McLean Evans (bookplate).

822. GLAUBER, JOHANN RUDOLF, 1604-1670. *Furni novi philosophici, sive Descriptio artis destillatoriæ novæ: nec non spirituum, oleorum, florum, aliorumque medicamentorum illius beneficio, facillimâ quâdam & peculiari viâ è vegetalibus, animalibus & mineralibus,*

conficiendorum & quidem magno cum lucro; agens quoque de illorum usu tâm chymico quàm medico / edita & publicata in gratiam veritatis studiosorum, per Johannem Rudolphum Glauberum.

Amsterodami: Prostant apud Johannem Janssonium, 1651. 67, [5], 145, [4], 55, [1], 83, [5], 54, [2], 72 p., [3] folded leaves of plates: ill.; 16 cm. Parts 2-6 have special title pages only; sixth part has title: Annotationes in appendicem quintæ partis Fornacum philosophicarum ... Vignettes on each t. p. decorated initials and borders throughout text. Ferguson, J. *Bib. chemica*, v. 1, p. 323-324. Includes indexes.

With the author's *Operis mineralis pars prima[-tertia]*. Amsterodami: prostant apud Joannem Janssonium, 1651-1652. Provenance: Bibliothèque de Cisteaux (giltstamped on cover); Herbert McLean Evans (bookplate).

823. GLAUBER, JOHANN RUDOLF, 1604-1670. *Miraculum mundi, sive Plena perfecta que descriptio admirabilis naturæ, ac proprietatis potentissimí subiecti, ab antiquis menstruum universale sive mercurius philosophorum dicti ... / in gratiam secretæ naturæ scrutatorum editum, à Johanne Rudolpho Glaubero, at que ex Germanico Latinum factum.*

Impressum Amsterodami: Apud Joannem Janssonium, 1653. 87 p.; 17 cm. Errors in pagination: p. 77 misnumbered as 57.

With the author's *Operis mineralis pars prima[-tertia]*. Amsterodami: prostant apud Joannem Janssonium, 1651-1652. Provenance: Bibliothèque de Cisteaux (lettering), Herbert McLean Evans (bookplate).

824. GLAUBER, JOHANN RUDOLF, 1604-1670. *Operis mineralis pars prima[-tertia] Inventa & publicata in gratiam studiosorum artis chymicæ per Johannem Rudolphum Glauberum.*

Amsterodami: Prostant apud J. Janssonium, 1651-1652. 3 v. 16 cm. Translation from German of *Operis mineralis*. Pars 1. Ubi docetur separatio auri è filicibus, arena, argillâ, aliisque fossilibus per salis spiritum, quae aliàs eliquari nequeunt. Item Panacea. – Pars 2. De ortu & origine omnium metallorum & mineralium, quo scilicet pacto illa per astra producantur ex aqua & terra corpus sibi suscipiant & multiplici forma formentur. – Pars 3. In qua titulo commentarii in libellum Paracelsi Coelum philosophorum. Ferguson, J. *Bib. chemica*, v. 1, p. 326.

Bound in 1 v. With: the author's *De auritinctura*. Amsterodami: prostant apud Joannem Janssonium, 1651; *Furni novi philosophici*. Amsterodami: prostant apud Joannem Janssonium, 1651; *Miraculum mundi*. Impressum Amsterodami: apud Joannem Janssonium, 1653; *Pharmacopoea spagyrica*. Impressum Amsterodami: apud Joannem Janssonium, 1654. Provenance: Bibliothèque de Cisteaux (lettering); Herbert McLean Evans (bookplate).

825. GLAUBER, JOHANN RUDOLF, 1604-1670. *Pharmacopoea spagyrica, sive Exacta descriptio, quâ ratione ex vegetabilibus, animalibus & mineralibus, modo haud usitato faciliorique, utilia, efficacia, & penetrantia medicamenta fieri præpararique possint... In usum afflictissimi generis humani in lucem prolata, per Joannem Rudolphum Glauberum.*

Impressum Amsterodami: Apud. J. Janssonium, 1654-1657. 3 v. in 1. 16 cm. Title varies. Translated from the German.

With: the author's *Operis mineralis pars prima[-tertia]*. Amsterodami: prostant apud Joannem Janssonium, 1651-1652. Provenance: Bibliothèque de Cisteaux (lettering); Herbert McLean Evans (bookplate).

826. GLAVNAIA ASTRONOMICHESKAIA OBSERVATORIIA (SOVIET UNION). *Librorum in bibliotheca Speculæ pulcovensis anno 1858 exeunte contentorum catalogus systematicus / edendum curavit et præfatus est Otto Struve.*

Petropoli: Eggers, 1860-1880. 2 v.; 28 cm. Vol. 2 has title: Librorum in bibliotheca Speculæ pulcovensis contentorum catalogus systematicus. Pars secunda ab Eduardo Lindemanno elaborata. Edendum curavit et præfatus est Otto Struve. On verso of t. p.: Typis Academiæ Imperialis Scientiarum Petropolitanæ. Includes indexes. Errata: v. 1, p. 967-970.

Provenance: [v. 1] Herschel Library, Collingwood (inkstamp).

827. GLAVNAIA ASTRONOMICHESKAIA OBSERVATORIIA (SOVIET UNION). *Librorum in bibliotheca Speculæ Pulcovensis contentorum catalogus systematicus: ex opere descriptionis Speculæ seorsim excudi curavit, indice alphabetico et præfatione / auxit F. G. W. Struve.*

Petropoli: Typis Academiæ Scientiarum, 1845. XLVIII, 437, [1] p.; 22 cm. Includes index.

828. Gleichen-Russwurm, Wilhelm Friedrich, Freiherr von, 1717-1783. *Das Neueste aus dem Reiche der Pflanzen, oder Mikroskopische Untersuchungen und Beobachtungen der geheimen Zeugungstheile der Pflanzen in ihren Blüten, und der in denselben befindlichen Insekten; nebst einigen Versuchen von dem Keim, und einem Anhang vermischter Beobachtungen, beschrieben, und mit Farben nach der Natur vorgestellt von Wilhelm Friedrich Freiherrn von Gleichen, genannt Russworm....*
p. l., 8, [4], 72, 40, [8], 26 p. col. plates. 42 cm. Errata: on last p. Plates signed: W. F. v. G. R. obs. et pinx., and J. C. Keller exc. Includes bibliographical references.

829. Gley, E. (Eugène), 1857-1930. *The internal secretions: their physiology and application to pathology, by E. Gley ... tr. from the French and ed. by Maurice Fishberg ... Authorized translation.*
New York: P. B. Hoeber, 1917. 241 p. 20 cm. Translation of *Les sécrétions internes.* 12 p. advertisements following text. Includes index.
Provenance: Ernest S. du Bray (inkstamp and inscription).

830. Glover, Richard, 1712-1785. *London: or, The progress of commerce. A poem. By Mr. Glover.*
London: Printed for T. Cooper, 1739. 1 p. l., 30 p. 26 cm. Foxon G198. Floral paper wrappers.
With: *Experiments and observations on electricity* / by Mr. Benjamin Franklin. London: printed and sold by E. Cave ..., 1751-1753. Provenance: L'Ab. Boyer (bookplate); Domus massiliensis (bookplate).

831. Goad, J. (John), 1616-1689. *Astro-meteorologica; or, Aphorisms and discourses of the bodies celestial, their natures and influences. Discovered from the variety of the alterations of the air, temperate, or intemperate ... and other secrets of nature. Collected from the observation at leisure times, of above thirty years; by J. Goad....*
London: Printed by J. Rawlins for O. Blagrave, 1686. 4 p. l., 509 [i.e. 511], [5] p. diagr. 30 cm. Errata: p. 509 [i.e. 511]. Advertisements: [5] p. at end. Errors in pagination; p. 511 misnumbered as 509. Wing G897. *Justin Wright collection,* no. 69.

832. Goddard, Robert Hutchings, 1882-1945. *Liquid-propellant rocket development [with 11 plates] by Robert H.Goddard ...*
City of Washington: The Smithsonian Institution, 1936. 1 p. l., 10 p. 11 pl. on 6 l., diagr. 25 cm. Smithsonian miscellaneous collections; v. 95, no. 3. Publication 3381.
Provenance: Forbes Library (inkstamp).

833. Goddard, Robert Hutchings, 1882-1945. *Rocket development; liquid-fuel rocket research, 1929-1941. Ed. By Esther C. Goddard and G. Edward Pendray.*
New York: Prentice-Hall, 1948. xx, 291 p. illus., ports. 24 cm.

834. Godfray, Hugh. *A treatise on astronomy: for the use of colleges and schools / by Hugh Godfray ... Third edition.*
London: Macmillan and Co., 1880. xvi, 320 p., [2] p. of plates: ill.; 23 cm. Includes bibliographical references.
Provenance: James D. Graham (book label & signature); ms. marginalia.

835. Gölicke, Andreas Ottomar, 1670?-1744? *Epistola anatomica, problematica nona ... Ad ... Fredericum Ruyschium De cursu arteriarum per piam matrem cerebrum involventem, de tertia cerebri meninge, de arteriis membranarum cavitates ossis frontis supranarium radices ... / authore Andrea Ottomaro Goelicke....*
Amstelædami: Apud Joannem Wolters, 1679 [i. e. 1697]. 13, [1] p., [1] leaf of plates: illus.; 22 cm. "Frederici Ruyschii responsio ...": p. [7]-13.
With: *Observationum anatomico-chirurgicarum centuria / Frederic Ruyschii.* Amstelodami: Apud Henricum & Viduam Theodori Boom, 1691.

836. Gompertz, Benjamin, 1779-1865. *The principles and application of imaginary quantities ... / by Benjamin Gompertz.*
London: Published for the author, by Davis and Dickson, 1817-1818. 2 v. in 1: ill.; 26 cm. Vol. 1 has subtitle: Book I; To which are added some observations

on porisms; being the first of a series of original tracts on various parts of the mathematics – v. 2: Book II; Derived from a particular case of functional projections: being the second of a series of original tracts on various parts of the mathematics. Errata for v. 1 on p. 35 (v. 1) and p. [iv] (v. 2); errata for v. 2: p.44 (v. 2).

837. Goodwin, Harold L. (Harold Leland), 1914- . *The real book about stars; illustrated by Paul Wenck.*

Garden City, N.Y.: Garden City Books, by arrangement with F. Watts, New York, 1951. 189 p. illus. 21 cm. Real Books. Bibliography: p. 181-183. Includes index.

838. Gore, J. Ellard (John Ellard), 1845-1910. *Astronomical curiosities: facts and fallacies / by J. Ellard Gore.*

London: Chatto & Windus, 1909. 370 p.: diagrs.; 20 cm. Includes bibliographical references and indexes.

839. Gore, J. Ellard (John Ellard), 1845-1910. *Astronomical essays historical and descriptive, by J. Ellard Gore ... With 6 illustrations.*

London: Chatto & Windus, 1907. ix, 342 p., 1 l. 6 pl. 20 cm. "Of the essays ... the following have appeared in *Knowledge:* The brightness of starlight, Stellar brightness and density, Holes in the heavens, The stellar universe, A possible celestial catastrophe, and The new cosmogony; and the following in the Observatory: The secular variation of stars, The number of visible stars, and The satellite of Sirius. The rest have not been hitherto published." cf. Pref. Includes bibliographical references and index.

Advertisements: [1] p. facing half-title; 4 p. at end. Provenance: W. H. Robinson (bookplate).

840. Gore, J. Ellard (John Ellard), 1845-1910. *Studies in astronomy by J. Ellard Gore....*

London: Chatto & Windus, 1904. x p., 1 l., 336 p. front., plates. 20 cm. "Most of the articles ... have been published ... in *The Gentleman's Magazine, Knowledge, The Observatory*, etc." – Pref. The size of the solar system. – Jupiter and its system. – Giant telescopes. – The distances of the stars. – The sun's journey through space. – The story of Gamma Virginis. – The Pleiades. – Globular star clusters. – The sun's stellar magnitude. – The suns of space. – Stellar satellites. – Spectroscopic binaries. – "The darkness behind the stars." – The nebular hypothesis. – Stellar evolution. – The construction of the visible universe. – The secular variation of starlight. – The Herschels and the nebulæ. – A chapter in the history of astronomy. – Messier's nebulæ. – The ring nebula in Lyra. – A great Belgian astronomer. – Some recent advances in astronomy. – The new star in Perseus. – The coming comet. – Immensity and minuteness. – Light, electricity, and the ether. – Appendix: Binary stars.

[2] p. of advertisements preceeding half-title.

841. Gore, J. Ellard (John Ellard), 1845-1910. *The visible universe; chapters on the origin and construction of the heavens, by J. Ellard Gore ... With stellar photographs and other illustrations....*

London: C. Lockwood and Son, 1892. x, 346 p. front., illus., pl. (partly fold.) 22 cm. Includes bibliographical references and index.

Advertisements: verso half-title; publisher's catalog dated August 1894 [48 p.] and another catalog [16 p.] at end.

842. Graaf, Reinier de, 1641-1673. *De mulierum organis generationi inservientibus tractatus novus: demonstrans homines & animalia caetera omnia, quae vivipara dicuntur, haud minus quàm ovipara ab ovo originem ducere.*

Lugduni Batav.: Ex Officina Hackiana, 1672. [24], 334, [14] p. port., xxvii plates (part fold.) 16 cm. Added title page, engraved. Includes index. Plate I signed: R.D.G. With this is bound the author's *Partium genitalium defensio.* Ludg. Batav., 1673.

Provenance: Wm. Oliver (armorial bookplate); Frederic Wood Jones (nameplate).

843. Graaf, Reinier de, 1641-1673. *Regneri de Graaf medici Delphensis Partium genitalium defensio: Societati Regiæ Londini ad scientiam naturalem promovendam institutæ, dicata.*

Lugd. Batav.: Ex officiana Hackiana, 1673. [8], 83 p.; 16 cm.

With: *Regneri de Graaf De mulierum organis generationi inservientibus tractatus novus.* Lugduni Batav.: Ex officinà Hackiana, 1672.

844. Graaf, Reinier de, 1641-1673. *A specimen of some observations made by a microscope, contrived by M. Leewenhoeck in Holland / lately communicated by Dr. Regnerus de Graaf.*
London : Printed by T. R. for John Martyn ..., 1674. p. 6037-6038 ; 23 cm. In: *Philosophical transactions /* Royal Society of London, v. 8 1673. Caption title. Date of publication from colophon. Letter from de Graaf "written from Delpht April 28. 1673". Burndy. *Science*, 189.

845. Graetz, Albrecht Heinrich, 1681-1713. *Epistola anatomica, problematica, quinta & decima ad ... Fredericum Ruyschium ... De vasorum sanguineorum extremitatibus, placentæ uterinæ, mammarumque structura, &c. / authore Alberto Hernico Grætz.*
Amstelædami: Apud Joannem Wolters, 1704. 15 p, [1] leaf of plates: illus.; 22 cm. "Frederici Ruyschii responsio": p. [7]-15. Plate numbered: XVIIII. Signed: C. Huijberts ad vivum sculp.
With: *Observationum anatomico-chirurgicarum centuria / Frederici Ruyschii.* Amstelodami: Apud Henricum & Viduam Theodori Boom, 1691.

846. Graetz, Johann Heinrich, fl. 1691-1697. *Epistola anatomica, problematica octava Ad ... Fredericum Ruyschium... De structura nasi cartilaginea, vasis sanguiferis arteriosis mebranæ & cavitatis tympani & ossiculorum auditus eorumque periostio / authore Johanne Henrico Grætz.*
Amstelædami: Apud Joannem Wolters, 1697. 13, [1] p., [1] leaf of plates: illus.; 22 cm. Statement of responsibility transposed. "Frederico Ruyschii responsio ...": p. 9-13. Plate is numbered 9.
With: *Observationum anatomico-chirurgicarum centuria / Frederici Ruyschii.* Amstelodami: Apud Henricum & ViduamTheodori Boom, 1691.

847. Graetz, Johann Heinrich, fl. 1691-1697. *Epistola anatomica, problematica septima Ad ... Fredericum Ruyschium ... De pia matre, e jusque processibus.*
Amstelædami: Apud Joannem Wolters, 1696. 14 p., [1] leaf of plates: illus.; 22 cm. "Frederici Ruyschii responsio ...": p. [7]-10. Plate is numbered 8.
With: *Frederici Ruyschii ... Observationum anatomico-chirurgicarum centuria.* Amstelodami: Apud Henricum & Viduam Theodori Boom, 1691.

848. Graetz, Johann Heinrich, fl. 1691-1697. *Epistola anatomica, problematica sexta ... ad ... Fredericum Ruyschium... de arteria & vena bronchiali, nec non de polypis bronchiorum ejectis, venæ & arteriæ pulmonalis ramos mentientibus / authore Johanne Henrico Grætz.*
Amstelaedami: Apud Joannem Wolters, 1696. 11, [3] p., [1] leaf of plates: illus.; 22 cm. Statement of responsibility transposed. Plate is numbered 7. "Frederici Ruyschii responsio ...": p. 10-12.
Plate with 1 blank leaf misbound behind Epistola anatomica, problematica septima. With: *Observationum anatomico-chirurgicarum centuria / Frederici Ruyschii.* Amstelodami: Apud Henricum & Viduam Theodori Boom, 1691.

849. Grant, Robert, 1814-1892. *History of physical astronomy: from the earliest ages to the middle of the 19th century, comprehending a detailed account of the establishment of the theory of gravitation by Newton, and its development by his successors; with an exposition of the progress of research on all the other subjects of celestial physics / by Robert Grant.*
London: H. G. Bohn, 1852. xx, xiv, 637 p.: ill., diagrs.; 23 cm. Imprint date from preface, p. xiv. Includes bibliographical references and index.
Provenance: Northern Church of England School (lettering); Theodore Williamson (inscription); Charles Atwood Kofoid (bookplate).

850. Grassmann, Hermann, 1809-1877. *Die lineale Ausdehnungslehre, ein neuer Zweig der Mathematik, dargestellt ... von Hermann Grassmann.*
Leipzig: O. Wigand, 1844. xxxii, 279 p. fold. plate. (diagrs.) 23 cm. Added t. p.: Die Wissenschaft der extensiven Grösse ... Erster Theil. [No more published].
Provenance: Ernst Mach (inkstamp); Herbert McLean Evans (bookplate).

851. Gratacap, L. P. (Louis Pope), 1851-1917. *The certainty of a future life in Mars / being*

the posthumous papers of Bradford Torrey Dodd; edited by L. P. Gratacap.

New York: Brentano's, 1903. 266 p.; 18 cm. Bradford Torrey Dodd is a fictitious character. Cf. *NUC pre-1956*, v. 210, p. 603. Posthumous papers of Bradford Torrey Dodd – Note by Mr. August Bixby Dodan – Note by the editor – The planet Mars / by Giovanni Schiaparelli.

852. Gravesande, Willem Jacob 's, 1688-1742. *Mathematical elements of natural philosophy confirm'd by experiments, or, An introduction to Sir Isaac Newton's philosophy... Written in Latin by William James 's Gravesande ... Translated into English by J. T. Desaguliers ... The 2d ed., corrected.*

London: Printed for J. Senex [etc.], 1726. 2 v. fold. plates. 21 cm. Translation of: *Physices elementa mathematica, experimentis confirmata.*

853. Gravesande, Willem Jacob 's, 1688-1742. *Mathematical elements of natural philosophy, confirm'd by experiments; or, An introduction to Sir Isaac Newton's philosophy ... Written in Latin by William James 's Gravesande ... Translated into English by J. T. Desaguliers ... The 4th ed.*

London: Printed for J. Senex [etc.], 1731. 2 v. fold. plates. 21 cm. Translation of: *Physices elementa mathematica, experimentis confirmata.* Gray, G. J. Newton, 83.

854. Gravesande, Willem Jacob 's, 1688-1742. *Mathematical elements of natural philosophy confirm'd by experiments: or, An introduction to Sir Isaac Newton's philosophy. Written in Latin by the late W. James s' Gravesande ... Translated into English by the late J. T. Desaguliers ... and published by his son J. T. Desaguliers. The 6th ed. greatly improved by the author and illustrated with 127 copper plates all new engraven....*

London: Printed for W. Innys, T. Longman [etc.], 1747. 2 v. 127 fold. plates. 26 cm. Translation of: *Physices elementa mathematica, experimentis confirmata.* Illustrated by J. Mynde. *Babson Newton Coll.* 69. Gray, G. J. *Newton,* 83.

855. Gravesande, Willem Jacob 's, 1688-1742. *Philosophiæ Newtonianæ institutiones, in usus academicos. Editio prima Italica auctior.*

Venetiis: Ex Typographia Remondini, 1749. 14 p.l., 571, [21] p. fold. plates. 18 cm. Title vignette.

Provenance: Charles Atwood Kofoid (bookplate).

856. Great Britain. *Anno regni Annæ Reginæ Magnæ Britanniæ, Franciæ, Hiberniæ, duodecimo: [An act for providing a publick reward for such person or persons as shall discover the longitude at sea.]: At the Parliament summoned to beheld at Westminster the twelfth day of November, Anno. Dom. 1713. in the twelfth year of the reign or Our Sovereign Lady Anne, by the grace of God, of Great Britain, France, and Ireland, Queen, Defender of the Faith, &c.: And by several writs of prorogation begun and holden on the sixteenth day of February, 1713.: Being the first session of this present Parliament.*

London: Printed by John Baskett, printer to the Kings Most Excellent Majesty, and by the assigns of Thomas Newcomb, and Henry Hills, deceas'd., 1714. [2], 355-357, [1] (blank) p.; 34 cm. Bracketed information in title area from caption title, which reads: Anno duodecimo Annæ Reginæ. An act for providing a publick reward for such person or persons as shall discover the longitude at sea. Title vignette (royal arms). *NUC pre-56* NSG 0048153. Horblit, H. D. *Grolier 100 science books,* 42a.

Provenance: Robert Honeyman IV (Honeyman sale).

857. Great Britain. Nautical Almanac Office. *The Nautical almanac and astronomical ephemeris for the year for the meridian of the Royal Observatory at Greenwich.*

Edinburgh [etc.] Printed for H.M. Stationery Office [etc.] v. fold. maps. 24 cm. 1767-1959. Includes supplements. 1767-1831 published by order of the Commissioners of Longitude; 1832-1833 by order of the Board of Admiralty. Beginning with issue for 1959 material is identical with *Ephemeris* pub. by U.S. Navy. Continued by: *Astronomical ephemeris.*

Library has: 1770-[1776]. Vols. for 1772-1774: Provenance: A. Shepherd (signature).

858. Great Britain. Poor Law Commissioners. *Report to Her Majesty's principal secretary of state for the Home Department, from the Poor Law Commissioners, on an inquiry into the sanitary condition of the labouring population of Great Britain; with Appendices. Presented to both houses of Parliament, by command of Her Majesty, July, 1842.*
London: Printed by W. Clowes, for H. M. Stationery Off., 1842. xxx, 457 p. plates, plans (part fold.) fold. diagr. 23 cm. Half-title (p. [xxi]) reads: Report on the sanitary condition of the labouring population of Great Britain. By Edwin Chadwick.

859. Green, A. H. (Alexander Green), 1832-1896. *The birth and growth of worlds: a lecture / by A. H. Green....*
London: Society for Promoting Christian Knowledge ...; E. & J. B. Young & Co., 1890. 61, [1], 10 p.: ill.; 17 cm. Romance of science. Bibliography: p. 60-61. Advertisements: 10 p. following text.

860. Greene, Dascom, 1825-1900. *An introduction to spherical and practical astronomy / by Dascom Greene.*
Boston, U.S.A.: Ginn, 1903. viii, 150, 8 p.: ill.; 22 cm. "Appendix: the method of least squares": p. 115-150. "Tables": 8 p. (3rd sequence).

861. Gregory, David, 1659-1708. *Astronomiæ, physicæ & geometricæ elementa. Auctore Davide Gregorio....*
Oxoniæ: E Theatro Sheldoniano, 1702. 6 p. l., 494, [2] p. diagrs. 36 cm. Title vignette. *Babson Newton Coll.* 71. Gray, G. F. *Newton,* 87.
Imperfect: t. p. missing, supplied in photocopy.

862. Gregory, David, 1659-1708. *The elements of physical and geometrical astronomy. By David Gregory. Done into English, with additions and corrections. To which is annex'd, Dr. Halley's synopsis of the astronomy of comets. The whole newly revised and compared with the Latin, and corrected throughout, by Edmund Stone.*
London: Printed for D. Midwinter, 1726. 2 v. 79 plates., diagr. 21 cm. Vol. 1 is 2d edition. Translation of: *Astronomiæ, physicæ, et geometricæ elementa.* Houzeau & Lancaster. *Astronomie* (1964 ed.) 9240.
Provenance: Henry Charles Howard (armorial bookplate).

863. Gregory, Olinthus, 1774-1841. *A treatise on astronomy: in which the elements of the science are deduced in a natural order from the appearances of the heavens to an observer on the earth, demonstrated on mathematical principles, and explained by an application to the various phenomena / by Olinthus Gregory...*
London: Printed for G. Kearsley ...: and sold by the author (and 8 others), 1802. xiii, [3], 522, [10] p.; 22 cm. Includes bibliographical references and index. "Addenda et corrigenda": p. [8-9] (last group). Advertisements on p. [xiv] and on final p. "Printed by T. Davison, White-Friars" – p. [9] (last group).
Binder: Homecrafters, Tucson, Ariz. (ticket). Imperfect: lacks p. 311-312.

864. Gregory, Richard, Sir, 1864-1952. *Discovery, or, The spirit and service of science / by Sir Richard Gregory.*
London: Macmillan, 1921. viii, 347 p., 8 leaves of plates: ill.; 19 cm. "First edition June 1916. Reprinted ... 1921." Includes indexes.

865. Grew, Nehemiah, 1641-1712. *The anatomy of plants: with An idea of a philosophical history of plants, and several other lectures, read before the Royal Society / by Nehemjah Grew....*
London: Printed by W. Rawlins, for the author, 1682. [22], 24, [10], 212, [4], 221-304, [20] p., 83 leaves of plates (some folded): ill.; 34 cm. Each part has a special t. p. Place of publication from second t. p. introducing the section of the work entitled "An idea of a philosophical history of plants. ..." Decorated initials throughout text. Includes index. Pritzel 3557. Wing G1945. Horblit, H. D. *Grolier 100 science books,* 43b. *Hunt botanical cat.,* 362. An idea of a philosophical history of plants ... The second edition. – The anatomy of plants, begun. With a general account of vegetation, grounded thereupon. The first book. ... The second edition. – The anatomy of roots; ... With an account of the vegetation of roots, grounded chiefly hereupon. The second book. ... The second edition. – The anatomy of trunks, with an account of their vegetation. Grounded thereupon. ... The third book. ... The second edition. – The anatomy of leaves, flowers, fruits and seeds. In four parts. The fourth

book. – Several lectures read before the Royal Society. ... The titles of the following lectures. I. Of the nature, causes, and power of mixture. The second edition. II. Of the luctation arising upon the mixture of several menstruum's with all sorts of bodies. The second edition. III. An essay, of the various proportions, wherein lixivial salts are found in plants. IV. Of the essential and marine salts of plants. V. Of the colours of plants. VI. Of the diversities and causes of tasts [sic]; chiefly in plants. With an appendix, Of the odours of plants. VII. Experiments in consort, upon the solution of salts in water.

866. Grew, Nehemiah, 1641-1712. *The anatomy of vegetables begun: With a general account of vegetation founded thereon. / By Nehemiah Grew....*

London: Printed for Spencer Hickman ..., 1672. [31], 198 [i.e. 186], [19] p. ([1-2] blank), [3] folded leaves ofplates: ill.; 16 cm. Errata: p. [31]. Page 186 misnumbered 198. Illustrated by W. Dolle. Pritzel, 3554. Wing, G1946. Osler, W. *Bibl. Osleriana*, 2837.

Ms. notes. Provenance: J. W. Blackler (inscription).

867. Grew, Nehemiah, 1641-1712. *An idea of a phytological history propounded. Together with a continuation of the Anatomy of vegetables, particularly prosecuted upon roots, and an account of the vegetation of roots grounded chiefly thereupon. By Nehemiah Grew.*

London: Printed by J. M. for R. Chiswell, 1673. 11 p. l., 144, [32] p. 7, [1] fold. pl. 19 cm.

Ms. notes on the plates. Provenance: Herbert McLean Evans (bookplate).

868. Grew, Nehemiah, 1641-1712. *Musæum Regalis Societatis; or, A catalogue & description of the natural and artificial rarities belonging to the Royal Society and preserved at Gresham College. Made by Nehemjah Grew ... Whereunto is subjoyned the Comparative anatomy of stomachs and guts. By the same author.*

London: Printed by W. Rawlins, for the author, 1681. [12], 386, [4], 43 p. front. (port.) 31 pl. (1 fold.) 33 cm. "The comparative anatomy of stomachs and guts" has special t. p. Errata: p. [12]

Provenance: Iohn Ward (armorial bookplate).

869. Griffith, C. J. *The romance of the sky: the story of star-gazing and star-tracing, being an introduction to the study of astronomy / by C. J. Griffith.*

London: G. Routledge & Sons; E. P. Dutton, 1907. viii, 166 p., [1] folded leaf of plates: ill; 19 cm. For date of imprint cf. BLC, v. 132, p. 455.

870. Grimthorpe, Edmund Beckett, Baron, 1816-1905. *Astronomy without mathematics / by Sir Edmund Beckett ... Sixth edition, revised for the results of the transit of Venus.*

London: Society for Promoting Christian Knowledge ...; Pott, Young & Co., 1876. viii, 412 p., [1] folded leaf: ill.; 18 cm. Table on [1] folded leaf at end. Includes bibliographical references and index.

Advertisements: 4 p. at end. Provenance: James Henry Parker (signature); ms. marginalia.

871. Gruson, Hermann, 1821-1895. *Im Reiche des Lichtes: Sonnen, Zodiakallichte, Kometen: Dämmerungslicht-Pyramiden nach den ältesten ägyptischen Quellen / von Hermann Gruson; mit achtundzwanzig Figuren und neun Tafeln, zum Theil in buntfarbiger Ausführung.*

Braunschweig: George Westermann; Haar & Steinert; Asher & Co., 1893. xii, 207, [1] p., ix leaves of plates (1 folded): ill. (some col.); 24 cm. Includes index.

872. Guericke, Otto von, 1602-1686. *Ottonis de Guericke Experimenta nova (ut vocantur) Magdeburgica de vacuo spatio primùm à R. P. Gaspare Schotto ... nunc verò ab ipso auctore perfectiùs edita, variisque aliis experimentis aucta. Quibus accesserunt simul certa quædam de aëris pondere circa terram; de virtutibus mundanis, & systemate mundi planetario; sicut & de stellis fixis, ac spatio illo immenso, quod tàm intra quam extra eas funditur.*

Amstelodami: Apud J. Janssonium à Waesberge, 1672. 8 p.l., 244, [4] p., 1 l. illus., 2 double pl., port., diagrs. 33 cm. Added t.-p., engr. liber I. De mundo ejusque systemate, secundum communiores philosophorum sententias. – liber 2. De vacuo spatio. – liber 3. De propriis experimentis. – liber 4. De virtutibus mundanis & aliis rebus inde dependentibus. – liber 5. De terraqueo globo & ejus sociâ quæ

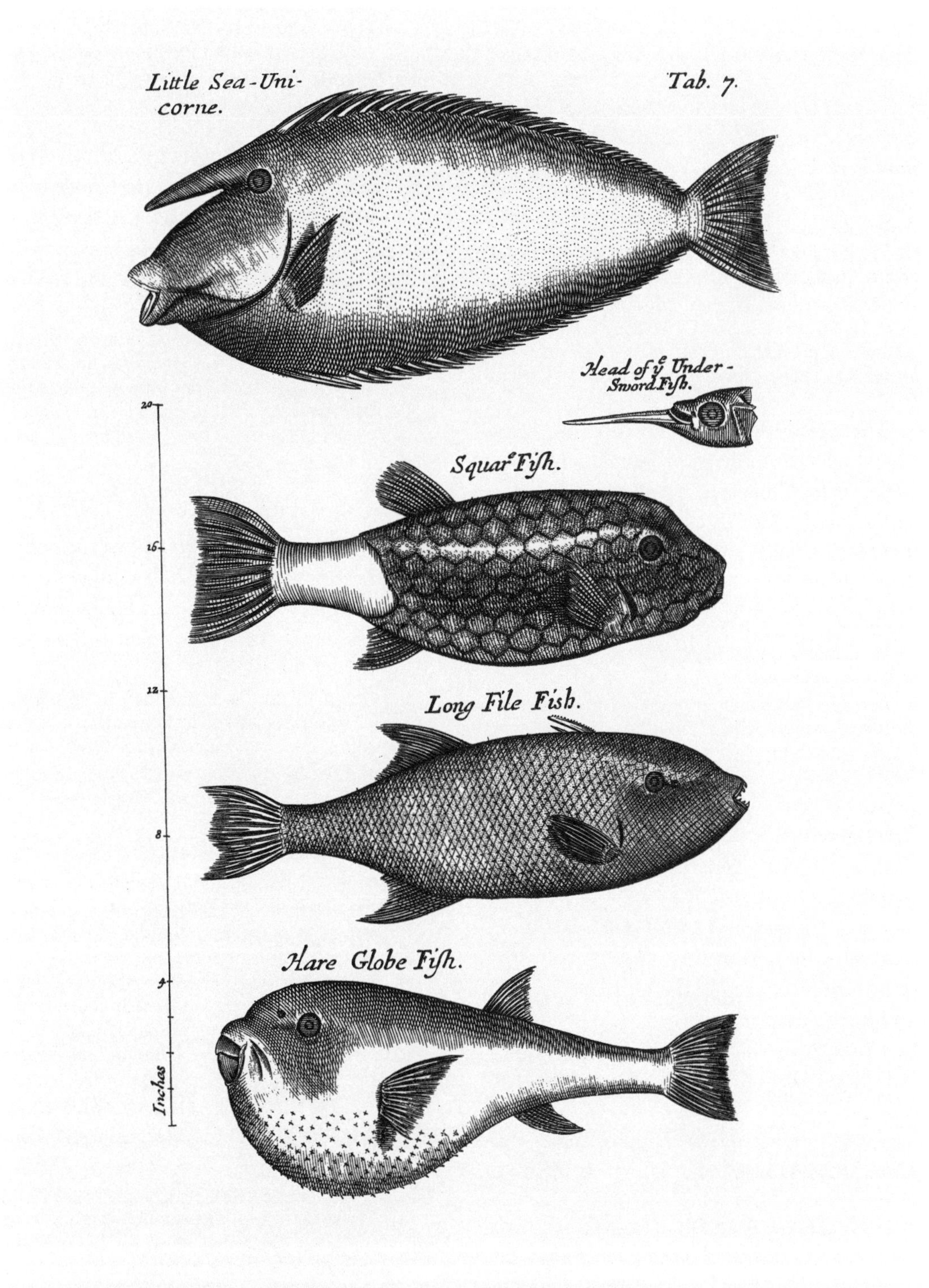

Grew, *Musæum Regalis Societatis*, 1681

vocaturluna. – liber 6. De systemate mundi nostri planetario. – liber 7. De stellis fixis & eo quod finit eas.

Provenance: Herbert McLean Evans (bookplate).

873. GUILLEMIN, AMÉDÉE, 1826-1893. *Le ciel: notions d'astronomie à l'usage des gens du monde et de la jeunesse / par Amédée Guillemin....*

Paris: Librairie de L. Hachette et Cie ..., 1864. [6], VI, 626 p., XII leaves of plates (1 folded): ill. (some col.); 28 cm. Includes bibliographical references.

Provenance: author's signed presentation inscription to W. H. Smyth; Admiral W. H. Smyth (armorial bookplate); presentation inscription [from Mrs. Smyth?] to Thereza Markeleyne.

874. GUILLEMIN, AMÉDÉE, 1826-1893. *Le ciel: notions élémentaires d'astronomie physique / par Amédée Guillemin. Cinquième édition, entièrement refondue, considérablement augmentée....*

Paris: Libraire Hachette et Cie ..., 1877. [6], IV, 969, [1] p., LIV [i.e. LXII] leaves of plates (4 folded): ill. (some col.); 28 cm. Includes bibliographical references. Errata: p. [970]. Plates numbered I-LIV; eight nos. repeated with bis.

Binder: Ch. Magnier (stamp). Binding: quarter morocco, brown & gilt pictorial cloth. Provenance: T. J. J. See (inkstamp).

875. GUILLEMIN, AMÉDÉE, 1826-1893. *The forces of nature: a popular introduction to the study of physical phenomena / by Amédée Guillemin; translated from the French by Mrs. Norman Lockyer; and edited, with additions and notes, by J. Norman Lockyer ... ; illustrated by eleven coloured plates and four hundred and fifty-five woodcuts.*

New York: Scribner, Welford & Armstrong, 1872. xxxix, 679, [1] p., xi leaves of plates: ill. (some col.); 26 cm. Translation of: *Les phénomènes de la physique.* Includes index.

Binder: Burn & Co. (ticket). Provenance: Charles Atwood Kofoid (bookplate).

876. GUILLEMIN, AMÉDÉE, 1826-1893. *The heavens: an illustrated handbook of popular astronomy / by Amédée Guillemin; edited by J. Norman Lockyer ...*

London: Richard Bentley ..., 1866. xxiii, [1], 524 p., [13] leaves of plates (1 folded): ill. (some col.); 28 cm. Translation of: *Le ciel.* "Appendix, by the editor": p. [505]-524. Includes bibliographical references.

Provenance: Spicer Library, Polytechnic Institute of Brooklyn (inkstamp).

877. GUILLEMIN, AMÉDÉE, 1826-1893. *The heavens: an illustrated handbook of popular astronomy / by Amédée Guillemin; edited by J. Norman Lockyer ... ; and revised by Richard A. Proctor ... An entirely new and revised edition (being the sixth).*

London: Richard Bentley & Son ..., 1876. x, [2], 436 p., [2] leaves of plates (1 folded): ill.; 23 cm. Translation of: *Le ciel.* Includes bibliographical references and index.

Provenance: New University Club (gilt stamp on binding).

878. GUILLEMIN, AMÉDÉE, 1826-1893. *The heavens: an illustrated handbook of popular astronomy / by Amédée Guillemin; edited by J. Norman Lockyer ... ; and revised by Richard A. Proctor ... An entirely new and revised edition (being the sixth).*

New York: Scribner, Welford, & Armstrong, 1876. x, [2], 436 p., [1] folded leaf of plates: ill.; 23 cm. Translation of: *Le ciel.* Includes bibliographical references and index.

Provenance: Vesta Bradburn (signature).

879. GUILLEMIN, AMÉDÉE, 1826-1893. *Le monde physique, par Amédée Guillemin....*

Paris: Hachette et Cie, 1880-1885. 5 v. illus., plates (part col.) maps (part double), ports. 29 cm. t. 1. La pesanteur et la gravitation universelle. Le son. – t. 2. La lumière. – t. 3. Le magnétisme et l'électricité. – t. 4. La chaleur. – t. 5. La météorologie, la physique moléculaire. Variously illustrated by Th. Deyrolle, P. Picart, C. Laplante, A. Jahandier, M. Rapine.

880. GUILLEMIN, AMÉDÉE, 1826-1893. *Les phénomènes de la physique / par Amédée Guillemin....*

Paris: Librairie de L. Hachette et Cie ..., 1868. [4], III, [1] (blank), 780 p., XI col. leaves of plates: ill.; 28 cm. Variously illustrated by: Blaise Desgoffe, R. H. Digeon, P. Richner, M. Rapine, C. Laplante, L. Crépon, E. Ronjat, B. Bonnafoux.

GUERICKE, *Experimenta nova*, 1672

881. GUILLEMIN, AMÉDÉE, 1826-1893. *Wonders of the moon. Tr. from the French of Amédée Guillemin by Miss M. G. Mead. Ed., with additions by Maria Mitchell....*
New York: C. Scribner's Sons, 1886. xxi, [23]-241 p. front., illus., 3 pl. 19 cm. Wonders of science. Advertisements: [4] p. at end.

882. GUMMERE, JOHN, 1784-1845. *An elementary treatise on astronomy. In two parts. The first containing, a clear and compendious view of the theory; the second, a number of practical problems. To which are added, solar, lunar, and other astronomical tables. By John Gummere ... 2d ed., enl. and improved.*
Philadelphia: Kimber & Sharpless, 1837. 1 p. l., vii, [1], [9]-373, 104 p. incl. tables. 62 diagrs. on 7 fold. pl. 23 cm.

883. GUMMERE, JOHN, 1784-1845. *An elementary treatise on astronomy; in two parts. The first containing, a clear and compendious view of the theory; the second, a number of practical problems. To which are added, solar, lunar, and other astronomical tables. By John Gummere ... 3d ed. improved.*

Philadelphia: Kimber & Sharpless, 1842. vii, [1], [9]-359, 112 p. incl. tables. 68 diagrs. on 8 fold. pl. 23 cm.

Provenance: Francis T. Bryan (signature); extensive ms. marginalia. Four of the plates are cut up, with the diagrams inserted as appropriate throughout the text.

884. GUNTHER, R. T. (ROBERT THEODORE), 1869-1940. *The astrolabes of the world: based upon the series of instruments in the Lewis Evans Collection in the old Ashmolean Museum at Oxford, with notes on astrolabes in the collections of the British Museum, Science Museum, Sir. J. Findlay, Mr. S. V. Hoffman, the Mensing Collection and in other public and private collections / by Robert T. Gunther, M. A., Hon. LL.D., curator of the Lewis Evans Collection in the Old Ashmolean Museum at Oxford.*

Oxford: Printed at the University Press, 1932. 2 v.: ill., port.; 30 cm. Paged continuously. Volume 1 has 68 leaves of plates; volume 2 has 85 leaves of plates. Volume 1 contains facsimile reprint of "Description of a planispheric astrolabe, constucted for Sháh Sultán Husain Safawí, King of Persia, and now preserved in the British Museum; comprising an account of the astrolabe generally, with notes illustrative and explanatory: to which are added, concise notices of twelve other astrolabes, eastern and European, hitherto undescribed. By William H. Morely. Williams and Norgate, 14, Henrietta Street, Covent Garden, London; 20, South Frederick Street, Edinburgh. Benj. Duprat, Paris. F. A. Brockhaus, Leipsig. MDCCCLVI." Bound in white cloth with gilt design of an astrolabe on front covers. "The literature": p. [565]-575. "Bibliography of the astrolabe": p. [576]-598.

885. GUY, JOSEPH, THE ELDER. *Guy's Elements of astronomy: and an abridgement of Keith's New treatise on the use of globes. New American edition, with additions and improvements, and an explanation of the astronomical part of the American almanac. Thirteenth edition.*

Philadelphia: Key & Biddle ..., stereotyped by L. Johnson, 1835. viii, 136, 173 p., 17 [i.e. 19] leaves of plates: ill.; 16 cm. Some other ed. published as *Elements of astronomy*. Plates are irregularly numbered. "A new treatise on the use of globes" has special t. p. and separate pagination.

Provenance: R. F. Beers (signature); Charles Atwood Kofoid (bookplate).

886. GUYNEMER, A. M. A. *Dictionnaire d'astronomie à l'usage des gens du monde, d'après W. et J. Herschel, Laplace, Arago, De Humboldt, Francur, Mitchell et autres savants français et étrangers, avec figures et un planisphère. Précédé de l'exposition d'un nouveau systême sur les formations planétaires, par A. M. A. Guynemer.*

Paris: Didot Frères, 1852. [6], 406 p. illus., chart. 23 cm. Errata: p. [5] (1st sequence).

Provenance: George Cornewall Lewis (armorial bookplate).

887. GUYTON DE MORVEAU, LOUIS BERNARD, BARON, 1737-1816. *Méthode de nomenclature chimique, / proposée par MM. de Morveau, Lavoisier, Bertholet, & de Fourcroy; on y a joint un nouveau systême de caractères chimiques, adaptés à cette nomenclature, par MM. Hassenfratz & Adet.*

À Paris: Chez Cuchet, Libraire ..., 1787. [4], 314 p., [7] folded leaves; 21 cm.

On spine: Lavoisier. Nomenclature chimique. Provenance: Herbert McLean Evans (bookplate); Joseph-Claude-Anthelme Recamier (booklabel).

888. HAAS, ARTHUR ERICH, 1884-1941. *Die Grundgleichungen der Mechanik: dargestellt auf Grund der geschichtlichen Entwicklung: Vorlesungen zur Einführung in die theoretische Physik, gehalten im Sommersemester 1914 an der Universität Leipzig / von Arthur Erich Haas.*

Leipzig: Veit & Co., 1914. iv, 216 p.: ill.; 24 cm. Bibliographisches "Namen verzeichnis": p. [211]-214. Advertisements: [2] p. on fly-leaf. Includes index.

Provenance: R. Hölzer (signature).

889. HAECKEL, ERNST HEINRICH PHILIPP AUGUST, 1834-1919. *Ernst Haeckels Wanderbilder: nach eigenen Aquarellen und Ölgemälden: erste und zweite Serie, Die Naturwunder der Tropenwelt, Ceylon und Insulinde.*

Gera-Untermhaus: W. Koehler, 1905. 1 portfolio ([88] p., [48] leaves of plates: ill. (some col.), ports.); 41 cm. Each plate is accompanied by explanatory text by the author.

890. HAECKEL, ERNST HEINRICH PHILIPP AUGUST, 1834-1919. *The evolution of man: a popular scientific study / by Ernst Haeckel; translated from the fifth (enlarged) edition by Joseph McCabe.*

London: Watts, 1905. 2 v. (xxiv, 905 p., xxx [i.e. xxviii] leaves of plates): ill. (some col.); 26 cm. Translation of: *Anthropogenie, odor, Entwicklungs Geschichte des Menschen.* "Issued for the Rationalist Press Association, Limited." Includes bibliographical references and index. V. I. Human embryology or ontogeny – v. II. Human stem-history orphylogeny.

Imperfect: lacks 1 plate, v. 2.

891. HAECKEL, ERNST HEINRICH PHILIPP AUGUST, 1834-1919. *Last words on evolution; a popular retrospect and summary. Tr. from the 2d ed. by Joseph McCabe.*

New York: Eckler, 1905. 179 p. ill., ports., 3 pl. 21 cm. A course of 3 lectures given at the Berlin Academy of Music, April 1905. Translation of *Der Kampf um den Entwickelungs-Gedanken.* The controversy about creation. – The struggle over our genealogical tree. – The controversy over the soul. – Appendix: evolutionary tables. – Postscript: evolution and Jesuitism.

Provenance: Mars Baumgardt (signature).

892. HAECKEL, ERNST HEINRICH PHILIPP AUGUST, 1834-1919. *Natürliche Schöpfungsgeschichte. Gemeinverständliche wissenschaftliche Vorträge über die Entwickelungslehre im Allgemeinen und diejenige von Darwin, Goethe, und Lamarck im besonderen, über die Anwendung derselben auf den Ursprung des Menschen ... / von Dr. Ernst Haeckel....*

Berlin : Verlag von Georg Reimer, 1868. xvi, 568 p., [3], VIII leaves of plates (2 folded): ill.; 22 cm. Includes index. Bibliography: p. 552-554.

893. HAHN, OTTO, 1879-1968. [Collection of reprints and journal articles from *Abhandlungen der Preussischen Akademie der Wissenschaften* / by Otto Hahn].

[1929-1944]. 4 pieces: ill.; 26-30 cm. Includes bibliographical references. (1) Atomumwandlungen und ihre Bedeutung für Chemie und Physik (1929) – (2) Über das Zerplatzen des Urankernes durch langsame Neutronen (1939) – (3) Einiges über die experimentelle Entwirrung der bei der Spaltung des Urans auf tretenden Elemente und Atomarten (1942) – (4) Die chemische Abscheidung der bei der Spaltung des Urans entstehenden Elemente und Atomwarten (allgemeiner Teil) 1944.

Provenance: (pieces 1 & 3) Herbert McLean Evans (bookplate).

894. HAHN, OTTO, 1879-1968. *Otto Hahn: a scientific autobiography / translated and edited by Willy Ley; introduction by Glenn T. Seaborg.*

New York: C. Scribner's Sons, [c1966]. xxiv, 296 p., [16] p. of plates: illus., ports.; 24 cm. Translation of *Vom Radiothor zur Uranspaltung.* Includes index. "Publications by Otto Hahn": p. [286]-292. Bibliographical footnotes.

895. HÁJEK Z HÁJKU, TADEÁS, 1525-1600. *Dialexis de nouae et prius incognitæ stellæ: inusitatæ magnitudinis & splendissimi luminis apparitione, & de eiusdem stellæ vero loco constituendo. Adiuncta est ibidem ratio inuestigandæ parallaxeos cuiuscunque phænomemi, eiúsque à centro terræ distantia, meteorologicam doctrinam mirificè illustrans / nunc primum conscripta & edita, per Thaddæum Hagecium ab Hayck ... ; accesserunt aliorum quoque doctissimorum virorum de eadem stella scripta....*

Francofurti ad Moenum: [s.n.], 1574. 176 p.: ill.; 23 cm. Includes index. Zinner, E. *Geschichte u. Bib. der Astr. Lit.* 2673.

With: *Tychonis Brahe De mundi aetherei recentioribus phænomenis liber secundus.* Vraniburgi Daniæ, 1603.

896. HALDANE, J. B. S. (JOHN BURDON SANDERSON), 1892-1964. *Possible worlds and other papers, by J. B. S. Haldane. 1st ed.*

New York, London: Harper & Brothers Publishers, 1928. viii, [2], 305, [1] p. 22 cm. On cover: A scientist looks at science.

Advertisements: [4] p. at end. Provenance: presentation inscription to John Calhoun Deager.

897. HALDANE, J. S. (JOHN SCOTT), 1860-1936. *Respiration, by J. S. Haldane.*

New Haven: Yale University Press [etc., etc.], 1922. xviii, 427 p. illus., plates, tables (part fold.) diagrs. 24 cm. Yale University. Mrs. Hepsa Ely Silliman Memorial Lectures.

Provenance: Ernest du Bray (inscription).

898. Hale, George Ellery, 1868-1938. *Beyond the milky way, by George Ellery Hale....*
New York, London: C. Scribner's Sons, 1926. xv, 105 p. incl. front., illus., diagrs. 20 cm. Includes bibliographical references. The oriental ancestry of the telescope. – Heat from the stars. – Beyond the milky way.

899. Hale, George Ellery, 1868-1938. *The depths of the universe, by George Ellery Hale....*
New York, London: C. Scribner's Sons, 1924. xv, 98 p. incl. front., illus., diagrs. 20 cm. "Appeared during the last two years as articles in *Scribner's Magazine.*" – Pref. The depths of the universe. – Barnard's dark nebulæ. – Sun-spots as magnets.
Provenance: William Andrews Clark, Jr. (bookplate).

900. Hale, George Ellery, 1868-1938. *The new heavens, by George Ellery Hale; with numerous illustrations.*
New York: C. Scribner's Sons, 1922. xv, 88 p. incl. front., illus., diagrs. 20 cm.

901. Hale, George Ellery, 1868-1938. *Signals from the stars, by George Ellery Hale.*
New York, London: C. Scribner's Sons, 1931. xx p., 1 l., 138 p. incl. front., illus., diagrs. 20 cm.

902. Hale, George Ellery, 1868-1938. *The Solar observatory of the Carnegie Institution of Washington, by George E. Hale.*
[Washington, D.C.: 1905]. 22 p. v pl., 2 plans. 26 cm. Contributions from the Solar Observatory, Mt. Wilson, California, no. 2. Title from cover. Pages also numbered 29-50. Includes bibliographical references.

903. Hale, George Ellery, 1868-1938. *The study of stellar evolution; an account of some recent methods of astrophysical research.*
Chicago: University of Chicago Press, 1908. xi, 252 p. 104 plates, diagrs. 23 cm. Decennial publications of the University of Chicago; v. 10. Includes index.
Provenance: E. W. Forthingham (signature).

904. Hale, George Ellery, 1868-1938. *Ten years' work of a mountain observatory; a brief account of the Mount Wilson solar observatory of the Carnegie institution of Washington, by George Ellery Hale.*
Washington, D. C.: Carnegie Institution of Washington, 1915. 98, [1] p. front., illus. 20 cm. Carnegie Institution of Washington. Publication; no. 235. "Published papers of the observatory": p. 92-98.

905. Hale, Matthew, Sir, 1609-1676. *Difficiles nugæ, or, Observations touching the Torricellian experiment: and the various solutions of the same, especially touching the weight and elasticity of the air.*
London: Printed by W. Godbid, for William Shrowsbury ..., 1674. [6], 304, [7] p., [2] folded leaves of plates: ill.; 17 cm. Errors of pagination: p. 151 misnumbered as 551, p. 179 as 176. Advertisements: p. [6-7].
Provenance: Thomas H. Ellis (inscription), Eric Hutchinson (donor).

906. Hale, Salma, 1787-1866. *History of the United States: from their first settlement as colonies, to the close of the war with Great Britain in 1815.*
New York: Stereotyped by H. & H. Wallis: Published by Collins and Hannay, 1826. [2], iv, [7]-281 p.; 18 cm. Sabin 29662.
Provenance: Sarah Maynard (inscription).

907. Hales, Stephen, 1677-1761. *Statical essays: containing vegetable staticks; or, an account of some statical experiments on the sap in vegetables ... read at several meetings before the Royal Society / by Steph. Hales ... The third edition, with amendments.*
London: Printed for W. Innys and R. Manby ... T. Woodward ... and J. Peele..., 1733-1738. 2 v.: ill.; 20 cm. Errors in pagination: p. 281 misnumbered as 821 [v. 1]; p. 255 as 225. Plates engraved by Simon Gribelin. Includes index. Errata: v. 2, p. [1] following text. Horblit, H. D. *Grolier 100 science books,* 45b (vol. 2).
Vol. 2 is 1st ed.: Statical essays: containing hæmastaticks / by Stephen Hales. London: Printed for W. Innys and R. Manby ... and T. Woodward ... 1733.
Provenance: B. Guy Phillips (armorial bookplate).

908. Hales, Stephen, 1677-1761. *La statique des végétaux, et l'analyse de l'air: expériences nouvelles lûes à la Societé Royale de Londres /*

par M. Hales ... ; ouvrage traduit de l'anglois, par M. de Buffon....

À Paris: Chez Debure l'Aîné ..., M. DCC. XXXV. [1735]. xviij, [8], 408, [2] p., [10] folded leaves of plates: ill.; 26 cm. Translation of: *Vegetable staticks.* "Appendice contenant plusieurs observations et plusieurs expériences qui ont rapport aux précédentes": p. [319]-400. Includes index. Errata: p. [7] of second group. Plates signed: Maisonneuve. Pritzel, 3700.

909. HALES, STEPHEN, 1677-1761. *Vegetable staticks: or, An account of some statical experiments on the sap in vegetables ... Also, a specimen of an attempt to analyse the air, by a great variety of chymio-statical experiments....*

London: W. and J. Innys [etc.], 1727. 4 p.l., ii-vii, [2], 376 p. plates. 20 cm. Reissued in 1731 as v. 1 of his *Statical essays.* Illustrated by Simon Gribelin. Horblit, H. D. *Grolier 100 science books,* 45a.

Provenance: John Hardves (inscription); Herbert McLean Evans (bookplate); Ph. Darell (inscription).

910. HALL, ASAPH, 1829-1907. *Observations and orbits of the satellites of Mars. With data for ephemerides in 1879. By Asaph Hall....*

Washington: Govt. Print. Off., 1878. 46 p. tables. 32 cm.

Provenance: Herbert McLean Evans (bookplate).

911. HALLER, ALBRECHT VON, 1708-1777. *Iconum anatomicarum quibus praecipuae partes corporis humani exquisita cura delineatae continentur. Fasciculus I. [-VIII. et ultimus].*

Gottingae: Typis Abrami Vandenhoeck ..., 1743-1782. [110], 63, [5], 14, [30], 52, [8], 71, [11], 58, [2], 94 p., [41] folded leaves of plates: ill.; 44 cm. Fasc. I: 1743; fasc. II: 1782; fasc. III: 1747; fasc. IV: 1749; fasc.V: 1752; fasc. VI: 1753; fasc. VII: 1754; fasc. VIII: 1756. Fasc. have separate t. p. with varying titles. Variously illustrated by C. J. Rollinus, G. D. Heumann, J. P. Kaltenhofer, J. v. d. Spyk, M. Rössler, C. Sepp, J. C. Schrader, J. C. G. Fritzsch.

P. 93-94 are bound in twice. Provenance: Liverpool Medical Institution (label). Choulant, L. Anatomic illustration, p. 289-291.

912. HALLEY, EDMOND, 1656-1742. *Astronomiae cometicae synopsis / autore Edmundo Halleio....*

London : Printed for S. Smith and B. Walford ..., 1706. p. 1882-1899 ; 23 cm. In: *Philosophical transactions* / Royal Society of London, v. 24. Caption title. English translation, *A synopsis of the astronomy of comets,* cited by *PMM,* no. 173, and Burndy, *Science,* no. 12.

913. HALLEY, EDMOND, 1656-1742. *Astronomical tables with precepts, both in English and Latin, for computing places of the sun, moon, planets, and comets. By Edmund Halley....*

London: Printed for W. Innys, MDCCLII. [385] p., front. (port.) tables, 29 x 24 cm. Tables have special t.-p.: Edmundi Halleii astronomi dum viveret regæ Tabulæ astronomicæ. Accedunt de usu tabularum praecepta. Londini, apud G. Innys, MDCCXLIX. (1st chi 1). Includes index. Errata: p. [385]. *Babson Newton Coll.* 350.

Collation matches Babson 350 but with addition of unnumbered 3 leaves at beginning, as well as [4] p. signed $2P^2$ inserted after 2O p^3; also different distribution of unnumbered leaves at end. Errata bound before index.

914. HAMILTON, JOSEPH, b. 1839. *Our own and other worlds / by Joseph Hamilton; introduction by W. H. Withrow.*

New York: Eaton & Mains; Cincinnati: Jennings & Graham, 1904. 203, [1] p., [6] leaves of plates: ill.; 20 cm. Date of publication supplied by *NUC pre-1956,* v. 228, p. 520. Includes index. Advertisement on p. [204].

915. HAMILTON, WILLIAM ROWAN, SIR, 1805-1865. *Elements of quaternions. By the late Sir William Rowan Hamilton ... Ed. by his son, William Edwin Hamilton....*

London: Longmans, Green, & Co., 1866. vi p., 1 l., lix, 762 p. diagr. 23 cm. Includes bibliographical references.

Provenance: J. D. Everett (signature), J. D. Barker (signature).

916. HAMILTON, WILLIAM ROWAN, SIR, 1805-1865. *Lectures on quaternions.*

Dublin, 1853. 736 p. 22 cm.

917. HANCOCK, BLITH. *The astronomy of comets: in two parts ... / by Blyth Hancock....*

Bury St. Edmunds: Printed by P. Gedge, for J. Murray ; ... London ..., 1786. xvi, 90, [2] (blank) p., [1] leaf

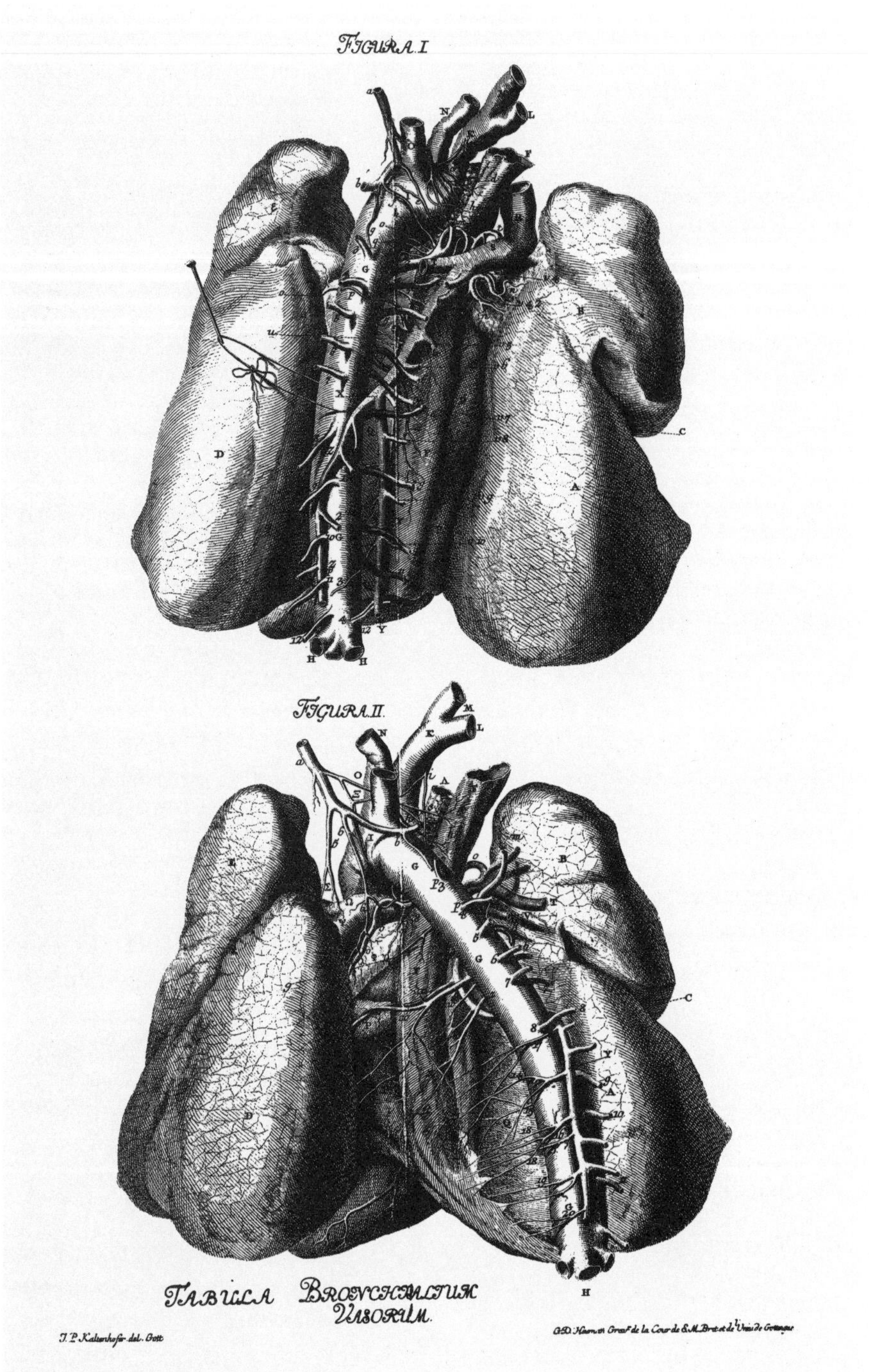

Haller, *Icones anatomicæ*, 1743-1782

of plates: 1 ill.; 22 cm. Signatures: A-C[8] D-K[4] L[2] (L2 blank). "Subscribers": p. [vii]-ix. Advertisement on p. [x]. Errata slip mounted on p. xiii. (From t. p.) Part I. Containing a physical account of the solar system, the whole theory of comets, with the rationale, or physical causes of these phenomena from the earliest ages to the present time – Part II. Containing the practical methods of calculation: first, by the properties of the parabola without tables: and secondly, by tables prefixed to the work ... the whole process of calculation exemplified in the comet which is expected to make its appearance in the year 1789.

Binder: Homecrafters, Tucson, Ariz. (ticket). Provenance: Samuel Horsley (inscription); H. Evans (signature). Imperfect? lacks A1. With: Of the valuation of the renewals of church leases. (England? : s.n., 1787).

918. HANCOCK, BLITH. *The doctrine of eclipses, both solar and lunar, containing short and easy precepts for computing solar and lunar eclipses ... With correct astronomical tables from a manuscript copy of the Tabulæ Dunelmenses, fitted to the meridian of Greenwich ... / by Blith Hancock.*

Norwich: Printed by J. Grouse for the author, 1782. xvi, 100 p.: plates (part fold.); 21 cm.

Binder: Homecrafters. Provenance: Evans (inscription).

919. *Handbuch der Astronautik, hrsg. von Karl Schütte und Hans K. Kaiser.*

Konstanz, Akademische verlagsgesellschaft Athenaion, A. Hachfeld [1958-]. v. 27 cm. Vol. 1 issued in parts [1958]-1964. Bd. 1, Heft 1. Die Geschichte des Raumfahrtgedankens von Willy Ley. – Die Schwerkraft und ihre Überwindung von Werner Schaub.

Library has: Bd. 1:Heft 1.

920. HARDING, CARL LUDWIG, 1765-1834. *Atlas nouus cœlestis: XXVII tabulis continens stellas inter Polum Borealem et trigesimum gradum declinationis Australis adhuc obseruatas / auctore Carolo Ludouico Harding.*

Gottingae: [s.n.], 1822. [1], XXVII folded leaves of plates: charts; 54 cm.

With ms. notes. Provenance: J. Lee (inscription).

921. HARLEY, TIMOTHY, d. 1904. *Lunar science: ancient and modern. By the Rev. Timothy Harley....*

London: S. Sonnenschein, Lowrey & Co., 1886. 4 p. l., 89 p. 22 cm. Notes, works referred to: p. 81-86. Includes index.

Advertisements: 5 p. at end. Provenance: Silas Bronson Library, Waterbury, Conn. (booklabel and embossed stamp).

922. HARLEY, TIMOTHY, d. 1904. *Moon lore. By the Rev. Timothy Harley ...*

London: S.Sonnenschein [etc.], 1885. xv, 296 p. incl. front., illus. 23 cm. "A contribution to light literature, and to the literature of light." – Pref. "Appendix. Literature of the lunar man": p. 259-260. "Notes: works referred to": p. 263-283. Includes index. I. Moon spots. – II. Moon worship. – III. Moon superstitions. – IV. Moon inhabitation.

Advertisements: 8 p. at end.

923. HARRIS, JOHN, 1667?-1719. *Astronomical dialogues between a gentleman and a lady: wherein the doctrine of the sphere, uses of the globes, and the elements of astronomy and geography are explain'd ... with a description of the famous instrument, called the orrery / by J.H. F.R.S. The second edition.*

London: Printed for John Horsfield ..., 1725. [2], vi, 184 p., [6] folded leaves of plates: ill.; 20 cm.

Provenance: James Brown (bookplate)

924. HARRIS, JOHN, 1667?-1719. *Lexicon technicum: or, An universal English dictionary of arts and sciences: explaining not only the terms of art, but the arts themselves./ by John Harris....*

London: Printed for Dan. Brown, Tim. Goodwin, John Walthoe, Tho. Newborough, John Nicholson, Tho. Benskin, Benj. Tooke, Dan. Midwinter, Tho. Leigh, and Francis Coggan, MDCCIV. [1704]-MDCCX., [1710]. 2 v.: ill., port.; 34 cm. Vol. 2 has variant publisher statement: Printed for Dan. Brown, Tim. Goodwin, J. Walthoe, Joh. Nicholson, Benj. Tooke, Dan. Midwinter, M. Atkins, and T. Ward. Vol. 1: [926] p., [8] leaves of plates (some folded); v. 2: [626], 44, [10], 120, [62] p., [7] leaves of plates (6 folded). "... earliest of the long list of English encyclopaedias..." – *Encyclopaedia Britannica,* 11th ed. Printed in double columns. Decorated initial at beginning of dedication to v. 2. "In this second volume ... the matter is entirely new and without any repetition ... of any thing in the former" – Introd. to v. 2. Subscribers' lists: p. [13-22] v. 1 and p. [13-24] (1st group) v. 2 Advertisements on p. [625]-[626] of 1st group of v. 2. Some plates signed by B. Lens, I. Sturt. Horblit,

H. D. *Grolier 100 science books*, 25a. *PMM* 171.

Provenance: Colonel Cooper (armorial bookplate). "Directions to the bookbinders": on v. 2 last p. Without port.

925. HARROW, BENJAMIN, 1888-1970. *Contemporary science, ed. with an introduction by Benjamin Harrow....*

New York: Boni and Liveright, [c1921]. 253 p. 17 cm. The modern library of the world's best books. Includes index. Modern physics, by R. A. Millikan. – The structure of atoms and its bearing on chemical valence, by Irving Langmuir. – Engineering before and after the war, by Sir Charles Parsons. – Methods of gas warfare, by S. J. M. Auld. – What are enzymes? by Benjamin Harrow. – Natural death and the duration of life, by Jacques Loeb. – The physiology of the aviator, by Yandell Henderson. – Twenty-five years of bacteriology: a fragment of medical research, by Simon Flexner. – Before and after Lister, by W. W.Keen. – The measurement and utilization of brain power in the Army, by R. M. Yerkes. – Conceptions and misconceptions in psychoanalysis, by Trigant Burrow. – Einstein's law of gravitation, by J. S. Ames.

Provenance: W. D. Trow (signature).

926. HARVEY, WILLIAM, 1578-1657. *The anatomical exercises of Dr. William Harvey, professor of physick and physician to the Kings Majesty, concerning the motion of the heart and blood / with the preface of Zachariah Wood, physician of Roterdam. To which is added Dr. James De Back his Discourse of the heart, physician in ordinary to the town of Roterdam.*

London: Printed by Francis Leach for Richard Lowndes ..., 1653. [40], 111, [21], 123, [1], 86 p. (the first leaf blank); 16 cm. Translation of: *De motu cordis* / William Harvey; *Dissertatio de corde* /Jacobus de Back; and *De circulatione sanguinis* / William Harvey. Translation of *Dissertatio de corde* has special t. p. with title: The discourse of James De Back ... Translation of *De circulatione sanguinis* (86 p. at end) has special t. p. with title: Two anatomical exercitations concerning the circulation of the blood ... The t. p. (2nd leaf) is a cancel in most copies. Cf. Keynes. Wing H1083. Keynes, G. *Harvey*, 19.

Provenance: Herbert McLean Evans (bookplate).

927. HARVEY, WILLIAM, 1578-1657. *Anatomical exercitations, concerning the generation of living creatures: to which are added particular discourses, of births, and of conceptions, &c. / By William Harvey....*

London: Printed by James Young, for Octavian Pulleyn, and are to be sold at his shop ..., 1653. [48], 566 [i.e. 556], [1] p.; 18 cm. Translation of: *De generatione animalium*. Page 556 erroneously numbered 566. Errata on p. [1] of last group. Wing H1085. Keynes, G. *Harvey*, 43. Osler, W. *Bib. Osleriana* 714.

Provenance: Jn. Swayne (inscription); Herbert McLean Evans (bookplate). First blank leaf missing.

928. HARVEY, WILLIAM, 1578-1657. *De motv locali animalivm, 1627. Edited, translated and introduced by Gweneth Whitteridge.*

Cambridge: Published for the Royal College of Physicians at the University Press, 1959. x, 162 p. diagrs., facsim. 26 cm. Parallel Latin and English text. "Transcription and translation of what appear to be the notes for a treatise on the physiology of movement which Harvey intended to write." The original is contained in the British Museum manuscript Sloane 486, ff. 69-118v. Includes index. Bibliography: p. 154-156.

929. HARVEY, WILLIAM, 1578-1657. *Exercitatio anatomica de motu cordis et sanguinis in animalibus by William Harvey, M.D.; with an English translation and annotations by Chauncey D. Leake.*

Springfield, Ill., Baltimore, Md.: C. C. Thomas, 1928. 6 p. l., fascim. (72, [2] p.) 154 p., 1 l. front., plates, ports.,facsim. 25 cm. Includes index. Coat of arms on t.-p. At head of title: Tercentennial edition. Pt. 1. Facsimile of the original Latin edition (1628) – pt. 2. The English translation. Keynes, G. *Harvey* (2nd ed.), 25a.

Provenance: Ernest S. du Bray (inscription).

930. HARVEY, WILLIAM, 1578-1657. *Exercitationes de generatione animalium. Quibus accedunt quædam De partu: De membranis ac humoribus uteri: & De conceptione....*

Londini: Typis Du-Gardianis; impensis Octaviani Pulleyn ... , 1651. [30], 301, [1] p.; 23 cm. Errata: p. [1] at end. Added engraved title page with title: *De generatione animalium*. Keynes, G. *Harvey*, 34. Wing H1091.

Engraved t. p. bound after t. p. First prelim. leaf (blank) missing. Provenance: Herbert McLean Evans (bookplate); Joa. Ge[?]bson (inscription).

931. HARVEY, WILLIAM, 1578-1657. *Guilielmi Harveii opera omnia: a Collegio Medicorum Londinensi edita : MDCCLXVI.*

[Londini: excudebat G. Bowyer, 1766]. 4 p. l., xxxviii p., 1 l., 673 p. front. (port.) 30 cm. Imprint taken from colophon. Port. signed: Corns. Jonson pinxt, J. Hall sculp.; plate signed: J. Mynde sc. Emendanda: p. [1] 2nd sequence, and p. 673. Osler, W. *Bib. Osleriana*, 717. Keynes, G. *Harvey* (2nd ed.), 47. Praefatio. – Harveii vita (auctore Thoma Lawrence) – Exercitatio de motu cordis et sanguinis. – Exercitationes duæ anatomicæ de circulatione sanguinis: ad Joannem Riolanum filium, Parisiensem. – Exercitationes de generatione animalium: quibus accedunt quaedam de partu, de membranis ac humoribus uteri; et de conceptione. – Anatomia Thomae Parri. – Guilielmi Harveii epistolae [IX] – Diploma patavinum Harveio concessum.

Provenance: Presented to Sir William Jenner, Bart. by the Royal College of Physicians, London (plate); Herbert McLean Evans (bookplate).

932. HARVEY, WILLIAM, 1578-1657. *Movement of the heart and blood in animals; an anatomical essays. Translated from the original Latin by Kenneth J. Franklin and now published for the Royal College of Physicians of London.*

Oxford, Blackwell Scientific Publications, 1957. xii, 209 p. illus., col. port. 23 cm. Originaly published: *De motu cordis.* English and Latin; added t. p. for each part has original (Frankfurt, 1628) imprint. Bibliography: p. vii.

Provenance: Herbert McLean Evans (bookplate).

933. HARVEY, WILLIAM, 1578-1657. *Prelectiones anatomiæ universalis / by William Harvey; edited with anautotype reproduction of the original by a committee of the Royal College of Physicians of London.*

London: J. & A. Churchill ..., 1886. viii, 98 [i.e. 195] p., [196] p. of plates: facsims.; 26 cm. The t. p. of the ms. is dated 1616. Numbering of p. repeated. Reproduced from Sloane ms. 230, A in the British Museum. Keynes, G. *Harvey* (2nd ed.), 52. Osler, W. *Bib. Osleriana*, 719. Scott, E.J.L. *Sloane ms.* p. 243.

Provenance: Herbert McLean Evans (bookplate).

934. HARVEY, WILLIAM, 1578-1657. *The works of William Harvey ... Tr. from the Latin, with a life of the author, by Robert Willis....*

London: Printed for the Sydenham Society, 1847. xcvi, 624 p. 22 cm. Preface. – Life of William Harvey. – Last will and testament of William Harvey. – An anatomical disquisition on the motion of the heart and blood in animals. – The first anatomical disquisition on the circulation of the blood, addressed to John Riolan. – A second disquisition to John Riolan; in which many objections to the circulation of the blood are refuted. – Anatomical exercises on the generation of animals; to which are added, essays on parturition; on the membranes, and fluids of the uterus; and on conception. – Anatomical examination of the body of Thomas Parr. – Letters.

Provenance: C. Hart Merriam (inscription).

935. HASLETT, ARTHUR WOODS. *Science in transition / by A. W. Haslett.*

London: The Scientific Book Club, 1949. iv, 252 p., [3] p. of plates: ill., port.; 22 cm. "For further reading": p. 239-241. Includes index.

936. HASSENFRATZ, J. H. (JEAN-HENRI), 1755-1827. *Cours de physique céleste, ou, Leçons sur l'exposition du système du monde: données a l'École polytechnique en l'an dix / par J. H. Hassenfratz....*

À Paris: A la Librairie Économique ...: De l'Imprimerie de Guilleminet, an 11, [1803]. xii, 379, [1] p., XXIX folded leaves of plates: ill. (some col.); 20 cm. Errata: p. (380).

Provenance: Massilia Soc. Jes. (inkstamp)

937. HAÜY, RENÉ JUST, 1743-1822. *Essai d'une théorie sur la structure des crystaux: appliquée à plusieurs genres de substances crystallisées / par M. l'abbé Haüy....*

À Paris: Chez Gogué & Née de la Rochelle ..., M.DCC.LXXXIV [1784]. [8], 236 p., VIII folded leaves of plates: ill.; 22 cm. Running title: De la structure des crystaux. Colophon: De l'imprimerie de Demonville ... 1783. Title vignette; decorative devices throughout text. Errata on p. [8] of 1st group. Plates signed: Fossier delin., Sellier sculp. Includes index. Horblit, H. D. *Grolier 100 Science Books* 47. Burndy. *Science* 92. California. *Epochal achievements* 65.

Provenance: Herbert McLean Evans (bookplate).

938. HAÜY, RENÉ JUST, 1743-1822. *Traité de minéralogie, par M. l'abbé Haüy. 2. éd., rev., corrigée, et considérablement augm. par l'auteur.*

Paris: Bachelier, 1822-23. 4 v. ill.; 23 cm. and atlas. 23 x 26 cm.

Binding: Académie de Paris prix du concours général (lettering on cover).

939. HAWKS, ELLISON, 1890- . *Astronomy/ by Ellison Hawks.*

London: T. C. & E. C. Jack, 1924. 294 p., [17] leaves of plates: ill. (1 col.); 21 cm. "Romance of reality" series.

940. HAWKS, ELLISON, 1890- . *The starry heavens, by Ellison Hawks....*

London and Edinburgh: T. Nelson & Sons, Ltd., T. C. & E. C. Jack, Ltd., 1934. x, 11-154 p. col. front., illus., XLIX pl. (part col.) 17 cm. "Shown" series. Second edition. First edition, 1910, published under title: *Stars shown to the children.* Includes index.

941. HAWKS, ELLISON, 1890- . *Stars shown to the children, by Ellison Hawks....*

London: T. C. & E. C. Jack; Platt & Peck Co., 1910. xii, 119 p. col. front., 49 pl. (7 col.) 17 cm. "Shown to the children" series; 9. Title vignette. Preface dated 1910. Includes index.

942. HAY, W. T. (WILLIAM THOMSON). *Through my telescope; astronomy for all, by W. T. Hay, F.R.A.S.; with an introduction by Sir Richard Gregory ... illustrations from drawings by the author.*

New York: E. P. Dutton & Co., Inc., [c1936]. xiii, 127, [1] p. incl. front., illus., diagrs. 20 cm. "First edition."

943. HEALD, FRANKLIN HERMANN, 1854- . *The procession of planets; a radical departure from former ideas of the processes of nature showing the true motion of matter, by Franklin H. Heald....*

Los Angeles, Cal.: Baumgardt Publishing Co., [c1906]. 12, 17-197 p. incl. front., illus., port. 20 cm. Includes index.

No. 14., signed by the author. Provenance: L. Sleigel (inscription).

944. HEATH, THOMAS LITTLE, SIR, 1861-1940. *A history of Greek mathematics / by Sir Thomas Heath.*

Oxford: Clarendon Press, 1960. 2 v.: ill.; 23 cm. "First published 1921. Reprinted lithographically from sheets of the first edition 1960" – T. p. verso. Includes bibliographical references and indexes. v. 1. From Thales to Euclid – v. 2. From Aristarchus to Diophantus.

945. HECKER, J. F. C. (JUSTUS FRIEDRICH CARL), 1795-1850. *The epidemics of the Middle Ages / from the German of J. F. C. Hecker ...; translated by B. G. Babington....*

London: George Woodfall and Son ..., 1846. xxviii, 380 p.; 23 cm. Translation of three works published originally as separates: *Der schwarze Tod im vierzehnten Jahrhundert; Die Tanzwuth; Der englische Schweiss.* "*Schwarze Tod* ... was published in 1832 ...; *Tanzwuth* ... came out shortly afterwards ...; *Englische Schweiss* ... appeared in 1834 ... The three treatises [are] now comprised for the first time under the title of The epidemics of the Middle Ages" – P. [v]-vii. "Reprinted 1846." Added engraved t.-p.: The Sydenham Society. The appendix consists of "A boke, or counseill against the disease commonly called The Sweate ... made by Jhon Caius ... 1552." General preface – Hecker's address – The Black Death – The dancing mania – The sweating sickness – Catalogue of works referred to by the author – Appendix.

946. HEISENBERG, WERNER, 1901-1976. *Die Einheit des naturwissenschaftlichen Weltbildes, von Werner Heisenberg.*

Leipzig: J. A. Barth, 1942. 31, [1] p. 20 cm. Leipziger Universitäts reden, Hft. 8. "Öffentlicher Vortrag ... gehalten im Auditorium maximum der Universität Leipzig am 26. november 1941."

947. HEISENBERG, WERNER, 1901-1976. *Die physikalischen Prinzipien der Quantentheorie.*

Leipzig: S. Hirzel, 1930. viii, 117, [1] p. [2] leaves of plates: 23 cm. Advertisements: [2] p. at end. Includes index. Bibliography: p. 114-115.

Provenance: Runge (signature).

948. HEISENBERG, WERNER, 1901-1976. *Two lectures.*

Cambridge [Eng.]: University Press, 1949. 51, [1] p. illus. 19 cm. "Delivered in December 1947 at the Cavendish Laboratory." "Literature": p. 25; page at end. The present situation in the theory of elementary particles. – Electron theory of superconductivity.

949. HELMHOLTZ, HERMANN VON, 1821-1894. *Beschreibung eines Augen-Spiegels zur Unter-*

suchung der Netzhaut im lebenden Auge / von H. Helmholtz....

Berlin: A. Förstnersche Verlagsbuchhandlung, 1851. 43, [5] p., [1] leaf of plates: ill.; 23 cm. Advertisements on lower wrapper. Plate signed: Helmholtz gez., Afinger gest.

950. HELMHOLTZ, HERMANN VON, 1821-1894. *Handbuch der physiologischen Optik / bearbeitet von H. Helmholtz....*

Leipzig: Leopold Voss, 1867. xiv, 874, [1] p., XI leaves of plates (2 folded): ill. (1 col.); 23cm. Allgemeine Encyklopädie der Physik; Bd. 9. Berichtigungen: final page. Illustrated by C. E. Weber. Includes bibliographical references and indexes. Horblit, H. D. *Grolier 100 science books,* 49b.

Bound in 2 v. Original printed wrapper bound in v. 2. Imperfect: plate XI missing. Provenance: F. B. Loring (bookplate); Edwd[?] Loring Jr. (signature).

951. HELMHOLTZ, HERMANN VON, 1821-1894. *Die Lehre von den Tonempfindungen als physiologische Grundlage für die Theorie der Musik. / Von H. Helmholtz....*

Braunschweig: Druck und Verlag von Friedrich Vieweg und Sohn., 1863. XI, [1], 600 p.: ill., music; 22 cm. Errata on p. [1] of 2nd group. Includes bibliographical references. Horblitt, H. D. *Grolier 100 science books,* 49a.

952. HELMHOLTZ, HERMANN VON, 1821-1894. *Die Mechanik der Gehörknöchelchen und des Trommelfells / von H. Helmholtz.*

Bonn: M. Cohen, 1869. 60 p.: ill.; 24 cm. "Separatabdruck aus *Pflüger's Archiv für Physiologie* I. Jahrgang." Includes bibliographical references.

953. HELMHOLTZ, HERMANN VON, 1821-1894. *The mechanism of the ossicles of the ear and membrana tympani. Tr. From the German with the author's permission by Albert H. Buck and Normand Smith.*

New York: Wood, 1873. 69 p. illus. 25 cm. Translation of: *Die Mechanik der Gehorknöchelchen und des Trommelfells,* originally published in *Pflüger's Archiv für Physiologie,* 1869.

Provenance: C. Hart Merriam (signature).

954. HELMHOLTZ, HERMANN VON, 1821-1894. *Popular lectures on scientific subjects. by H. Helmholtz ... Tr. by E. Atkinson ... With an introduction by Professor Tyndall.*

London: Longmans, Green, and Co., 1873. xvi, 397 p. illus. 21 cm. Advertisements: [2] p. following text. I. On the relation of natural science to science in general. Tr. By H. W. Eve. – II. On Goethe's scientific researches. Tr. by H. W. Eve. – III. On the physiological causes of harmony in music. Tr. by A. J. Ellis. – IV. Ice and glaciers. Tr. by Dr. Atkinson. – V. On the interaction of the natural forces. Tr. By Professor Tyndall. – VI. The recent progress of the theory of vision. Tr. by Dr. Pye-Smith. – VII. On the conservation of force. Tr. by Dr. Atkinson. – VIII. On the aim and progress of physical science. Tr. by Dr. W. Flight.

955. HELMHOLTZ, HERMANN VON, 1821-1894. *Populäre wissenschaftliche Vorträge. Drittes Heft / von H. Helmholtz.*

Braunschweig: Druck und Verlag Friedrich Vieweg und Sohn, 1876. VII, [3], 139 p.: ill.; 22cm.

No. 9 in a v. of 11 items with binder's title: Geometrie. Provenance: Ernst Mach (inkstamp).

956. HELMHOLTZ, HERMANN VON, 1821-1894. *Über die Erhaltung der Kraft, eine physikalische Abhandlung: vorgetragen in der Sitzung der physikalischen Gesellschaft zu Berlin am 23sten Juli 1847 / von H. Helmholtz.*

Berlin: G. Reimer, 1847. 72 p.; 22 cm. Berichtigung: p. 72. Horblit, H. D. *Grolier 100 science books,* 48.

Provenance: Herbert McLean Evans (bookplate).

957. HELMHOLTZ, HERMANN VON, 1821-1894. *Über das Sehen des Menschen: ein populärwissenschaftlicher Vortrag, gehalten zu Königsberg in Pr. zum Besten von Kant's Denkmal am 27. Februar 1855 / von H. Helmholtz.*

Leipzig: L. Voss, 1855. 42, [2] p. ; 23 cm.

958. HELMHOLTZ, HERMANN VON, 1821-1894. *Über die Thatsachen, die der Geometrie zu Grunde liegen / von H. Helmholtz.*

Göttingen: [s.n.], 1868. p. (193)-221; 22 cm. Nachrichten d. k. Gesellschaft d. W. zu Göttingen, 1868 Juni 3.

No. 1 in a v. with binder's title: Geometrie, I., containing 18 items of which 8 are offprints from journals.

959. HELMONT, JEAN BAPTISTE VAN, 1577-1644. *Opuscula medica inaudita. Joanais Baptistæ Van Helmont ... Opuscula medica inaudita. Editio secunda multo emendatior.*

Amsterodami: Apud Ludovicum Elzevirium, 1648. [8], 110, 115, [1], 88 p.; 22 cm. Edited by F. M. van Helmont. "Scholarum humoristarum passiva deceptio atque ignorantia ...": p. 68-115 of part [2] has caption title. With (as issued) the author's *Ortus medicinæ*. Amsterodami, 1648. Separately paged pts. have special title pages. Printed in double columns. Osler, W. *Bib. Osleriana*, 2932. (From t. p.) I. De lithias: – II. De febrius – III. De humoribus Galeni – IV De peste.

960. HELMONT, JEAN BAPTISTE VAN, 1577-1644. *Ortus medicinæ, id est Initia physicæ inaudita: progressus medicinæ novus, in morborum ultionem, ad vitam longam / authore Ioanne Baptista Van Helmont ...; edente authoris filio Francisco Mercurio Van Helmont, cum ejus præfatione ex Belgico translatâ.*

Amsterodami: Apud Ludovicum Elzevirium, 1648. [36], 800 [i.e. 806] p.: ill., ports.; 20 cm. Errors in pagination: p. 87-88 repeated, p. 119 misnumbered as 127, p. 159-160 omitted, p. 175-176 repeated, p. 207 misnumbered as 107, p. 373-382 repeated, p. 443 misnumbered as 343, p. 453-456 omitted, p. 540-541 misnumbered as 538-539, p. 544 misnumbered as 542. Printed in double columns. With the author's: *Opuscula medica inaudita*. Amsterodami: Apud Ludovicum Elzevirium, 1648. Osler, W. *Bib. Osleriana*, 2929.

961. HENISCH, GEORG, 1549-1618. *Tablulæ institutionum astronomicarum / Georgii Henischii Bartfeldensis; adiuncta est Sphæra Procli cum textu Græco à regione in Latinam linguam conuerso.*

Augustæ Vindelicorum: Ex officina typographica Michaëlis Mangeri, 1575. [69] p.; 20 cm. Signatures: A-I^4 (I2 is printed as A2). Adams H224. Houzeau & Lancaster. *Astronomie* (1964 ed.) 2714.

Provenance: Monast. Lambacens. (stamp).

962. HENLE, JACOB, 1809-1885. *Allgemeine Anatomie: Lehre von den Mischungs- und Formbestandtheilen des menschlichen Körpers / von J. Henle....*

Leipzig: Verlag von Leopold Voss, 1841. xxiv, 1048, [2] p., 5 folded leaves of plates: ill.; 22 cm. Added t. p.: Samuel Thomas von Sömmering Vom Baue des menschlichen Körpers: neue umgearbeitete und vervollständigte Original-Ausgabe ...Sechster Band. Leipzig: Verlag von Leopold Voss, 1841. Illustrated by J.D.L. Franz Wagner. "Verzeichniss der mit Abkürzung citirten Schriften": p. [xiii]-xxiv. Includes index. Errata: [2] p. at end. Garrison-Morton (4th ed.), 543.

Errata bound after p. xxiv. Provenance: Mendelsohn, Berlin (booklabel).

963. HENLEY, CARRA DEPUY. *A man from Mars / by Carra Depuy Henley.*

Los Angeles, Cal.: Printed by B. R. Baumgardt & Co., [c1891]. [8], 15-66, [1] p.; 19 cm.

Binding: grey illustrated boards.

964. HERO, OF ALEXANDRIA. *Heronis Alexandrini Spiritalium liber / a Federico Commandino Vrbinate, ex Græco nuper in Latinum conuersus.*

Paris: Apud Ægidium Gorbinum ..., 1583. 163 p.: ill.; 21 cm. Original title: *Pneumatica*. Errors in pagination: p. 127 misnumbered as 217. Adams, H370.

Provenance: P. Guiraud (bookplate). T. p. damaged.

965. HERSCHEL, CAROLINE LUCRETIA, 1750-1848. *Catalogue of stars, taken from Mr. Flamsteed's observations contained in the second volume of the Historia Cœlestis, and not inserted in the British Catalogue. With an index, to point out every observation in that volume belonging to the stars of the British Catalogue. To which is added, a collection of errata that should be noticed in the same volume. By Caroline Herschel. With introductory and explanatory remarks to each of them. By William Herschel, LLD. F.R.S. Published by order, and at the expence, of the Royal Society.*

London: Sold by Peter Elmsly, Printer to the Royal Society, MDCCXCVIII. 136 p., 2 l. tables 44 cm. First edition; the astronomer's first printed work. Errata on last leaf.

966. HERSCHEL, JOHN F. W. (JOHN FREDERICK WILLIAM), SIR, 1792-1871. *Astronomy / by Sir John F. W. Herschel....*

London: Printed for Longman, Rees, Orme, Brown, Green & Longman ..., and John Taylor ..., 1833. viii, 422, [2] p., 3 leaves of plates: ill.; 18 cm. The Cabinet cyclopædia / conducted by the Rev. Dionysius Lardner ...; 43. Natural philosophy. Series statement at head of title. Added engraved t. p. has title: A treatise on astronomy. Added t. p., [2] page at end, has series title: The cabinet of natural philosophy / conducted by the Rev. Dionysius Lardner ... Includes bibliographical references and index.

Advertisements: 16 p. preceding half-title. Provenance: John Nash (booklabel and signature).

967. Herschel, John F. W. (John Frederick William), Sir, 1792-1871. *Catalogue of nebulæ and clusters of stars / by Sir John Frederick William Herschel, Bart.....*

London: Royal Society of London, 1864. 137 p.; 30 cm. Caption title. "Received October 16, – Read November 19, 1863." Detached from the Royal Society's *Philosophical transactions,* 1864.

Provenance: Herbert McLean Evans (bookplate). Lower journal wrapper attached.

968. Herschel, John F. W. (John Frederick William), Sir, 1792-1871. *Familiar lectures on scientific subjects / by Sir John F. W. Herschel....*

London and New York: Alexander Strahan ..., 1867. [2], viii, 507 p.: ill.; 20 cm.

969. Herschel, John F. W. (John Frederick William), Sir, 1792-1871. *A Manual of scientific enquiry: prepared for the use of Her Majesty's Navy: and adapted for travellers in general. / Edited by Sir John F. W. Herschel, Bart. Published by authority of the Lords Commissioners of the Admiralty.*

London: John Murray ..., 1849. [2], xi, [1], 96, 96a-b, 97-488 p., [3] leaves of plates (2 folded): ill., maps; 21 cm. Maps signed: J. & C. Walker sculpt. Advertisements on inside front and back covers and fly-leaves. Includes bibliographical references.

970. Herschel, John F. W. (John Frederick William), Sir, 1792-1871. *Observations of nebulæ and clusters of stars: made at Slough, with a twenty-feet reflector, between the years 1825 and 1833 / by Sir John Frederick William Herschel, Knt. Guelp.....*

London: Royal Society of London, 1833. p.359-505, [8] leaves of plates: ill.; 30 cm. Caption title. Detached from the Royal Society's *Philosophical transactions,* 1833. "Received July 1, – Read November 21, 1833." Plates signed "Js. Basire."

Provenance: Herbert McLean Evans (bookplate). Lower journal wrapper attached.

971. Herschel, John F. W. (John Frederick William), Sir, 1792-1871. *Outlines of astronomy / by Sir John F. W. Herschel ... Seventh edition.*

London: Longman, Green, Longman, Roberts & Green, 1864. xxiv, 729, [1] p., [9] leaves of plates (1 folded): ill.; 24 cm. "The work here offered ... is based upon ... a treatise on the same subject forming part 43 of the *Cabinet cyclopædia,* published in the year 1833" – P. [vii]. Errata slip tipped in. Includes bibliographical references.

972. Herschel, John F. W. (John Frederick William), Sir, 1792-1871. *Outlines of astronomy / by Sir John F. W. Herschel ... Tenth edition.*

London: Longmans, Green and Co., 1869. xxviii, 753, [1] p., [9] leaves of plates (1 folded): ill.; 24 cm. "The work here offered ... is based upon and may be considered as an extension ... of a treatise on the same subject, forming Part 43 of the *Cabinet cyclopædia,* published in the year 1833" – P. [vii]. Includes bibliographical references and index.

973. Herschel, John F. W. (John Frederick William), Sir, 1792-1871. *Outlines of astronomy / by Sir John F. W. Herschel, Bart., K.H. ... New edition.*

London: Longmans, Green, and Co., 1883. xxviii, 753 p., vi, [3] plates: ill.: 22 cm. Last 3 plates numbered A-C. Illustrated by H. Adlard. Includes index.

Provenance: Benjamin Davies (1st prize in Viaduct Institute, Earlestown examinations)

974. Herschel, John F. W. (John Frederick William), Sir, 1792-1871. *Outlines of astronomy / by Sir John F. W. Herschel.*

New York: P. F. Collier, 1901. 2 v. (926 p., [10] leaves of plates (1 folded)): ill.; 21 cm. Library of universal literature. Pt. 1, Science; 19-20. "The work here offered ... is based upon and may be considered as an extension ... of a treatise on the same subject, forming Part 43 of the *Cabinet cyclopædia*, published in the year 1833" – P. 11. Includes bibliographical references.

975. HERSCHEL, JOHN F. W. (JOHN FREDERICK WILLIAM), SIR, 1792-1871. *Results of astronomical observations made during the years 1834, 5, 6,7, 8, at the Cape of Good Hope; being the completion of a telescopic survey of the whole surface of the visible heavens, commenced in 1825, by Sir John F. W. Herschel, bart.*

London: Smith, Elder, 1847. xx, 452 p. illus., 17 plates (4 fold.) tables, diagrs. 32 cm. Plates signed: J.F.W. Herschel delint., and J. Basire sc. Advertisements: [2] p. at the end.

976. HERSCHEL, JOHN F. W. (JOHN FREDERICK WILLIAM), SIR, 1792-1871. *The telescope. (From the* Encyclopædia Britannica.*) By Sir John F. W. Herschel....*

Edinburgh: A. and C. Black, 1861. vii, 190 p. illus., diagrs. 18 cm.

Advertisements: 16 p. at end.

977. HERSCHEL, JOHN F. W. (JOHN FREDERICK WILLIAM), SIR, 1792-1871. *Traité d'astronomie / par Sir John F.-W. Herschel ...; traduit de l'anglais et suivi d'une addition sur la distribution des orbites comètaires dans l'espace par Augustin Cournot....*

Paris: Paulin ..., 1834. [4], III, [1] (blank), 529 p., [1] folded leaf of plates: ill.; 17 cm. Addition: p. 493-524. Advertisement on lower wrapper. Includes bibliographical references.

978. HERSCHEL, JOHN F. W. (JOHN FREDERICK WILLIAM), SIR, 1792-1871. *Traité d'astronomie / de Sir John Herschel fils ...; traduit de l'anglais par M. Peyrot ...; les figures sont gravées par Gallé.*

À Paris: Chez l'auteur ...: Mansut fils ..., 1834. 224 p., 15 leaves of plates: ill.; 23 cm. Translation of: *Treatise on astronomy.* "Cet ouvrage fait partie de l'Encyclopédie de Cabinet sous la direction du docteur Lardner."

Provenance: College Royal de Henri IV, Université de France (binding).

979. HERSCHEL, WILLIAM, SIR, 1738-1822. [Collection of articles detached from the Royal Society's *Philosophical transactions* / by Sir William Herschel].

[1780-1818]. 60 pieces: ill.; 27-30 cm. Includes bibliographical references. Poggendorff, 1: 1087-1089. (From caption titles) (1) Astronomical observations on the periodical star in Collo Ceti (1780) – (2) Astronomical observations relating to the mountains of the moon (1780) – (3) Astronomical observations on the rotation of the planets round their axes (1781) – (4) Account of a comet (1781) – (5 & 6) On the parallax of the fixed stars; Catalogue of double stars (1782) – (7) Description of a lamp-micrometer, and the method of using it (1782) – (8) A paper to obviate some doubts concerning the great magnifying powers used (1782) – (9 & 10) A letter from William Herschel, Esq. ... to Sir Joseph Banks, Bart. ...; On the diameter and magnitude of the Georgium Sidus (1783) – (11) On the proper motion of the sun and solar system (1783) – (12) On the remarkable appearances at the polar regions of the planet Mars (1784) – (13) Account of some observations tending to investigate the construction of the heavens (1784) – (14) Catalogue of double stars (1785) – (15) On the construction of the heavens (1785 (not in Pogg.)) (16 & 17) Catalogue of one thousand new nebulæ and clusters of stars; Investigation of the cause of the indistinctness of vision which has been ascribed to the smallness of the optic pencil (1786) – (18) An account of three volcanoes in the moon (1787) – (19) On the Georgian planet and its satellites (1788) – (20) Observations on a comet (1789) – (21) Catalogue of a second thousand of new nebulæ and clusters of stars (1789) – (22) Account of the discovery of a sixth and seventh satellite of the planet Saturn (1789) – (23) On the satellites of the planet Saturn (1790) – (24) On nebulous stars, properly so called (1791) – (25) Observations on the planet Venus (1793) – (26) Observations of a quintuple belt on the planet Saturn (1794) – (27 & 27A) Account of some particulars observed during the late eclipse of the sun (1794) (2 copies – one of which is large paper and lacking plate = 27A) – (28) On the rotation of the planet Saturn upon its axis (1794) – (29) On the nature and construction of the sun and fixed stars (1795). (30) On the method of observing the changes that happen to the fixed stars ... to which is added, a catalogue of comparative brightness, for ascertaining the permanency of the lustre of stars (1796) – (31) On the periodical star (Alpha) Herculis ... to which is added a second catalogue of the comparative brightness of

J F W Herschel delin^t
G.H. Ford, lithog^r
SITE OF THE TWENTY FEET REFLECTOR AT FELDHAUSEN,
Cape of Good Hope Sepr 1834.
London, Smith, Elder & Co 65 Cornhill 1847.

HERSCHEL, *Results of Astronomical Observations ... at the Cape of Good Hope*, 1847

the stars (1796) – (32) A third catalogue of the comparative brightness of the stars (1797) – (33) Observations of the changeable brightness of the satellites of Jupiter,and the variation in their apparent magnitudes (1797) – (34) A fourth catalogue of the comparative brightness of the stars (1799) – (35) On the power of penetrating into space by telescopes (1800) – (36 & 37) Investigation of the powers of the prismatic colours to heat and illuminate objects; Experiments of the refrangibility of the invisible rays of the sun (1800) – (38 & 39) Experiments on the solar and on the terrestrial rays that occasion heat, part I & II (1800) – (40) Observations tending to investigate the nature of the sun (1801) – (41) Observations on the two lately discovered celestial bodies (1802) – (42) Observations of the transit of Mercury over the disk of the sun (1803) – (43) Account of the changes that have happened, during the last twenty-five years, in the relative situation of double-stars (1803) – (44) Continuation of an account of the changes that have happened in the relative situation of double stars (1804? (not in Pogg.)) – (45) Experiments for ascertaining how far telescopes will enable us to determine very small angles (1805) – (46) On the direction and velocity of the motion of the sun, and solar system (1805) – (47) Observations on the singular figure of the planet Saturn (1805) – (48) On the quantity and velocity of the solar motion (1806) – (49) Observations and remarks on the figure, the climate, and the atmsophere of Saturn, and its ring (1806) – (50) Observations on the nature of the new celestial body discovered by Dr. Olbers (1807) – (51) Observations of a comet, made with a view to investigate its magnitude,and the nature of its illumination (1808) – (52) Continuation of experiments for investigating the cause of coloured concentric rings, and other appearances of a similar nature (1809) – (53) Supplement to the first and second part of the paper of experiments, for investigating the cause of coloured concentric rings between object glasses, and other appearances of a similar nature (1810) – (54) Astronomical observations relating to the construction of the heavens (1811) – (55) Observations of a comet, with remarks on the construction of its different parts (1812) – (56) Observations of a second comet (1812) – (57) Astronomical observations relating to the sidereal part of the heavens (1814) – (58) A series of observations of the satellites of the Georgian planet (1815) – (59) Astronomical observations and experiments tending to investigate the local arrangement of the celestial bodies in space (1817) – (60) Astronomical observations and experiments, selected for the purpose of ascertaining the relative distances of clusters of stars (1818).

980. HERSCHEL, WILLIAM, SIR, 1738-1822. *Observations and remarks on the figure, the climate, and the atmosphere of Saturn, and its ring / by William Herschel....*

London: Printed by W. Bulmer and Co. ..., 1806. 15 p., [1] leaf of plates: ill.; 27 cm. "From the *Philosophical transactions.*" "Read before the Royal Society, June 26, 1806" – p. [3]. Plate signed: Basire sc. Includes bibliographical references.

Provenance: author's presentation inscription.

981. HERSCHEL, WILLIAM, SIR, 1738-1822. *The scientific papers of Sir William Herschel, knt. ... including early papers hitherto unpublished; collected and edited under the direction of a joint committee of the Royal Society and the Royal Astronomical Society; with a biographical introduction compiled mainly from unpublished material, by J. L. E. Dreyer....*

London: The Royal Society and the Royal Astronomical Society, 1912. 2 v. fronts., illus., plates (part fold.) ports., facsims., tables, diagrs. 31 cm. Includes bibliographical references and index.

982. HERTZ, HEINRICH, 1857-1894. *Ueber sehr schnelle electrische Schwingungen; Nachtrag zu der Abhandlung über sehr schnelle electrische Schwingungen; Ueber einen Einfluss des ultravioletten Lichtes auf die electrische Entladung / von H. Hertz.*

Leipzig: Verlag von Johann Ambrosius Barth, 1887. p. 421-448, 543-544, 983-1000: ill.; 23 cm. *Annalen der Physik und Chemie;* n. F., Bd. 31, No. 7, 8b. Caption titles. Includes bibliographical references.

983. HERTZ, HEINRICH, 1857-1894. *Untersuchungen über die Ausbreitung der elektrischen Kraft.*

Leipzig: J. A. Barth, 1892. vi, 295 p. diagrs. 23 cm. Includes index.

Provenance: W. Kohlrausch (inkstamp); Edmund Neusser (bookplate).

984. HEVELIUS, JOHANNES, 1611-1687. *Johannis Hevelii Annus climactericus, sive Rerum uranicarum observationum annus quadragesimus nonus exhibens diversas occultationes, tam planetarum, quàm fixarum post editam Machinam cœlestem; nec non plurimas altitudines meridianas solis, ac distantias planetarum, fixarumque, eo anno, quousque divina concessit benignitas, impetratas: cumamicorum non nullorum epistolis, ad rem istam spectantibus: & continuatione historiæ novæ stellæ in collo Ceti, ut & annotationum rerum celestium....*

Gedani: Sumptibus auctoris, typis D. F. Rhetii, 1685. [12], 24, 196 p., [7] plates: ill., port.; 36 cm. Errata: p. 189. Plates numbered A-F. Includes index. Port. signed: A. Stech pinxit, Lambertus Visscher sculp. Plates signed: Observator sculpsit.

985. HEVELIUS, JOHANNES, 1611-1687. *Johannis Hevelii Cometographia: totam naturam cometarum; utpote sedem, parallaxes, distantias, ortum & interitum ... exhibens....*

Gedani: Auctoris typis, & sumptibus, imprimebat Simon Reiniger, 1668. [38], 913, [46] p., [38] leaves of plates: ill. ; 36 cm. Half-title: J. Hevelii Cometographia. Added engraved t. p. Illustrated by A. Stech, L. Visscher and the author. Errata: p. [46] at end. Includes index.

Provenance: Bibliotheca in Keszthely (inkstamp). With: *Johannis Hevelii Mercurius in sole visus Gedani.* Gedani: Autoris typis et sumptibus imprimebat S. Reiniger, 1662; and *Observatio eclipseos solaris Gedani* / à Johanne Hevelio peracta. [Danzig? : s.n., 1652].

986. HEVELIUS, JOHANNES, 1611-1687. *Johannis Hevelii Firmamentum Sobiescianum, sive, Uranographia: totum coelum stellatum ... exhibens....*
Gedani: Typis Johannis-Zachariæ Stollii, 1690. [2], 21, [1] p., [57] folded leaves of plates: ill.; 40 cm. Added t. p. dated 1687. The plates and added t. p. engraved by C. de La Haye after A. Stech. Plates numbered: A-3F. With: *Johannis Hevelii Prodromus astronomiæ*. Gedani: Typis Johannis-Zachariæ Stollii, 1690.
Text is bound to precede *Prodromus astronomiæ*.

987. HEVELIUS, JOHANNES, 1611-1687. *Mercurius in Sole visus. Johannis Hevelii Mercurius in Sole visus Gedani, anno ... MDCLXI, d. III Maji, st. n. cum aliis quibusdam ... observationibus ... Cui annexa est Venus in Sole pariter visa, anno 1639, d. 24 Nov. st. v. Liverpoliae, a Jeremia Horroxio, nunc primùm edita ... quibus accedit ... Historiola, novæ illius, ac miræ stellæ in collo Ceti....*
Gedani: Autoris typis et sumptibus; imprimebat S. Reiniger, 1662. 181 p. 10 plates 36 cm. Illustrated by the author. Includes index.
With: *Johannis Hevelii Cometographia*. Gedani: Auctoris typis, & sumptibus, imprimebat Simon Reiniger, 1668. Imperfect: t. p. defective.

988. HEVELIUS, JOHANNES, 1611-1687. *Johannis Hevelii Prodromus astronomiæ: exhibens fundamenta, quæ tam ad novum planè & correctiorem stellarum fixarum catalogum construendum, quàm ad omnium planetarum tabulas corrigendas omnimodè spectant ... quibus additus est uter[que] catalogus stellarum fixarum....*
Gedani: Typis Johannis-Zachariæ Stolli, 1690. [20], 350, [2] p., [3] leaves of plates (1 folded): ill., port.; 40 cm. Half title: J. Hevelii Prodromus astronomiæ cum catalogo fixarum, & Firmamentum Sobiscianum. Port. signed: A. Stech, Lambertus Visscher. Includes index. With: *Johannes Hevelii Firmamentum Sobiescianum, sive Uranographia*. Gedani: Typis Johannes-Zachariæ Stollii, 1690. Houzeau & Lancaster. *Astronomie*. (1964 ed.), 12781.

989. HEVELIUS, JOHANNES, 1611-1687. *Machina coelestis. Machinæ coelestis pars prior[-posterior].*
Gedani: Auctoris typis & sumptibus imprimebat S. Reiniger, 1673-79. 2 v. plates, port. 37-41 cm. Some plates by the author; some by I. Saal after A. Stech. Added engr. t. p. (repeated in vols., by J. Falck after A. Boy. Portrait in v. 2) by L. Visscher after A. Stech. Includes indexes.

990. HEVELIUS, JOHANNES, 1611-1687. *Observatio eclipseos solaris Gedani, anno æræ Christianæ 1652, die 8. Aprilis ... à Johanne Hevelio peracta.*
[Danzig?: s.n., 1652]. [8] p. illus. 35 cm. Title from tables on p. [4] and [5]. Illustrated by the author. Letter to Pierre Gassendi and Ismael Boulliau.
With: *Johannis Hevelii Cometographia*. Gedani: Auctoris typis, & sumptibus, imprimebat Simon Reiniger, 1668.

991. HEVELIUS, JOHANNES, 1611-1687. *Selenographia: sive, Lunæ descriptio; atque accurata ... delineatio. In quâ simul cæterorum omnium planetarum nativa facies, variæque observationes ... figuris accuratissimè æri incisis, sub aspectum ponuntur ... Addita est, lentes expoliendi nova ratio....*
Gedani: Autoris sumtibus, typis Hünefeldianis, 1647. [30)], 563 p. illus., port. 35 cm. Errata: p. 563. Includes index. Engraved t. p. signed: Adolf Boij delineav., J. Falck Polonus Sculps. Plates drawn by the author.
Letterpress t. p. missing. Provenance: author's presentation copy to the Senate [of Gdansk?] (inscriptions); Nicolai Pabl. Borus. (inscription).

992. HICKEY, JAMES C. *Introducing the universe; illustrated with photos and endpaper maps.*
New York: Dodd, Mead, 1951. xii, 154 p. illus. 21 cm.

993. HILL, JOHN, 1714?-1775. *Essays in natural history and philosophy. Containing a series of discoveries, by the assistance of microscopes.*
London: Printed for J. Whiston [etc.], 1752. 4 p. l., 415 p. 21 cm. Head- and tailpieces; initials.

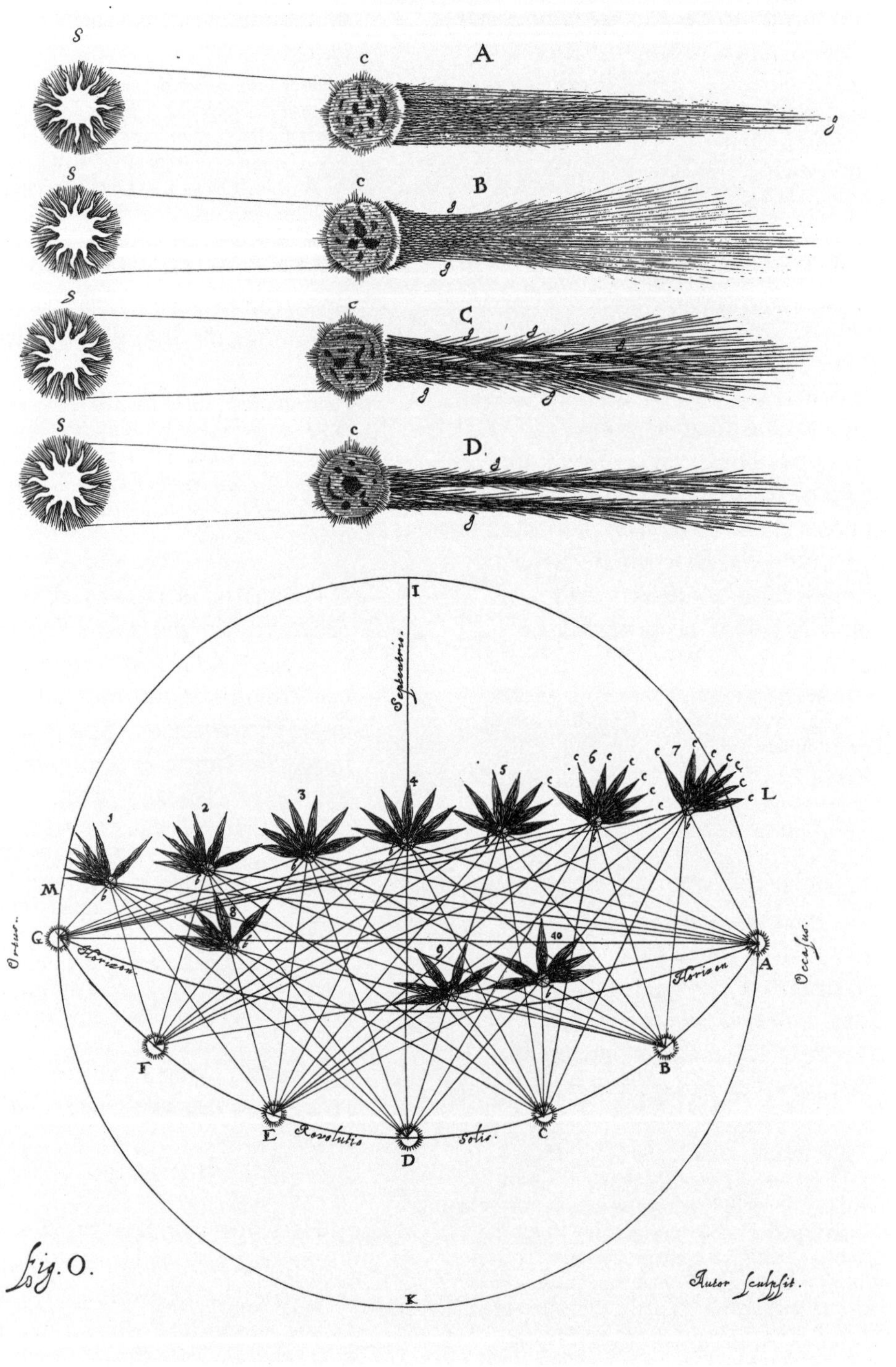

Hevelius, *Cometographia*, 1668

994. HILL, JOHN, 1714?-1775. *Urania or, A compleat view of the heavens: containing the antient and modern astronomy, in form of a dictionary ... / by John Hill....*

London: Printed for T. Gardner ..., 1754. [1240] columns, [13] folded leaves of plates: ill.; 25 cm. Signatures: pi^2 A-4H^4. Special t. p.: Urania ... vol. I. Being the first of a compleat system of natural and philosophical knowledge. No more published. Cf. *NUC pre-1956*, v. 246, p. 76. Houzeau & Lancaster. *Astronomie* (1964 ed.) 9366.

Provenance: Iames Hustler (armorial bookplate).

995. HIND, J. RUSSELL (JOHN RUSSELL), 1823-1895. *The comet of 1556: being popular replies to every-day questions referring to its anticipated re-appearance, with some observations on the apprehension of danger from comets / by J. Russell Hind.*

London: J. W. Parker, 1857. xii, 69, [1], 2 p.; 19 cm. Advertisements: 2 p. (last group).

996. HIND, J. RUSSELL (JOHN RUSSELL), 1823-1895. *The comets: a descriptive treatise upon those bodies. With a condensed account of the numerous modern discoveries respecting them; and a table of all the calculated comets, from the earliest ages to the present time. By J. Russell Hind....*

London: J. W. Parker and Son, 1852. viii, 184 p. 20 cm. Includes index.

Provenance: E. Brown (signature); F. A. Lloyd Philipps (signature). Ms. notes on lower fly-leaf concerning "The great comet of 1861."

997. HIND, J. RUSSELL (JOHN RUSSELL), 1823-1895. *An introduction to astronomy, to which is added an astronomical vocabulary containing an explanation of terms in use at the present day. By J. R. Hind ... 3d ed., rev. and greatly enl.*

London: H. G. Bohn, 1863. viii, 216 p. illus., diagrs. 18 cm.

Advertisements: 2-15 p. before and after text, including paste-down endpapers. Provenance: Frank Stewart (signature).

998. HIPPARCHUS, fl. 190-127 B.C. *Ipparchou Bithynou ton Aratou kai Eudoxou Fainomenon exegeseon biblia g' ... = Hipparchi Bithyni in Arati et Eudoxi Phænomena libri III. Eiusdem liber asterismorum. Achillis Statii in Arati Phænomena. Arativita, & fragmenta aliorum veterum in eius poema.*

Florentiae: In officina Iuntarum, Bernardi filiorum, M D LXVII, [1567]. [8], 123 p.; 30 cm. Some errors in pagination. Colophon reads: Florentiæ: Apud heredes Bernardi Iantæ, 1567. Edited by Pietro Vettori. Houzeau & Lancaster. *Astronomie* (1964 ed.), 774.

999. HIPPOCRATES. *Hapanta ta tou / Hippokratous = Omnia opera / Hippocratis.*

Venetiis: In ædibus Aldi & Andreæ Asulani soceri, Mense Maii, 1526. [6], 233, [1] leaves; 32 cm. Imprint from colophon. Title romanized. Includes index. Errors in foliation: leaf 16 misnumbered as 15, 35 as 36, 81 as 61. Stillwell, M. B. *Science*, 405. Osler, W. *Bib. Osleriana*, 142.

Ms. notes in Greek. Provenance: Starkensteid (bookplate).

1000. HIPPOCRATES. *Hippocratis Coi medicorum omnium facilè principis opera quæ extant omnia / Iano Cornario medico physico interprete; nouis & argumentis in singulos libros, & indice copiosissimo per Ioan. Culman. Geppingen. editis, illustrata....*

Lugduni: Apud Hæredes Iacobi Iunctæ, 1564. [6], 588, [114] p.; 34 cm. Colophon reads: Lugduni: Excudebat Symphorianus Barbier. Printed in double columns. Includes index. *Wellcome cat. of printed books*, 3184.

1001. HOEFER, M. (JEAN CHRÉTIEN FERDINAND), 1811-1878. *Histoire de l'astronomie depuis ses origines jusqu'à nos jours, par Ferdinand Hoefer.*

Paris: Hachette, 1873. 2 p. l., 631 p. diagrs. 18 cm. Histoire universelle. Includes bibliographical references.

Provenance: Charles Atwood Kofoid (bookplate); Lees-Museum Bibliotheck te Amsterdam (inkstamp).

1002. HOEK, MARTIN, 1834-1873. *De l'influence des mouvements de la terre sur les phénomènes fondamentaux de l'optique dont se sert l'astronomie.*

La Haye: M. Nijhoff, 1861. viii, 71, [1] p. II pl. (diagrs.) 31 cm. *Recherches astronomiques de l'Observatoire d'Utrecht;* 1. Livre. Errata: p. [72].

Hevelius, *Firmamentum Sobiescianum*, 1690

1003. Hoek, Martin, 1834-1873. *Perturbations de Proserpine, dépendantes de la première puissance de la masse perturbatrice de Jupiter.*
La Haye: M. Nijhoff, 1864. viii, 94 p. incl. tables (part fold.) 31 cm. *Recherches astronomiques de l'Observatoire d'Utrecht;* 2. Livre. Preface signed: M. Hoek.

1004. Hoek, Martin, 1834-1873. *Recherches sur la quantité d'éther contenue dans les liquides, par M. Hoek et A. C. Oudemans....*
La Haye: M. Nijhoff, 1864. viii, 71, [1] p. pl. 30 cm. *Recherches astronomiques de l'Observatoire d'Utrecht;* 1 livre., addition. Advertisements on p. [4] of wrapper.

1005. Hoff, J. H. van't (Jacobus Henricus van't), 1852-1911. *Acht Vorträge über physikalische Chemie: gehalten auf Einladung der Universität Chicago 20. bis 24. Juni 1901 / von J. H. van't Hoff.*
Braunschweig: F. Vieweg und Sohn, 1902. 81 p.: ill.; 23 cm. Title on spine: Physikalische Chemie.

1006. Hoff, J. H. van't (Jacobus Henricus van't), 1852-1911. *Études de dynamique chimique, par J. H. van't Hoff.*
Amsterdam, F. Muller, 1884. 2 p. l., iv, 214 p., 1 l. illus., diagrs. 24 cm.

1007. HOFF, J. H. VAN'T (JACOBUS HENRICUS VAN'T), 1852-1911. *The arrangement of atoms in space, by J. H. van't Hoff. 2d rev. and enl. ed. with a preface by Johannes Wislicenus ... and an appendix, Stereochemistry among inorganic substances, by Alfred Werner ... Tr. and ed. by Arnold Eiloart.*
London: Longmans, Green and Co., 1898. xi, 211 p. tables, diagrs. 19 cm. Translation of: *Lagerung der Atome im Raume.* Advertisements: 32 p. following text. Includes bibliographical reference and index.

1008. HOFF, J. H. VAN'T (JACOBUS HENRICUS VAN'T), 1852-1911. *Lois de l'équilibre chimique dans l'état dilué, gazeux ou dissous. Par J. H. van't Hoff....*
Stockholm: P. A. Norstedt & Söner, 1886. 58 p. diagrs. 31 cm. *Kongl. Svenska vetenskaps-akademiens handlingar;* Bd. 21, no. 17. Includes bibliographical references.

1009. HOFFMANN, ERICH, 1868- . *Die Ätiologie der Syphilis / von Erich Hoffmann.*
Berlin: J. Springer, 1906. 58 p., ii leaves of plates: ill.; 25 cm. "Sonderabdruck aus den *Verhandlungen der Deutschen Dermatologischen Gesellschaft: Neunter Kongress in Bern*" – T. p. verso. Includes bibliographical references.
In original printed wrappers, with [2] p. of advertisements on lower wrapper. Provenance: [?] Kirchhoff (signature); ms. marginalia.

1010. HOLDEN, EDWARD SINGLETON, 1846-1914. *The family of the sun: conversations with a child / by Edward S. Holden.*
New York, London: D. Appleton, 1912. xxiv, 252 p.: ill., port.; 19 cm. Appleton's Home Reading Books.

1011. HOLDEN, EDWARD SINGLETON, 1846-1914. *Hand-book of the Lick Observatory of the University of California / by Edward S. Holden....*
San Francisco: The Bancroft Company, [c1888]. [2], 128 p.: ill., ports.; 19 cm. Includes index. Advertisements: t. p. verso, p. [126].
Provenance: Author's proof copy; extensive ms. marginalia.

1012. HOLDER, WILLIAM, 1616-1698. *A discourse concerning time, with application of the natural day and lunar month and solar year as natural; and of such as are derived from them, as artificial parts of time, for measures in civil and common use. For the better understanding of the Julian year and calendar. The first column also in our church-calendar explained, with other incidental remarks.*
London: Printed by J. Heptinstall for L. Meredith, 1694. 120 p. 17 cm. Corrigenda: p. 120. Wing H2385.
Provenance: Edward Smith (inscription).

1013. HOLLAND, CHARLES J. *Rational philosophy of astronomy, by Chas. J. Holland.*
[Stockton, Calif.: Muldowney Printing Co., 1947]. 68 p. 20 cm.

1014. HOLLIS, H. P. (HENRY PARK), b. 1858. *Chats about astronomy / by H. P. Hollis.*
Philadelphia: J. B. Lippincott; T. Werner Laurie, 1910. 226 p., [6] leaves of plates: ill.; 19 cm. Date of publication from *U.S. Cat.*, 1910, p. 266. Includes index.

1015. HOLMAN, ADDIE A. DE GRAFFENRIED, "MRS. JESSE B. HOLMAN," 1862- . *An easy guide to astronomy, by Mrs. Jesse B. Holman ... containing an explanation of the zodiac, with maps and illustrations. Locating the principal constellations, and giving Greek myths connected with them. It also contains information of all other heavenly bodies, including its phenomena.*
San Antonio, Tex.: The Naylor Company, [c1940]. xi, 235 p. front., illus., plates, diagr. 21 cm. A new edition of the author's *The zodiac, the constellations and the heavens,* published 1924. Includes index.

1016. HOLMES, OLIVER WENDELL, 1809-1894. *Boylston prize dissertations for the years 1836 and 1837 / by Oliver Wendell Holmes.*
Boston: C. C. Little and J. Brown, 1838. xiv, [2], 371 p., [1] folded leaf of plates: ill., map; 25 cm. Includes bibliographical references. Facts and traditions respecting the existence of indigenous intermittent fever in New England – On the nature and treat-

ment of neuralgia – On the utility and importance of direct exploration in medical practice.

Provenance: Tho. C. Brintwade (signature).

1017. HOME, EVERARD, SIR, 1756-1832. *Lectures on comparative anatomy; in which are explained the preparations in the Hunterian Collection.*

London: G. and W. Nicol, 1814-28. 6 v. front. (port.) 371 plates. 32 cm. Vol. 2, 4 and 6 made up entirely of plates and explanatory letterpress. Some plates signed: Wm. Clift del., Js. Basire sculp. Vol. 5-6: "Supplement ... London, Longman, Rees, Orme, Brown, and Green, 1828." "A synopsis of the classes and orders of the animal kingdom" v. 3, p. [459]-576.

Presentation copy from the Royal College of Surgeons to the Earl of Liverpool.

1018. HOMER. *Homeri poetæ clarissimi Ilias / per Laurentiu[m] Vallensem Romanum e Græco in Latinum translata; [et] nuper accuratissime emendata.*

[Venice]: Impressum opus hoc emendatissimum Venetiis, accuratissima dexteritate, & impensa Ioannis Tacuini de Tridino, 1502, die xxv. Februarii. LXXXXVI leaves; 31 cm. Imprint taken from colophon. Adams, H781.

Ms. notes on margins.

1019. HOMER. *Homerou Ilias, e mallon hapanta ta sozomena. Homeri Ilias, Sev Potivs omnia eius quæ extant opera. Studio & cura Ob. Giphanii I. C. quàm emendatissimè edita, cum eiusdem scholijs & indicibus nouis.*

Argentorati: Excudebat Theodosius Rihelius, 1572. 2 v. (893, [73]; 827, [52] p.) 18 cm. Brunet, III: 272. Ritter, F. *Livres du 16.s. á la Bib. nat. de Strasbourg,* 1186, 1199. Vol. 2 has special t. p. only (Greek portion romanized): Homerou Odysseia, Homeri Odyssea, eiusdem Batrachomyomachia, Hymni, aliaq; eius opuscula, seu catalecta ... Dedication to vol. 1 dated XIIII. Kalend. Aprilis. A.D. 1572. Greek (text of H. Estienne) and Latin (text of J. Crespin's edition, Geneva, 1560-67) on opposite pages. Woodcut printer's devices on title pages.

Provenance: Francis James Rennell Rodd (bookplate, v. 2).

1020. HOOD, PETER, 1905- . *Observing the heavens / by Peter Hood.*

London: Oxford University Press, 1957. 64 p., ill. (some col.), charts, map; 24 cm. Oxford Visual Series. Bibliography: p. 64.

1021. HOOGERWERFF, J. A. (JOHN ADRIAN), b. 1860. *Magnetic observations at the United States Naval Observatory 1888 and 1889 / by Ensign J. A. Hoogerwerff....*

Washington: Government Printing Office, 1890. [4], 100 p., 14 folded leaves of plates: ill.; 30 cm. Washington observations, 1886; Appendix I. Chiefly tables. "Publication approved by the chief of Bureau of Equipment Navy Department."

1022. HOOKE, ROBERT, 1635-1703. *An attempt for the explication of the phænomena, observable in an experiment published by the Honourable Robert Boyle, esq.; in the XXXV. experiment of his epistolical discourse touching the aire. In confirmation of a former conjecture made by R. H.....*

London: Printed by J. H. for Sam. Thomson ... 1661. 3 p. l., 50 p. fold. plate. 17 cm. First edition. Dedication to Robert Boyle signed: Robert Hooke. Signatures: A-C8, D4. Cf. Oxford Bibliographical Society. *Proceedings & papers.* 1933. v. 3, p. 149, no. 260. *ESTC (RLIN)*, R015266.

With: Boyle, Robert. *New experiments physico-mechanicall, touching the spring of the air, and its effects.* Oxford: Printed by H. Hall ... for Tho. Robinson, 1660.

1023. HOOKE, ROBERT, 1635-1703. *An attempt to prove the motion of the earth from observations made by Robert Hooke....*

London: Printed by T. R. for John Martyn, printer to the Royal Society, at the Bell in St. Paul's churchyard, 1674. [8], 28 p., [1] leaf of plates (folded); 24 cm. Signatures: A-D4 E2. Colophon: London, printed for John Martyn, printer to the Royal Society. 1674. The epistle dedicatory to Sir John Cutler, signed Robert Hooke and dated: Gresham College, March 25, 1674. Folding plate inserted at the end with diagrams; figs. 1-8 illustrate Hooke's theory of parallax. First Cutlerian lecture; on p. 1: Numb. 1. Keynes, G. *Hooke,* no. 16.

With: *New experiments and observations on electricity. Part II* / by Benjamin Franklin. – The second edition. London: printed and sold by D. Henry and R. Cave ..., 1754. Provenance: Darwin family (inscription), G. H. Hare (signature).

1024. HOOKE, ROBERT, 1635-1703. *Micrographia, or, Some physiological descriptions of minute bodies made by magnifying glasses.: With observations and inquiries thereupon. / By R. Hooke....*

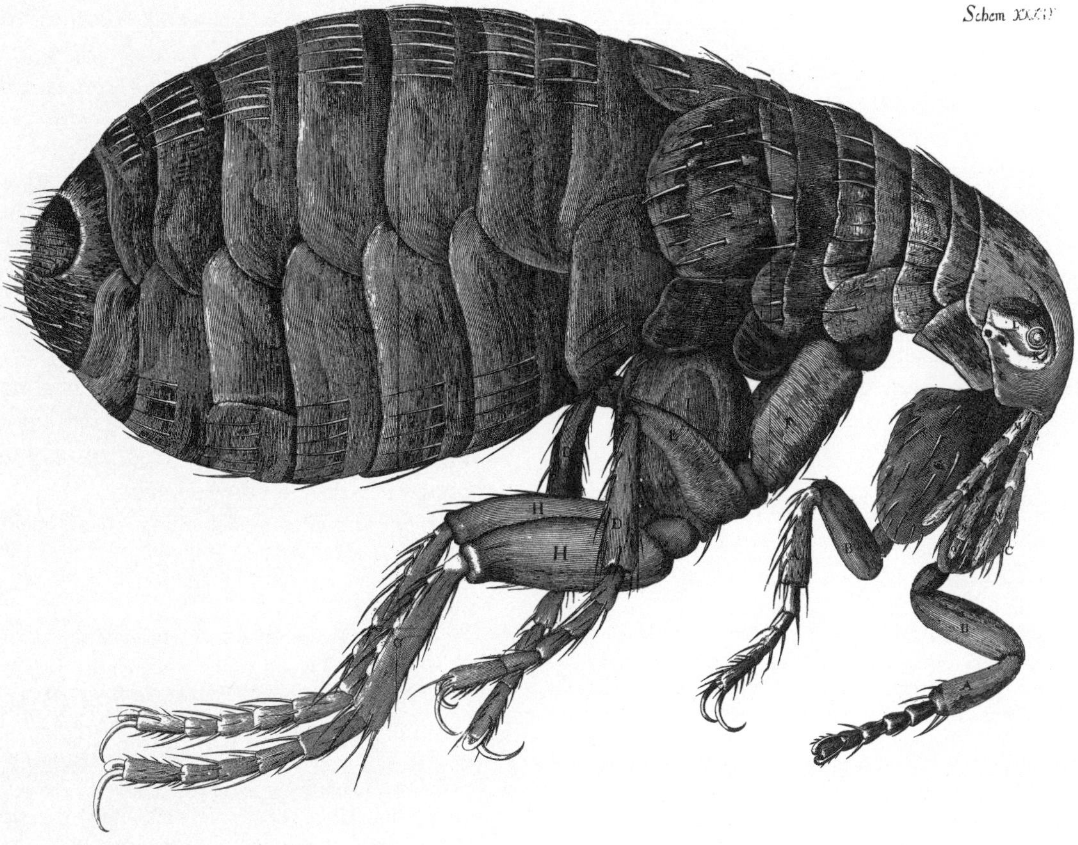

Hooke, *Micrographia*, 1665

London: Printed by Jo. Martyn and Ja. Allestry ... [for] the Royal Society ..., MDCLXV, [1665]. [35], 246, [10] p., XXXVIII leaves of plates (some folded): ill. (engravings), coat of arms; 31 cm. T. p. in red and black, with engraving of the Royal Society's coat of arms. Signatures: [pi]^2 A^2 a-q^2 B-C^2 D-Z^4 Aa-Kk^4 Ll-Mm^2. Errata: p. [10] at end. Plate 16 out of numerical order, facing descriptive text, p. 163. Wing H2620. Keynes, G. *Hooke,* 6. Horblit, H. D. *Grolier 100 science books,* 50. Goldschmidt, E. P. *Catalogue 165,* 87.

Provenance: William Gregory (inscription); Rob Raymond (inscription).

1025. Hooke, Robert, 1635-1703. *The posthumous works of Robert Hooke ... containing his Cutlerian lectures, and other discourses, read at the meetings of the illustrious Royal Society ... Illustrated with sculptures. To these discourses is prefixt the author's life, giving an account of his studies and employments ... Publish'd by Richard Waller....*

London: Printed by S. Smith and B. Walford, 1705. 4 p. l., xxviii, 572 [i.e. 506], [10] p., 1 l. 15 pl. (5 fold.) 33 cm. Errors in paging. The dedication is to Sir Isaac Newton. I. The present deficiency of natural philosophy ... with the methods of rendering it more certain and beneficial. – II. The nature, motion and effects of light ... particularly that of the sun and comets. – III. An hypothetical explication of memory; how the organs made use of by the mind in its operation may be mechanically understood. – IV. An hypothesis and explication of the cause of gravity, or gravitation, magnetism, &c. – V. Discourses of earthquakes, their causes and effects, and histories of several; to which are annext, physical explications of several of the fables in Ovid's Metamorphoses, very different from other mythologick interpreters. – VI. Lectures for improving navigation and astronomy, with the descriptions of several new and useful instruments and contrivances; the whole full of curious disquisitions and experiments.

Imperfect: lacks half title.

1026. HORNER, DONALD W. (DONALD WILLIAM). *Easy astronomy. Horner's Easy astronomy / by Donald W. Horner; with an introduction by W. F. Denning.*

Glasgow: Brown, Son & Ferguson, 1942. xv, 140 p., VIII, [1] leaves of plates: ill., charts; 19 cm. "Mr. Horner has designed his work to meet the particular requirements of seafaring men..." – p. vii. Includes index.

Provenance: Pvt. Donald E. Keeler (signature).

1027. HORROCKS, JEREMIAH, 1617?-1641. *Jeremiæ Horroccii Liverpoliensis Angli, ex Palatinatu Lancastriæ Opera posthuma....*

Londini: Prostant venales apud Mosem Pitt ..., 1678. [2], 496, [14], 69, [2] p.,]3?] folded leaves of plates: ill.; 21 cm. Errata: p. 496, and last p. Errors in pagination: 127 misnumbered as 227, 134 as 334, 246 as 311 (1st group), p. 56 as 54 (2nd group). Separate pts. have special title pages with varying imprints, dated 1672 and 1673. Includes bibliographical references. (From t. p.): Astronomia Kepleriana, defensa & promota – Excerpta ex epistolis ad Crabtræum suum – Observationum cœlestium catalogus – Lunæ theoria nova – Guilielmi Crabtræi Observationes cœlestes – Johannis Flamstedii De temporis æquatione diatriba. Numeri ad lunæ theoriam Horroccianam – Johannis Wallisii De cometarum distantiis investigandis. De rationum & fractionum reductione. De periodo Juliana. Wing H2869.

Imperfect: t. p. to pt. 8 and 2[?] plates missing, photocopies supplied. 7 prelim. leaves with running title: Epistola nuncupatoria are bound behind p. 496.

1028. HORROCKS, JEREMIAH, 1617?-1641. *The transit of Venus across the sun: a translation of the celebrated discourse thereupon / by the Rev. Jeremiah Horrox, curate of Hoole, (1639), near Preston; to which is prefixed a memoir of his life and labours, by the Rev. Arundell Blount Whatton....*

London: William Macintosh ... , 1859. xvi, 216 p., [3] leaves of plates (1 folded): ill. ; 20 cm. Preface dated July 26th, 1859. Translation of: *Venus in sole visa.*

Provenance: Herbert McLean Evans (bookplate).

1029. HOWARD, JOHN, 1726-1790. *Appendix to The state of the prisons in England and Wales, &c. / by John Howard ... ; containing a farther account of foreign prisons and hospitals, with additional remarks on the prisons of this country.*

Warrington: Printed by William Eyres; and sold by T. Cadell ... and N. Conant ... London, 1780. [4], 205, [9] p.,[7] leaves of plates (6 folded): ill.; 29 cm. Some plates signed: M. Fischer del., Isaac Taylor sculp. Includes index.

Provenance: Sir Henry Burdett (inkstamp).

1030. HOWARD, JOHN, 1726-1790. *The state of the prisons in England and Wales: with preliminary observations, and an account of some foreign prisons / by John Howard.*

Warrington: Printed by William Eyres, and sold by T. Cadell ... and N. Conant ... London, 1777. [6], 489, [1] (blank), [22] p., [3] folded leaves of plates: ill.; 29 cm. Includes index.

Provenance: Sir Henry Burdett (inkstamp).

1031. HUBBLE, EDWIN POWELL, 1889-1953. *The realm of the nebulæ / by Edwin Hubble....*

New Haven: Yale University Press; H. Milford, Oxford University Press, 1936. xii p., 1 l., 210 p. front. illus., xiv pl., diagrs. 28 cm. Yale University. Mrs. Hepsa Ely Silliman memorial lectures (1935). Includes index. "This book consists of the Silliman lectures, delivered at Yale University in ... 1935, with the addition of an introductory chapter." – Pref.

Provenance: Mars Baumgardt (author's signed presentation inscription).

1032. HUES, ROBERT, 1553-1632. *A learned treatise of globes, both celestiall and terrestriall: with their several uses / written first in Latine, by Mr. Robert Hues, and by him so published; afterward illustrated with notes, by Jo. Isa. Pontanus; and now lastly made English, for the benefit of the unlearned by John Chilmead Mr. of A. Christ-Church in Oxon.*

London: Printed by J. B. for Andrew Kemb, and are to be sold at his shop, on S. Margarets-hill in Southwark, 1659. [40], 209, 220-241, 142-186, [2] p. : ill. ;

17 cm. Translation of: *Tractatus de globis,* and 1st published in English, London, (1638). Translation attributed to Edmund Chilmead. cf. *Dictionary of national biography,* v. 10, p. 257-258. Signatures: A-V⁸ (-V8) (C3 verso, C4 and V7 verso blank). Several errors of pagination. Brown Univ. *JCB Library catalogue,* 3:14. Wing H3298. Contains numerous references to American geography.

Provenance: Dan. Fleming (inscription).

1033. Huggins, Lady, d. 1915. *Agnes Mary Clerke, and Ellen Mary Clerke; an appreciation by Lady Huggins....*

[S.l.] Printed for private circulation, 1907. xi, 54 p. front., ports. 23 cm. "Foreword" signed: Aubrey St. John Clerke. "List of papers contributed to Edinburgh review by Agnes Mary Clerke": p. 37-38. "A list of the works of Ellen Clerke": p. 52-53.

1034. Hulme, Nathaniel, 1732-1807. *Oratio de re medica cognoscenda et promovenda: habita apud Societatem Medicam Londinensem, die XVIII Januarii, anno MDCCLXVII / auctore Nathanēle Hulme ... ; cui accessit via tuta et jucunda calculum solvendi in vesica urinaria inhaerentem; ab historia calculosi hominis confirmata.*

Londini: Prostant apud G. Robinson ... et P. Elmsley ..., 1777. [2], 47, [1] p. ; 23 cm. Errata on t. p. verso. Advertisements on last p. Includes bibliographical references.

With: *New experiments and observations on electricity Part II* / by Benjamin Franklin.-The second edition. London: printed and sold by D. Henry, and R. Cave ... , 1754. Provenance: Darwin family.

1035. Humboldt, Alexander von, 1769-1859. *Cosmos: a sketch of a physical description of the universe / by Alexander von Humboldt; translated from the German by E. C. Otté.*

London: Harper & Brothers ..., [between 1850 and 1870]. 5 v.: port.; 20 cm. Vol. 4 translated by E. C. Otté and B. H. Paul, v. 5 translated by E. C. Otté and W. S. Dallas. Includes bibliographical references and indexes.

1036. Humboldt, Alexander von, 1769-1859. *Cosmos: essai d'une description physique du monde / par Alexandre de Humboldt; traduit par H. Faye ... et par Ch. Galusky.*

Bruxelles: C. W. Froment ..., 1851-1853. 4 v.; 19 cm. Vol. 1-2: 1852; v. 3: 1851 on t. p. and 1852 on upper wrapper; v. 4: 1853. Includes bibliographical references.

Bound in 3 v.

1037. Humboldt, Alexander von, 1769-1859. *Essai sur la géographie des plantes; accompagné d'un tableau physique des régions équinoxiales, fondé sur des mesures exécutées, depuis le dixième degré de latitude boréale jusqu'au dixième degré de latitude australe, pendant les années 1799, 1800, 1801, 1802 et 1803. Par Al. de Humboldt et A. Bonpland. Rédigé par Al. de Humboldt.*

Paris: Levrault, Schoell et Compagnie, 1805. xii, [13]-155 p. tab. 33 cm. Engr. dedicatory page added. Horblit, H. D. *Grolier 100 science books,* 51. Pritzel, 4327.

Imperfect? lacks engr. dedicatory page.

1038. Humboldt, Alexander von, 1769-1859. *Kosmos; Entwurf einer physischen Weltbeschreibung, von Alexander von Humboldt.*

Stuttgart: J. G. Cotta, 1845-62. 5 v. fold. table. 24 cm.

Provenance: Henry Eickhoff (signature); Ludovici (inscription).

1039. Humboldt, Alexander von, 1769-1859. *Kosmos. Entwurf einer physischen Weltbeschreibung, von Alexander von Humboldt ... Amerikanische Jubiläums-Ausgabe....*

Philadelphia: F. W. Thomas & Söhne, 1869. VI, 7-923, [1], XII p. front. (port.) 24 cm. "Namens-Verzeichniss der Subscribenten": XII p. Includes bibliographical references.

Advertisements: [3] p. at end. Provenance: Professor Falk (inscription); ms. annotations.

1040. [Humboldt Library of Popular Science Literature: Selections.]

[1879-1892]. 3 v.: ill.; 24 cm. Collection of various nos. of the series, published by Humboldt Publishing Company, New York. Most individual works lack title page. Binder's title: (v. 1) Science essays; (v. 2-3) Scientific essays. Includes bibliographical references. (v. 1) The romance of astronomy, by R. Kalley Miller; with an appendix by Richard A. Proctor. The forms of water: in clouds and rivers, ice and glaciers, by John Tyndall. The wonders of the heavens, by Camille Flammarion, from the French, by Mrs. Norman Lockyer. Light science for leisure hours: a series of familiar essays on scientific subjects, natural phenomena, etc., by Richard A. Proctor. The sun: its constitution, its phenomena, its condition, by Nathan T. Carr; with an appendix. Six lectures on light, by Prof. John Tyndall. Notes on earthquakes: with thirteen miscellaneous essays, by Richard A. Proctor. The unseen universe; philosophy of the pure sciences, by Wm. Kingdon Clifford. (v. 2) The childhood of the world: a simple account of man in early times, by Edward Clodd. Scientific aspects of some familiar things, by W. M. Williams. The mystery of matter. The philosophy of ignorance. The formation of vegetable mould, through the action of worms: with observations of their habits [Charles Darwin]. Scientific methods of capital punishment, by J. Mount Bleyer. The factors of organic evolution, by Herbert Spencer. Cosmic emotion; also [Virchow on] The teaching of science, by William Kingdon Clifford. Nature studies, by F. R. Eaton Lowe, Dr. Robert Browne, Geo. G. Chisholm, James Dallas. English past and present, by Richard Chenevix Trench. Modern science and the science of the future: with an essay on defence of criminals, by Edward Carpenter. The study of languages brought back to its true principles, by C. Marcel. The romance of astronomy, by R. Kalley Miller; with an appendix by Richard A. Proctor. Scientific sophisms: a review of current theories concerning atoms, apes and men, by Samuel Wainwright. (v. 3) Town geology, by the Rev. Charles Kingsley. The data of ethics, by Herbert Spencer. The wonders of the heavens, by Camille Flammarion; from the French, by Mrs. Norman Lockyer. Familiar essays on scientific subjects: viz., oxygen in the sun, sun-spot, storm and famine, new ways of measuring the sun's distance, drifting light-waves, the new star which faded into star-mist, star-grouping, star-drift, and star-mist, by Richard A. Proctor. On the study of words, by Richard Chenevix Trench. Geological sketches at home and abroad, by Archibald Geikie. Current discussions in science, by W. Mattieu Williams. The sun: its constitution, its phenomena, its condition, by Nathan T. Carr; with an appendix.

1041. Hume, David, 1711-1776. *An enquiry concerning the principles of morals. By David Hume....*

London: Printed for A. Millar, 1751. [8], 253, [3] p. 18 cm. Errata: p. [7] (1st count). Publisher's advertisements: p. [1-3] at end. Jessop, T. E. Hume, p. 22.

Leaf L3 is not a cancel. Provenance: St. Andren Ward (bookplate).

1042. Hunter, John, 1728-1793. *Observations on certain parts of the animal œconomy / by John Hunter.*

London: [s.n.], 1786. [6], 225 p., [18] leaves of plates: ill.; 27 cm. Nine papers reprinted with additions from the *Philosophical transactions* of the Royal Society. Variously illustrated by W. Skelton, W. Bell, P. C. Canot, J. V. Riemsdyk. Errata on p. [6]. Includes bibliographical references.

1043. Hunter, John, 1728-1793. *A treatise on the venereal disease / by John Hunter.*

London: [s.n], 1786. [12], 398, [26] p., 7 leaves of plates: ill.; 27 cm. Plates signed: Wm Bell del., Wm. Sharp sc.; Jas. Roberts sculp. Includes bibliographical references and index.

Provenance: Herbert McLean Evans (bookplate).

1044. Hunter, William, 1718-1783. *Anatomia uteri humani gravidi tabula illustrata, auctore Gulielmo Hunter. The anatomy of the human gravid uterus exhibited in figures, by William Hunter.*

Birmingham: Printed by J. Baskerville; S. Baker and G. Leigh, 1774. [40] p. 34 pl. 67 cm. Preface and descriptive text in Latin and English in parallel columns. Plates drawn by I. V. Rymsdyk.

1045. Huntington, Ellsworth, 1876-1947. *Earth and sun, an hypothesis of weather and sunspots, by Ellsworth Huntington, with a chapter by H. Helm Clayton.*

New Haven: Yale University Press, 1923. xxv, 296 p., 1 l. tables (part fold.) diagrs. (1 fold.) 24 cm. "The present volume is the sixth work published by the Yale University Press on the Theodore L. Glasgow Memorial Publication Fund."

1046. Hutchins, Robert Maynard, 1899- . *The atomic bomb versus civilization, by Robert M. Hutchins.*

Washington, Chicago: Human Events Inc., 1945. 14 p. illus. (port.) 22 cm. "Published in conjunction with the National Foundation for Education in American Citizenship".

1047. Hutton, Charles, 1737-1823. *A mathematical and philosophical dictionary: containing an explanation of the terms, and an account of the several subjects, comprized under the heads mathematics, astronomy, and philosophy both natural and experimental: with an historical account of the rise, progress, and present state of these sciences: also memoirs of the lives and writings of the most eminent authors, both ancient and modern, who by their discoveries or improvements have contributed to the advancement of them ... With many cuts and copper-plates. By Charles Hutton....*

London: Printed by J. Davis, for J. Johnson; and G. G. and J. Robinson, 1795-96 (v. 1, 1796). 2 v. illus., xxxvii pl., tables, diagrs. 28 x 22 cm. In double columns.

1048. HUTTON, CHARLES, 1737-1823. *Mathematical tables: containing the common, hyperbolic, and logistic logarithms. Also sines, tangents, secants, & versed sines ... / by Charles Hutton ... The fourth edition.*

London: Printed for G. and J. Robinson, and R. Baldwin ..., by S. Hamilton ..., 1804. xi, [1] (blank), 179, [1] (blank), 344 p.: ill.; 23 cm.

Provenance: Wm. J. Davies (signature).

1049. HUTTON, JAMES, 1726-1797. *The theory of rain; Theory of the earth, or, An investigation of the laws observable in the composition, dissolution, and restoration of land upon the globe / by James Hutton....*

[Edinburgh: Printed for J. Dickson ...: Sold in London by T. Cadell ..., 1788. p. 41-86, 209-304, [1], II leaves of plates: ill.; 27 cm. *Transactions of the Royal Society of Edinburgh;* v. 1. Caption title. Vol. 1 printed by T. Cadell. Includes bibliographical references.

1050. HUTTON, JAMES, 1726-1797. *Theory of the earth with proofs and illustrations ... / by James Hutton....*

Edinburgh: Printed for Messrs Cadell [etc.], 1795-1899. 3 v.: ill., 6 fold. pl.; 22 cm. Vol. 3 ed. by Sir Archibald Geikie and pub. by the Geological Society, London, 1899. No more published. Horblit, H. D. *Grolier 100 science books,* 52a.

Provenance: Herbert McLean Evans (bookplate).

1051. HUXLEY, THOMAS HENRY, 1825-1895. *Darwiniana: essays / by Thomas H. Huxley.*

London: Macmillan ..., 1899. x, [2], 475, [1] p.; 19 cm. Collected essays / by T. H. Huxley; v. 2. "First edition printed 1893. Reprinted ... 1899" – T. p. verso. Includes bibliographical references. The Darwinian hypothesis (1859) – The origin of species (1860) – Criticisms on "The origin of species" (1864) – The genealogy of animals (1869) – Mr. Darwin's critics (1871) – Evolution in biology (1878) – The coming of age of "The origin of species" (1880) – Charles Darwin (1882) – The Darwin memorial (1885) – Obituary (1888) – Six lectures to working men "On our knowledge of the causes of the phenomena of organic nature" 1863.

Advertisements: [2] p. at end. Provenance: M. Bottermann (signature).

1052. HUXLEY, THOMAS HENRY, 1825-1895. *Evidence as to man's place in nature / by Thomas Henry Huxley....*

[London]: Williams and Norgate ... London and ... Edinburgh, 1863. [8], 159 p., [1] leaf of plates: ill.; 23 cm. Title vignette. Includes bibliographical references. I. On the natural history of the man-like apes – II. On the relations of man to the lower animals – III. On some fossil remains of man.

Advertisements: 8 p. at end; [6] p. on endpapers. Binder: Edmonds & Remnants (ticket). Provenance: Herbert McLean Evans (bookplate); Herbert Nash (armorial bookplate and signature).

1053. HUXLEY, THOMAS HENRY, 1825-1895. *Method and results: essays / by Thomas H. Huxley.*

London; New York: Macmillan, 1901. viii, 430 p.; 19 cm. Collected essays / by T. H. Huxley; v. 1. "First edition, 1893. Reprinted ... 1901" – T. p. verso. Includes bibliographical references. Autobiography – On the advisableness of improving natural knowledge (1866) – The progress of science (1887) – On the physical basis of life (1868) – On Descartes' "Discourse touching the method of using one's reason rightly and of seeking scientific truth" (1870) – On the hypothesis that animals are automata, and its history (1874) – Administrative nihilism (1871) – On the natural inequality of men (1890) – Natural rights and political rights (1890) – Government: anarchy or regimentation (1890).

Advertisements: [2] p. at end. Newspaper photo of Huxley tipped in.

1054. HUXLEY, THOMAS HENRY, 1825-1895. *On our knowledge of the causes of the phenomena of organic nature. By Professor Huxley....*

London: B. Hardwicke, 1862. 4 p. l., [5]-157 p. illus. 19 cm. Half-title: Professor Huxley's lectures to working men. Advertisements: [2] p. following text.

1055. HUXLEY, THOMAS HENRY, 1825-1895. *Science and Christian tradition: essays / by Thomas H. Huxley.*

Macmillan, 1909. xxxiv, [2], 419, [1] p.; 19 cm. Collected essays / by T. H. Huxley; v. 5. "First edition, 1894. Reprinted ... 1909" – T. p. verso. Includes bibliographical references. Prologue (controverted questions, 1892) – Scientific and pseudo-scientific realism (1887) – Science and pseudo-science (1887) – An Episcopal trilogy (1887) – The value of witness to the miraculous (1889) – Possibilities and impossibilities (1891) – Agnosticism (1889) – Agnosticism: a rejoinder (1889) – Agnosticism and Christianity (1889) – The keepers of the herd of swine (1890) – Illustrations of Mr.Gladstone's controversial methods (1891).

Provenance: Cecil Grantham Page (presentation inscription from W. G. P., and armorial bookplate).

1056. HUXLEY, THOMAS HENRY, 1825-1895. *Science and Hebrew tradition; essays by Thomas H. Huxley.*

New York: D. Appleton and Company, 1897. 1 p. l., [v]-xvi, 372 p. ill. 19 cm. "Authorized edition." Includes bibliographical references. On the method of Zadig (1880) – The rise and progress of palæontology (1881) – Lectures on evolution (New York, 1876) – The interpreters of Genesis and the interpreters of nature (1885) – Mr. Gladstone and Genesis (1886) – The lights of the church and the light of science (1890) – Hasisadra's adventure (1891) – The evolution of theology: an anthropological study (1886)

Provenance: Fred & Ethlyn Whittier (bookplate).

1057. HUXLEY, THOMAS HENRY, 1825-1895. *The scientific memoirs of Thomas Henry Huxley, ed. by Michael Foster and by E. Ray Lankester.*

London: Macmillan; D. Appleton, 1898-1902. 4 v. illus., ports.,129 pl. (part fold.) 2 fold maps, diagrs. 27 cm. Papers contributed to scientific societies and periodicals arranged in chronological order with the name and date of the publication in which each first appeared.

Provenance: Arnold Peskind (nameplate).

1058. HUXLEY, THOMAS HENRY, 1825-1895. *The scientific memoirs of Thomas Henry Huxley. Supplementary volume, ed. by Professor Sir Michael Foster ... and by Professor E. Ray Lankester....*

London: Macmillan and Co., Limited; D. Appleton and Company, 1903. 6 p. 1., 90 p. 11 pl. (part fold.) 27 cm. Advertisements: [2] p. following text.

Provenance: Arnold Peskind (nameplate).

1059. HUYGENS, CHRISTIAAN, 1629-1695. *Abhandlung über die Ursache der Schwere / von Christian Huyghens; Deutsch herausgegeben von Rudolf Mewes.*

Berlin: Verlag von Albert Friedländer's Druckerei, 1893. [2], X, 46, [1] p.: ill.; 24 cm. Translation of: *Discours de la cause de la pesanteur.* Advertisements on wrappers.

Provenance: Herbert McLean Evans.

1060. HUYGENS, CHRISTIAAN, 1629-1695. *The celestial worlds discover'd: or, Conjectures concerning the inhabitants, plants and productions of the worlds in the planets. Written in Latin by Christianvs Hvygens, and inscrib'd to his brother Constantine Hvygens....*

London: Printed for T. Childe, 1698. vi, 160 p. 5 folded pl. 18 cm. Translation of *Kosmotheoros; sive, De terris cœlestibus earumque ornatu conjecturæ. Babson Newton Coll.* 353.

Provenance: Thomas Philip Earl de Grey (armorial bookplate); Henry Duke of Kent (armorial bookplate). Spine title: Planetary worlds.

1061. HUYGENS, CHRISTIAAN, 1629-1695. *Christiani Hugenii Zulichemii, Const. f., Horologium oscillatorium, siue, De motu pendulorum ad horologia aptato demonstrationes geometricæ.*

Parisiis: Apud F. Muguet ..., 1673. [14], 161, [1] p.: ill.; 33 cm. (fol.). Signatures: a⁴ e⁴ (-e4) A-V⁴ X1. Corrigenda: last p. Lalande, J. *Bib. astronomique,* p. 280. Harrison, J. *Newton,* 820. Horblit, H. D. *Grolier 100 science books,* 53.

Provenance: author's presentation copy to I.Newton (shaved inscription), John Huggins, Charles Huggins, James Musgrave (armorial bookplate), Herbert McLean Evans (bookplate).

1062. HUYGENS, CHRISTIAAN, 1629-1695. *Christiani Hugenii Zulichemii, dum viveret Zelemii toparche Opera varia.*

Lugduni Batavorum: Apud Janssonios Van der Aa, 1724. 4 v. in 1, 56 fold. plates, port v. 2, 26 cm. Vol. 1-2 have individual t.-p. Collation: [18], 308, [11], 316-

THE

Celeſtial Worlds

DISCOVER'D:

OR,

CONJECTURES

Concerning the

INHABITANTS,

PLANTS and PRODUCTIONS

OF THE

Worlds in the Planets.

Written in Latin by

CHRISTIANUS HUYGENS,

And inſcrib'd to his Brother

CONSTANTINE HUYGENS,

Late Secretary to his Majeſty K. *William.*

LONDON,

Printed for TIMOTHY CHILDE at the White Hart at the Weſt-end of St. *Paul's* Church-yard. MDCXCVIII.

HUYGENS, *The Celestial Worlds Discover'd*, 1698

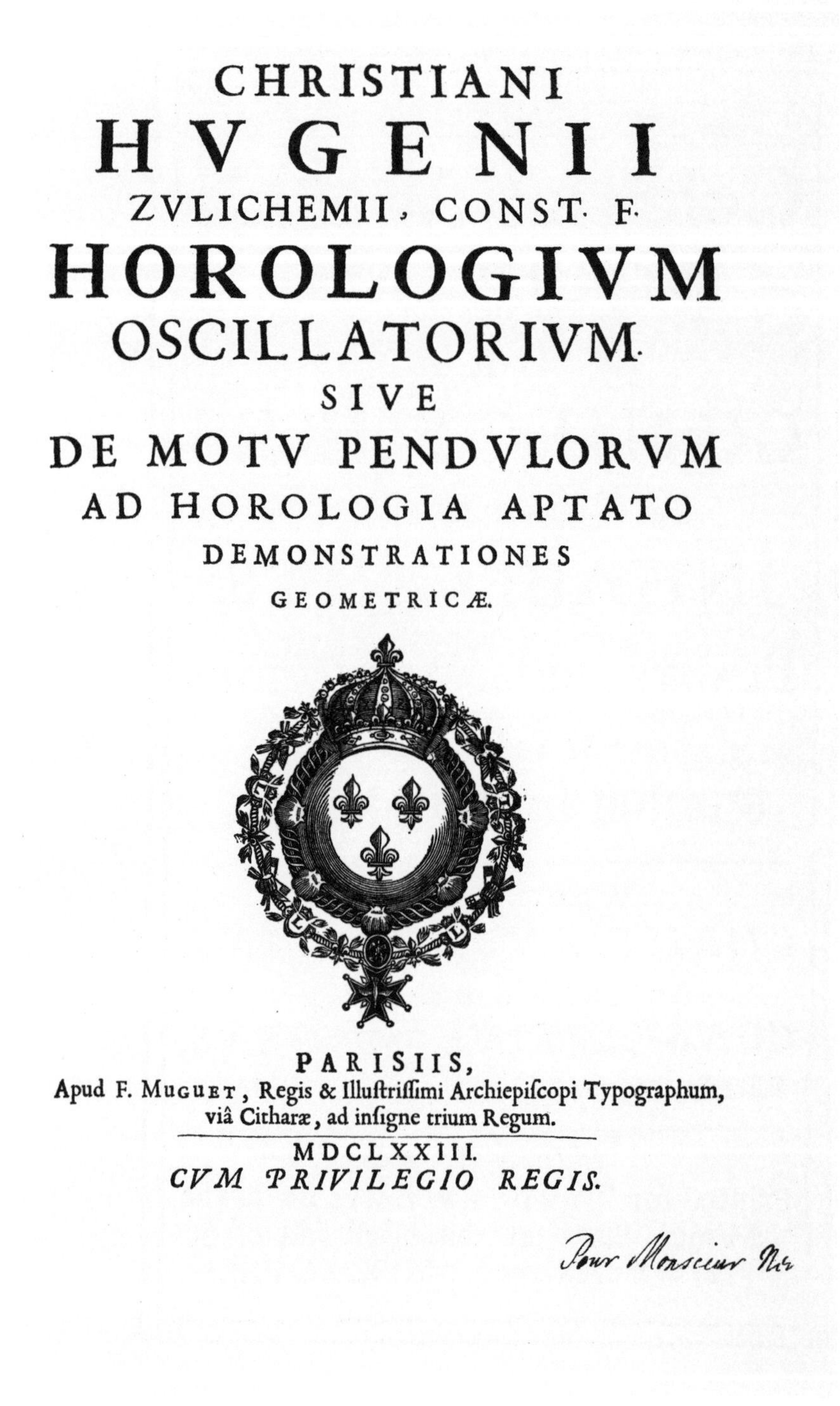

CHRISTIANI
HVGENII
ZVLICHEMII, CONST. F.
HOROLOGIVM
OSCILLATORIVM.
SIVE
DE MOTV PENDVLORVM
AD HOROLOGIA APTATO
DEMONSTRATIONES
GEOMETRICÆ.

PARISIIS,
Apud F. MUGUET, Regis & Illustrissimi Archiepiscopi Typographum,
viâ Citharæ, ad insigne trium Regum.
MDCLXXIII.
CVM PRIVILEGIO REGIS.

Pour Monsieur

HUYGENS, *Horologium*, 1673

520, [4], 523-722, [4], 725-776, [18] p. Hugenii vita: p. [10-16]. Port. by Fr. Ottens.

Provenance: J. L. E. Dreyer (armorial bookplate).

1063. HUYGENS, CHRISTIAAN, 1629-1695. *Cristiani Hugenii Zulichemii, Const. f. Systema Saturnium, sive, De causis mirandorum Saturni phænomenôn, et comite ejus planeta novo.*

Hagæ-Comitis: Ex Typographia A. Vlacq, 1659. 6 p. l., 4 [i.e. 84] illus., diagrs. 20 cm. Error in paging: 84 incorrectly numbered 4. Errata: p. [12] (1st group). Binder's blanks at end.

1064. HUYGENS, CHRISTIAAN, 1629-1695. *Traité de la lumière. Où sont expliquées les causes de ce qui luy arrive dans la réflexion, & dans la réfraction. Et particulièrement dans l'etrange réfraction dv cristal d'Islande. Par C.H.D.Z. Avec un discours de la cause de la pesanteur.*

À Leide: Chez Pierre vander Aa, 1690. 4 p.l., 180 p. 21 cm. The "Discovrs de la cavse de la pesantevr" has special t. p. Title in red and black; title vignette (printer's device); headpieces; initials. There exist two states of the title leaves for this first edition, one with the full name of the author, the other bearing only his initials, "C.H.D.Z. " Fautes à corriger: on p. 180. Horblit, H. D. *Grolier 100 science books,* 54.

Provenance: T. J. J. See (inkstamp); Herbert McLean Evans (bookplate).

1065. HYGINUS. *C. Iulii Higini, Augusti liberti, Poeticon astronomicon....*

Salingiaci: Opera et impensa Ioannis Soteris, 1539, mense Martio. [100] p.: ill.; 28 cm. Signatures: a^6 b-m^4.

With: *Nicolai Copernici Torinensis De revolutionibus orbium celestium.* Norimbergæ: Apud Ioh. Petreium, 1543. Provenance: Herbert McLean Evans (bookplate).

1066. HYGINUS. *Hygini Astronomica; texte du manuscrit tironien de Milan, publié par Émile Chatelain [et] Paul Legendre avec 8 planches en héliogravure.*

Paris: H. Champion, 1909. 4 p. l., xix, [1] 48 p. 2 l. 8 fold. facsim. 25 cm. *Bibliothèque de l'École des hautes études, Sciences historiques et philologiques;* 180 fasc. "Le manuscrit M. 12 sup. de la Bibliothèque Ambrosienne de Milan." Advertisements on wrappers.

Provenance: Presentation copy from E. Chatelain to S. De Vries (inscription).

1067. HYMERS, JOHN, 1803-1887. *The elements of the theory of astronomy. By J. Hymers ... 2d ed. rev. and improved.*

Cambridge: For J. and J. J. Deighton; [etc., etc.], 1840. vii, [1], 354 p. diagrs. on 4 fold. pl. 23 cm. Advertisements on paste-down endpapers.

1068. HYRTL, JOSEPH, 1811-1894. *Lehrbuch der Anatomie des Menschen: mit Rücksicht auf physiologische Begründung und praktische Anwendung / von Dr. Jos. Hyrtl....*

Prag: Verlag von Friedrich Ehrlich, 1846. [4], XVI, 718, [2] p.; 24 cm. Errata: p. [1] at end. Includes bibliographies. Advertisements: p. [1]-[2] preceding half-title.

1069. HYRTL, JOSEPH, 1811-1894. *Onomatologia anatomica; Geschichte und Kritik der anatomichen Sprache der Gegenwart, mit besonderer Berücksichtigung ihrer Barbarismen, Widersinnigkeiten, Tropen und grammatikalischen Fehler.*

Wien: W. Braumüller, 1880. xvi, 626 p. 24 cm. Includes bibliographical references.

1070. IBN ABI AL-RIJAL, ABU AL-HASAN 'ALI, fl. 1016-1040. *Albohazen Haly filii Abenragel libri de iudiciis astrorum, / summa cura & diligenti studio de extrema barbarie uindicati, ac Latinitati donati, per Antonium Stupam Rhœtum Prægalliensem. Additus est huic authori index capitum singularum octo partium, seu librorum, quò lector faciliùs inueniat quæstionem sibi oblatam.*

Basileæ: Ex Officina Henrichi Petri., Mense Martio M.D.LI., [1551]. [20], 410, [2] p.; 33 cm. Translation of: *Al-bari' fi a'hkam al-nujum.* Publication date from colophon on p. 410. Signatures: a^4 b^6 (b6 blank) A-$2K^6$ $2l^8$. Title vignette. Adams A69; Grässe, I, p. 59; BM *STC German,* 1455-1600, p. 21; Houzeau & Lancaster. *Astronomie* (1964 ed.), 3870; Zinner, E. *Geschichte und Bib. der astronomischen Lit.* (1964 ed.), 2007; Lalande, J. J. le F. de. *Bib. astronomique,* p. 73 (also p. 72).

With: *Iulii Firmici Materni ... Astronomicon libri VIII.* Basileæ: Per Ioannem Heruagium, 1551. Provenance: Universitäts-Sternwarte Strassburg (inkstamp).

1071. IBN ABI AL-RIJAL, ABU AL-HASAN 'ALI, fl. 1016-1040. *El libro conplido en los iudizios de las estrellas, por Aly aben Ragel. Traducción hecha en la corte de Alfonso el Sabio. Introducción y edición por Gerold Hilty. Prólogo de Arnald Steiger.*

Madrid: Real Academia Española, 1954. lxvii, 272 p. col. facsim. 29 cm. Translation, probably by Judah ben Moses, ha-Kohen, of *al-Bari' fia'hkam al-nujum.* Latin title: *Liber de judiciis astrorum.* Bibliography: p. [xiii]-xv.

1072. IBN EZRA, ABRAHAM BEN MEÏR, 1092-1167. *El libro de los fundamentos de las tablas astronómicas. Edición crítica, con introducción y notas por José M. a Millás Vallicrosa.*

Madrid: 1947. 171 p. illus., facsim. 26 cm. (Publicación), ser. D – Consejo superior de investigaciones científicas. Instituto Arias Montano; no. 2. Printed from mss. no. 10053 of the Biblioteca Nacional, Madrid, Digbyno. 40 of the Bodleian Library, Oxford, no. 16648 of the Bibliothèque National, Paris and Vesp. F II (p. 27999) of the British Museum, London. Cf. p. 69. Text in Latin; critical material in Spanish. Includes bibliographical references.

1073. IDELER, LUDWIG, 1766-1846. *Untersuchungen über den Ursprung und die Bedeutung der Sternnamen. Ein Beytrag zur Geschichte des gestirnten Himmels, von Ludewig Ideler....*

Berlin: J. F. Weiss, 1809. lxxii, 452 p. 20 cm. Includes bibliographical references and indexes. Einleitung. – Zakaria Ben Mahmud El-Kazwini. Gestirnbeschreibung deutsch, mit Erläuterungen die Sternnamen betreffend. – Anhang. – Zakaria Ben Mahmud El-Kazwini. Gestirnbeschreibung arabisch. – Über die Gestirne der Araber.

Provenance: armorial bookplate with motto: Carpe diem.

1074. INGENHOUSZ, JAN, 1730-1799. *Experiments upon vegetables, discovering their great power of purifying the common air in the sunshine, and of injuring it in the shade and at night. To which is joined, a new method of examining the accurate degree of salubrity of the atmosphere. By John Ingen-Housz....*

London: Printed for P. Elmsly and H. Payne, 1779. lxviii, 302, (17) p. col. pl. 22 cm. Port. signed: A. L. L. ad vivum delin, Cunego inc.; plate signed: T. Bowen sct. Includes index. Horblit, H. D. *Grolier 100 science books,* 55.

Provenance: Charles J. Dimsdale (armorial bookplate).

1075. INSTITUTS SOLVAY. CONSEIL DE PHYSIQUE (1ST : 1911 : BRUSSELS, BELGIUM). *La théorie du rayonnement et les quanta. Rapports et discussions de la réunion tenue à Bruxelles, du 30 octobre au 3 novembre 1911, sous les auspices de M. E. Solvay. Pub. par MM. P. Langevin et M. de Broglie.*

Paris, Gauthier Villars, 1912. 461 p. incl. illus., diagrs. 25 cm. Includes: La loi du rayonnement noir et l'hypothèse de quantités élémentaires d'action / par M. Max Planck (p. [93]-114); and L'état actuel du problème des chaleurs spécifiques / par M. A. Einstein (p. [407]-435). Advertisements on lower wrapper. Bibliographical foot-notes.

1076. *The International control of atomic energy: scientific information transmitted to the United Nations Atomic Energy Commission June 14, 1946-October 14, 1946.Prepared in the office of Mr. Bernard M. Baruch....*

[Washington, D.C.]: Department of State, 1946. 195 p.; 24 cm. Department of State publication; 2661. United States and the United Nations Report Series; 5. Bibliography: p. 103-119.

1077. IRMINGER, GOTTFRIED. *Zurcherishe Seidenwebschule : 1. & 2. Kurs. Schuljahre 1906/07. & 1907/08.*

Zurich: [s.n.], 1906-1907. 5 v.: ill. 2 Text- and 3 Atlas volumes. v. 1. Geschichte der Seidenindustrie – v. 2. Rohmaterialien – v. 3. Kurs: Bindungslehre und Dekomposition der Schaft-Gewebe – v. 4. Kurs: Theorie & Dekomposition der Jacquard-Gewebe – v. 5. Farbenlehre u. Musterzeichnen.

1078. IRVING, EDWARD, 1856- . *How to know the starry heavens; an invitation to the study of suns and worlds, by Edward Irving; with charts, coloured plates, diagrams, and many engravings of photographs.*

New York: F. A. Stokes Company, 1904. xvi, 313 p. col. front., illus., plates (part. col.) diagrs., charts (part. col.) 21 cm. Includes index.

Provenance: Edward Irving (signature).

1079. ISIDORE, OF SEVILLE, SAINT, d. 636. *Isidori Iunioris Hispalensis Episcopi liber Etimologiarum ad Braulionem Cesaraugustanum Episcopum scriptus incipit foeliciter.*

[Augsburg]: Per Gintherum Zainer ex Reutlingen progenitum literis impressi ahenis., 19 die mensis Noue[m]bris, 1472. [528] p.: ill.; 28 cm. Title from p. [15]. Place of publication cited from BM *15th cent.*; publisher and date from colophon, p. [528]. "Capitula in librum primum" (table): p. [1]-[8]. "Isidori Iunioris Hispalensis Episcopi Epistola ad Braulionem Cesaraugustanum Eiscopum incipit" – p. [9]. Gatherings unsigned. Capital spaces; spaces for Greek words in the text. Woodcut diagrams,and full-page illustrations on p. [260]-[262]. BM *15th cent.*, II, p. 317 (IB.5438). Goff (rev.) I-181. Hain 9273*. *ISTC*, ii00181000. Polain 2135.

Rubrication: capitals added in red ink; dated at end by rubricator, 1473. Binding: stamped vellum over boards; 2 fore-edge clasps. Binder's title: Isidori episcopi Hispalæ Ethimolog. lib. XX. Provenance: Bibliote. ssrm Alexandri A. [Th?]eod. in Ottobeurni (inscription); Cvno Schongauiani Carmel Disc. 177[?] (inscription); ms. marginalia. Imperfect: final leaf trimmed and mounted; margins trimmed, with loss of ms. notes.

1080 J., FRÈRE. *Éléments de cosmographie / par F. J.*

Tours: A. Mame; Ch. Poussielgue, 1910. vii, 239 p., [1] folded leaf of plates: ill., chart; 19 cm. Collection d'ouvrages classiques. Cours de mathématiques élémentaires. One of a series of texts issued by the Christian Brothers. "No. 273" – Half-title.

1081. JACKSON, JAMES, 1777-1867. *Letters to a young physician just entering upon practice. By James Jackson.*

Boston: Phillips, Sampson; J. C. Derby, 1855. iv, 344 p. 19 cm. Errata slip inserted. Includes index.

1082. JACKSON, JOHN BAPTIST, 1701-1780? *An essay on the invention of engraving and printing in chiaro oscuro, as practised by Albert Durer, Hugo di Carpi, &c. and the application of it to the making paper hangings of taste, duration, and elegance.*

London: A. Millar, 1754. 19 p. col. plates. 27 cm.

Imperfect: plates missing. Provenance: L'Ab. Boyer (bookplate); Domus Massiliensis (bookplate). With: *Experiments and observations on electricity*, by Mr. Benjamin Franklin. London, printed and sold by E. Cave ..., 1751-1753.

1083. JACOBI, C. G. J. (CARL GUSTAV JAKOB), 1804-1851. *Fundamenta nova theoriæ functionum ellipticarum, auctore d. Carolo Gustavo Iacobo Iacobi....*

Regiomonti: Sumtibus fratrum Borntræger; [etc., etc.], 1829. vi, 191 p. fold. tab. 26 cm. Corrigenda: p. 189-191. Advertisements: p. [192].

Provenance: Edmund Neusser (bookplate); Alex. Brill (inscription).

1084. JACOBY, HAROLD, 1865-1932. *Astronomy: a popular handbook / by Harold Jacoby.*

New York: Macmillan, 1917. xiii, 435 p., 32 leaves of plates: ill. (1 col.); 22 cm. Includes bibliographical references and index.

Advertisements: [9] p. at end.

1085. JAEGER, GEORG VON, 1785-1866. *Ehrengedächtniss des Königl. Würtembergischen Staatsraths von Kielmeyer / von Dr. G. Jaeger....*

[Jena: F. Frommann, 1845]. p. [XVII]-XCII; 29 cm. Detached from: *Novorum actorum Academiae Caesareae Leopoldino Carolinae germanicae naturae curiosorum*, v. 21, pt. 2 1845. Cf. *DSB*, v. 7, p. 369. Includes bibliographical references.

Provenance: Herbert McLean Evans (bookplate).

1086. *Jahrbuch der Radioaktivität und Elektronik....*

Leipzig, S. Hirzel, 1905-24. 20 v. ill., plates, fold. tab., diagrs. 24 cm. 1. -20. Bd.; 1904-18. März 1924. Editors: Johannes Stark, 1904-June 1920; Rudolf Seeliger Sept. 1920-Mar. 1924. Vols. 1-16 include section "Literatur der Elektronik". Absorbed by: *Physikalische Zeitschrift*.

Library has: 4, 1907.

1087. JAMES, WILLIAM, 1842-1910. *The principles of psychology / by William James....*

London: Macmillan & Co., 1890. 2 v.: ill.; 22 cm. Includes bibliographical references and index.

Provenance: F.M.R. Walshe (bookplate).

1088. JAMES, WILLIAM, 1842-1910. *The principles of psychology / by William James.*
New York: H. Holt, 1890. 2 v.; 22 cm. American Science series. Advanced course. Also published same year London: Macmillan & Co. Advertisements: 8 p. in v. 2 following text. Includes index. Horblit, H. D. *Grolier 100 science books,* 100b.
Provenance: Arnold Green (bookplate).

1089. JAMIESON, ALEXANDER. *A celestial atlas: comprising a systematic display of the heavens in a series of thirty maps: illustrated by scientific description of their contents and accompanied by catalogues of the stars and astronomical exercises / by Alexander Jamieson.*
London: G. & W. B. Whittaker, 1822. [4], 64 p., xxx leaves of plates: ill., 30 col. maps; 23 x 29 cm. Illustrated by the author.

1090. JANSKY, KARL G. [Four papers on radio astronomy / Karl Jansky].
[New York: Institute of Radio Engineers, 1932-1939]. 4 pieces: ill.; 23-28 cm. *Proceedings of the Institute of Radio Engineers;* v. 20, no. 12 & v. 21, no. 10 & v. 25, no. 12. *Proceedings of the IRE;* v. 27, no. 12. Binder's title. Includes bibliographical references. (1) v. 20, no. 12. Directional studies of atmospherics at high frequencies (1932) – (2) v. 21, no. 10. Electrical disturbances apparently of extraterrestrial origin (1933) – (3) v. 25, no. 12. Minimum noise levels obtained on short-wave radio receiving systems (1937) – (4) v. 27, no. 12. An experimental investigation of the characteristics of certain types of noise (1939).
4 v. in slipcase, 30 cm., with binder's [?] stamp: Atmore Beach. Provenance: no. 3: Goldsmith (signature); no. 2:O.[?] Levinson (signature).

1091. JEANS, H. W. (HENRY WILLIAM), 1804-1881. *Hand-book for the stars: containing rules for finding the names and positions of all the stars of the first and second magnitude / by H. W. Jeans ... Second edition.*
London: Printed by Levey, Robson and Franklyn ..., 1848. vi, [46], 15, [1], 2 p.: ill.; 25 cm. Advertisements: [2] p. at end.

1092. JEANS, JAMES HOPWOOD, SIR, 1877-1946. *À travers l'espace et le temps / par Sir James Jeans; traduit del'anglais par A. Caffi.*
Paris: Hermann, 1935. xv, 261 p., liii p. of plates: ill.; 25 cm. Translation of: *Through space & time.* Based on the Royal Institution Lectures, Christmas, 1933. Cf. Avant-propos, p. [vii]. Includes index.

1093. JEANS, JAMES HOPWOOD, SIR, 1877-1946. *The astronomical horizon, by Sir James Jeans.*
London, New York: H. Milford, Oxford University Press, 1945. 23 p. illus., plates. 23 cm. Philip Maurice Deneke Lecture; 1944.

1094. JEANS, JAMES HOPWOOD, SIR, 1877-1946. *Astronomy and cosmogony, by J. H. Jeans....*
Cambridge [Eng.]: The University Press, 1928. x, 420 p. XVI pl., diagrs. 28 cm. "In a sense the book constitutes a sequel to my *Problems of cosmogony and stellar dynamics* of ten years ago." – Pref.

1095. JEANS, JAMES HOPWOOD, SIR, 1877-1946. *Cosmogony and stellar evolution / by J. H. Jeans.*
Washington: GPO, 1923. p. 153-164: ill.; 24 cm. Publication; 2677. "From the *Smithsonian Report* for 1921."

1096. JEANS, JAMES HOPWOOD, SIR, 1877-1946. *The dynamical theory of gases....*
Cambridge [Eng.]: The University Press, 1904. vi, [2], 352 p. illus., diagrs. 27 cm. Includes index.
Provenance: Herbert McLean Evans (bookplate).

1097. JEANS, JAMES HOPWOOD, SIR, 1877-1946. *Eos; or, The wider aspects of cosmogony.*
London: K. Paul, Trench, Trubner & Co., Ltd; E. Dutton & Co., 1928. 88 p. VI pl. (incl. front.) diagr. 17 cm. To-day and to-morrow. "While the 'To-day and to-morrow' series has been the medium of publication of many brilliant flights of imagination, the present book is limited to scientific facts and such inferences as I think may properly be drawn from them." - Foreword.
"Second impression, November 1928" – T. p.verso. Advertisements: 24 p. following text.

1098. JEANS, JAMES HOPWOOD, SIR, 1877-1946. *Gegenwartsprobleme der Astronomie / James H. Jeans.*
Leipzig; Wien: Akademische Verlagsgesellschaft,

1937. 15 p.; 24 cm. Cover title. "Sonderdruck aus den *Monatsheften für Mathematik und Physik.*" "Achtzehnter Gastvortrag gehalten am 29. April 1936 in Wien auf Einladung des Komitee zur Veranstaltung von Gastvorträgen ausländischer Gelehrter der exakten Wissenschaften, Wien."

1099. JEANS, JAMES HOPWOOD, SIR, 1877-1946. *The growth of physical science / Sir James Jeans. Rev. ed.*
London: Readers Union; University Press, 1950. x, 364 p., 13 p. of plates: ill.; 19 cm. Includes bibliographical references and index.

1100. JEANS, JAMES HOPWOOD, SIR, 1877-1946. *Man and the stars; or, The wider aspects of cosmogony, by Sir James H. Jeans.*
New York: E. P. Dutton & Co., Inc., 1931. 2 p. l., 9-88 p. VI pl. (incl. front.) diagr. 18 cm. "Copyright, 1929, under the title Eos ... Reprinted, April, 1931."

1101. JEANS, JAMES HOPWOOD, SIR, 1877-1946. *The mysterious universe, by Sir James Jeans ... decorations by Walter T. Murch.*
New York: The Macmillan Company; The University Press, 1931. viii p., 2 l., 163 p. incl. illus., plates, diagrs., front. 21 cm. "An expansion of the Rede Lecture delivered before the University of Cambridge in November 1930" – Foreword. "Published November, 1930. Reprinted ... February , 1931." Includes index.

1102. JEANS, JAMES HOPWOOD, SIR, 1877-1946. *The new background of science, by Sir James Jeans.*
Cambridge: The University Press, 1933. viii, 303 p. front., illus., diagrs. 20 cm.

1103. JEANS, JAMES HOPWOOD, SIR, 1877-1946. *Problems of cosmogony and stellar dynamics ... being an essay to which the Adams prize of the University of Cambridge for the year 1917 was adjudged.*
Cambridge [Eng.]: The University Press, 1919. vii, [1], 293 p. 5 fold. plates, diagrs. 27 cm. Includes bibliographical references and index.

1104. †JEANS, JAMES HOPWOOD, SIR, 1877-1946. *Report on radiation and the quantum-theory / by J. H. Jeans.*
London: "The Electrician" Printing & Publishing Co., 1914. iv, 90 p.: ill.; 23 cm. At head of title: The Physical Society of London. "Principal references other than the detailed papers referred to in the text": p. iv.
Binding: original printed wrappers. Advertisements on p. [3] of wrapper. Provenance: S. H. Brass [?] (signature).
Provenance: A. O. Rankine (signature).

1105. JEANS, JAMES HOPWOOD, SIR, 1877-1946. *Science & music / by Sir James Jeans.*
Cambridge [Eng.]: University Press, 1953. x, 258 p., [10] leaves of plates: ill.; 20 cm. First impression 1937, reprinted 1953. Bibliography: p. x. Includes index.

1106. JEANS, JAMES HOPWOOD, SIR, 1877-1946. *The stars in their courses / by Sir James Jeans.*
New York: Macmillan; Cambridge, England: University Press, 1944. x, 173 p., [49] p. of plates (2 folded): ill., maps; 20 cm. Includes index.

1107. JEANS, JAMES HOPWOOD, SIR, 1877-1946. *Through space & time / by Sir James Jeans.*
New York: Macmillan, 1934. xiv, 224 p., liii p. of plates: ill.; 23 cm. "Based on the Royal Institution Lectures, Christmas 1933." Includes index.

1108. JEANS, JAMES HOPWOOD, SIR, 1877-1946. *Through space & time / by Sir James Jeans.*
Cambridge: University Press, 1940. xiv, 224 p., liii p. of plates: ill.; 21 cm. "Based on the Royal Institution Lectures, Christmas 1933." "First edition 1934. Reprinted 1940" – T. p. verso. Includes index.
Provenance: Edward Whitlock (signature).

1109. JEANS, JAMES HOPWOOD, SIR, 1877-1946. *L'univers / Sir James Jeans; traduit de l'anglais par George Gros.*
Paris: Payot, 1930. 287 p., 24 p. of plates: ill.; 23 cm. Bibliothèque scientifique. Translation of: *Universe around us.* Advertisements on lower wrapper.

1110. JEANS, JAMES HOPWOOD, SIR, 1877-1946. *The universe around us, by Sir James Jeans....*
New York: The Macmillan Company; Cambridge, Eng.: The University Press, [c1929]. x p., 1 l., 341 p. XXIV pl. on 18 l., diagrs. 23 cm.
"Reprinted November, 1929" – T. p. verso. Provenance: I. Jacy[?] (signature).

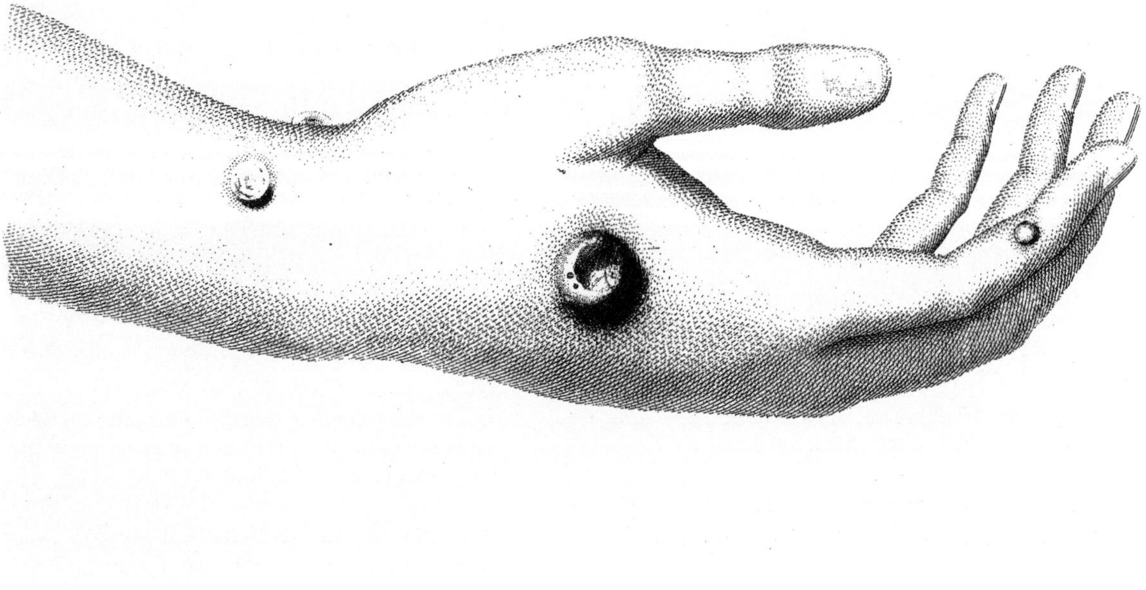

JENNER, *An Inquiry into the Causes and Effects of the Variolae Vaccinae*, 1798

1111. JEANS, JAMES HOPWOOD, SIR, 1877-1946. *The universe around us, by Sir James Jeans....*
Cambridge: The University Press, 1929. x, 352 p.: XXIV plates, diagrs.; 23 cm. Substance of lectures and wireless talks delivered to university and other audiences. cf. Pref. Includes index.
Provenance: Isabel G. Bnixner (signature).

1112. JEANS, JAMES HOPWOOD, SIR, 1877-1946. *The universe around us / by Sir James Jeans. 3rd ed.*
Cambridge: University Press, 1933. x, 380 p., xxiv, [1] p. of plates: ill.; 23 cm. Includes index.

1113. JENNER, EDWARD, 1749-1823. *An inquiry into the causes and effects of the variolae vaccinae: a disease discovered in some of the western counties of England, particularly Gloucestershire, and known by the name of the cow pox / by Edward Jenner.*
London: Printed for the author by Sampson Low ..., 1798. [2], iv, 75, [3] p., [4] leaves of plates: col. ill.; 29 cm. Errata: p. [2] at end. Plates signed: Willm. Skelton, and Edwd. Pearce. Horblit, H. D. *Grolier 100 science books*, 56. Garrison-Morton, no. 5423.
Provenance: Thomas Wright (inscription).

1114. JENNER, EDWARD, 1749-1823. *The note-book of Edward Jenner, in the possession of the Royal college of physicians of London, with an introduction on Jenner's work as a naturalist, by F. Dawtrey Drewitt....*
London, Oxford university press, H. Milford, 1931. vi, [1], 49, [1] p. front. (port.) 22 x 17 cm. "The Note-Book, which covers the period from 1787 to 1806, records various observations made by Jenner concerning the habits of the Cuckoo, the presence of Hydatids in the bodies of various animals, and concerning the Distemper in Dogs." – Preface.

1115. JENNINGS, DAVID, 1691-1762. *An introduction to the use of globes, and the orrery: also, the application of astronomy to chronology ... with an appendix attempting to explain the account of the first and fourth days work of creation in the first chapter of Genesis / by David Jennings ... The third edition.*
London: Printed for J. Nourse ... J. Buckland ... and E. and C. Dilly ..., 1766. xi, [1], 127 [i.e. 172], 10] p., [5] leaves of plates (3 folded): ill.; 22 cm. Errors in pagination: p. 109 misnumbered as 106, 172 as 127. Includes index.
Ms. notes.

1116. JEVONS, WILLIAM STANLEY, 1835-1882. *The principles of science: a treatise on logic and scientific method / by W. Stanley Jevons.*
London: Macmillan, 1924. xliv, 786 p.: 1 ill.; 23 cm. Colophon reads: Printed in Great Britain by Richard Clay & Sons, Limited ... Includes bibliographical references and index.
Advertisements: 2 p. at end. Ms. marginalia.

1117. JOHNSON, GAYLORD. *The sky movies, by Gaylord Johnson ... with over one hundred pictures....*
New York: The Macmillan Company, 1922. viii p., 1 l., 170 p. illus., diagrs. 18 cm.

1118. JOHNSON, S. J. (SAMUEL JENKINS), b. 1845. *Historical and future eclipses: with notes on planets, double stars, and other celestial matters / by Rev. S. J. Johnson ... New edition.*
[London]: James Parker and Co. ... London and ... Oxford, 1896. viii, 178 p., 12 p. of plates: ill.; 19 cm. Errata slip tipped in between p. viii and [1].

1119. JOHNSTON, ALEXANDER KEITH, 1804-1871. *Atlas of astronomy: comprising, in eighteen plates a complete series of illustrations of the heavenly bodies ... / by Alex. Keith Johnston ... ; edited by J. R. Hind....*
Edinburgh and London: William Blackwood and Sons, 1855. [4], 16 p., 18 leaves of plates: col. ill., maps; 35 cm. Plates signed by W. & A. K. Johnston.
Provenance: Ignacio Avilez (inkstamp).

1120. JOHNSTON, SWIFT P. (SWIFT PAINE). *Notes on astronomy: a complete elementary handbook, together with a collection of examination questions / by Swift P. Johnston ...; edited by James Lowe ... New and enl. ed.*
London: John Heywood ..., 1892. 86 p.: ill.; 22 cm. Ed. statement from cover. Date from preface.

1121. JONES, H. SPENCER (HAROLD SPENCER), 1890- . *Life on other worlds. (2d ed.)*
London: English Universities Press, 1952. xi, [1], 259 p. illus., plates. 20 cm. Includes index.

1122. JONES, H. SPENCER (HAROLD SPENCER), 1890- . *A picture of the universe.*
London: Raven Books Limited, 1947. 88 p. illus. 18 cm.

1123. JONES, H. SPENCER (HAROLD SPENCER), 1890- . *Worlds without end, by H. Spencer Jones....*
London: The English Universities Press, Ltd., 1935. xv, 262 p. front., illus., plates, diagrs. 20 cm. Includes index.

1124. JOULE, JAMES PRESCOTT, 1818-1889. [Collection of journal articles detached from the *Report of the British Association for the Advancement of Sciences* / by James Prescott Joule].
[1842-1850]. 6 pieces; 22 cm. Includes bibliogaphical references. (1) On the electric origin of the heat of combustion (1842) – (2) On the calorific effects of magneto-electricity, and the mechanical value of heat (1843) – (3) On specific heat (1844) – (4) On the mechanical equivalent of heat (1845) – (5) On the mechanical equivalent of heat, as determined by the heat evolved by the agitation of liquids (1847) – (6) On some amalgams 1850.

1125. *Journal d'histoire naturelle, par une société de naturalistes et rédigé par MM. Lamarck, Bruguière, Olivier, Haüy et Pelletier: prospectus.*
[Paris]: De l'imprimerie du Cercle social, rue du Théâtre françois, no. 4, [1791?]. 4 p.; 22 cm. "Ce journal ... devroit par oitre au premier janvier 1792 ..." – p. 3.

1126. *Journal für Chemie und Physik.*
Nuremberg, 1811-1823; Halle, 1824-33. 69 v. fronts, plates ports., maps, tables, diagrs. 21 cm. 1.-69. Bd.; 1811-1833. Vols. 31-69 have added t.-p.: v.31-60 read, *Jahrbuch der Chemie und Physik* v. 1-30; v. 61-69 read: *Neues Jahrbuch der Chemie und Physik,* bd. 1-9. With supplements. Vol. 1-26, 39-44, edited by J.S.C. Schweigger; vol. 27-38, by J. S. C. Schweigger and Meinecke; vol. 45-54, by J. S. C. Schweigger and Fr. W. Schweigger - Seidel; vol. 54-69, by Fr. W. Schweigger-Seidel. Continues: *Journal für die Chemie, Physik und Mineralogie.* Continued by: *Journal für praktische Chemie.*
Library has: 44, 1825; 46, 1826. Vol. 44 and 46: Provenance: Academy of Natural Sciences of Philadelphia (inkstamp and presentation bookplate from Dr. T. B. Wilson).

1127. *The Journal of science, and annals of astronomy, biology, geology, industrial arts, manufactures, and technology. Quarterly journal of science 1864-70. Quarterly journal of sci-*

ence, and annals of mining, metallurgy, engineering, industrial arts, manufactures, and technology 1871-Jan. 1879. Monthly journal of science, and annals of biology, astronomy, geology, industrial arts, manufactures, and technology Feb.-Dec. 1879.

London, J. Churchill and Sons. 22 v. ill., plates (part col.) ports., maps. 22 cm. Monthly, 1879-85 Quarterly, 1864-79. v. 1-7, 1864-70; v. 8-15 (new ser., v. 1-8),1871-78; v.16-22 (3rd ser., v. 1-7), 1879-85. Editors: 1864-70, James Samuelson, William Crookes and others. – 1871-79, William Crookes. Absorbed: *Edinburgh new philosophical journal* July 1864.

vol. V-VI: Provenance: Library, Royal College of Surgeons in Ireland (inkstamp).

1128. Joyce, Jeremiah, 1763-1816. *Scientific dialogues: intended for the instruction and entertainment of young people: in which the first principles of natural and experimental philosophy are fully explained / by the Rev. J. Joyce; with corrections and improvements by Dr. Olinthus Gregory. A new edition, containing the recent additions to science / by Charles V. Walker....*

London: Baldwin and Co. [and 8 others], 1846. xii, 436 p.: ill.; 19 cm. Includes index.

Provenance: W. Johnson (signature).

1129. Joyce, Jeremiah, 1763-1816. *Scientific dialogues: for the instruction and entertainment of young people: in which the first principles of natural and experimental philosophy are fully explained and illustrated / by the Rev. J. Joyce. A new and enlarged edition, with questions for examination and other additions / by William Pinnock. Revised and completed to the present state of knowledge, with an additional chapter on recent discoveries / by J. W. Griffith....*

London: Bell & Daldy ..., 1866. [6], x, 583, [4] p.: ill.; 19 cm. Advertisements: [6] p. preceding t. p., [4] p. at end, and front and back paste-down endpapers. Includes index.

Page 583 duplicated. Provenance: Charles Atwood Kofoid (bookplate); E. Disc[ou?] to Alfred G. Dixon (presentation inscription).

1130. Jubilee of Relativity Theory (1955: Bern, Switzerland). *Verhandlungen. Actes. Proceedings. Publiés par André Mercier et Michel Kervaire.*

Basel: Birkhäuser, 1956. 286 p. illus. 23 cm. *Helvetica physica acta. Supplementum;* 4. Includes bibliographies.

1131. Jussieu, Antoine Laurent de, 1748-1836. *Genera plantarum, secundum ordines naturales disposita, juxta methodum in Horto Regio Parisiensi exaratam, anno M. DCC. LXXIV.*

Parisiis: Apud Viduam Herissant, typographum ... et Teophilum Barrois ..., 1789. 24, lxxii, 498 p., [1] l. 20 cm. "Extrait des registres de l'Académie royale de sciences ...": p. 5-11; "Extrait des registres de la Société royale de médecine ...": p. 12-24, in French. Errata: p. [1] at end. Horblit, H. D. *Grolier 100 science books,* 68b.

Provenance: Herbert McLean Evans (bookplate).

1132. Kahn, Fritz, 1888-1968. *Die Milchstrasse, von Dr. Fritz Kahn. Mit einem farbigen Umschlag und zahlreichen Abbildungen nach Photographien u. Zeichnungen, von Georg Helbig, R. Oeffinger und andern.*

Stuttgart: Kosmos, Gesellschaft der Naturfreunde, 1914. 101, [3] p. illus., diagrs. 21 cm. Includes index. Advertisements on [3] p.

Binder: F. G. Koster, Amsterdam (ticket). Provenance: Lees Museum Amsterdam (inkstamp); Charles Atwood Kofoid (bookplate).

1133. Kaiser, Friedrich, 1814-1874. *De geschiedenis der ontdekkingen van planeten; als een tafereel van het wezen en den toestand der sterrekunde, in de taal van het dagelijksche leven voorgedragen, door F. Kaiser.*

Amsterdam: J.C.A. Sulpke, 1851. xxix, 764 p. 23 cm.

1134. Kaiser, Friedrich, 1814-1874. *De sterrenhemel. Eerste deel / door F. Kaiser ... Tweede druk.*

Te Amsterdam: bij C. G. Sulpke, 1847. [6], XV, (1), 499 p.; 24 cm. Separate t. p. for complete work. Errata slip following text.

1135. Kant, Immanuel, 1724-1804. *Critik der reinen Vernunft / von Immanuel Kant.*
Riga [Latvia]: J. F. Hartknoch, 1781. 856 p.; 21 cm.
Provenance: Herbert McLean Evans (bookplate).

1136. Keeler, James Edward, 1857-1900. *Photographs of nebulæ and clusters made with the Crossley reflector, by James Edward Keeler, director of the Lick Observatory, 1898-1900.*
[Sacramento: W. W. Shannon, Superintendent of State Printing, 1908]. 46 p. front., 70 pl. 30 x 24 cm. *Publications of the Lick Observatory of the University of California;* v. 8. "Note" on plates of subjects 10 and 12 tipped in. Includes bibliographical references.
Provenance: presentation inscription to Edward D. Adams from John A. Brashear.

1137. Keerwolff, Bartholomaeus, fl. 1693-1697. *Epistola anatomica, problematica decima ... ad ... Fredericum Ruyschium ... De auricularum cordis, earumque fibrarum motricium structura.*
Amsteledami: Apud Joannem Wolters, 1697. 10 p., [1] leaf of plates: illus.; 22 cm. "Frederici Ruyschii responsio ...": p. 5-7. Plate numbered: 11.
Imperfect: t. p. missing. With: *Observationum anatomico-chirurgicarum centuria / Frederici Ruyschii.* Amstelodami: Apud Henricum & Viduam Theodori Boom, 1691.

1138. Keill, John, 1671-1721. *Institutions astronomiques, ou Leçons élémentaires d'astronomie, pour servir d'introduction à la physique céleste, & à la science des longitudes, avec de nouvelles tables d'équation corrigées; et particulièrement les tables du soleil, de la lune & des satellites; précédées d'un essai sur l'histoire de l'astronomie moderne.*
Paris: Chez H.-L. Guerin, & J. Guerin, 1746. 4 p. l., lxiv, 660 p. 15 fold. pl. (incl. maps) tables, diagrs. 29 x 22cm. Translaton of: *Introductio ad veram astronomiam.* Translated by P. C. Le Monnier.

1139. Keill, John, 1671-1721. *An introduction to the true astronomy: or, Astronomical lectures read in the Astronomical School of the University of Oxford / by John Keill. 2d ed.*
London: Printed for Bernard Lintot, 1730. [6], xiv, [4], 396, [20] p., xxvii [i.e. 28] leaves of plates: diagrs., maps; 21 cm. Includes index. Plate no. xvii omitted and 2 unnumbered plates facing p. 108. Advertisements: [8] p. at end. Plates signed: I. Senex sculpt.

1140. Keill, John, 1671-1721. *Introductiones ad veram physicam et veram astronomiam. Quibus accedunt Trigonometria. De viribus centralibus. De legibus attractionis.*
Mediolani: Excudit F. Agnelli, 1742. 4 p. l., 5-636, [10] p. 47 fold. plates. (incl. maps) 25 cm. Includes index. Title vignette.
Provenance: Charles Atwood Kofoid (bookplate).

1141. Keith, Thomas, 1759-1824. *A new treatise on the use of globes, or, A philosophical view of the earth and heavens: comprehending an account of the figure, magnitude, and motion of the earth ...: preceded by an extensive selection of astronomical and other definitions ...: designed for the instruction of youth / by Thomas Keith ... The third American, from the last London improved edition.*
New York: Published by Samuel Wood & Sons ... ; [Balitmore]: And Samuel S. Wood & Co. ...Baltimore, 1819. xvi, 352 [i.e. 343] p., V folded leaves of plates: ill.; 23 cm. Errors in pagination: nos. 328-337 omitted, 296 repeated. Includes bibliographical references. Shaw & Shoemaker, 48409.
Provenance: Sarah Ann Bergh (signature).

1142. Kellaway, Francis William. *Splitting the atom, by F. W. Kellaway....*
[Bognor Regis and London]: J. Crowther, 1945. 32 p. illus., diagrs. 18 cm. On cover: A simple explanation of the atomic bomb and its principles. Text on p. [2] of cover.

1143. Kemplay, Christopher. *Comets: their constitution & phases; being an attempt to explain the phenomena on known principles of physical laws, by Christopher Kemplay.*
London: Longman, Brown, Green, Longmans & Roberts [etc.], 1859. 1 p.l., vii, [1], 118 p. 22 cm.

1144. Kepler, Johannes, 1571-1630. *Ad Vitellionem paralipomena, quibus astronomiæ pars optica traditvr: potissimùm de artificiosa observatione et aestimatione diametrorvm deliquiorumq[ue] solis & lunæ cvm exemplis insignivm*

eclipsivm. Habes hoc libro, lector, inter alia multa noua, tractatum luculentum de modo visionis, & humorum oculi vsu, contra opticos & anatomicos / avthore Ioanne Keplero....
Francofvrti: Apud Claudium Marnium & Haeredes Ioannis Aubrii, 1604. [16], 449, [18] p.: ill., plates (2 folded); 22 cm. Signatures:)(, (:) A-Z Aa-Zz Aaa-Mmm4 Nnn2. Includes index. Errata: last[2] p. Printer's device on the title page. Caspar, M. *Kepler* (2. Aufl.), 18.
2 leaves: plate by F. Plater and its explanation bound at the end instead of between p. 176 and 177. Provenance: Leonardo Lapiccirella (bookplate).

1145. KEPLER, JOHANNES, 1571-1630. *Astronomia nova aitiologētos, seu Physica cœlestis, tradita Commentariis de motibvs stellæ Martis, ex observationibus G. V. Tychonis Brahe: Jussu & sumptibus Rudolphi II. Romanorum imperatoris &c: Plurium annorum pertinaci studio elaborata Pragæ, / a Sæ. Cæ. Mtis. Sæ. mathematico Joanne Keplero, cum ejusdem Cæ. Mtis. privilegio speciali anno æræ Dionysianæ MDCIX.*
[Heidelberg: G. Voegelinus, 1609]. [44], 337, [3] p. (the first three and last leaves blank), [1] folded leaf of plates: ill.; 36 cm. (fol.) Third word of title is in Greek letters. Signatures: [*]4?, [**]-[****]6, A-2E6 [chi]2 (*1[-3?] and [chi]2 blank). Horblit, H. D. *Grolier 100 science books,* 57. Brunet, III, 652; Caspar, M. *Bib. Kepleriana,* no. 31; Grässe, v. 4, p. 11; Houzeau & Lancaster. *Astronomie* (1964 ed.), 11830; Zinner, E. *Geschichte und Bib. der astronomischen Lit.* (1964 ed.), 4237; Lalande. *Bib. astronomique,* p. 149. Publication date in Roman numerals with backward C to indicate the right stroke of M. Imprint from: Caspar, M. *Bib. Kepleriana*; and Zinner. Lalande and Houzeau & Lancaster give Prague as place of publication. Errata: p. [43]-[44] of 1st group.
Provenance: G. P. C (bookplate); R. B. (bookplate); Herbert McLean Evans (bookplate). Imperfect copy: lacks first two blanks ([*]1-2). 41 cm.

1146. KEPLER, JOHANNES, 1571-1630. *De cometis libelli tres ... / autore Iohanne Keplero....*
Augustæ Vindelicorum: Typis Andreæ Apergeri, sumptibus Sebastiani Mylii bibliopolæ Augustani, 1619. [8], 98, [6], 99-110, [5], 110-138 p., [5] folded leaves of plates: ill.; 21 cm. Special t. p.: Libellus secundus: Cometarum physiologia nova ...; and: Libellus tertius: De significationibus cometæ qui anno MDCVII conspectus est ... 1620. Pt. 3 is rev. translation of: *Aussführlicher Bericht von dem newlich... erschienenen ... Cometen* ... 1608. (From t. p.) I. Astronomicus, theoremata continens de motu cometarum ...qui annis 1607. & 1618. conspecti sunt ... II. Physicus ... III.Astrologicus. Caspar, M. *Kepler.* (2. Aufl.), 60.
Ms. note.

1147. KEPLER, JOHANNES, 1571-1630. *Epitome astronomiae Copernicanæ: usitatâ formâ quæstionum & responsionum conscripta inq[ue] VII. libros digesta, quorum tres hi priores sunt de doctrina sphæricâ ... Avthore Joanne Kepplero....*
Lentijs ad Danubium: excudebat Johannes Plancus, Anno MDCXVIII-[M. DC. XXII] [1618]. 7 v. in 1: ill.; 16 cm. Signatures: *6 ** ***4 A-Z Aa-Bb8 Cc Cc6(Cc6 blank) Aaa-Mmm8 6 Aaaa-Ssss8 Tttt2, Vuuu8 (Diii numb. Diiii; signatures in Roman and Arabic). Full extent: [28], 400, 409-417, [5] (4 of these blank), 419-622, [14] (2 of these blank), 641-932, [16] p., [1] folded leaf of plates. Includes indexes. V. 4 has separate title page with imprint: Lentiis ad Danubium, impensis Godefridi Tampachii excudebat Iohannes Plancus. Anno M. DC.XXII; v. 5-7 have separate title pages with imprint: Francofvrti, Sumptibus Godefridi Tampachij. Anno M. DC. XXI. Numerous errors in pagination; some verso numbers are on the right side of the page. Placed on the *Index Librorum Prohibitorum* in 1619. Errata :p. [27]-[28] (1st group) and last [3] p. Caspar, M. *Kepler.* (2. Aufl.), 55, 66, 69.
Provenance: Herbert McLean Evans (bookplate). Imperfect copy: p. 413-416 missing.

1148. KEPLER, JOHANNES, 1571-1630. *Epitome astronomiæ Copernicanæ vsitatâ formâ quæstionum & responsionum conscripta: inque VII. libros digesta, quorum tres hi priores sunt de doctrina sphæricâ... / authore Ioanne Keplero....*
Francofurti: Impensis Ioannis Godefridi Schönwetteri excudebat Iohan Fridericus Weissius, MDCXXXV [1635]. [18], 400, 409-417, [3], 419-622, [14], 641-932, [14] p., [1] folded leaf of plates: ill.; 17 cm. Book IV has special t.-p.; books V-VII have collective t.-p. Many irregularities in paging. Includes indexes. Caspar, M. *Kepler.* (2. Aufl.), 87.
Ms. note on fly-leaf.

1149. KEPLER, JOHANNES, 1571-1630. *Ioannis Kepleri mathematici Cæsarei Dissertatio cum Nuncio sidereo: nuper ad mortales misso à Galilæo Galilæo mathematico Patavino.*

Pragæ: Typis Danielis Sedesani, 1610. [6], 34, [1] p.; 23 cm. Caspar, M. *Kepler* (2. Aufl.), 34.

1150. KEPLER, JOHANNES, 1571-1630. *Ioannis Kepleri Sæ. Cæ. Mtis. mathematici Dioptrice seu Demonstratio eorum quæ visui & visibilibus propter conspicilla non ita pridem inventa accidunt: præmissæ epistolæ Galilæi de ijs, quæ post editionem Nuncij siderij ope perspicilli, nova & admiranda in cœlo deprehensa sunt: examen præfationis Ioannis Penæ Galli in Optica Euclidis, de usu optices in philosophia.*

Augustae Vindelicorum: Typis Davidis Franci, 1611. [8], 28, 80, [4] p.: ill.; 21 cm. Signatures:)(^{4} a-c^4 d^2 A-K^4. Caspar, M. *Kepler* (2. Aufl.) 40.

Provenance: Richard Towneley (armorial bookplate); Herbert McLean Evans (bookplate). Note on conservation by Don Etherington pasted on flyleaf. Imperfect: last 2 unnumbered leaves missing.

1151. KEPLER, JOHANNES, 1571-1630. *Ioannis Keppleri Harmonices mvndi libri v. Qvorvm primus geometricvs, de figurarum regularium, quæ proportiones harmonicas constituunt, ortu & demonstrationibus. Secundus architectonicvs, seu ex geometria figvrata, de figurarum regularium congruentia in plano vel solido: Tertius propriè harmonicvs, de proportionum harmonicarum ortu ex figuris; deque naturâ & differentiis rerum ad cantum pertinentium, contra veteres: Quartus metaphysicvs, psychologicvs & astrologicvs, de harmoniarum mentali essentiâ earumque generibus in mundo; præsertim de harmonia radiorum, ex corporibus cœlestibus in terram descendentibus, eiusque effectu in natura seu anima sublunari & humana: Quintus astronomicvs & metaphysicvs, de harmoniis absolutissimis motuum cœlestium, ortuque eccentricitatum ex proportionibus harmonicis. Appendix habet comparationem huius operis cum Harmonices Cl. Ptolemæi libro III. cumque Roberti de Fluctibus, dicti Flud. medici oxoniensis speculationibus harmonicis, operi de Macrocosmo & microcosmo insertis.*

Lincii Austriæ: sumptibus Godofredi Tampachii excudebat Ioannes Plancvs, 1619. 4 p. l., 52, 55-66, 255 p. illus. (music) 4 pl., diagrs. 31 cm. Books 1-2 are paged continuously, as are books 3-5. Books 1, 4 and 5 have special title-pages, included in the paging. Emendanda: p. 255. Caspar, M. *Kepler* (2. Aufl.), 58.1. Horblit, H. D. *Grolier 100 science books*, 58.

Provenance: Herbert McLean Evans (bookplate).

1152. KEPLER, JOHANNES, 1571-1630. *Joannis Keppleri Sac. Cæs. Majest. Mathematici De stella nova in pede Serpentarii: et qui sub ejus exortum de novo iniit, trigono igneo. Libellus astronomicis, physicis, metaphysicis, meteorologicis & astrologicis disputationibus ... Accesserunt I. De stella incognita Cygni: narratio astronomica. II. De Jesu Christi servatoris vero anno natalitio....*

Pragae: Typis Pauli Sessii, impensis authoris, M.DC.VI 1606. [12], 212, 35, [5] p. (the last leaf blank), [1] folded leaf of plates: ill.; 22 cm. Parts 2-4 have special title pages; part 4 has separate pagination. Part 3 has imprint: Francofurti, 1606; part 4 has imprint: Francofurti: In officina typographica Wolfgangi Richteri, 1606. Errata: p. [11]. Caspar, M. *Kepler* (2. Aufl.), 27 (2nd variant). Yale. Cushing Coll. K43. Joannis Keppleri ... De stella nova in pede Serpentarii – Joannis Keppleri ... De stella tertii honoris in Cygno – Joannis Keppleri ... De stella nova in pede Serpentarii, pars altera – Ioannis Kepleri ... De Iesu Christi seruatoris nostri vero anno natalitio.

Copious ms. notes. Provenance: Hans Ludendorff (bookplate).

1153. KEPLER, JOHANNES, 1571-1630. *Opera omnia; ed. Ch. Frisch.*

Frankofurti am M.: Heyder & Zimmer, 1858-1871. 8 v. in 9 illus., diagrs., facsims., tables. 28 cm. "Vita Johannis Kepleri": v. 8:2.

1154. KEPLER, JOHANNES, 1571-1630. *Prodromus dissertationum cosmographicarum: continens Mysterium cosmographicum de admirabili proportione orbium cœlestium ... /*

a M. Ioanne Keplero, Wirtembergico ...; Addita est erudita Narratio M. Georgii Ioachimi Rhetici de Libris reuolutionum ... Nicolai Copernici.

Tubingæ: Excudebat Georgius Gruppenbachius, 1596. [2], 181 p., [5] folded leaves of plates: ill.; 21 cm. Includes: De dimensionibus orbium et sphærarum cœlestium / Appendix Michaelis Maestlini. Caspar, M. *Kepler.* (2. Aufl.), 6.

Provenance: Hans Ludendorff (bookplate); Herbert McLean Evans (bookplate). Bound in music ms. fragment.

1155. KEPLER, JOHANNES, 1571-1630. *Prodromus dissertationvm cosmographicarvm, continens mysterivm cosmographicvm de admirabili proportione orbium cœlestium: deque causis coelorum numeri, magnitudinis, motuumque periodicorum genuinis & propiis, demonstratum per quinque regularia corpora geometrica. Libellus primum Tübingæ in lucem datus anno Christi M. D. XCVI. / à M. Ioanne Keplero VVirtembergico, tvnc temporis illustrium styriæ prouincialium mathematico. Nunc vero post annos 25. ab eodem authore recognitus, & notis notabilissimis partim emendatus, partim explicalia cognati argumenti opera, quæ author ex illo tempore sub duorum Impp. Rudolphi & Matthiæ auspiciis; etiamq[ue] in illustr. ord. Austriæ supr-anisanæ clientela diuersis locis editit. Potissemum ad illustradas occasiones operis, harmonice mundi, dicti, eiusque progressum in materia & methodo; addita est erudita Narratio M. Georgii Ioachimi Rhetici, de libris reuolutionum, atque admirandis de numero, ordine, & distantiis sphærarum mundi hypothesibus, excellentissimi mathematici, totiusque astronomiae restauratoris D. Nicolai Copernici. Item, eiusdem Ioannis Kepleri pro suo opere harmonices mundi apologia aduersus demonstrationem analyticam cl. v. D. Roberti de Fluctibus, medici Oxoniensis. Cum priuilegio ad annos XV.*

Francofvrti: Recusus typis Erasmi Kempferi, sumptibus Godefridi Tampachii, Anno M.DC. XXI [1621]. 4 leaves, 163, 50 p.: ill., fold. plate; 31 cm. Signatures:):(^{4} A-V^4 (G2 numb. G3). Caspar, M. *Kepler.* (2. Aufl.), 67.

His *Pro svo opere Harmonices mvnde apologia*, is separately paged, has its own title page, dated 1622. Provenance: Herbert McLean Evans (bookplate).

1156. KEPLER, JOHANNES, 1571-1630. *Tabulæ Rudolphinæ: quibus astronomicæ scientiæ, temporum longinquitate collapse restauratio continetur: a phœnice illo astronomorum Tychone, ex illustri & generosa Braheorum ... familiâ ... primum animo concepta et destinata anno Christi MDLXIV: exinde observationibus siderum accuratissimis, post annum præcipue MDLXXII ... seriò affectata ... / tabulas ipsas ... morte authoris sui anno MDCI desertas ... continuavit; deindè ... perfecit, absolvit; ad[que] causarum & calculi perennis formulam traduxit Ioannes Keplerus ... Opus hoc ad usus præsentium posteritatis, typis, numericis, proprijs, cæteris & prælo.*

[Ulm]: ...Jonae Saurii, Reip. Ulmanæ typographi ..., 1627. [18], 120, 115 [i.e. 119] p., [1] folded leaf of plates: ill., map; 34 cm. Historiated half-title, engr., signed by Georg Cöler. Error in pagination: p. 119 (2nd group) misnumbered 115. Map of the world: curavit Philippus Eckebrecht, sculpsit J. P. Walch. Caspar, M. *Kelper.* (2. Aufl.), 79. 2

Imperfect: with the folded "Mappa mundi universalis" but without the "Sportula". Provenance: David Christian Hafner (inscription); Herbert McLean Evans (bookplate).

1157. KERSEY, JOHN, 1616-1690? *The elements of that mathematical art commonly called algebra, expounded in four books....*

London: Printed by William Godbid, for Thomas Passinger, and Benjamin Hurlock, [1673-74]. 2 v. in 1 front. (port.) 32 cm. Wing, K 352. Titles in red and black within double line border. The third & fourth books have separate t. p. With imprint: London: Printed by William Godbid for Thomas Passinger, 1674. Port. engraved by W. Faithorne; headpieces; initials.

Imperfect: port. missing.

1158. KEYNES, JOHN MAYNARD, 1883-1946. *The general theory of employment, interest and*

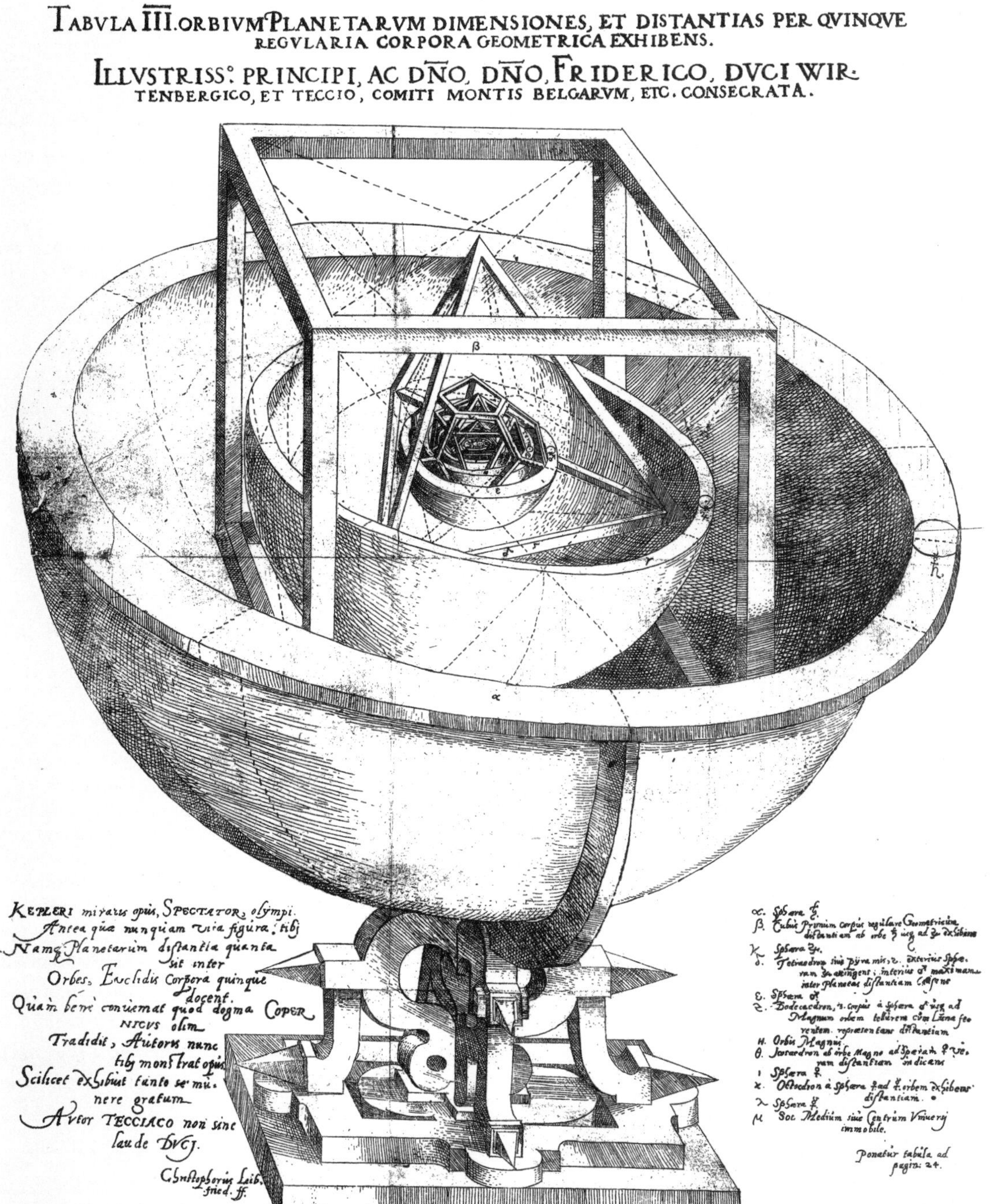

KEPLER, *Mysterium cosmographicum*, 1596

money, by John Maynard Keynes....
London: Macmillan and Co., Limited, 1936. xii, 403 p. diagrs. 22 cm. Includes index.
Erratum on p. 403.

1159. KIDD, JOHN, 1775-1851. *A geological essay on the imperfect evidence in support of a theory of the earth, deducible either from its general structure or from the changes produced on its surface by the operation of existing causes. By J. Kidd.*
Oxford: At the University Press for the author, 1815. xv, 269, [1] p. 23 cm. Errata: last p. "Books referred to in the following essay, arranged in the order of their reference": p. [ix]-xii.
Provenance: Margaret Brown (signature).

1160. KIDDLE, HENRY, 1824-1891. *A short course in astronomy and the use of the globes / by Henry Kiddle ... New edition, revised and corrected.*
New York; Cincinnati; Chicago: American Book Company, [1871?]. vi, [7]-190, [2] p.: ill.; 18 cm. Based on, and in part an abridgement of, the author's *New Manual of the Elements of Astronomy*. Advertisements: [2] p. at end.

1161. KINCKHUYSEN, GERARD, fl. 1645-1663. *Algebra ofte stel-konst, beschreven tot dienst van de leerlinghen, door Gerard Kinckhuysen.*
Tot Haerlem: By Passchier van Wesbusch, boeck-verkooper op de marckt, in den beslaghen Bybel, Anno 1661. 110, [2] p. diagr. 20 cm. Colophon: Te Haerlem, Ghedruckt by Isaac van Wesbusch, boeck-drucker in de korte Zijl-straet, in de groote druckery, 1661. Illustrated t.-p.; tail-pieces.
With: *De grondt der meet-konst* / door Gerard Kinckhuysen. Te Haerlem: By Passchier van Wesbusch, 1660.

1162. KINCKHUYSEN, GERARD, fl. 1645-1663. *De grondt der meet-konst, ofte een korte verklaringe der keegel-sneeden, met een by-voeghsel. Door Gerard Kinckhvysen.*
Haerlem: Passchier van Wesbusch, 1660. 2 p.l., 91, [1] p. diagrs. 19 cm. Title vignette, engraved. With his *Algebra ofte Stel-konst*. Haerlem, 1661.

1163. KING, HENRY C. *The background of astronomy.*
London: Watts, 1957. 254 p. 23 cm. Bibliography: p. 241-46. Includes index.

1164. KIPPAX, JOHN R. (JOHN ROBERT), 1849-1922. *The call of the stars; a popular introduction to a knowledge of the starry skies, by John R. Kippax ... Fifty-four illustrations.*
New York, London: G. P. Putnam's Sons, 1914. xviii p., 1 l., 431 p. col. front., illus., plates, charts. 24 cm. "Some authorities consulted": p. xvii-xviii.

1165. KIRCHER, ATHANASIUS, 1602-1680. *Athanasii Kircheri e Soc. Iesu Scrutinium physico-medicum contagiosæ luis, quæ pestis dicitur: quo origo, causæ, signa, prognostica pestis, nec non insolentes malignantis naturæ effectus, qui statis temporibus, cælestium influxuum virtute & efficacia, tum in elementis, tum in epidemijs hominum animantiumque morbis elucescunt, vnà cum appropriatis remediorum antidotis nouâ doctrinâ in lucem eruuntur.*
Romæ: Typis Mascardi, 1658. [16], 252, [16] p. (last p. blank); 22 cm. Text was the first treatise to "state explicitly the theory of contagion by animalculæ as the cause of infectious disease" – Garrison-Morton. Signatures: +-2+^{4} A-2I^4 2K^6. "Ad Alexandrum VII, Pont. Opt. Max". Woodcuts: Arms of Pope Alexander VII on verso of t. p.; headpieces, tailpieces and initial letters throughout. Garrison-Morton (3rd ed.), 5118. Manchester University Library. *Cat. of medical books*, 1367. Includes index. "Errores": p. [15] (3rd group).

1166. KIRCHER, ATHANASIUS, 1602-1680. *Athanasii Kircheri e Soc. Jesu Mundus subterraneus, in XII libros digestus: quo divinum subterrestris mundi opificium, mira ergasteriorum naturæ in eo distributio, verbo pantamorphon Protei regnum, universæ denique naturæ majestas & divitiæ summa rerum varietate exponuntur. Abditorum effectuum causæ acri indagine inquisitæ demonstrantur; cognitæ per artis & naturæ conjugium ad humanæ vitæ necessarium usum vario experimentorum apparatu, necnon novo modo, & ratione applicantur.*

Ex Libris Davidis Christiani Hafner 1641.

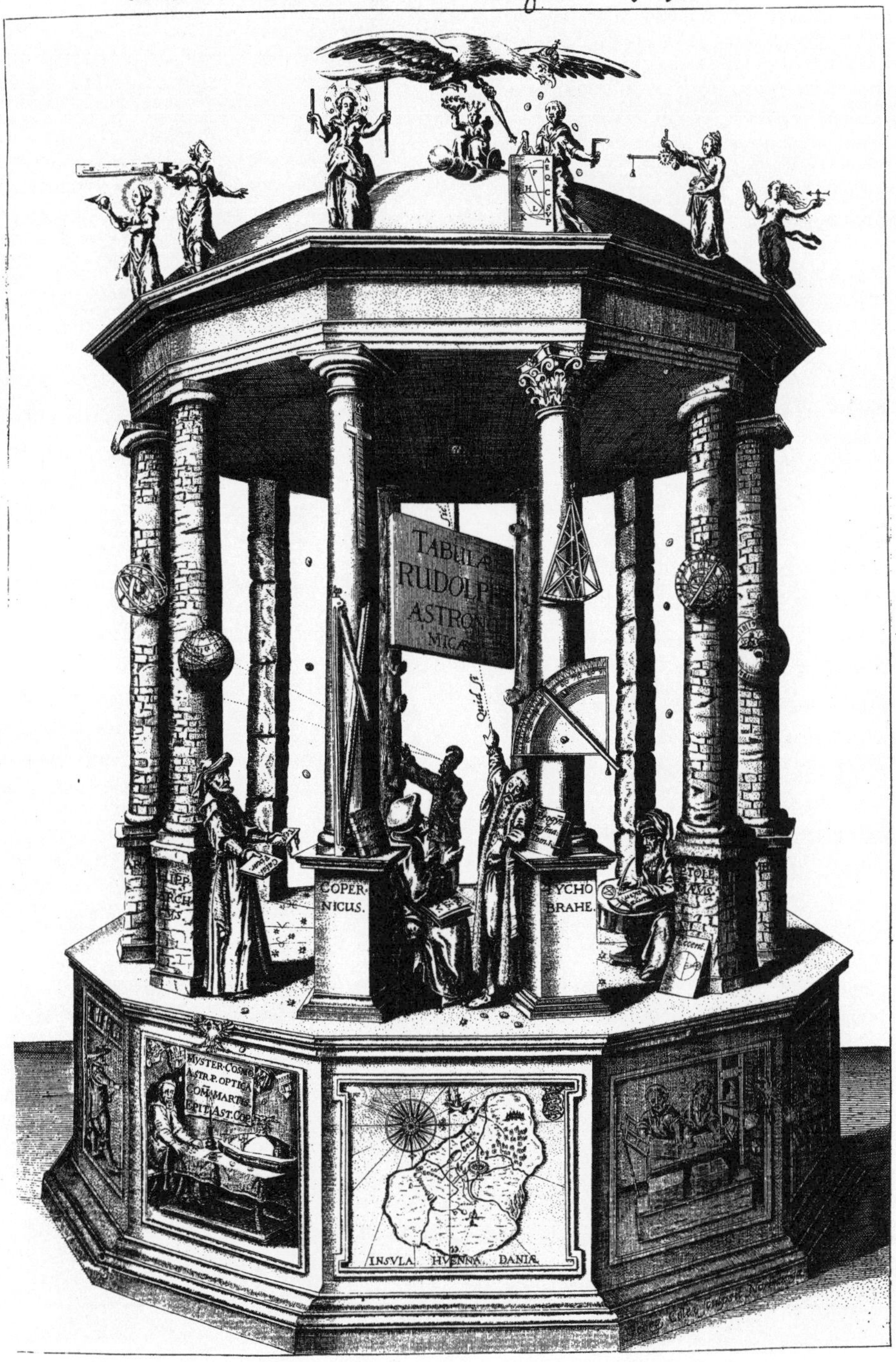

Kepler, *Tabulae Rudolphinae*, 1627

Amstelodami: Apud Joannem Janssonium & Elizeum Weyerstraten, MDCLXV. [1665]. 2 v.: ill., maps, ports., volvelles; 42 cm. Second part has special t. p.: Athanasii Kircheri ... Mundi subterraneitomus Tomus IIus. In V. libros digestus quibus mundi subterranei fructur exponuntur, et quidquid tandem rarum, insolitum, et portentosum in foecundo naturæ utero continetur, ante oculos ponitur curiosi lectoris. Bound in 1 v.; v. 1: [30], 346, [6] p., [17] leaves of plates (most folded); v. 2: [12], 487, [9] p. [12] leaves of plates (some folded). Added engraved t. p.; title vignette; decorated initials; some tail-pieces. Includes indexes. Errata on p. [6] of last group of v. 1. Engraved title pages by: Jo. Paul. Schor, Theod. matham, C. vande Pas, A. Sioutsma. Yale. *Cushing Coll.*, K91.

Provenance: Bibliotheca Reuvensiana (bookplate); Albert Vial (bookplate); Tis[s?]ot, M.D. (inscription).

1167. KIRCHER, ATHANASIUS, 1602-1680. *Athanasii Kircheri Fuldensis Buchonii, e Soc. Jesu ... Magnes siue De arte magnetica opus tripartitum, quo præterquam quod universa magnetis natura, eiusque in omnibus artibus & scientijs usus noua methodo explicetur, è viribus quoque & prodigiosis effectibus magneticarum, aliarumq[ue] abditarum naturæ motionum in elementis, lapidibus, plantis & animalibus elucescentium multa hucusque incognita naturæ arcana per physica, medica, chymica & mathematica omnis generis experimenta recluduntur. Editio secunda post Romanam multò correctior.*

Coloniæ Agrippinæ: Apud Iodocum Kalcoven, 1643. [14] p. l., 797, [39] p. illus., 28 pl. (1 fold.) incl. 2 volvelles, tables, diagrs. 21 cm. Added engraved t. p. has title: Magnes, siue De arte magnetica libritres.

Provenance: Dr. P. Maisonneuve (inkstamp); Bibliotheca Carmelitarum Andegauensium (inscription).

1168. KIRCHER, ATHANASIUS, 1602-1680. *Iter extaticum cœleste, quo mundi opificium ... novâ hypothesi exponitur ad veritatem, interlocutoribus Cosmiele et Theodidacto; hac secundâ editione prælusionibus & scholiis illustratum, ac schematismis necessariis, qui deerant, exornatum, nec non à mendis ... expurgatum, ipso auctore annuente, a P. Gaspare Schotto ... Accessit ejusdem auctoris Iter exstaticum terrestre & synopsis mundi subterranei.*

Herbipoli: Sumptibus Joh. Andr. & Wolffg. jun. Endterorum hæredibus, prostat Norimbergæ apud eosdem, 1660. [24], 689, [18] p., XII leaves of plates. illus., map, 21 cm. Added illustrated t. p., engr., with title: Iter exstaticum Kircherianum. First ed. of the *Iter extaticum cœleste* appeared in 1656 under title: *Itinerarium exstaticum.* "Iter extaticum II" (the Iter exstaticum terrestre ...): p. [513]-689. Errata: on p. [17-18] at end. Includes index and bibliographical references.

Provenance: J. V. Manecke (signature); Friedericus Nicolaus (bookplate).

1169. KIRCHHOFF, G. (GUSTAV), 1824-1887. *Researches on the solar spectrum, and the spectra of the chemical elements. By G. Kirchhoff ... Translated with the author's sanction from the* Transactions of the Berlin Academy *for 1861. By Henry E. Roscoe....*

Cambridge, London: Macmillan and Co., 1862. iv, 36 p. III pl. (2 double) 28 x 22 cm. Translation of: *Untersuchungen über das Sonnenspectrum.*

1170. KIRCHHOFF, G. (GUSTAV), 1824-1887. *Untersuchungen über das Sonnenspectrum und die Spectren der chemischen Elemente / von G. Kirchhoff. 2. durch einen Anhang vermehrte Ausgabe.*

Berlin: Ferd. Dümmler's Verlagsbuchhandlung, (1862-1863). 2 v.: ill.; 30 cm. "Besonderer Abdruck aus den *Abhandlungen der Königl. Akademie der Wissenschaften zu Berlin*, 1861[-1862]" – T. p. Vol. 2 lacks edition statement. Vol. 2 has imprint: Berlin: Gedruckt in der Druckerei der Königl. Akademie der Wissenschaften: in Commission bei F. Dümmlers Verlags-Buchhandlung, Harrwitz und Gossmann. Vol. 1: [4], 43, [1] p., III leaves of plates (2 folded); v. 2: 16 p.,[2] folded leaves of plates. Vol. 2 also issued with paging [225]-240 and variant statement on t. p.: Aus den *Abhandlungen der Königl. Akademie der Wissenshaften zu Berlin* 1862. "Anhang. Über das Verhältniss zwischen dem Emissionsvermögen und dem Absorptionsvermögen der Körper für Wärme und Licht": v. 1, p. [22]-43. Includes bibliographical references. Advertisements on p. [4] of cover, v. 1. Horblit, H. D. *Grolier 100 science books*, 59 (variant).

Vol. 2 is variant issue. V. 1-2 in slipcase. Provenance: Robert Honeyman (Honeyman sale).

Kircher, *Magnes*, 1643

1171. Kirwan, Richard, 1733-1812. *Essai sur le phlogistique, et sur la constitution des acides / traduit de l'anglois de M. Kirwan; avec des notes de MM. de Morveau, Lavoisier, de La Place, Monge, Berthollet, & de Fourcroy.*
À Paris: Rue et hôtel Serpente, 1788. xij, 344, [4] p.; 21 cm. Translation of *Essay on phlogiston, and the constitution of acids* by Marie-Anne-Pierrette Lavoisier. Cf. BM. Signatures: $[pi]^2$ a^4 $A\text{-}X^8$ Y^6. Includes bibliographical references.

1172. Kitchiner, William, 1775?-1827. *Practical observations on telescopes, opera-glasses and spectacles / by William Kitchiner ... Third edition.*
London: Printed for S. Bagster ... , 1818. [8], 165 p., [2] leaves of plates: ill.; 20 cm. Frontispiece by Rose. Price list of telescopes made by Messrs. Dollond on p. 99-101.

1173. Klaproth, M. H. (Martin Heinrich), 1743-1817. *Analytical essays towards promoting the chemical knowledge of mineral substances. By Martin Henry Klaproth ... Tr. from the German.*
London: T. Cadell, jun. and W. Davies, 1801-1804. 2 v. 21 cm. Errata: last p. Includes bibliographical references.
Provenance: Herbert McLean Evans (bookplate); William Peet (inscription).

1174. Klebs, Arnold C. (Arnold Carl), 1870-1943. *Incunabula scientifica et medica / Arnold C. Klebs.*
Hildesheim: G. Olms, 1963. 359 p.; 25 cm. "Reprografischer Nachdruck der Ausgabe *Osiris*, vol. IV, s. 1-359, Bruges 1938".

1175. Klein, Felix, 1849-1925. *Vergleichende Betrachtungen über neuere geometrische Forschungen.*
Erlangen: A. Deichert, 1872. 48 p. 24 cm. Programm zum Eintritt in die Philosophische Facultät und den Senat der K. Friedrich-Alexanders-Universität zu Erlangen.

1176. Klein, Hermann J. (Hermann Joseph), 1844-1914. *Star atlas: containing maps of all the stars from 1 to 6.5 magnitude between the North Pole and 34° South declination, and of all nebulæ and star clusters in the same region which are visible in telescopes of moderate powers: with explanatory text / by Hermann J. Klein; translated by Edmund McClure; with eighteen maps printed by E. A. Funke. 3rd ed., rev. and enl.*
London: Society for Promoting Christian Knowledge; E. & J. B. Young, 1901. viii, 74, [1] p., xviii folded leaves of plates: ill., maps; 32 cm. Translation of: *Stern-Atlas für Freunde der Himmelsbeobachtung.* "Published under the direction of the General Literature Committee." "Printed by William Clowes and Sons, Limited" – Colophon.

1177. Klinkerfues, W. (Wilhelm), 1827-1884. *Theoretische Astronomie / von Dr. W. Klinkerfues....*
Braunschweig: Druck und Verlag von Friedrich Vieweg und Sohn, 1871-1872. 2 v. (VI, 473, [2], VIII-XII p.): ill.; 23 cm. Vol. 2 lacks t. p. "Tafel der Gauss'schen Constanten für die nicht identischen Kometenbahnen": p. [453]-473.
Advertisements: on lower wrappers; [2], 6, [2] p. at end, v. 1.

1178. Koch, Robert, 1843-1910. *Die Aetiologie der Milzbrand-Krankheit, begründet auf die Entwicklungsgeschichte des Bacillus anthracis / von Dr. Koch....*
[Breslau: J. U. Kern's Verlag (Max Müller), 1876]. p. 277-310, [5] leaves of plates: ill.; 22 cm. *Beiträge zur Biologie der Pflanzen;* Bd. 2. Caption title. At head of title: Untersuchungen über Bacterien. Includes bibliographical references.

1179. Koch, Robert, 1843-1910. *Die Bekämpfung der Infektionskrankheiten insbesondere der Kriegsseuchen: Rede, gehalten zur Feier des Stiftungstages des Militärärztlichen Bildungsanstalten am 2. August 1888 / von R. Koch.*
Berlin: Verlag von August Hirschwald ..., 1888. 40 p.; 24 cm. Advertisements on lower wrapper.

1180. Koch, Robert, 1843-1910. *Über bakteriologische Forschung: Vortrag in der 1. Allgemeinen Sitzung des X. Internationalen Medicinischen Congresses am 4. August 1890/ von R. Koch.*
Berlin: Verlag von August Hirschwald, 1890. 15 p.;

24 cm. Advertisements on back cover. Published in: *Verhandlungen des X. Internationalen Medicinischen Congresses.* Berlin, A. Hirschwald, 1891. Bd. 1, p. 35-47.

1181. KOCH, ROBERT, 1843-1910. *Über die Milzbrandimpfung: eine Entgegnung auf den von Pasteur in Genf gehaltenen Vortrag / von Dr. R. Koch....*
Kassel und Berlin: Verlag von Theodor Fischer, 1882. 37, [3] p.; 23 cm. Advertisements on last [2] p.

1182. KOCH, ROBERT, 1843-1910. *Untersuchungen über die Aetiologie der Wundinfectionskrankheiten / von Dr. Robert Koch ...*
Leipzig: Verlag von F.C.W. Vogel, 1878. [4], 80 p., V leaves of plates (some folded): ill.; 24 cm. Includes bibliographical references.
Provenance: Herbert McLean Evans (bookplate).

1183. KOEBEL, JACOB, d. 1533. *Astrolabii declaratio: eiusdemque vsus mire iuncundus ... / à Iacobo Koebelio....*
Coloniae Agrippinae: Apud Henricum Falckenburg, 1594. 31, [1] leaves, [1] folded leaf of plates: ill.; 16 cm. Leaf 21 misnumbered as 22, 26 as 16, 27 as 30, 29 as 23. Colophon reads: Coloniæ Agrippinæ: typis Lamberti Andreæ, 1594. Houzeau & Lancaster. *Astronomie.* (1964 ed.), 3257.

1184. KOENIGSBERGER, LEO, 1837-1921. *Repertorium der literarischen Arbeiten aus dem Gebiete der reinen und angewandten Mathematik. "Originalberichte der Verfasser," gesammelt und hrsg. von dr. Leo Koenigsberger ... und dr. Gustav Zeuner....*
Leipzig: B. G. Teubner, 1877-79. 2 v. 23 cm.
Provenance: Herbert McLean Evans (bookplate).

1185. KOVALEVSKII, A. O. (ALEKSANDR ONUFRIEVICH), 1840-1901. *Entwickelungsgeschichte der einfachen Ascidien. Von A. Kowalevsky. (Mit 3 tafeln.) Der Akademie vorgelegt am 1. November, 1866.*
St. Petersburg: Commissionäre der kaiserlichen Akademie der Wissenschaften, Eggers et Cie und H. Schmitzdorff; [etc., etc., 1866]. 1 p. l., 19 p. III pl. 33 cm. *Mémoires de l'Académie Impériale des Sciences de St.-Pétersbourg.* VIIe série; t. 10, no. 15. Includes bibliographical references.

1186. KOVALEVSKII, MARIAN ALBERTOVICH, 1821-1884. *Recherches sur la réfraction astronomique. Par M. Kowalski....*
Kasan: Imprimerie de l'Université, 1878. xi, 172 p., 1 l., ii p. incl. tables. 24 cm. Errata: p. [173].
Provenance: M. Hoüel (presentation inscription by the author); Cornell University Library (lettering).

1187. KRIEGER, JOHANN NEPOMUK, 1865-1902. *Joh. Nep. Kriegers Mond-Atlas; nach seinen an der Pia-Sternwarte in Triest angestellten Beobachtungen unter Zugrundelegung der hinterlassenen Zeichnungen und Skizzen. Bearbeitet und mit Unterstützung der kaiserl. Akademie der Wissenschaften in Wien aus den Mitteln der Treitl-Stiftungherausgegeben von Rudolf König. Neue Folge.*
Wien: E. H. Mayer, 1912. 2 v. plates, port., 32 cm.

1188. KROGH, AUGUST, 1874-1949. *The anatomy and physiology of capillaries, by August Krogh....*
New Haven: Yale University Press; [etc., etc., 1922]. xvii, 276 p. ill. 24 cm. Yale University. Mrs. Hepsa Ely Silliman Memorial Lectures. Bibliography: p. [268]-276.
Provenance: Ernest S. du Bray (inscription).

1189. KUIPER, GERARD PETER, 1905- . *Orthographic atlas of the moon. Supplement no. 1- to the Photographic lunar atlas. Edition A, showing the standard orthographic coordinate grid.*
Tucson: University of Arizona Press, 1960. -pts. in (chiefly photos.) 47 x 59 cm. Arizona University Lunar and Planetary Laboratory. Contributions no.1. "Produced with the technical assistance of the Aeronautical Chart and Information Center." no. 1. pt. 1. Central area, compiled by D. W. G. Arthur and E. A. Whitaker.

1190. KUIPER, GERARD PETER, 1905- . *Photographic lunar atlas, based on photographs taken at the Mount Wilson, Lick, Pic du Midi, McDonald, and Yerkes Observatories. With the collaboration of D. W. G. Arthur [and others].*
[Chicago]: University of Chicago Press, 1960. 23 p. tables. 28 cm. and atlas (230 photos.) 56 cm. Issued in a portfolio.

1191. La Caille, Nicolas Louis de, 1713-1762. *A catalogue of 9766 stars in the southern hemisphere: for the beginning of the year 1750 / from the observations of the Abbé de Lacaille made at the Cape of Good Hope in the years 1751 and 1752. Reduced at the expense of the British association for the advancement of science, under the immediate superintendence of the late Professor Henderson ...and printed at the expense of Her Majesty's government, under the direction of the late Francis Baily, esq. With a preface by Sir J. F. W. Herschel....*
London: R. and J. E. Taylor, 1847. xi, 299, [1] p. tables. 22 cm.
Provenance: Conservative Club (bookplate) and armorial binding. Binder: J. Kelley (label).

1192. La Caille, Nicolas Louis de, 1713-1762. *Clarissimi viri d. de La Caille ... Lectiones elementares astronomiæ, geometricæ, et physicæ / ex editione Parisina anni MDCCLV in Latinum traductæ a C. S. e S. J.*
Viennæ & Pragæ: Typis et sumtibus Joannis Thomæ Trattner ..., 1757. [10], 280, [6] p., IX folded leaves of plates: ill.; 24 cm. Translation of: *Leçons élémentaires d'astronomie, géométrique et physique.* Errata: p. [6] at the end. Includes index. With the author's *Lectiones elementares opticæ.* Viennæ Austriæ: Typis Joannis Thomæ Trattner, 1757.
Provenance: Országos Könyvtári Központszegedi raktárából (inkstamp).

1193. La Caille, Nicolas Louis de, 1713-1762. *Clarissimi viri d. de La Caille ... Lectiones elementares opticæ exeditione Parisina anni MDCCLVI in Latinum traductæ a C.S. e S.J. quibus auctarii loco accessit Brevis theoria micrometri objectivi a R. P. Rogerio Josepho Boscovich ... concinnata....*
Viennæ, Austriæ: J. T. Trattner, 1757. [8], 150, [1] p.: 98 diagrs. on xiii pl.; 24 cm. Translation of: *Leçons élémentaires d'optique.* Errata: p. [1] following text. With his: *Lectiones elementares astronomiæ, geometricæ, et physicæ...* 1757.
Provenance: Országos Könyvtári Központszegedi raktárából (inkstamp).

1194. La Condamine, Charles-Marie de, 1701-1774. *Mesure des trois premiers degrés du méridien dans l'hémisphere austral: tirée des observations de MM. de l'Académie Royale des Sciences, envoyés par le roi sous l'équateur / par M. de La Condamine.*
À Paris: De l'Imprimerie Royale, 1751. [12], 266, x p., III folded leaves of plates: ill.; 26 cm. Fautes à corriger: on p. [3-4]. Includes index. Plate signed: R. Brunet scup. Engraved title vignette.

1195. La Hire, Philippe de, 1640-1718. *La gnomonique ou méthodes universelles, pour tracer des horloges solaires où cadrans sur toutes sortes de surfaces / par M. de la Hire....*
Paris: T. Moette, 1698. [24], 274 [i.e. 275] p.: fold. plates; 15 cm. First published (1682) under title: *La gnomonique; ou, L'art de tracer des cadrans.* Errors of pagination: p. 269 misnumbered as 279, p. 275 as 274.

1196. Laennec, R. T. H. (René Théophile Hyacinthe), 1781-1826. *De l'auscultation médiate, ou, Traité du diagnostic des maladies des poumons et du coeur: fondé principalement sur ce nouveau moyen d'exploration / Par. R. T. H. Laennec ... Tome premier [-seconde].*
À Paris: Chez J.-A. Brosson et J.-S. Chaudé ..., 1819. 2 v.: ill.; 21 cm. Vol. 1: [iii]-xlviii, 456 p.; v. 2: xvi, 472, [8] p., 4 folded leaves of plates. Includes bibliographical references and index. Garrison, F. H. *Medical bibl.* 2673. Yale. *Cushing Coll.* L5.
Plates and [8] p. explanations bound in v. 1. Provenance: Dr. Denizet (bookplate); Herbert McLean Evans (bookplate).

1197. Lagrange, J. L. (Joseph Louis), 1736-1813. *Méchanique analitique.*
Paris: Chez la Veuve Desaint, 1788. xij, 512 p. 26 cm. Colophon reads: À Paris: De l'Imprimerie de Philippe-Denys Pierres ... Horblit, H. D. *Grolier 100 science books,* 61.
Provenance: École Polytechnique (inkstamp); Adolphe Robin (bookplate); Herbert McLean Evans (bookplate). 29 cm.

1198. Lagrange, J. L. (Joseph Louis), 1736-1813. *Théorie des fonctions analytiques: contenant les principes du calcul différentiel,*

dégagés de toute considération d'infiniment petits ou d'évanouissans, de limites ou de fluxions, et réduits a l'analyse algébrique des quantités finies / par J. L. Lagrange....
À Paris: De l'Imprimerie de la République, prairial an 5 [i.e. 1797]. [4], viii, 276 p.; 26 cm. Also published in 1797 in an edition of 278 p.
Provenance: Herbert McLean Evans (bookplate).

1199. LALANDE, JOSEPH JÉRÔME LE FRANÇAIS DE, 1732-1807. *Astronomie, par Jérôme Le Français [La Lande]. 3. éd. rev. et augm.*
Paris: Chez la Veuve Desaint, 1781-92. 4 v. 48 fold. plates (incl. map) tables. 28 cm. T. 1-3: 1792; t. 4 is 1st edition: 1781. t. 1-3. Astronomie. – t. 4. Traité du flux et du reflux de la mer. Mémoire sur l'origine des constellations & sur l'explication de la fable, par le moyen de l'astronomie, par M. Dupuis. Supplemens pour l'Astronomie, publiée à Paris en 1771.
Provenance: J. J. Gonzenbach v. Hauptweil (bookplate).

1200. LALANDE, JOSEPH JÉRÔME LE FRANÇAIS DE, 1732-1807. *Astronomie des dames, par Jérôme de Lalande ... Nouv. éd.*
Paris: Chez Salmon, Libraire, 1824. 1 p.l., [5]-182 p. fold. pl. 11 cm.
Plate by Boblet. With: *Histoire del'Inquisition*, par Gilles de Witte. Paris, Chez Carpentier et Compagnie, 1826.

1201. LALANDE, JOSEPH JÉRÔME LE FRANÇAIS DE, 1732-1807. *Bibliographie astronomique: avec l'histoire de l'astronomie depuis 1781 jusqu'à 1802 / par Jérôme de La Lande....*
Paris: De l'Imprimerie de la République, an XI, 1803. 2, viii, 915, [1] p.; 27 cm.
Provenance: Royal Astronomical Society (inkstamp).

1202. LAMARCK, JEAN BAPTISTE PIERRE ANTOINE DE MONET DE, 1744-1829. *Histoire naturelle des animaux sans vertèbres ... précédée d'une introduction offrant la détermination des caractères essentiels del'animal, sa distinction du végétal et des autres corps naturels, enfin, l'exposition des principes fondamentaux de la zoologie. Par M. de Lamarck....*
Paris: Verdière, 1815-1822. 7 v. in 8; 22 cm. Vol. 6 in 2 parts. Imprint varies. T. 4-5: Paris, Chez Deterville ..., Verdière ...; t.. 6-7: Paris, Chez l'auteur ...
Provenance: Palaeontologisches Museum und Institut der Universität Bonn (inkstamp). Ms. notes tipped in, v. 4-7.

1203. LAMARCK, JEAN BAPTISTE PIERRE ANTOINE DE MONET DE, 1744-1829. *Philosophie zoologique; ou, Exposition des considérations relatives à l'histoire naturelle des animaux; à la diversité de leur organisation et des facultés qu'ils en obtiennent; aux causes physiques qui maintiennent en eux la vie et donnent lieu aux mouvemens qu'ils exécutent; enfin, à celles qui produisent, les unes le sentiment, et les autres l'intelligence de ceux qui en sont doués; par J.-B.-P.-A. Lamarck.*
À Paris: Chez Dentu ... [et] L'Auteur ... 1809. 2 v.; 23 cm. [8 vo].
Provenance: Herbert McLean Evans (bookplate).

1204. LAMARCK, JEAN BAPTISTE PIERRE ANTOINE DE MONET DE, 1744-1829. *Recherches sur les causes des principaux faits physiques, et particulièrement sur celles de la combustion, de l'élévation de l'eau dans l'état de vapeurs ... de l'origine des composés et de tous les minéraux; enfin de l'entretien de la vie des êtres organiques, de leur accroissement, de leur état de vigueur, de leur dépérissement et de leur mort. Avec une planche. Par J. B. Lamarck....*
Paris: Maradan, seconde année de la République. [1794]. 2 v. pl., fold. tab. 21 cm.

1205. LAMARCK, JEAN BAPTISTE PIERRE ANTOINE DE MONET DE, 1744-1829. *Système des animaux sans vertèbres, ou tableau général des classes, des ordres et des genres de ces animaux ... précédé du discours d'ouverture du cours de zoologie, donné dans le Muséum national d'histoire naturelle l'an 8 de la République. Par J. B. Lamarck.*
Paris: Chez Deterville, 1801. viii, 432 p. ill. 21 cm. First ed. Includes index.

1206. LAMBERT, ARMAND. ...*L'astronomie.*

Paris: A. Michel, [c1922]. 192 p., 1 l. plates, diagrs. 18 cm. Bibliothèque Cosmos; petite bibliothèque de culture générale.

1207. LAMBERT, JOHANN HEINRICH, 1728-1777. *Cosmologische Briefe über die Einrichtung des Weltbaues / ausgefertigt von J. H. Lambert.*

Augspurg: Bey Eberhard Kletts Wittib., 1761. xxviii, 318 p.: ill., tab. (fold.); 20 cm. Contains "Edmund Halley[s] Tafel der Laufbahn, der von ihme berechneten Cometen." Later rewritten and publ. under title: *Systême du monde,* Berlin, 1770. Steck, M. *Bib. Lambertiana,* I.6.

Provenance: C. Easton (inkstamp).

1208. LAMBERT, JOHANN HEINRICH, 1728-1777. *I. H. Lambert Academiæ Scientiarum Electoralis Boicæ ... Photometria, siue, De mensura et gradibus luminis, colorum et umbræ.*

Augustae Vindelicorum: Sumptibus Viduæ Eberhardi Klett, typis Christophori Petri Detleffsen, 1760. [16], 547, [13] p., VIII folded leaves of plates: diagrams; 21 cm. Signatures:)([8] A-2M[8]. Includes index. Steck, M. *Bib. Lambertiana,* I.4. Horblitt, H. D. *Grolier 100 science books,* 62. Includes index.

Provenance: Robert Honeyman IV (bookplate).

1209. LAMBERT, JOHANN HEINRICH, 1728-1777. *Systême du monde / par M. Lambert; publié par M. Mérian ... Seconde édition.*

Bouillion: Et se vend a Paris chez la ve. Duchesne ... Durand neveu ... et a Geneve chez Barthelemi Chirol ..., 1784. viij, 180 p. 23 cm. French edition of: *Cosmoligische Briefe.* Steck, M. *Bib. Lambertiana,* II.5.

1210. LANA TERZI, FRANCESCO, 1631-1687. *Podromo ouero saggio di alcune inuentione nuoue premesso all'arte maestra ... per mostrare li piu reconditi principij della naturale filosofia, riconosciuti con accurata teorica nelle piu segnalate inuentioni, ed isperienze sin' hora ritrouate da gli scrittori di questa materia & altra nuoue dell'autore medesimo. / Opera che prepara il P. Francesco Lana.*

In Brescia: Per li Rizzardi, M.DCLXX [1670]. [8], 252 p., [20] leaves of plates: ill., music (engravings); 33 cm. Statement of responsibility transposed. Proemio, in cui l'autore dichiara qual sia per essere l'opera che'promette (Magisterium naturæ, et artis. Brescia, 1684) p. 1-17 – cap. 1. Nuoue inuentioni di scrivere in cifera – cap. 2. In qual modo un cieco nato possa imparare a scriuere ... – cap. 3. In qual modo si possa parlare senza mandar ne lettere, ne messagiere – cap. 4. Come si possa insegnare a parlare ad vno, che per esser nato sordo sia nuto ... – cap. 6. Frabricare vna naue, che camini sostentata sopre l'aria a remi. – cap. 16. L'Arte maestra d'agricoltura – cap. 20. L'Arte maestra di chimica – cap. 21. L'Arte maestra di medicina – cap. 22. L'Arte maestra di aritmetica – L'Arte maestra sopra l'arte della pittura (4 chap.) L'Arte maestra presriue alcune regole ... per fabricare molte sorti di cannocchiali, e microscopij (8 chap.).

Provenance: E. N. da C. Andrade (bookplate).

1211. LANDSTEINER, KARL, 1868-1943. *Die Spezifizität der serologischen Reaktionen, von dr. K. Landsteiner....*

Berlin: J. Springer, 1933. 2 p. l., 123, [1] p. 24 cm. "Die vorliegende Schrift beabsichtigt die Untersuchungen des Verfassers und seiner Mitarbeiter über Antigene zusammenzufassen." – Prelim. note. Includes bibliographies and index.

Provenance: Siegwart Hermann (inkstamp and bookplate).

1212. LANGLEY, S. P. (SAMUEL PIERPONT), 1834-1906. *The new astronomy / by Samuel Pierpont Langley....*

Boston: Houghton, Mifflin and Company: The Riverside Press, Cambridge, 1891. xii, 260 p.: ill.; 25 cm. Originally published in *Century Magazine,* 1884-1887. Includes index.

1213. LANKESTER, EDWIN, 1814-1874. *Half-hours with the microscope: a popular guide to the use of the microscope as a means of amusement and instruction / by Edwin Lankester... . Eighteenth edition.*

London: W. H. Allen & Co. ..., 1892. XX, 130 p., 8 leaves of plates: ill. (some col.); 17 cm. Appendix by Thomas Ketteringham: p. 119-130. Plates signed: F. G. Kitton, del. ad nat. and Tuffen West sc. ad nat.

1214. LAPLACE, PIERRE SIMON, MARQUIS DE, 1749-1827. *Elementary illustrations of the Celestial mechanics of Laplace. Part the first, comprehending the first book.*

London: Printed for J. Murray, 1821. 3 p. l., iv p., 1 l., 344 p. diagrs. 23 cm. "A mosaic work" combining Thomas Young's translation of parts of Laplace's *Celestial mechanics* with Young's own work. cf. Pref. No more published. Cf. *NUC pre-1956*, v. 316, p. 90.

1215. LAPLACE, PIERRE SIMON, MARQUIS DE, 1749-1827. *Essai philosophique sur les probabilités / par M. le comte Laplace....*
Paris: Mme. Ve. Courcier ..., 1814. [4], 96, [2] p.; 26 cm. Errata: p. [1] at end.
4 p. advertisements at end. Provenance: Herbert McLean Evans (bookplate).

1216. LAPLACE, PIERRE SIMON, MARQUIS DE, 1749-1827. *Exposition du systême du monde.*
Paris: Imprimerie du Cercle-social, an IV [1796]. 2 v. 20 cm.

1217. LAPLACE, PIERRE SIMON, MARQUIS DE, 1749-1827. *Exposition du systême du monde / par P. S. Laplace ... Seconde édition, revue et augmentée par l'auteur.*
À Paris: De l'Imprimerie de Crapelet: chez J. B. M. Duprat ..., an 7, 1799. viij, 351 p.; 26 cm.
Imperfect: half title missing.

1218.LAPLACE, PIERRE SIMON, MARQUIS DE, 1749-1827. *Exposition du systême du monde / par le M. le marquis de Laplace ... Cinquième édition / revue et augmentée par l'auteur.*
Paris: Bachelier ..., 1824. viij, 418, [1] p., [1] leaf of plates: port.; 25 cm. Errata: p. [1] following text.

1219. LAPLACE, PIERRE SIMON, MARQUIS DE, 1749-1827. *Mécanique céleste. By the Marquis de La Place ... Tr., with a commentary, by Nathaniel Bowditch....*
Boston: Hillard, Gray, Little, and Wilkins, 1829-39. 4 v. ports. 28 cm. Translation of: *Traité de mécanique céleste.* On t. p. of v. 4: With a memoir of the translator, by his son, Nathaniel Ingersoll Bowditch. Boston, C. C. Little and J. Brown. vol. I. 1st book. On the general laws of equilibrium and motion. 2d book. On the law of universal gravitation and the motions of the centres of gravity of the heavenly bodies. – vol. II 3d book. On the figures of the heavenly bodies. 4th book. On the oscillations of the sea and atmosphere. 5th book. On the motions of the heavenly bodies about their own centres of gravity. – vol. III. 6th book. Theory of the planetary motions. 7th book. Theory of the moon. Appendix, presented by the author of the Board of Longitude of France, August 17, 1808. Appendix by the translator. Tables. – vol. IV. 8th book. Theory of the satellites of Jupiter, Saturn,and Uranus. 9th book. Theory of comets. 10th book. On the several subjects relative to the system of the world. Supplement to the tenth book: On capillary attraction. Supplement to the theory of capillary attraction. *Babson Newton Coll.* 82.

1220. LAPLACE, PIERRE SIMON, MARQUIS DE, 1749-1827. *Supplément à la Théorie analytique des probabilités. Sur l'application du calcul des probabilités à la philosophie naturelle.*
[Paris]: De l'Imprimerie de Mme Ve Courcier ... , [1816?]. 54 p.; 27 cm. Caption title. Authorship and date of publication from *DSB*, v. 15, p. 395. Publisher statement from colophon.

1221. LAPLACE, PIERRE SIMON, MARQUIS DE, 1749-1827. *The system of the world, by P. S. Laplace. Translated from the French by J. Pond.*
London: Printed for R. Phillips, 1809. 2 v. 21 cm. Translation of: *Exposition du systême du monde.* Advertisements: v. 2, p. 377-880 [i.e. 380].
Provenance: Charles Atwood Kofoid (bookplate).

1222. LAPLACE, PIERRE SIMON, MARQUIS DE, 1749-1827. *Théorie analytique des probabilités; par m. le comte Laplace....*
Paris: Ve Courcier, 1812. 2 p. l., 464 p., 1 l. 26 cm. I. Calcul des fonctions génératrices. II. Théorie générale des probabilités. Errata: p. 5.
Errata leaf bound behind p. [4]. Ms. notes. Provenance: Herbert McLean Evans (bookplate), binder: Jas. Macdonald Co. N.Y. (stamp).

1223. LAPLACE, PIERRE SIMON, MARQUIS DE, 1749-1827. *Traité de mécanique céleste, tome premier-[cinquième] / par P. S. Laplace....*
À Paris: De l'Imprimerie de Crapelet: Chez J.B.M. Duprat ..., an 7, [1798-1827]. 5 v. ill.; 28 cm. Author statement and imprint vary: v. 4: Par M. Laplace ... A Paris: Chez Courcier ...; v. 5: Par M. le Marquis de Laplace ... Paris: Bachelier (successeur de Mme Ve Courcier) ... Horblit, H. D. *Grolier 100 science books*, 63. t. 1. (an VII [1798]) livre I. Des lois générales de l'équilibre et du mouvement. livre II. De la loi de la pesanteur universelle, et du mouvement des centres de gravité des corps célestes. – t. 2. (an VII [1798]) livre III. De la figure des corps célestes. livre IV. Des

oscillations de la mer et de l'atmosphère. livre V. Des mouvements des corps célestes, autour de leurs propres centres de gravité. – t. 3. (an XI [1802]) livre VI. Théorie des mouvements planétaires. livre VII. Théorie de la lune. Supplément au IIIe volume présenté au Bureau des Longitudes, le 17 août 1808. – t. 4. (an XIII-1805) livre VIII. Théorie des satellites de Jupiter, de Saturne et d'Uranus. livre IX. Théorie des comètes. livre X. Sur différens points relatifs au système du monde. Supplément au Xe livre: Sur l'action capillaire. Supplément à la théorie de l'action capillaire. t. 5. (1825) Notice historique des travaux des géométres sur la mécanique céleste, et nouvelles recherches sur le système du monde. livre XI. De la figure et de la rotation de la terre. livre XII. De l'attraction et de la répulsion des sphères et des lois de lui libre et du mouvement des fluides élastiques. livre XIII. Des oscillations des fluides qui recouvrent les planètes. livre XIV. Des mouvements des corps célestes autour de leur centre de gravité. livre XV. du mouvement des planètes et des comètes. livre XVI. Du mouvement des satellites. Supplément au 5e volume ... / par M. le marquis de Laplace; imprimé sur le manuscrit trouvé dans ses papiers. 1827.

Imperfect: lacks 2nd suppl., v. 4. Supplement to v. 5 (35 p.) bound separately, in wrappers.

1224. LARDNER, DIONYSIUS, 1793-1859. *Handbook of astronomy / by Dionysius Lardner ... Fourth edition / revised and edited by Edwin Dunkin ...*

London: Lockwood & Co. ..., 1875, [i.e. 1878]. xxii, 528, 32, 16 p., XXXVII leaves of plates (2 fold.): ill, charts.; 19 cm. Advertisements: 32 p. (3rd group), dated November, 1878, and 16 p. (4th group). Includes index.

1225. LARTET, ÉDOUARD AMAND ISIDORE HIPPOLYTE, 1801-1871. *Reliquiæ Aquitanicæ; being contributions to the archæology and palæontology of Périgord and the adjoining provinces of southern France. By Edouard Lartet and Henry Christy. Ed. by Thomas Rupert Jones. Illustrated with 87 plates, 3 maps, and 132 woodcuts. 1865-75.*

London: Williams & Norgate, 1875. xxii, 302, 204 p. illus., maps, 87 plates. 33 cm. Note inserted between p. 212 and 213. Four of the plates are each accompanied by leaf with descriptive text not included in paging. Includes index. A collection of essays originally published 1865-1875. Variously illustrated by: Louveau, G. De Wilde, W. Tipping.

1226. LAUE, MAX VON, 1879-1960. *Das Relativitätsprinzip, von dr. M. Laue ... mit 14 in den Text eingedruckten Abbildungen.*

Braunschweig: F. Vieweg & Sohn, 1911. x, 208 p. diagrs. 22 cm. Die Wissenschaft ...; 38 Hft. Includes indexes. Advertisements: [36] p. following text and on endpapers. "Literatur": p. [201]-205.

Provenance: Herbert McLean Evans (bookplate).

1227. LAVOISIER, ANTOINE LAURENT, 1743-1794. *Traité élémentaire de chimie, présenté dans un ordre nouveau et d'après les découvertes modernes; avec figures / par M. Lavoisier....*

Paris: Cuchet, 1789. 2 v. XIII fold. pl., tables (2 fold.) 21 cm. Paged continuously. Plates engraved by Mme. Lavoisier. Title vignette, head and tail-pieces. Errata: [2] p. at end, v. 2. Horblit, H. D. *Grolier 100 science books*, 64.

Provenance: ms. note in v. 1, signed Edouard Grimaux, states that copy belonged to Lavoisier. Title pages repaired; no loss of text.

1228. †LAVOISIER, ANTOINE LAURENT, 1743-1794. *Traité élémentaire de chimie, présenté dans un ordre nouveau et d'après les découvertes modernes, par M. Lavoisier. Nouvelle édition, à la quelle on a joint la nomenclature ancienne & moderne... différens mémoires de MM. Fourcroy & Morveau, & le rapport de MM. Baumé, Cadet, Darcet & Sage, sur la necessité de réformer & de perfectionner la nomenclature chimique. Avec figures & tableaux....*

Paris: Chez Cuchet, Libraire, rue & hôtel Serpente, 1789. 3 v. (322, 326, 259 p.) 13 fold. plates; tables (part fold.) 20.7 cm. Tome 3 has title: Nomenclature chimique ou synonymie ancienne et moderne... The 13 plates (all in tome 3) engraved by Paulze Lavoisier.

Provenance: Dr. Lejeune (inkstamp); Herbert McLean Evans (bookplate).

1229. LAVOISIER, ANTOINE LAURENT, 1743-1794. *Traité élémentaire de chimie: présenté dans un ordre nouveau et d'après les découvertes modernes ... / par M. Lavoisier ... Seconde édition.*

À Paris: Chez Cuchet ... , 1793. 2 v.: ill; 21 cm. Vol. 1: xliv, 322 p., [2] folded leaves of plates; v. 2: viij, 331 p.,

XIII folded leaves of plates. Colophon reads: De l'Imprimerie de Chardon, rue de la Harpe, 1792. Plates signed: Paulze Lavosier sculp. Grolier Club. *Lavoisier*, 43.

1230. LE CLERC, DANIEL, 1652-1728. *Bibliotheca anatomica, sive recens in anatomia inventorum thesaurus locupletissimus: in quo integra atque absolutissima totius corporis humani descriptio ... tum hactenus in lucem editis, tum etiam ineditis, concinnata exhibetur. Adiecta est partium omnium administratio anatomica, cum variis earundem præparationibus curiosissimis. / Digesserunt, tractatus suppleuerunt, argumenta, notulas, & observationes anatomico-practicas addiderunt Daniel Le Clerc & I. Iacobus Mangetus ... Cum indicibus necessariis, figurisque æneis. Tomus primus [-secundus].*
Genevæ: Sumptibus Joannis Anthonii Chovet, M.DC.LXXXV, [1685]. 2 v.: ill.; 37 cm. Title pages printed in red and black, with engraved vignettes. Vol. 1: [32], 763, [1] p. (last page blank), [40] leaves of plates; v. 2: 1106, [2] p. (last leaf blank), [48] leaves of plates. Printed in double columns. Osler, W. *Bib. Oslerianna*, 3192. Yale. *Cushing Coll.*, L111. Includes index.
Provenance: Herbert McLean Evans (bookplate), Mario Donati (inscription), Bernardini Ramazzini Mutinensis (signature).

1231. LE VERRIER, U.-J. (URBAIN J.), 1811-1877. *Recherches sur les mouvements de la planète Herschel / par U.-J. Le Verrier.*
Paris: Bachelier, Imprimeur-libraire, 1846. [2], 254 p.; 25 cm. "Extrait de la *Connaissance des temps pour 1849*" – p. 254.
With: *Théorie géométrique de la variation des éléments des planètes* / par M. Lespiault. Paris: Gauthier-Villars..., 1868 – *Mémoire sur le mouvement des noueds de la lune* / par M. G. Lespiault. Paris: Chez Mallet-Bachelier, Libraire-éditeur ..., 1861.

1232. LE VERRIER, U.-J. (URBAIN J.), 1811-1877. *Recherches sur les mouvements de la planète Herschel, (dite Uranus) / par U.-J. Le Verrier.*
[Paris: Bachelier ..., Nov., 1846]. 254 p.; 25 cm. *Connaissance des temps, ou des mouvements célestes, a l'usage des astronomes et des navigateurs pour l'an ...; 1849*. Caption title. Half-title: Additions à la Connaissance des temps, 1849.

1233. LEADBETTER, CHARLES, fl. 1728. *Astronomy; or, the true system of the planets demonstrated ... By Charles Leadbetter....*
London: Printed for J. Wilcox [etc.], 1727. 2 p. l., viii p., 1 l., [2], 120 p. fold. plates, tables, diagr. 24 cm.,

1233A LEAHY, GEORGE VINCENT, 1869- . *Astronomical essays, by the Rev. George V. Leahy....*
Boston: Washington Press, 1910. ix, [1], 274 p. 19 cm. "Compiled from a series of articles originally published in the *Boston Pilot* over the pen-name Catholicus." – Foreword.

1234. *Lectures delivered at the celebration of the twentieth anniversary of the foundation of Clark University, under the auspices of the Department of Physics, by Vito Volterra, Ernest Rutherford, Robert Williams Wood, Carl Barus, Worcester, Mass., September 7-11, 1909.*
[Worcester]: Clark University, 1912. v. p., 1 l., 161 p. III pl., diagrs. 24 cm. Volterra, V. Sur quelques progrès récents de la physique mathématique. – Rutherford, E. History of the alpha rays from radioactive substances. – Wood, R. W. The optical properties of metallic vapors. – Barus, C. Physical properties of the iron carbides.
Provenance: Herbert McLean Evans.

1235. LEDGER, EDMUND. *The sun: its planets and their satellites. A course of lectures upon the solar system. Read in Gresham College, London, in the years 1881 and 1882, pursuant to the will of Sir Thomas Gresham. By Edmund Ledger ... Illustrated by 94 woodcuts, a chart of Mars, and eight woodbury and lithographic plates....*
London: E. Stanford, 1882. xiv, [2], 432 p. illus., ix pl. (incl. fold. front.: chart) diagrs. 21 cm. Gresham Lectures; 1881-1882. I-II. The sun. – III-IV. The moon. – V. Ptolemy versus Copernicus. – VI. The planet Mercury. – VII. The planet Venus. – VIII-IX. The earth. – X. The planet Mars. – XI. The minor planets. – XII. The planet Jupiter. – XIII. The satellites of Jupiter. – XIV. The planet Saturn. – XV. The planets Uranus and Neptune.

1236. LEE, OLIVER JUSTIN, b. 1881. *Beyond yonder, by Oliver Justin Lee....*
Boston: Chapman & Grimes, [c1939]. 169 p. incl. front., illus. plates, diagrs. 20 cm.

1237. LEE, OLIVER JUSTIN, b. 1881. *Measuring our universe from the inner atom to outer space.*
New York: Ronald Press Co., 1950. x, 170 p. illus. 22 cm. Humanizing Science Series.

1238. LEEUWENHOEK, ANTONI VAN, 1632-1723. *Arcana naturæ detecta....*
Delphis Batavorum: Apud Henricum a Krooneveld, 1695. [8], 568, [14] p.: front. (port.), illus., plates.; 20 cm. Added engraved title page. Port. signed: J. Verkolje pinx., A. de Blois fec. Includes index. Emendanda: p. [14]. Dobell, C. *Leeuwenhoek,* 25.
Variant of p. 15-16 inserted in front of the port.

1239. LEEUWENHOEK, ANTONI VAN, 1632-1723. *Ontdekkingen en ontledingen van sout-figuren: van verscheyden souten... vervat in twee brieven, geschreven aan de Wijt-vermaarde Koninglijke Wetenschap-soekende Societeyt tot Londen in Engelandt / door Antoni van Leeuwenhoek....*
Tot Leyden: By Cornelis Boutesteyn ..., 1685. 76 p., [1] folded leaves of plates: ill.; 22 cm. Letter 44-45. Dobell, C. *Leeuwenhoek,* 6.
With the author's: *Ontledingen en ontdekkingen van de onsigtbare verborgentheden.* Tot Leyden: By Cornelis Boutesteyn, 1685.

1240. LEEUWENHOEK, ANTONI VAN, 1632-1723. *Ontledingen en ontdekkingen van de cinnaber naturalis: en bus poeder; van her maaksel van been en huyd ... vervat in verscheide brieven, geschreven aan de Wyd-vermaarde Koninglyke Wetenschap-zoekende Societeit tot Londen / door Antoni van Leeuwenhoek....*
Tot Leyden: By Cornelis Boutesteyn ..., 1686. 109, [1] p., [1] folded leaves of plates: ill.; 22 cm. Errors in pagination: p. 51 misnumbered as 37. Letters 48-52. Dobell, C. *Leeuwenhoek,* 9.
With the author's *Ontledingen en ontdekkingen van de onsigtbare verborgentheden.* Tot Leyden: By Cornelis Boutesteyn, 1685.

1241. LEEUWENHOEK, ANTONI VAN, 1632-1723. *Ontledingen en ontdekkingen van de onsigtbare verborgentheden: vervat in verscheyde brieven geschreven aan de Wyd-vermaarde Koninklijke Wetenschap-soekende Societeyt tot Londen in Engeland / door Antoni van Leeuwenhoek....*
Tot Leyden: By Cornelis Boutesteyn ..., 1685. [2], 94 [i.e. 88] p.: ill.; 22 cm. Errors in pagination: p. 46 misnumbered as 6, p. 73-78 omitted. Additional engraved t. p.: Ontdeckte onsigtbaarheeden. Signed by R. DeHooghe. With the author's: *Ontledingen en ontdekkingen van levende dierkens in de teel-deelen van verscheyde dieren, vogelen en visschen.* Tot Leyden: By Cornelis Boutesteyn, 1686; *Ontledingen en ontdekkingen van het begin der planeten in de zaden van boomen.* Tot Leyden: By Cornelis Boutesteyn, 1685; *Ontdekkingen en ontledingen van sout-figuren.* Tot Leyden: By Cornelis Boutesteyn, 1685; *Ontledingen en ontdekkingen van de cinneber naturalis.*Tot Leyden: By Cornelis Boutesteyn, 1686. Letters 38, 42, 43. Dobell, C. *Leeuwenhoek.,* 5.
Ms. notes.

1242. LEEUWENHOEK, ANTONI VAN, 1632-1723. *Ontledingen en ontdekkingen van het begin der planten in de zaden van boomen ... : vervat in twee brieven, geschreven aan de Wijd-vermaarde Koninglijke Wetenschap-soekende Societeit tot Londen in England / door Antoni van Leeuwenhoek....*
Tot Leyden: By Cornelis Boutesteyn ..., 1685. 78 p., [1] folded leaves of plates: ill.; 22 cm. Letters 46-47. Dobell, C. *Leewenhoek.,* 7.
With the author's *Ontledingen en ontedekkingen van de onsigtbare verborgentheden.* Tot Leyden: By Cornelis Boutesteyn, 1685.

1243. LEEUWENHOEK, ANTONI VAN, 1632-1723. *Ontledingen en ontdekkingen van levende dierkens in de teel-deelen van verscheyde dieren, vogelen en visschen; van het hout met der selver menigvuldige vaaten ... : vervat in verscheyde brieven, geschreven aan de Wyt-vermaarde Koninglijke Wetenschap-zoekende Societeit, tot Londen in Engeland / door Antoni van Leeuwenhoek....*
Tot Leyden: By Cornelis Boutesteyn ..., 1686. [3]-40,

35 p., [3] leaves of plates (2 folded): ill.; 22 cm. Letters 28, 29, 30, 31, 34, 35, 36. Dobell, C. *Leeuwenhoek.*, 8. With the author's *Ontledingen en ontdekkingen van de onsigtbare verborgentheden.* Tot Leyden: By Cornelis Boutesteyn, 1685.

1244. LEEUWENHOEK, ANTONI VAN, 1632-1723. *The select works of Antony van Leeuwenhoek, containing his microscopical discoveries in many of the works of nature.*

London: Printed for the translator by G. Sidney and sold by G. and W. Nicol ... [and 3 others], 1800-1807. 2 v. plates 28 cm. Translated from the Dutch and Latin editions published by the author, by Samuel Hoole. Port. engraved by Anker Smith after L. Verkolje. Imprint of v. 2: London: Printed by the Philantropic Society, and sold by G. and W. Nicol ...; J. White ...; and J. & A. Arch ... Includes index.

Bound in 1 v.

1245. LEEUWENHOEK, ANTONI VAN, 1632-1723. [Werken / Leeuwenhoek.]

[1686-1718] 4 v.: ill., port.; 21 cm. Title and statement of responsibility from spine. Engraved t. p. by J. Goeree; port. by J. Verkolje and A. de Blois. Includes indexes. Vol.1: *Send-brieven.* Delft: A. Beman, 1718 (Dobell, C. *Leeuwenhoek* 19) – v. 2.: *Register der saaken – Ontledingen en ontdekkingen ... van het hout.* Den tweeden druk. 1696 (Dobell 8a) – *Ondervindingen en beschouwingen der onsigtbare geschapene waarheden.* Delft: H.v. Kroonevelt, 1694 – 37ste missive (Dobell 2a) – *Ontledingen en ontdekkingen van de onsigtbare verborgentheden.* Leyden: C. Boutesteyn, 1698 (Dobell 5b) – (D'Heer Francois Aston) p. 11-28 – 40ste missive (Dobell 3a) – 41ste missive. Delft: H.v. Kroonevelt, 1698 (Dobell 17) – *Ontdekkingen en ontledingen van Sout-figuren.* Leiden: C. Boutestein, 1696 (Dobell 6a) – *Ontledingen en ontdekkingen van het begin der planten.* Leyden: C. Boutesteyn, 1697 (Dobell 7a) – *Ontledingen en ontdekkingen van de cinnaber.* Leyden: C. Boutesteyn, 1686 (Dobell 9) – *Vervolg der Brieven* (t. p. & prelims missing); v. 3: *Natuurs verborgentheden ontdekt.* Den tweeden druk. Delft: H.v. Kroonevelt, 1697 (Dobell 12a) – *Derde vervolg der brieven.* Delft: H.v. Kroonevelt, 1693 (Dobell 13) – *Vierde vervolg der brieven.* Delft: H.v. Kroonevelt, 1694 (Dobell 14); v. 4: *Vijfde vervolg der brieven.* Delft: H.v. Kroonevelt, 1696 (Dobell 15) – *Sesde vervolg der brieven.* Delft: H.v. Krooneveld, 1697 (Dobell 16) – *Sevende vervolg der brieven.* Delft: H.v. Krooneveld, 1702 (Dobell 18) – *Register.* Leiden: C. Boutesteyn, 1695. Horblit, H. D. *Grolier 100 science books,* 65 (variant).

Provenance: Herbert McLean Evans (bookplate). Letters bound in numerical order.

1246. LEIBNIZ, GOTTFRIED WILHELM, FREIHERR VON, 1646-1716. *Nova methodus pro maximus & minimis, itemque tangentibus, quæ nec fractas, nec irrationales quantitates moratur, & singulare pro illis calculi genus / per G. G. L.*

[Lipsiae: Prostant apud J. Grossium & J. F. Gletitschium: Typis Christophori Güntheri, 1684]. p. 467-473; 22 cm. *Acta eruditorum;* 1684. Caption title. Variant to Horblit 66a.

1247. LEIBNIZ, GOTTFRIED WILHELM, FREIHERR VON, 1646-1716. *Protogaæ. Summi polyhistoris Godefridi Guilielmi Leibnitii Protogaæ: siue de prima facie telluris et antiquissimæ historiæ vestigiis in ipsis naturæ monumentis dissertatio ex schedis manuscriptis viri illustris / in lucem edita a Christiano Ludovico Scheidio.*

Goettingae: Sumptibus Ioh. Guil. Schmidii ..., MDCCXXXXVIIII, [1749]. [4], xxvi, [2], 86 p., XII folding leaves of plates: ill. (engravings); 24 cm. Title in red and black, with engraved vignette.

1248. LEIBNIZ, GOTTFRIED WILHELM, FREIHERR VON, 1646-1716. *Virorum celeberr. Got. Gul. Leibnitii et Johan. Bernoullii Commercium philosophicum et mathematicum.*

Lausannæ ; Genevæ: sumpt. Marci M. Bousquet & Socior., 1745. 2 v. 129 diagr. on XXIII pl. 26 cm. Includes index. Title in red and black; vignette [printer's device?] with motto: Supra invidiam. Port. signed: Gravé par Ficquet. t. 1. Ab anno 1694 ad annum 1699. – t. 2. Ab anno 1700 ad annum 1716. Wallis & Wallis. *Newton,* 259. *Babson Newton Coll.* 196. Gray, G. J. *Newton,* 259.

1249. LÉMERY, NICOLAS, 1645-1715. *Cours de chymie, contenant la manière de faire les opérations qui sont en usage dans la médecine, par une méthode facile. Avec des raisonnemens sur chaque opération, pour l'instruction de ceux qui veulent s'appliquer à cette science ... 8. éd., rev., corr. & augm. par l'auteur.*

Paris: Éstienne Michallet, 1693. [16], 768 p. [1] folded leaf of plates: 19 cm. Includes index.

Provenance: Dominique Francisci De Scavini (inscription).

1250. LESPIAULT, G. (GASTON), 1823-1904. *Mémoire sur le mouvement des noueds de la lune: et sur l'inégalité en latitude qui donne la mesure de l'aplatissement de la terre / par M. G. Lespiault.*
Paris: Chez Mallet-Bachelier, Libraire-éditeur ..., 1861. 54 p.: ill.; 25 cm. "Extrait des *Mémoires de la Société des Sciences Physiques et Naturelles de Bordeaux.*" Includes bibliographical references.
With: *Recherches sur les mouvements de la planète Herschel* / par U.-J. Le Verrier. Paris: Bachelier, Imprimeur-libraire ..., 1846.

1251. LESPIAULT, G. (GASTON), 1823-1904. *Théorie géométrique de la variation des éléments des planètes / par M. Lespiault ...*
Paris: Gauthier-Villars ..., 1868. 29 p.: ill.; 25 cm. "Extrait des *Mèmoires de la Société des Sciences Physiques et Naturelles de Bordeaux,* 2e cahier, 1867."
With: *Recherches sur les mouvements de la planète Herschel* / par U.-J. Le Verrier. Paris: Bachelier, Imprimeur-libraire ..., 1846. Provenance: author's presentation inscription.

1252. *A letter to a friend in the country.*
London: Printed for T. Cooper, 1740. 31 p.; 26 cm. Errors in pagination: p. 14 misnumbered 15. Erratum: on p. 31.
With: *Experiments and observations on electricity,* by Mr. Benjamin Franklin. London: printed and sold by E. Cave ..., 1751-1753. Provenance: L'Ab. Boyer (bookplate); Domus Massiliensis (bookplate).

1253. *Letters relating to a theorem of Mr. Euler, of the Royal Academy of Sciences at Berlin ... : for correcting the aberrations in the object-glasses of refracting telescopes.*
London: Royal Society, 1753. p. 287-296; 23 cm. Caption title. English or French. Detached from: *Philosophical transactions* of the Royal Society of London, v. 48 (1753). Includes bibliographical references. A letter from Mr. James Short ... to Peter Daval ... – A letter from Mr. John Dollond to James Short ... – Mr. Euler's letter to Mr. James Short ... – A Monsieur Dollond.

1254. LEVITT, I. M. (ISRAEL MONROE), 1908- . *Star maps for beginners, by I. M. Levitt ... and Roy K. Marshall....*
Philadelphia: The authors, 1942. 1 p. l., 32, [2] p., illus. (charts) 28 x 22 cm. Reproduced from typewritten copy. "A brief bibliography": p. 6.

1255. LEWIS, GEORGE CORNEWALL, SIR, 1806-1863. *An historical survey of the astronomy of the ancients. By the Right Hon. Sir George Cornewall Lewis.*
London: Parker, Son, and Bourn, 1862. viii, 527, [1] p. 22 cm. Advertisements: 8 p. following text. Includes bibliographical references and index.

1256. LEWIS, GILBERT NEWTON, 1875-1946. *The anatomy of science, by Gilbert N. Lewis....*
New Haven, Yale University Press; London, H. Milford, Oxford University Press, 1926. ix p., 1 l., 221 p. illus., diagrs. 21 cm. Yale University. Mrs. Hepsa Ely Silliman memorial lectures.

1257. LEWIS, ISABEL MARTIN, b. 1881. *Astronomy for young folks, by Isabel Martin Lewis....*
New York: Duffield and Company, 1922. xiv, 267 p. front., illus., plates. 21 cm.

1258. LEWIS, ISABEL MARTIN, b. 1881. *A handbook of solar eclipses, by Isabel Martin Lewis, A.M. (Corrected with the* Nautical Almanac, *Office of the U.S. Naval Observatory.)*
New York: Duffield & Company, 1924. xi, 118 p. incl. maps. front., plates. 21 cm.

1259. LEY, WILLY, 1906-1969. *Rockets, missiles, and space travel. Rev. and enl. ed., with additional satellite data.*
New York: Viking Press, 1958. xvi, 528 p. illus., ports., maps, tables. 22 cm. First published in 1944 under title: *Rockets.* Bibliography: p. 489-520.

1260. LEYBOURN, WILLIAM, 1626-1716. *Cursus mathematicus. Mathematical sciences, in nine books....*
London: Printed for T. Basset [etc.], 1690. 8 p. l., 440 p., 441-526 l., [2], 547-904, [92] p. front. (port.), maps, plates (part fold.) 34 cm. Title in red and black. Each book has special t. p. Port. by R. White. Wing L-1911.
Imperfect: plate following p. 554 supplied in photocopy. Provenance: John Toplis, Wm. Star, Peter Hill, F. Partridge (inscriptions).

1261. Leybourn, William, 1626-1716. *Pleasure with profit: consisting of recreations of divers kinds, viz. numerical, geometrical, mechanical, statical, astronomical, horometrical, cryptographical, magnetical, automatical, chymical, and historical ... By William Leybourn ... To this work is also annext, A treatise of algebra... applied to numerical questions and geometry ... By R. Sault....*
London: Printed for Richard Baldwin and John Dunton ..., 1694. 1 v. (various pagings) illus., [2] fold. plates. 32 cm. Each of the twelve sections has separate pagination. Wing L-1931.
Imperfect: lacks treatise by R. Sault.

1262. Liais, Emmanuel, 1826-1900. *L'espace céleste et la nature tropicale. Description physique del'univers d'après des observations personnelles faites dans les deux hémisphères. Préface de M. Babinet. Dessins de Yan' Dargent.*
Paris: Garnier Frères, 1865. xiii p., 1 l., 606 p. front. (port.) illus., plates (partly col.) 28 cm. Title vignette.
Provenance: Charles Atwood Kofoid (bookplate).

1263. Liais, Emmanuel, 1826-1900. *Traité d'astronomie: appliquée à la géographie et à la navigation suivi de la géodésie pratique: par Emm. Liais....*
Paris: Garnier Frères ..., 1867.

1264. Library of Congress. *Catalogue of the Library of Congress, in the Capitol of the United States of America, December, 1839.*
City of Washington: Printed by order of Congress (by Langtree and O'Sullivan), 1840. vii, [9]-747 p. 23 cm. Classified catalog, representing about 30,000 volumes; with an "Index to the names of authors and annotators: and to the publications of learned societies, to encyclopædias, newspapers, reviews, magazines, &c." (p. [687]-747) Supersedes the 1830 catalog and its annual supplements, 1831-35 (pub. 1831-37). "Chapters" 18-23 were issued separately in advance under half-title Catalogue of books in the Law department of the Library of Congress, January 1, 1839.
Provenance: J. Howe Watts (inscription); J. S. Candelario (inkstamp).

1265. Libri, Guillaume, 1803-1869. *Histoire des sciences mathématiques en Italie, depuis la renaissance des lettres jusqu'à la fin du dix-septième siècle.*
Paris: J. Renouard et Cie, 1838-41. 4 v. 22 cm. "La 1re édition du 1re volume ayant été consumée par une incendie en 1835, l'auteur a refondu entièrement ce volume." – Lorenz, *Cat. gén. de la librairie française.* Includes bibliographical references. Errata to v. 1-2: p. [531]-534, v. 2. Errata to v. 1-4: [4] p. at end, v. 4.

1266. Lick Observatory. *Studies of the nebulæ made at the Lick Observatory, University of California, at Mount Hamilton, California and Santiago, Chile.*
Berkeley: University of California Press, 1918. 5 p. l., 11-268 p. L pl., tables (part fold.) diagrs. 31 cm. Publications of the Lick Observatory of the University of California; v. 13. Includes bibliographical references. pt. I. Descriptions of 762 nebulæ and clusters photographed with the Crossley reflector, by H. D. Curtis. – pt. II. A study of occulting matter in the spiral nebulæ, by H. D. Curtis. – pt. III. The planetary nebulæ, by H. D. Curtis. – pt. IV. The spectrographic velocities of the bright line nebulæ, by W. W. Campbell and J. H. Moore. – pt. V. The radial velocity of the Greater Magellanic Cloud, by R. E. Wilson. – pt. VI. The wave-lengths of the nebular lines and general observations of the spectra of the gaseous nebulæ, by W. H. Wright.

1267. Liebig, Justus, Freiherr von, 1803-1873. *1842. Animal chemistry, or Organic chemistry in its applications to physiology and pathology / by Justus Liebig ...; edited from the author's manuscript by William Gregory ...*
London: Printed for Taylor and Walton ..., 1842. xxiv, 354 p.; 23 cm. Translation of: *Thier-Chemie.* Half title: Animal chemistry, &c. Includes index. Advertisements: [2], 8 p. following text.
Provenance: Herbert McLean Evans (bookplate).

1268. Liebig, Justus, Freiherr von, 1803-1873. *Anleitung zur Analyse organischer Körper. Von Dr. Justus Liebig....*
Braunschweig: F. Vieweg und Sohn, 1837. 2 p.l., 72, [2] p. diagrs. on III pl. (2 fold.) fold tab. 21 cm. Plate II signed: Guinand sc. Reprint of the article "Organische Analyse" in the *Handwörterbuch der Chemie,* with table added. Horblit, H. D. *Grolier 100 science books,* 67.

1269. Liebig, Justus, Freiherr von, 1803-1873. *Chemische Briefe / von Justus Liebig.*
Heidleberg: Akademische Verlagshandlung von E. F. Winter, 1844. XI, [1], 342 p.; 19 cm. Verbesserungen: p. [XII].

1270. Liebig, Justus, Freiherr von, 1803-1873. *Chemistry and physics in relation to physiology and pathology / by Baron Justus Liebig....*
London: H. Baillière ..., 1846. [4], 116, 11 p.; 22 cm. Advertisements: 11 p. before and after text including end sheets. Translation of *Thier-Chemie,* Abth. 1, Th. 2.
Provenance: Herbert McLean Evans (bookplate); Lapworth (stationer's label).

1271. Liebig, Justus, Freiherr von, 1803-1873. *Die organische Chemie in ihrer Anwendung auf Agricultur und Physiologie. / Von Justus Liebig.*
Braunschweig: Verlag von Friedrich Vieweg und Sohn, 1840. xii, 352, [1] p.; 22 cm. Errata: p. [1] at end.
Provenance: A. Koenig (signature).

1272. Liebig, Justus, Freiherr von, 1803-1873. *Die organische Chemie in ihrer Anwendung auf Physiologie und Pathologie.*
Braunschweig: F. Vieweg, 1842. xvi, 342, [1] p. 21 cm. Druckfehler: p. [1] at end. Later editions published as: *Die Thier-Chemie, oder, Die organische Chemie in ihrer Anwendung auf Physiologie und Pathologie. GV* 88, p. 235.
Provenance: Adolf Lieben (inkstamp).

1273. Lilienthal, Otto, 1848-1896. *Der Vogelflug als Grundlage der Fliegekunst. Ein Beitrag zur Systematik der Flugtechnik. Auf Grund zahlreicher von O. und G. Lilienthal ausgeführter Versuche bearb. von Otto Lilienthal ... Mit 80 Holzschnitten, 8 lithographierten Tafeln und 1 Titelbild in Farbendruck.*
Berlin: R. Gaertner, 1889. viii, 187 p. col. front., illus., VIII fold. diagr. 24 cm.
Provenance: signed presentation inscription from Max Rittberger to Hans Richter.

1274. Linné, Carl von, 1707-1778. *Caroli Linnæi ... Philosophia botanica; in qva explicantur fundmenta botanica cum definitionibus partium, exemplis terminorum, observationibus rariorum, adjectis figuris æneis....*
Stockholmi: Apud Godofr. Kiesewetter, 1751. 3 p.l., 362 p. illus., IX pl. 21 cm. Pritzel, 5426. *Hunt botanical cat.,* 541.
Includes portrait (front.) by J. M. Bernigeroth, dated 1749. Provenance: Dahlstrom (signature); Herman Knoche (embossed stamp).

1275. Lister, Martin, 1638?-1712. *Martini Lister Conchyliorum bivalvium utriusque aquæ exercitatio anatomica tertia. Huic accedit Dissertatio medicinalis de calculo humano....*
Londini: Sumptibus Authoris impressa, 1696. xliii, 173, 51 p., 9 plates (part fold.) 21 cm. "M.L. Dissertatio medicinalis de calculo humano" has special t. p. and separate paging.

1276. Lister, Martin, 1638?-1712. *Martini Lister Exercitatio anatomica: in qua de cochleis maximà terrestribus & limacibus, agitur....*
Londini: Sumptibus Sam. Smith & Benj. Walford, 1694. [4], xi, [1], 208 p., [1], 7 folded leaves of plates: ill.; 20 cm. Errata: p. [XII]. Wing (2nd ed.) 2520.

1277. Littrow, J. J. (Joseph Johann), 1781-1840. *Atlas des gestirnten Himmels. Für freunde der Astronomie hrsg. Von J. J. v. Littrow....*
Stuggart: Hoffmann, 1839. 2 p. l., xxxvi p., 18 double pl. 24 cm. Includes index.
Provenance: Gerling (bookplate), E. W. Barlow (inscription); 2 ms. notes inserted between plates xxxi-xxxii & xxxiii-xxxiv.

1278. Littrow, J. J. (Joseph Johann), 1781-1840. *Theoretische und practische Astronomie / von J. J. Littrow....*
Wien: Gedruckt und im Verlage bey J. B. Wallishausser, 1821-1827. 3 v.: ill.; 22 cm.
Provenance: Mathem. Verein Univers. Berlin (inkstamp); Max-Planck Schule (inkstamp); E. Husserl (inscription).

1279. Livingstone, David, 1813-1873. *Missionary travels and researches in South Africa;*

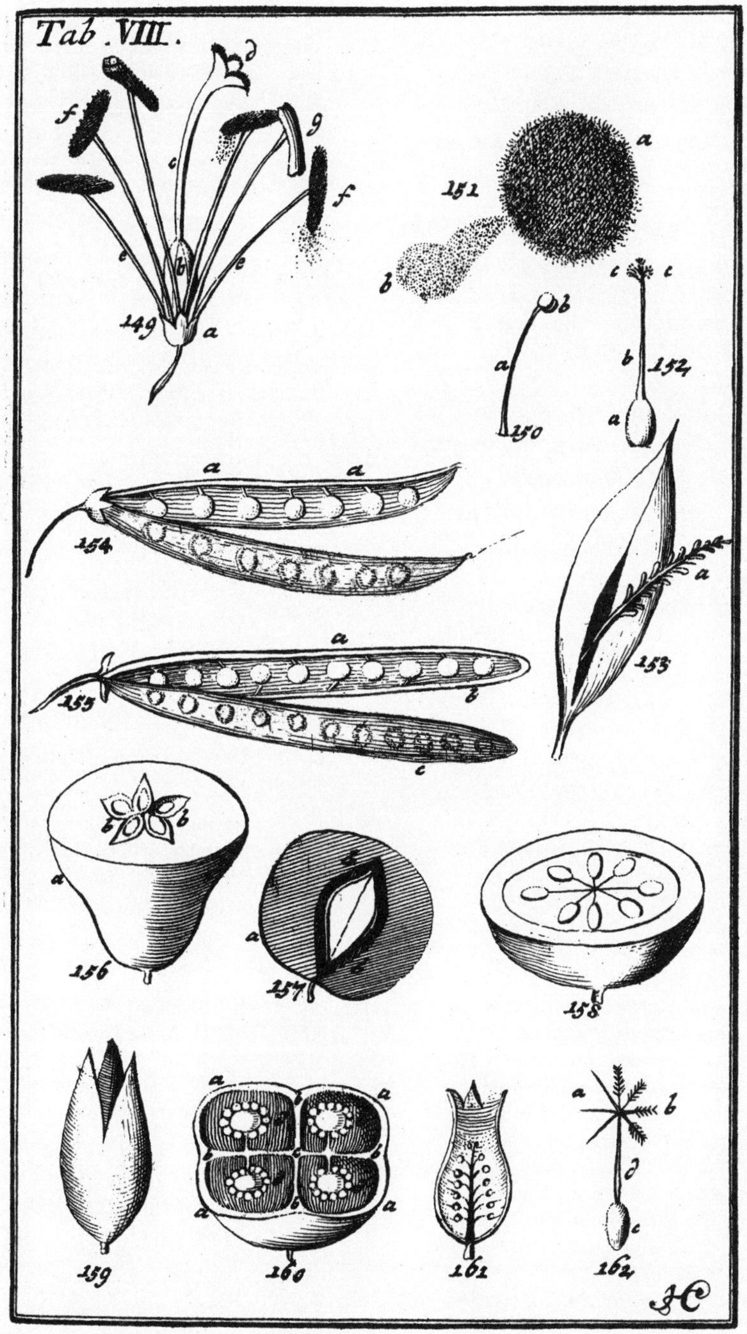

Linné, *Philosophia botanica*, 1751

including a sketch of sixteen years' residence in the interior of Africa, and a journey from the Cape of Good Hope to Loanda, on the west coast; thence across the continent, down the river Zambesi, to the eastern ocean ... With portrait; maps by Arrowsmith; and numerous illustrations.

London: J. Murray, 1857. ix, [1], 687, [1] p. illus., plates (part col. & fold.), 2 fold. maps 24 cm. Colophon: London: Printed by W. Clowes and Sons ...

Advertisements: publisher's catalog (8 p.) at end. Binder: Edmonds & Remnants (ticket). Binding: brown cloth. One fold. map in pocket.

1280. Lobachevskii, N. I. (Nikolaæi Ivanovich), 1792-1856. *Études géométriques sur la théorie des parallèles. Traduit de l'allemand par J. Hoüel. Suivi d'un extrait de la correspondance de Gausset de Schumacher.*

Paris: Gauthier-Villars, 1866. iv, 42 p. diagrs. 22 cm. Errata: on p. iv. Includes bibliographical references.

No. 17 in a v. with binder's title: Geometrie, I.

1281. L'Obel, Matthias de, 1538-1616. *Plantarum seu stirpium icones.*

Antuerpiae : Ex officina Christophori Plantini, Architypographi regij, 1581. 2 v. ([8], 816; 280, [36] (last p. blank) p.) : chiefly ill. ; 19 x 23 cm. Collection combining the ill. published in Plantin's editions of the works of R. Dodoens, C. Clusius and L'Obel, classified by the latter. L'Obel's name in publisher's dedication, p. [3-4], the only text besides the table of contents, the captions in Latin, and the index in Latin, Dutch, German, French, Italian, Spanish, Portuguese and English. Vol. 2 has caption title only: Iconum stirpium tomus secundus. Signatures: v. 1: ***4 A-Z8 a-z8 2A-2E8; v. 2: 2A-2R8 2S-2X4 2Y6. Plantin's compass device on t.p.; ornamental initials. Illustrations: 2176 prints, various sizes. Count is according to Voet; other authorities give slightly different totals, owing to the difficulty of determining whether adjoining ill. are from a single block. "Sana Sancta Indorum, siue Nicotiana Gallorum": v. 1, p. 584. Cut reprinted from *Stirpium adversaria nova* by Pierre Pena and L'Obel (London, 1571; Plantin's ed., 1576, has title: *Nova stirpium adversaria*). Described as the first recorded ill. of the tobacco plant in Arents, G. *Tobacco*, I, no. 13 (reproduced, p. 240). Small fig. at side depicts man smoking via a coiled funnel. "Tabacum siue Herba Sancta minor" and "Tabacum siue Sana Sancta minima": p. 585. Pritzel 5549. Adams L-1383. *Hunt botanical cat.*, I, 138. Nissen, C. *Botanische Buchillustration*, II, 1220. *Bib. Belgica*, L120. Voet, L. *Plantin Press*, 1580. Contents: t. 1. Icones graminum. Icones frumentorum. Icones stirpium – t. 2. Iconum stirpium tomus secundus. Index synonymicus stirpium (p. [281]-[315]).

Provenance: Theophilus Kentmanus (signature); Dno Georgio Mosero (inscription); Museo Doctr Levade (bookplate); Bibliothèque botanique Emile Burnat (bookplate and withdrawal stamp); The Horticultural Society of New York (bookplate); W C O (engraved on upper cover).

1282. †Locke, John, 1632-1704. *An essay concerning humane understanding. In four books.*

London, Printed [by Elizabeth Holt] for T. Basset, and sold by E. Mory, 1690. 6 p. l., 362, [22] p. 33 cm. Pforzheimer 600. Wing L 2739.

1283. Locke, John, 1632-1704. *Essai philosophique concernant l'entendement humain: ou l'on montre quelle est l'etendu de nos connoissances certaines, et la manière dont nous y parvenons / par M. Locke; traduit de l'anglois par M. Coste. Seconde édition, revûe, corrigée, & augmentée de quelques addition importantes de l'auteur qui n'ont paru qu'après sa mort, & de quelques remarques du traducteur.*

À Amsterdam: Chez Pierre Mortier, 1729. XLVI, 595, [16] p.: ill., port.; 27 cm. Translation of: *Essay concerning human understanding.* Port. by J. Greenhill, engraved by P. van Gunst. Includes index.

1284. Lockyer, Norman, Sir, 1836-1920. *Astronomy. By J. Norman Lockyer....*

New York: D. Appleton and Company, 1875. 3 p. l., [ix]-xv, 120 p. incl. front., illus., diagrs. pl. 16 cm. Science primers; 7. Series note also at head of t.-p. Advertisements: [4] p. of endpapers.

1285. Lockyer, Norman, Sir, 1836-1920. *The dawn of astronomy: a study of the temple-worship and mythology of the ancient Egyptians / by J. Norman Lockyer....*

London, Paris, and Melbourne: Cassell and Company Limited, 1894. xvi, 432 p., [1] folded leaf of plates: ill., plans; 24 cm. Includes bibliographical references and index.

Provenance: Charles Atwood Kofoid (bookplate). Errata slip inserted before p. [1].

1286. Lockyer, Norman, Sir, 1836-1920. *Elementary lessons in astronomy / by J. Norman Lockyer....*

London: Macmillan and Co., 1868 [i.e.1869]. xiv, [2], 347, [1], [4], 51, [1] p., [7] leaves of plates (some fold.): ill. (1 col.); 16 cm. Macmillan's School Class Books. "Macmillan's School Class Books" – verso of half title. Colophon reads (p. [1], 4th group and verso of t. p.) read: London: R. Clay, Son, and Taylor, printers, Bread Street Hill. Advertisements: 4 p. (5th group) and 51 p. at end, dated October, 1869. Includes index.

Provenance: [Mary?] Smith for Prof. Guyot's Lecture (inscription).

1287. Lockyer, Norman, Sir, 1836-1920. *Elements of astronomy: accompanied with numerous illustrations, a colored representation of the solar, stellar, and nebular spectra, and celestial charts of the northern and southern hemisphere. By J. Norman Lockyer ... American ed. rev....*

New York: D. Appleton and Company, 1870. 312 p. fold. col. front., illus., fold. map, diagrs. 20 cm.

1288. Lockyer, Norman, Sir, 1836-1920. *The movements of the earth / by J. Norman Lockyer....*

London and New York: Macmillan and Co., 1887. xvi, 130 p.: ill.; 20 cm. At head of title: Outlines of physiography.

Provenance: Radcliffe Library, Oxford University Museum (inkstamp). Bodl. Lib. (inkstamp).

1289. Lockyer, Norman, Sir, 1836-1920. *Recent and coming eclipses, by Sir Norman Lockyer ... Second edition, containing an account of the observations made at Viziadrug, in India, in 1898 and of the conditions of the eclipses visible in 1900, 1901 and 1905.*

London: Macmillan and Co., Ltd., 1900. xiv, 236 p. front., illus. 24 cm.

1290. Lockyer, Norman, Sir, 1836-1920. *The spectroscope and its applications / by J. Norman Lockyear ... Second edition.*

London: Macmillan and Co., 1873. 4, xii, 127 p., [1] folded leaf of plates: ill. (1 col.); 19 cm. Nature Series. Series title also at head of t.-p. On verso of t.-p.: London: R. Clay, Sons, and Taylor, printers, Bread Street Hill. Advertisements: p. 2-4 (1st group), p. 119-127.

1291. Lockyer, Norman, Sir, 1836-1920. *Stonehenge and other British stone monuments astronomically considered, by Sir Norman Lockyer....*

London: Macmillan and Co., Limited, 1906. xii, 340 p. illus., diagrs. 24 cm. Includes index.

1292. Lockyer, Thomazine Mary Browne, Lady. *Life and work of Sir Norman Lockyer, by T. Mary Lockyer and Winifred L. Lockyer, with the assistance of H. Dingle and contributions by Charles E. St. John [and others].*

London: Macmillan and Co., 1928. xii, 474, [2] p. illus., XVII pl. (incl. front., ports.) diagrs. 23 cm. Advertisements: [2] p. at end.

1293. Lohrmann, Wilhelm Gotthelf, 1796-1840. *Topographie der sichtbaren Mondoberfläche / von Wilhelm Gotthelf Lohrmann.*

Dresden, Leipzig: Bei J. F. Hartknoch, 1824. [10], 110, [2], XVIII, [1] p., [6] leaves of plates: ill., maps; 29 cm. Berichtigungen: on p. [9]. No more published. Cf. *NUC pre-1956*, V. 338, p. 673. Variously illustrated by: G. Borger, W. G. Lohrmann, G. Zumpe, Hajeck.

1294. Lomonosov, Mikhail Vasilevich, 1711-1765. *Oratio de origine lucis....*

Petropoli: Typis Academiae Scientiarum, [1756?]. [2], 40 p. Translated by Gregorio Kositzki.

Author's name on spine: Lomonsow.

1295. Long, Roger, 1680-1770. *Astronomy, in five books. By Roger Long....*

Cambridge: Printed for the author, 1742-85. 2 v. fronts., tables, diagrs. on 97 pl. (partly folded) 28 x 20 cm. Paged continuously. Vol. 2 has imprint: Cambridge, Printed for the author, 1764; Cambridge, Sold by J. Deighton; [etc., etc.] 1785. Bibliographical footnotes. "In the year 1764, Dr. Long published the third book of his *Astronomy*, as a part only of his second volume. Before the time of his death he had finished and printed off the fourth, and a small part of the fifth book... Mr. Dunthorn made ... a rough draft of the remaining part ... After his death, Mr. Wales ... was prevailed upon to revise and correct Mr.

Dunthorn's continuation, and to complete it upon the original plan." – Advertisement, v. 2.

Provenance: Philip Worsley Wood.

1296. LOOMIS, ELIAS, 1811-1889. *Elements of astronomy: designed for academies and high schools / by Elias Loomis....*

New York: Harper & Brothers ..., 1880. viii, [9]-254 p.: ill.; 20 cm. Includes index.

1297. LOOMIS, ELIAS, 1811-1889. *An introduction to practical astronomy: with a collection of astronomical tables / by Elias Loomis....*

London: Sampson Low, Son, & Co. ...; Harper and Brothers, 1859. xi, [12]-497 p.: ill.; 24 cm. "Catalogue of astronomical instruments by different makers, with their prices": p. [491]-497.

Provenance: Thomas Sebastian Bazley (armorial bookplate and signature).

1298. LOOMIS, ELIAS, 1811-1889. *An introduction to practical astronomy: with a collection of anatomical tables / by Elias Loomis ... Seventh edition.*

New York: : Harper & Brothers ..., 1894. [xiii], [13]-505 p.: ill.; 25 cm. "Catalogue of astronomical instruments by several different makers, with their prices": p. [497]-505.

1299. LOOMIS, ELIAS, 1811-1889. *The recent progress of astronomy; especially in the United States. 3d ed., mostly rewritten, and much enlarged.*

New York: Harper & Bros., 1856. viii, [9]-396 p. illus., plates, port. 20 cm.

Provenance: Orton Williams (inscription); Charles Atwood Kofoid (bookplate).

1300. LOOMIS, ELIAS, 1811-1889. *A treatise on astronomy. By Elias Loomis....*

New York: Harper & Brothers, 1868. 1 p.l., viii, [9]-338 p. illus., 8 pl. (incl. front) diagrs. 24 cm.

1301. LOOMIS, ELIAS, 1811-1889. *A treatise on astronomy / by Elias Loomis.*

New York: Harper & Brothers, 1887. [2], viii, [9]-346 p., VIII leaves of plates: ill., map; 24 cm. Loomis's series of text-books. Includes index. Advertisement on t. p. verso.

1302. LOOMIS, ELIAS, 1811-1889. *A treatise on meteorology. With a collection of meteorological tables. By Elias Loomis....*

New York: Harper & Brothers, 1868. viii, [9]-305 p. illus., III pl., diagrs. 24 cm. "Works on meteorology": p. [296]-299.

Provenance: Taylor Library, Sidney College (inkstamp).

1303. LOOMIS, WILLIAM ISAACS, 1810-1888. *Discovery of the origin of gravitation, and the majestic motive force which generated the diurnal and yearly revolutions of the heavenly bodies. In two parts. By William Isaacs Loomis.*

Martindale Depot, N. Y.: T. Holman, printer, 1866. 3 p.l., 82 p. diagrs. 24 cm.

1304. LORENTZ, H. A. (HENDRIK ANTOON), 1853-1928. *Abhandlungen über theoretische Physik, von H. A. Lorentz ... 1. Bd. Mit 40 Figuren im Text.*

Leipzig and Berlin: B. G. Teubner, 1906-07. 2 v. (489, [1] p.) diagrs. 26 cm. No more published.

1305. LORENTZ, H. A. (HENDRIK ANTOON), 1853-1928. *Beginselen der natuurkunde, door H. A. Lorentz. 5. druk. Bewerkt door H. A. Lorentz en L. H. Siertsema.*

Leiden: E. J. Brill, 1908-09. 2 v. illus., diagrs. 24 cm. Includes index. Advertisements on p. [4] of wrapper. Addenda: 12 p. at end of v. 2.

Original printed wrappers bound in. Provenance: Horatio B. Williams (signature & inkstamp).

1306. LORENTZ, H. A. (HENDRIK ANTOON), 1853-1928. *The Einstein theory of relativity; a concise statement, by Prof. H. A. Lorentz....*

New York: Brentano's, [c1920]. 64 p. 19 cm. First published in the *Nieuwe Rotterdamsche Courant* of November 19, 1919.

1307. LORENTZ, H. A. (HENDRIK ANTOON), 1853-1928. *Ergebnisse und Probleme der Elektronentheorie: Vortrag gehalten am 20. Dezember 1904 im Elektrotechnischen Verein zu Berlin / von H. A. Lorentz.*

Berlin: J. Springer, 1905. 62 p.: ill.; 22 cm. Advertisements: 2 p. following text and on lower wrapper.

1308. Lorentz, H. A. (Hendrik Antoon), 1853-1928. *Das Relativitätsprinzip; drei Vorlesungen gehalten in Teylers Stiftung zu Haarlem, von H. A. Lorentz; bearb. von W. H. Keesom.*

Leipzig: B. G. Teubner, 1914. 52 p. diagrs. 25 cm. *Beihefte zur Zeitschrift für mathematischen und naturwissenschaftlichen Unterricht aller Schulgattungen;* Nr. 1. Includes bibliographical references.

Original printed wrappers bound in. Advertisements: p. [2-4] of wrappers. Provenance: Karl Horovitz (signature).

1309. Lorentz, H. A. (Hendrik Antoon), 1853-1928. *Das Relativitätsprinzip, eine Sammlung von Abhandlungen, mit Anmerkungen von A. Sommerfeld und Vorwort von O. Blumenthal.*

Leipzig, Berlin: B. G. Teubner, 1913. 2 p.l., 89, [1] p. front. (port.) diagrs. 25 cm. Fortschritte der mathematischen Wissenschaften in Monographien, hrsg. von Otto Blumenthal, hft. 2. At head of title: H. A. Lorentz, A. Einstein, H. Minkowski.

1310. Lorentz, H. A. (Hendrik Antoon), 1853-1928. *Das Relativitätsprinzip, eine Sammlung von Abhandlungen, mit einem Beitrag von H. Weyl und Anmerkungen von A. Sommerfeld, Vorwort von O. Blumenthal. 4., verm. Aufl.*

Leipzig, Berlin: B. G. Teubner, 1922. 2 p. l., 159 p. 24 cm. Fortschritte der mathematischen Wissenschaften in Monographien, Hft. 2. At head of title: H. A. Lorentz, A. Einstein, H. Minkowski.

Provenance: Thos.[?] Seumaur[?] (inscription); Dr. Elshout, M.[?] (signature & bookplate).

1311. Lorentz, H. A. (Hendrik Antoon), 1853-1928. *Sichtbare und unsichtbare Bewegungen: Vorträge auf Einladung des Vorstandes de Departements Leiden der Maatschappij tot nut van't algemeen im Februar und März 1901 / gehalten von H. A. Lorentz; unter Mitwirkung des Verfassers aus dem Holländischen ubersetzt von G. Siebert.*

Braunschweig: F. Vieweg und Sohn, 1902. 6, 123 p.: ill.; 23 cm. I. Geradlinige Bewegungen. – II. Krummlinige Bewegungen – III. Schwingende Bewegungen. Lichtstrahlen – IV. Lichtschwingungen – V. Molekular-Bewegungen – VI. Elektrische Erscheinungen – VII. Die Erhaltung der Energie.

Provenance: Edmund Neusser (bookplate).

1312. Lorentz, H. A. (Hendrik Antoon), 1853-1928. *Über positive und negative Elektronen / von H. A. Lorentz.*

Leipzig : S. Hirzel, 1908. p. [125]-131 ; 25 cm. In: *Jahrbuch der Radioaktivität und Elektronik,* 4. Bd. (1907). Caption title. At head of title: Originalabhandlungen.

1313. Lorentz, H. A. (Hendrik Antoon), 1853-1928. *Versuch einer Theorie der elektrischen und optischen Erscheinungen in bewegten Körpern / von H. A. Lorentz.*

Leiden: E. J. Brill, 1895. [4], 138, [1] p. 24 cm.

1314. Lorentz, H. A. (Hendrik Antoon), 1853-1928. *Versuch einer Theorie der electrischen und optischen Erscheinungen in bewegten Körpern, von H. A.Lorentz.... Unveränderter Abdruck der 1895 bei E. J. Brill in Leiden erschienenen ersten Auflage.*

Leipzig: B. G. Teubner, 1906. 2 p. l., 138 p., 1 l, 24 cm. [2] p. advertisements preceding text.

1315. Lowell, Percival, 1855-1916. *The evolution of worlds, by Percival Lowell....*

New York: The Macmillan Company, 1909. xiii, 262 p. front., illus., plates, diagrs. 23 cm.

With [2] p. of advertisements at end. Provenance: Victor H. Wood (inkstamp).

1316. Lowell, Percival, 1855-1916. *Mars / by Percival Lowell....*

Boston and New York: Houghton, Mifflin and Company: The Riverside Press, Cambridge, [c1895]. [2], x, 228 p., XXVI leaves of plates (1 folded): ill. (1 col.); 23cm. "Fifth impression" – T. p. verso. Includes indexes. Advertisements on p. [2] (1st sequence).

Provenance: Mars Baumgardt (signature).

1317. Lowell, Percival, 1855-1916. *Mars and its canals, by Percival Lowell....*

New York, London: The Macmillan Company, [1911, c1906]. xv, 393 p. front., illus., plates (part col.) maps 23 cm. "Third thousand." Includes index.

Advertisements: [2] p. at end.

1318. LOWELL, PERCIVAL, 1855-1916. *Mars as the abode of life / by Percival Lowell.*

New York: Macmillan, [1909, c1908]. xix, 288 p., [8] leaves of plates: ill. (1 col.); 23 cm. Eight lectures delivered at the Lowell Institute, published in six papers in the *Century Magazine*. Cf. Pref., p. vii. Includes index. The genesis of a world – The evolution of life – The sun dominant – Mars and the future of the earth – The canals and oases of Mars – Proofs of life on Mars – Notes.

Provenance: L. A. Thompson (signature).

1319. LOWER, RICHARD, 1631-1691. *The method observed in tran[s]fusing the bloud out of one animal into another.*

In the Savoy [London]: Printed by T. N. for John Martyn ... and James Allestry ..., 1667. p. 353-358 ; 23 cm. In: *Philosophical transactions* / Royal Society of London, v. 1 (1665-1666). Caption title. Date of publication from colophon. "It was first practised by Dr. Lower in Oxford, and by him communicated to the Honourable Robert Boyl, who imparted it to the Royal Society, as follows."

1320. LUCRETIUS CARUS, TITUS. *T. Lucretii Cari De rerum natura: libri VI.*

[Impressum Florentiae Sumptibus Philippi Giuntæ ..., 1512 mense Martio]. [8], cxxv, [13] l.; 16 cm. Edited by Petrus Candidus [i. e. Pier Candido Decembrio]. Imprint taken from colophon. Emendationes: on leaf [12].

Provenance: Abraham Auguste Rolland (inkstamp).

1321. LUYS, JULES BERNARD, 1828-1897. *Recherches sur le système nerveux cérébro-spinal, sa structure, ses fonctions et ses maladies, par J. Luys. Accompagné d'un atlas de 40 planches.*

Paris: J.-B. Baillière, 1865. xv, 660 p. 24 cm + atlas (2 p. 1., 80 p. XL pl. 24 cm.) Plates engraved by Léveillé after J. Luys.

1322. LUYTEN, WILLEM JACOB, 1899- . *The pageant of the stars, by Willem J. Luyten....*

Garden City, New York: Doubleday, Doran & Company, 1929. xvii p., 1 l., 300 p. incl. illus., plates. front. 21 cm.

1323. LYELL, CHARLES, SIR, 1797-1875. *Principles of geology, being an attempt to explain the former changes of the earth's surface, by reference to causes now in operation. By Charles Lyell....*

London: J. Murray, 1830-1833. 3 v. fronts. (2 col.) ill., maps (part fold.) diagrs. 23 cm. Vol. 1 has on t.-p.: In two volumes; v. 2 has on t.-p.: Volume the second. "The author has found it impossible to compress into two volumes, according to his original plan, the wide range of subjects which must be discussed ... it will therefore be necessary to extend the 'Principles of geology' to three volumes" – v. 2, Preface. Vol. 3 was issued for the first time in 1833, a little after the 2d edition of v. 1-2, with which it is usually placed, as no 2d edition of v. 3 ever appeared. Appendices: I. Tables of fossil shells by Monsieur G. P. Deshayes. II. Lists of fossil shells chiefly collected by the author in Sicily and Italy, named by M. Deshayes. Includes bibliographical references and indexes. Illustrated by T. Bradley and P. Oudart. Horblit, H. D. *Grolier 100 science books*, 70.

Advertisements: final p., v. 1; final 3 p. and 16 p. bound in front, v. 3. Provenance: Sir J. Hall (signature).

1324. LYELL, CHARLES, SIR, 1797-1875. *Principles of geology, being an attempt to explain the former changes of the earth's surface, by reference to causes now in operation. By Charles Lyell ... The 2d ed.*

London: J. Murray, 1832-33. 3 v. fronts. (2 col.) illus., plates, maps (part fold.) diagrs. 22-23 cm. Vol. 2 is second edition corrected. Vol. 3 was contemplated when the first edition of v. 2 appeared, but was published for the first time in 1833 a little after the second edition of v. 1-2. No second edition of v. 3 was issued. Variously illustrated by: T. Bradley, P. Oudart, J. Gardner. Includes indexes.

16 p. advertisements preceding text in v. 1 and v. 3. Newspaper cutting from *The Times*, Nov. 22, 1865 pasted in.

1325. LYELL, CHARLES, SIR, 1797-1875. *Principles of geology; or, The modern changes of the earth and its inhabitants considered as illustrative of geology, by Sir Charles Lyell ... 10th and entirely rev. ed.*

London: J. Murray, 1867-68. 2 v. illus., maps (part fold.) 23 cm. Includes bibliographical references and indexes.

Advertisements: publisher's catalogue (32 p.) dated January 1866 at end, v. 1; [2] p. at end, v. 2. Binder: Edmonds & Remnants, London (ticket). Provenance: author's presentation inscription to Sir John F. W. Herschel; Herbert McLean Evans (bookplate).

Lyell, *Principles of Geology*, 1832-1833

1326. Lyell, Charles, Sir, 1797-1875. *Principles of geology; or, The modern changes of the earth and its inhabitants, considered as illustrative of geology. 12th ed.*

London: J. Murray, 1875. 2 v. illus.,maps. 23 cm. Includes bibliographical references and index. "List of the dates of publication of successive editions of the 'Principles', 'Elements' and the 'Antiquity of man'": v. 1, p. xi-xii.

Advertisements: 20 p. at end, v. 2. Provenance: Herbert McLean Evans (bookplate); Robt. B. Gibson (signature).

1327. Lyonnet, Pieter, 1707-1789. *Traité anatomique de la chenille: qui ronge le bois de saule / par Pierre Lyonet....*

À la Haye: Aux depends de l'auteur, se vend chez Pierre de Hondt [and 2 others], 1760. XXIJ, [2], 587, [4] p., XVIII folded leaves of plates: ill.; 27 cm. Illustrated by the author. Includes index.

Provenance: Herbert McLean Evans (bookplate).

1328. Lyttleton, Raymond Arthur. *The modern universe. With line diagrams by A. Spark.*

London: Harper, [1957, c1956]. 207 p.: illus.; 22 cm.

1329. Lyttleton, Raymond Arthur. *The modern universe / Raymond A. Littleton; with line drawings by A. Spark....*

New York: Readers Union, Hodder & Stoughton, 1957 [i.e. 1958]. 207 p., [16] p. of plates: ill.; 21 cm. Includes bibliographies.

1330. Macfarlane, Alexander, 1851-1913. *The fundamental theorems of analysis generalized for space. By Alexander Macfarlane....*

Boston: Norwood Press: J. S. Cushing & Co., printers, 1893. 1 p.l., 31 p. diagrs. 22 cm. "Read before the New York Mathematical Society, May 7, 1892." "Appendix: Note on plane algebra": p. 28-31. Appendix is from *Proceedings of the Royal Society of Edinburgh,* 1883.

No. 12 in a v. with binder's title: Geometrie, I.

1331. Mackenzie, J. S. F. (James Stuart Fraser), b. 1843. *A night raid into space: the story of the heavens told in simple words/ by J. S. F. Mackenzie....*

Philadelphia: J. B. Lippincott Company; Henry Hardingham, [1920?]. x, [11]-143 p.: 20 ill.; 18 cm. Includes index. Cover-title: A night raid into space seeing stars. Colophon: The Whitefriars Press, Ltd., London and Tonbridge.

1332. Mackey, S. A. (Sampson Arnold). *The mythological astronomy: in three parts / by S. A. Mackey.*

London: Published by Hunt and Clarke ..., 1827. [4], viii, [v]-viii, 263 p., [3] leaves of plates: ill, map; 20 cm. Includes bibliographical references and index. The third plate is a volvelle. Mythological astronomy – Mythological astronomy of the Hindoos – Analysis of the writings of the Jews.

Includes a loose astrological chart with Cyclob thiad at head. Provenance: Wm. Brookes (signature).

1333. MacLaurin, Colin, 1698-1746. *An account of Sir Isaac Newton's philosophical discoveries, in four books. By Colin Maclaurin ... Published from the author's manuscript papers, by Patrick Murdoch....*

London: Printed for the author's children: and sold by A. Millar, and J. Nourse; [etc., etc.], 1748. [28], xx, 392 p. diagrs. on 6 fold. plates. 29 cm. "An account of the life and writings of the author": [i]-xx. "A list of ... the subscribers names": p. [9-28] (1st group). Advertisements and errata on p. [28] (1st group). *Babson Newton Coll.* 85. Gray, G. J. *Newton,* 112.

Subscribers' list bound after p. xx. Provenance: Hans Sloane (armorial bookplate).

1334. MacLaurin, Colin, 1698-1746. *An account of Sir Isaac Newton's philosophical discoveries, in four books. By Colin Maclaurin ... Published from the author's manuscript papers, by Patrick Murdoch ... 2d ed.*

London: Printed for A. Millar, 1750. 5 p. l., xxvi, 412 p. diagrs. on VI fold. pl. 22 cm. "An account of the life and writings of the author": p. [i]-xxvi. *Babson Newton Coll.* 87. Gray, G. J. *Newton,* 112.

Provenance: Theo Vincent Gould (inscription). Imperfect: lacks half-title.

1335. MacLaurin, Colin, 1698-1746. *Exposition des découvertes philosophiques de m. le chevalier Newton. Par m. Maclaurin ... Ouvrage traduit de l'anglois par m. Lavirotte....*

Paris: Durand [etc.], 1749. lvij, [3], 422, [2] p. 6 fold. pl., fold. map. 27 cm. Title vignette; head pieces; ini-

tials. From the 1st English ed., 1748. Gray, G. J. *Newton*, 113.
Imperfect: map missing, title vignette cut out.

1336. MACPHERSON, HECTOR, b. 1888. *Practical astronomy with the unaided eye, by Hector Macpherson, jun.....*
London: T. C. & E. C. Jack; [etc., etc., 1913]. 94 p. illus. 17 cm. People's Books.
Provenance: Frederick Hutton Getman (bookplate); [2] p. of advertisements at end.

1337. MACPHERSON, HECTOR, b. 1888. *The romance of modern astronomy: describing in simple but exact language the wonders of the heavens / by Hector Macpherson....*
London: Seeley, Service & Co., 1919. 332 p., [16] leaves of plates: ill.; 21 cm. Library of Romance. Includes index. Advertisements: p. [3]-[4] at end.

1338. MACPHERSON, HECTOR, b. 1888. *Through the depths of space; a primer of astronomy, by Hector Macpherson, jun.....*
Edinburgh and London: W. Blackwood and Sons, 1908. vi p., 2 l., 123 p. front., 7 pl. 20 cm.

1339. MACROBIUS, AMBROSIUS AURELIUS THEODOSIUS. *Macrobii Aurelii Theodosii viri consularis In Somnium Scipionis libri II. Saturnaliorum libri VII. Nunc denuo recogniti, & multis in locis aucti.*
Excud. Lugd.: Seb. Gryphius Germ., 1532. [48], 590, [2] p.: ill., map; 17 cm. Known as: *Commentarii in Somnium Scipionis.* Includes index.
Provenance: Gymnasial Bibliothek Freising (inkstamp).

1340. MACROBIUS, AMBROSIUS AURELIUS THEODOSIUS. *Macrobii Ambrosii Aurelii Theodosii viri consularis, & illustris, In Somnium Scipionis, lib. II. Saturnaliorum, lib. VII. Ex uarijs, ac uetustissimis codicibus recogniti, & aucti.*
Lugduni: Apud Seb. Gryphium, 1548. 567, [73] p.: ill., map; 18 cm. Known as: *Commentarii in Somnium Scipionis.* Errors in pagination: p. 129 misnumbered as 139, p. 132-133 as 142-143, p. 136-137 as 146-147, 140-141 as 150-151, p. 144 as 154, p. 299 as 399. Includes index.
Ms. notes.

1341. MÄDLER, JOHANN HEINRICH, 1794-1874. *Astronomische Briefe / von Dr. J. H. Mädler ...*
Mitau: Verlag von G. A. Reyher, 1844-1846. 3 v. (494 p.): ill.; 21 cm. Druckfehler: p. 494. 1. Lfg.: vi, [1]-129, [1]; 2. Lfg.: 129-343; 3. Lfg.: [iv], 343-494.
Provenance: E. de Wahl (bookplate and signature).

1342. MÄDLER, JOHANN HEINRICH, 1794-1874. *Geschichte der Himmelskunde von der ältesten bis auf die neueste Zeit, von Dr. J. H. v. Mädler....*
Braunschweig: G. Westermann, 1873. 2 v. 24 cm. Includes bibliographies and indexes.
Advertisements: [2] p. at end, v. 2.

1343. MAESTLIN, MICHAEL, 1550-1631. *Epitome astronomiæ: qua breui explicatione omnia, tam ad sphæricam quàm theoricam eius partem pertinentia ... / conscripta per M. Michaelem Mæstlinum Goeppingensem ... Iam nunc ab ipso autore diligenter recognita.*
Tubingae: Excudebat Georgius Gruppenbachius, 1588. [32], 509 p., [6] folded leaves of plates: ill., maps; 17 cm. Errors in pagination: p. 70 misnumbered 68, 425 as 325.
P. 471 repaired with slight loss of text. With: *Elementale Ebræum* / autore M. Conrado Neandro Bergens. Lipsiæ: Excudebat Abraham Lamberg, 1588.

1344. MAETERLINCK, MAURICE, 1862-1949. *The magic of the stars, by Maurice Maeterlinck; translated by Alfred Sutro.*
New York: Dodd, Mead & Company, 1930. 4 p. l., 3-147 p. 20 cm. Discussions of modern astronomical theory. Translation of: *La grande férie.* Introduction. – The immensity of the universe. – The earth. – Sidereal influences.

1345. MAGALOTTI, LORENZO, CONTE, 1637-1712. *Saggi di naturali esperienze / fatte nell'Accademia del cimento sotto la protezione del serenissimo principe Leopoldo di Toscana e descritte del segretario di essa Accademia.*
In Firenze: Per Giuseppe Cocchini ..., 1666, [i.e. 1667]. [16], CCLXIX, [17] p., [1] leaf of plates: ill., port.; 34 cm. The secretary of the Accademia del cimento was conte Lorenzo Magalotti. Cf. *DSB* vol. 9, p. 3. Dedication is dated: 14. luglio 1667. Port. signed: Franciscus Spierre Lotaringus sculpebat. Includes index.
Provenance: Herbert McLean Evans (bookplate).

1346. MAGINI, GIOVANNI ANTONIO, 1555-1617. *Nouæ cœlestium orbium theoricæ congruentes cum obseruationibus N. Copernici / Auctore Io. Antonio Magino Pat.....*

Venetiis: Ex officina Damiani Zenarij., MDLXXXIX., [1589]. [14], 115 leaves; ill.; 25 cm. Title within engraved ornamental border; some decorated borders and initials. Errata on leaf [11] of 1st group. Houzeau & Lancaster. *Astronomie,* 12741. Grässe, v. 4, p. 336.

Provenance: Cynerij Clementis (inscription).

1347. MAILLET, BENOÎT DE, 1656-1738. *Telliamed ou entretiens d'un philosophe indien avec un missionnaire françois sur la diminution de la mer, la formation de la terre, l'origine de l'homme, &c. / Mis en ordre sur les mémoires de feu M. de Maillet. Par J.A.G*** Tome premier [-second].*

À Amsterdam: Chez L'honoré & Fils, Libraires., M.DCC.XLVIII, [1748]. 2 v.; 21 cm. The title is an anagram of the author's name. Title page of v. 2 has author's name as: M. de Maille. Half title which precedes v. 2 reads: Système de Telliamed. Edited by Jean Antoine Guer (J.A.G***). Vol. 1: [10], cxix [i.e. lxix], [9], 208, [3] p.; v. 2: [2], 231 p. Vol. 1 has numerous errors in paging. Title vignettes. Sabin 43891. Cioranescu, A. 18. s., 41376. Errata statement in v. 1, p. [3] at the end.

Bound in 1 v.

1348. MAIN, ROBERT, 1808-1878. *Rudimentary astronomy: by the Rev. Robert Main....*

London: J. Weale, 1852. xx, 156 p. incl. front., illus., diagrs. 18 cm.

Provenance: Wm. Birnie, Jr. (bookplate); 12 p. of advertisements at end.

1349. †MAIRAN, DORTOUS DE, 1678-1771. *Traité physique et historique de l'aurore boréale / par Mr. De Mairan.*

À Paris: De l'Imprimerie Royale, 1733. [8], 281 p., XV folded leaves of plates: ill.; 26 cm. Suite des *Mémoires de l'Académie royale des sciences;* année M.DCCXXXI. Title vignette. Plates signed: Ph. Simonneau. Quérard, V: 449.

1350. MAIRE, CHRISTOPHER, 1697-1767. *Voyage astronomique et géographique dans l'État de l'Église: entrepris par l'ordre et sous les auspices du Pape Benoit XIV: pour mesurer deux dégrés du méridien, & corriger la Carte de l'État ecclésiastique / par les PP. Maire & Boskovich de la Compagnie de Jesus; traduit du Latin, augmenté de notes & d'extraits de nouvelles mesures de dégrés faites en Italie, en Allemagne, en Hongrie & en Amérique; avec une nouvelle carte des États du Pape levée géométriquement.*

À Paris: Chez N. M. Tilliard ..., 1770. xvi, 526 p., [1], 4 leaves of plates (4 folded): ill., map (engravings); 26 cm. Translation of: *De litteraria expeditione per pontificiam ditionem ad dimentiendos duos meridiani.* Half-title. Errata on p. 525-526. The work consists of five books, the first, fourth and fifth by Boskovic, the second and third by Maire. Plates signed: De Bellay sculp. Backer-Sommervogel, I, col. 785, #39. BN, v. 16, col. 652. Includes bibliographical references and index.

Map missing.

1351. MALPIGHI, MARCELLO, 1628-1694. *Marcelli Malpighii ... Anatome plantarum. Cui subjungitur appendix, iteratas & auctas ejusdem authoris de ovo incubato observationes continens. Regiæ societati, Londini ad scientiam naturalem promovendam institutæ, dicata.*

Londini: impensis Johannis Martyn, 1675-79. 2 v. 102 pl. (incl. front.) 36 cm. Title in red and black; title vignette; added t.-p., engr. Pt. 1, liv pl.; appendix, vii pl.; pt. 2, xxxix pl. Appendix follows pt. 1 and has separate paging and t.-p. dated 1675. "Catalogus librorum latinorum qui prostant venales apud Joannem Martyn...": [2] p. following text, v. 2. Wing M-345. Osler, W. *Bib. Osleriana,* 985. Horblit, H. D. *Grolier 100 science books,* 43a.

Provenance: Jean Baptiste Colbert (armorial binding).

1352. MALPIGHI, MARCELLO, 1628-1694. *Marcelli Malpighii philosophi & medici Bononiensis Dissertatio epistolica de bombyce: Societati Regiæ, Londini ad Scientiam Naturalem Promovendam Institutæ, dicata.*

Londini: Apud J. Martyn & J. Allestry, Regiæ Societatis typographos, 1669. [9], 100 p. 12 fold. pl. 24 cm. Preface by H. Oldenburg. Errata: on p. [6].

Provenance: R. Walpole (inscription); Herbert McLean Evans (bookplate).

1353. Malpighi, Marcello, 1628-1694. *Marcelli Malpighii philosophi & medici Bononiensis, e Regia Societate Opera omnia ... tomis duobus comprehensa....*

Londini: Apud Robertum Littlebury ..., 1686-1687. 2v. ill.; 38 cm. Additional engraved t. p.: Marcelli Malpighii Anatome plantarum. Signed: R. White sculp. Imprint of t. 2: Londini: Typis M. F. impensis R. Littlebury, R. Scott, Tho. Sawbridge, & G. Wells, 1686. Errors in pagination: p. 82 misnumbered as 78 (1st sequence), p. 1-4 as 65-68 (4th sequence). Collation: v. 1: [8], 15, [6], 78 [i.e. 82], [2], 35 p. [1], LIV, VII leaves of plates; v. 2: [8], 72, [4], 65 [i.e. 1]-44, [4], 20, [2], 144 p., XXXIX, XII, IV, [4] leaves of plates. T. 1 continet: Plantarum anatomes partem primam – Epistolas varias ad Oldenburgum & Sponium. T. 2 continet; Plantarum anatomes partem secundam – De bombyce – De formatione pulli in ovo – De cerebro – De lingua – De externo tactûs organo – De omento, pinguedine & adiposis ductibus – Exercitationem anatomicam de viscerum structura – Dissertationes de polypo cordis & de pulmonibus. T. 1 Plantarum anatomes partem primam. Epistolas varias ad Oldenburgum & Sponium – T. 2 Plantarum anatomes partem secundam. De bombyce. De formatione pulli in ovo. De cerebro. De lingua. De externo tactûs organo. De omento, pinguedine & adiposis ductibus. Exercitationem anatomicam de viscerum structura. Dissertationes de polypo cordis & de pulmonibus.

Plate XXXVI bound before plate XXXV (1st sequence) Bound in one v.

1354. Malpighi, Marcello, 1628-1694. *Marcelli Malpighii philosophi & medici Bononiensis e Regia Societat Lond. Opera posthuma ... quibus præfixa est ejusdem vita à seipso scripta.*

Londini: Impensis A. & J. Churchill ..., 1697. [5], 110, 187, [1] (blank) [2], 10 p., XIX leaves of plates ill., port. 37 cm. The "Morborum exitialium tyrannica sævitia ... in medicam historiam redacta a Johanne Baptista Gyraldo" and "De structura glandularum conglobatarum ... epistola ... Londini, Apud Richardum Chiswell, 1697" have special title pages. Port. signed: I. Kip sculp. Osler, W. *Bib. Osleriana*, 987.

1355. Malus, E. L. (Etienne Louis), 1775-1812. *Théorie de la double réfraction de la lumière dans les substances cristallisées, mémoire couronné par l'Institut, dans la séance publique, du 2 janvier 1810, par E. L. Malus....*

Paris: Garnery, 1810. 302 p. 24 diagr. on 3 fold. pl. 26 x 20 cm.

1356. Mangard, Petrus. *Disputatio astronomica inauguralis, de systemate Copernicano: quam ... pro Artium Liberalium Magisterio, et gradu Doctoratus in Philosophia ... / submittit Petrus Mangard, Ultrajectinus, ad diem 3. Julii MDCCXLIV H.L.Q.S.*

Lugduni Batavorum: Apud Bernhardum Jongelyn, 1744. [4], 40, [12] p.; 22 cm. Errata: p. [2] following text. Thesis (doctoral) – Rijksuniversiteit te Leiden, 1744. Includes bibliographical references.

1357. Manilius, Marcus. *The five books of M. Manilius, containing a system of the ancient astronomy and astrology: together with the philosophy of the Stoicks. Done into English verse. With notes.*

London: Printed for J. Tonson, 1697. 3 p. l., 68, 134, 88, [6] p., 1 l. front., diagrs. 20 cm. Translator's preface signed: T. C. [i. e. Thomas Creech] Errata: p. [7] at end. Includes index. Frontispiece signed: M. Burg sculp. Half title: Manilius in English. Wing M430. *Justin Wright collection*, no. 119.

1358. Manilius, Marcus. *M. Manili Astronomicon / a Iosepho Scaligero ex vetusto codice Gemblacensi infinitis mendis repurgatum; eiusdem Iospehi Scaligeri notæ, quibus auctoris prisca astrologia explicatur, castigationum caussæ redduntur, portentosæ transpositiones in eo auctore antiquitus commissæ indicantur.*

[Leiden]: Ex officina Plantiniana, apud Christophorum Raphelengium, Academiæ Lugduno-Batauæ typographum, 1600. [32], 131, [5], [20], 510, [2] p.: ill; 20 cm. Colophon reads: Lugd. Batavorum excudebat Christophorus Raphelengius Academiæ typographus, expensis Ioannis Commelini. Anno M.D.C. Title vignette. "Iosephi Scaligeri ... Castigationes et notæ" has special t. p. and separate paging. Includes indexes. Signatures: [alpha-delta]^4 A-R^4 *-**^{4} ***^{2} a-z^4 2A-3S^4. Adams M-365.

Provenance: Gottfridus Oleavius, Adolphus Vorski, F. Stern (signatures); presentation inscription from C. Leeson Prince to the Royal Astronomical Society.

1359. MANILIUS, MARCUS. *M. Manili Astronomicon libri quinque/ Iosephus Scaliger Iul. Cæs. F. recensuit, ac pristino ordini suo restitutit; eiusdem Ios. Scaligeri Commentarius in eosdem libros, & castigationum explicationes; lectiones variæ e ms. Bibliothecæ Palatinæ, et aliis, cum notis F. Iuni Biturigis.*
[Heidelberg]: In officina Sanctandreana, 1590. [4], 136, [6] 415, [15], 131, [4] p.; 17 cm. Iosephi Scaligeri ... *In Manilii quinque libros Astronomicon commentarus & castigationes* has special t. p. Reprint of Paris 1579 ed. – cf. Grässe. Adams M362.

1360. MANILIUS, MARCUS. *M. Manilii Astronomicon / interpretatione et notis ac figuris illustravit Michael Fayus ...; jussu Christianissimi regis, in usum serenissimi Delphini; accesserunt v. ill. Petri Danielis Huetii animadversiones, ad Manilium & Scaligeri notas.*
Parisiis: Apud Fredericum Leonard ..., 1679. [28], 448, [68], 88 p.: ill.; 25 cm. Title vignette. "De vita Marci Manilii": p. 19-24 (1st group). Includes index. Errata: p. [67-68] (3rd group). Signatures: $*a^4*e^4*i^4*o^2$ A-3K^4 a-g^4 h^6. Houzeau & Lancaster (1964 ed.), 1037.
Imperfect: lacks *a1 [frontispiece?]

1361. MANILIUS, MARCUS. *The sphere of Marcus Manilius made an English poem: with annotations and an astronomical appendix / by Edward Sherburne, esquire.*
London: Printed for Nathanael Brooke, at the sign of the Angel in Cornhill, near the Royal Exchange, MDCLXXV, 1675. [19], 68, [2], 221, [9] p.: tables, front., maps, plates, diagrs. (part double); 42 cm. Head-pieces; initials. A translation of the first book of the *Astronomicon*. "A catalogue of the most eminent astronomers, ancient & modern": p. 6-126. Includes index. Errata: last p. Added engraved t. p. signed: W. Hollar fecit.

1362. MARCET, MRS. (JANE HALDIMAND), 1769-1858. *Conversations on natural philosophy: in which elements of that science are familiarly explained, and adapted for the comprehension of young pupils ... / by the author of Conversations on chemistry, and Conversations on political economy; improved by appropriate questions, for the examination of scholars, also by illustrative notes, and a dictionary of philosophical terms, by ... J. L. Blake ... Boston stereotype ed.*
Boston: Gould, Kendall & Lincoln ..., 1841. viii, 9-276 p., [1], XXVII leaves of plates: ill.; 19 cm. Author's name taken from preface. Title on frontispiece: Blake's improved edition of *Conversations on philosophy*.
Provenance: Minott Leroy Beardsley (inscription); ms. notes throughout. Spine title: Blake's natural philosophy. Advertisements: 12 p. preceding text.

1363. MARCILE, THÉODORE, 1548-1617. *Theodori Marcilii professoris eloquentiæ Regii, Ad Q. Horatii Flacci opera omnia, quotidiana & emendatæ lectiones.*
Parisiis: Apud Bartholomæum Macæum ... , 1604. [6], 163, [1] p.; 33 cm. Errors in pagination: p. 147 misnumbered as 144. Printed in double columns. Includes bibliographical references and indexes.
With: *Marci Minutii Felicis Octavius*, 1612; and *Tychonis Brahe Astronomiæ instauratæ mechanica.* Noribergæ: Apud Levinum Hulsium, 1612.

1364. MARCUSE, ADOLF, 1860-1930. *Astronomie in ihrer bedeutung für das praktische leben, von dr. Adolf Marcuse ... Mit 26 abbildungen im text.*
Leipzig: B. G. Teubner, 1912. 2 p. l., 99, [1] p. illus., diagrs. 19 cm. Aus Natur und Geisteswelt; 378. Bdchn.
[23] p. of advertisements at end.

1365. MAREY, ETIENNE-JULES, 1830-1904. *Physiologie du mouvement. Le vol des oiseaux.*
Paris: C. Masson, 1890. xvi, 394, [1] p., I leaf of plates: ill.; 25 cm. Includes index. Colophon: Corbeil. Imprimerie Crété. Errata: last p. Advertisements: half title verso and lower wrapper.

1366. MARFELD, A. F. (ALEXANDER FRIEDRICH). *El universo y nosotros: pasado y presente del universo, la tierra y el hombre / A. F. Marfeld; traducción del alemán por José M. A. Vidal Llenas ..., Ramón Margalef ..., Francisco Payarals....*
Barcelona: Editorial Labor, S.A., 1961. 366, [8] p.,

XXXII leaves of plates: ill.; 23 cm. Translation of: *Das Weltall und wir.* Includes bibliography and index. Advertisements: [8] p. at end.

1367. MARGOLLÉ, ÉLIE, 1816-1884. *Les météores, par Margollé et Zurcher. Ouvrage illustré de 23 vignettes sur bois par Lebreton. 2. éd.*
Paris: L. Hachette et Cie, 1867. vii, 334 p. incl. illus., plates. 18 cm. Bibliothèque des merveilles. Series title also at head of t.-p.

1368. MARINONI, GIOVANNI JACOPO DE, 1676-1755. *De astronomica specula domestica et organico apparatu astronomico libri duo, Reginæ dicati a Joanne Jacobo Marinonio.*
Viennæ Austriæ: L. J. Kaliwoda, 1745. 11 p.l., 210, [4] p. illus., diagrs., plates (part fold.), tables. 41 cm. Engraved frontispiece by A. D. Bertoli and J. J. Sedelmayr, title vignette by Jo. Christ. Winnckler.
Without the last leaf.

1369. MARIUS, SIMON, 1573-1624. *Mundus Iovialis: anno MDCIX detectus ope perspicilli Belgici, hoc est quatuor Jovialium planetarum, cum theoria, tum tabulæ ... / jnventore & authore Simone Mario Guntzenhusano....*
Noribergensis: Sumptibus & typis Iohannis Lauri ..., 1614. [76] p.: ill., port.; 20 cm. Signatures:)(^{4}2)(^{4}3)(^{2}A-G^4 (G4 blank). Errata: G3 verso. Zinner, E. *Geschichte u. Bib. astr. Lit.*, 4474.
Ms. notes. Provenance: G. W. Cook (bookplate)

1370. MARSHALL, C. K. *A key, with general observations, explanations and questions, for the use of parents and teachers: designed to accompany the Astronomical atlas/ by C. K. Marshall.*
Philadelphia: T. K. and P. B. Collins, printers, 1847. [2], 184, [2] p.; 19 cm. Includes bibliographical references. Cover title: Key to Marshall's Astronomical atlas. Advertisements: [2] p. at end.
Provenance: David Richardson (signature).

1371. MARTIN, BENJAMIN, 1705-1782. *Biographia philosophica: being an account of the lives, writings, and inventions, of the most eminent philosophers and mathematicians who have flourished from the earliest ages of the world to the present time / by Benjamin Martin.*
London: Printed and sold by W. Owen ... and by the author ..., 1764. [4], 565, [3] p., [1] leaf of plates: port.; 21 cm. Includes index.

1372. MARTIN, BENJAMIN, 1705-1782. *The description and use of both the globes, the armillary sphere, and orrery: exemplified in a large and select variety of problems ... / by Benj. Martin. The second edition corrected, and enlarged with the addition of many useful subjects; and an appendix of chronology, or the doctrines of time.*
London: Printed for, and sold by the author ..., [176-?]. viii, 242 [i.e. 258], [2], 243-257 [i.e. 274] p., 5, [1] leaves of plates: ill.; 22 cm. Errors in pagination: p. 167-176, 184-185, 235-236, 237-242, and 257 repeated. Frontispiece signed: Emanl. Bowen sculpt. Advertisements: [2] p. Colophon on p. 242 reads: From the press of Bigg and Cox ... Houzeau & Lancaster. *Astronomie.* (1964 ed.) 9754.
Provenance: William Freer (armorial stamp).

1373. MARTIN, BENJAMIN, 1705-1782. *Philosophia Britannica: or, A new and comprehensive system of the Newtonian philosophy, astronomy, and geography, in a course of twelve lectures, with notes: containing the physical, mechanical, geometrical, and experimental proofs and illustrations of all the principal propositions in every branch of natural science ... 4th ed.....*
London: Printed for J., F., C. Rivington [etc.] 1788; [v. 3, 1787). 3 v. fold. plates, fold. maps, tables. 22 cm. Includes index. "A catalogue of the principal books made use of"; v. 1, 10th-12th prelim. leaf. Vol. 3 was probably also published in 1788.
Provenance: Mrs. W. Belcher (inscription).

1374. MARTIN, BENJAMIN, 1705-1782. *The theory of comets; illustrated in four parts ... The whole adapted to, and exemplified in the orbit of the comet of the year 1682, whose return is now near at hand.*
London: Printed for the author, 1757. 2 p.l., 57,[3] p. fold. plate. 27 cm. "A catalogue of philosophical, optical, and mathematical instruments, made and sold by B. Martin": [3] p. at end.

With: *Astronomy explained upon Sir Isaac Newton's principles ...* / by James Ferguson. London: Printed for and sold by the author, 1756.

1375. MARTIN, MARTHA EVANS, d. 1925. *The friendly stars, by Martha Evans Martin; with an introduction by Harold Jacoby.*

New York, London: Harper & Brothers, 1907. ix, [1] p., 2 l., 264, [1] p. illus., II pl. (1 double) 20 cm. Title in red and black, imprint date on t. p. Also published same year but t. p. varies: imprint date appears on verso of t. p.; t. p. printed in black.

Provenance: Carrie C. McLenegan (signature); W. E. Jackson (inkstamp); Jessie M. Jackson (signature).

1376. MARTIN, MARTHA EVANS, d. 1925. *The friendly stars / by Martha Evans Martin; with an introduction by Harold Jacoby.*

New York; London: Harper & Brothers, 1907. ix, [5], 264, [1] p.: ill.; 20 cm. Imprint date appears on verso of t. p.; t. p. printed in black. Also published same year but t. p. varies, printed in red and black, with date appearing on recto. Includes index.

1377. MARTIN, MARTHA EVANS, d. 1925. *The ways of the planets, by Martha Evans Martin....*

New York, London: Harper & Brothers, 1912. 3 p.l., 272, [1] p. front., illus., plates, double map. 20 cm.

1378. MARTIN, THOMAS HENRI, 1813-1884. *Histoire des hypothèses astronomiques grecques, qui admettent la sphéricité de la terre. 1re section: hypothèses les plus simples, mais dans les quelles beaucoup de faits importants sont méconnus. 2: hypothèse astronomique de Parménide / par M. Th. H. Martin.*

[À Paris: Chez G. Martin, Jean-Baptiste Coignard, H.-L. Guerin, 1879]. p. [305]-318; 27 cm. Caption title. Detached from: *Mémoires de l'Acadèmie Royale des Sciences del'Institut de France,* t. XXIX, 2e ptie (1879). Includes bibliographical references.

1379. *Marvels of the universe: a popular work on the marvels of the heavens, the earth, plant life, animal life, the mighty deep / edited by Walter Hutchinson; with an introduction by Lord Avebury; and with contributions by leading specialists, including Sir Harry Johnston ... [et al.].*

New York: G. P. Putnam, 1913. 2 v. (viii, 1162 p., [56] leaves of plates): ill. (64 col.); 29 cm. "Printed in Great Britain" – T. p. verso. Includes index. Erratum slip tipped in, v. 2, facing p. [vi].

1380. MASCAGNI, PAOLO, 1755-1815. *Vasorum lymphaticorum corporis humani historia et ichnographia, autore Paulo Mascagni.*

Senis: P. Carli, 1787. 138 p. 27 [i.e. 41] pl. 60 cm. Title vignette. Illustrated by Cyrus Sanctius. Numbering of some plates duplicated. Includes bibliographical references. Choulant, L. *Anatomic illustration,* p. 315-316.

Provenance: Ralph Hermon Major (bookplate); Herbert McLean Evans (bookplate).

1381. MASHA'ALLAH, 730?-815? *Messahalæ antiquissimi ac laudatissimi inter Arabes astrologi, Libri tres ... / editi à Ioachimo Hellero Noribergensium mathematico.*

Norimbergæ: Apud Ioannem Montanum, & Vlricum Neuberum, 1549. [139] p.: ill.; 21 cm. Translated by Joannes Hispalensis. Cf. *NUC pre-1956,* v. 366, p. 665. Signatures: A^6 B-R^4. Liber primus de reuolutione annorum mundi – Liber secundus, de significatione planetarum in natiuitatibus – Liber tertius, de receptione.

1382. MATTERSDORF, LEO, 1903- . *Insight into astronomy.*

New York: Lantern Press, in collaboration with Sky Pub. Corp., Cambridge, Mass, 1952. 223 p. illus. 21 cm.

1383. MATTIOLI, PIETRO ANDREA, 1500-1577. *Kreutterbuch dess ... Herrn D. Petri Andreae Matthioli: jetzt widerumb mit viel schönen neuwen Figuren, auch nützlichen Artzneyen, und andern guten Stücken ... / gemehret und verfertiget durch Joachimum Camerarium ... ; sampt dreyen wolgeordneten nützlichen Registern, der Kreutter lateinische und deutsche Namen ... innhaltendt.*

Gedruckt zu Franckfurt am Mayn: In Verlegung Sigmund Feyerabends, Peter Fischers vnd Heinrich Dacken, 1586. [8], 460, [37] leaves ; ill. ; 38 cm. Translated by G. H. Handsch. Imprint from colophon. Errata on leaf Rrrr3; colophon on verso. Deurling 3019. Includes indexes in Latin and German.

Imperfect: 1st signature incomplete: lacks t.p.; 1st leaf is blank, followed by)(2-5 signed, 2 unsigned, leaves; hole in leaf)(4 with loss of text; leaves 176, 215, 292 lacking. Leaves Ooo03, Oooo2 bound between leaves Llll and Llll2. Final signature, Rrrr, lacks 4th leaf – blank bound 1st? Provenance: ms. annotations and underscoring.

1384. Mattison, Hiram, 1811-1868. *An elementary astronomy for academies and schools: illustrated by numerous original diagrams, and adapted to use either with or without the author's large maps / by H. Mattison. Fifth edition – twelfth thousand.*

New York: Published by Huntington and Savage ...; Cincinnati: H. W. Derby & Co., 1849. 243, [1] p., [20] leaves of plates: ill., charts (some col.); 17 cm. On cover: Mattison's elementary astronomy for academies and schools. Fifth edition – illustrated. Includes bibliographical references. Some plates are hand-colored. Advertisement on p. [244], and p. [4] of cover.

Advertisements: [1], 16-22 p. at end. Provenance: William Patton (signature). Imperfect: lacks 2 plates.

1385. Mattison, Hiram, 1811-1868. *A high-school astronomy: in which the descriptive, physical, and practical are combined ... by Hiram Mattison....*

New York: F. J. Huntington [etc.], 1853. 240 p. illus., diagrs. 19 cm. "Astronomical works": p. [4]. Substantially a rev. ed. of the *Elementary astronomy*, with extensive additions and improvements. cf. Pref.

Imperfect: t. p. wanting.

1386. Mauduit, Antoine-René, 1731-1815. *A new & complete treatise of spherical trigonometry: in which are contained the orthographic, analytical & logarithmical solutions of the several cases of spherical triangles ... a comprehensive theory of the fluxions of these triangles ... Carefully tr. from the French of Mr. Mauduit, by W. Crakelt.*

London: Printed by W. Adlard, 1768. xv, [1], 216 p. 37 diagrs. on ii fold. plates. 21 cm. Translation of: *Principes d'astronomie sphérique.* Errata: [1] p.

Provenance: Edwd. Banbury (inscription).

1387. Maunder, E. Walter (Edward Walter), 1851-1928. *The astronomy of the Bible: an elementary commentary on the astronomical references of Holy Scripture / by E. Walter Maunder ... 4th ed.*

London: Epworth Press, 1922. xvi, 430 p., [2] leaves of plates: ill.; 19 cm. Imprint date supplied from *NUC*, v. 370, p. 369. Includes bibliographical references and indexes.

Provenance: John C. Deagan (signature).

1388. Maunder, E. Walter (Edward Walter), 1851-1928. *Astronomy without a telescope; a guide to the constellations, and introduction to the study of the heavens with the unassisted sight. By E. Walter Maunder ... Illustrated by star maps and key diagrams.*

London: "Knowledge" Office, 1903. xx, xii, 280 p. incl. front., illus. pl. 23 cm.

1389. Maunder, E. Walter (Edward Walter), 1851-1928. *The science of the stars, by E. Walter Maunder....*

London and Edinburgh: T. C. & E. C. Jack, 1912. vii, 9-95 p. 17 cm. People's Books; 15. "Books to read": p. 91-92.

Provenance: H. James Yates (bookplate): with [2] p. of advertisements at end.

1390. Maupertuis, 1698-1759. *La figure de la terre, déterminée par les observations de Messieurs de Maupertuis, Clairaut, Camus, Le Monnier ... & de M. l'Abbé Outhier ...accompagnés de M. Celsius ... faites par ordre du roy au cercle polaire, par M. de Maupertuis.*

Paris: Imprimerie Royale, 1738. xxiv, [4], 184 p. 9 fold. plates, fold. map, tables. 21 cm. Map by Delahaye. *Babson Newton Coll.* 94.

1391. Maupertuis, 1698-1759. *Œurves de Mr de Maupertuis. Nouv. éd. cor. & augm.....*

Lyon: J. M. Bruyset, 1756. 4 v. front. (port.) map, diagrs. 20 cm. Title in red and black. Port. engraved by J. Daullé after Tourniere. t. 1. Essai de cosmologie. Discours sur les différentes figures des astres. Essai de philosophie morale. Réflexions philosophiques, sur l'origine des langues et la signification des mots. – t. 2. Venus physique: 1. ptie. Sur l'origine des animaux. 2. ptie. Variétés dans l'espèce humaine.

k Maxwell's Electricity, Vol. I.

FIG. I.

Art. 118.

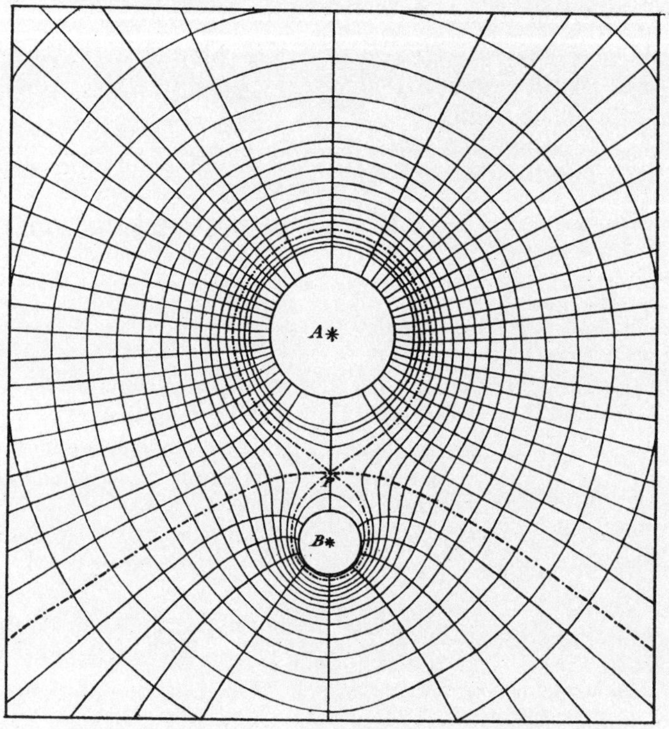

Lines of Force and Equipotential Surfaces.

A = 20. *B* = 5. *P*, Point of Equilibrium. $AP = \frac{2}{3} AB$.

For the Delegates of the Clarendon Press.

MAXWELL, *A Treatise on Electricity and Magnetism*, 1873

Systême de la nature. Réponse aux objections de M. Diderot. Lettres. Lettre sur le progrès des sciences. – t. 3. Éléments de géographie. Relation du voyage fait par ordre du roi au cercle polaire pour déterminer la figure de la terre. Relation d'un voyage au fond de la Lapponi pour trouver un ancien monument. Lettre sur la comète, qui paroissoit en 1742. Discours académiques. Dissertation sur les différents moyens dont les hommes se sont servis pour exprimer leurs idées. – t. 4. Accord de différentes loix de la nature qui avoient jusqu'ici paru incompatibles. Recherche des loix du mouvement. Loi du repos. Astronomie nautique, ou Éléments d'astronomie. Discours sur la parallaxe de la lune. Opérations pour déterminer la figure de la terre & les variations de la pesanteur. Autres mesures.

1392. MAURY, MATTHEW FONTAINE, 1806-1873. *The physical geography of the sea / by M. F. Maury.*

New York: Harper & Bros., 1855. 274 p., [8] folded leaves of plates: ill., maps; 25 cm. Plates are numbered: V-XII. Horblit, H. D. *Grolier 100 science books,* 71.

Provenance: James E. Robinson (signature).

1393. MAXWELL, JAMES CLERK, 1831-1879. *A dynamical theory of the electromagnetic field / J. Clerk Maxwell....*

[London: Royal Society, 1865]. p. 459-512; 30 cm. Caption title. Detached from: *Philosophical transactions,* v. 155. Includes bibliographical references.

Provenance: Cavendish Laboratory, Cambridge (inkstamp).

1394. MAXWELL, JAMES CLERK, 1831-1879. *A treatise on electricity and magnetism / by James Clerk Maxwell....*

Oxford: Clarendon Press, 1873. 2 v.: 20 pl., diagrs.; 23 cm. Clarendon Press series. Includes index. Horblit, H. D. *Grolier 100 science books,* 72.

Provenance: Rob. Rawson (signature); H. S. White (inscription). Advertisements: 15 p. at end of v. 2. Errata slip inserted.

1395. MAYER, JULIUS ROBERT VON, 1814-1878. *Die organische Bewegung in ihren Zusammenhange mit dem Stoffwechsel. Ein Beitrag zur Naturkunde von Dr. J. R. Mayer.*

Heilbronn: C. Drechsler, 1845. 1 p.l., 112 p., 1 l. 21 cm. Druckfehler: p. [113].

Provenance: Herbert McLean Evans (bookplate).

1396. MAYER, TOBIAS, 1723-1762. *Tabulæ motuum solis et lunæ, novæ et correctæ; auctore Tobia Mayer: quibus accedit methodus longitudinum promota, eodem autore. Editæ jussu præfectorum rei longitudinariæ.*

Londini: typis Gulielmi et Johannis Richardson, 1770. vii, 136, cxxx, [2] p. 2 fold. pl. 28 x 22 cm. Latin and English. Edited by Nevil Maskelyne, astronomer royal.

Provenance: Joachim Carnicer (inscription). 29 cm.

1397. MAYHEW, HENRY, 1812-1887. *The story of the peasant-boy philosopher; or, "The child gathering pebbles on the sea-shore." (Founded on the early life of Ferguson, the shephard-boy astronomer, and intended to show how a poor lad became acquainted with the principles of natural science.) By Henry Mayhew.*

London: D. Bogue, 1854. xvi, 484 p. front., illus., plates, 17 cm. Plates signed: H. Vizetelly sc.

16. p. of advertisements follow text. Binder: Leighton Son & Hodge.

1398. MAYORA, MIGUEL DE. *Cosmometro, ó tratado de las medidas de la naturaleza / por Miguel de Mayora.*

Barcelona: Imprenta y Libreria Politécnica de Tomás Gorchs ..., 1855. xvi, 390 p., [2] folded leaves of plates: ill.; 25 cm. Correcciones: p. 386.

Provenance: Ministère de l'intérieur (inkstamp).

1399. MCCABE, JOSEPH, 1867-1955. *The end of the world, by Joseph McCabe....*

London: G. Routledge & Sons, Ltd.; E. P. Dutton & Co., 1920. vi p., 1 l., 267 p. front., plates, diagrs. 19 cm.

1400. MCCABE, JOSEPH, 1867-1955. *Evolution: a general sketch from nebula to man / by Joseph McCabe....*

New York: Frederick A. Stokes, [1910?]. v, 124 p., [8] leaves of plates: ill.; 20 cm. XXth Century Science series. Includes bibliographical references and index.

1401. MCCABE, JOSEPH, 1867-1955. *The wonders of the stars, by Joseph McCabe.*

New York: G. P. Putnam's Sons, 1923. viii, 134 p. front., illus., plates. 19 cm.

[6] p. of advertisements at end.

1402. McDowell, Ephraim, 1771-1830. *Three cases of extirpation of diseased ovaria / by Ephraim M'Dowell....*

[Philadelphia: Published by Thomas Dobson and Son ...: William Fry, printer, 1817]. p. 242-244; 22 cm. *Eclectic repertory and analytical review, medical and philosophical;* v. 7. Caption title.

1403. McFee, Inez N. (Inez Nellie Canfeld), b. 1879. *Secrets of the stars, by Inez N. McFee....*

New York: Thomas Y. Crowell Company, [c1922]. xii, 273 p. front., plates 21 cm. Part of plates printed on both sides. Maps on lining-papers.

1404. McLennan, Evan. *Cosmical evolution; a new theory of the mechanism of nature, by Evan McLennan .... .*

Chicago: Donohue, Henneberry & Co., 1890. xxii, 23-399 p. incl. tables, diagrs. 20 cm.

Provenance: Presentation copy from (Orry?) Leslie to Dr. T. V. Meacham; Grove House for Convalescents (inkstamp).

1405. McMillan, Edwin M. (Edwin Mattison), 1907-. *Lecture series in nuclear physics / by E. M. McMillan ... [et al.]*

Washington, D.C.: United States Government Printing Office, 1947. 132 p. : ill. ; 26 cm. (MDDC ; 1175). "Prepared in September 1943 for use at the Los Alamos Scientific Laboratory as LA-24 ... Declassified October 3, 1945 and assigned the number MDDC 1175. The 41 chapters of the present document are equivalent to the 46 of the original LA document; the decrease results from combining material in the last 10 chapters of the original series." At head of title: United States Atomic Energy Commission. Oak Ridge Operations. Includes bibliographical references.

Provenance: R. Kennedy (inkstamp).

1406. McMillan, Edwin Mattison, 1907- . *The synchrotron: a proposed high energy particle accelerator; Radiation from a group of electrons moving in a circular orbit / Edwin M. McMillan.*

[New York: Macmillan, 1945]. 3 p.; 27 cm. "Reprinted from the *Physical Review,* vol. 68, nos. 5 and 6, 143-145, September 1 and 15, 1945."

With author's signature.

1407. Meckel, J. F. (Johann Friedrich), 1781-1833. *System der vergleichenden Anatomie.*

Halle: In der Rengerschen Buchhandlung, 1821-33. 6 v. in 7. 21 cm. Includes bibliographical references.

Provenance: P. Lohnmann (signature); Herbert McLean Evans (bookplate).

1408. Meitner, Lise, 1878-1968. [Collection of articles on nuclear physics / by Lise Meitner, O. R. Frisch, et al.]

[1924-1939]. 5 pieces: ill; 24-27 cm. Includes bibliographical references. (1) Der Zusammenhang zwischen (beta)- und (gamma)-Strahlen / Lise Meitner (1924) – (2) On the products of the fission of uranium and thorium under neutron bombardment / Lise Meitner (1939) – (3) Disintegration of uranium by neutrons / Lise Meitner and O. R. Frisch – (4) Physical evidence for the division of heavy nuclei under neutron bombardment / O. R. Frisch (1939) – (5) Liberation of neutrons in the nuclear explosion of uranium / H. von Halban [et al.] (1939).

1409. Melville, Herman, 1819-1891. *Moby-Dick; or, The whale.*

New York: Harper & Brothers, 1851. xxiii, 634, [8] p. 20 cm. "[Ahab] sat and smoked ... 'How now,' he soliloquized ... 'this smoking no longer soothes ... I'll smoke no more-' He tossed the still lighted pipe into the sea": p. 141-142 (chapter XXX: The pipe). Publisher's advertisements: p. [635-642]. First published in London with title: *The whale.* In the original black cloth ("first binding" - Blanck) with brown-orange end papers. *BAL* 13664.

Provenance: Kathryn and Joe E. Brown (bookplate). In slipcase.

1410. Mendel, Gregor, 1822-1884. *Versuche über Pflanzen-Hybriden / von Gregor Mendel.*

[Brünn: Im Verlag des Vereines, 1865]. p. 3-47 (Abhandlungen); 26 cm. Naturforschender Verein in Brünn. *Verhandlungen des naturforschenden Vereines in Brünn;* Bd. 4. Caption title. Horblit, H. D. *Grolier 100 science books,* 73a.

1411. Mendeleyev, Dmitry Ivanovich, 1834-1907. *The principles of chemistry, by D. Mendeléeff. Translated from the Russian (5th ed.) by George Kamensky. Ed. by A. J. Greenaway.*

London, New York: Longmans, Green, (1891). 2 v. illus. 23 cm. Includes indexes.

Advertisements, dated April 1895: 24 p. at end, v. 2. Provenance: M. O. Farrar, Metallurgy, Mining, Chemistry (inkstamp).

1412. MENDELEYEV, DMITRY IVANOVICH, 1834-1907. *Sootnoshenie svoistv s atomnym viesom elementov / D. Mendelieva.*

[Sanktpeterburg: Tipografiia Tovarishchestva "Obshchestvennaia Polza", 1869]. p. 60-77; 22 cm. *Zhurnal russkago khimicheskago obshchestva;* t.1. Horblit, H. D. *Grolier 100 science books,* 74.

1413. MENZEL, DONALD HOWARD, 1901- . *Stars and planets; exploring the universe, by Donald H. Menzel....*

New York: The University Society, Incorporated, [c1938]. iv, p., 2 l., 129 p. illus., diagrs. 24 cm. The University series: Highlights of Modern Knowledge. Astronomy. "First trade edition 1935." "Third edition ... a complete revision." – Pref. "Suggestions for further reading": p. 118-119.

1414. MERCATOR, GERHARD, 1512-1594. *Chronologia hoc est supputatio temporum: ab initio mundi ex eclipsibus & obseruationibus astronomicis & sacræ scripturæ firmissimis testimonijs demonstrata / Gerardo Mercatore, & Matthaeo Beroaldo authoribus; accessit & Isidori Hispalensis Epi. Chronologia....*

Basileæ: Per Thomam Guarinum, 1577. [14], 292, 631, [22] p.; 18 cm. Includes index.

Bound partially in music ms. fragment.

1415. MERCATOR, NICOLAUS, 1620-1687. *Nicolai Mercatoris ... Institutionum astronomicarum libri duo, de motu astrorum communi & proprio, secundum hypotheses veterum et recentiorum præcipuas; deque hypotheseon ex observatis constructione: cum Tabulis Tychonianis solaribus, lunaribus, lunæ-solaribus, et Rudolphinis solis, fixarum, et quinque errantium; earumque usu præceptis & exemplis commonstrato. Quibus accedit appendix de iis, quæ novissimis temporibus coelitus innotuerunt.*

Londini: Typis G. Godbid, sumptibus S. Simpson, 1676. [16], 288, 64 p. diagrs. 19 cm. Errata: p. [16] (1st sequence). Wing (2nd ed.), M-1729. Houzeau & Lancaster. *Astronomie* (1964 ed.), 9235.

With: *Astronomia geometrica* / authore Setho Wardo ... Londini: Typis Jacobi Flesher, 1656. Provenance: Michael Chasles (bookplate).

1416. MERCURIALE, GIROLAMO, 1530-1606. *De arte gymnastica, libri sex: in quibus exercitationum omnium vetustarum genera, loca, modi, facultates, & quidquid denique ad corporis humani exercitationes pertinet, diligenter explicatur. Secunda editione aucti, & multis figuris ornati....*

Parisiis: Apud Jacobum du Puys, 1577. [4], 201 [i. e. 200], [13] l. illus., 2 plans. 24 cm. Leaf no. 197 omitted. Many other errors in foliation. The woodcut illustrations are crude copies of those designed for the author by Pirro Ligorio and cut by Cristoforo Coriolani. Cf. note on the Venice 1573 ed., of which this is a reprint. Adams, M1321.

Imperfect: 3G3 & 3G4 missing and supplied in ms. 3G6 (blank) missing. Index bound before text.

1417. MERRILL, PAUL W. (PAUL WILLARD), 1887-1961. *The nature of variable stars [by] Paul W. Merrill.*

New York: Macmillan, 1938. vii p., 1 l., 134 p. 2 pl., diagrs. (1 double) 21 cm. "First printing." "Part of the material has been taken from a series of articles in *Popular Astronomy.*" – Pref.

1418. MERSENNE, MARIN, 1588-1648. *Harmonie universelle: contenant la théorie et la pratique de la musique: où il est traité de la nature des sons, & des mouuemens, des consonances, des dissonances, des genres, des modes, de la composition, de la voix, des chants, & de toutes sortes d'instrumens harmoniques / par F. Marin Mersenne....*

À Paris: Chez Sébastien Cramoisy ..., 1636-1637. 2 v. in 1: ill., music; 38 cm. "Les caracteres de musique sont de l'impression de Pierre Ballard imprimeur de la musique du Roy" – T. p. verso, v. 1. Vol. 2 has title and imprint: Seconde partie de l'Harmonie universelle... À Paris: Par Pierre Ballard ..., 1637. Many irregularities in pagination. Collations of this work differ. Cf. *NUC pre-1956,* v. 377, p. 635. Includes index. Traitez de la nature des sons et des mouuements de toutes sortes de corps – Traité de

HARMONIE
VNIVERSELLE

Ex antiquo marmore Illustrissimi Marchionis Mathei Romæ.

Nam & ego confitebor tibi in vasis psalmi veritatē tuam:
Deus psallam tibi in Cithara, sanctus Israel. Psalme 70.

MERSENNE, *Harmonie universelle*, 1636-1637

mechanique – Traitez de la voix et des chants – Traitez des consonances, des dissonances, des genres, des modes, & de la composition – Traité des instrumens a chordes – Liure cinquiesme, Des instrumens a vent – Liure sixiesme, Des orgues – Liure septiesme, Des instrumens de percussion – Liure de l'utilité de l'harmonie – Nouuelles obseruations physiques et mathématiques – Tables des propositions des dix-neuf liures de l'Harmonie uniuerselle – Table des XIX liures de musique. Horblit, H. D. *Grolier 100 science books,* 75. Brunet, III:1661.

For collation and irregularities in pagination, see Horblit. Provenance: royal armorial bookplate; Monsieur de Mets (inscription); Vincens [?] (inkstamp); Harrison D. Horblit (booklabel).

1419. MESMER, FRANZ ANTON, 1734-1815. *Mémoire sur la découverte du magnétisme animal / par M. Mesmer....*

À Geneve; et se trouve à Paris: Chez P. Fr. Didot le jeune ..., M.DCC.LXXIX., [1779]. [2], vj, 85, [3] p.; 18 cm. With half-title. Last leaf blank.

1420. MESSIER, CHARLES. *Catalogue de nébuleuses et des amas d'étoiles / observées à Paris par M. Messier....*

[À Paris: De l'Imprimerie Royale, 1781]. p.227-269; 19 cm. *Connoissance des temps, ou connoissance des mouvements célestes pour l'année bissextile ...* ; 1784. Caption title.

1421. METCHNIKOFF, ELIE, 1845-1916. *Études sur la nature humaine; essai de philosophie optimiste, par Élie Metchnikoff.*

Paris: Masson, 1903. ii, 399 p. ill. 22 cm. Includes bibliographical references.

Presentation copy from the author to G. Bertrand.

1422. METIUS, ADRIAAN ADRIAANSZ, 1570-1635. *Adriani Metii Alcmar D. M. et matheseos profess. ordin. Primum mobile: astronomicæ, sciographicæ, geometricæ et hydrographicæ....*

Amstelodami: Apud Ioannem Ianssonium, 1631. 4 v.: ill.; 20 cm. First t. has caption title: *Doctrinæ sphæriæ* with a special t. p. for liber V. dated 1630. T. 2-3 have titles, *Exercitationes astronomiæ* and T. 3 is dated 1630. T. 4 has title *Institutionis astronomicæ*. T. 2-4 have separate pagination. Special title pages: [t. 1], liber 5: Geographicus. Franekeræ: Apud Vldericum Balck, 1630; Exercitationis astronomicæ tomus secundus astrolabium. Franecaræ: Excudebat Vldericus Balck; Exercitationis astronomicæ tomus tertius, sive historia astronomica. Franekeræ: Excudebat Vldericus Balck, 1630; Institutionis astronomicæ tomus quartus. Franequeræ: Apud Vldericum Balck, 1631.

Bound in 1 v.

1423. MEUNIER, STANISLAS, 1843-1925. *Le ciel géologique; prodrome de géologie comparée, par Stanislas Meunier.*

Paris: F. Didot Frères, Fils et Cie, 1871. 3 p.l., 247 p. 23 cm. Includes bibliographical references and index.

1424. M'EWAN, DUNCAN. *An easy and concise guide to the starry heavens. with maps, key maps, scales and diagrams, arranged as a companion to the Umbrella star map and Revolving star dome, for instruction in astronomy, by D. M'Ewan....*

London: K. Paul, Trench, Trübner & Co., Ltd., 1910. 140, [4] p., incl. front., illus., diagrs. (1 fold.) 22 cm.

Provenance: University Club of Chicago (raised stamp and bookplate).

1425. MEYER, LOTHAR, 1830-1895. *Grundzüge der theoretischen Chemie / von Lothar Meyer....*

Leipzig: Druck und Verlag von Breitkopf & Härtel, 1890. XI, [1], 206 p., [2] folded leaves of plates: ill.; 23 cm. Includes index. Errata: p. [XII].

Advertisements: [1] p. at end.

1426. MEYER, M. W. (MAX WILHELM), 1853-1910. *The end of the world / by M. Wilhelm Meyer; translated by Margaret Wagner.*

Chicago: Charles H. Kerr & Co., 1914. 140 p., [7] leaves of plates: ill.; 18 cm.

Provenance: L. A. Thompson (signature).

1427. MEYER, M. W. (MAX WILHELM), 1853-1910. *Die Welt der Planeten, von dr. M. Wilh. Meyer. Mit zahlreichen Abbildungen.*

Stuttgart: Kosmos, Gesellschaft der Naturfreunde, 1910. 104 p. illus. 21 cm.

[8] p. of advertisements and 1 commercial mail order coupon at end.

1428. MICHELI, PIER ANTONIO, 1679-1737. *Nova plantarvm genera iuxta Tovrnefortii methodvm disposita quibus plantae MDCCCC recensentur, scilicet fere MCCCC nondum observatæ, reliquæ suis sedibus restitutæ; quarum vero figuram exhibere visum fuit, eæ al DL æneis tabulis CVIII. graphice expressæ sunt; adnotationibus, atque observationibus, præcipue fungorum, mucorum, affiniumque plantarum sationem, ortum, & incrementum spectantibus, interdum adiectis ... avctore Petro Antonio Michelio.*

Florentiae: Typis B. Paperinii, 1729. 12 p. l., 234 p. 108 pl. 35 cm. "Syllabus auctorum quorum nomina brevioribus notis compendii caussa citata sunt": prelim. leaves 10-12. Includes indexes. *Hunt botanical cat.* 480. Pritzel 6202*

1429. MICHELSON, ALBERT ABRAHAM, 1852-1931. *Experimental determination of the velocity of light / made at the U.S. Naval Academy, Annapolis, by Albert A. Michelson....*

[Washington: U.S. Nautical Almanac Office, 1882]. p. 109-145: ill; 30 cm. Title from cover. Also published in: U.S. Nautical Almanac Office. *Astronomical Papers,* v. 1, pt. 3.

1430. MICHELSON, ALBERT ABRAHAM, 1852-1931. *Light waves and their uses, by A. A. Michelson....*

Chicago: The University of Chicago Press, 1903. 6 p. l., 166 p. illus., 3 col. pl., diagrs. 23 cm. (Chicago. University) The Decennial Publications. 2d series, v. 3. "This series of eight lectures ... was delivered in the spring of 1899 at the Lowell Institute." – Pref. Includes index. Wave motion and interference. – Comparison of the efficiency of the microscope, telescope, and interferometer. – Application of interference methods to measurements of distances and angles. – Application of interference methods to spectroscopy. – Light waves as standards of length. – Analysis of the action of magnetism on light waves by the interferometer and the echelon. – Application of interference methods to astronomy. – The ether.

Provenance: Harvard University, Library of the Chemical Department (bookplate).

1431. MIDDLETON, J. (JAMES). *Astronomy and the rise of the globes: for schools and families ... / by J. Middleton ... Third edition.*

London: Jarrold & Sons ...: Whittaker & Co. ..., 1862. xvi, 198 p., [1] leaf of plates: ill.; 19 cm. Cover title: Middleton's astronomy and use of globes. Advertisements: p. [viii].

Provenance: I. Littlefield (signature). Newspaper clippings pasted onto some pages.

1432. MIHILL, RICHARD. *A treatise on the various lengths of the days, nights and twilights: with tables of latitude and longitude of the most eminent towns, harbours, headlands, and islands in the world ... / by Richard Mihill....*

London: Printed by D. Henry and R. Cave, for the author ... , 1755. iv, [2], 57 p.: ill., volvelles; 25 cm.

With : *Astronomy explained upon Sir Isaac Newton's principles ...* / by James Ferguson. London: Printed for, and sold by the author, 1756.

1433. MILHAM, WILLIS I. (WILLIS IBISTER), b. 1874. *How to identify the stars / by Willis I. Milham....*

New York: Macmillan, 1917. v, 38, [4] p., [16] leaves of plates: ill., charts; 20 cm. Advertisements: [4] p. at end. Includes bibliography.

1434. *The Milky Way / by Flammarion, Miller and Carr.*

New York: Humboldt Pub. Co., [1900?]. [51]-128, [397]-450, [1]-47 p.: ill., charts; 24 cm. Humboldt Library Series. Includes: translation of: *Les merveilles célestes* / Camille Flammarion; Miller's *Romance of astronomy;* and Carr's *Sun.*

"Catalogue of the Humboldt Library of Popular Science.": [46] p. at end. Provenance: Arthur T. Vance (bookplate).

1435. MILLER, WILLIAM, S. S. C. *The heavenly bodies: their nature and habitability / by William Miller....*

London: Hodder and Stoughton ..., 1883. xiv, [2], 347 p.; 21 cm. Includes bibliographical references.

Provenance: Wilson Noble (armorial bookplate).

1436. MILLIKAN, ROBERT ANDREWS, 1868-1953. *High frequency rays of cosmic origin / by R. A. Millikan ... ; introduction by C. G. Abbot.*

Washington: United States Government Printing Office, 1927. p. 193-201; 23 cm. Smithsonian publication; 2884. Includes bibliographical references.

"From the *Smithsonian report* for 1926, pages 193-201." First published in the *Proceedings of the National Academy of Sciences,* v. 12, no. 1, January, 1926.

1437. MILLIKAN, ROBERT ANDREWS, 1868-1953. *On the elementary electrical charge and the Avogadro constant / by R. A. Millikan.*
Lancaster, Pa.: American Institute of Physics, 1913. p. [109]-143: ill.; 26 cm. Title from cover. "Reprinted from the *Physical review,* N. S., Vol. II, No.2, August, 1913." Includes bibliographical references.
Provenance: Author's presentation inscription to Professor Carl Barus; ms. marginalia.

1438. MILNE-HOME, DAVID, 1805-1890. *Essay on comets, which gained the first of Dr. Fellowes's prizes, proposed to those who had attended the University of Edinburgh within the last twelve years. By David Milne....*
Edinburgh: Printed for A. Black; [etc., etc.], 1828. xii p., 1 l., 189, [3] p. diagrs. 28 cm. Advertisements: p. [2]-[3]. Includes bibliographical references.
Provenance: York Subscription Library (bookplate).

1439. MINKOWSKI, H. (HERMANN), 1864-1909. *Mémoire sur la théorie des formes quadratiques à coefficients entiers / par M. Minkowski.*
[Paris: Imprimerie Nationale, 1887]. 180 p.; 29 cm. Caption title. At head of title: *Mémoires présentés par divers savants à l'Académie des Sciences de l'Institut National de France.* Tome XXIX -No. 2. Poggendorff, Bd. 4, p. 1015.

1440. MINKOWSKI, H. (HERMANN), 1864-1909. *Raum und Zeit / H. Minkowski.*
[Leipzig: F. C. W. Vogel, 1909]. p. 4-9; 25 cm. Gesellschaft Deutscher Naturforscher und Ärzte. *Verhandlungen der Gesellschaft Deutscher Naturforscher und Ärzte,* 2. T., 1. Hälfte.

1441. MINKOWSKI, H. (HERMANN), 1864-1909. *Zwei Abhandlungen über die Grundgleichungen der Elektrodynamik, mit einem Einführungswort von Otto Blumenthal.*
Leipzig und Berlin: B. G. Teubner, 1910. 82 p. 26 cm. *Fortschritte der mathematischen Wissenschaften in Monographien,* Hft. 1. Advertisements: p. [83-84].
Provenance: Karl Horovitz (inscription).

1442. M'INTIRE, JAMES, 1799-1879. *A new treatise on astronomy, and the use of globes: in two parts ... / by James M'Intire....*
New York: Published by A. S. Barnes & Burr ..., 1860. xii, [13]-326 p., [1] leaf of plates: ill.; 20 cm. "Designed for the use of high schools and academies." Includes index.
Provenance: College of the Holy Names, Oakland, California (raised stamp).

1443. MINUCIUS FELIX, MARCUS. *Marci Minutii Felicis Octavius / Geverhartus Elmenhorstius recensuit et librum commentarium adiecit.*
[Hamburg?: s.n, 1612]. [4], 41, [1] (blank), XCII, [1] p. 33 cm. Commentary includes quotations in Greek. Includes bibliographical references and indexes.
With: *Theodori Marcilii ... Ad. Q. Horatii Flacci opera omnia ... lectiones.* Parisiis: Apud Bartholomæum Macæum, 1604.

1444. MITCHEL, O. M. (ORMSBY MACKNIGHT), 1809-1862. *The astronomy of the Bible / by O. M. Mitchel ...; with a biographical sketch.*
New York: Oakley, Mason and Co. ..., 1871. xi, [1] (blank), [13]-322 p., [1] leaf of plates: port.; 19 cm.
Provenance: Library of Gettysburg College (donor bookplate); presentation inscription from Brother Jim to George Barnes.

1445. MITCHEL, O. M. (ORMSBY MACKNIGHT), 1809-1862. *The orbs of heaven, or, The planetary and stellar worlds: a popular exposition of the great discoveries and theories of modern astronomy / by O. M. Mitchell ... New edition, with numerous illustrations.*
London: George Routledge and Sons ..., [1892?]. [2], viii, 304, [8] p., [12] leaves of plates: ill. (some col.), ports.; 19 cm. Added engraved t. p. Text and format the same as the author's, *The planetary and stellar worlds: a popular exposition of the great discoveries and theories of modern astronomy,* but with more illustrations and a different appendix. Imprint date from *BLC.* Advertisements: [8] p. at end.

1446. MITCHEL, O. M. (ORMSBY MACKNIGHT), 1809-1862. *The planetary and stellar worlds: a popular exposition of the great discoveries and theories of modern astronomy / by O. M. Mitchel....*

New York: Wm. L. Allison Company, 1848. 264 p., [16] leaves of plates: ill.; 20 cm. Scientific Series. The same text and format as the author's, *The orbs of heaven, or, the planetary and stellar worlds,* but with fewer illustrations and a different appendix. Preface dated 1848.

1447. MITCHELL, S. A. (SAMUEL ALFRED), 1874-1960. *Eclipses of the sun, by S. A. Mitchell....*

New York: Columbia University Press, 1923. xvii, 425 p. col. front., plates (part. col.) diagrs. 23 cm.

1448. MITTON, G. E. (GERALDINE EDITH). *The book of stars: for young people / by G. E. Mitton....*

New York: Macmillan, 1928. xii, 212 p., [15] leaves of plates: ill. (some col.), map; 21 cm.

1449. MIZAULD, ANTOINE, 1510-1578. *Antonii Mizaldi Monsluciani Cometographia: crinitarum stellarum quas mundus nunquam impunè vidit, aliorumq[ue] ignitoru[m] aëris phænomen[o]n, natura[m] & portenta duobus libris philosphicè iuxtà ac astronomicè expediens: & de variis præteritorum sæculorum obseruatonibus, gentiumq̃ue ac regnorum historijs accuratè demonstrans & confirmans: Habes insuper Catalogum visorum cometarum & ignitorum aëris spectrorum, vsque ad annum 1540 cum portentis & euentis quæ secuta sunt.*

Parisiis: Excudebat Christianus Wechelus, ... , Anno salutis humanæ, M.D.XLIX., 1549. 265, [3] p.; 20 cm. Signatures: A-2I^{4} 2K^{6}. Text in italic script, headings and marginal notes in roman script. BM *STC French,* 1470-1600, p. 314. Grässe, v. 4, p. 553. BN, v. 116, columns 111-112. Lalande, *Bib. astronomique,* p. 68. Errata: p. (267).

1450. MIZAULD, ANTOINE, 1510-1578. *Ephemeridum aeris perpetuarum, seu popularis et rusticæ tempestatum astrologiæ: ubique terrarum & veræ & certæ, libelli seu classes quinque ... / autore Antonio Mizaldo Monluciano.*

Ambergæ: Typis Schönfeldianis, 1604. [8], 267 p.; 13 cm. Errors in pagination: p. 162 misnumbered as 164, p. 192 as 190. Includes bibliographical references and index.

Provenance: Sion College Library (inkstamp).

1451. MOHL, HUGO VON, 1805-1872. *Principles of the anatomy and physiology of the vegetable cell. By Hugo von Mohl ... Translated ... by Arthur Henfrey. With an illustrative plate and numerous woodcuts.*

London: J. Van Voorst, 1852. viii, 158, [2] p. illus. 23 cm. Translation of *Grundzüge der Anatomie und Physiologie der vegetabilischen Zelle.* Includes bibliographical references. Advertisements: [2] final p. Pritzel, 6351.

Provenance: W. H. Smith & Son Library (embossed stamp).

1452. MOHL, HUGO VON, 1805-1872. *Vermischte Schriften botanischen Inhalts.*

Tübingen: L. F. Fues, 1845. viii, 442 p. 13 plates (part col.) 28 cm. Contains 31 of the author's works, reprinted from various sources. Includes bibliographical references.

Provenance: Dr. Schilling (inscription).

1453. MOHOROVICIC, ANDRO. *Potres od 8. X. 1909 / napisao A. Mohorovicic = Das Beben vom 8. X. 1909 / von A. Mohorovicic.*

Zagreb: Naklada Kr. Hrv.-Slav.-Dalm. Zem. Vlade, Odjela za Bogostovje i Nastavu, 1910. 63 p., [2] folded leaves of plates: ill.; 23 cm. *Godisnje Izvjesce;* vg. 9 dio 4, polovina 1. Text in romanized Serbo-Croatian and German.

1454. [Monographs astronomical].

[1860-1878].1 v. (various pagings): ill.; 30 cm. Binder's title. Collection of 12 journal articles on practical and geodetic astronomy. Includes bibliographical references. Appendix no. 9: determination of time by means of the transit instrument, prepared for the *Coast Survey manual* by C. A. Schott ... Appendix no. 10: determination of the astronomical latitude of a station by means of the zenith telescope, prepared ... by C. A. Schott ... Appendix no. 11: determination of the astronomical azimuth of a direction, prepared ... by C. A. Schott ... Appendix no. 36: formulæ, tables, and example for the geodetic computation of latitudes, longitudes, and azimuths of trigonometrical points, as used in the *United States*

Coast Survey. Longitude by lunar culminations, by Lieut. James Mercur ... Memoranda relating to the field-work of the secondary triangulation, prepared by Richard D. Cutts ... Report on the results from the observations made at the magnetical observatory on Capitol Hill ...between 1867 and 1669 [sic], by Charles A. Schott ... Notes on measurements of terrestrial magnetism, prepared ... by Charles A. Schott... Instructions for observing the transit of Venus, December 8-9, 1874, prepared by the commission authorized by Congress ... Instructions for observing the transit of Mercury, 1878, May 5-6. Report on the difference of longitude between Washington and Havana, by William Harkness and Cecilio Pujazon. Report on the difference of longitude between Washington and Detroit, Michigan, Carlin, Nevada, and Austin, Nevada, by J. R. Eastman....

1455. Montucla, Jean Étienne, 1725-1799. *Histoire des mathématiques dans laquelle on rend compte de leurs progrès depuis leur origine jusqu'à nos jours; où l'on expose le tableau et le développement des principales découvertes dans toutes les parties des mathématiques, les contestations qui se sont élevées entre les mathématiciens, et les principaux traits de la vie des plus célèbres. Nouv. éd., considérablement augm., et prolongée jusque vers l'époque actuelle. Par J. F. [!] Montucla....*

Paris: H. Agasse, ([1799]-1802). 4 v. front. (port.) diagrs. on fold. plates. 27 x 21 cm. Vol. 3-4 "achevé et publié par Jérôme de Lalande." First edition in 2 v., published 1758. Portrait of Lalande, v. 4, engraved by A. de St. Aubin. Plates signed: G. Benard. List of the most important Arabian mathematicians with titles of their works: v. 1, p. 403-412. Works on Chinese astronomy arranged chronologically, with titles translated in Latin: v. 1, p. 479-480. "Sur la vie et les ouvrages de Montucla": v. 4, p. [662]-672.

1456. Moore, Jonas, Sir, 1617-1679. *A new systeme of the mathematicks ... composed by Sir Jonas Moore ... and designed for the use of the Royal Foundation of the Mathematical School in Christ-Hospital.*

London: Printed by A. Godbid and J. Playford, for Robert Scott, 1681. 2 v. illus., fold. maps, plates (part fold.), volvelle 24 cm. "By His Majesty's special command." Conceived and in part written by Moore; sections on algebra, Euclid, and navigation written by P. Perkins; astronomical tables and "The doctrine of the sphere" by J. Flamsteed; "A new geography" in part by E. Halley; the whole edited posthumously by W. Hanway and J. Potenger. Some parts have special title pages, dated 1680. Added illustrated t. p., engr., in v. 1. Signed: N Yeates sculp. Errata: follows index. Wing M2579, P1542, F1137.

Provenance: Zach. Webb (inscription). Bound in 1 v., "Arithmetick in species, or algebra" bound before "The doctrine of the sphere."

1457. Moore, Patrick. *Suns, myths, and men.*

London: F. Muller, 1954. 192 p. illus. 21 cm.

1458. Moore, Patrick Alfred. *Naked-eye astronomy. Line diagrams by Warwick MacCallum.*

New York: Norton, [1966, c1965]. 253 p. illus. 22 cm. Amateur Astronomer's Library.

1459. Morden, Robert, d. 1703. *An introduction to astronomy, geography, navigation, and other mathematical sciences: made easie by the description and uses of the cœlestial and terrestrial globes. In seven parts ... / by Robert Morden.*

London: Printed for R. Morden ... R. Smith ..., 1702. [24], 184, 87 p., [8] leaves of plates (3 folded): ill., maps; 19 cm. Houzeau & Lancaster. *Astronomie* (1964 ed.), 8823.

Provenance: John Pinney (armorial bookplate)

1460. Moreux, Théophile, 1867-1954. *Astronomy to-day / by the Abbé Th. Moreux ...; translated by C. F. Russell ...*

London: Methuen & Co., 1926. xiv, 256, 8 p. [1] leaf of plates: ill.; 20 cm. Translation of *Où en est l'astronomie?* Advertisements: 8 p. at end. Includes bibliographical references and index.

Provenance: William Andrews Clark, Jr. (giltbook label)

1461. Moreux, Théophile, 1867-1954. *Pour observer le ciel; astronomie pratique, par l'Abbé Th. Moreux ... avec figures dans le texte.*

Paris: G. Doin & Cie, 1938. 2 p. l., [7]-204 p. illus., diagrs. 18 cm. Bibliothèque d'Education Scientific. Collection des Pour Comprendre. "Renseignements d'ordre pratique pour les observateurs": p. [190].

Advertisements on verso of half-title, t. p., and [2] p. at end.

1462. MORGAGNI, GIAMBATTISTA, 1682-1771. *Jo. Baptistæ Morgagni P. P. P. P. De sedibus, et causis morborum per anatomen indagatis libri quinque: Dissectiones, et animadversiones, nunc primum editas, complectuntur propemodum innumeras, medicis, chirurgis, anatomicis profuturas. Multiplex præfixus est index rerum, & nominum accuratissimus. Tomus primus [-secundus].*

Venetiis: Ex typographia Remondiniana, MDCCLXI, [1761]. 2 v.: port.; 40 cm. Bound in 1 volume. Vol. 1: xcvi, 298, [2] p. (last leaf blank); v. 2:452 p. Title page of vol. 1 in red and black, with engraved vignette. Portrait by Jean Renard. Includes bibliographical references and indexes. Osler, W. *Bib. Osleriana,* 1178. Waller 6672. Garrison, F. H. *Medical bibl.* 2151.

Provenance: E. B. Krumbhaar (inscription); Herbert McLean Evans (bookplate).

1463. MORGAGNI, GIAMBATTISTA, 1682-1771. *The seats and causes of diseases investigated by anatomy; in five books, containing a great variety of dissections, with remarks. To which are added ... copious indexes ... Translated from the Latin ... by Benjamin Alexander....*

London: A. Millar; and T. Cadell, his successor [etc.], 1769. 3 v.; 27 cm. Translation of *De sedibus et causis morborum.* Includes bibliographical references and indexes. Contents. – v. 1. Book I. Of disorders of the head (Letters 1-14) Book II. Of disorders of the thorax (Letters 15-27) – v. 2. Book III. Of disorders of the belly (Letters 28-48) – v. 3. Book IV. Of chirurgical and universal disorders (Letters 49-59) Book V. Of such things as may be added to the former books (Letters 60-70).

1464. MORGAN, SYLVANUS, 1620-1693. *Horologiographia optica. Dialling universall and particular: speculative and practicall ... Illustrated by diverse opticall conceits, taken out of Augilonius, Kercherius, Clavius, and others. Lastly, Topothesia, or, A feigned description of the court of art ... Together with many usefull instruments and dials in brasse, made by Walter Hayes... Written by Silvanus Morgan.*

London: Printed by R. & W. Leybourn for A. Kemb and R. Boydell, 1652. 8 p.l., 144 p. illus., tables. 18 cm. Added t.-p.,engraved. Errata: p. [15]. Wing (2nd ed.) M2741.

Provenance: George Gibson Hartt (inscription).

1465. MORGAN, THOMAS HUNT, 1866-1945. *The physical basis of heredity, by Thomas Hunt Morgan ... 117 illustrations.*

Philadelphia and London: J. B. Lippincott Company, [c1919]. 305 p. illus., plates, diagrs. 21 cm. Monographs on experimental biology. Includes index. "Literature": p. 274-300.

1466. MORO, ANTONIO LAZZARO. *De' crostacei e degli altri marini corpi che si truovano su' monti; libri due di Anton Lazzaro Moro.*

Venezia: S. Monti, 1740. 7 p.l., 452 p., 8 pl. 26 cm. Title vignette. Includes bibliographical references and index.

Provenance: Herbert McLean Evans (bookplate).

1467. MORSE, EDWARD SYLVESTER, 1838-1925. *Mars and its mystery / by Edward S. Morse....*

Boston: Little, Brown, 1913. viii, 192 p., [13] leaves of plates: ill., ports.; 22 cm. Includes index.

Provenance: signed presentation copy from the author to Mr. John M. Clarke; Charles Atwood Kofoid (bookplate).

1468. MOSELEY, H. G. J. (HENRY GWYN JEFFREYS), 1887-1915. *The high-frequency spectra of the elements. Part [I]-II / by H. G. J. Moseley.*

[London: Taylor and Francis: Sold By Simpkin, Marshall, Hamilton, Kent and Co., 1913-1914]. p. 1024-1034, 703-713, leaf of plate XXIII: ill.; 23 cm. *London, Edinburgh and Dublin Philosophical Magazine and Journal of Science,* Sixth series, v. 26, no. 156 & v. 27, no. 160. Includes bibliographical references.

1469. MOULTON, FOREST RAY, 1872-1952. *Astronomy, by Forest Ray Moulton....*

New York: The Macmillan Company, 1931. xxiii, 549 p., front., illus., double plates, diagrs. 23 cm. Bibliography at end of most of the chapters.

Provenance: [W.?] A. Clark, Jr. (signature); C. C. Parker (signature).

1470. MOULTON, FOREST RAY, 1872-1952. *An introduction to astronomy, by Forest Ray Moulton....*

New York: The Macmillan Company; Macmillan & Co., Ltd., 1906.

With [4] p. of advertisements at end.

1471. MOUNT WILSON SOLAR OBSERVATORY. *Report of director of the Solar Observatory, Mount Wilson, California / by George E. Hale.*

Washington D. C.: Judd & Detweiler, 1906. p. 56-77, 2 leaves of plates: ill.; 25 cm. "Extracted from the *Fourth Year Book* of the Carnegie Institution of Washington." Includes bibliographical references.

1472. MOXON, JOSEPH, 1627-1700. *A tutor to astronomy and geography. Or an easie and speedy way to know the use of both the globes, celestial and terrestrial ... With an appendix shewing the use of the Ptolomaick sphere. The 3d ed. cor. and enl.*

London: Printed by T. Roycroft, for J. Moxon, 1674. 271 p. illus. 21 cm. Added t.-p. engraved: Ductor ad astronomiam & geographiam, vel usus globi ... "The ancient stories of the several stars and constellations ...Collected from Dr. Hood": p. 208-232.

Additional engraved t. p. missing. Ms. notes.

1473. MOYE, MARCEL, 1873-1939. *L'astronomie: observations, théorie et vulgarisation générale / par Marcel Moye: avec 43 figures dan le texte et 4 planches hors texte.*

Paris: O. Doin et Fils, 1913. viii, 395, xii p., [4] leaves of plates: ill.; 19 cm. Encyclopedie scientifique. Bibliothèque d'astronomie et de physique cæleste. Includes bibliographies and index.

Imperfect: 4 plates wanting.

1474. MÜLLER, FRITZ, 1822-1897. *Für Darwin. Von Fritz Müller.*

Leipzig: Wilhelm Engelmann, 1864. [4], 91, [1] p. illus. 25 cm.

1475. MÜLLER, JOH., 1801-1858. *Bildungsgeschichte der Genitalien aus anatomischen Untersuchungen an Embryonen des Menschen und der Thiere, nebst einem Anhang über die chirurgische Behandlung der Hypospadia / von Dr. Johannes Müller....*

Düsseldorf: Arnz, 1830. xviii, 152 p., IV leaves of plates: ill.; 27 cm. Plates signed: Dr. Müller ad not. del. Includes bibliographical references.

Provenance: C. Toldt (embossing); Charles Atwood Kofoid (bookplate); Herbert McLean Evans (bookplate).

1476. MÜLLER, JOH., 1801-1858. *Über den Bau und die Lebenserscheinungen des Branchiostoma lubricum Costa, Amphioxus lanceolatus Yarrel: gelesen in der Königlichen Akademie der Wissenschaften zu Berlin am 6. December 1841 / von J. Müller.*

Berlin: Gedruckt in der Druckerei der Königlichen Akademie der Wissenschaften, 1844. 40 p., V leaves of plates: ill.; 35 cm. Plates signed: Joh. Müller, and C. Haas. Includes bibliographical references.

Provenance: Charles Singer (signature).

1477. MÜLLER, JOH., 1801-1858. *Ueber die phantastischen Gesichtserscheinungen: Eine physiologische Untersuchung mit einer physiologischen Urkunde des Aristoteles über den Traum, den Philosophen und Aerzten gewidmet ... / von Dr. Johannes Müller....*

Coblenz: Bei Jacob Hölscher, 1826. x, 117, [1] p.; 23 cm. German translation of Aristotle's *De insomniis*: p. [107]-117. Garrison, F. H. *Medical bibl.* 1456. Horblit, H. D. *Grolier 100 science books*, 76. Waller. *Bibl. Walleriana* 6733.

Provenance: Charles Singer (signature).

1478. MÜLLER, JOH., 1801-1858. *Zur vergleichenden Physiologie des Gesichtssinnes des Menschen und der Thiere; nebst einem Versuch über die Bewegungen der Augen und über den menschlichen Blick / von Dr. Johannes Müller....*

Leipzig: Bei C. Cnobloch, 1826. xxxii, 462, [2] p., VIII, [1] folded leaves of plates: ill. (some col.); 21 cm. Includes bibliographical references. Variously engraved by J. F. Schröter, W. Engels, Schubert; some ill .drawn by the author.

1479. MÜLLER, JOHANN HEINRICH JACOB, 1809-1875. *Atlas zu Joh. Müller's Lehrbuch der kosmischen Physik. Fünfte umgearbeitete und vermehrte Auflage / von Dr. C. F. W. Peters....*

Braunschweig: Druck und Verlag von Friedrich Vieweg und Sohn, 1894. [6] p., [1] folded leaf, LX leaves of plates (19 folded): ill., maps (some col.); 26 cm. "Enthaltend 60 zum Theil in Farbendruck ausgeführte Tafeln."

Provenance: P. de Riencourt (booklabel and signature).

1480. MÜLLER, ROLF, 1898- . *Astronomisches ABC für Jedermann.*
Leipzig: J. A. Barth, 1938. 158 p. illus., 6 plates. 21 cm.
[2] p. of advertisements at end. Provenance: Charles Atwood Kofoid (bookplate).

1481. MURCHISON, RODERICK IMPEY, SIR, 1792-1871. *Outline of the geology of the neighbourhood of Cheltenham. By Roderick Impey Murchison....*
Cheltenham: H. Davies; [etc., etc.], 1834. 40 p. illus., fold. col. pl. 21 cm. Errata on last p. Includes bibliographical references.
Disbound.

1482. MURCHISON, RODERICK IMPEY, SIR, 1792-1871. *The Silurian system, founded on geological researches in the counties of Salop, Hereford, Radnor, Montgomery, Caermarthen, Brecon, Pembroke, Monmouth, Gloucester, Worcester, and Stafford; with descriptions of the coal-fields and overlying formations. By Roderick Impey Murchison....*
London: John Murray, 1839. 2 v. illus., plates (partly fold., partly col.) maps. 31 x 27 cm. And portfolio of 2 fold. maps. 32 x 25 cm. Paged continuously. "Printed by Richard and John E. Taylor" – T. p. verso. Illustrated by G. Scharf, T. Webster and others; lithography by Day and Haghe. List of subscribers: v. 1, p. [vii]-xii. Includes index.
Larger map in 2 parts, mounted on cloth and folded. Provenance: D.C.M. (armorial bookplate); Institute of Geographical Exploration, Harvard University (donor bookplate).

1483. MURPHY, EDGAR GARDNER, 1869-1913. *A beginner's guide to the stars, based on A beginner's star book, by Kelvin McKready (Edgar Gardner Murphy) arranged by Maud King Murphy....*
London, New York: G. P. Putnam's Sons, 1924. v, 86 p. incl. illus., plates, tables. 19 cm.
With [4] p. advertisements at end.

1484. MURPHY, EDGAR GARDNER, 1869-1913. *A beginner's star-book; an easy guide to the stars and to the astronomical uses of the opera-glass, the field-glass and the telescope, by Kelvin McKready [pseud.]; with charts of the moon, tables of the planets, and star maps on a new plan, including seventy illustrations.*
New York and London: G. P. Putnam's Sons, 1912. vii, 148 p. front., illus., (incl. maps) 2 double pl. 27 cm. "A list of books": p. 144-146.

1485. MURPHY, EDGAR GARDNER, 1869-1913. *A beginner's star-book; an easy guide to the stars and to the astronomical uses of the opera-glass, the field-glass, and the telescope, by Kelvin McKready (Edgar Gardner Murphy) with charts of the moon, tables of the planets, and star maps on a new plan. 2d ed. rev., including seventy illustrations.*
London, New York: G. P. Putnam's Sons, 1923. vii, 150 p. front., illus., 2 double pl. 27 cm. "Third impression, revised edition, 1923." "A list of books": p. 146-148.
Provenance: Edward A. Meyer

1486. MURPHY, EDGAR GARDNER, 1869-1913. *A beginner's star-book: an easy guide to the stars and to the astronomical uses of the opera-glass, the field-glass and the telescope / by Kelvin McKready (Edgar Gardner Murphy); with charts of the moon, tables of the planets, and star maps on a new plan. 2nd ed., rev.*
New York: G. P. Putnam's Sons, 1927. vii, 150 p., [3] leaves of plates (2 folded): ill., maps; 27 cm. "Fourth impression, October, 1927" – t. p. verso. Includes bibliographical references and indexes.

1487. NACCARI, GIUSEPPE, 1856- . *Atlante astronomico, opera fondata dal prof. Giuseppe Naccari. 3. ed. rinnovata ed ampliata dal dott. Attilio Colacevich ... con prefazione del prof. Giorgio Abetti....*
Milano: F. Vallardi, 1935. xvi, 136 p. LXXI pl. (part fold., part col.) 33 cm. Il sole. – La luna. – La terra. – Il sistema solare. – Le comete e le meteore cosmiche. – L'universo stellare. – Strumenti e osservatori astronomici.

1488. NAPIER, JOHN, 1550-1617. *A description of the admirable table of logarithmes: with a declaration of the most plentifull, easie, and speedy vse thereof in both kinds of trigonometry*

... / inuented and published in Latine by ... Iohn Nepair, Baron of Marchiston, and translated into English by ... Edward Wright; with an addition of the instrumentall table ... described in the end of the booke by Henrie Brigs....

London: Printed for Simon Waterson, 1618. [2], 16, [22], 89, [87], 8, p., [1] folded leaf of plates: ill.; 15 cm. Pages [1-2] (3rd group), and p. [87] (5th group) are blank. Errata: on last p. Translation of *Mirifici logarithmorum canonis descriptio* first published in 1616. *Napier tercentenary*, 13. *STC* 18352.

A6a: "and maintaine" scored out. T. p. torn with initial article "A" on title missing. Provenance: Standfast Library (bookplate).

1489. NAPIER, JOHN, 1550-1617. *Logarithmorum canonis descriptio, seu, Arithmeticarum supputationum mirabilis abbreuiatio: Eiusque vsus in vtraque trigonometria vt etiam in omni logistica mathematica, amplissimi, facillimi & expeditissimi explicatio / authore ac inuentore Ioanne Nepero....*

Lugdini: Apud Barth. Vincentium, 1620. 2 v. in 1 ([8], 56, [92] p.): ill.; 21 cm. Originally published in 1614 with the title: *Mirifici logarithmorum canonis descriptio*. Pt. 2 has separate t. p.: Sequitur tabula canonis logarithmorum seu arithmeticarum supputationum. *Napier tercentenary*, 12.

With: *Mirifici logarithmorum canonis constructio*/ John Napier. Lugduni: Apud Bartholomæum Vincentium ..., 1620. Bound in ms. fragments.

1490. NAPIER, JOHN, 1550-1617. *Mirifici logarithmorum canonis constructio: et eorum ad naturales ipsorum numeros habitudines; vnà cum appendice ... quibus accessere propositiones ad triangula sphærica faciliore calculo resoluenda: vna cum annotationibus aliquot doctissimi D. Henrici Briggii ... / authore & inuentore Ioanne Nepero, Barone Merchistonii, &c. Scoto.*

Lugdini: Excudebat Andreas Hart, 1619. 67 p.: ill.; 19 cm. With the author's: *Mirifici logarithmorum canonis descriptio*. Edinburgi: Excudebat Andreas Hart, 1619. Horblit, H. D. *Grolier 100 science books*, 77b.

Binder: James Macdonald Co. (stamp on slipcase). Provenance: Lord Napier (armorial bookplate); Robert Honeyman IV (bookplate); Mr. Laing (inscription).

1491. NAPIER, JOHN, 1550-1617. *Mirifici logarithmorum canonis constructio: et eorum ad naturales ipsorum numeros habitudines; vna cum appendice, de alia eâque præstantiore logarithmorum specie condenda: quibus accessere propositiones ad triangula sphærica faciliore calculo resoluenda: vnà cum annotationibus aliquot doctissimi D. Henrici Briggii in eas, & memoratam appendicem / authore & inuentore Ioanne Nepero....*

Edinburgi: Apud Bartholomæum Vincentium ..., 1620. 62, [1] p.: tables, diagrs.; 21 cm.

With: *Logarithmorum canonis descriptio* / John Napier. Lugduni: Apud Bartholomæum Vincentium ..., 1620.

1492. NAPIER, JOHN, 1550-1617. *Mirifici logarithmorum canonis descriptio: ejusque usus, in utraque trigonometria; ut etiam in omni logistica mathematica, amplissimi, facillimi, & expeditissimi explicatio / Authore ac inventore, Ioanne Nepero....*

Edinburgi: Ex officinâ Andreæ Hart ..., M.DC.XIV., [1614]. [8], 57, [90] p.: ill.; 20 cm. First edition, first issue, with verso of t. p. blank. Without "Admonitio" at end. Title within ornamental border; some decorated initials. Pages 14 and 15 incorrectly numbered 22 and 23. Signatures: A-H^4 I^1, a-l^4 m^1. Errata: p. 57. STC 18349. Horblit, H. D. *Grolier 100 science books*, 77a. Dibner Lib. *Science*, 106.

Provenance: William Stirling (bookplate). Ms. note in Dutch attached.

1493. NAPIER, JOHN, 1550-1617. *Mirifici logarithmorum canonis descriptio: ejusque usus, in utraque trigonometria ... accesserunt opera posthuma ... / autore ac inventore Ioanne Nepero, Barone Merchistonii, &c. Scoto.*

Edinburgi: Excudebat Andreas Hart, 1619. [8], 57, [91] p.: ill.; 19 cm. Errors in pagination: p. 14-15 misnumbered as 22-23. Admonitio on m1 verso. Originally published in 1614. With the author's *Mirifici logarithmorum canonis constructio*. Edinburgi: Excudebat Andreas Hart, 1619. *STC* 18350. *Napier tercentenary*, 10.

Binder: James Macdonald Co. (stamp on slipcase). Provenance: Lord Napier (armorial bookplate); Robert Honeyman IV (bookplate); Mr. Laing (inscription). Ms. notes. Some p. shaved.

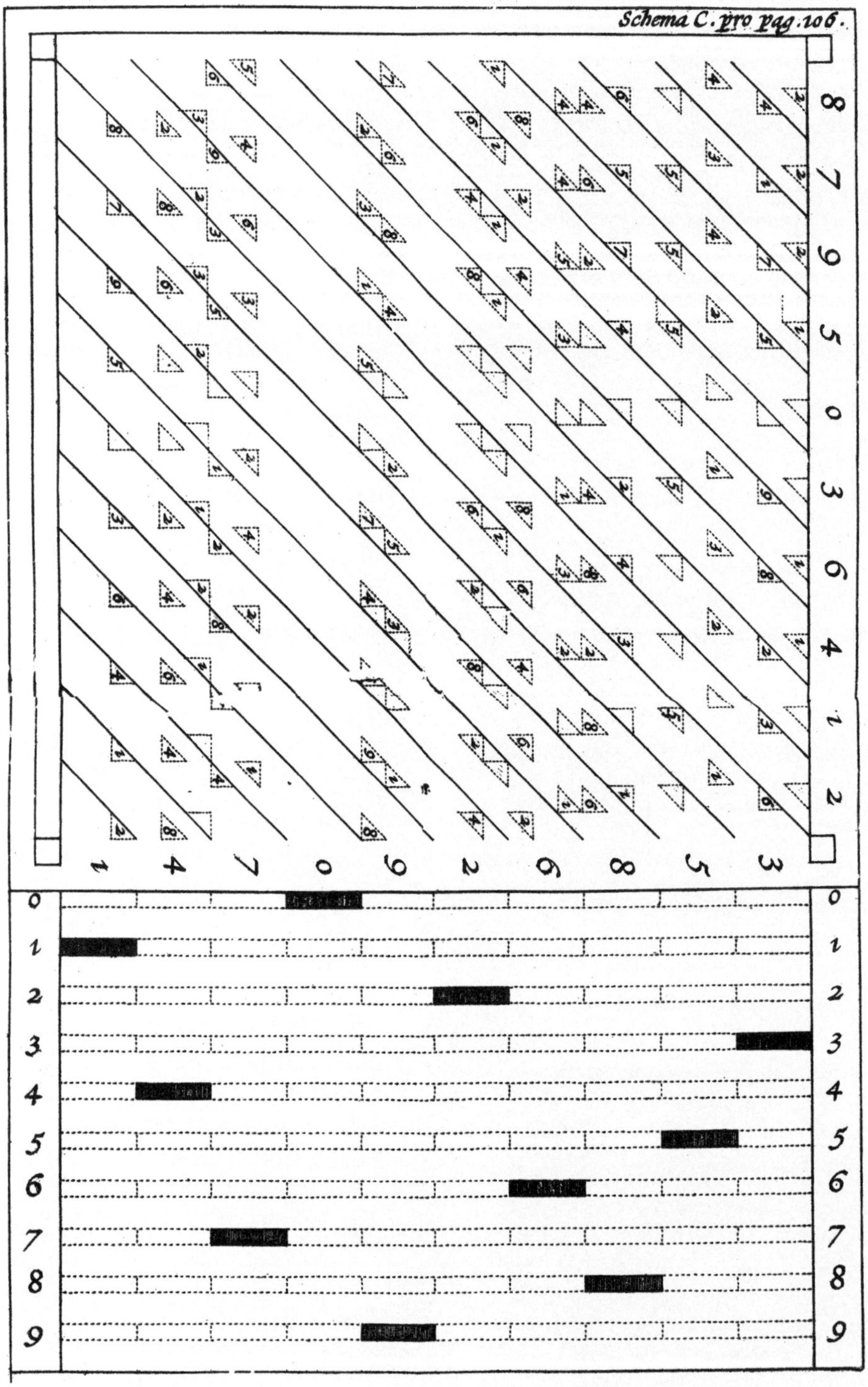

Napier, *Rabdologiæ*, 1617

1494. Napier, John, 1550-1617. *Rabdologiæ, seu, Numerationis per virgulas libri duo: cum appendice de expeditissimo multiplicationis promptuario; Quibus accessit & arithmeticæ localis liber vnus / authore & inventore Ioanne Nepero, Barone Merchistonii, &c. Scoto.*
Edinburgi: Excudebat Andreas Hart, 1617. 12, 154 p., [4] folded leaves of plates: ill.; 15 cm. Signatures: [Paragraph mark]^{6}, A-F^{12}, G^{5}. *STC* 18357. *Napier tercentenary*, 16.
Provenance: Patrick Hume, Earl of Marchmont, etc. (armorial bookplate).

1495. *Narrative of the surveying voyages of His Majesty's ships* Adventure *and* Beagle: *between the years 1826 and 1836, describing their examination of the southern shores of South America, and the* Beagle's *circumnavigation of the globe....*
London: Henry Colburn ... , 1839. 4 v.: ill., maps; 25 cm. Variously illustrated by: P. P. King, T. Landseer, C. Martens, J.W. Cook, A. Earle, S. Bull, T. Hair, T. A. Prior, R. N. Hammond, R. FitzRoy, J. C. Wickham. In each v., 2 of the plates are folded and placed in front pockets. Vols. 1-3 have indexes. v. 1. Proceedings of the first expedition, 1826-1830, under the command of Captain P. Parker King – v. 2. Proceedings of the second expedition, 1831-1836, under the command of Captain Fitz-Roy – v. 3. Journal and remarks, 1832-1836. By Charles Darwin – v. 4. Appendix to the second volume.
Provenance: A. Park (signature), Herbert McLean Evans (bookplate). Advertisements bound in with Appendix.

1496. Narrien, John, 1782-1860. *An historical account of the origin and progress of astronomy. With plates illustrating, chiefly, the ancient systems....*
London: Baldwin and Cradock, 1833. xiv p., 1 l., 520 p. diagrs. on 5 fold.plates. 23 cm. Illustrated by J. W. Lowry.
Binder: Verrico. Provenance: Captain Straith (author's presentation inscription); Radcliffe Observatory, Oxford (inkstamp).

1497. Nasmyth, James, 1808-1890. *The moon considered as a planet, a world, and a satellite / by James Nasmyth and James Carpenter ... ; with twenty-four illustrative plates of lunar objects, phenomena, and scenery, numerous woodcuts, &c.*
London: J. Murray, 1874. xvi, 189 p., [1], XXIII leaves of plates: ill. (1 col.); 29 cm. Illustrated by Nasmyth.
Advertisements: [2] p. at end, dated 1873. Provenance: presentation inscription from Mary Wood to Rev. Th. Murray Gorman.

1498. Nasmyth, James, 1808-1890. *The moon considered as a planet, a world, and a satellite / by James Nasmyth and James Carpenter ... ; with twenty-six illustrative plates of lunar objects phenomena and scenery, numerous diagrams, etc. 4th ed.*
New York: : James Pott & Co., 1903. xviii, 315 p., [53] leaves of plates (1 folded): ill. (some col.), map; 21 cm.
Provenance: Dr. Mars Baumgardt (signature).

1499. National Academy of Sciences (U.S.). *Proceedings of the National Academy of Sciences of the United States of America.*
[Washington, D.C. etc.]: National Academy of Sciences [etc.] v. ill. 26 cm. Semimonthly 1982-. Former frequency: Monthly v. 1- Jan. 1915-. This series of *Proceedings* is independent of the earlier one of the same title, published in 3 parts, 1877-95. Vols. for 1980-1984 issued in two parts: Biological sciences, and, Physical sciences. Vols. 1- issued by the academy under a variant name: National Academy of Sciences of the United States of America. Indexes: Vols. 1-10, 1915-24, in v. 13 (Includes list of academy publications, 1863-1926, and list of publications of the National Research Council, 1916-25); Author index: Vols. 1-50, 1914-63. 1 v.
Library has: 45, 1959. Vol. 45: Provenance: HME [i.e. Herbert McLean Evans] (signature).

1500. *Nature a poem: being an attempt towards a vindication of providence, in the seemingly most exceptionable things of the natural world (1748).*
London: Printed for M. Cooper ... and sold by J. Fletcher ... , 1748. v, [6]-22 p.; 26 cm.
With: *Experiments and observations on electricity*, by Mr. Benjamin Franklin. London: printed and sold by E. Cave ... , 1751-1753. Provenance: L'Ab. Boyer (bookplate); Domus Massiliensis (bookplate).

1501. *Nature (London, England).*
[London, etc., Macmillan Journals ltd.] v. ill. (part col.) ports. 26-28 cm. v. 1- Nov. 4, 1869-. Subtitle varies. Supplements accompany many numbers. Founded and for many years edited by Sir J. N. Lockyer. Vol. 229-246, Jan. 1971-Dec. 1973, issued in three parts. The two new parts, *Nature: new biology,*

and *Nature: physical sciences,* continued the volume numbering of *Nature* in addition to carrying their own issue numbering. With vol. 246, Dec. 1973, *Nature: new biology,* and *Nature: physical sciences,* ceased publication and were absorbed by *Nature.*

Library has: 171, 1953. Vol. 171: Provenance: Twyford Laboratories Ltd. (inkstamp).

1502. NATURFORSCHENDER VEREIN IN BRÜNN. *Verhandlungen des naturforschenden Vereines in Brünn.*

Brünn, Czechoslovakia : Verlage des Vereines, v. : ill.; 25 cm. Description based on: Bd. 4; 1866. Horblit, H. D. *Grolier 100 science books,* 73a. Volumes 8, 12, 15 each in 2 parts, having special t.-p. and separate pagination. Volumes 21-24 each in two parts. The 2d parts are entitled "Flora von Mähren und österr. Schlesien ... von A. Oborny". List of members in volumes 1-13, 18, 25, 28.

Library has: 4, 1865.

1503. NEANDER, CONRAD, fl. 1584-1594. *Elementale Ebræum: viam rectam quàm breuissimè monstrans Tyronibus, perfectè legendi Ebraica ... / autore M. Conrado Neandro Bergensi.*

Lipsiæ: Excudebat Abraham Lamberg, 1588. [38] p., [1] folded leaf of plates; 17 cm. Signatures: A-B^{8}C^4 (C4 blank).

With: *Epitome astronomiæ* / per M. Michaelem Mæstlinum. Tubingæ: Excudebat Georgius Gruppenbachius, 1588.

1504. NEEDHAM, WALTER, 1631?-1691? *Disquisitio anatomica de formato foetu / authore Gualtero Needham.*

Londoni: Typis G. Godbid, prostantq[ue] venales apud Radulphum Needham..., 1667. [24], 205, [3] (blank), [15] p., 7 folded leaves of plates: ill.; 17 cm. Wing N411.

Provenance: Heinr. Jos. Tortz (inscription); Herbert McLean Evans (bookplate).

1505. NEISON, EDMUND. *The moon and the condition and configurations of its surface, by Edmund Neison....*

London: Longmans, Green and Co., 1876. xviii, 576 p. front., plates, maps (part fold.) 24 cm. Includes indexes.

Advertisements: [2] p. preceding half-title. Provenance: H. C. Leadbeater (signature).

1506. NERNST, WALTHER, 1864-1941. *Theoretische Chemie vom Standpunkte der Avogadro'schen Regel und der Thermodynamik / von Dr. Walther Nernst....*

Stuttgart: Verlag von Ferdinand Enke, 1893. XIV, 589 p.: ill.; 24 cm. Naturwissenschaftliche Lehrbücher. Includes bibliographical references and indexes.

Provenance: Herbert McLean Evans (bookplate); Ernst Mach (inkstamp).

1507. NERNST, WALTHER, 1864-1941. *Die theoretischen und experimentellen Grundlagen des neuen Wärmesatzes/ von W. Nernst.*

Halle (Saale): W. Knapp, 1918. vii, 218 p.: ill.; 25 cm. Bibliography: p. 210-215. Includes index.

1508. *Neurologisches Centralblatt.*

Berlin: J. Springer, 1882-1921. 40 v. : ill. ; 24 cm. 1. Jahrg., Nr. 1 (Jan. 1882)-40. Jahrg. (Jan. 1921). Previous publisher: Verlag von Veit. Editors: vol. 1-26, E. Mendel; vol. 26-40, K. Mendel. Absorbed by: *Zentralblatt für die gesamte Neurologie und Psychiatrie.*

Library has: 12, 1893. Vol XII: Provenance: Institut für allgemeine und experimentelle Pathologie in Wien (inkstamp).

1509. NEWCOMB, SIMON, 1835-1909. *Astronomy for everybody. A popular exposition of the wonders of the heavens.*

Garden City, New York: Garden City Publishing Co., Inc., 1902. xv, 333 p. incl. front., illus. diagrs. 21 cm. Star series.

1510. NEWCOMB, SIMON, 1835-1909. *Astronomy for everybody: a popular exposition of the wonders of the heavens / by Simon Newcomb.*

New York: McClure, Phillips & Co., 1907. xv, 333 p.: ill.; 21 cm. Science for Everybody. Includes bibliographical references.

Provenance: L. A. Thompson (signature).

1511. NEWCOMB, SIMON, 1835-1909. *Elements of astronomy, by Simon Newcomb....*

New York, Cincinnati: American Book Company, 1900. 1 p.l., 240 p. front., illus. 19 cm.

Rust, green, and gold stamped binding; "W.P.I" on verso of t. p., "Typography by J. S. Cushing & Co., Norwood, Mass," p. 240. Provenance: L. D. Jones (signature). [copy 1].

Rust, light blue and gold stamped binding; "W.P. 4"

on verso of t. p. Provenance: L. D. Jones (signature). [copy 2].

1512. NEWCOMB, SIMON, 1835-1909. *Newcomb-Engelmanns Populäre Astronomie. 4. Aufl. in Gemeinschaft mit den herren Prof. Eberhard, Prof. Ludendorff, Prof. Schwarzschild hrsg. von Prof. dr. P. Kempf ... Mit 213 Abbildungen im Text und auf 21 Tafeln.*

Leipzig: W. Engelmann, 1911. xvi, 772 p. illus., XXI pl., diagrs. 25 cm. "Biographische Skizzen": p. [679]-726.

[8] p. of advertisements at end.

1513. NEWCOMB, SIMON, 1835-1909. *Popular astronomy / by Simon Newcomb ... School edition.*

New York: Harper & Brothers, [1880?]. xviii, 571, [3], 8 p.: ill., maps, charts: 21 cm. "Five maps of the stars" are in a pocket. "Synopsis of papers on the solar parallax, 1854-1877": p. 546-549. "List of astronomical works, most of which have been consulted ... in the preparation of the present work": p. 550-556. "Glossary of technical terms": p. 557-566. "Preface to the third edition": p. [vii]. Advertisements: 8 p. at end. Includes bibliographies and index.

Imperfect: maps of the stars wanting; imprint and copyright date erased.

1514. NEWCOMB, SIMON, 1835-1909. *Popular astronomy / by Simon Newcomb. Fifth edition revised.*

New York: Harper & Brother Publishers ..., 1884. xviii, [1] - 577, [1], 12 p., [5] folded leaves of plates: ill., charts; 23 cm. Advertisements: 12 p. at end. Includes bibliographies and index.

1515. NEWCOMB, SIMON, 1835-1909. *The reminiscences of an astronomer, by Simon Newcomb.*

Boston and New York: Houghton, Mifflin and Company, 1903. x p., 1 l., 424 p., 1 l. front. (port.) 23 cm. Includes index.

Provenance: presentation inscription from Stella; Charles Atwood Kofoid (bookplate).

1516. NEWCOMB, SIMON, 1835-1909. *The stars; a study of the universe.*

New York: G. P. Putnam's Sons, 1901. 2 p.l., xi, 333 p. front., illus., diagrs. 22 cm. Science series, [9]. Frontispiece accompanied by guard sheet with descriptive letterpress. Includes index.

Advertisements: [4] p. at end.

1517. NEWCOMB, SIMON, 1835-1909. *The stars: a study of the universe / by Simon Newcomb....*

New York: G. P. Putnam's Sons, 1902. xi, 333, [5] p., [1] leaf of plates: ill.; 22 cm. Science series. Advertisements: [4] p. at end. Includes bibliographical references and index.

Provenance: Harold B. Curtis (signature).

1518. NEWELL, A. (ANDREW). *Darkness at noon, or, The great solar eclipse of the 16th of June, 1806 described and represented in every particular....*

Boston, printed – New York reprinted: [s.n.], June, 1806. iv, [5]-36 p.: ill.; 17 cm. Attributed to Andrew Newell. Cf. Halkett & Laing, v. 2, p. 8.

1519. †NEWLANDS, JOHN A. R. *On the discovery of the periodic law, and on relations among the atomic weights. By John A. R. Newlands....*

London, New York: E. & F. N. Spon, 1884. viii, 39 p. 2 fold. tab. 19 cm. Colophon: London: Printed by Wm. Clowes and Sons, Limited....

Advertisements: publisher's catalog (15, [1] p.) at end. Provenance: presentation inscription "From the author" to the British Association for the Advancement of Science.

1520. NEWTON, ISAAC, SIR, 1642-1727. *Analysis per quantitatum series, fluxiones, ac differentias: cum enumeratione linearum tertii ordinis.*

Londoni: Ex Officina Pearsoniana, M.DCC.XI. [14], 101 p. 2 fold. tab., diagrs. 24 cm. Engraved title vignette; head and tail pieces. Author's name in preface; preface signed: W. Jones. Title vignette by J. Nutting. De analysi per æquationes infinitas. – Fragmenta epistolarum. – De quadrata curvarum. – Enumeratio linearum tertii ordinis. – Methodus differentialis. Wallis & Wallis. *Newton,* 293. Horblit, H. D. *Grolier 100 science books,* 66b.

Provenance: Bibliotheca Acad. Georgiæ Augustæ (inkstamp); Ernst Mach (inkstamp).

1521. NEWTON, ISAAC, SIR, 1642-1727. *Arithmetica universalis; sive De compositione et resolutione arithmetica liber. Cui accessit*

Halleiana æquationum radices arithmetice inveniendi methodus. In usum juventutis Academicæ.

Cantabrigiæ: Typis Academicis. Impensis B. Tooke, Bibliopolæ, 1707. 4 p. l., 343 p. diagrs. 20 cm. Running title: p.18-343: Algebræ elementa. "Ad lectorem" signed: G. W. [i.e. W. Whiston]. *Babson Newton Coll.* 199. Gray, G. J. *Newton,* 277. Wallis & Wallis. *Newton,* 277.

Provenance: Herbert McLean Evans (bookplate).

1522. NEWTON, ISAAC, SIR, 1642-1727. *The chronology of ancient kingdoms amended. To which is prefix'd, a short chronicle from the first memory of things in Europe, to the conquest of Persia by Alexander the Great.*

London: Printed for J. Tonson ..., and J. Osborn and T. Longman ... 1728. xiv, [2], 376 p. 3 fold. plates. 30 cm. Large paper copy. Dedication "To the Queen" signed: John Conduit. *Babson Newton Coll.* 214.

Provenance: Robert Townley Woodman (bookplate); Caroline Charleton (inscription).

1523. NEWTON, ISAAC, SIR, 1642-1727. *The first three sections of Newton's Principia, with an appendix; and the ninth and eleventh sections. Edited by John H. Evans ... 4th ed.*

Cambridge [Eng.]: Deighton, Bell, and Co., [etc., etc.] 1855. 96 p. diagrs. 24 cm. Gray, G. J. *Newton,* 35.

Advertisments: 8 p. at end. Provenance: W. M. Richardson (signature); F. Heal (signature).

1524. NEWTON, ISAAC, SIR, 1642-1727. *The first three sections of Newton's Principia; with copious notes and illustrations, and a great variety of deductions and problems. Designed for the use of students. By the Rev. John Carr ... 2d ed., imp. and enl.*

Cambridge: Printed for Deighton and Sons, 1826. iv, [5]-183 p. diagrs. on 6 fold. pl. 22 cm.

Provenance: George Hamilton (bookplate). Gray, G. J. *Newton,* 33.

1525. NEWTON, ISAAC, SIR, 1642-1727. *Four letters from Sir Isaac Newton to Doctor Bentley. Containing some arguments in proof of a deity.*

London: Printed for R. and J. Dodsley, 1756. 2 p. l., 35 p. 21 cm. *Babson Newton Coll.* 226. Gray, G. J. *Newton,* 345.

Provenance: presentation inscription from Edward Montagu to J. Beattie.

1526. NEWTON, ISAAC, SIR, 1642-1727. *Isaaci Newtoni, eq. aur. in Academia Cantabrigiensi matheseos olim professoris Lucasiani Lectiones opticæ, annis MDCLXIX, MDCLXX & MDCLXXI. in scholis publicis habitæ: et nunc primum ex mss. in lucem editæ.*

Londini: Apud G. Innys, 1729. xii, 152, 145-291, [5] p. fold. diagrs. 23 cm. Errata: [5] p. at end. Wallis & Wallis. *Newton,* 191.

Spine title: Academ. Cantab.

1527. NEWTON, ISAAC, SIR, 1642-1727. *A letter of Mr. Isaac Newton ... containing his new theory about light and colors : sent by the author to the publisher from Cambridge, Febr. 6, 1671/72 in order to be communicated to the R. Society.*

London : Printed for John Martyn ..., 1671. p. 3075-3087 : ill. ; 23 cm. In: *Philosophical transactions /* Royal Society of London, v. 6. Caption title. Horblit, H. D. *Grolier 100 science books,* 79a. Burndy. *Science,* 144.

1528. NEWTON, ISAAC, SIR, 1642-1727. *Isaaci Newtoni opera quæ exstant omnia. Commentariis illustrabat Samuel Horsley....*

Londini: Excudebat J. Nichols, 1779-85. 5 v. plates (3 fold.) tables, 2 fold. diagr. 31 x 24 cm. v. 1. I. Arithmetica universalis. II. Tractatus de rationibus primis ultimisque. III. Analysis per æquationes numero terminorum infinitas. IV. Excerpta quædam ex epistolis ad series fluxionesque pertinentia. V. Tractatus de quadraturâ curvarum. VI. Geometria analytica sive specimina artis analyticæ. VII. Methodus differentialis. VIII. Enumeratio linearum tertii ordinis. Editoris: 1. Logistica infinitorum. 2. De geometria fluxionum sive additamentum tractatûs Newtoniani de Rationibus primis ultimisque. – v. 2. Philosophiæ naturalis principia mathematica: Principiorum libri priores duo, De motu corporum. – v. 3. I. Principiorum liber tertius, De systemate mundi. II. De mundi systemate. III. Theoria lunæ. IV. Lectiones opticæ. Editoris: De viribus centralibus quæ rationem triplicatæ distantiarum a centro contrariam inter se constanter servant. v. 4. I. Opticks. II. Letters on various subjects in natural philosophy, published from the originals in the archives of the Royal Society of London. I. Relating to reflecting telescopes. II. Relating

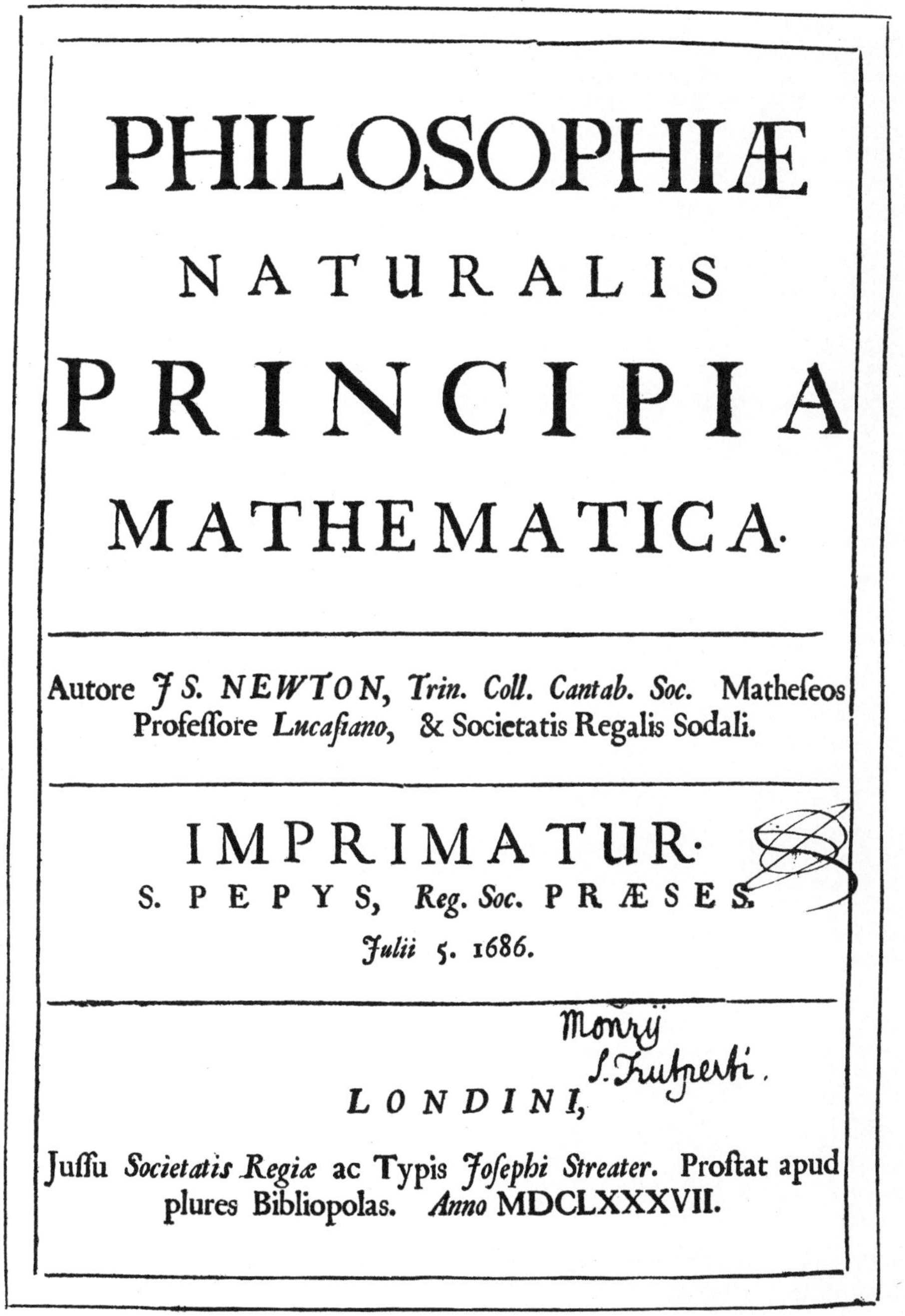

PHILOSOPHIÆ

NATURALIS

PRINCIPIA

MATHEMATICA.

Autore *J S.* NEWTON, *Trin. Coll. Cantab. Soc.* Matheseos Professore *Lucasiano*, & Societatis Regalis Sodali.

IMPRIMATUR.

S. PEPYS, *Reg. Soc.* PRÆSES.

Julii 5. 1686.

LONDINI,

Jussu *Societatis Regiæ* ac Typis *Josephi Streater*. Prostat apud plures Bibliopolas. *Anno* MDCLXXXVII.

NEWTON, *Principia*, 1687

to the theory of light and colours. III. Relating to the excitation of electricity in glass. III. Letter to Mr. Boyle, on the cause of gravitation. IIIa. De natura acidorum. IV. Tabulæ duæ, calorum altera, altera refractionum. V. De problematibus Bernoullianis. VI. Propositions for determining the motion of a body urged by two central forces. VII. Four letters to Dr. Bentley containing some arguments in proof of a deity. VIII. Commercium epistolicum. IX. Additamenta commercii epistolici ex historia fluxionum Raphsoni. – v. 5. I. The chronology of ancient kingdoms amended. II. A short chronicle from a ms. the property of the Rev. Dr. Ekins, dean of Carlisle. III. Observations upon the prophecies of Holy writ, particularly the prophecies of Daniel and the Apocalypse of St. John. IV. An historical account of two notable corruptions of Scripture. In a letter to a friend.

Provenance: Joshua Smith (armorial bookplate). Vol. 5, p. 491 not a cancel, additional leaf of p. 491 inserted at the end. *Babson Newton Coll.* 8. Gray, G. J. *Newton*, 1.

1529. Newton, Isaac, Sir, 1642-1727. *The mathematical principles of natural philosophy. By Sir Isaac Newton. Translated into English by Andrew Motte. To which are added, The laws of the moon's motion, according to gravity. By John Machin....*

London: Printed for B. Motte, 1729. 2 v. front. illus., tables (part fold.) diagrs. (part fold). 20 cm. Translation of: *Principia*. Title of v. 2 reads: The mathematical principles of natural philosophy. By Sir Isaac Newton. Translated into English. "The laws of the moon's motion according to gravity," [71 p.] with half-title, is appended to v. 2. Includes index. Frontispieces by A. Motte. Wallis & Wallis. *Newton*, 23. *Babson Newton Coll.* 20. Gray, G. J. *Newton*, 23.

1530. Newton, Isaac, Sir, 1642-1727. *Newton's Principia. The mathematical principles of natural philosophy, by Sir Isaac Newton; translated into English by Andrew Motte. To which is added Newton's System of the world; with a portrait taken from the bust in the Royal Observatory at Greenwich. 1st American ed., carefully rev. and cor., with a life of the author by N. W. Chittenden....*

New-York: D. Adee, 1848. 4, [v]-vii, [9]-581 p. front. (port.) diagrs. 24 cm. Includes index. Life of Sir Isaac Newton: p. 9-61. Wallis & Wallis. *Newton*, 26. Todd, W. B. *Principia*, EE6.

Variant 1. Cf. I. B. Cohen. "The American editions of Newton's Principia." *Harvard Lib. Bull.* 1970, v. 18, pp. 345-358.

1531. *Newton, Isaac, Sir, 1642-1727. Observations upon the prophecies of Daniel, and the Apocalypse of St. John. In two parts....*

London: Printed by J. Darby and T. Browne, and sold by J. Roberts [etc.] 1733. vi p.,1 l.,323 p. 26 x 21 cm. *Babson Newton Coll.* 224. Gray, G. J. *Newton*, 328. Wallis & Wallis. *Newton*, 328.

1532. Newton, Isaac, Sir, 1642-1727. *Optice: sive de reflexionibus, refractionibus, inflexionibus & coloribus lucis libri tres. Authore Isaaco Newton ... Latine reddidit Samuel Clarke ... Accedunt tractatus duo ejusdem authoris de speciebus & magnitudine figurarum curvilinearum, latine scripti.*

Londini: impensis S. Smith & B. Walford, 1706. 7 p. l., 348 p., 1 l., 24 p., 1 l., 43 [i.e. 47] p. 1 illus., 19 fold. diagr. 25 x 20 cm. P. numbers 21-24 (last group) repeated.

Provenance: Royal Society of Literature (bookplate). *Babson Newton Coll.* 137. Gray, G. J. *Newton*, 179.

1533. Newton, Isaac, Sir, 1642-1727. *Optice: sive de reflexionibus, refractionibus, inflexionibus et coloribus lucis, libri tres ... Latine reddidit Samuel Clarke ... Editio novissima.*

Lausannæ & Genevæ: Sumpt. M. M. Bousquet & Sociorum, 1740. 2 p. l., xxxii, 363, [1] p. 12 fold. plates, port. 25 x 19 cm. Errata: last p. Title vignette. Port. by Daudet. *Babson Newton Coll.* 141. Gray, G. J. *Newton*, 181. Wallis & Wallis. *Newton*, 182.

1534. Newton, Isaac, Sir, 1642-1727. *Opticks: or, A treatise of the reflexions, refractions, inflexions and colours of light. Also two treatises of the species and magnitude of curvilinear figures.*

London: Printed for S. Smith, and B. Walford, 1704. 2 p. 1., 144, 211 [i.e. 213] [1] p. fold. plates. 25 x 21 cm. Versos of p. 137 and 138 (2nd group) are blank and unpaged. Errata: last p. *Babson Newton Coll.* 132. Gray, G. J. *Newton*, 174. Horblit, H. D. *Grolier 100 science books*, 79b.

Provenance: Herbert McLean Evans (bookplate).

1535. Newton, Isaac, Sir, 1642-1727.
Philosophiæ naturalis principia mathematica. Autore Is. Newton ... Imprimatur. S. Pepys, Reg. Soc. præses. Julii 5. 1686.
Londini: Jussu Societatis Regiæ ac Typus Josephi Streater. Prostat apud plures Bibliopolas, Anno 1687. 4 p. l., 383, 400-510 p., 1 l. fold. pl., diagrs. 25cm. Signatures: [A]-Z^4, (H2 lettered G2), Aa-ZZ^4, ****4, Aaa-Ooo^4. The second and third books were apparently printed by different printers as indicated by the different type in the headings and the break in paging between the two books. *Babson Newton Coll.* 10. Gray, G. J. *Newton,* 6. Horblit, H. D. *Grolier 100 science books,* 78. Wallis & Wallis. *Newton,* 6.
Provenance: Herbert McLean Evans (bookplate).

1536. Newton, Isaac, Sir, 1642-1727.
Philosophiæ naturalis principia mathematica ... Editio secunda auctior et emendatior.
Cantabrigiae: 1713. 2 p. l., [24], 484, [8] p. fold. plate, diagrs. 25 cm. Title vignette. Edited by R. Cotes. "Corrigenda": p. [8] (last group). *Babson Newton Coll.* 12. Gray, G. J. *Newton,* 8.
Binding error: p. 231-2 misbound after p. 224.

1537. Newton, Isaac, Sir, 1642-1727.
Philosophiæ naturalis principia mathematica. Auctore Isaaco Newtono, equite aurato. Editio ultima, auctior et emendatior.
Amstælodami: Sumptibus Societatis, 1714. 14 p. l., 484, [7] p. fold. pl., diagrs. 25 x 21cm. Reprinted from the 2d edition, Cambridge, 1713. cf. Gray. Edited by R. Cotes. Gray, G. J. *Newton,* 11. Wallis & Wallis. *Newton,* 11.
Provenance: Louis Antoine Lacroix [?] (prize from École Centrale de l'Ardèche); Darbigny (signature). Imperfect: plate missing.

1538. Newton, Isaac, Sir, 1642-1727.
Philosophiæ naturalis principia mathematica ... Editio tertia aucta & emendata.
Londini: Apud. Guil. & Joh. Innys, Regiæ Societatis Typographos, 1726. 17 p. l., 530, [6] p. front. (port.) diagrs. 31 cm. Large quarto, thick paper issue. "The third edition ... appeared in three sizes: the ordinary ... 24 x 18.5 cm.; a large-paper edition 28.0 x 21.6 cm measured on my copy ...; and a magnificent largest-paper, printed for presentation, of page-size 32.6 x 23.4 cm." – Andrade, E. N. da C. "A Newton collection." *Endeavor,* v. 12, no. 46. Edited by Henry Pemberton. Portrait signed: "I. Vanderbank pinxit 1725, Geo. Vertue sculpsit 1726." *Babson Newton Coll.* 14. Gray, G. J. *Newton,* 10.
Advertisements: [2] p. at end. Binding variant: Privilege (verso) leaf precedes half-title; trimming results in a 28.8 cm. page size; binding size 30 cm. Provenance: Tiberio Cavallo (inscription). Imperfect: lacks portrait.

1539. Newton, Isaac, Sir, 1642-1727.
Philosophiæ naturalis principia mathematica ... Editio tertia aucta & emendata.
Londini: Apud. Guil. & Joh. Innys, 1726. 17 p.l., 530, [6] p. front. (port.), illus. 25 cm. Title in red and black. Edited by Henry Pemberton. Quarto edition. Collation: pi^5 a-c p^4 B-$3Y^4$. Portrait signed: "I. Vanderbank pinxit 1725; Geo. Vertue sculpsit 1726." *Babson Newton Coll.* 13. Gray, G. J. *Newton,* 9.
Preliminary leaves vary with respect to half-title being first leaf. No advertisements. Provenance: Stillman Drake (bookplate); Richard Prime (bookplate and shelf-mark).

1540. Newton, Isaac, Sir, 1642-1727.
Philosophiæ naturalis principia mathematica; auctore Isaaco Newtono, eq. aurato; perpetuis commentariis illustrata, communi studio p. p. Thomæ Le Seur & Francisci Jacquier, ex gallicana Minimorum familiâ, matheseos professorum. Editio altera longè accuratior & emendatior....
Coloniæ Allobrogum: sumptibus C. & A. Philibert, 1760. 3 v. diagrs. 26 x 21 cm. "Traité sur le flux et reflux de la mer. Par mr. Daniel Bernoulli": v. 3, p. 133-246. "De causa physica fluxus et refluxus maris ad d. Mac-Laurin": v. 3, p. 247-282. "Inquisitio physica in causam fluxus ac refluxus maris ad d. Euler": v. 3, p. 283-374. *Babson Newton Coll.* 31. Gray, G. J. *Newton,* 14.

1541. Newton, Isaac, Sir, 1642-1727. *Sir Isaac Newton's Mathematical principles of natural philosophy and his System of the world, translated into English by Andrew Motte in 1729. The translations revised, and supplied with an historical and explanatory appendix by Florian Cajori....*
Berkeley, Calif: University of California Press, 1934. xxxv, 680 p. incl. front. (port), facsim, diagrs. 26 cm. With reproduction of the t.-p. of the 1st edition of the *Principia,* London, 1687. "Editor's note to the present

OPTICKS:

OR, A

TREATISE

OF THE

REFLEXIONS, REFRACTIONS, INFLEXIONS and COLOURS

OF

LIGHT.

ALSO

Two TREATISES

OF THE

SPECIES and MAGNITUDE

OF

Curvilinear Figures.

LONDON,
Printed for SAM. SMITH, and BENJ. WALFORD, Printers to the Royal Society, at the *Prince's Arms* in St. *Paul's* Church-yard. MDCCIV.

NEWTON, *Opticks*, 1704

revision" signed: R. T. Crawford. *Babson Newton Coll.* 26.

Half-title: "One of 25 copies printed on 100% rag paper." Provenance: Herbert McLean Evans (bookplate); presentation slip from the University of California Press.

1542. NEWTON, ISAAC, SIR, 1642-1727. *1871. Sir Isaac Newton's Principia reprinted for Sir William Thomson ... and Hugh Blackburn....*

Glasgow: James Maclehose ... printed by Robert Maclehose, 1871. xxxvi, 538 p. diagrs. 27 cm. Includes reprint of t.-p.: *Philosophiæ naturalis principia mathematica.* Auctore Isaaco Newtono, eq. aur. Editio tertia aucta & emendata. Londini, apud G. & J. Innys, 1726. "Finding that all the editions of the *Principia* are now out of print, we have been induced to reprint Newton's last edition without note or comment, only introducing the 'Corrigenda' of the old copy and correcting typographical errors." – Editors' notice. *Babson Newton Coll.* 35. Gray, G. J. *Newton,* 15.

Provenance: W. Harvey (prize bookplate).

1543. NEWTON, ISAAC, SIR, 1642-1727. *Traité d'optique: sur les réflexions, réfractions, inflexions, et couleurs de la lumière / par M. le Chev. Newton; traduit de l'anglois par M. Coste. Sur la seconde edition, augmenté par l'auteur.*

À Amsterdam: Chez Pierre Humbert, 1720. 2 v. (XV, [1], 583, [17] p., 5 leaves of plates): ill.; 17 cm. Number of plates from Babson. Fautes à corriger: on p. 583. Catalogue des livres imprimes chez Pierre Humbert: [17] p. following text. *Babson Newton Coll.* 139. Wallis & Wallis. *Newton,* 186.

Bound in 1 v. Imperfect: plates missing.

1544. NEWTON, ISAAC, SIR, 1642-1727. *A treatise of the system of the world. By Sir Isaac Newton. Translated into English. The 2d ed., wherein are interspersed some alterations and improvements.*

London: Printed for Fayram, 1731. vi, [9], 152 p. 2 plates, diagrs. 21 cm. The Latin edition, published in 1728 with title: *De mundi systemate,* was originally intended to form Book III of Newton's *Principia.* Translation ascribed to Andrew Motte. Gray, G. J. *Newton,* 31. Wallis & Wallis. *Newton,* 31.

1545. NEWTON, WILLIAM, 1786-1861. *A Familiar introduction to the science of astronomy: illustrated by numerous diagrams: to which are added Problems on the use of the globes, and A description of the orrery and armillary sphere / by W. Newton ... Third edition, revised.*

London: Sherwood, Gilbert and Piper ...: Simpkin, Marshall and Co.: Newton and Son..., 1845. iv, [2] (2nd blank), 144 p.: ill.; 18 cm. Spine title: Newton's astronomy. Includes index. Later edition published in 1854 with title: *The use of globes: with a familiar introduction to the science of astronomy.*

Advertisements: [1] p. preceding t. p.

1546. NICHOL, J. P. (JOHN PRINGLE), 1804-1859. *Contemplations on the solar system / by J. P. Nichol ... Third edition.*

Edinburgh: John Johnstone ..., 1847. xxxvi, [4], 219, [1] p.; [1], XV leaves of plates (some folded): ill. (some col.); maps; 22 cm. Advertisements on half title verso. Errata: p. [xxxviii]. 3rd ed. of the author's *Phenomena and order of the solar system.*

Binder: Homecrafters.

1547. NICHOL, J. P. (JOHN PRINGLE), 1804-1859. *The phenomena and order of the solar system / by J. P. Nichol ... From the last Edinburgh ed.*

New-York: Published by Dayton & Newman, 1843. vi, [7], 14-165, [1] p., XXI leaves of plates (some folded): ill.; 20 cm. Advertisements: 18 p. following text.

Provenance: R. O. Parker (inscription).

1548. NICHOL, J. P. (JOHN PRINGLE), 1804-1859. *The stellar universe: views of its arrangements, motions, and evolutions. By J. P. Nichol....*

Edinburgh and London: J. Johnstone, 1848. xii p., 1 l, [15]-257 p. illus., v pl. (incl. front.) 17 cm. Appendix. The telescope: p. (231)-257.

Imperfect: lacking p. 15-16, the leaf preceding, and all plates but I and III. Provenance: J. Metcalf (signature)

1549. NICHOL, J. P. (JOHN PRINGLE), 1804-1859. *Views of the architecture of the heavens: in a series of letters to a lady / by J. P. Nichol ... Second edition.*

Edinburgh: William Tait ..., J. & D. Nichol, Montrose, Simpkin, Marshall and Company, London, and John Cumming, Dublin, 1838. xii, [2], 222 p., XXIII leaves of plates: ill.; 20 cm. Additions and corrections: p. 222. Half title: The architecture of the heavens.

1550. Nichol, J. P. (John Pringle), 1804-1859. *Views of the architecture of the heavens: in a series of letters to a lady / by J. P. Nichol. 3rd ed.*
Edinburgh: William Tait, 1839. xii, 219 p., [23] leaves of plates: ill.; 22 cm.
Provenance: Camer (signature)

1551. Nicholas, of Cusa, Cardinal, 1401-1464. *Hæc accurata recognitio trium voluminum operum / clariss. P. Nicolai Cusæ Card. ...*
[Paris]: Vaenundantur cum caeteris eius operibus in aedibus Ascensianis, 1514. 3 v.: ill.; 28 cm. Edited by Jacques Lefèvre d'Etaples. Vol. 3 is: De co[n]cordantia catholica libri tres. Colophon of v. 2 reads: Emissum est hoc librorum Cusaeopus egregium Parisiis: ex Officina Ascensiana ... 1514. Errata: last 4 p. of v. 2. Includes index. Adams C3130, C3132.
v. 3 bound with v. 1. Provenance: Robert Honeyman IV (bookplate).

1552. †Nicholson, William, 1753-1815. *An introduction to natural philosophy, illus. with copper plates. 2d ed., with improvements....*
London: Printed for J. Johnson, 1787. 2 v. 25 fold plates. 22 cm. Title vignettes engraved. Includes indexes.
Provenance: John Hamilton (signature).

1553. Nicomachus, of Gerasa. *Nikomachou Gerasinou Arithmetikes biblia dyo. = Nicomachi Gerasini Arithmeticæ libri duo. / Nunc primùm typis excusi, in lucem eduntur.*
Parisiis: In Officina Christiani Wecheli., M.D.XXXVIII, [1538]. 77 [i.e. 76] p.; 23 cm. Also cited as: *Introductio arithmetica.* Title vignette. Errors in pagination: p. 49 misnumbered as 46, 67 as 97, 68 omitted. Adams N257. Smith, D. E. *Rara arithmetica* (4th ed.), p. 596. Grässe, IV, p. 672. BM *STC French,* 1470-1600, p. 325. BN, v. 124, columns 607-608.

1554. Nieremberg, Juan Eusebio, 1595-1658. *Ioannis Eusebii Nierembergii Madritensis ex Societate Iesu ... Historia naturae, maxime peregrinae, libris XVI. distincta ... Accedunt De miris & miraculosis naturis in Europâ libri duo: item de iisdem in terrâ Hebraeis promissâ liber vnus.*
Antuerpiae: Ex officina Plantiniana Balthasaris Moreti, 1635. [8], 502, [104] p. illus. 36 cm. Tail-pieces, initials. Title in red and black. Title vignette.

1555. Nierop, Dirck Rembrantsz van, 1610-1682. *Nederduytsche astronomia, dat is: onderwijs van den loop des hemels ... : hier by gevoeght een aen-hangh, dienende tot naeder verklaeringhe over den loop des hemels. Als oock eenighe voorbeelden der son-eclipsen ... / beschreven door Dirck Rembrantsz van Nierop ... Ende nu met den tweeden druck, overghesien, verbetert ende vermeerdert/ by den zelfden autheur, als oock een gedruckten planeet-wyser.*
t'Amsterdam: By Gerrit van Goedesbergh ..., 1658. [12], 105 [i.e. 207], [1] (blank), 65 [i.e. 63], [1], 112, [3] p., [1] folded leaf of plates: ill.; 24 cm. Plate signed: gemackt door Dirck Rembrantsz van Nierop. Errata: p. [113]. Errors in pagination first sequence: p. 7 misnumbered as 9, 73 as 37, 79 as 97, 199-200 repeated, 205 misnumbered as 105; second sequence: 57-58 omitted. Verbeterde figuren ... pasted in following aen-hangh.

1556. Nightingale, Florence, 1820-1910. *Notes on nursing: what it is, and what it is not / by Florence Nightingale.*
London: Harrison ..., 1859. 79 p.; 22 cm. Various issues/states of this title exist. cf. Osler 1667 and 7737-8. This is the issue numbered 7737 in Osler identified by: "(The right of translation is reserved)" on the t. p.; blank verso; no colophon; side note on p. 69 reads: "Average rate of mortality tells us only that so many percent will die ..."; advertisements on end-papers include notices of annuals for 1860. Osler, W. *Bib. Osleriana,* 7737.

1557. Noble, William, Captain. *Hours with a three-inch telescope / by Capt. Wm. Noble....*
London and New-York: Longmans, Green and Co. ..., 1887. vi, [2], 122 p., [1] folded leaf of plates: ill., map; 20 cm. "The following pages are ... a reprint of a series of papers ... for the columns of 'Knowledge' in which they originally appeared" – p. [v].

1558. Nollet, Abbé (Jean Antoine), 1700-1770. *Essai sur l'électricité des corps / par M. l'Abbé Nollet ... Seconde édition.*
À Paris: Chez les Frères Guerin ..., 1765. xxiij, [1], 276 p., [1], 5 leaves of plates (4 folded): ill.; 17 cm.

1559. Nordmann, Charles. *The kingdom of the heavens; some star secrets, by Charles Nordmann, tr. by E. E. Fournier d'Albe.*
New York: D. Appleton and Co., 1923. 261, [1] p. 23 cm. Translation of: *Royaume des cieux un peu du secret des étoiles.*
Provenance: William Andrews Clark, Jr. (leather book label)

1560. Norie, J. W. (John William), 1772-1843. *A new and complete epitome of practical navigation: containing all necessary instruction for keeping a ship's reckoning at sea ... to which is added a new and correct set of tables ... / by J. W. Norie. Third edition.*
London: Printed for the author and for William Heathes ..., 1810. xii, 304, xxviii, 259, [1], 4 p., [1], IX leaves of plates: ill, maps; 22 cm. Plates signed: J. Norie delint.; Stephenson sc.
Provenance: John Ralph Blois (signature). Advertisements: 4 p. at the end.

1561. Norton, William A. (William Augustus), 1810-1883. *A treatise on astronomy, spherical and physical: with astronomical problems, and solar, lunar, and other astronomical tables: for the use of colleges and scientific schools / by William A. Norton ... Fifth edition, revised and enlarged.*
New York: John Wiley & Sons ..., 1881. 457, [1], 115 [1] p., [15] leaves of plates: ill.; 24 cm.

1562. Nunes, Pedro, 1502-1578. *Obras. Nova ed., rev. e anotada por una comissão de sócios da Academia das Ciências.*
Lisboa: Imprensa Nacional, 1940- . v. illus., diagrs., facsims. 33 cm. Latin and Portugese. Includes bibliographical references. v. I. Tratado da sphera & Astronomici introductorii de spæra epitome. – v. II. De crepusculis. – v. III. De Erratis Orontii Finaei. – v.VI. Libro de algebra en arithmetica y geometria.
Provenance: Galvão Mendes (signature). Vols.1 & 2 bound together; printed wrappers bound in.

1563. Ocellus, Lucanus. *Ocellus Lucanus, De la nature de l'univers; Timée de Locres, De l'âme du monde; Lettre d'Aristote à Alexandre sur le systême du monde / avec la traduction françoise & des remarques, par M. l'Abbé Batteux....*
À Paris: Chez Saillant ..., 1768. viij, 118, [4], 130, [4], 150, [1] p.; 20 cm. No collective t. p. Each part has special t. p. Greek and French on facing pages. Errata, for all 3 works: final page. Includes bibliographical references. Houzeau & Lancaster. *Astronomie.* (1964 ed.), 797, 800, 810.

1564. *Of the valuation of the renewals of church leases.*
[England?: s.n., 1787].[2], 13 p.; 22 cm. Title from half-title page. Publication date inferred from text, p. 2.
With: *The astronomy of comets,* by Blyth Hancock. Bury St. Edmunds: Printed by P. Gedge, for J. Murray ... London..., 1786.

1565. Ohm, Georg Simon, 1789-1854. [Collection of articles in *Journal für Chemie und Physik,* 1825-1826 on electric circuits and Ohm's law / by Georg Simon Ohm].
[1825-1826] 4 pieces in 2 v.: 23 cm. *Journal für Chemie und Physik;* Bd. 44, 46. Caption titles. Includes bibliographical references. (1) Leitung der Electricität (1825), Bd. 44, p. 110-118 – (2) Über Leitungsfähigkeit der Metalle für Elektricität (1825), Bd. 44, p. 245-247 – (3) (Letter concerning electrical conductors) (1825), Bd. 44, p. 370-373 – (4) Bestimmung des Gesetzes, nach welchem Metalle die Contaktelektricität leiten, nebst einem Entwurfe zu einer Theorie des Voltaischen Apparates und des Schweiggerschen Multiplicators (1826), Bd. 46, p. 137-166.

1566. Ohm, Georg Simon, 1789-1854. *Die galvanische Kette, mathematisch bearbeitet von Dr. G. S. Ohm....*
Berlin: T. H. Riemann, 1827. iv, 245, [1] p. plate. 21 cm. Verbesserungen: on p. 245. Horblit, H. D. *Grolier 100 science books,* 81.

1567. Oken, Lorenz, 1779-1851. *Die Zeugung / von Dr. Oken.*
Bamberg u. Wirzburg: Bei Joseph Anton Goebhardt, 1805. viii, 216 p.; 20 cm. Engraved t. p. signed "Vogel fec."
Provenance: Wilhelm Heyden (ink stamp); Herbert McLean Evans (bookplate).

1568. Olbers, W. (Wilhelm), 1758-1840. *Abhandlung über die leichteste und bequemste Methode die Bahn eines Cometen aus einigen Beobachtungen zu berechnen ... Mit einem Kupfer und Tafeln.*

Weimar: Industrie-Comptoirs, 1797. xxxii, 106, 80 p. diagrs. on fold. plate., tables. 20 cm.
Provenance: C. L. Gerling (signature).

1569. Olbers, W. (Wilhelm), 1758-1840. *Dr. Wilhelm Olbers' Abhandlung über die leichteste und bequemste Methode die Bahn eines Cometen zu berechnen: mit Berichtigung und Erweiterung der Tafeln im Jahre 1847 von neuem herausgegeben von J. F. Encke ... Dritte Ausgabe, vermehrt mit einem Anhange, die Fortsetzung und Ergänzung des Cometen-Verzeichnisses bis zum Jahre 1864 enthaltend / von Dr. J. G. Galle....*
Leipzig: Voigt & Günther, 1864. VIII, [III]-XXIV, 334 p., [1] leaf of plates: port.; 24 cm. Includes bibliographical references. Previously published as *Abhandlung über die leichteste und bequemste Methode die Bahn eines Cometen aus einigen Beobachtungen zu berechnen* ... Weimar: Industrie-Comptoirs, 1797.
Extensive ms. additions throughout, and ms. list of bibliographic references on preliminary and end pages; 1 page of ms. mathematical computations tipped in between p. 4 and 5. Provenance: Charles N. Haskins (bookplate)

1570. Olcott, William Tyler, 1873-1936. *The book of the stars for young people, by William Tyler Olcott....*
New York, London: G. P. Putnam's Sons, 1923. xx, 411 p. front., illus., plates, diagrs. 21 cm. Includes index.
Advertisements: [2] p. at end.

1571. Olmsted, Denison, 1791-1859. *A compendium of astronomy: adapted to the use of schools and academies. By Denison Olmsted ... Rev. by E. S. Snell....*
New York: Collins & Brother, 1868. 2 p. 1, [vii]-xi, [13]-194 p. front, illus., pl., diagr. 20 cm. At head of title: Snell's Olmsted's school astronomy.
Provenance: Jno. V. Eckenrode, Colbert College, New Windsor, Md. (prize bookplate).

1572. Olmsted, Denison, 1791-1859. *An introduction to astronomy: designed as a text book for the students of Yale College / by Denison Olmsted ... Third edition.*
New York: Collins, Keese & Co., 1843. XV, [1], 284 p.: ill., map; 24 cm. Includes bibliographical references.

1573. Olmsted, Denison, 1791-1859. *An introduction to astronomy: designed as a text-book for the use of students in college / by Denison Olmsted ... Third stereotype edition / revised by E. S. Snell....*
New York: Collins & Brother, Publishers ..., 1878. [6], 228 p., IV, [1] leaves of plates: ill.; 24 cm.
Provenance: O. E. Hotchkiss (signature).

1574. Olmsted, Denison, 1791-1859. *Letters on astronomy, addressed to a lady: in which the elements of the science are familiarly explained in connexion with its literary history. With numerous engravings. By Denison Olmsted....*
Boston: Marsh, Capen, Lyon and Webb, 1840. 419 p. front., illus., plates, diagrs. 20 cm. Includes index.
Provenance: Author's presentation copy to Prof. Silliman (inscription); Yale University Library (bookplate).

1575. O'Neill, John J. (John Joseph), 1889- . *Almighty atom; the real story of atomic energy, by John J. O'Neill.*
New York, I. Washburn, 1945. 2 p. l., [3]-94 p. ; 27 cm.

1576. *De Oorsaak van het door-wateren en het inbreken der zee-dyken: en door wat middelen dit te verbeteren is.*
Tot Utrecht: by Herman Hardenberg ... , 1702. 8 p.; 20 cm.
With: *De oorsaak van de beweeging en de beginsselen der vaste lichamen,* door D. S. J. Tot Utrecht: by Herman Hardenberg, 1703.

1577. Oppolzer, Theodor, Ritter von, 1841-1886. *Lehrbuch zur Bahnbestimmung der Kometen und Planeten, von Theodor P. Oppolzer....*
Leipzig: W. Engelmann, 1870-80. 2 v. tables, diagrs. 28 cm.
Presentation copy from the author. Bound in 1 v. Binder: R. Lechner (gilt stamped on spine).

1578. Oppolzer, Theodor, Ritter von, 1841-1886. *Lehrbuch zur Bahnbestimmung der Kometen und Planeten. Erster Band. Zweite und völlig umgearbeitete Auflage.*

Leipzig: W. Engelmann, 1882. xii, 683, [1] p. tables. 28 cm.
Binder: R. Lechner, Wien (stamp on spine).

1579. ORFILA, MATTHIEU JOSEPH BONAVENTURE, 1787-1853. *Éléments de chimie: appliquée a la médecine et aux arts / par M. Orfila. Cinquième édition, revue, corrigée et augmentée.*
Paris: Librairie de Crochard ..., 1831. 2 v.: ill.; 21 cm. Errata: in each v. following text. Includes bibliographical references and index.

1580. ORIGANUS, DAVID, 1558-1628. *Novæ motuum cœlestium ephemerides Brandenburgicæ, annorum LX, incipientes ab anno 1595, & desinentes in annum 1655: calculo duplici luminarium, Tychonico & Copernicæo, reliquorum planetarum posteriore elaboratæ, & varijs diversarum nationum calendarijs accommodatæ, cum introductione hac pleniore, in qua chronologica, astronomica & astrologica ex fundamentis ipsis tractantur, / autore Davide Origano Glacense....*
Francofurti cis Viadrum: Typis Ioannis Eichornij apud Davidem Reichardum ..., 1609. [108], 790, [1] p.,: ill.; 25 cm. Chiefly tables. Signatures: (a)-(i)6 A-3V6. The engraved t. p. has an architectural border. Zinner, E. *Geschichte und Bib. der astronomischen Lit.* (1964 ed.), 4247. Houzeau & Lancaster. *Astronomie* (1964 ed.), 14952. Lalande. *Bib. astronomique,* p. 150. "Errata": p. [69] of 1st group (leaf [f] 5 recto).

1581. ØRSTED, HANS CHRISTIAN, 1777-1851. *Experimenta circa effectum conflictus electrici in acum magneticam.*
[Hafniae]: Typis Schultzianis, 1820. 4 p.; 27 cm. No t. p. Caption title. Printer from colophon. Horblit, H. D. *Grolier 100 science books,* 3b.
Provenance: Herbert McLean Evans (bookplate on slipcase.)

1582. ØRSTED, HANS CHRISTIAN, 1777-1851. *Experiments on the effect of a current of electricty on the magnetic needle / by John Christian Oersted....*
[London: Printed by C. Baldwin ... for Baldwin, Cradock, and Joy ..., 1820]. p. 273-276; 24 cm. *Annals of Philosophy, or, Magazine of Chemistry, Mineralogy, Mechanics, Natural History, Argriculture, and the Arts;* v. 16. Caption title.

1583. ØRSTED, HANS CHRISTIAN, 1777-1851. *The soul in nature, with supplementary contributions. By Hans Christian Oersted. Tr. from the German by Leonora and Joanna B. Horner.*
London: H. G. Bohn, 1852. xiv, 465 p. incl. front. (port.) 18 cm. Bohn's scientific library; [16]. Translation of: *Geist in der Natur. The life of H. C. Oersted:* p. [vii]-xxii. Advertisements: p. 2b-[8b]; p. 1e-7e.

1584. OSBORN, FREDERICK HENRY, 1889- . *Atomic impasse, 1948; a collection of speeches.*
[Washington, U.S. Govt. Print. Off., 1948]. iv, 48 p. 23 cm. Department of State publication; 3272. International Organization and Conference series; III, 14.

1585. OSBORN, L. M. *Astronomy for the senior class in Madison University / L. M. Osborn.*
Hamilton, N.Y.: University Press Print, [1881?]. [1], 84 leaves; 23 cm. Publication date inferred from text, p.73. Recto of most leaves blank, with text on verso.
Provenance: author's signed presentation inscription to Robert Bruce; Charles Atwood Kofoid (bookplate); Ms. notations and diagrams on blank pages.

1586. OSLER, WILLIAM, SIR, 1849-1919. *An Alabama student and other biographical essays, by William Osler....*
New York: Oxford University Press American branch; [etc., etc.] 1908. 4 p.l., 334 p., 1 l. inc. facsisms. front., plates, ports. 23 cm. Printed in Great Britain. Preface – An Alabama student (John Y. Bassett, reprinted from the *Johns Hopkins Hospital Bulletin,* no. 58, Jan., 1896) – Thomas Dover, physician and buccaneer. (*Johns Hopkins Hospital Bulletin,* no. 58, Jan.,1896) – John Keats, the apothecary poet. (*Johns Hopkins Hospital Bulletin,* no. 58, Jan. 1896) – Oliver Wendell Holmes. – John Locke as a physician. (*The Lancet,* Oct. 20, 1900) – Elisha Bartlett, a Rhode Island philosopher. (*Transactions of the Rhode Island Medical Society*) – A backwood physiologist (William Beaumont) – The influence of Louis on American medicine. (*Johns Hopkins Hospital Bulletin,* nos. 77-78, August-September, 1897) – William Pepper. – Alfred Stillé. (*University of Pennsylvania Medical Bulletin,* June, 1902) – Sir Thomas Browne. (The Library, Jan., 1906) - Fracastorius. (*Proceedings of the Charaka Club,* vol. II) – Harvey and his discovery (Harveian oration delivered at the Royal College of Physicians, London, Oct. 18, 1906)
Provenance: L. Rosencrantz (signature)

1587. OSSERVATORIO ASTRONOMICO DI TORINO. *Atlante di carte celesti, contenenti le 634 stelle principali visibili alla latitudine boreale di 45o proiettate stereograficamente sull'orizzonte di due in due ore siderali coi circoli e paralleli di declinazione di 10 in 10 gradi, e catalogo delle posizioni medie di dette stelle per l'anno 1880.*

Torino: Stamperia Reale, 1871. [2] p. XII pl. (maps) tables (2 p.) 40 x 56 cm. Cover title. At head of title: Reale Accademia delle Scienze di Torino. Regio Osservatorio. Explanations of tables and plates in *Memorie della R. Accademia*, ser. 2, vol. XXVI. Plates signed: Alessandro Dorna, direttore dell'Osservatorio.

Lacks cover; plates folded and bound to 37 x 24 cm. Provenance: Marchese Giuseppe de Luca (donor's label).

1588. OVENDEN, MICHAEL W. (MICHAEL WILLIAM). *Looking at the stars / Michael Ovenden.*

London: Phoenix House, 1957. 192 p., [17] p. of plates: ill. Excursion series; v. 14. Bibliography: p. 182-183. Includes index.

1589. OWEN, RICHARD, 1804-1892. *On the anatomy of the Indian rhinoceros / by Professor Owen....*

London: Printed by Richard Taylor ..., 1852. [2], 31-58 p., [14] leaves of plates: ill.; 32 cm. "From the *Zoological Society's Transactions*, Vol. IV, Part II." Illustrated by J. Erxleben. Plates numbered 9-22. Includes bibliographical references.

Provenance: author's presentation inscription to Professor Dr. Brandt.

1590. OWEN, RICHARD, 1804-1892. *On the anatomy of vertebrates.*

London: Longmans, Green, 1866-68. 3 v. illus. 23 cm. Title on spine: Comparative anatomy and physiology of vertebrates. Includes bibliographies and indexes. v. 1. Fishes and reptiles. – v. 2. Birds and mammals. – v. 3. Mammals.

Advertisements: 24 p. at end, v. 3. Binder: Westleys & Co., London (ticket). Provenance: James Giles (booklabel).

1591. OWEN, RICHARD, 1804-1892. *On the archetype and homologies of the vertebrate skeleton.*

London: Van Voorst, 1848. viii, 203 p., [9] leaves of plates (5 folded): ill.; 23 cm. Includes bibliographical references.

Provenance: Herbert McLean Evans (bookplate). Advertisements pasted in at end.

1592. OWEN, RICHARD, 1804-1892. *On the classification and geographical distribution of the mammalia, being the lecture on Sir Robert Reade's foundation, delivered before the University of Cambridge ... May 10, 1859. To which is added an appendix "On the gorilla," and "On the extinction and transmutation of species." By Richard Owen....*

London: J. W. Parker and Son, 1859. 2 p.l., 103 p. illus. 22 cm. Advertisements: [4] p. following text. Includes bibliographical references. Wood, C. *Vertebrate zoology*, 1859.

Provenance: Robert Fisher Tomes, Charles Atwood Kofoid, Herbert McLean Evans (bookplates).

1593. OWEN, RICHARD, 1804-1892. *On the dodo. Part II: notes on the articulated skeleton of the dodo (didus ineptus, Linn.) in the British Museum / by Professor Owen....*

[London: Zoological Society, 1871]. p. 513-525, [3] leaves of plates: ill.; 33 cm. *Transactions of the Zoological Society of London*; v. 7, pt. 7. Caption title. "Read April 18th, 1871." Plates numbered 64-66. Illustrated by J. Erxleben and G. H. Ford; engraved by M. and N. Hanhart. Includes bibliographical references.

Provenance: Herbert McLean Evans (bookplate). With: *On the osteology of the dodo (didus ineptus, Linn.)* / by Professor Owen ... London: Printed for the Society: and sold at their house ...and by Messrs. Longmans, Green, Reader, and Dyer ..., 1867.

1594. OWEN, RICHARD, 1804-1892. *On the nature of limbs: a discourse delivered on Friday, February 9, at an evening meeting of the Royal Institution of Great Britain / by Richard Owen.*

London: Van Voorst, 1849. [2], 119 p., [7], II leaves of plates (2 folded): ill.; 23 cm. Plate signed J. Erxleben.

Provenance: Herbert McLean Evans (bookplate).

1595. OWEN, RICHARD, 1804-1892. *On the osteology of the dodo (didus ineptus, Linn.) / by Professor Owen....*

London: Printed for the Society: and sold at their house ... and by Messrs. Longmans, Green, Reader, and Dyer ..., 1867. p. 49-85, [10] leaves of plates (1 folded): ill.; 33 cm. *Transactions of the Zoological Society of London;* v. 6, pt. 2. Caption title. "Read January 9th, 1866." Imprint from cover. Plates numbered 15-24. Illustrated by J. Erxleben, F. W. Robinson and J. Smit; plates engraved by W. West and M. and N. Hanhart.

Provenance: Herbert McLean Evans (bookplate). With: *On the dodo.* Part II. / by Professor Owen ... [London: Zoological Society], 1871.

1596. PACCHIONI, ANTONIO, 1665-1726. *Antonii Pacchioni Regiensis philosophi, & medici De Duræ meningis fabrica & usu disquisitio anatomica....*

Romae: Typis D. A. Herculis ... 1701, [16], 139, 5 leaves of plates (3 folded): ill; 17 cm. Half title: De dura meninge.

With the author's *Dissertatio epistolaris de glandulis conglobatis duræ meningis humanæ.* Romæ: Typis Io. Francisci Buagni, 1705.

1597. PACCHIONI, ANTONIO, 1665-1726. *Dissertatio epistolaris: de glandulis conglobatis duræ meningis humanæ, indeque ortis lymphaticis ad piam meningem productis. Lucæ Schrokio ... Antonius Pacchionus Regiensis....*

Romæ: Typis Io. Francisci Buagni, 1705. 32 p., I folded leaf of plates: ill.; 17 cm. Plate signed: Dom.us Moratori delin., Nicolaus Oddi sculp.

With the author's *De duræ meningis fabrica & usu disquisitio anatomica.* Romæ: Typis D. A. Herculis, 1701.

1598. PALINGENIO STELLATO, MARCELLO, ca. 1500-ca. 1543. *Marcelli Palingenii Stellati poëtæ doctissimi Zodiacus vitæ: hoc est, De hominis vita, studio, ac moribus optimè instituendis, libri XII. Cum indice locupletissimo.*

Lvgdvni: Apud Ioannem Tornæsium, 1576. 366, [81] p. 13 cm. Signatures: a-z^8, aa-ee^8. Title within border of printer's ornaments; initials. The initial letters of the first 29 lines of the first book "Aries" form an acrostic of the author's pseudonym Marcellus Palingenius Stellatus, said by Facciolati to be the anagram of Pier Angelo Manzolli, of Stellata in Ferrara. Also attributed to Marc Antonio Flamini, and to others. Includes index.

Provenance: Bibliotheca Cortiniana (armorial bookplate).

1599. PALMA CAMARILLO, FRANCISCO. *Eclipse total de sol: del día 10 de septiembre de 1923 / por el pbro. Francisco Palma Camarillo.*

Mejico: H. Barrales, 1923. 29 p.: ill.; 22 cm. At head of title: Conferencia.

1600. PANDER, CHRISTIAN HEINRICH, 1794-1865. [Vergleichende Osteologie.]

Bonn: In Commission bei Eduard Weber, 1821-1838. 14 pts.: ill.; 47 x 52 cm. bound to 52 cm. Binder's title. 1. Abth. (Lfg. 1) Das Riesen-Faulthier, *Bradypus giganteus,* abgebildet, beschrieben, und mit den verwandten Geschlechtern verglichen, von Chr. Pander und E. d'Alton – (Lfg. 2) Die Skelete der *Pachydermata* abgebildet, beschrieben und verglichen, von C. Pander und E. d'Alton – (Lfg. 3) Die Skelete der Raubthiere, abgebildet und verglichen, von Chr. Pander und E. d'Alton – (Lfg. 4) Die Skelete der Wiederkäuer, abgebildet und verglichen, von Chr. Pander und E. d'Alton – (Lfg. 5-6) Die Skelete der Nagethiere, abgebildet und verglichen, von Chr. Pander und E. d'Alton – (Lfg. 7) Die Skelete der Vierhänder, abgebildet und verglichen von Chr. Pander und E. d'Alton – (Lfg. 8) Die Skelete der zahnlosen Thiere, abgebildet und verglichen von Chr. Pander und E. d'Alton – (Lfg. 9) Die Skelete der Robben und Lamantine, abgebildet und verglichen, von Chr. Pander und E. d'Alton – (Lfg. 10) Die Skelete der Cetaceen, abgebildet und beschrieben, von Chr. Pander und E. d'Alton – (Lfg. 11) Die Skelete der Beutelthiere, abgebildet und beschrieben, von Chr. Pander und E. d'Alton – (Lfg. 12) Die Skelete der Chiropteren und Insectivoren, abgebildet und beschrieben, von E. d'Alton, d.Ä – und E. d'Alton, d.J. – 2. Abth. (Lfg. 1) Die Skelete der straussartigen Vögel, abgebildet und beschrieben, von E. d'Alton, d.J. – (Lfg. 2) Die Skelete der Raubvögel, abgebildet und beschrieben, von E. d'Alton, d.Ä und E. d'Alton, d.J.

Provenance: Herbert McLean Evans (bookplate); Fran. Coppi (lettering on spine).

1601. PANNEKOEK, ANTON, 1873-1960. *Die nördliche Milchstrasse / von A. Pannekoek.*

Haarlem: J. Enschedé en Zonen, 1920. 115 p., ix leaves of plates: ill.; 30 cm. *Annalen van de Sterrewacht te Leiden;* d. 11, 3. Stuk. Includes bibliographical references.

1602. PANSER, SYMON. *Verklaringe over den loop van Mercurius ... Verklaringe van de verduysteringe der mane ... / Symon Panser....*

[Amsterdam: 1736]. 1 sheet: ill.; 52 x 63 cm. Fig. 1: De loop van Mercurius om de zonne des jaars 1736 beneffens de verschyning in dezelve den 11 November des s'middags. Fig. 2: Vertooninge van een aanmerkelyke maan eclips gevallende A 1736 den 26 Maart savonts. Fig. 3: Vertooninge van de tweede geheele maans verduysteringe A 1736 tuschen den 19 en 20 September snagts. Fig. 4: Vertooninge van de maarkwaardige zons verduysteringe, invallende op den 4 October savonts.

With: *Atlas cœlestis* / a Ioh. Gabriele Doppelmaiero. Norimbergæ: Sumptibus heredum Hommannianorum, 1742.

1603. PANSER, SYMON. *Vertoning van de merkwaardige zons-verduistering of te grootezon-eclips ... 13 Mey 1733 ... / door Symon Panser....*

Gedrukt 't Amsterdam: By Reinier & Iosua Ottens, 1733. 1 sheet: ill., maps; 53 x 86 cm. folded to 53 x 27 cm. Text begins: Generale aanwyzing.

With: *Atlas cœlestis* / a Ioh. Gabriele Doppelmaiero. Norimbergæ: Sumptibus heredum Homannianorum, 1742.

1604. PAPPUS, OF ALEXANDRIA. *Commentaires de Pappus et de Théon d'Alexandrie sur l'Almageste, texte établie et annoté par A. Rome.*

Roma: Biblioteca Apostolica Vaticana, 1931-1943. 3 v. diagrs. 25 cm. Studi e testi (Biblioteca apostolica vaticana); 54, 72, 106. Paged continuously. Vol. 2-3 published in Città del Vaticano. I. *Pappus d'Alexandrie. Commentaire sur les livres 5 et 6 del'Almageste.* -II-III *Théon d'Alexandrie. Commentaire sur les livres 1 - 4 de l'Almageste.*

Provenance: Library of the University of California (inkstamp).

1605. PARACELSUS, 1493-1541. *Operum medicochimocorum sive paradoxorum tomus genuinus primus-[duodecimus]. Recenter latine factus, & in usum asselclarum novæ & veteris philosophiæ foras datus.*

In Francofurto: A Collegio Musarum Palthenianarum, 1603-05. 12 v. illus., port. 25 cm. Each volume has special title page only. Vol. 12 has title: *Bertheonea; sive, Chirvrgia minor* [etc.] and was pub. separately by the Palthen Press in 1603. It here has an added half-title: Prodevnt Opera Theophrasti Latini, quorum cum Chirurgia minor partes duodecim. Includes index. Sudhoff, no. 258-263; 269-274.

1606. PARÉ, AMBROISE, 1510?-1590. *Die Behandlung der Schusswunden (1545) Eingeleitet, übersetzt und herausgegeben von Henry E. Sigerist....*

Leipzig: J. A. Barth, 1923. 87 p. 18 cm. Klassiker der Medizin; Bd. 29. Reprint of title and text of the original, *La méthode de traicter les playes faictes par hacqvebvtes et avltres bastons à feu*: p. [49]-87. Includes bibliographical references. Doe, J. Paré, 6.

Provenance: John Farquhar Fulton.

1607. PARÉ, AMBROISE, 1510?-1590. *The workes of that famous chirurgion Ambrose Parey translated out of Latine and compared with the French. By Th. Johnson.*

London: Printed by Th. Cotes and R. Young, 1634. [14], 1173 [i.e. 1101], [22] p. illus. (incl. port.) 35 cm. Engraved and illustrated t.-p. engraved by J. Cecill, with portrait of Paré. Many errors in pagination. Printers' device on p. 1083 (end of 26th book); head pieces; initials. "It seems ... more than probable that Thomas Johnson, apothecary, finished the translation ... begun by George Baker ... doing much work on the latter's manuscript and making his own translation of more than half of the whole." Cf. *A bib. of the works of A. Paré* / Janet Doe. Chicago, 1937, p. 180-181. Waller, E. *Bib. Walleriana*, 7177. *STC* 19189. Doe, J. *Paré*, 51.

Provenance: Herbert McLean Evans (bookplate). "The authors epistle dedicatorie" is bound behind the t. p.

1608. PARK, MUNGO, 1771-1806. *Travels in the interior districts of Africa: performed under the direction and patronage of the African Association, in the years 1795, 1796, and 1797 / by Mungo Park ... ; with an appendix, containing geographical illustrations of Africa by Major Rennell.*

London: Printed by W. Bulmer ... for the author; and sold by G. and W. Nicol... , 1799. xxviii, 372, xcii, [3] p., [9] leaves of plates (some folded): ill.,maps, port., music; 28 cm. Appendix has special t. p. "A vocabulary of the Mandingo language.": p. [365]-372. Illustrated by H. Edridge, T. Dickinson, J. C. Bassow, McKenzie, J. Walker, W. C. Wilson, J. Mills. Subscribers' names: p. xxi-xxviii.

Provenance: Oxford & Cambridge University Club (inkstamp).

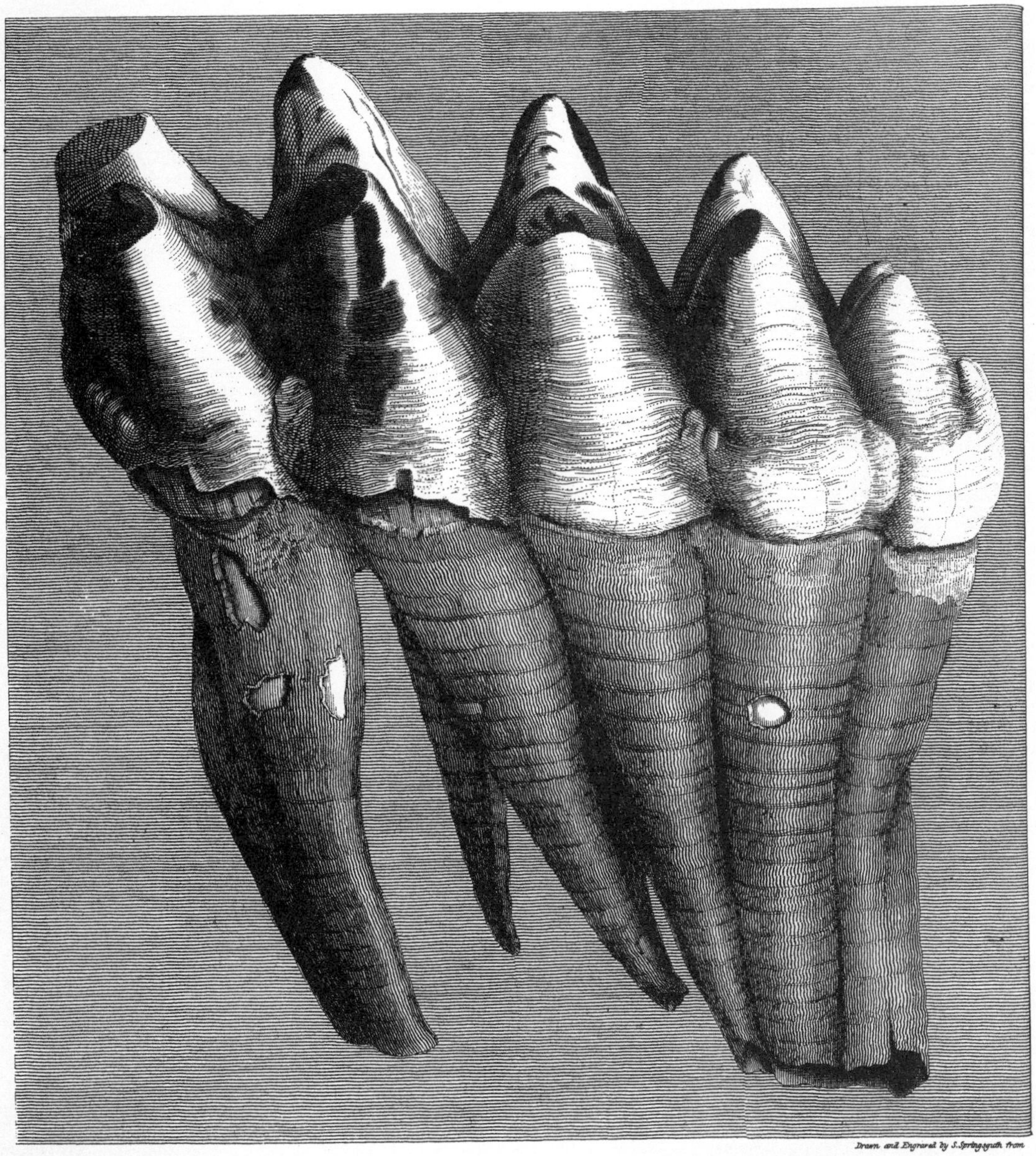

Drawn and Engraved by S. Springsguth from

The back grinding tooth of the MAMMOTH or MASTODON of Ohio.—— weight. 4 lb. 7 oz.

London Published as the Act directs, by James Parkinson, Hoxton, September 2nd 1811.

PARKINSON, *Organic Remains of a Former World*, 1804-1811

1609. Parker, William Harwar, 1826-1896. *Familiar talks on astronomy, with chapters on geography and navigation, by William Harwar Parker....*
Chicago: A. C. McClurg and Company, 1889. xiii, [15]-264 p. incl. diagrs. 18 cm. Includes index.

1610. Parkinson, James, 1755-1824. *Organic remains of a former world. An examination of the mineralized remains of the vegetables and animals of the antediluvian world; generally termed extraneous fossils. By James Parkinson.....*
London: J. Robson [etc.], 1804-11. 3 v. fronts., col. plates. 28 x 23 cm. "Printed by C. Whittingham." Plates drawn and engraved by S. Springsguth. Includes bibliographical references and indexes. The vegetable kingdom. – The fossil zoophytes. – The fossil starfish, echini, shells, insects, amphibia, mammalia, &c.
Advertisements: [3] p. at end, v. 1; final p., v. 2.

1611. Parsons, Albert Ross, 1847-1933. *The road map of the stars: a pocket folding chart of the heavens, from horizon to zenith / by Albert Ross Parsons; the 48 star views specially drawn for this work by Annette Weaver Peck.*
London: Mitchell Kennerley, 1911. ix, 31 p., [48] leaves of plates: charts; 19 cm.

1612. Pascal, Blaise, 1623-1662. *Traitez de l'équilibre des liqueurs, et de la pesanteur de la masse de l'air: contenant l'explication des causes de divers effets de la nature qui n'avoient point esté bien connus jusques ici, & particulierème[n]t de ceux que l'on avoit attribuez à l'horreur du vuide / Par monsieur Pascal.*
À Paris: Chez Guillaume Desprez ..., 1663. [28], 232, [8] p., [2] folded leaves of plates: ill.; 15 cm. Errata on p. [28] of 1st group. Burndy. *Science,* 143. Osler, W. *Bib. Osleriana,* 3625.
Provenance: Herbert McLean Evans (bookplate); De Cayrol (inkstamp).

1613. Pasch, Moritz, 1843-1930. *Vorlesungen über neuere Geometrie.*
Leipzig: B. G. Teubner, 1882. iv, 201, [1] p. ill., 24 cm. Advertisements: [2] p. following text.

1614. Pasteur, Louis, 1822-1895. [Collection of articles in *Comptes Rendus,* 1880-1881 on vaccination / by Louis Pasteur]
[1880-1881] 8 pieces; 32 cm. *Comptes rendus hebdomadaires des séances de l'Académie des Sciences;* v. 90-92. In linen case, with binder's title: Louis Pasteur in *Comptes Rendus,* 1880-1881. Advertisements (2 p.) loosely inserted. Includes bibliographical references. t. 90, no. 17. Sur le choléra des poules: études des conditions de lanon-récidive de la maladie et de quelques autres de ses caractères (1880) – t. 90, no. 18. De l'extension de la théorie des germes à l'étiologie de quelques maladies communes (1880) – t. 91, no. 2. Sur l'étiologie du charbon (1880) – t. 91, no. 10. Sur l'étiologie des affections charbonneuses (1880) – t. 91, no. 17. De l'atténuation du virus du choléra des poules (1880) – t. 92, no. 12. De la possibilité de rendre les moutons réfractaires au charbon par la méthode des inoculations préventives (1881) – t. 92, no. 12. Le vaccin du charbon (1881) – t. 92, no. 24. Compte rendu sommaire des expériences faites à Pouilly-le-Fort, près Melun, sur la vaccination charbonneuse (1881).

1615. Pasteur, Louis, 1822-1895. *Études sur la maladie des vers à soie, moyen pratique assuré de la combattre et d'en prévenir le retour, par M. L. Pasteur....*
Paris: Gauthier-Villars, successeur de Mallet-Bachelier, 1870. 2 v. front. (v. 1) illus., plates (part col.) 23 cm. Includes bibligraphical references. t. I. La pébrine et la flacherie. – t. II. Notes et documents.

1616. Pasteur, Louis, 1822-1895. *Études sur le vinaigre,: sa fabrication, ses maladies, moyens de les prévenir: nouvelles observations sur la conservation des vins par la chaleur; / par M. L. Pasteur....*
Paris: Gauthier-Villars ...; Victor Masson et Fils ..., 1868. viii, 119, [1] p.: ill.; 24 cm. Garrison, F. H. *Medical bibl.* 2480.

1617. Pasteur, Louis, 1822-1895. *Mémoire sur la fermentation appelée lactique / par M. L. Pasteur (extrait par l'auteur).*
[Paris: Mallet-Bachelier, Imprimeur-Libraire ..., 1857]. p. 913-916; 29 cm. *Comptes rendus hebdomadaires des séances de l'Académie des Sciences;* t. 45. Caption title. Horblit, H. D. *Grolier 100 science books,* 82.

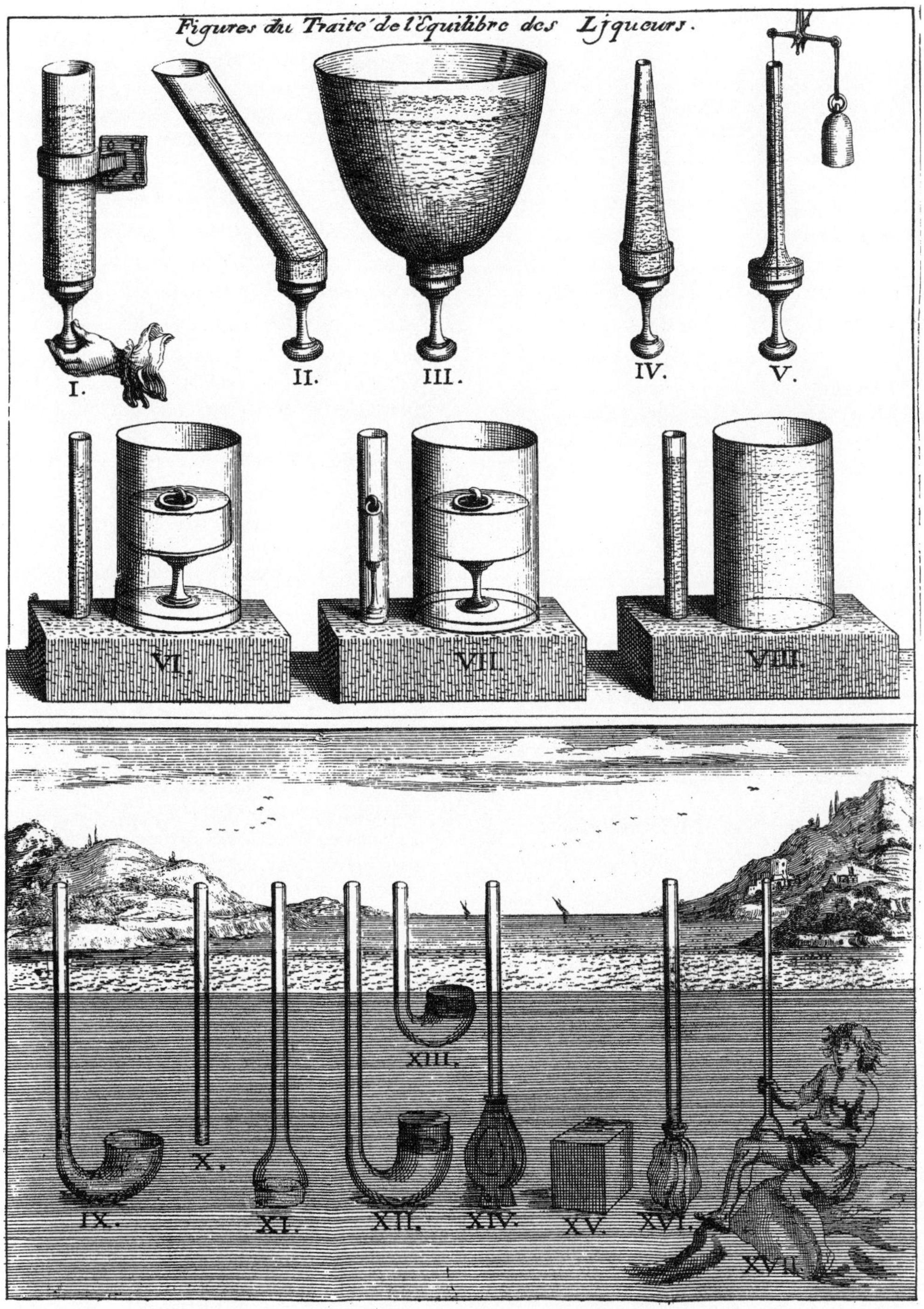

Pascal, *Traitez de l'équilibre des liqueurs, et de la pesanteur de la masse de l'air*, 1663

1618. Pasteur, Louis, 1822-1895. *Mémoire sur la fermentation appelée lactique / par M. L. Pasteur....*

[Lille: s.n., 1858]. p. [13]-26; 25 cm. Caption title. "Séance du 3 août 1857." Detached from *Mémoires de la Société Impériale des Sciences, del'Agriculture et des Arts de Lille,* 2nd. ser., 5 1858. Includes bibliographical references.

Provenance: Bibliothèque de la Feuille des Jeunes Naturalistes (inkstamp).

1619. Pasteur, Louis, 1822-1895. *Note relative au penicillium glaucum et à la dissymétrie moléculaire des produits organiques naturels / par M. L. Pasteur.*

[Paris: Mallet-Bachelier, Imprimeur-Libraire ..., 1860]. p. 298-299; 28 cm. *Comptes rendus hebdomadaires des séances de l'Académie des Sciences;* t. 51. Caption title.

1620. Pasteur, Louis, 1822-1895. *Nouvelles expériences relatives aux générations dites spontanées / par M. L. Pasteur.*

Paris: Mallet-Bachelier, 1860. p. 348-352 ; 27 cm. In: *Comptes rendus hebdomadaires des séances de l'Académie des sciences,* t. 51. Caption title. In the same volume: Suite à une précédente communication relative aux générations dites spontanées / par M. L. Pasteur (p. 675-678). *PMM,* 336.

1621. Pasteur, Louis, 1822-1895. *Nouvelles observations sur l'étiologie et la prophylaxie du charbon / par M. Pasteur.*

Paris : Gauthier-Villars, 1880. p. [697]-701 ; 27 cm. In: *Comptes rendus hebdomadaires des séances de l'Académie des sciences,* t. 91. Caption title.

1622. Pasteur, Louis, 1822-1895. *Recherches sur la putréfaction / par M. L. Pasteur.*

Paris : Mallet-Bachelier, 1863. p. 1189-1194 ; 27 cm. In: *Comptes rendus hebdomadaires des séances de l'Académie des sciences,* t. 56. Caption title. *PMM,* 336.

1623. Pasteur, Louis, 1822-1895. *Researches on the molecular asymmetry of natural organic products, by Louis Pasteur (1860).*

Edinburgh: W. F. Clay; London: Simpkin, Marshall, Hamilton, Kent & Co., Ltd., 1905. 46, [2] p. 19 cm. Alembic Club reprints; no. 14. "Lectures ... given at the invitation of the Council of the Société Chimique of Paris." – Introd. Published by the Société Chimique of Paris in a volume entitled *Leçons de chimie professées en 1860,* Paris, 1861.

Advertisements: [2] p. at end, dated April, 1905. Provenance: R. G. Neville (signature); Taunton's School, Senior Library. Southampton (inkstamp).

1624. Pasteur, Louis, 1822-1895. *Sur la longue durée de la vie des germes charbonneux et sur leur conservation dans les terres cultivées: note / de M. Pasteur; avec la collaboration de MM. Chamberland et Roux.*

Paris: Gauthier-Villars, 1881. p. [209]-211 ; 27 cm. In: *Comptes rendus hebdomadaires des séances de l'Académie des sciences,* t. 92. Caption title.

1625. Pauli, Wolfgang, 1900-1958. *Relativitätstheorie / von W. Pauli Jr.*

Leipzig: B. G. Teubner, 1921. p. [539]-775; 26 cm. *Encyklopädie der mathematischen Wissenschaften;* Bd. V. 2, Hft. 4. Caption title. Bibliography: p. 542-543. Advertisements on p. [4] of wrapper.

1626. Pavlov, Ivan Petrovich, 1849-1936. *Die Arbeit der Verdauungsdrüsen; Vorlesungen von J. P. Pavlov. Autorisierte Übersetzung aus dem Russischen, von A. Walther. Mit einem Vortwort und Zusätzen des Verfassers.*

Wiesbaden: Bergmann, 1898. xii, 199 p. illus. 25 cm. Translation of *Lektsii o rabotie glavnykh pishchevaritelnykh zhelez.* Includes index. Bibliography: p. [197]-199.

1627. Pavlov, Ivan Petrovich, 1849-1936. *Lektsii o rabote glavnykh pishchevaritelnykh zhelez. / professor I. P. Pavlov.*

S.-Peterburg: Tipografia Ministerstva Putei Soobsheniia ... , 1897. [6], II, 223 p.: ill.; c 20 cm. Statement of responsibility transposed. T. p. romanized. Bibliography: p. 221-223. Horblit, H. D. *Grolier 100 science books,* 83.

Provenance: O. Assonovoi (signature); Vsesoiuznaia Bibl-ka imeni V. I. Lenina.

1628. Pavlov, Ivan Petrovich, 1849-1936. *The work of the digestive glands / lectures by ... J. P. Pawlow ... ; translated into English by W. H. Thompson....*

London: Charles Griffin; Chicago: J. B. Lippincott, 1902. xii, 196 p.: ill.; 23 cm. At head of title: Sole authorised English translation. Includes index. Translation of: *Lektsii o rabote glavnykh pishchevaritelnykh zhelez*. Bibliography: p. 187-189.
Provenance: Otto Orren Fisher (bookplate).

1629. PAYEN, A. F. (ANTOINE FRANÇOIS). *Selenelion ou apparition luni-solaire en l'isle de Gorgone: obserué... le xvj. iuin MDCLXVI ... / [A. F. Payen].*
À Paris: Chez L. Bilaine ... & I. Cusson ..., 1666. [4], 118, [4] p.: ill.; 24 cm. Statement of responsibility from preliminaries. Illustrated by F. Lapointe. Ænigma astronomicum: p. 33-[122].
Disbound.

1630. PAZ SOLDÁN, MATEO, b. 1814. *Tratado elemental de astronomía teórica y práctica / por el doctor don Mateo Paz Soldán....*
Paris: Imprenta de Crapelet ..., 1848. 2 v.: ill.; 28 cm. Errata: p. IV [v. 1].

1631. PEARSON, KARL, 1857-1936. *The grammar of science.*
London: Walter Scott; Scribner, 1892. xvi, 493 p. illus. 19 cm. Contemporary Science series. Includes bibliographies and index.
Advertisements: publisher's catalog, 8 p. at end. Provenance: Herbert McLean Evans (bookplate).

1632. PEARSON, W. (WILLIAM), 1767-1847. *An introduction to practical astronomy ... By the Rev. W. Pearson....*
London: Printed for the author, (1824-29). 2 v. XXXI pl. (1 fold.) tables, diagrs. 33 x 25 cm. Colophon: G. Woodfall, printer ..., London. V. I: Tables, recently computed, for facilitating the reduction of celestial observations; and a popular explanation of their construction and use. – V. II: Descriptions of the various instruments, that have been usefully employed in determining the places of heavenly bodies, with an account of the methods of adjusting and using them.
Binder: Verrico (ticket).

1633. PECK, WILLIAM G. (WILLIAM GUY), 1820-1892. *Text-book of popular astronomy: for the use of colleges, academics, and high-schools / by William G. Peck....*
New York and Chicago: A. S. Barnes & Company, [c1883]. iv, [5]-380 p.: ill., charts; 19 cm. Peck's academic and collegiate course; v. 8. Cover title: Astronomy. Includes index.

1634. PECKHAM, JOHN, D. 1292. *Ioannis Archiepiscopi Cantuariensis, Perspectivæ communis libri tres. Jam postremo correcti....*
Coloniae Agrippinae: Apud hæredes Arnoldi Birckmanni, 1580. 47 l.; 21 cm. A reprint of the 1542 edition, edited by Georg Hartmann. The illustrations are by Paschasius Hamellius.

1635. PELL, JOHN, 1611-1685. *Controversiæ de verâ circuli mensurâ anno 1644 exortæ: inter Christianum Severini, Longomontanum ... et Ioannem Pellium ... Pars prima.*
Amstelodami: Apud Ioannem Blaeu, [1647]. [2], 96 p.: ill.; 20 cm. No more published. Cf. *NUC pre-1956*, v. 447, p. 637. Date in title transcribed into Arabic numerals. Special title pages: p. 37 with imprint: Haviniæ, 1644; p. 63 with imprint: Literis viduæ Salomonis Sartorii, 1645. Claudii Mydorgii sententia pro I. Pellio: p. 90-94. Iacobi Golii sententia pro I. Pellio: p. 95-96. Includes bibliographical references.
Provenance: Jo. Farrington (inscription).

1636. PELTIER, LESLIE C., 1900- . *Starlight nights; the adventures of a star-gazer, by Leslie C. Peltier. Illustrated by the author. [1st ed.]*
New York: Harper & Row, [1965]. x, 236 p. illus. 22 cm.

1637. PEMBERTON, HENRY, 1694-1771. *A view of Sir Isaac Newton's philosophy.*
London: Printed by S. Palmer, 1728. 25 p. l., 407 p. 12 fold. pl. 29 cm. Title vignette; head and tail pieces; initials. Dedication signed: Henry Pemberton. A poem on Sir Isaac Newton, by R. Glover: [15] p. following the preface. *Babson Newton Coll.* 98. Gray, G. J. *Newton*, 132.

1638. PENCK, ALBRECHT, b. 1858. *Die Alpen im Eiszeitalter, von Albrecht Penck ... und Eduard Brückner ... Von der Sektion Breslau des Deutschen und österreichischen Alpenvereins gekrönte Preisschrift ...*
Leipzig: C. H. Tauchnitz, 1909. 3 v. front., illus., plates (part fold., part col.) maps (part fold.) diagrs. 27 cm. 1. Bd. Die Eiszeiten in den nördlichen

Perrault, *Mémoires pour servir à l'histoire naturelle des animaux*, 1676

Ostalpen. – 2. Bd. Die Eiszeitenin den nördlichen Westalpen. – 3. Bd. Die Eiszeiten in den Südalpen und im Bereich der Ostabdachung der Alpen.

Provenance: Hellmut Schnitter (inkstamp).

1639. PERRAULT, CLAUDE, 1613-1688. *Mémoires pour servir a l'histoire naturelle des animaux / dressez par M. Perrault ...*

À Paris: De l'Imprimerie Royale, 1676. [16], 205, [3] p., [29] leaves of plates: ill.; 50 cm. Illustrated by Sile Clerc. Corrections: on p. [207]. Includes index. Colophon reads: À Paris: De l'Imprimerie Royale, par Sébastien Mabre -Cramoisy ..., 1676. Brunet v. 4, column 507.

Joa. du [J?]illion, 1728 (inscription); Paul R[icher?] (presentation inscription to "Henri"); unidentified armorial bookplate; ms. notes.

1640. PERRIN, JEAN, 1870-1942. *Les atomes, par Jean Perrin ... avec 13 figures.*

[Paris]: F. Alcan, 1913. 3 p. l., xvi, 295, [1] p. illus. 19 cm. Nouvelle Collection Scientifique.

Presentation copy (signed inscription by the author).

1641. PERRIN, JEAN, 1870-1942. *Die Brown'sche Bewegung und die wahre Existenz der Moleküle / von J. Perrin; Deutsch von J. Donau.*

Dresden: T. Steinkopff, 1910. 84 p.: ill.; 24 cm. Translated from the French, first published 1909 in *Annales de Chimie et de Physique*, 8me série. "Sonderausgabe aus *Kolloidchemische Beihefte, Monographien zur reinen und angewandten Kolloidchemie*, herausgegeben von Dr. Wolfgang Ostwald, Band I." Includes bibliographical references.

In original printed wrappers. Advertisements on p. [2-4] of wrappers.

1642. PETAU, DENIS, 1583-1652. *Dionysii Petauii Aurelianensis e Societate Iesu Opus de doctrina temporum: diuisum in partes duas, quarum prior ta technika temporum, posterior ta historoumena complectitur.*

Lutetiae Parisiorum: Sumptibus Sebastiani Cramoisy ..., 1627. 2 v. : ill. ; 36 cm. Greek words in title transliterated. Includes indexes. Errata: on last printed p. of each v. Library has: parts 1-2 [in 1 v.]

1643. PETAU, DENIS, 1583-1652. *Vranologion, siue systema variorum avthorum: qui de sphæra, ac sider ibus, eorumque motibus græcè commentati sunt; sunt autem horum libri ... omnia vel Græcè ac Latinè nunc primùm edita, vel ante non edita; cura & studio Dionysii Petavii Aurelianensis œe Societate Iesu....*

Lutetiæ Parisiorum: Sumptibus Sebastiani Cramoisy ... M. DC. XXX, [1630]. [21], 424, [12] p., 338, [9] p.: ill.; 37 cm. Engraved title vignette. Text in Greek and Latin. Includes indexes. Errata p. [a] at the end. Houzeau & Lancaster. *Astronomie.* (1964 ed.), 786. Gemini Isagoge / Interprete Edone Hilderico – Ptolemæus de Apparentiis inerrantium / Interprete Dionysio Petauio – Ptolemæi inerrantium significationes / Latinè per Nicolaum Leonicu – Calendarium vetus Romanum cum ortu occasùque stellarum ex Ouidio, Columella, Plinio / A Dionysio Petauio confectum – Calendarium Romanum / ab Ioanne Georgio Hervuart editum – Achillis Tatij Isagoge ad Arati Phænomena – Eiusdem Tatij fragmenta Græca – Hipparchi Bithyni ad Arati, & Eudoxi Phænomena libri tres – Achillis Tatij ad Arati Phænomena, qui liber falsò Eratostheni tribuitur – Arati genus, & vita – Theodorus Gaza de mensibus/ Interprete Ioanne Perrello – S. Maximi computus – Isaaci Argyri Computus – Eiusdem Computus alter – S. Andræ Computus / Interprete Dionysio Petauio – Fragmentum Græcum de Paschate – Notæ Dionysij Petauij ad Geminum, Ptolemæum, & Hipparchum – Fragmentum Aetij de significationibus stellarum / interprete Cornario – Index rerum memorabilium – Subiecti sunt variorum dissertationum libri VIII, authore Dionysio Petauio.

Provenance: J. T. Voemel (bookplate.)

1644. PETERS, C. F. W. (CARL FRIEDRICH WILHELM), 1844-1894. *Die Entfernung der Erde von der Sonne. Von Dr. C.F.W. Peters ...*

Berlin: C. G. Lüderitz, 1873. 30 p. 21 cm. Sammlung gemeinverständlicher wissenschaftlicher Vorträge; 8. Serie, Hft. 173. Pages also numbered [151]-180.

Provenance: Lees-Museum te Amsterdam, Bibliotheek (inkstamp); Charles Atwood Kofoid (bookplate).

1645. PETERSON, HANNAH MARY BOUVIER, 1811-1870. *Bouvier's Familiar astronomy; or, An introduction to the study of the heavens. Illustrated by celestial maps, and upwards of 200 finely executed engravings. To which is added a treatise on the globes, and a comprehensive astronomical dictionary...By Hannah M. Bouvier.*

Philadelphia: Childs & Peterson, [etc., etc.], 1857. 499 p. front. (fold. col. charts) illus., tables, diagrs. 22 cm. Includes index. History of astronomy: p. 320-343.

11 p. of Recommendations precede text, [12] p. of advertisements follow text.

1646. PEURBACH, GEORG VON, 1423-1461. *Theoricæ novæ planetarum Georgii Purbachij fœliter incipiunt. Figura nouem sphærarum & elementorum ordinem designans.*

Parisiis: Apud Christianum Wechelum, 1543. 127, [1] p.: ill., diagrs. (2 fold.); 17 cm. Title vignette (diagram).

Imperfect: p. 97-98 missing. Disbound.

1647. PEURBACH, GEORG VON, 1423-1461. *Theoricæ nouæ planetarum / Georgii Purbachij Germani; quibus accesserunt: Ioannis de Monte Regio Disputationes, super deliramenta Theoricarum Gerardi Cremonensis. Item, Ioannis Essler Maguntini tractatus utilis ... cui titulum fecit Speculum astrologorum ... Qaestiones vero in Theoricas planetarum Purbachij, authore Christiano Vrstisio....*

Basileae: Ex Officina Henricpetrina, Mense Martio, 1573. [16], 226 [i.e. 262], [18], 430, [2] p., [10] folded leaves of plates: ill.; 16 cm. Imprint taken from colophon. *Quæstiones nouæ* has separate t. p. Errata: p. 15 (4th sequence). Errors in pagination: p. 262 misnumbered as 226.

Imperfect: p. 5-12 and 135-138 missing.

1648. *Philosophical collections. Numb. 1. containing an account of such physical, anatomical, ... experiments and observations as have lately come to the publishers hands.*

London: ...Printed for John Martyn ... , 1679. 44 p., [1] folded leaf of plates: ill.; 23 cm. Includes bibliographical references. First of seven numbers published as a substitute for the *Philosophical transactions,* Royal Society of London, no volumes of which were issued from 1679-82.

With: *New experiments and observations on electricity* Part II [-III], by Benjamin Franklin. The second edition. London: printed and sold by D. Henry and R. Cave ..., 1754. Provenance: Darwin family; G. J. Hare (signature).

1649. *Philosophical magazine; a journal of theoretical, experimental and applied physics. Philosophical magazine 1798-1813. Philosophical magazine and journal 1814-26. Philosophical magazine; or, Annals of chemistry, mathematics, astronomy, natural history and general science 1827-32. London and Edinburgh philosophical magazine and journal of science 1832-40. London, Edinburgh and Dublin philosophical magazine and journal of science 1840-1944.*

London, Taylor & Francis. v. ill. 22-26 cm. v. 1-68, June 1798-Dec. 1826; new ser., v. 1-11, Jan. 1827-June 1832; 3* ser., v. 1-37, July 1832-Dec.1850; 4th ser., v. 1-50, Jan. 1851-Dec. 75; 5th ser., v. 1-50, Jan. 1876-Dec. 1900; 6th ser., v. 1-50, Jan. 1901-Dec. 1925; 7th ser., v. 1-46, 1926-56; 8th ser., v. 1-v. 36; 1956-1977 Vols. for 1976-77 have no series designation but constitute part of 8th ser. Other slight variations in title. "Europhysics journal" (varies slightly), -1977. Supplements accompany some numbers. Absorbed: *Journal of natural philosophy* 1814. *Annals of philosophy* 1827. *Edinburgh journal of science* 1832. Split into: *Philosophical magazine. A, Physics of condensed matter, defects and mechanical properties* 1978. *Philosophical magazine. B, Physics of condensed matter, electronic, optical, and magnetic properties* 1978.

Library has: ser. 6: [26-27, 1913-14]. Vol. 26, no. 156 (Dec. 1913): Provenance: Herbert McLean Evans (bookplate). Vol. 26, nos. 156 and 160 in cases.

1650. *Physical review.*

Lancaster, Pa. [etc.] Published for the American Physical Society by the American Institute of Physics [etc.] 223 v. ill. 25-28 cm. Frequency varies. v. 1-35, July 1893-Dec. 1912; ser. 2, v. 1-188, no. 5, Jan. 1913-Dec. 25, 1969. "A journal of experimental and theoretical physics." Vols. 133-140 issued in two sections: A and B. Vols. for 1903- include *Proceedings of the American Physical Society*. Published for Cornell University, July 1893-Jan. 1903. General index: Vol. 1-ser. 2, v. 16, 1893-1920. 1 v. Author indexes: Vols. 101-120, 1956-60 (includes index to *Physical review letters*) 1 v.; Vols. 121-140, 1961-65 (includes index to *Physical review letters*) 1 v.; Vols. 141-188, 1966-69 (includes index to *Physical review letters*) 1 v. Subject index: Vols. 17-80, 1921-50. 1 v. Split into: *Physical review. A. General physics,* ISSN 0556-2791; *Physical Review. B. Solid state physics,* ISSN 0556-2805; *Physical review. C. Nuclear physics,* ISSN 0556-2813; *Physical review. D. Particles and fields,* ISSN 0556-2821. Superseded partly by: *Physi-*

cal review letters ISSN:0031-9007 1958-.
Library has: ser.2: [74, 1948]; ser.2: [112, 1958].

1651. *Physikalisch-Technische Reichsanstalt: Aufruf.*
Berlin: [s.n.], 1912. 1 v. ; 24 cm.

1652. *Physikalische Zeitschrift.*
Leipzig, S. Hirzel. 45 v. ill. 28 cm. Semimonthly Former frequency: Weekly, v. 1-2 1.-45. Jahrg.; 1. Oct. 1899-1945. Editors: Oct. 1899-Dec. 1914, E. Riecke, H. T. Simon; Jan. 1915- P. Debye (with H. T. Simon, 1915-18; M. Born, 1921-). Includes section "Besprechungen". Absorbed: *Jahrbuch der Radioaktivität und Elektronik.*
Library has: 10, 1909. Vol. 10: Provenance: Cornell University Library (bookplate and stamps); Henry W. Sage (gift bookplate).

1653. Piazzi, Giuseppe, 1746-1826. *Præcipuarum stellarum inerrantium positiones mediæ ineunte seculo XIX: ex observationibus habitis in Specula Panormitana ab anno 1792 ad annum 1802.*
Panormi: Typis Regiis, 1803. XL, [698], 76 p.: ill.; 37 cm. Authorship assigned Brunet. Title decoration and ill. signed: F. Ognibene. Includes bibliographical references. Brunet v. 4. col. 507.

1654. Piccolomini, Alessandro, 1508-1578. *De la sfera del mondo: Libri quattro in lingua Toscana: i quali non per via di traduttione, nè à qual si voglia particolare scrittore obligati: ma parte da i migliori raccogliendo; e parte di nuouo producendo; contengano in se tutto quel ch'intorno à tal materia si possa desiderare; ridotti à ta[n]ta ageuolezza, & à cosi facil modo di dimostrare che qual si voglia poco essercitato negli studij di matemmatica potrà ageuolissimamente & con prestezza intenderne il tutto; De le stelle fisse. Libro uno con le sue figure, e con le sue tauole: doue co[n] marauigliosa ageuolezza potrà ciascheduno conoscere qualunque stella dele XLVIII immagini del cielo stellato, e le fauole loro integramente: & sapere in ogni tempo del'anno, à qual si voglia hora di notte, in che parte del cielo si truouino, non solo le dette immagini, ma qualunq[ue] stella di quelle.*

In Venetia ... Per Giouanantonio & Domenico Fratelli de Volpini da Castelgiufredo, ad instantia de Andrea Ariuabeno ..., Del mese de Aprile MDXL. 1540. [12], 5-176 [i.e. 178], [2] leaves: ill.; 22 cm. Author's name in dedication: Alisandro Piccolomini altrimenti Lo Stordito Intronato. "De le stelle fisse" has separate t. p. Vignette on both title pages; some decorated initials. Publisher from colophon on leaf [2] of last group. Numbers 103-106 repeated and numbers 166-167 omitted in foliation. Errata on leaf [2] of 1st group and leaves [1]-[2] of last group. *Renaissance books of science from the collection of Albert E. Lownes* 31.
"De le stelle fisse" is bound before "De la sfera del mondo." Provenance: Liechtensteinianis (bookplate); Amerigo Antinor (inscription).

1655. Piccolomini, Alessandro, 1508-1578. *La prima parte delle theoriche, oueru speculationi de i pianeti / di M. Alessandro Piccolomini.*
In Venetia: Appresso Giouanni Varisco, & Paganino Paganini, 1558. [10], 62, [2] leaves: ill.; 21 cm. Imprint date taken from leaf [3] verso. Adams P1119.

1656. Pichot, J. (Jules), 1820- . *Traité élémentaire de cosmographie / par J. Pichot.*
Paris: Librairie de L. Hachette et Cie ..., 1867. [4], 351, [1] p., [1], XVIII leaves of plates (2 folded, some col.): ill., maps; 22 cm. Variously illustrated by: Le Breton, E. Salle, C. Laplante, Bonnofoux, Max. Rapine, W. de la Rue.
Presented to M. Bouquets by the author (inscription)

1657. Pickering, James S. (James Sayre). *The stars are yours.*
New York: Macmillan Co., 1948. x, 264 p. illus., charts. 21 cm. Bibliography: p. 255-256. Includes index.

1658. Pickering, William H. (William Henry), 1858- . *The moon: a summary of the existing knowledge of our satellite, with a complete photographic atlas / by William H. Pickering.*
New York: Doubleday, Page & Co., 1904, c1903. viii, 103 p., A-K, 1A-16E, [9] leaves of plates: ill., maps; 33

cm. Includes bibliographical references.

Ms. marginalia. Newspaper clipping tipped in.

1659. PIERRE DE SAINTE MARIE MAGDELAINE. *Traitté d'horlogiographie: contenant plusiers manieres de construire, sur toutes surfaces, toutes sortes de lignes horaires ... / par Dom Pierre de Ste. Marie Magdelaine ... Reueu, corrigé & augmenté en cette troisième edition, de plusiers propositions & figures.*

À Paris: Chez Iean du Puis ..., 1663. [16], 312 [i.e. 294] p., 72 [i.e. 71] leaves of plates (1 folded): ill.; 16 cm. Errors of pagination: p. 81-100 omitted, p. 259-260 repeated. Plates 71 and 72 are 1 leaf of plates.

Plate 20 bound between 17 and 18.

1660. PIETZKER, FRIEDRICH, 1844-1916. *Die Gestaltung des Raumes: kritische Untersuchungen über die Grundlagen der Geometrie / von F. Pietzker....*

Braunschweig: Verlag von Otto Salle, 1891. V, [3], 110, [2] p.; 23 cm. Druckfehler-Berichtigung: p. [1] following text. Includes bibliographical references.

No. 8 in a v. of 11 items with binder's title: Geometrie. Provenance: Ernst Mach (inkstamp).

1661. PIKE, NICOLAS, U.S. CONSUL, PORT LOUIS, MAURITIUS. *Sub-tropical rambles in the land of aphanapteryx. Personal experiences, adventures, and wanderings in and around the island of Mauritius. By Nicolas Pike.*

New York: Harper & Brothers, 1873. 3 p. l., [v]-xviii, 509 p., 1 l. front. (port.), illus., plates, fold. maps 22 cm. Half-title: The island of Mauritius. Advertisements: 4 p. following text.

1662. PISA (ITALY). SPECOLA ACCADEMICA. *Observationes siderum habitae Pisis in Specula academica.*

Pisis, excudebat A. Landius [etc.] 17 -1795. v. 27 cm. Quaderennial. -1786/90. Issues for -1778/82 printed by A. Raphaellius; 1782/86 by C. Mugnainius. Editors: -1782/86, Josephus Slop de Cadenburg. – 1786/90, Franciscus Slop de Cadenburg. No more published.

Library has: 1778/82.

1663. PITATI, PIETRO, 16th cent. *Compendium Petri Pitati Veronensis ... : super annua solaris, atque lunaris anni quantitate ... ortu quoque, et occasu stellarum fixarum, in tres diuisum tractatus....*

Venetiis: Apud Dominicum Nicolinum, 1564. 130 [i.e. 134], [1] leaves; 22 cm. Errors in foliation: leaf 6 misnumbered as 8, 81 as 80, 87 as 86, 84-86 repeated. Houzeau & Lancaster. *Astronomie.* (1964 ed.), 13751.

1664. PITISCUS, BARTHOLOMÄUS, 1561-1613. *Bartholomæi Pitisci Grunbergensis Silesij Trigonometriæ siue De dimensione triangulos libri quinque: item problematum varioru[m] ... libri decem. Editio tertia cui recens accessit problematum architectonicorum liber unus.*

Francofurti: Typis Nicolai Hofmanni sumptibus Ionæ Rosæ, 1612. [8], 183, [1] (blank), 270, [227] p.: ill.; 21 cm. *Problematum variorum* and *Canon triangulorum emendatissimus* have separate title pages. Errata: last [5] p.

Binder's blanks printed fragments.

1665. PLANCK, MAX, 1858-1947. *Acht Vorlesungen über theoretische Physik, gehalten an der Columbia University in the city of New York im Frühjahr 1909, von dr. Max Planck... mit fünf Figuren.*

Leipzig: S. Hirzel, 1910. 4 p. l., 127 p. diagrs. 23 cm.

Provenance: Herbert McLean Evans (bookplate).

1666. PLANCK, MAX, 1858-1947. [Collection of offprints and journal articles / by Max Planck].

[1901-1926]. 8 pieces: ill.; 23-27 cm. Includes bibliographical references. (1) Über die Elementarquanta der Materie und der Elektricität (1901) – (2) Zur elektromagnetischen Theorie der Dispersion in isotropen Nichtleitern (1902) – (3) Zur elektromagnetischen Theorie der selectiven Absorption in isotropen Nichtleitern (1903) – (4) Über die Extinction des Lichtes in einem optisch homogenen Medium von normaler Dispersion (1904) – (5) Über die mechanische Bedeutung der Temperatur und der Entropie (1904) – (6) Normale und anomale Dispersion in nichtleitenden Medien von variabler Dichte (1905) – (7) Zur Hypothese der Quantenemission (1911) – (8) Über die Begründung des zweiten Hauptsatzes der Thermodynamik (1926).

1667. Planck, Max, 1858-1947. *Dynamische und statistische Gesetzmässigkeit: Rede, gehalten bei der Feier zum Gedächtnis des Stifters der Berliner Friedrich-Wilhelms-Universität am 3. August 1914 / von Max Planck.*
Leipzig: J. A. Barth, 1914. 31 p.; 21 cm. Title from cover.

1668. Planck, Max, 1858-1947. *Die Einheit des physikalischen Weltbildes; Vortrag gehalten am 9. Dezember 1908 in der Naturwissenschaftlichen Fakultät des Studentenkorps an der Universität Leiden, von Max Planck.*
Leipzig: S. Hirzel, 1909. 33 p. 21 cm. Advertisements on lower wrapper.
Provenance: Karl Horovitz (inscription)

1669. Planck, Max, 1858-1947. *Kausalgesetz und Willensfreiheit. Öffentlicher Vortrag gehalten in der Preussischen Akademie der Wissenschaften am 17. Februar 1923, von Max Planck.*
Berlin: J. Springer, 1923. 52 p. 21 cm. Advertisements on lower wrapper.

1670. Planck, Max, 1858-1947. *Die Physik im Kampf um die Weltanschauung; Vortrag gehalten am 6. März 1935 im Harnack-Haus Berlin-Dahlem, von Dr. Max Planck....*
Leipzig: J. A. Barth, 1935. 32 p. 21 cm.

1671. Planck, Max, 1858-1947. *Physikalische Gesetzlichkeit im Lichte neuerer Forschung: Vortrag gehalten am 14. Februar 1926 in den Akademischen Kursen von Düsseldorf / von Max Planck.*
Leipzig: J. A. Barth, 1926. 48 p.; 21 cm. Title from cover.

1672. †Planck, Max, 1858-1947. *Physikalische Rundblicke: gesammelte Reden und Aufsätze, von Max Planck.*
Leipzig: S. Hirzel, 1922. 2 p. l., 168 p. 22 cm. Bibliography in "Anmerkungen". Die Einheit des physikalischen Weltbildes. – Die Stellung der neueren Physik zur mechanischen Naturanschauung. – Neue Bahnen der physikalischen Erkenntnis. – Dynamische und statistische Gesetzmüssigkeit. – Das Prinzip der kleinsten Wirkung (Sonderdruck aus *Kultur der Gegenwart* Leipzig, 1915). – Verhältnis der Theorien zueinander (Sonderdruck aus *Kultur der Gegenwart.* Leipzig, 1915). – Das Wesen des lichts. – Die Entstehung und bisherige Entwicklung der Quantentheorie.
[2] p. of advertisements on lower endpapers.

1673. Planck, Max, 1858-1947. *Scientific autobiography, and other papers; with a memorial address on Max Planck, by Max von Laue. Tr. from German by Frank Gaynor.*
New York: Philosophical Library, 1949. 192 p. port. 22 cm. A scientific autobiography. – Phantom problems in science. – The meaning and limits of exact science. – The concept of causality in physics. – Religion and natural science.

1674. Planck, Max, 1858-1947. *Die Stellung der neueren Physik zur mechanischen Naturanschauung: Vortrag gehalten am 23. September 1910 auf der 82. Versammlung Deutscher Naturforscher und Ärzte in Königsberg i. Pr. / von Max Planck.*
Leipzig: S. Hirzel, 1910. 33 p.; 23 cm.
Provenance: Karl Horovitz (inscription).

1675. Planck, Max, 1858-1947. *Treatise on thermodynamics, by Dr. Max Planck. Tr. with the author's sanction by Alexander Ogg.*
London: Longmans, Green, and Co., 1903. xii, 272 p. diagr. 23 cm. Translaton of: *Vorlesungen über Thermodynamik.* Includes index. "Catalogue of the author's publications on thermodynamics, excluding the applications to electricity, with a reference to the paragraphs of this book, which deal with the same point": p. [264]-265.

1676. Planck, Max, 1858-1947. *Über eine Verbesserung der Wien'schen Spectralgleichung / von M. Planck.*
Leipzig: J. A. Barth, 1900. p. 202-204; 23 cm. Cover title. "Sonderabdruck aus den *Verhandlungen der Deutschen Physikalischen Gesellschaft,* II. Jahrg. Nr. 13." Includes bibliographical references.
Provenance: author's inscription and signature; Herbert McLean Evans (bookplate).

1677. Planck, Max, 1858-1947. *Über neuere thermodynamische Theorien (Nernstsches*

Wärmetheorem und Quantenhypothese): Vortrag gehalten am 16. Dezember 1911 in der Deutschen Chemischen Gesellschaft in Berlin / von Max Planck.
Leipzig: Akademische Verlagsgesellschaft, 1912. 34 p.; 22 cm. Advertisements on lower wrapper.

1678. PLANCK, MAX, 1858-1947. *Vorlesungen über die Theorie der Wärmestrahlung, von dr. Max Planck....*
Leipzig: J. A. Barth, 1906. viii, 222 p. diagrs. 24 cm. Advertisements: 2 p. following text. Bibliography: p. 221-222.
Provenance: Herbert McLean Evans (bookplate).

1679. PLANCK, MAX, 1858-1947. *Vorlesungen über Thermodynamik / von Dr. Max Planck ...; mit fünf Figuren im Text.*
Leipzig: Veit & Comp., 1897. vi, [2], 248 p.: ill.; 24 cm. Advertisements on flyleaves and inside covers. "Verzeichniss der thermodynamischen Schriften des Verfassers"; p. 248.
Provenance: Albert Lessing (ink stamp).

1680. PLANCK, MAX, 1858-1947. *Vorlesungen über Thermodynamik / von Max Planck. 2. verb. Aufl.*
Leipzig: Veit, 1905. vii, 256 p.; 24 cm. Bibliography: p. 255-256.

1681. PLANCK, MAX, 1858-1947. *Wege zur physikalischen Erkenntnis: Reden und Vorträge / von Max Planck.*
Leipzig: S. Hirzel, 1933. ix, 280 p.; 23 cm. "Die vorliegende Sammlung ... war ursprünglich gedacht als eine neue Auflage meiner in dem nämlichen Verlag erschienenen 'Physikalischen Rundblicke,' ergänzt durch Aufnahme einiger inzwischen erschienener Aufsätze allgemeineren Inhalts." – Geleitwort. Later edition (1949, c1933) published under title: *Vorträge und Erinnerungen.* Die Einheit des physikalischen Weltbildes. – Neue Bahnen der physikalischen Erkenntnis. – Dynamische und statistische Gesetz mässigkeit. – Die Entstehung und bisherige Entwicklung der Quantentheorie. – Kausalgesetz und Willensfreiheit. – Vom Relativen zum Absoluten. – Physikalische Gesetzlichkeit. – Das Weltbild der neuen Physik. – Positivismus und reale Aussenwelt. – Die Kausalität in der Natur. – Ursprung und Auswirkung wissenschaftlicher Ideen.

1682. PLANCK, MAX, 1858-1947. *Das Wesen des Lichts: Vortrag gehalten in der Hauptversammlung der Kaiser-Wilhelm-Gesellschaft am 28. Oktober 1919 / von Max Planck.*
Berlin: Julius Springer, 1920. 22 p.; 22 cm. Advertisements: 2 p. following text, and lower wrapper.

1683. PLANCK, MAX, 1858-1947. *Where is science going? [By] Max Planck. With a pref. by Albert Einstein. Translated and edited by James Murphy.*
London: G. Allen & Unwin, 1933. 224 p. port. 23 cm. Includes index.

1684. PLANCK, MAX, 1858-1947. *Wissenschaftliche Selbstbiographie: mit einem Bildnis und der von Max von Laue gehaltenen Traueransprache / Max Planck.*
Leipzig: J. A. Barth, 1948. 33 p., [1] leaf of plates: port.; 21 cm. Cover title.

1685. PLANCK, MAX, 1858-1947. *Zur Theorie des Gesetzes der Energieverteilung im Normalspectrum / von M. Planck.*
[Leipzig: J. A. Barth, 1900]. p.237-245: ill.; 24 cm. Caption title. Detached from: *Verhandlungen der Deutschen Physikalischen Gesellschaft* im Jahre 1900, zweiter Jahrgang, Nr. 17. "Vorgetragen in der Sitzung vom 14. December 1900." Includes bibliographical references. Horblit, H. D. *Grolier 100 science books,* 26a.

1686. *The Planetary system.*
London: T. Nelson and Sons, [187-?].vi, [7]-118, [2] p.: ill. (some col.); 17 cm. Wonders of the heavens. Includes bibliographical references. [2] p. of advertisements at end.
Provenance: First Presbyterian Sunday School Library, Portland, Oregon, No. 525 (inkstamp).

1687. PLASSMANN, JOSEPH, 1859- . *Himmelskunde: Versuch einer methodischen Einführung in die Hauptlehren der Astronomie / von Joseph Plassmann. 2. und 3., verb. Aufl.*
Freiburg im Breisgau: Herdersche Verlagshandlung, 1913. xiv, 571 p., [10] leaves of plates (some folded): ill., map, charts; 25 cm. Illustrierte Bibliothek der Länder und Völkerkunde. Folded chart in pocket. Includes bibliographical references and index.
Advertisements: [4] p. at end. Provenance: Dr. Charles Maechling (inkstamp).

ΠΛΑΤΩΝΟΣ

ΑΠΑΝΤΑ ΤΑ ΣΩΖΟΜΕΝΑ.

PLATONIS

opera quæ extant omnia.

EX NOVA IOANNIS SERRANI INterpretatione, perpetuis eiusdẽ notis illustrata: quibus & methodus & doctrinæ summa breuiter & perspicuè indicatur.

EIVSDEM *Annotationes in quosdam suæ illius interpretationis locos.*

HENR. STEPHANI de quorundam locorum interpretatione iudicium, & multorum contextus Græci emendatio.

EXCVDEBAT HENR. STEPHANVS,
CVM PRIVILEGIO CÆS. MAIEST.

PLATO, *Platonis opera*, 1578

1688. Plato. *Hapanta Platonos meth ypomnematon Proklou eis ton Timaion ... = Platonis Omnia opera cum commentariis Procli in Timæum & Politica....*

Basileae: Apud Ioan. Valderum, 1534. 2 v.; 33 cm. Title and imprint of v. 1 from *NUC -pre 56*. Edited by Simon Grynaeus and Johann Walder. Adams P2139.

1689. Plato. *Platonos hapanta ta sozomena = Platonis opera quæ extant omnia / ex nova Ioannis Serrani interpretatione, perpetuis eiusde[m] notis illustrata; quibus & methodus & doctrinæ summa breuiter & perspicuà indicatur; eiusdem annotationes in quosdam suæ illius interpretationis locos; Henr. Stephani de quorundam locorum interpretatione iudicium, & multorum contextus Græci emendatio.*

[Geneva?]: Excudebat Henr. Stephanus, 1578. 3 v.; 39 cm. Includes index. Printer's device on the t. p. of v. 1. Imprint date part of the printer's device. The Greek text is from the Aldine 1513 edition collated with the Basel 1534 and 1556, and for the Laws, the Louvain 1531 edition. The Latin is a new translation by Jean de Serres revised and corrected by Estienne. Includes three dedicatory prefaces: the first vol. is dedicated to Queen Elizabeth, the second to James VI of Scotland, the third to the Republic of Berne. Greek and Latin in parallel columns. Vols. 2 and 3 have half-title only. Adams P-1439. Schreiber, F. *Estiennes*, no. 201.

v. 1 & 3 bound together. Provenance: Colonel Cooper (armorial bookplate); Markree Library (booklabel).

1690. Playfair, John, 1748-1819. *Illustrations of the Huttonian theory of the earth / by John Playfair....*

London: Cadell and Davies; Edinburgh: William Creech, 1802, (Edinburgh: Neill & Co.). xx, 528 p.; 22 cm. Includes bibliographical references. Horblit, H. D. *Grolier 100 science books*, 52b.

Provenance: presentation inscription from [Ben?] Waters to Chas. Anderson.

1691. Playfair, John, 1748-1819. *The works of John Playfair ... with a memoir of the author....*

Edinburgh: A. Constable & Co.; [etc., etc.], 1822. 4 v. viii pl. 23 cm. Edited by James G. Playfair. v. 1. Biographical memoir. Illustrations of the Huttonian theory of the earth. -v. 2. Dissertation, exhibiting a general view of the progress of mathematical and physical science since the revival of letters in Europe. -v. 3. On the arithmetic of impossible quantities. On the causes which affect the accuracy of barometrical measurements. Remarks on the astronomy of the Brahmins. On the origin and investigation of porisms. Observations on the trigonometrical tables of the Brahmins. Theorems relating to the figure of the earth. On the solids of greatest attraction. On the progress of heat in spherical bodies. Account of a lithological survey of Schehallien. On the naval tactics of the late John Clerk. -v. 4. Biographical account of Matthew Stewart. Biographical account of James Hutton. Biographical account of John Robinson. Review of Mudge's *Account of the trigonometrical survey of England*. Review of Mechain et Delambre, *Base du système mérique décimal*. Review of Laplace, *Traité de mécanique céleste*. Review of *Le Compte rendu* par l'Institut de France. Review of Lambton's *Measurement of an arch of the meridan*. Review of Laplace, *Essai philosophique sur les probabilitiés*. Review of Baron de Zach, *Attraction des montagnes*. Review of Kater, *On the pendulum*.

1692. Pliny, the Elder. *Plinii Secvndi Historia mvndi, denvo sic emendata, vt in svperiori æditione, quæ tamen fuit accuratissima, præ hac dormitatum uideri possit. In illa longo interuallo uiceramus cæteros, in hac longiore uicimus nos ipsos, potissimum adiuti tribus optimæ fidei peruetustis exemplaribus, tum opera cuiusdam eruditi, qui sibi sumpserat hanc prouinciam, nonnihil etiam Beati Rhenani doctissimis annotationibus, quas utinam absoluisset ... Adiunctus est index copiosissimus.*

Basileae: In officina Frobeniana, 1530. [36], 671, [177] p. 34 cm. Also known as: *Naturalis historia*. At head of title: Hieronymvs Frobenivs amico lectori s. d. Based on Erasmus' edition issued by Froben in 1525; index based on that of Joannes Camers. Index has special t. p.

Provenance: British School of Rome (inkstamp); presentation inscription from Charles Godfrey Leland to Rev. J. Wood Brown; ms. marginalia.

1693. Pliny, the Elder. *Caii Plinii Secundi Historia naturalis / ex recensione I. Harduini et recentiorum adnotationibus.*

Augustae Taurinorum: Ex typis Iosephi Pomba, 1829-1834. 11 v.; 23 cm. Indexes: v. 10-11, by Angelo Pihan Delaforest. Includes bibliographical references.

Provenance: Bibliotheca Carmelitarum Merkelbeek (inkstamp).

1694. Pliny, the Elder. *Caio Plinio Veronese Libro De l'historia naturale.*

Impresso in Venesia: Per Vbertino da Vercelli, 1501. die. xxx. di octobre. [1032] columns; 31 cm. Signatures: $2a^6a^6b\text{-}q^8r\text{-}s^6A^6B\text{-}N^8O\text{-}P^6$. Imprint from $P6a^1$. Includes indexes. Adams P 1591.

Imperfect: t. p. missing, a fragment pasted on a blank leaf is supplied (this used as t. p. substitute); a6, s1 missing.

1695. Pliny, the Elder. *The historie of the world: commonly called, the Naturall historie / of C. Plinius Secundus; translated into English by Philemon Holland....*

London: Printed by Adam Islip, and are to be sold by Iohn Grismond ..., 1635. 2 v.; 34 cm. Preface dated 1601. Imprint of v. 2: London: Printed by Adam Islip, 1634. Includes indexes. *STC* 20030a

Bound in 1 v.

1696. Pliny, the Elder. *Libros naturalis historiae nouitiu[m] Cam[a]enis Q[ui]ritiu[m] tuo[rum] opus natu[m] apud me proxima f[a]etura licentiore epistola narrare co[n]stitui tibi iocu[n]dissime imperator.*

Restituit Venetis: me nuper Spira Ioannes ..., 1469. [712] p.; 41 cm. Text begins: Plinus secundus nouocomensis equestribus militiis industri[a]e functus ... Title from line 12 onwards. Imprint from colophon. *ISTC* gives date as (before 18 Sept.) 1469. Spaces left for capitals, headings, and for Greek words in text. Gatherings unsigned. BM *15th cent.*, V, p. 153 (IC. 19506) (variant setting). Goff (rev.) P-786. Hain-Copinger-Reichling, 13087. Horblit, H. D. *Grolier 100 science books,* 84. *ISTC,* ip00786000.

Rubrication: 2 large decorated initials, one with human figure and floral border, in blue, red, green, brown, mauve, white & gold ink; most large spaces blank; smaller capitals added in red or blue; initial-strokes, some headings in red. Signatures (cf. BM *15th cent.*) added in pencil. Imperfect: lacks final blank (p. [711]-[712]). Binding: full calf, gilt spine; red edges. Binder's title: C. Plinii Historia natur. de anno 1468. Provenance: Christophorus Pirchaimer Viennensis (inscription); facsim. of Hilprand Brandenburg of Biberach's bookplate depicting an angel holding shield with bull.

1697. Pliny, the Younger. *C. Plinii Caecilii Secundi Epistolarum libri decem et Panegyricus: cum notis variorum.*

Augustae Taurinorum: Ex typis Iosephi Pomba, 1828. 2 v.; 23 cm. Includes bibliographical references and indexes. Praefatio Schaeferi: p. iii-xiv. Vita C. Plinii Caecilii Secundi auctore Christophoro Cellario: p. xl-lviii.

Provenance: Bibliotheca Carmelitarum Merkelbeek (inkstamp).

1698. Plot, Robert, 1640-1696. *The natural history of Oxford-shire,: being an essay toward the natural history of England. / By R. P.....*

[Oxford]: Printed at the theater in Oxford, and are to be had there: and in London at Mr. S. Millers ..., 1677. [12], 358, [12] p., [17] leaves of plates (1 folded): ill., map, coats of arms; 33 cm. Title vignette. Plates by Michael Burghers. Includes index. Errata: p. [1] at end. Wing P2586. Yale. *Ornithological books,* p. 229.

Provenance: William Thorn (signature); Herbert McLean Evans (bookplate). 4 leaves inserted containing in ms.: The publisher to the reader, a short account of the author, the contents of the chapters of the second edition, and the additions to the second edition of Plots Oxfordshire.

1699. Pluche, Noèl Antoine, 1688-1761. *Le spectacle de la nature, ou, Entretiens sur les particularités de l'histoire naturelle: qui ont parus les plus propres à rendre les jeunes-gens curieux, & à leur former l'esprit....*

À Paris: Chez les Frères Éstienne ..., 1764-1770. 8 v. in 9: ill.; 17 cm. Plates engraved by J. P. Le Bas.

Vol. 5-7 are nouv. éd.

1700. Plücker, Julius, 1801-1868. *Analytisch-geometrische Entwicklungen.*

Essen: bey G. D. Baedeker, 1828-1831. 2 v. plates. 28 cm. Verbesserungen: in v. 2 following text.

1701. Plücker, Julius, 1801-1868. *Neue Geometrie des Raumes gegründet auf die Betrachtung der geraden Linie als Raumelement.*

Leipzig: 1868-1869. 2 v. in 1. 29 cm. Paged consecutively. Abth. 1, mit einem Vorwort von A. Clebsch; Abth. 2, hrsg. von Fleix Klein.

With: *Étude des élassoïdes* /par Albert Ribaucour. Bruxelles: F. Hayez, 1881.

1702. PLÜCKER, JULIUS, 1801-1868. *On the spectra of ignited gases and vapours: with especial regard to the different spectra of the same elementary gaseous substance / by Dr. J. Plücker ... and Dr. J. W. Hittorf....*

[London: Royal Society, 1865]. 29 p., III folded leaves of plates: ill. (1 col.); 30 cm. Caption title. "Received February 23, read March 3, 1864." At head of title: Philosophical transactions. Detached from: *Philosophical transactions of the Royal Society*, v. 155 1865. Includes bibliographical references.

Provenance: authors' presentation inscription to Fizeau; Herbert McLean Evans (bookplate).

1703. PLUMMER, JOHN ISAAC. *Introduction to astronomy: for the use of science classes and elementary and middle class schools / by John Isaac Plummer....*

London and Glasgow: William Collins, Sons, and Company, 1873. vii, [1], [9]-174, [2] p., [1] leaf of plates: ill.; 17 cm. Collins' Elementary Science series. Includes index. Advertisements: [2] p. at end.

Ms. marginalia.

1704. PLUTARCH. *The lives of the noble Grecians & Romans / compared together by ... Plutarch of Chæronea; translated out of Greek into French by James Amiot ... ; with the lives of Hannibal & Scipio African, translated out of Latin into French by Charles del'Escluse, and out of French into English by Sir Thomas North ...; hereunto are added the lives of Epaminondas, of Philip of Macedon, of Dionysius the elder ... of Augustus Cæsar, of Plutarch, and of Seneca, with the lives of nine other excellent chieftains ... collected out of Æmylius Probus by S.G.S. and Englished by the afore said translator; and now also in this edition are further added the lives of twenty selected eminent persons, of ancient and latter times, translated out of the work of ... Andrew Theuet; to which ... are subjoyned notes and explications upon Plutarch's Lives, collected out of Xylander, Cruserus, Henry Stephanus and others....*

Printed by Abraham Miller, and are to be sold by William Lee ..., 1657. [48], 1031 [i.e. 1027], [3], [24], 76, [2] p.: ports; 34 cm. The biographies here attributed to Aemylius Probus are by Cornelius Nepos. "The lives of Epaminondas, of Philip of Macedon ..." (p. [913]-1031) has special t. p. dated 1656. "Prosopographia, or, Some select pourtraitures and lives of ancient and modern illustrious personages ...originally compiled ... by Andrew Thevet ...; newly translated into English by some learned and eminent persons, and generally by Geo. Gerbier, alias D'Ouuilly ..." ([4], 76 p.) has special t. p. dated 1657. Added engraved t. p., dated 1656, signed: Francis Barlow inventer. Signatures: A^8 *-2*^{6} 3*^{4} B-4S^6 4T^4 4U^6 5A-5K^4. Pagination: nos. 97-100, 444-445 omitted, 797-798 repeated; numerous other errors. Wing (2nd ed.), P-2633. "An alphabeticall table of the principallest things...": p. [17]-[48] (1st sequence). "Notes & explications upon Plutarch's Lives...": p. [3]-[22] (4th sequence). Publisher's advertisements on final [2] p.

Imperfect: lacks "The frontispice explain'd" (=A1?), B3.4, and 5H1, 2.3; 3I2, 3.4 and 5E1 torn with loss of text; added engraved t. p., and 5K2, 3.4 repaired.

Provenance: Roy Vernon Sowers (booklabel); Gerard (signature).

1705. POBLACIÓN, JUAN MARTÍNEZ. *De vsu astrolabi compe[n]dium: schematibus commodissimis illustratum / authore Ioanne Martino Poblacion.*

Parisiis: Ex typographia Ioannis Barbæi, prostat apud Iacobum Gazellum ..., 1546. 64 leaves: ill.; 16 cm. Procli Diadochi Fabrica ususque astrolabi / Georgio Valla Placentino interprete – Gregoræ Nicephori Astrolabus / eodem interprete.

Imperfect: leaves 10 & 15 are missing. Disbound.

1706. POINCARÉ, HENRI, 1854-1912. *Science and method. Translated by Francis Maitland. With a pref. by the Hon. Bertrand Russell.*

London, New York: T. Nelson, 1914. 288 p. 20 cm.

1707. POINCARÉ, HENRI, 1854-1912. *La science et l'hypothèse / par H. Poincaré.*

Paris: Flammarion, [1905?]. 284 p.; 19 cm. Bibliothèque de philosophie scientifique. Le nombre et la grandeur – L'espace – La force – La nature. Advertisements: t. p. verso, dated 1905.

Provenance: S. E. Yaggy (signature); ms. marginalia.

1708. POINCARÉ, HENRI, 1854-1912. *La valeur de la science par H. Poincaré....*

Paris: E. Flammarion, [1905?]. 2 p. l., 278 p. 19 cm. Bibliothèque de philosophie scientifique. "Huitième mille" – Cover.

Advertisements: [2] p. at end of text and [1] p. on

lower wrapper. Provenance: Herbert M. Evans (shipping label loosely inserted).

1709. PONCELET, M. (JEAN VICTOR), 1788-1867. *Traité des propriétés projectives des figures, ouvrage utile à ceux qui s'occupent des applications de la géométrie descriptive et d'opérations géométriques sur le terrain / par J. V. Poncelet....*

Paris: Bachelier, 1822. xlvi, 426, [2] p.: diagrs. on XII fold. pl.; 28 cm. Errata: p. [427]. Plates signed: J. V. Poncelet del., Dembour sculp.

1710. POOR, CHARLES LANE, 1866- . *The solar system: a study of recent observations / by Charles Lane Poor.*

London: John Murray, 1908. x, 310 p., [6] leaves of plates (1 folded): ill., maps; 22 cm. Progressive Science series. "This work grew out of a series of lectures delivered at Columbia University" – P. iii. Includes bibliographical references and index. Also published in same year: New York & London: G. P. Putnam's Sons.

Advertisements: 10 pages at end.

1711. PORTER, JERMAIN G. (JERMAIN GILDERSLEEVE), b. 1852. *The stars in song and legend / by Jermain G. Porter; with illustrations from the drawings of Albrecht Dürer.*

Boston: Ginn & Co., [1902, c1901]. xvi, 129 p., [19] leaves of plates: ill., plan; 19 cm. Includes index.

1712. *Practical astronomy, navigation, nautical astronomy, and meteorology: being a guide to the scenery of the heavens, the planetary and stellar movements, the practice of navigation, and phenomena of the atmosphere / by J. R. Young ..., Hugh Breen ..., John Scoffern ... and E. J. Lowe.*

London: Houlston and Stoneman ...: Wm. S. Orr and Co. ..., 1856. viii, 598, [2] p.: ill.; 21 cm. Orr's circle of the science; v. 7. Advertisements on [2] p. at end. Includes indexes. *Nautical astronomy and navigation* / J. R. Young – *Practical and physical astronomy* / (Hugh Breen) – *Meteorology* / (John Scoffern) – *Practical meteorology* / (E. J. Lowe).

Provenance: H. C. Perkins (signature); extensive ms. marginalia; newspaper clippings and ms. notes tipped in.

1713. PRAETORIUS, JOHANN, 1537-1616. *De cometis qui antea visi sunt: et de eo, qui nouissime mense nouembri apparuit, narratio / a Iohanne Prætorio Ioachimico, Reip. Noribergensis....*

Noribergæ: In Officina Typographica Catharinæ Gerlachin, & hæredum Iohannis Montani, 1578. [22] p.; 20 cm. Imprint taken partly from colophon. Signatures: A-C^4 (C4 blank).

1714. PRESCOT, BARTHOLOMEW. *The inverted scheme of Copernicus; with the pretended experiments upon which his followers have founded their hypotheses of matter and motion, compared with facts, and with the experience of the senses, and the doctrine of the formation of worlds out of atoms, by the power of gravity and attraction, contrasted with the formation of one world by divine power, as it is revealed in the history of creation. To which is prefixed a letter to Sir Humphry Davy.*

Liverpool: 1822-1823. 2 v. front. (v. 2) diagrs. (part. fold.) 21 cm. Errata: last p. Vol. 2 has title: The system of the universe.

With the author's: *The motion of the sun in the ecliptic.* London, Published by C. & J. Rivington ... and by G. Riebau... , 1825. Ms. notes. Binder: Homecrafters.

1715. PRESCOT, BARTHOLOMEW. *The motion of the sun in the ecliptic, proved to be uniform in a circular orbit: and tables of the equations, directly and accurately calculated from the true distances; with preliminary observations on the fallacy of the solar system, in a series of letters / by Bartholomew Prescott....*

London: Published by C. & J. Rivington ... and by G. Riebau ..., 1825. 70 p.; 22 cm. Errata: p. 70. Imprint date taken from p. 70.

With v. 2 of the author's: *The inverted scheme of Copernicus.* Liverpool, 1822-1823. Binder: Homecrafters.

1716. PRIESTER, WOLFGANG. *Radiobeobachtungen des ersten künstlichen Erdsatelliten, von Wolfgang Priester, Hans-Gerhard Bennewitz und Peter Lengrüsser.*

Köln: Westdeutscher Verlag, 1958. 38 p. illus. 25 cm. Wissenschaftliche Abhandlungen der Arbeitsgemeinschaft für Forschung des Landes Nordrhein-Westfalen; Bd. 1. Bibliography: p. 38.

1717. PRIESTLEY, JOSEPH, 1733-1804. *Experiments and observations on different kinds of air. / By Joseph Priestley....*

London: Printed for J. Johnson ..., MDCCLXXIV-MDCCLXXVII [1774-1777]. 3 v.: ill.; 22 cm. Vol. 1: 1774; v. 2: 1775; v. 3: 1777. Continued as the author's *Experiments and observations relating to various branches of natural philosophy*, 3 vols. (London, 1779-1786). Signatures: v. 1: $pi^1a^8b^4c^2B\text{-}X^8Y^4$; v. 2: $a\text{-}b^8c^4d^2B\text{-}2D^8$; v. 3: $a\text{-}b^8c^4B\text{-}2D^82E^4$. Vol. 1: [2], xxiii, [5], 324, [4] p., [2] folded leaves of plates; v. 2: xliv, 399, [17] p., III leaves of plates; v. 3: xxxiv, [6], 411, (13)p., [1] folded leaf of plates. Errata: v. 1: p. [1] at end; v. 2: p. [1] at end; v. 3: p. [9] at end. Includes indexes. Publisher's advertisements: v. 1: last three unnumbered pages; v. 3: last four unnumbered pages. Crook, R. E. *Priestley*, S/451-453. Horblit, H. D. *Grolier 100 science books*, 85.

Imperfect: v. l last [4] p. missing. Provenance: Ralph Hermon Major (bookplate); presented to R. C. B. by Cecil Reddie (inscription).

1718. PRIESTLEY, JOSEPH, 1733-1804. *Observations on different kinds of air / by Joseph Priestley....*

London : Printed for Lockyer Davis ..., 1772. p. 147-264, [1] folded leaf of plates : ill. ; 23 cm. In: *Philosophical transactions* / Royal society of London, v. 62. Caption title. "Read March 5, 12, 19, 26, 1772". Crook. *Priestley*, Per/672. *PMM*, 217. Burndy. *Science*, 40.

1719. *The Principle of relativity: a collection of original memoirs on the special and general theory of relativity / by H. A. Lorentz, A. Einstein, H. Minkowski and H. Weyl; with notes by A. Sommerfeld; translated by W. Perrett and G. B. Jeffery.*

New York: Dodd, Mead, 1923. viii, 216 p.: ill.; 23 cm. Translated, with the exception of one article, from the German collection entitled *Das Relativitätsprinzip* (Teubner, 4th ed., 1922). Cf. p. v. Includes bibliographical references. "Printed in Great Britain" – T. p. verso.

Provenance: William Howell Williams (bookplate).

1720. PROCTOR, MARY, b. 1862. *Comets; their nature, origin, and place in the science of astronomy, by Mary Proctor ... and Dr. A.C.D. Crommelin....*

London: The Technical Press Ltd., 1937. xi, 203, [1] p. front., illus., 2 pl., diagrs. 23 cm. Includes bibliographical references and index.

1721. PROCTOR, MARY, b. 1862. *Everyman's astronomy, by Mary Proctor....*

London: J. Gifford Limited, 1939. vi p. 2 l., 245, [1] p. front., plates. 22 cm. "First published, 1939."

Provenance: Percy Marshall (inscription).

1722. PROCTOR, MARY, b. 1862. *Half-hours with the summer stars, by Mary Proctor....*

Chicago: A. C. McClurg & Co., 1911. xxiii p., 1 l., 232 p. front., 9 pl. 17 cm. Cover title: *Half hours with summer stars.* Includes index.

1723. PROCTOR, MARY, b. 1862. *Legends of the stars, by Mary Proctor ... illustrated by Dorothy Newsome.*

London: G. G. Harrap & Co. Ltd., 1922. 128 p. incl. front., illus., plates 19 cm. All time tales. Includes bibliographical references.

1724. PROCTOR, MARY, b. 1862. *The romance of comets, by Mary Proctor....*

New York and London: Harper & Brothers, 1926. xiii, 210 p. front., plates, ports., diagr. 20 cm. Includes bibliographical references.

1725. PROCTOR, MARY, b. 1862. *Romance of the moon, by Mary Proctor ... illustrated with charts, and photographs taken at the leading observatories.*

New York and London: Harper & Brothers, 1928. xii p.,1 l., 262 p. front., plates, map. 20 cm. Includes bibliographical references and index.

1726. PROCTOR, MARY, b. 1862. *Romance of the planets, by Mary Proctor ... illustrated with photographs taken at the leading observatories, drawings and a chart.*

New York, London: Harper & Brothers, 1929. xii p., 1 l., 272 p. front., plates. 20 cm. Includes bibliographical references and index.

1727. PROCTOR, MARY, b. 1862. *Romance of the sun, by Mary Proctor.*

New York, London: Harper & Brothers, 1927. xii p., 1 l., 266 p. front., plates, map. 20 cm. Includes bibliographical references and index.

1728. PROCTOR, MARY, b. 1862. *Wonders of the sky, by Mary Proctor ... with eleven illustrations.*

London & New York: F. Warne & Co. Ltd., (c1932). 96 p. illus. 20 cm. Warne's "Recreation" books. Books recommended for reading. p. 10.

1729. PROCTOR, MARY, b. 1862. *The young folks book of the heavens / Mary Proctor.*
[Boston: Little, Brown and Co., 1900?]. xiv, 256 p., [18] leaves of plates: ill. (some col.), charts, maps; 23 cm. Romance of knowledge. Star charts on endpapers. Includes bibliographical references and index.
Imperfect: lacks title page. Provenance: Alexander Hamilton Junior High School Library (inkstamp).

1730. PROCTOR, RICHARD A. (RICHARD ANTHONY), 1837-1888. *The borderland of science: a series of familiar dissertations on stars, planets, and meteors; sun and moon; earthquakes; flying-machines; coal; gambling; coincidences; ghosts; &c. By Richard A. Proctor ... With a portrait of the author.*
Philadelphia: J. B. Lippincott & Co.; [etc., etc.], 1874. vii p., 1 l., 438 p. front. (port.) 20 cm. "Reprinted from the *Cornhill magazine.*"

1731. PROCTOR, RICHARD A. (RICHARD ANTHONY), 1837-1888. *Easy star lessons / by Richard A. Proctor ... A new edition.*
London: Chatto and Windus ..., 1883. 239 p.: ill., charts; 19 cm.
Advertisements: half-title verso; at end publisher's catalog, 32 p., dated October, 1886. Binding: publisher's blue cloth. Provenance: Charles Atwood Kofoid (bookplate).

1732. PROCTOR, RICHARD A. (RICHARD ANTHONY), 1837-1888. *Essays on astronomy: a series of papers on planets and meteors, the sun and sun-surrounding space, stars and star cloudlets: and a dissertation on the approaching transits of Venus: preceded by a sketch of the life and work of Sir John Herschel / by Richard A. Proctor....*
London: Longmans, Green, and Co.; Scribner, Welford, and Armstrong, 1872. xiv, [2], 401 p., X leaves of plates (some folded): ill., charts; 23 cm.
Advertisements: [2] p. at end. Provenance: Sara P. Lowell (signature).

1733. PROCTOR, RICHARD A. (RICHARD ANTHONY), 1837-1888. *The expanse of heaven: a series of essays on the wonders of the firmament. By R. A. Proctor....*
New York: D. Appleton and Company, 1874. 2 p. l., [iii]-iv, 305 p. 19 cm. Includes bibliographical references.
Binder: Homecrafters, Tucson, Ar. (ticket).

1734. PROCTOR, RICHARD A. (RICHARD ANTHONY), 1837-1888. *Flowers of the sky / by Richard A. Proctor. New ed.*
London: Chatto & Windus, 1903. 295 p.: ill., charts, maps; 20 cm.

1735. PROCTOR, RICHARD A. (RICHARD ANTHONY), 1837-1888. *The moon: her motions, aspect, scenery, and physical condition, by Richard A. Proctor ... With three lunar photographs by Rutherfurd (enlarged by Brothers) and many plates, charts, etc.*
London: Longmans, Green & Co., 1873. xv, [1], 394, [6] p. front., illus., 24 pl. (incl. 2 fold. maps, fold. chart) tables. 20 cm. Errata on p. [xvi]. Advertisements: [6] p. at end. Includes bibliographical references.

1736. PROCTOR, RICHARD A. (RICHARD ANTHONY), 1837-1888. *The moon: her motions, aspect, scenery, and physical condition / by Richard A. Proctor ...; with two lunar photographs by Rutherfurd and many illustrations. Second edition.*
London: Longmans, Green, and Co., 1878. x, [2], 314 p., [8] leaves of plates (1 folded): ill., maps; 20 cm. Includes bibliographical references.
Advertisements: [2] p. at end.

1737. PROCTOR, RICHARD A. (RICHARD ANTHONY), 1837-1888. *The moon: her motions, aspect, scenery, and physical condition / by Richard A. Proctor ...; with photographs by Rutherfurd and many illustrations. [2nd ed.]*
New York: D. Appleton and Company, 1896. x, [2], 314 p., [8] leaves of plates (1 folded): ill., maps; 20 cm. "Authorized edition" – T. p. verso. Preface to

2nd ed. p. [5], dated 1878. Includes bibliographical references.
Provenance: John H. Comstock (signature).

1738. PROCTOR, RICHARD A. (RICHARD ANTHONY), 1837-1888. *Myths and marvels of astronomy / by Richard A. Proctor ...*
New York: R. Worthington ..., 1880. vi, [2], 363 p.; ill.; 23 cm. Includes bibliographical references.

1739. PROCTOR, RICHARD A. (RICHARD ANTHONY), 1837-1888. *A new star atlas: for the library, the school, and the observatory: in twelve circular maps / by Richard A. Proctor; revised and corrected by T. E. Espin (1895).*
London: Longmans, Green and Co., 1915. xii, 36 p., [14] folded leaves of plates: ill., charts; 20 cm. "Twenty-third impression." "This atlas is reduced from my large star atlas" – p. [v]. Includes bibliographical references.

1740. PROCTOR, RICHARD A. (RICHARD ANTHONY), 1837-1888. *Old and new astronomy. By Richard A. Proctor ... Completed by A. Cowper Ranyard. With numerous plates and woodcuts.*
London: Longmans, Green and Co., 1892. viii, 816 p. illus., XXXI pl. (incl. front.) maps, diagrs. 30 cm. Issued in twelve parts with a supplementary part. Includes bibliographical references and index.
Provenance: Evelyn Peel (signature).

1741. PROCTOR, RICHARD A. (RICHARD ANTHONY), 1837-1888. *The orbs around us: a series of familiar essays on the moon and planets, meteors and comets, the sun and coloured pairs of suns / by Richard A. Proctor ... New edition.*
London and New York: Longmans, Green, and Co. ..., 1894. viii, [4], 336 p.: ill., map; 19 cm. Includes bibliographical references.
Advertisements: [2], 24 p. at end.

1742. PROCTOR, RICHARD A. (RICHARD ANTHONY), 1837-1888. *Other worlds than ours: the plurality of worlds studied under the light of recent scientific researches / by Richard A. Proctor; with an introductory note by Frank Parsons.*
New York: A. L. Burt, [1890]. 328 p., [3] leaves of plates (2 folded): ill., charts, port.; 20 cm. Burt's library of the world's best books. Date of publication supplied by *NUC pre-1956*, v. 472, p. 342.
Advertisements: [8] p. at end. Provenance: B. R. Baumgardt (booklabel).

1743. PROCTOR, RICHARD A. (RICHARD ANTHONY), 1837-1888. *Our place among infinities; a series of essays contrasting our little abode in space and time with the infinities around us. To which are added essays on the Jewish sabbath and astrology, by Richd. A. Proctor.*
New York: D. Appleton and Company, 1883. 3 p.l. 323 p. 21 cm. "Most of these essays have been reprinted from current periodicals."
Advertisements: [6] p. at end.

1744. PROCTOR, RICHARD A. (RICHARD ANTHONY), 1837-1888. *Our place among infinities: a series of essays contrasting our little abode in space and time with the infinities around us: to which are added essays on the Jewish sabbath and astrology / by Richd. A. Proctor....*
New York: D. Appleton and Company ..., 1897. [6], 323 p.; 21 cm.
Advertisements: [6] p. at end. Provenance: L. H. Thompson (signature).

1745. PROCTOR, RICHARD A. (RICHARD ANTHONY), 1837-1888. *Pleasant ways in science / by Richard A. Proctor ... New edition.*
London and New York: Longmans, Green and Co., 1895. viii, 402 p.: ill.; 20 cm. Includes bibliographical references.
Advertisements: half-title verso, 32 p. atend.

1746. PROCTOR, RICHARD A. (RICHARD ANTHONY), 1837-1888. *The poetry of astronomy: a series of familiar essays on the heavenly bodies, regarded less in their strictly scientific aspect than as suggesting thoughts respecting infinities of time and space, of varitey, of vitality, and of development / by Richard A. Proctor....*

Philadelphia: J. B. Lippincott & Co.; Smith, Elder, & Co., 1881. vi, [2], 447 p.; 21 cm. "Reprinted, with additions, from the *Cornhill magazine, Belgravia,* and the *Contemporary review*" – T. p. verso.

Provenance: Peabody Library Association of Georgetown D. C. (inkstamp)

1747. PROCTOR, RICHARD A. (RICHARD ANTHONY), 1837-1888. *The sun: ruler, fire, light, and life of the planetary system. By Richard A. Proctor ... With ten lithographic plates (seven colored) and one hundred and six drawings on wood. 2d ed.*

London: Longmans, Green, and Co., 1872. xxviii, 503 p. illus., x pl. (part col., part fold.; incl. front.) diagrs. 21 cm. Appendix A: The approaching transits of Venus and the best means for observing them. Includes bibliographical references.

Advertisements: 32 p. at end.

1748. PROCTOR, RICHARD A. (RICHARD ANTHONY), 1837-1888. *Transits of Venus. A popular account of past and coming transits, from the first observed by Horrocks A. D. 1639 to the transit of A. D. 2012.*

London: Longmans, Green, 1874. xiv, 236 p. illus., XX plates (part col. part fold.) 21 cm.

Advertisements: 4, 32 p. at end.

1749. PROCTOR, RICHARD A. (RICHARD ANTHONY), 1837-1888. *The universe and the coming transits: presenting researches into and new views respecting the constitution of the heavens: together with an investigation of the conditions of the coming transits of Venus ... / By Richard A. Proctor....*

London: Longmans, Green, and Co., 1874. xiv, 303, 23 leaves of plates (some folded): ill. (some col.), charts, maps; 23 cm. Advertisements: [2] p. at beginning. Includes bibliographical references.

Provenance: L. L. Rice (bookplate and signature).

1750. PROCTOR, RICHARD A. (RICHARD ANTHONY), 1837-1888. *The universe of stars: presenting researches into and new views respecting the constitution of the heavens / by Richard A. Proctor ... Second edition.*

London: Longmans, Green, and Co., 1878. [12], 230 p., XII leaves of plates (some folded): ill., charts; 23 cm. First edition appeared in 1874 under title: *The Universe and the coming transits.* The second edition contains only the first part.

Advertisements: 24 p. at end. Provenance: Rev.d Alfred Sells (bookplate).

1751. PROCTOR, RICHARD A. (RICHARD ANTHONY), 1837-1888. *The universe of suns: and other science gleanings / by Richard A. Proctor....*

New York: R. Worthington ... 1884. vi, 401 p., 1 folded leaf of plates: ill.; 19 cm. Includes bibliographical references.

1752. PTOLEMY, 2nd cent. *Almagestu[m] Cl. Ptolemei Pheludiensis Alexandrini astronomo[rum] principis. Opus ingens ac nobile omnes celoru[m] motus continens. Felicibus astris eat in luce[m]: ductu Petri Liechtenstein Colonie[n]sis Germani.*

[Venice]: Anno virginei partus 1515. Die 10. Ja. Venetijs, exofficina eiusdem litteraria. Cum privilegio. 2 p. l., 152, [1] l. diagrs., tables. 31 cm. Printer's device on verso of last leaf, in red and black.

1753. PTOLEMY, 2nd cent. *Cl. Ptolomaei Pheludiensis Alexandrini philosophi et mathematici excelentissimi Phænomena, stellarum MXXII. fixarum ad hanc ætatem reducta ... / nunc primum edita, interprete Georgio Trapezuntio; adiecta est isagoge Ioannis Nouiomagi ad stellarum inerrantium longitudines ac latitudines; cui etiam accessere imagines sphæræ barbaricæ duodequinquaginta Alberti Dureri.*

Excusum Coloniæ Agrippinæ: [s.n.], 1537 octauo Calendas Septembres, [Aug 25]. [51] p.: ill.; 28 cm. Books 7-8 of the *Almagest.* Signatures: A^4B-D^6E^4. Plates by Dürer were probably never published. Cf. *BLC* v. 267, p. 137.

With: *Nicolai Copernici Torinensis De revolutionibus orbium cœlestium.* Norimbergae: Apud Ioh. Petreium, 1543. Provenance: Herbert McLean Evans (bookplate).

1754. PTOLEMY, 2nd cent. *Claudii Ptolemaei Pelusiensis Alexandrini omnia quæ extant opera, præter Geographiam ... / castigata ab Erasmo Osualdo Schrekhenfuchsio, & ab eodem Isagoica [sic] in Almagestum præfatione, & fidelissimis in priores libros annotationibus illustrata....*

Basileæ: In officina Henrichi Petri, [1551]. [88], 447, [1] p. 2 folded leaves of plates: ill.; 32 cm. Two columns to the page. Includes index. Proclus's *Hypotyposis astronomicarum positionum* is in fact the second item, following the *Almagest,* and not the last. Imprint partially taken from colophon. (From t. p. verso) Almagesti seu Magnæ compositionis mathematicae opus, / à Georgio Trapezuntio tralatum, lib. XIII. – De iudicijs astrologicis, aut, ut uulgò uocant, Quadripartitæ co[n]structionis, lib. IIII. / Quorum priores duo à Ioachimo Camerario Latinitate donati sunt: ... – Centum sententiæ, quod Centiloquium dicunt, / à Iouiano Pontano uersæ. – Inerrantium stellarum seu fixarum significationes, / per Nicolaum Leoni cum traductæ. – Procli Diadochi Hypotoposes astronomicarum positionum, quod est omnium, quæ in Almagesto demonstrantur, epitome & compendium, ad reminiscentiam rerum plurimum conducens, / Georgio Valla Placentino interprete.

Provenace: James Whatman Bosanquet (armorial bookplate).

1755. PTOLEMY, 2nd cent. *Claudii Ptolemaei Pheludiensis Alexandrini Almagestum seu Magnae constructionis mathematicae opus plane diuinum / Latina donatum lingua ab Georgio Trapezuntio usquequaq. doctissimo.; Per Lucam Gauricum Neapolit. diuinae matheseos professorem egregium in alma urbe Veneta orbis regina recognitum anno salutis M D XXVIII labente.....*

In Vrbe Veneta: Calcographica Luceantonii Iu[n]ta officina aere proprio, ac typis excussa ..., Anno Chr[isti], 1528. [6], 143, [1] leaves (the last leaf blank): ill. (woodcuts); 33 cm. First printed edition of the Latin translation of the *Almagest,* from the Greek by George of Trebizond. Cf. Sarton. This edition has been observed in at least three states; cf. *NUC pre-1956* NP 0630147 and NP 0630149 (both at Harvard University) and RLIN record for Brown University Library copy. Imprint from colophon on leaf 143 verso. Signatures: A^6 a-s^8 (s8 blank). Adams P2214; Grässe, VI, p. 498; BM *STC Italian,* 1465-1600, p. 542; BN, v. 143, column 743; Hoffmann, S.F.W. *Bibliographisches Lexicon der gesammten Litt. Der Griechen* (2. Aufl.), III, p. 321; Sarton, G. *Introd. to hist. of science,* I, p. 274; Errata: leaf 143 verso.

State or variant copy with leaf 90 missigned m3 and with three-line register on verso of leaf 143. Binding: Hebrew ms. leaf.

1756. PTOLEMY, 2nd cent. *Composition mathématique; traduite pour la première fois du grec en français par M. Halma (avec le text grec) et suivie des notes de M. Delambre ... (Réimpression facsimilé).*

Paris: J. Hermann, 1927. 2 v. front., tables, diagrs. 24 cm. Cover-title (at head of title: Ptolémée). Vol. 1 has title: Klaudiou Ptolemaiou Mathematike syntaxis. Composition mathématique de Claude Ptolémée ... Paris, H. Grand, 1813; v. 2.: ... (livre I-VI) Composition mathématique ... ou Astronomie ancienne ... (livre VII-XIII) Paris, Imp. de J.-M. Eberhart, 1816. Greek and French in parallel columns. Vol. 1. Greek title romanized. Reprint of the French translation of the *Almagest,* originally published: 1813-1816.

Binder: Verrico.

1757. PTOLEMY, 2nd cent. *État des étoiles fixes au second siècle / par Claude Ptolemée, comparé à la position des mêmes étoiles en 1786, avec le texte grec & la traduction françoise par M. l'Abbé Montignot.*

Strasbourg: Librairie Académique, 1787. vj, 192, [1] p.: 2 fold. plates; 27 cm. Greek and French in parallel columns. Tables in Greek and French on opposite pages. Includes chapters 1-4, Bk. VII of the *Almagest.*

1758. PTOLEMY, 2nd cent. *Kl. Ptolemaiou Megales syntaxeos : bibl. 13, Thenos Alexandreos Eis ta auta hypomnematon bibl. 11. = Claudii Ptolemaei Magnæ constructionis, id est, Perfectæ cœlestium motuum pertractionis, lib. XIII. : Theonis Alexandrini in eosdem commentariorum Lib. XI.*

Basileæ: Apud Ioannem VValderum, 1538. 2 v.: ill.; 33 cm. Known as the *Almagest.* Greek text, editors' prefaces in Latin. Both Greek titles precede the Latin titles. Vol. [2] has title: Theonos Alexandreos eis ten tou Ptolemaiou Megalen syntaxin hypomnematon bibl. ia = Theonis Alexandrini in Claudii Ptolemaei Magnam constructionem commentariorum lib. XI. Vol. (1) edited by Simon Grynaeus; v. [2] by Joachim Camerarius. Authorship of pts. 5-6 of the *Commentarii* is ascribed to Pappus of Alexandria. Cf. *Oxford classical dict.* Vol. [1]: [16], 327, [1] (blank) p.; v. [2]: [8],

189

ΚΛΑΥΔΙΟΥ ΠΤΟΛΕ
ΜΑΙΟΥ ΜΑΘΗΜΑΤΙΚΗΣ ΣΥΝΤΑΞΕΩΣ
ΒΙΒΛΙΟΝ ΟΓΔΟΟΝ.

ΕΚΘΕΣΙΣ ΚΑΝΟΝΙΚΗ ΤΟΥ ΚΑΤΑ ΤΟ ΝΟΤΙΟΝ ἡμισφαίριον ἀστερισμοῦ.

ΤΩΝ ΕΝ ΤΩ ΖΩΔΙΑΚΩ ΝΟΤΙΩΝ ΖΩΔΙΩΝ ΑΣΤΕΡΙΣ. μῆκ. πλάτ. μέγεθ.

ΧΗΛΩΝ ΑΣΤΕΡΙΣΜΟΣ						
τῶν ἐπ᾽ ἄκρας τῆς νοτίου χηλῆς ὁ λαμπρὸς	ζυγ	ιγ	βο	γ´	β	
ὁ βορειότερος αὐτοῦ καὶ ἀμαυρότερος	ζυγ	ιζ	βο	β ς´	ε	
τῶν ἐπ᾽ ἄκρας τῆς βορείου χηλῆς ὁ λαμπρὸς	ζυγ	κβ ς´	βο	η ς´ γ´	β	
ὁ προηγούμενος αὐτοῦ καὶ ἀμαυρὸς	ζυγ	ιζ γ´	βο	η ς´	ε	
ὁ ἐν μέσῃ τῇ νοτίῳ χηλῇ	ζυγ	κδ	νο	α γ´	δ	
ὁ τούτου προηγούμενος ἐπὶ τῆς αὐτῆς χηλῆς	ζυγ	κα γ´	βο	α δ´	δ	
ὁ ἐν μέσῃ τῇ βορείῳ χηλῇ	ζυγ	κζ ς´ γ´	βο	δ ς´ δ´	δ	
ὁ ἑπόμενος αὐτῷ ἐπὶ τῆς αὐτῆς χηλῆς	σκορ	γ	βο	γ ς´	δ	ἐλάσσων
ἅπαντ. ἀστέρες η̄, ὧν δευτέρου μεγέθους β̄, τετάρτου δ̄, πέμπτου β̄.						
ΟΙ ΠΕΡΙ ΤΑΣ ΧΗΛΑΣ ΑΜΟΡΦΩΤΟΙ						
τῶν βορειοτέρων τῆς βορείου χηλῆς γ̄ ὁ προηγούμενος	ζυγ	κς ς´	βο	θ	ε	
τῶν ἑπομένων β̄ ὁ νότιος	σκορ	γ γ´	βο	ς γ´	δ	ἐλάσσων
ὁ βόρειος αὐτῶν	σκορ	δ γ´	βο	θ δ´	δ	ἐλάσσων
τῶν μεταξὺ τῶν χηλῶν γ̄ ὁ ἑπόμενος	σκορ	γ ς´	βο	ς´	ε	
τῶν λοιπῶν β̄ καὶ προηγουμένων ὁ βόρειος	σκορ	δ γ´	βο	δ γ´	ε	
ὁ νότιος αὐτῶν	σκορ	α ς´	νο	α ς´	δ	
τῶν νοτιωτέρων τῆς νοτίου χηλῆς γ̄ ὁ προηγούμενος	ζυγ	κγ	νο	ζ ς´	γ	
τῶν λοιπῶν καὶ ἑπομένων β̄ ὁ βορειότερος	σκορ	α ς´	νο	η ς´	δ	
ὁ νοτιώτερος αὐτῶν	σκορ	β	νο	δ γ´	δ	
ἅπαντ. ἀστέρες θ̄, ὧν τρίτου μεγέθους ᾱ, δ΄ ε̄, ε΄ β̄, ς΄ ᾱ.						
ΣΚΟΡΠΙΟΥ ΑΣΤΕΡΙΣΜΟΣ						
τῶν ἐν τῷ μετώπῳ λαμπρῶν γ̄ ὁ βόρειος	σκορ	ς γ´	βο	α γ´	γ	
ὁ μέσος αὐτῶν	σκορ	ε γ´	νο	α γ´	γ	
ὁ νοτιώτερος τῶν τριῶν	σκορ	ε γ´	νο	ε	γ	
ὁ τούτου ἔτι νοτιώτερος ἐφ᾽ ἑνὸς τῶν ποδῶν	σκορ	ς	νο	ζ ς´ γ´	γ	
τῶν β̄ τῶν παρακειμένων τῷ βορειοτάτῳ τῶν λαμπρῶν ὁ βόρειος	σκορ	ζ	βο	α γ´	δ	
ὁ νότιος αὐτῶν	σκορ	ς γ´	βο	ς´	δ	
τῶν ἐν τῷ σώματι τριῶν λαμπρῶν ὁ προηγούμενος	σκορ	ι γ´	νο	γ ς´ δ´	γ	
ὁ μέσος αὐτῶν καὶ ὑπόκιρρος καλούμενος ἀντάρης	σκορ	ιβ γ´	νο	δ	β	
ὁ ἑπόμενος τῶν τριῶν	σκορ	ιδ ς´	νο	ε ς´	γ	
τῶν ὑπὸ αὐτοὺς β̄ ὡς ἐπὶ τοῦ ἐσχάτου ποδὸς ὁ ἡγούμενος	σκορ	θ γ´	νο	ς ς´	ε	
ὁ ἑπόμενος αὐτῶν	σκορ	ι γ´	νο	ς γ´	ε	
ὁ ἐν τῷ ᾱ ἀπὸ τοῦ σώματος σπονδύλῳ	σκορ	ιη ς´	νο	ια	γ	
ὁ μετὰ τοῦτον ἐν τῷ δευτέρῳ σπονδύλῳ	σκορ	ιη ς´ γ´	νο	ιε	γ	
τοῦ ἐν τῷ τρίτῳ σπονδύλῳ διπλοῦ ὁ βόρειος	σκορ	κ	νο	ιη γ´	δ	
ὁ νοτιώτερος τοῦ διπλοῦ	σκορ	κ ς´	νο	ιη	δ	
ὁ ἐφεξῆς ἐν τῷ τετάρτῳ σπονδύλῳ	σκορ	κγ ς´	νο	ιθ ς´	γ	
ὁ μετ᾽ αὐτὸν ἐν τῷ πέμπτῳ σπονδύλῳ	σκορ	κη ς´	νο	ιη ς´ γ´	γ	

π 4

Ptolemy, *Almagest*, 1538

275, 267-291, 293-425, [3] p. Adams P-2209.
Bound in 1 v. Provenance: Herbert McLean Evans (bookplate).

1759. PTOLEMY, 2nd cent. *Ptolemaei mathematicæ constructionis liber primus græce & latinee ditus. Additæ explicationes aliquot locorum ab Erasmo Rheinholt Salueldensi.*
VVittebergae: ex officina Iohannis Lufft, 1549. 8 p.l., 123, [1] p., 1 l. tables, diagrs. 16 cm. Book 1 of the *Almagest.* Adams P2210. Houzeau & Lancaster. *Astronomie.* (1964 ed.), 866.
Provenance: Ex Bibl. ad deo. Mar. Magdal (inkstamp).

1760. PUTNAM, EDMUND W. (EDMUND WHITMAN), 1881-1940. *The essence of astronomy; things everyone should know about the sun, moon, and stars, by Edward W. Price [pseud.]....*
New York and London: G. P. Putnam's Sons, 1914. (New York: Knickerbocker Press). xiv, 1 l., 207 p. front., plates, diagrs. 20 cm. "A brief bibliography": p. 198-207.
Advertisements: [4] p. at end. Provenance: William Andrews Clark, Jr. (bookplate).

1761. RADCLIFFE OBSERVATORY. *The Radcliffe catalogue of 6317 stars, chiefly circumpolar reduced to the epoch 1845.0; formed from the observations made at the Radcliffe Observatory, under the superintendence of Manuel John Johnson, M.A., late Radcliffe observer. With introduction by the Rev. Robert Main, M.A., Radcliffe observer. Published by order of the Radcliffe trustees.*
Oxford: J. H. and J. Parker, 1860. 3 p.l., xiii, 363 p. tables. 26 cm.
Imperfect? Lacks all but 1 of prelim. leaves called for but has [4] p. of errata at end of text [?- missing 2 leaves?].

1762. RADCLIFFE OBSERVATORY. *Second Radcliffe catalogue, containing 2386 stars; deduced from observations extending from 1854 to 1861, at the Radcliffe Observatory, Oxford; and reduced to the epoch 1860. Under the superintendence of the Rev. Robert Main, M.A., Radcliffe observer. Pub. by order of the Radcliffe trustees.*
Oxford: J. Parker and Co., 1870. xx, 139 p. tables. 26 cm.
Signed holograph letter by Robert Main inserted.

1763. RAMAZZINI, BERNARDINO, 1633-1714. *De morbis artificium / diatriba Bernardini Ramazzini....*
Mutinæ: Typis Antonii Capponi ..., 1700. viii, 360 p.; 18 cm. Includes bibliographical references and index. Osler, W. *Bib. Osleriana,* 3760.

1764. RAMBOSSON, JEAN PIERRE, 1827-1886. *Astronomy; translated by C. B. Pitman.*
London: Chatto and Windus, 1878. xiii, 385 p. illus. (some col.), ports. 21 cm. Translation of: *Astres.*
Advertisements: 36 p. at end. Binder: Homecrafters.

1765. RAMSEY, MILTON WORTH. *Elements of astronomy, containing several new theories, and is illustrated. By Milton W. Ramsey.*
Minneapolis: Travis Brothers, 1883. 160 p. tab., diagr. 19 cm.

1766. †RATHKE, HEINRICH. *Abhandlungen zur Bildungs- und Entwickelungs Geschichte des Menschen und der Thiere.*
Leipzig: F. C. W. Vogel, 1832-33. 2 pts. in 1 v. 14 plates (part. col.) 27 cm. Druckfehler: 2. Theil, p. 102. Plates signed: Rathke ad nat. del., J. F. Schröter del. Includes bibliographical references.
Provenance: Herbert McLean Evans (bookplate); Kölliker (signature and inkstamp).

1767. RAY, JOHN, 1627-1705. *Historia plantarum: species hactenus editas aliasque insuper multas noviter inventas & descriptas complectens: in qua agitur primò de plantis in genere, earúmque partibus, accidentibus & differentiis: deinde genera omnia tum summa tum subalterna ad species usque infimas, notis suis certis & characteristicis definita, methodo naturæ vestigiis insistente disponuntur: species singulæ accurate describuntur, obscura illustrantur, omissa supplentur, superflua resecantur, synonyma necessaria adjiciuntur: vires denique & usus recepti compendiò traduntur / auctore Joanne Raio....*

Londini: Typis Mariæ Clark: Prostant apud Henricum Faithorne & Joannem Kersey..., 1686-1704. 3 v.; 37 cm. T. p. in red and black, v. 1 & 3. Text in Latin, selected terms also in English (identified in black letter). Vol. 2 has title & imprint: Joannis Raii Historiæ plantarum tomus secundus: cum duplici indice, generali altero nominum & synonymorum præcipuorum, altero affectuum & remediorum: accessit Nomenclator botanicus Anglo-Latinus. Londini: Typis Mariæ Clark: Prostant apud Henricum Faithorne, Regiæ Societatis typographum ..., 1688. Vol. 3 has title & imprint: Joannis Raii, Societatis Regiæ Socii, Historiæ plantarum tomus tertius: qui est supplementum duorum præcedentium: species omnes vel omissas, vel post volumina illa evulgata editas, præter innumeras fere novas & indictas ab amicis communicatas complectens: cum synonymis necessariis, et usibus in cibo, medicina, & mechanicis: addito ad opus consummandum generum indice copioso: accessit Historia stirpium Ins. Luzonis & reliquarum Philippinarum / a R. P. Geo. Jos. Camello, Moravo-Brunensi, S.J. conscripta; item D. Jos. Pitton Tournefort, ... Corollarium institutionum rei herbariæ. Londini: Apud Sam. Smith & Benj. Walford, Reg. Soc. typographos ..., 1704. Vol. 1: [24], 58, [59]-[62], 59-983, [1] p. (the last page blank); v. 2: [8], 985-1350, [2], 1351-1944, [36] p. (the last page blank); v. 3: [2], ix, [1] (blank), 40, 43-666, 135, [1] (blank), 112, 225-255, [9] p. (the last page blank). Vol. 3, p. 666, has mounted slip headed "Botanologiæ finis". Includes indexes. Errata: v. 1, p. [14] of 1st group, v. 2, p. [8] of 1st group, and v. 3, p. [8] of last group. Camellus's contribution (v. 3, p. 1-96, 8th group) has caption title: Appendix. Herbarum aliarumque stirpium in insulâ Luzone Philippinarum primariâ nascentium / a Revdo Patre Georgio Josepho Camello, S. J. observatarum & descriptarum syllabus; ad Joannem Raium transmissus ... The extracts from Tournefort's "Corollarium institutionum rei herbariae" (v. 3, p. 97-112 of 8th group) have running title: Appendix. Plantæ orientales à D. Jos. Pit. Tournefort observatæ. "Explicatio nominum abbreviatorum & recensio operum ab eisdem autoribus editorum": v. 1, p. [9]-[14] of 1st group. Horblit, H. D. *Grolier 100 science books,* 87 (variant). Pritzel, 7436 (variant).

Provenance: Herbert McLean Evans (bookplate).

1768. Ray, John, 1627-1705. *Miscellaneous discourses concerning the dissolution and changes of the world. Wherein the primitive chaos and creation, the general deluge, fountains, formed stones, sea-shells found in the earth, subterraneous trees, mountains, earthquakes, vulcanoes, the universal conflagration and future state, are largely discussed and examined. By John Ray....*

London: S. Smith, 1692. 14 p.l., 259 p. 18 cm. Errata: p. [23]. Advertisements: p. [260]. Bibliography: p. [21]-[22]. Wing R397.

Provenance: Herbert McLean Evans (bookplate).

1769. Rayet, Georges Antoine Pons, 1839-1906. *Notes sur l'histoire de la photographie astronomique, par M. G. Rayet....*

Paris: Gauthier-Villars, 1887. 63, [1] p. 26 cm. "Extrait du *Bulletin astronomique de l'Observatoire de Paris,* IV: 1887." Includes bibliographical references.

Original printed wrappers bound in. Provenance: author's signed presentation inscription to Mr. Fruillient.

1770. Rayleigh, John William Strutt, Baron, 1842-1919. *Argon, a new constituent of the atmosphere. By Lord Rayleigh and Professor William Ramsay.*

Washington: Smithsonian Institution, 1896. 2 p.l., 43 p. illus. 34 cm. Smithsonian contributions to knowledge; [v. 29, art. 4]. Smithsonian Institution publication 1033. At head of title: Hodgkins fund.

1771. Razi, Abu Bakr Muhammad ibn Zakariya, 865?-925? *Rhazes de variolis et morbillis: Arabice et Latine; cum aliis nonnullis eiusdem argumenti / cura et impensis Iohannis Channing, natu et civitate Londinensis.*

Londini: Excudebat Guilielmus Bowyer, 1766. xiv, [2], 276 p.; 22 cm. Arabic title: *Jadari wa-al-hasbah.* Errata: [2] p. Includes bibliographical references. Osler, W. *Bib. Osleriana,* 455.

1772. Razi, Abu Bakr Muhammad ibn Zakariya, 865?-925? *A treatise on the small-pox and measles / by Abú Becr Mohammed ibn Zacaríyá ar-Rází (commonly called Rhazes); translated from the original Arabic by William Alexander Greenhill.*

London: Printed for The Sydenham Society, 1848. vii, 212, 40 p.; 22 cm. Translation of: *Jadari wa-al-*

hasbah. Arabic index: p. [179]-197. Bibliography: p. 5-9, 83, 100. Treatise on the small-pox and measles – Liber ad Almansorem (lib. x, cap. 18) – Divisio morborum (cap. 149) – Liber continens (lib. xviii, cap. 8, cap. 4) Notes and illustrations – Indices.

Provenance: C. Hart Merriam (inscription). Binder: Westleys & Co. (ticket).

1773. Réaumur, René-Antoine Ferchault de, 1683-1757. *Mémoires pour servir à l'histoire des insectes. Par m. de Rèaumur....*

Paris: De l'Imprimerie Royale, 1734-1929. 7 v. 267 fold. pl. 26 cm. Vol. 7, published as *Encyclopédie entomologique,* (no. 11) has imprint: Paris, R. Lechevalier, 1928; added t.-p. 1929. "(Tome 7) publiée pour la première fois, d'après le manuscrit original." cf. *Bibl. de la France,* nov. 9, 1928, *Annonces,* p. 5338. Illustrated by Simonneau, Cl. Lucas, Filloeul and Haussard. 1. Sur les chenilles & sur les papillons. – 2. Suite de l'histoire des chenilles & des papillons; et l'histoire des insectes ennemis des chenilles. – 3. Histoire des vers mineurs des feuilles, des teignes, des fausses teignes, des pucerons, des ennemis der pucerons, des faux pucerons, & l'histoire des galles des plantes, & de leurs insects. – 4. Histoire des gallinsectes, des progallinsectes, & des mouches à deux aîles. – 5. Suite de l'histoire des mouches à deux aîles, & l'histoire de plusieurs mouches à quatre aîles, sçavoir, des mouches à scies, des cigales, & des abeilles. – 6. Suite de l'histoire des mouches à quatre âiles, avec un supplément à celle des mouches à deux aîles. – 7. Histoire des formis, par m. de Réaumur ... Introduction de E. L. Bouvier... avec notes de Charles Pérez.

1774. Redi, Francesco, 1626-1698. *Esperienze intorno a diverse cose naturali, e particolarmente a quelle, che ci son portate dall'Indie ... scritte in vna lettera al ... Atanasio Chircher....*

Firenze: All'insegna della Nave, 1671. [6], 152 p. plates. 24 cm. Osler, W. *Bib. Osleriana,* 3776.

With the author's: *Esperienze intorno alla generazione degl'insetti.* In Firenze, 1668. T. p. and prelim. matter misbound. Provenance: Herbert McLean Evans (bookplate).

1775. Redi, Francesco, 1626-1698. *Esperienze intorno alla generazione degl'insetti / fatte da Francesco Redi ...e da lui scritte in una lettera all'illustrissimo signor Carlo Dati.*

In Firenze: All'Insegna della Stella., MDCLXVIII, [1668]. [8], 228 p. (the first leaf blank), 29 leaves of plates (3 folded): ill. (engravings); 24 cm. Text in Italian, with quotations in Latin or Greek. "Prima edizione" – Prandi, Unnumbered plates are included in paging. Title in red and black, with vignette. Horblit, H. D. *Grolier 100 science books,* 88. Prandi, D. *Redi,* 7. Burndy. *Science,* 188. Osler, W. *Bib. Osleriana,* 3775. Gamba, B. *Testi di lingua,* 814. Includes index. "Errori [e] correzioni": p. 228.

With the author's: *Esperienze intorno a diverse cose naturali.* In Firenze, 1771. T. p. and prelim. matter misbound. Provenance: Herbert McLean Evans (bookplate).

1776. Reed, Lucas Albert. *Astronomy and the Bible; the empire of creation seen in the dual light of science and the Word, by Lucas A. Reed....*

Mountain View, Cal., Kansas City, Mo., etc.: Pacific Press Publishing Assn., [c1919]. 206 p. incl. front, illus. plates 19 cm. Plates printed on both sides.

[2] p. of advertisements at end.

1777. Rees, Abraham, 1743-1825. *The cyclopædia; or, Universal dictionary of arts, sciences and literature. By Abraham Rees ... with the assistance of eminent professional gentlemen....*

London: Longman, Hurst, Rees, Orme & Brown [etc.], 1819. 39 v. front. (port.) illus. (music) forms. 28 cm. "Printed by A. Strahan ... London" – T. p. verso.

1778. Rees, Abraham, 1743-1825. *The cyclopædia, or, Universal dictionary of arts, sciences, and literature: plates / by Abraham Rees ...; with the assistance of eminent professional gentlemen; illustrated with numerous engravings by the most distinguished artists.*

London: Printed for Longman, Hurst, Rees, Orme & Brown ... [and 26 others], 1820. 6 v.: all ill., maps; 28 cm. "Printed by A. Strahan ... London" – Half-title verso. Plates engraved by W. Lowry, T. Wilson, and others; drawn by J. Farey, Syd. Edwards, and others. Some plates are folded. V. I. Agriculture-astronomical instruments – v. II. Bassorelievo-horology – v. III. Hydraulics-naval architecture – v. IV. Navigation-writing by cipher – v. V. Natural history – v. VI. Ancient and modern atlas.

Spine title: Rees's Cyclopædia; vols. Numbered 40-45.

Regiomontanus, *Epitoma in Almagestum,* 1496

1779. REGIOMONTANUS, JOANNES, 1436-1476. *Doctissimi viri et mathematicarum disciplinarum eximii professoris Ioannis de Regio Monte De triangvlis omnimodis libri qvinqve: quibus explicantur res necessariæ cognitu, uolentibus ad scientiarum astronomicarum perfectionem deuenire: quæ cum nusqua[m] alibi hoc tempore expositæ habeantur, frustra sine harum instructione ad illam quisquam aspirarit. Accesserunt huc in calce pleraq[ue] d. Nicolai Cusani De quadratura circuli, ... Omnia recens in lucem edita, fide & diligentia singulari.*

Norimbergæ: in ædibus Io. Petrei, 1533. 2 pts. in 1 v. diagrs. 28 cm. Title vignette (diagram). Edited by Johann Schöner. Errata: p. [94] at the end. Colophon reads: "Excudebatur Norimbergae per Ioh. Petreium anno MDXXXIII mense Augusto."

Imperfect: pt. 2, p. 1-4 missing and supplied in photocopy.

1780. REGIOMONTANUS, JOANNES, 1436-1476. *Epytoma Ioa[n]nis de Mo[n]te Regio in Almagestu[m] Ptolomei.*

Venetijs: Iohannis Ha[m]man de Landoia, dictus Hertzog ... , 1496. Currente pridie Caleñ. Septembris [31 Aug.]. [216] p.: ill.; 31 cm. Imprint from colophon. Begun by Georg von Peurbach. Some copies contain the text of a 2-leaf letter by Giovanni Abiosi, the editor, dated 15 Aug. 1496, and inserted between sigs. a1 and a2. Signatures: a^{10} b-n [alternate 8s and 6s] o^6 p^8 (p8 blank). Xylographic title page; woodcut initials; diagrams in margins. Full page woodcut on p. [6] (a3v) showing armillary sphere crossed by the signs of the zodiac, with the figures of Ptolemy and the author. Printer's mark on p. [214] (p7v). BM *15th cent.*, V, p. 427 (IB.23380). Goff (rev.) R-111. Hain 13806*. Horblit, H. D. *Grolier 100 science books*, 89. *ISTC*, ir00111000. Rhodes 1506.

Without the letter of Abiosi. Binding: full vellum, with fold-over front edges. Provenance: Teodoro Becu (bookplate); ms. annotations. Par. marks and initial strokes added in red up to p. [26].

1781. REGIOMONTANUS, JOANNES, 1436-1476. *Tabule directionu[m] profectionu[m]q[ue] famosissimi viri Magistri Ioannis Germani de Regiomonte in natiuitatibus multum vtiles. [Tabella sinus recti, per gradus [et] singula minuta divisa: ad tabulas directionu[m] M[a]g[ist]ri Iohannis de Regiomonte necessarias cum quibus exemplis].*

[Augsburg]: Erhardiq[ue] Ratdolt mira imprimendi arte, qua nuper Venetijs nunc Auguste Vindelicorum excellit nominatissimus, 4 nonas Ianuarij (2 Jan.), 1490. [312] p.; 20 cm. Titles from p. [1] and p. [281]. Imprint from explicit, p. [278] (s5v). "Opus tabularum directionum profectionumq[ue] pro reuerendissimo d[omi]no Ioanne archiep[iscop]o Strigonien[si] ... per Magistrum Ioannem de Regiomonte composita[rum] anno d[omi]ni 1467 explicit feliciter. Magistri Ioannis Angeli viri p[er]itissimi dilige[n]ti correctione" – P.[278]. BM *15th cent.*, II, p. 383 (IA.6698). Goff (rev.) R-112. Hain 13801*. *ISTC*, ir00112000. Klebs 834.1.

Imperfect: p. [61]-[278] (e-r p8 s s p5 s) only. Titles and signatures from BM *15th cent.* Binding: blue wrappers.

1782. REH, FRANK. *Astronomy for the layman, by Frank Reh; foreword by Clyde Fisher ...drawings by the author.*

New York, London: D. Appleton-Century Company, Incorporated, (1936). Xvii p., 2 l., 3-308 p. front., illus., plates, map, diagrs. 21 cm. Illustrated lining-papers.

Biographical note on author tipped in on front paste-down endpaper.

1783. REID, HUGO, 1809-1872. *Elements of astronomy: adapted for private instruction and use in schools / by Hugo Reid ...; illustrated by fifty-six engravings on wood.*

Edinburgh: Published by Oliver & Boyd ...; Simpkin, Marshall & Co., 1842. 168, 24 p.: ill.; 18 cm.

Provenance: Robert Carswell (signature). Advertisements: p. 166-168 and [1]-24 at end, and on front and back paste-down endpapers.

1784. REISCH, GREGOR, d. 1525. *Margarita philosophica.*

[Freiburg i. Br.?]: Rursus exaratum [pro]puigili, noua, ite[m]que secu[n]daria hac opera Joannis Schotti Argentinen[sis] chalchographi ciuis: ad 17. k[a]l[endis] Apriles [16 March] Anno gratie, 1504. [660] p., [3] folded leaves of plates: ill., map, music; 23 cm. Author's name appears on p. [2]. Place of publication from Alden. Printer's name and date of publication from colophon, p. [652]. *JCB Lib. cat.*, pre-1675, 1:39. Adams R333. Alden, J. E. *European Americana*, 504/3. BM *STC German, 1455-1600*, 731.

Errata statement, p. [655-657]. Includes index. Imperfect: e8, n7, 2d1, 2d3, 2t7 missing, 2d8 misbound as 2d1. Plates missing.

1785. REISER, ANTON. *Albert Einstein, a biographical portrait, by Anton Reiser, with a foreword by Albert Einstein.*
London: T. Butterworth, Ltd., 1931. 223 p. front. (port.) 22 cm.
Provenance: Charles Atwood Kofoid (bookplate).

1786. REMAK, ROBERT, 1815-1865. *Galvanothérapie; ou, De l'application du courant galvanique constant au traitement des maladies nerveuses et musculaires. Tr. de l'allemand par Alp. Morpain, avec les additions de l'auteur.*
Paris: Baillière, 1860. xx, 467 p. Translation of *Galvanotherapie der Nerven- und Muskelkrankheiten.* Includes bibliographical references.

1787. REMAK, ROBERT, 1815-1865. *Ueber ein selbständiges Darmnervensystem / von Dr. Robert Remak.*
Berlin: Verlag von G. Reimer, 1847. [6], 37 [1] p., 2 leaves of plates: ill.; 44 cm. Plates signed: Gez. v. J. D. L. Franz Wagner, Gest. v. C. Haas.
Provenance: Herbert McLean Evans (bookplate).

1788. RENOUARD, P.-V. (PIERRE-VICTOR), b. 1798. *History of medicine from its origin to the nineteenth century, with an appendix containing a philosophical and historical review of medicine to the present time. Trans. from the French by Cornelius G. Comegys.*
Cincinnati: Moore, Wilstach, Keys, 1856. xxii, 719 p. 24 cm.
Provenance: L. M. Van Meter (inscription); J. Frazier Rumbold (signature).

1789. REUSS, JEREMIAS DAVID, 1750-1837. *Repertorium commentationum a societatibus litterariis editarum. Secundum disciplinarum ordinem.*
Gottingae: apud Henricum Dieterich, 1801-21. 16 v. in 15. 22 cm. Includes indexes. T. V. Astronomia.

1790. REVERHORST, MAURITS VAN, 1666-1722. *Epistola anatomica, problematica, quarta & decima ... Ad ...Fredericum Ruyschium. De nova artuum decurtandorum methodo / authore Mauritio à Reverhorst....*
Amstelædami: Apud Joannem Wolters, 1701. 21 p., [2] folded leaves of plates: ill.; 24 cm. Statement of responsibility transposed. Plates numbered: XVIII, XVII. Signed: C. Huijberts ad vivum sculpsit.
With: *Observationum anatomico-chirurgicarum centuria* / Frederici Ruyschii. Amstelodami: Apud Henricum & Viduam Theodori Boom, 1691.

1791. RHÄTICUS, GEORG JOACHIM, 1514-1576. *Opvs palatinvm de triangvlis a Georgio Ioachimo Rhetico coeptvm: L. Valentinvs Otho principis Palatini Friderici IV. electoris mathematicvs consvmmavit.*
[Neostadii in Palatinatv Excudebat Matthæs Harnisius] An. sal. hvm. [M] [D] XCVI, [1596]. 10 p.l., 85 p., 1 l., 86-104, 140, 341 p., 1 l., 121 p., 1 l., 554, 181 p. diagrs. 37 cm. Colophon (on (Vvv' recto): Neostadii in Palatinatv. Excudebat Matthæus Harnisius. (Device of Mathes Harnisch, Neustadt an der Hardt) Anno salutis. 1596 Imprint taken from colophon. Imprint date in Roman numerals. Engraved and illustrated t.-p.; each part has special t.-p. or half-title. Head and tail pieces; initials. Many errors in pagination. (1) Georgii Ioachimi Rhetici libri tres De fabrica canonis doctrinæ triangvlorvm. Georgii Ioachimi Rhetici De triqvetris rectarvm linearvm in planitie liber vnvs. – (2) Georgii Ioachimi Rhetici De trianvlis globi cvm angvlo recto. – (3) L. Valentini Othonos Parthenopolitani. De triangvlis globi sine angvlo recto libri qvinqve. – (4) L. Valentini Othonis Parthenopolitani. Meteoroscopivm nvmerorvm primvm-(tertium) – (5) Georgii Ioachimi Rhætici Magnvs canon doctrinæ triangvlorvm ad decades secvndorvm scrvpvlorvm et ad partes J0000000000. – (6) Tertia series Magni canonis doctrinae triangvlorvm.

1792. RHÄTICUS, GEORG JOACHIM, 1514-1576. *Thesaurus mathematicus, sive, Canon sinuum ad radium 1.00000.00000.00000. et ad dena quaeque scrupula secunda quadrantis: una cum sinibus primi et postremi gradus, ad eundem radium, et ad singula scrupula secunda quadrantis: adiunctis ubique differentiis primis et secundis: atq[ue] vbi res tulit, etiam tertijs / iam olim quidem incredibili labore & sumptu à Georgio Joachimo Rhetico supputatus; at nunc primum in lucem editus, & cum viris doctis communicatus a Bartholomaeo Pitisco ...;*

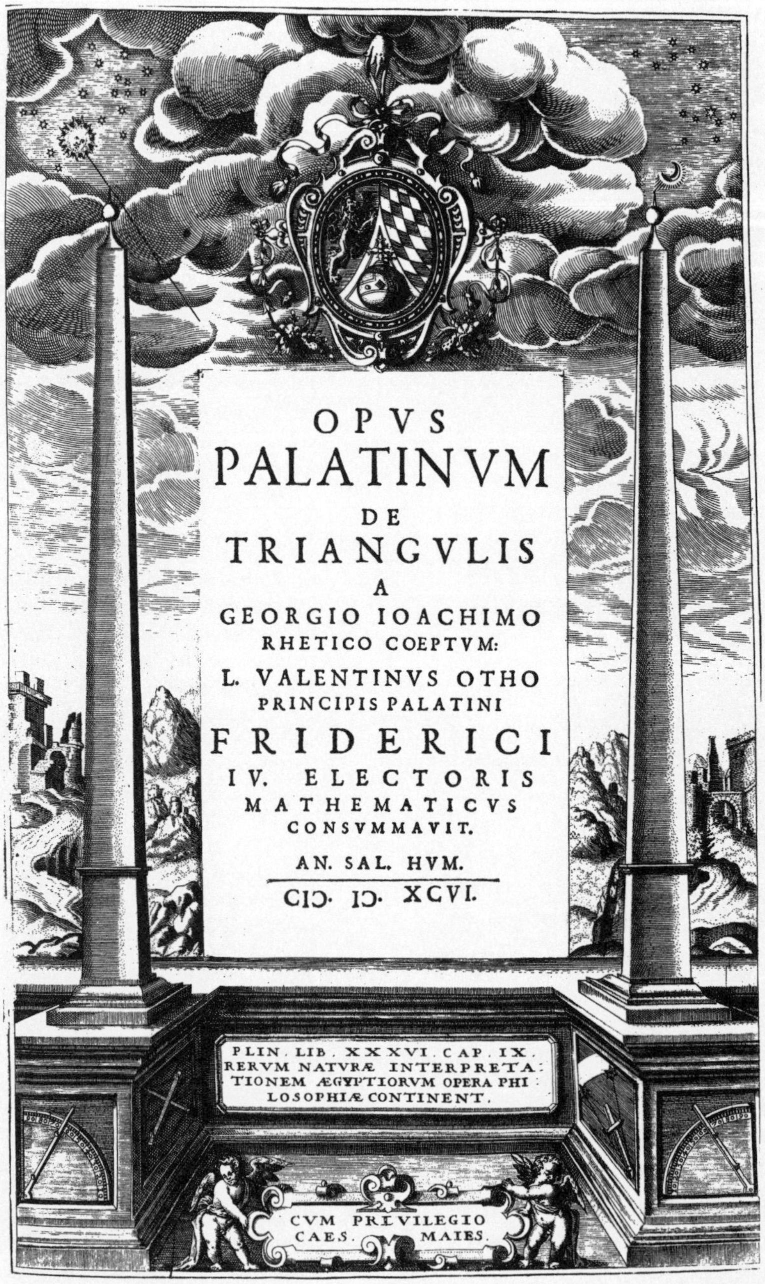
OPVS
PALATINVM
DE
TRIANGVLIS
A
GEORGIO IOACHIMO
RHETICO COEPTVM:
L. VALENTINVS OTHO
PRINCIPIS PALATINI
FRIDERICI
IV. ELECTORIS
MATHEMATICVS
CONSVMMAVIT.
AN. SAL. HVM.
CIↃ. IↃ. XCVI.
PLIN. LIB. XXXVI. CAP. IX.
RERVM NATVRÆ INTERPRETA:
TIONEM ÆGYPTIORVM OPERA PHI:
LOSOPHIÆ CONTINENT.
CVM PRIVILEGIO
CAES. MAIES.

Rhäticus, *Opus palatinum de triangulis*, 1596

cuius etiam accesserunt: I. Principia sinuum... II. Sinus decimorum....

Francofurti: Excudebat Nicolaus Hoffmannus, sumptibus Jonae Rosae, 1513 [i.e. 1613]. [8], 271, [1], 61, [1], (2 blank), [15] p.; 35 cm. Title in red and black within border. "Sinus primi et postremi gradus" has special t. p. and separate paging (61, [1] p.). "Principia sinuum adradium" and "Sinus decimorum" have separate t. p.s but continuous paging ([15] p.). The additional t. p.'s are all dated 1613. After the death of Rheticus, his pupil, Otho, finished this work and published it in 1598. Brunet, t. 4, col. 1265.

Provenance: Robert Honeyman (Honeyman sale). In slipcase signed: James Macdonald Co.

1793. RIBAUCOUR, ALBERT, 1845-1893. *Étude des élassoïdes, ou surfaces a courbure moyenne nulle / par Albert Ribaucour....*

Bruxelles: F. Hayez ..., 1881. [4], VI, 236 p.; 29 cm. "Couronné par l'Académie dans la séance publique du 16 décembre 1880." "Extrait du t. 44 des *Mémoires couronnés et mémoires des savants étrangers*, 1881."

With: *Neue Geometrie des Raumes* / von Julius Pluecker. Leipzig: Druck und Verlag von B. G. Teubner, 1868.

1794. RICCIOLI, GIOVANNI BATTISTA, 1598-1671. *Almagestum nouum: astronomiam veterem nouamque complectens observationibus aliorum, et propriis nouisqve theorematibus, problematibus, ac tabulis promotam, opus absolutum ... / auctore P. Joanne Baptista Ricciolo Societatis Iesu Ferrariensi....*

Bononiæ: Nunc autem Francofurti apud Joannem Beyerum per venales habentur, 1653. 2 v.: ill., maps; 37 cm. Engraved t. p. signed by F. Curtus. Moon; map by P. Grimaldus. Colophon reads: Bononiæ: Typis hæredis Victorij Benatij, 1651. Printed in double columns. Errata: on last p. of both v. Epitome genealogiæ Grimaldæ gentis: v. 2, p. [I]-IX. Houzeau & Lancaster. *Astronomie* (1964 ed.), 9223.

Provenance: presented to the Society of Jesus by Petrus Daniel Huetius (bookplate).

1795. RICCIOLI, GIOVANNI BATTISTA, 1598-1671. *Astronomiaæ reformatæ tomi duo, quorum prior observationes, hypotheses, et fundamenta tabularum, posterior præcepta pro usu tabularum astronomicarum, et ipsas tabulas astronomicas CII. continet ... Auctore P. Ioanne Baptista Ricciolo....*

Bononiæ: Ex typographia hæredis V. Benatij, 1665. 2 v. in 1. ill., 2 double plates, tables. 36 cm. Added t. p. in red and black: Astronomia reformata ad serenissimum d. Ferdinandum Mariam, Bavariæ etc. Ducem. Vol. 2 has special t. p.: Astronomiæ reformatæ tomus II. cuius pars prior præcepta pro usu tabularum, posterior tabulas ipsas astronomicas CII. noualmagestica continet. Text printed in double columns; title vignette (arms); head- and tailpieces; initials.

Provenance: Le Chier de Fleurieu.

1796. RICHARDSON, O. W. (OWEN WILLANS), 1879-1959. *The electron theory of matter, by O. W. Richardson.*

Cambridge, The University press, 1914. vi, 612 p. illus. diagrs. 22 cm. (Cambridge physical series). Includes bibliographical references and index.

Provenance: Henry R. Cu[rm?]e (signature).

1797. RIEMANN, BERNHARD, 1826-1866. *Bernhard Riemann's gesammelte mathematische Werke und wissenschaftlicher Nachlass; hrsg. unter Mitwirkung von Richard Dedekind, von Heinrich Weber.*

Leipzig: B. G. Teubner, 1876. viii, 526 p. port. 25 cm. Bernhard Riemann's Lebenslauf: p. [507]-526.

Contains no port. Provenance: Ella C. Williams (inscription); Harry J. Sternberg (signature).

1798. RITTER, ERASMUS, 1726-1805. *Preissschrift über die 1768 von der Oekonomischen Gesellschaft in Bern aufgegebere Frage: welches ist die beste Theorie der Küchenherde und Stubenöfen, zu ersparung des Holzes und anderer Feurungsmittel? / von Hrn. Ritter....*

Bern: In Verlag der neuen Buchhandlung, 1771. 52 p., VI folded leaves of plates: ill.; 21 cm. Half title: Theorie der Stubenöfen und Küchenherde. Plates signed: Ritter inv. del.; Rein sc. A. V. Also published in French with title: *Théorie des foyers de cuisine et des poêles.*

With: *Abhandlung von den verbesserten dioptrischen Fernröhren* / Roger Joseph Boscovich. Wien: Gedruckt bey Johann Thomas Edlen von Trattnern, 1765.

1799. Ritter, Franz, d. 1641. *Speculum solis, das ist, Sonnenspiegel: Beschreibung und Unterricht derer in das Kupffer gestochenen Sonnenuhren ... / durch M. Franciscum Ritter....*

Gedruckt zu Nürnberg: Durch Christoff Lochner, in Verlegung Balthaser Camoxen, 1609. [15] p.; 20 cm. Signatures: A-B4.

1800. Rivard, M. (Dominique François), 1697-1778. *Traité de la sphère et du calendrier / par M. Rivard ... Cinquième édition / revue et augmentée par Jérome de Lalande....*

À Paris: Chez Guillaume ..., an 6 [1797 or 1798]. [2], vij, [1], 238 p., [1], 3 folded leaves of plates: ill.; 21 cm. Plate [1] included in pagination as p. 229.

Provenance: Sir Velters Cornewall, Bart. (armorial bookplate.)

1801. Rixson, M. E., Mrs., 1872- . *Glorious stars, by M. E. Rixson....*

New York, London: G. P. Putnam's Sons, [c1933]. xiii, p., 1 l., 17-80 p. illus., 2 fold. pl. 17 cm. Bibliography: p. 76-80.

1802. Roberts, Isaac, 1829-1904. *A selection of photographs of stars, star-clusters and nebulae, together with information concerning the instruments and the methods employed in the pursuit of celestial photography.*

London: Universal Press, 1893-1899. 2 v. plates. 33 cm. Vol. 2, published by Knowledge Office, has title: Photographs of stars, star-clusters and nebulae, together with records of results obtained in the pursuit of celestial photography. On spine: Celestial photographs.

1803. †Robinet, J. B. (Jean Baptiste), 1735-1820. *Considerations philosophiques de la gradation naturelle des formes de l'être, ou, Les essais de la nature qui apprend a faire l'homme ... Par J. B. Robinet....*

Paris: C. Saillant, 1768. 2 p. l., 260 p. X pl. 20 cm. Published also with title: *Vue philosophique de la gradation naturelle des formes de l'être, ou Les essais ...* Amsterdam, E. van Harrevelt, 1768. Plates engraved by J. v. Schley and B. de Bakker.

Provenance: armorial bookplate with motto "Tu deus fortitudo mea."

1804. Robinson, Horatio N. (Horatio Nelson), 1806-1867. *A treatise on astronomy: descriptive, theoretical and physical, designed for schools, academies, and private students / by H. N. Robinson... University edition, revised and enlarged.*

New York: Ivison, Phinney; Chicago: Blakeman & Co.; S. C. Griggs & Co., 1866. x, 11-357, [1], 55 p.: ill.; 23 cm.

1805. Rodés, Luis, 1881- . *El firmamento, por Luis Rodés.*

Barcelona: Salvat editores, s.a., 1927. 2 p. l., iv, 585, [1] p. illus., plates (part col., part double) tables, diagrs. 26 cm.

1806. Rohault, Jacques, 1618-1672. *Rohault's system of natural philosophy, illustrated with Dr. Samuel Clarke's notes taken mostly out of Sir Isaac Newton's philosophy, with additions ... Done into English by John Clarke....*

London: Printed for J. Knapton, 1723. 2 v. fold. plates. 20 cm. Translation of: *Traité de physique.* Includes index. *Babson Newton Coll.* 103.

1807. Rokitansky, Karl, Freiherr von, 1804-1878. *Die Defecte der Scheidewände des Herzens: Pathologisch-anatomische Abhandlung / von Dr. Carl Frieherrn von Rokitansky.*

Wien: Wilhelm Braumüller, 1875. vi, [1], 156, [1] p.: ill. (some col.); 33 cm. Illustrated by C. Heitzmann, W. Bader, F. Froning. Berichtigungen: p. [1] at the end.

Provenance: Herbert McLean Evans (bookplate).

1808. Rolfe, W. J. (William James), 1827-1910. *Handbook of the stars: for school and home use / by W. J. Rolfe and J. A. Gillet....*

Boston: Woolworth, Ainsworth & Co.; A. S. Barnes & Co., 1868. vi, 224 p.; [1], xvii leaves of plates: ill. (1 col.); 20 cm. Includes bibliographical references and index.

Binder: Homecrafters.

1809. Romé de l'Isle, Jean Baptiste Louis de, 1736-1790. *Essai de cristallographie; ou, Description des figures géométriques, propres à différens corps du règne minéral, connus vulgairement sous le nom de cristaux, avec figures et développemens. Par M. de Romé Delisle...*

Paris: Didot Jeune [etc.], 1772. 2 p. l., [vii]-xxxii, 427, [1] p., 1 l. x pl., 2 fold tab. 21 cm. Illustrated by Bresse and Sellier. "Table alphabétique des principaux auteurs qui ont écrit sur les cristaux ...": p. xvii-xviii. Errata: p. 385-390.

Provenance: Herbert McLean Evans (bookplate).

1810. RONDELET, GUILLAUME, 1507-1566. *Gulielmi Rondeletii Doctoris medici et medicinae in schola Monspeliensi professoris regii Libri de piscibus marinis: in quibus veræ piscium effigies expressæ sunt....*

Lugduni: Apud Matthiam Bonhomme, 1554-1555. 2 v.: ill., port.; 34 cm. Vol. 2 has title: ... Vniuersæ aquatilium historiæ pars altera, cum veris ipsorum imaginibus ... Vol. 1: [16], 583, [24] p.; v. 2: [12], 242, [9] p. Nissen. *Schöne Fischbücher,* 105. Osler, W. *Bib. Osleriana* 3831. Errata: on v. 2, p. 242. Includes indexes.

Provenance: Bartholdus O. Gambrinus (inscription), Johannes D. von Quakkenbusch (inscription). Bound in 1 v.

1811. RÖNTGEN, WILHELM CONRAD, 1845-1923. *Eine neue Art von Strahlen / von Dr. Wilhelm Konrad Röntgen ... 5. Auflage.*

Würzburg: Verlag und Druck der Stahel'schen K. B. Hof. und Universitätsbuch- und Kunsthandlung, 1896. 12 p.; 23 cm. Advertisements on lower wrapper. Aus den *Sitzungsberichten der Würzburger physik. - medic. Gesellschaft* 1895.

Upper wrapper missing.

1812. RÖNTGEN, WILHELM CONRAD, 1845-1923. *Eine neue Art von Strahlen: [I]-II Mitteilung / von Dr W. Röntgen ...*

Würzburg: Verlag und Druck der Stahel'schen K. B. Hof. und Universitätsbuch- und Kunsthandlung, (1895-1896). 2 v. (10; 9, [3] p.); 23 cm. Caption title: Ueber eine neue Art von Strahlen. Cover title for pt. 1. "Aus den *Sitzungsberichten der Würzburger Physik. - Medic. Gesellschaft*". Advertisements on wrappers and [3] p. following text of pt. 2. Horblit, H. D. *Grolier 100 science books,* 90.

In slipcase. Provenance: Herbert McLean Evans (bookplate); F. Roever (ink stamp)

1813. ROSENBUSCH, H. (HARRY), 1836-1914. *Mikroskopische Physiographie der petrographisch wichtigen Mineralien: ein Hülfsbuch bei mikroskopischen Gesteinstudien / von H. Rosenbusch.*

Stuttgart: E. Schweizerbart'sche Verlagshandlung (E. Koch), (1873-1877). 2 v.: ill., col. plates; 23 cm. Second vol. has also title: *Mikroskopische Physiographie der Mineralien und Gesteine.* Later editions published under title: *Mikroskopische Physiographie der Mineralien und Index.* Includes bibliographies and index. (Bd. 1) Mikroskopische Physiographie der petrographisch wichtigen Mineralien. – Bd. 2 Mikroskopische Physiographie der massigen Gesteine.

1814. ROSENTHAL-SCHNEIDER, ILSE, 1891- . *Das Raum-Zeit-Problem bei Kant und Einstein / von Ilse Schneider.*

Berlin: J. Springer, 1921. 75 p.; 22 cm. Advertisements on lower wrapper. Includes bibliographical references.

1815. ROST, JOHANN LEONHARD, 1688-1727. *Der aufrichtige Astronomvs. Welcher von verschiedenen, so wol zur doctrina sphaerica als zur Bewegung der Cometen und zu den observationibvs astronomicis gehörigen Materien, einen ausführlichen Unterricht ertheilet....*

Nürnberg: Bey P. C. Monath, 1727. 336, 24 p. illus., charts. 25 cm. Supplement to the author's *Astronomisches Handbuch.* Cf. C. G. Jöcher. *Allg. Gelehrten-Lex.* Includes index. Plates engraved by Sebastian Dorn.

1816. ROUSSEAU, PIERRE, 1905- . *Man's conquest of the stars. Translated from the French by Michael Bullock. (1st American ed.).*

New York: W. W. Norton, 1961. 355 p. illus. 21 cm. Translation of *À la conquête des étoiles.* Includes index.

1817. ROWLAND, HENRY AUGUSTUS, 1848-1901. *The highest aim of the physicist / by Henry A. Rowland.*

[New Haven: J. D. & E. S. Dana, 1899]. p. [401]-411; 24 cm. Title from cover. "Address delivered to the Physical Society of America by the president at its meeting in New York, October 28, 1899." "From the

American Journal of Science, Vol. VIII, December, 1899."

Provenance: G. Stanley Hall (inkstamp); Herbert McLean Evans (bookplate).

1818. ROWLAND, HENRY AUGUSTUS, 1848-1901. *Preliminary table of solar spectrum wave-lengths, by Henry A. Rowland.*

Chicago: The University of Chicago Press, 1896-1898. 2 v. in 1. 24 cm. "Reprinted from the *Astrophysical Journal,* vol. I, no. 1, January 1896 to vol. V, no. 3, March 1897, and vol. VI, no. 5, December 1897."

Provenance: Herbert McLean Evans (bookplate).

1819. ROWNING, J. (JOHN), 1701?-1771. *A compendious system of natural philosophy: with notes, containing the mathematical demonstrations, and some occasional remarks. In four parts. By J. Rowning.*

London: S. Harding, 1744. 2 v. fold. diagrs. 21 cm. Consists of 8 sections, each with special t.-p. Includes index.

Part 1, 4th ed., with additions: 1745; pt. 2, 4th ed.: 1745; pt. 2, continued, 3rd ed.: 1745; pt. 3, 2nd ed.: 1743; pt .3, continued: 1738; pt. 4: 1742; pt. 4, continued: 1743.

1820. ROYAL ASTRONOMICAL SOCIETY. *Memoirs of the Royal Astronomical Society. Memoirs of the Astronomical Society of London v. 1-4.*

London, The Society. v. ill. 22-28 cm. v. 1-85; 1821-1978. Supplements and appendices accompany some volumes. Vols. 1821-1830/31 issued by the Society under its earlier name: Astronomical Society of London. Indexes: Vols. 1-10, 1821-1836/38 in v. 10; vols. 11-24, 1839/40-1854/55 in v. 24; vols. 1-38, 1821/71. 1 v. 22 cm.; vols. 39-54, 1870/71-1899/1901 in v. 54; vols. 39-60, 1870/71-1911/15 with v. 60; vols. 1-64, 1821-1925/29 (issued as appendix to v. 65) with v. 64. Vols. for 1847/48-1874/75 supplemented by the Society's monthly notices for the same period. With vols. 1858/59-1866/67, are also published the Society's monthly notices. Beginning with 1978, papers which would have appeared as *Memoirs* are issued in microfiche enclosed with the Society's Monthly notices.

Library has: 41, 1879. Vol. XLI: Provenance: A. Brothers (presentation inscription from A. C. R. [i.e. A. C. Ranyard, Sec. R.A.S.], vol. XLI being his collation of "Observations made during total solar eclipses," and bearing a spine title to this effect.)

1821. ROYAL OBSERVATORY, CAPE OF GOOD HOPE. *Catalogue of 4,810 stars for the epoch 1850; from observations made at the Royal Observatory, Cape of Good Hope, during the years 1849 to 1852, under the direction of Sir Thomas Maclear ... Reduced and published under the direction of David Gill ... Published by order of the Board of Admiralty in obedience to Her Majesty's command.*

[London: Printed by Eyre and Spottiswoode, for H. M Stationery off., 1884]. 1 p. l., xvii, 215, [l] p. tables. 25 cm. Publisher's lettering: Cape catalogue of stars, 1850. Imprint from colophon, date from p. ii. Errata: p. i-ii.

1822. ROYAL OBSERVATORY, GREENWICH. *Catalogue of double stars from observations made at the Royal Observatory, Greenwich, with the 28-inch refractor during the years 1893-1919, under the direction of Sir Frank Watson Dyson; Astronomer Royal.*

London: H. M. Stationery Off., 1921. xvii, 229 p. diagrs. 31 x 25 cm.

1823. ROYAL SOCIETY (GREAT BRITAIN). *Philosophical transactions.*

London, Royal Society of London. 177 v. ill. 23-30 cm. v. 1-177; 1665/66-1886. Title varies slightly. For fuller bibliographical notes consult the *Library of Congress catalog of printed books.* Horblit, H. D. *Grolier 100 science books,* 95b. Vols. 1-46, 1665-1750, issued as no. 1-497. Issues for 1792-1852 have no vol. designations but constitute vols. 82-142. Publication suspended 1679-82; for this period Robert Hooke published seven numbers of *Philosophical collections* (bound with v. 12 of the *Transactions*). From 1887 the transactions have been divided into two series: *Series A,* containing papers of a mathematical or physical character; *Series B,* containing papers of a biological character. *The Croonian lectures on muscular motion* for 1738, 1744-1747 were published as separately paged supplements to v. 40, 43 and 44 of the *Transactions.*

Library has: 1-95, 1665/66-1805. Vol. 1-95: Provenance: Kinnaird (armorial bookplate); ms. armorial drawing bearing motto "Noc=ce te ipsum." [copy 1]

Vol. 1: Provenance: Denis Duveen (bookplate). [copy 2]

1824. ROYAL SOCIETY OF EDINBURGH. *Transactions – The Royal Society of Edinburgh.*
Edinburgh, The Society. v. ill., plates (part fold., part col.), maps, tables, diagrs., 28 cm. v. 1-v.70, no. 13/14; 1783/85-1979. Includes *Proceedings of the Society* for 1783-1803. Indexes: v. 1-34. 1783-1888. 1890.; v. 35-46. 1889-1908. 1910. Continued by: *Transactions of the Royal Society of Edinburgh.* Earth sciences ISSN:0263-5933.
Library has: 1, 1783/85. Vol. I: Provenance: Wm. Constable (bookplate).

1825. RUDAUX, LUCIEN, 1874-1947. *How to study the stars: Astronomy with small telescopes and the naked eye and notes on celestial photography / by L. Rudaux; translated by A. H. Keane; with 79 illustrations.*
New York: Frederick A. Stokes, [1909?]. 360 p.: ill.; 21 cm. Translation of: *Comment étudier les astres.* Includes index.
Provenance: William Andrews Clark, Jr. (bookplate).

1826. RUDEL, K. *Über eine Gattung von Körpern höherer Dimension: (Separatabdruck) / von K. Rudel....*
Fürth: Verlag von Friedrich Essmann, 1887. 32 p.; 22 cm.
No. 5 in v. with binder's title: Geometrie, I.

1827. RUDEL, K. *Die Verwertung der Symmetrie im Geometrieunterrichte / von K. Rudel....*
[Nürnberg: Heerdegen-Barbeck, 1890]. 47 p.; 22 cm. *GV* 1700-1910 v. 120, p. 223. Includes bibliographical references.
No. 10 in a collection of 18 items bound together with binder's title: Geometrie, I.

1828. RUDEL, K. *Vom Körper höherer Dimension: Beiträge zu den Elementen einer n-dimensionalen Geometrie / von K. Rudel....*
Kaiserslautern: In Kommission bei Herrmann Kaysers Verlagsbuchhandlung, 1882. 56 p.; 22 cm. Errata: on t. p. verso. At head of title: Wissenschaftliche Beigabe zum *Jahresberichte der Kgl. Industrie-Schule in Kaiserslautern für das Schuljahr 1881/82.*
p. 41-56 are bound in front. No. 15 in v. with binder's title: Geometrie I.

1829. RUMFORD, BENJAMIN, GRAF VON, 1753-1814. *An inquiry concerning the source of the heat which is excited by friction / by Benjamin Count of Rumford....*
London : Sold by Peter Elmsly ..., 1798. p. 80-102, [1] leaf of plates : ill. ; 23 cm. In: *Philosophical transactions* / Royal Society of London, v. 88. Caption title. "Read January 25, 1798". Burndy. *Science,* 151.

1830. RUSSELL, BERTRAND, 1872-1970. *The ABC of atoms / by Bertrand Russell.*
London: Kegan Paul; New York: Trench, Trubner; E. P. Dutton, (1923). 175 p.; 20 cm.

1831. RUSSELL, BERTRAND, 1872-1970. *The ABC of atoms, by Bertrand Russell....*
New York: E. P. Dutton & Company, [c1923]. v p., 1 l., 162 p. diagrs. 20 cm. "Third printing, March, 1924."
Provenance: Charles Atwood Kofoid (bookplate).

1832. RUSSELL, BERTRAND, 1872-1970. *The analysis of matter, by Bertrand Russell, F. R. S.*
London: K. Paul; New York: Trench, Trubner & Co. Ltd.; Harcourt, Brace & Company, Inc., 1927. viii, 408 p. diagrs. 23 cm. International library of psychology, philosophy and scientific method. Includes bibliographical references and index.
Advertisements: 14, [1] p. at end. Provenance: Society of Writers to His Majesty's Signet (bookplate).

1833. RUSSELL, BERTRAND, 1872-1970. *Introduction to mathematical philosophy, by Bertrand Russell.*
London: G. Allen & Unwin, Ltd.; The Macmillan Co., 1919. viii, 208 p. 23 cm. Library of philosophy. Includes bibliographical references and index.

1834. RUSSELL, BERTRAND, 1872-1970. *Introduction to mathematical philosophy, by Bertrand Russell.*
London: G. Allen & Unwin; New York: The Macmillan Co., 1938. xv, 208 p. 22 cm. Library of philosophy. "First published May 1919. Second edition April 1920. Reprinted February 1938." Advertisements: p. iv-v.
Provenance: Arthur Lanyon Blair (armorial bookplate).

1835. RUTHERFORD, ERNEST, 1871-1937. *Heating effect of the radium emanation / by E. Rutherford and H. T. Barnes.*
[London: Taylor & Francis, 1904]. p. [202]-219: ill.;

22 cm. Title from cover. "From the *Philosophical Magazine* for February 1904." Includes bibliographical references.

Provenance: authors' presentation inscription.

1836. RUTHERFORD, ERNEST, 1871-1937. *The natural and artificial disintegration of the elements; an address by Professor Sir Ernest Rutherford ... on the occasion of the centenary celebration of the founding of the Franklin Institute and the inauguration exercises of the Bartol Research Foundation, September 17, 18, 19, 1924.*

Philadelphia: The Franklin Institute, [1924?]. 24 p. 25 cm.

1837. RUTHERFORD, ERNEST, 1871-1937. *The newer alchemy; based on the Henry Sidgwick memorial lecture delivered at Newnham College, Cambridge, November, 1936, by Lord Rutherford.*

Cambridge [Eng.]: The University Press, 1937. viii, 67 p., xiii p. of plates illus. 19 cm. Printed in Great Britain.

Provenance: Library, Northern Montana College (inkstamp).

1838. RUTHERFORD, ERNEST, 1871-1937. *Present problems of radioactivity / by Ernest Rutherford.*

[Boston: Houghton Mifflin, 1906]. p. [157]-186; 24 cm. Caption title. Extracted from: Congress of Arts and Science. *Universal exposition, St. Louis,* 1904. Vol. 4, 1906. Cf. *NUC pre-1956,* v. 512, p. 96. Includes bibliographical references.

1839. RUTHERFORD, ERNEST, 1871-1937. *Radiations from radioactive substances, by Sir Ernest Rutherford, James Chadwick, and C. D. Ellis. (Reprinted with corrections.)*

Cambridge [Eng.]: University Press, 1951. xi, 588 p. illus. 24 cm. Includes indexes. Reprint. Originally published: 1930.

1840. RUTHERFORD, ERNEST, 1871-1937. *Radioactivity. By E. Rutherford.*

Cambridge: University Press, 1904. viii, [2]. 399 p. illus., pl., diagrs. 23 cm. Cambridge Physical series. Includes bibliographical references and index. Horblit, H. D. *Grolier 100 science books,* 91.

Provenance: Herbert McLean Evans (bookplate).

1841. RUTHERFORD, ERNEST, 1871-1937. *Radioactive substances and their radiations, by E. Rutherford....*

Cambridge [Eng.]: The University Press, 1913. vii, [1], 699, [1] p. illus., plates, diagrs. 22 cm. Includes index.

Provenance: H. J. E. Bailey (inscription).

1842. RUTHERFORTH, T. (THOMAS), 1712-1771. *Ordo institutionum physicarum: in privatis lectionibus / Tho. Rutherforth ... Editio secunda.*

Cantabrigiae: Typis Academicis excudebat J. Bentham, impensis Gul. Thurlbourn & J. Woodyer ...; [London]: Prostant apud J. Beecroft Londini; [Oxford]: Fletcher & Prince Oxonii., MDCCLVI, 1756. [12], 99, [1] p., XXXI leaves of plates: ill.; 27 cm. With half-title. Blank leaves interleaved. Bibliography: p. [12]. Publisher's advertisements: verso of half-title and p. [1] at the end. Errata: p. [11] of first count.

Provenance: Harry Arnold (bookplate); Hon. Robinson (inscription).

1843. RUTHERFORTH, T. (THOMAS), 1712-1771. *A system of natural philosophy, being a course of lectures in mechanics, optics, hydrostatics, and astronomy; which are read in St. Johns College Cambridge.*

Cambridge [Eng.]: Printed by J. Bentham for W. Thurlbourn, 1748. 2 v. (12 p. l., 1105, [6] p.) fold. plates. 27 cm. Vol. 1 has half-title and title-page not included in numbering. Includes index. Subscribers names: p. [9-18].

Provenance: Royal College of Physicians (bookplate); N. Griffinhoofe (inscription).

1844. RUTHERFORD, ERNEST, 1871-1937. *Über Masse und Geschwindigkeit des von Radium und Aktinium ausgesandten [Alpha]-Teilchens / von E. Rutherford.*

Leipzig : S. Hirzel, 1908. p. [1]-6 ; 25 cm. In: *Jahrbuch der Radioaktivität und Elektronik,* 4. Bd. 1907. Caption title. At head of title: Originalabhandlungen.

1845. RUYSCH, FREDERIK, 1638-1731. *Observationum anatomico-chirurgicarum centuria.*

Frederici Ruyschii anatomes, chirurg., & botanices professoris, observationum anatomico-chirurgicarum centuria: accedit Catalogus rariorum, quae in Museo Ruyschiano asservantur; adjectis ubique iconibus æneis naturalem magnitudinem repræsentantibus.

Amstelodami: Apud Henricum & viduam Theodori Boom ..., 1691. [16], 138, [4], 120 p., [46] leaves of plates (4 folded): ill; 24 cm. Part [2] has special title page: Museum anatomicum Ruyschianus; sive, Catalogus rariorum. *Bib. Walleriana.* 8337.

Plate to p. 45 of pt 2 misbound in pt. 1. With: *Johannis Gaubii Epistola problematica.* Amstelædami: Apud Johannem Wolters, 1696; and 13 other letters. Pencilled ms. notes attached.

1846. RUYSCH, FREDERIK, 1638-1731. *Frederici Ruyschii responsio ad Godefridi Bidloi libellum, cui nomen vindiciarum inscripsit.*

Amstelædami: Apud Joannem Wolters, 1697. 47, [1] p.; 22 cm. Errata: p. [1].

With: *Frederici Ruyschii ... Observationum anatomico-chirurgicarum centuria.* Amstelodam: Apud Henricum & Viduam Boom, 1691

1847. RYAN, JAMES. *The new American grammar of the elements of astronomy: on an improved plan; in three books ... / by James Ryan....*

New York: W. E. Dean ..., 1839. 342 p., [8] leaves of plates (1 folded): ill.; 16 cm. Originally published in 1825. I. The use of the terrestrial globe in the solution of geographical and astronomical problems – II. The use of the celestial globe in the solution of problems, relative to the sun, planets, and fixed stars – III. The solar system, and the firmament of fixed stars.

1848. RYDBERG, JOHANNES ROBERT, 1854-1919. *Recherches sur la constitution des spectres d'émission des éléments chimiques, par J. R. Rydberg. Avec quatre planches....*

Stockholm: P. A. Norstedt & Söner, 1890. 155 p. IV fold. pl. (diagrs.) 31 cm. *Kongl. Svenska vetenskaps-akademiens handlingar;* Bd. 23, no. 11. "Table de littérature des déterminations de longueurs d'onde": p.151.

1849. RYPMA, ENNO. *Dissertatio astronomico-geographica: de solis et umbræ stili retrogradatione, singulis aliquando diebus in quibusdam terræ locis conspicua .. sub præsidio Friderici Adami Widderi ... / publica defendendam suscipit Enno Rypma.*

Groningæ: Apud Hajonem Spandaw ..., 1760. [6], 34, [2] p., [1] folded leaf of plates: ill.; 20 cm. Plate signed: A. Durleu sculpsit. Includes bibliographical references. Thesis – Rijks-Universiteit te Groningen.

Provenance: G. Telghuis (Presentation copy inscribed by author).

1850. SACRO BOSCO, JOANNES DE, fl. 1230. *Habeslector [sic] Johannis de Sacro Busto Sphere textum / vna cum additionibus non aspernandis Petri Ciruelli. D. (a vero tamen textu apparenter distinctis) cu[m] ipsiusmet sublimi [et] lucule[n]tissima expositio[n]e aliquot figuris nouiter adiu[n]ctis decorata; Intersertis p[rae]terea q[uae]stio[n]ib[us D[omi]ni Petri de Alliaco; Omnia peruigili cura ad amussim castigata. Et rursus coipressa.*

[Paris]: Iehan Petit: Venundantur Parrhisius a Iohan[n]e Paruo ..., 1515 in me[n]se Augusti. lxxxi [i.e. lxxix], [1] (blank) leaves: ill.; 28 cm. Running title: Sphere mundi. Previous ed. published under title: *Vberrimum Sphere mundi comme[n]tum, intersertis etia[m] questionibus Petri de Aliaco, nuper magna cu[m)]dilige[n]tia castigatu[m].* (Parisius: Impensis I. Petit, 1508). That ed. in turn was reprinted from an earlier ed. with similar title, published by Guy Marchant for Jean Petit, Paris, in 1498. Cf. *Essays honoring L. C. Wroth,* p. 139-141; BN, v. 78, columns 454-456; and *NUC pre-1956* NS0014983-0014984. Name of publisher from his device on t. p. (title vignette). Publication date from colophon (leaf lxxvii, i.e. lxxvi, verso), which reads: Et sic finis hui[s] egregij Tractat[us] de sphera mundi Iohannis de Sacro Busco ... vnacum textualibus, optimis[que] additionibus: ...Impressum est hoc opusculum Anno Dominice Natiuitatis. 1515. in me[n]se Augusti Parisius. Impensis Iohannis Petit commora[n]te in vico Diui Iacobi ad intersignium Lilij aurei. Many errors in foliation. Signatures: a-m^6 n-o^4. Printed in double columns. Houzeau & Lancaster. *Astronomie* (1964 ed.), 1643; *NUC pre-1956* NS 0014666.

1851. SACRO BOSCO, JOANNES DE, fl. 1230. *Iohannis de Sacrobusto, Anglici, uiri clarissimi, Spera mundi feliciter incipit. [Gerardi Cremonensis, uiri clarissimi, Theorica planetaru[m] feliciter incipit].*

COMPENDIVM

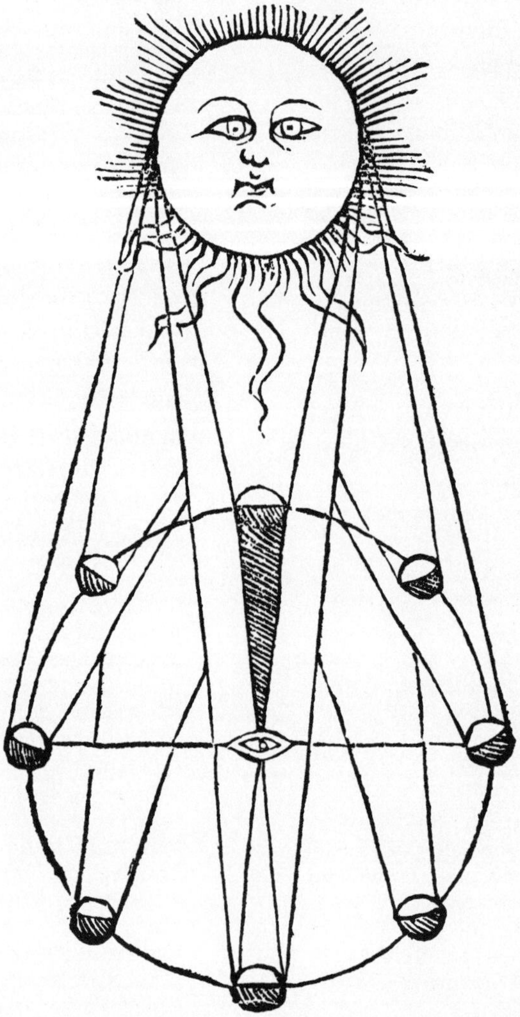

QVID NOX, QVID DIES SIT.

NEque illud ignorandum eſt, diem aut à tempore, aut à qualitate intelligi. à tempore

Sacro Bosco, *Sphaera mundi*, 1552

Impressa Venetijs: Per Franciscu[m] Renner de Hailbrun, 1478. [96] p.: diagrams (woodcuts); 21 cm. Titles from p. [1], [57] (incipits, printed in red). The *Theorica planetarum* is usually considered to be by the Cremona astrologer Gherardo da Sabbioneta, although some authorities ascribe it to the Gerardus Cremonensis who died 1187. Cf. *Dict. of scientific biog.*, suppl., p. 189 for a summary of the evidence. Both works were first printed in 1472. Cf. *The awakening interest in science during the first cent. of printing* / Margaret Bingham Stillwell. no. 63, 70. Imprint from colophon. Signatures: a-b^8 c-d^6 e-f^{10}. BM *15th cent.*, V, p. 195 (IA.19869). Goff (rev.) J-402. Hain-Copinger 14108*. *ISTC*, ij00402000.

Binding: gilt mottled calf. Provenance: Henry de Cessole (signature); ms. marginalia.

1852. Sacro Bosco, Joannes de, fl. 1230. *Sphaera / Ioannis de Sacro Bosco, typis auctior quàm antehac, atq[ue] ex diligenti manuscriptorum impressorúmque codicum collatione castigatior, cum annotationibus, & scholijs doctissimi uiri. Eliæ Vineti...; præmissa Philippi Melanchtonis doctiss. præfatione ...; adiunximus huic libro compendium in Sphæram per Pierium Valerianum Bellunensem.*

Parisiis: Apud Gulielmum Cauellat ..., 1552. 104 leaves: ill., maps; 16 cm. Error in foliation: leaf 85 misnumbered 75.

1853. Sacro Bosco, Joannes de, fl. 1230. *Sphera: cum commentis in hoc volumine contentis videlicet....*

Venetijs: Impensa heredum quondam Domini Octauiani Scoti Modoetiensis ac sociorum., 19. Januarij, 1518. 180, 201-253, [1] leaves: ill.; 30 cm. By Joannes de Sacro Bosco. Publication statement from colophon. Signatures: A^4 B-2F^8 2G^6 (2G6 blank) (G2 and G3 missigned F2 and F3). Errors in foliation: leaves 92, 97 misnumbered 192, 81. "Bartholomei Vespuccii Flore[n]tini ... Oratio habita in celeberrimo Gymnasio Patauino ...": leaves 2-3. Panzer, VIII, 944. Riccardi, P. *Bib. matematica*, I: 447-449. Houzeau & Lancaster. *Astronomie* (1964 ed.), I, 1: 755. (From t. p.) Cichi Esculani cum textu – Expositio Joannis Baptiste Capuani in eandem – Jacobi Fabri Stapulensis – Theodosij de Speris – Michaelis Scoti – Q[uaesti]ones Reuere[n]dissimi D[omi]ni Petri de Aliaco [et]c – Roberti Linchoniensis Compendium – Tractatus de sphera solida – Tractatus de sphera campani – Tractatus de computo maiori eiusdem – Disputatio Joannis de Monte Regio – Textus Theorice cu[m] exp[ositi]one Joa[n]nis Baptiste Capuani – Ptolomeus de speculis.

Addenda: [4] leaves at end (gathering signed (section mark)4) includes *Tebith de imaginatione sphere* and *Theorica planetarum* Joa[n]nis Cremonensis. Ms. marginalia throughout.

1854. Salk, Jonas, 1914- . *The use of adjuvants to facilitate studies on the immunologic classification of poliomyelitis viruses / by Jonas E. Salk ... [et al.]*

[Baltimore: The Johns Hopkins Press, 1951]. p. 157-173; 27 cm. *American Journal of Hygiene;* v. 54, no. 2. Caption title. Includes bibliographical references.

1855. Salusbury, Thomas. *Mathematical collections and translations: the first tome. In two parts ... By Thomas Salusbury, esq.*

London: Printed by W. Leybourne, 1661. 2 pts. in 1 v. illus., 4 fold. pl., diagrs. 35 cm. Collation: pt. 1: 8 p. l., 503, [24] p.; pt. 2: 7 p. l., 118, [5] p. On t.-p. of pt. 2 the words "The second tome. The second part" should read "The first tome. The second part." Half-title: Mathematical collections and translations: in two tomes. The work was published in two volumes, 1661-65. It is rarely found complete, as most of the copies of vol. 2 were destroyed in the great fire of London. t. 1, 1st pt. I. Galileus Galileus, his System of the world. II. Galileus, his epistle to the Grand Dutchesse mother concerning the authority of Holy Scripture in philosophical controversies. III. Johannes Keplerus, his reconciling of Scripture texts, &c. IV. Didacus à Stunica, his reconcilings of Scripture texts, &c. V. P. A. Foscarinus, his epistle to Father Fantonus, reconciling the authority of Scripture, and judgements of divines alledged against this system. – t. 1, 2d pt. I. D. Benedictus Castellus, his Discourse of the mensuration of running waters. II. His geometrical demonstrations of the measure of running waters. III. His letters and considerations touching the draining of fenns, diversions of rivers, &c. IV. D. Corsinus, his relation of the state of the inundations, &c. in the territories of Bologna, and Ferrara. Wing S-517

1856. Sarton, George, 1884-1956. *Ancient science and modern civilization.*

[Lincoln]: University of Nebraska Press, 1954. 111 p. diagr. 23 cm. Montgomery lectureship on contemporary civilization; 1954. Includes bibliographical references. Euclid and his time. – Ptolemy and his time. – The end of Greek science and culture.

1857. Sarton, George, 1884-1956. *A guide to the history of science; a first guide for the study of the history of science, with introductory essays on science and tradition.*

GALILÆUS Galilæus Lyncæus, HIS SYSTEME OF THE WORLD.

The Firſt Dialogue.

INTERLOCUTORS.

SALVIATUS, SAGREDUS, and SIMPLICIUS.

SALVIATUS.

IT was our yeſterdayes reſolution, and agreement, that we ſhould to day diſcourſe the moſt diſtinctly, and particularly we could poſſible, of the natural reaſons, and their efficacy that have been hitherto alledged on the one or other part, by the maintainers of the Poſitions, *Ariſtotelian*, and *Ptolomaique*; and by the followers of the *Copernican Syſtème*: And becauſe *Copernicus* placing the Earth among the moveable Bodies of Heaven, comes to conſtitute a Globe for the ſame like to a Planet; it would be good that we began our diſputation with the examination of what, and how great the energy of the *Peripateticks* arguments is, when they demonſtrate, that this *Hypotheſis* is impoſ-

Copernicus *reputeth the Earth a Globe like to a Planet.*

A fible

SALUSBURY, *Mathematical Collections and Translations*, 1661

Waltham, Mass.: Chronica Botanica Co., 1952. xvii, 316 p. illus. 24 cm. At head of title: Horus. Classified and annotated. Includes bibliography and index.

1858. SARTON, GEORGE, 1884-1956. *A history of science.*

Cambridge: Harvard University Press, 1952-59. 2 v. illus., maps, facsims. 25 cm. No more published. Bibliographical footnotes. Bibliography: v. 1, p. [615]; v. 2, p. 528. Includes indexes. (1) Ancient science through the Golden Age of Greece. – (2) Hellenistic science and culture in the last three centuries B.C.

1859. SARTON, GEORGE, 1884-1956. *The life of science; essays in the history of civilization. Foreword by Max H. Fisch.*

New York: H. Schuman, 1948. vii, 197 p. 22 cm. Life of science library. "Selected from the author's writings over a period of some thirty years." – p. 187.

1860. SARTON, GEORGE, 1884-1956. *Sarton on the history of science, essays. Selected and edited by Dorothy Stimson.*

Cambridge: Harvard University Press, 1962. xvi, 383 p. 25 cm. Includes bibliographical references and index.

1861. SARTON, GEORGE, 1884-1956. *Six wings: men of science in the Renaissance.*

Bloomington: Indiana University Press, 1957. xiv, 318 p. illus. ports. 24 cm. Patten lectures; 1955. Bibliographical references included in "Notes" [p. 239-309]. Includes index.

1862. SARTON, GEORGE, 1884-1956. *The study of the history of science by George Sarton.*

Cambridge, Mass.: Harvard University Press, 1936. 75 p.: ill.; 22 cm. "The study of the history of science; being the substance of the inaugural lecture of the seminary on the history of science in Harvard University delivered on October 4, 1935." Bibliography: p. [53]-70. Includes index.

Provenance: author's signed presentation inscription to H. M. Evans; Herbert McLean Evans (bookplate).

1863. SAUNDERSON, NICHOLAS, 1682-1739. *The method of fluxions applied to a select number of useful problems: together with the demonstration of Mr. Cotes's forms of fluents in the second part of his Logometria; the analysis of the problems in his Scholium generale; and an explanation of the principal propositions of Sir Isaac Newton's philosophy. By Nicholas Saunderson....*

London: Printed for A. Millar [etc.], 1756. xxiv, 309, [1] p. diagrs. on XII fold. pl. 22 cm. *Babson Newton Coll.* 111. Gray, G. J. *Newton,* 147.

Provenance: University of London (inkstamp).

1864. †SAUSSURE, HORACE BÉNÉDICT DE, 1740-1799. ... *Essais sur l'hygrométrie ... / par Horace-Bénédict de Saussure.*

À Neuchatel: Chez Samuel Fauche Pere et Fils ..., 1783. XXIV, 367 p., II leaves of plates: ill.; 29 cm. Published in the same year in an edition of 524 p. Cf. *NUC pre-1956,* v. 522, p. 91, and Quérard, v. 8, p. 476. Description d'un nouvel hygrometre comparable – Théorie de l'hygrométrie – Théorie de l'évaporation – Application des théories précédentes à quelques phénomenes de la météorologie.

1865. SAUSSURE, NICOLAS THÉODORE DE, 1767-1845. *Recherches chimiques sur la végétation / par Théod. De Saussure.*

Paris: Chez la Ve. Nyon, an 12, 1804. viii, 327, [9] p., [16] folded leaves, [1] folded leaf of plates: ill.; 21 cm. "Tables des incinérations et des analyses": [16] folded leaves. Includes bibliographical references. Errata: p. [328]. "De l'Imprimerie de Didot jeune" – Colophon.

1866. SAVERY, THOMAS, 1650?-1715. *An account of Mr. Tho. Savery's engine for raising water by the help of fire.*

London : Printed for S. Smith and B. Walford ..., 1700. p. 228, [1] folded leaf of plates : ill. ; 23 cm. In: *Philosophical transactions* / Royal Society of London, v. 21, 1699. Caption title. "Mr. Savery, June 14. 1699". Burndy. *Science,* 177.

1867. SAVICH, ALEKSEI NIKOLAEVICH, 1810-1883. *Abriss der practischen Astronomie, vorzüglich in ihrer Anwendung auf geographische Ortsbestimmung, aus dem Russischen übersetzt von dr. W. C. Goetze. Mit mehreren im Originalwerke nicht vorhandenen vom Herrn Verfasser nachgelieferten Zusätzen und Erweiterungen.*

Hamburg: Perthes-Besser & Mauke, 1850-1851. 2 v. tables. 23 cm. Verbesserungen: v. 2, p. [2].

Bound in 1 v. Ms. note inserted between p. 12 and 13.

1868. SCHAUDINN, FRITZ RICHARD, 1871-1906. *Vorläufiger Bericht über das Vorkommen von Spirochaeten in syphilitischen Krankheitsprodukten und bei Papillomen / von Fritz Schaudinn und Erich Hoffmann.*
Berlin: Springer, 1905. p. (527)-534: ill.; 28 cm. Caption title. Detached from Bd. 22, Hft. 2, of: *Arbeiten aus dem Kaiserlichen Gesundheitsamte.* Berlin: J. Springer, 1905. Includes bibliographical references. Garrison-Morton (4th ed.), 2399.
Printed wrappers bound in.

1869. SCHAWLOW, ARTHUR L., 1921- . *Infrared and optical masers / A. L. Schawlow and C. H. Townes.*
[Lancaster, Pa.: Published for the *American Physical* Society by the American Institute of Physics, c1959]. p. 1940-1949; 27 cm. *Physical review;* 2nd ser., v. 112, no. 6. Caption title. Includes bibliographical references.

1870. SCHEELE, CARL WILHELM, 1742-1786. *Carl Wilhelm Scheele's d. Königl. Schwed. Acad. d. Wissenschaft Mitgliedes, Chemische Abhandlung von der Luft und dem Feuer / nebst einem Vorbericht von Torbern Bergman....*
Upsala und Leipzig: Verlegt von Magn. Swederus ... zu finden bey S. L. Crusius, 1777. [6], 16, 155, [1] p., [1] folded leaf of plates: ill.; 17 cm. Advertisements: p. [1] at the end. Horblit, H. D. *Grolier 100 science books,* 92.
Provenance: Josephus Andreas Freyherr von Beretzko (armorial bookplate). With: Christian Ernst Bornemann's *Versuch einer systematischen Abhandlung von den Kohlen.* Göttingen: bey Johann Christian Dieterich, 1776.

1871. SCHEELE, CARL WILHELM, 1742-1786. *Chemical observations and experiments on air and fire. By Charles-William Scheele ... with a prefatory introduction by Torbern Bergman; tr. from the German by J. R. Forster ... To which are added notes, by Richard Kirwan ... with a letter to him from Joseph Priestley....*
London: J. Johnson, 1780. xl, 259 p. front. 22 cm. Translaton of: *Chemische Abhandlung von der Luft und dem Feuer.* Advertisements: p. [260].
Provenance: William Brodie of Brodie (armorial bookplate).

1872. SCHEELE, CARL WILHELM, 1742-1786. *Mémoires de chymie de M. C. W. Schéele, tirés des Mémoires de l'Académie royale des sciences de Stockholm, tr. du suédois & de l'allemand....*
Dijon: Chez l'éditeur, et se trouve à Paris, Chez T. Barrois, jeune [etc.], 1785. 2 v. fold. pl. 18 cm. Translated (with the exception of *Mémoires* 2, 11, 12 and 13) by Mme. Guyton de Morveau. Faute à corriger: v. 1, on p. 269. Includes index.
In 1 v. Provenance: Herbert McLean Evans (bookplate).

1873. SCHEINER, CHRISTOPH, 1575-1650. *Rosa Vrsina sive Sol ex admirando facularum & macularum suarum phœnomeno varius,: necnon circa centrum suum & axem fixum ab occasu in ortum annua, circaq. alium axem mobilem ab ortu in occasum conuersione quasi menstrua, super polos proprios, libris quatuor mobilis ostensus / a Christophoro Scheiner Germano Sueuo, e societate Iesu.*
Bracciani [i.e. Bracciano, Italy]: Apud Andream Phæum typographum ducalem, Impressio cœpta anno 1626. finita vero 1630. Id. Iunij., 1626-1630. [40], 784 [i.e. 838], [38] p.: ill., 1 port.; 39 cm. Added engraved t. p. Signatures: [pi]^4 a-b^6 c^4 A-E^6 F^4 G-R^6 2a-2s^6 2t^4 2u-2x^6 2y^4 2A-4M^6 (leaves F4, R6 and 4I6 are blank). Title vignette. Partly foliated: sigs. L6-P5 numbered 125-148; P6-R5 each numbered 149. Illustration on p. 150 signed: Daniel Widman sculpt. "Principis Federici Caesii ... De caeli vnitate, tenuitate, fusaque & peruia stellarum motibus natura ... ad ... Robertum Bellarminum ...epistola": p. [775]-782. Backer-Sommervogel, v. 7, columns 738-739; Grässe, v. 6, p. 298. Includes index. Erratorum correctio": p. [37]-[38] of last group. Includes illustrations of author's Keplerian telescope.
Imperfect: 4 prelim. leaves (pi^4), p. 219-220 (2g1), p. 229-230 (2g6), p. 257-258 (2k2), p. 263-264 (2k5), p. 305-306 (2o2), p. 311-312 (2o5), p. 362-383 (2t^{4}2u^6) are missing, some blank leaves substituted. P^6 is bound behind R6.

1874. SCHEINER, J. (JULIUS), 1858-1913. *Populäre Astrophysik, von dr. J. Scheiner ... 2., durch einige Nachträge ergänzte Aufl., mit 30 Tafeln und 210 Figuren im Text.*
Leipzig und Berlin: B. G. Teubner, 1912. vi, 722, [2] p. illus., xxx pl. (partly col., incl. front.) 24 cm.
8 p. of advertisements at end.

1875. SCHELLEN, HEINRICH, 1818-1884. *Spectrum analysis in its application to terrestrial substances and the physical constitution of the heavenly bodies. Familiarly explained by Dr. H. Schellen ... Tr. from the 2d. enl. and rev. German ed. by Jane and Caroline Lassell. Ed., with notes, by William Huggins ... With numerous woodcuts and coloured plates; also Ångström's and Kirchhoff's maps.*

London: Longmans, Green & Co.; New York: Scribner, Welford & Co., 1872. xxvi, 662 p. illus., XIII pl. (part col., incl. front.) diagrs. 23 cm. Translation of: *Spektralanalyse in ihrer Anwendung auf die Stoffe der Erde und die Natur der Himmelskörper.* "List of works on spectrum analysis": p. [635]-662.

Provenance: Charles Atwood Kofoid (bookplate).

1876. SCHELLEN, HEINRICH, 1818-1884. *Spectrum analysis in its application to terrestrial substances, and the physical constitution of the heavenly bodies; tr. from the 2d enl. And rev. German ed. by Jane and Caroline Lassell; edited with notes, by William Huggins....*

New York: D. Appleton, 1872. xviii, 455 p. illus. (part col.) 25 cm. "List of works on spectrum analysis": p. [440]-455.

Advertisements; [2] p. at end. Provenance: John C. Garner (book label). Imperfect? lacks p. [v-vi].

1877. SCHELLEN, HEINRICH, 1818-1884. *Spectrum analysis in its application to terrestrial substances and the physical constitution of the heavenly bodies / familiarly explained by the late Dr. H. Schellen ...; translated from the third enlarged and revised German edition by Jane and Caroline Lassell; edited, with notes, by Captain W. de W. Abney ...; with numerous woodcuts, coloured plates, and Ångström's and Cornu's maps. Second edition.*

London: Longmans, Green & Co., 1885. xxiv, 626 p., XIV leaves of plates (some col., some folded): ill.; 23 cm. Translation of: *Spektralanalyse in ihrer Anwendung auf die Stoffe der Erde und die Natur der Himmelskörper.* Includes index.

Advertisements: publisher's catalog: 24 p. at end.

1878. SCHEUCHZER, JOHANN JAKOB, 1672-1733. *Piscium querelae et vindiciae / expositæ à Johanne Jacobo Scheuchzero....*

Tiguri: Sumtibus authoris, typis Gessnerianis, 1708. [2], 36 p., V folded leaves of plates: ill.; 22 cm. Plates signed by Joh. Hen. Huber. Includes bibliographical references.

Provenance: Herbert McLean Evans (bookplate).

1879. SCHIAPARELLI, G. V. (GIOVANNI VIRGINIO), 1835-1910. *Osservazioni astronomiche e fisiche sull'asse di rotazione e sulla topografia del pianeta Marte fatte nelle Reale specola in Milano ... / del socio G. V. Schiaperelli.*

Roma, 1878- . v. plates. 29 cm. Memoria [1]- . At head of title: Reale accademia dei Lincei.

Library has: 1-7. [I]-VII: Provenance: Herzögliche Sternwarte, Gotha; v. 2 and 7 bear presentation inscription from the author with v. 7 addressed to G. Celoria.

1880. SCHIAPARELLI, G. V. (GIOVANNI VIRGINIO), 1835-1910. *Le più belle pagine di astronomia popolare / Giovanni Schiaparelli; scelte e ripubblicate da Luigi Gabba. 2a ed., con tavole e illustrazioni.*

Milano: Ulrico Hoepli, 1927. viii, 456 p., [13] leaves of plates: ill. (some col.), port.; 20 cm. Includes bibliographical references. I. Lettera autobiografica a Onorato Roux – II. Sul metodo del lavoro intellettuale – III. Le stelle cadenti – IV. La cometa – V. La cometa del 1882 – VI. Orbite cometarie, correcti cosmiche meteoriti – VII. Il pianeta Marte ed i moderni telescopi – VIII. Il piantete Marte – IX. La vita sul pianete Marte – X. Il pianete Marte – XI. Sulla rotazione e sulla sostitusione fisica del pianeta Mercurio – XII. Dimensioni terrestri e cosmiche – XIII. Gli abitanti di altri mondi – XIV. Il movimento dei poli di rotazione sulla superfice del blobo – XV. Sulle anomalie della gravità – XVI. Come i Greci arrivarono al primo concetto del sistema planetario eliocentrico detto oggi copernicano.

1881. SCHINDLER, ROBERT. *The mechanic of the moon. Dedicated to the astronomers and astrophysicists / by Robert Schindler....*

Lucerne, Switz.: The author, 1906-1912. 2 v.: ill., port.; 18 cm. [Pt. I] English edition. 250 copies; pt. II.

English edition, 300 copies. Part II has title: The mechanics of the moon.

Provenance: author's presentation inscription to B. R. Baumgardt [v. 1]; to T. J. J. See [v. 2].

1882. SCHLEGEL, GUSTAAF, 1840-1903. *Uranographie chinoise; ou, Preuves directes que l'astronomie primitive est originaire de la Chine, et qu'elle a été empruntée par les anciens peuples occidentaux à la sphère chinoise: ouvrage accoumpagné d'un altas céleste chinois et grec, par Gustave Schlegel, Pub. par l'Institut royal pour la philologie, la géographie et l'ethnologie des Indes-Orientales néerlandaises à la Haye.*

La Haye: Librairie de M. Nijhoff; 1875. 2 v. illus., tables (1 fold.) diagrs. 28 cm. Paged continuously. Title in red and black. Chinese caption, with transliteration: Sing chin khao youen. Atlas has title: Uranographie chinoise. Atlas céleste chinois et grec d'après le Tien-youen-lì-li. Dessiné par Gustave Schlegel. Errata: p. 928-929. Includes bibliographical references.

Provenance: E. F. Thijssen (inkstamp).

1883. SCHLEGEL, VICTOR, 1843-1908. *Ueber den sogenannten vierdimensonalen Raum / von Dr. V. Schlegel.*

Berlin: Ferd. Dümmlers Verlagsbuchhandlung, 1889. 28, [2] p.; 22 cm. Advertisements: p. [1] following text.

No. 3 in a v. with binder's title: Geometrie I. Original imprint reads: Berlin: Verlag von Hermann Riemann, 1888 (covered by label).

1884. SCHLEIDEN, M. J. (MATTHIAS JACOB), 1804-1881. *Grundzüge der wissenschaftlichen Botanik: nebst einer methodologischen Einleitung als Anleitung zum Studium der Pflanze / von M. J. Schleiden....*

Leipzig: Verlag von Wilhelm Engelmann., 1842-1843. 2 v.; 22 cm. Vol. 1: XXVI, 289, [3] p.; v. 2: XVIII, 564, [3] p. Errata on p. [2]-[3] of 3rd group of v. 1 and [559]-564 of 2nd group of v. 2. Horblit, H. D. *Grolier 100 science books,* 93b. Pritzel, G. A. *Thesaurus lit. botanicae* 8224. Includes bibliographical references.

Bound in 1 vol. Only [2] p. advertisements follow v. 2, p. 564. Provenance: L. Bandau (signature).

1885. SCHLICK, MORITZ, 1882-1936. *Space and time in contemporary physics, an introduction to the theory of relativity and gravitation, by Moritz Schlick. Rendered into English by Henry L. Brose, with an introduction by F. A. Lindemann.*

New York, Oxford University Press, 1920. x, 89 p. 24 cm. Translation of: *Raum und Zeit in der gegenwartigen Physik.* "Bibliographical note": p. [ix]-x.

1886. SCHNELL, ALBERT FREDERICK. *Schnell astronomy; being a treatise on the origin of the planets and daylight by vibration ... with engravings illustrating the different parts.*

New York and San Francisco, Cal.: A. F. Schnell, 1909. 201, [1] p., 1 l. incl. plates, diagrs., 19 cm.

Provenance: L. A. Thompson (signature).

1887. SCHOTT, GASPAR, 1608-1666. *Organum mathematicum libris IX. explicatum à P. Gaspare Schotto, e Societate Jesu, quo per paucas ac facillimè parabiles tabellas, intra cistulam ad modum organi pnevmatici constructam reconditas, pleræque mathematicæ disciplinæ, modo novo ac facili traduntur ... Opus posthumum.*

Herbipoli: Sumptibus Johannis Andreæ Endteri, & Wolfgangi jun. hæredum, excudebat J. Hertz; [etc., etc.], 1668. 18 p.l., 858, [8] p., 1 l. illus., plates, port., tables, diagrs., music, 22 x 17 cm. Added t.-p., engr.: Organum mathematic. ... Explicatum à P. Gaspare Schotto, Soc. Jesu. Errata: last p. Includes index. Port. signed: C. Dittman pin., Cornelis Nicolas Schurz sculp. liber 1. Arithmeticus. – liber 2. Geometricus. – liber 3. Fortificatorius. – liber 4. Chronologicus. – liber 5. Horographicus. – liber 6. Astronomicus. – liber 7. Astrologicus. – liber 8. Steganographicus. – liber 9. Musicus.

Imperfect: additional engraved t. p. missing.

1888. SCHOTT, GASPAR, 1608-1666. *P. Gasparis Schotti Regiscuriani e Societate Jesu olim in Panormitano Siciliæ, nunc in Herbipolitano Franconiæ ejusdem Societatis Jesu gymnasio matheseos professoris Cursus mathematicus, sive, Absoluta omnium mathematicarum disciplinarum encyclopædia: bin libros XXVIII. digesta, eoque ordine disposita, ut quivis, vel*

SCHOTT, *Cursus mathematicus*, 1661

mediocri prædītus ingenio, totam mathesin à primis fundamentis proprio marte addiscere possit: Opus desideratum diu, promissum à multis, à non paucis tentatum, à nullo numeris omnibus absolutum. Accesserunt in fine Theoreses mechanicæ novæ.

Herbipoli [Würzburg]: Sumptibus Hæredum Joannis Godefridi Schönwetteri bibliopolæ Francofurtensis.: Excudebat Jobus Hertz typographus Herbipolensis., 1661. [24], 660, [56] p., [43] leaves of plates (2 folded): ill.; 36 cm. (fol.). Title page varies from others published same year in that the "Excudebat" in the imprint is spelled correctly. Title on added t. p. (engraved by And. Frölich): Cursus mathematicus ad augustissimum imperatorem Leopoldum I. / auctore P. Gaspare Schotto e Soc: Iesu. Signatures:) (-2) (^{6} A-M^6 N^8 O-3H^6 3I^4 a-d^6 e^4. Two columns to a page; the pagination does not include the added t. p., which is counted as a leaf of plates. Backer-Sommervogel, VII, columns 907-908 (no. 6); Houzeau & Lancaster. *Astronomie* (1964 ed.), 9324; Lalande, J. J. Le F. de. *Bib. astronomique,* p. 250, 253; Grässe, VI, p. 314; BN, v. 167, column 403. For list of contents, see record for 1677 ed. in *NUC pre-1956* NS0272885 (wording of one title varies slightly). "Analecta mathematica, sive Theoreses mechanicæ novæ", by Adam Kochánski: p. 621-657. Cf. *Polski sownik biograficzny,* v. 13, p. 205. Includes index. Errata: p. 56 (3rd group).

Provenance: Comes de Cho[rm?]sky L. B. de Ledske (armorial bookplate).

1889. Schott, Gaspar, 1608-1666. *P. Gasparis Schotti e Societate Jesu Schola steganographica: in classes octo distributa, quibus, praeter alia multa, ac jucundissima, explicantur artificia nova, queis quilibet, scribendo epistolam qualibet de re, & quocunque idiomate, potest alteri absenti, eorundem artificiorum conscio, arcanum animi sui conceptum, sine ulla secreti latentis suspicione manifestare, & scriptam ab aliis eâdem arte, quacunque linguâ, intelligere, & interpretari ... : cum figuris aeri incisis....*

[Nuremberg]: Sumptibus Johannis Andreae Endteri & Wolfgangi Junioris haeredum excudebat Jobus Hertz, typographus Herbipol.; Prostant Norimbergae : Apud dictos Endteros, anno 1665. [36], 346, [10] p., [11] folded leaves of plates : ill. (engravings) ; 21 cm. Added engraved t.p. Signatures:)(-4)(^{4} 5)(^{2} A-2X^4 2Y^2. Includes index. Errata: p. [351-352]; Lectori meo: p. [353-354]; Catalogus librorum à P. Gasparo Schotto Societatis Jesu hactenus editorum: p. [355]; Nota lector: p. [356].

Provenance: Bibliotheca Mon[aste]rij Schwartzacensis (inscription).

1890. †Schott, Gaspar, 1608-1666. *Technica curiosa. P. Gasparis Schotti ... Technica curiosa, sive Mirabilia artis, libris XII. comprehensa .... .*

Norimbergæ: Sumptibus J. A. Endteri, & Wolfgangi junioris hæredum, excudebat J. Hertz, typographus herbipol., 1664. 20 p. l., 1044, [16] p. illus., 61 plates (part folded) port., tables, diagrs. 22 x 17 cm. Added t.-p., engraved. Includes index. Errata: p. [12]-[14] (last sequence). The last two pages contain a list of Schott's works. pars I. I. Mirabilia magdeburgica. II. Mirabilia anglicana. III. Mirabilia varia. IV. Scrutinium physicum præcedentium experimentorum. V. Mirabilia hydrotechnica. VI. Mirabilia mechanica. Appendix ad librum VI: Specula melitensis encyclica ... auctore R. P. Athanasio Kirchero. VII. Mirabilia graphica. – pars II. VIII. Mirabilia cyclometrica. IX. Mirabilia chronometrica. X. Mirabilia automatica. XI. Mirabilia miscellanea. XII. Mirabilia cabalistica. Waller, E. *Bib. Walleriana,* 20243.

Provenance: F. Melborne (signature).

1891. Schröter, Johann Hieronymus, 1745-1816. *Selenotopographische Fragmente zur genauern Kenntniss der Mondfläche: ihrer erlittenen Veränderungen und Atmosphäre, sammt den dazu gehörigen Specialcharten und Zeichnungen / von Johann Hieronymus Schroeter....*

Lilienthal: Auf Kosten des Verfassers, bey demselben und in Commission bey Carl. Gottfr. Fleckeisen ... in Helmstädt. Gedruckt in Göttingen bey Joh. Georg Rosenbusch ..., 1791. [12], XX, 676 p., XLIII folded leaves of plates: ill., maps; 27 cm. Illustrated by the author and G. Fischbein.

1892. Schüler, Wilhelm Friedrich. *Das Imaginäre in der analytischen Geometrie: und das Problem der stationären Strömung in der unendlichen Ebene / von Wilhelm Friedrich Schüler.*

Freising: Buchdruckerei von Anton Fellerer, 1882. [4], 29 p.; 22 cm. "Programm zum Jahresberichte der kgl. Realschule Freising pro 1892." Includes bibliographical references.

No. 14 in a v. with binder's title: Geometrie, I.

1893. SCHWANN, THEODOR, 1810-1882. *Microscopical researches into the accordance in the structure and growth of animals and plants. Tr. from the German of Dr. Th. Schwann, by Henry Smith.*
London: The Sydenham Society, 1847. xx, 268 p. 6 plates 23 cm. Translation of: *Mikroskopische Untersuchungen über die Uebereinstimmung in der Struktur und dem Wachsthum der Thiere und Pflanzen.* "Contributions to phytogenesis, translated from the German of Dr. M. J. Schleiden": p. [229]-268.
Provenance: C. Hart Merriam (inscription).

1894. SCHWANN, THEODOR, 1810-1882. *Mikroskopische Untersuchungen über die Uebereinstimmung in der Struktur und dem Wachsthum der Thiere und Pflanzen / von Dr. Th. Schwann; mit vier Kupfertafeln.*
Berlin: Verlag der Sander'schen Buschhandlung (G. E. Reimer), 1839. XVIII, 270 p., IV folded leaves of plates: ill; 21 cm. Illustrated by the author; plates engraved by C. E. Weber. Garrison-Morton (4th ed.), 113. Horblit, H. D. *Grolier 100 science books,* 93a. Yale. *Cushing Coll.* S160.
Provenance: Herbert McLean Evans (bookplate); St. St. Joanneums Bibliotheck (inkstamp).

1895. *Scientiæ baccalaureus.*
[S.n. : s.l.], 1890-1891. 1 v. : ill. ; 25 cm. Vol. 1, no. 1 (June 1890)-v. 1, no. 4 (June 1891). Title from caption.
Library has: 1, 1890/91. Imperfect: original covers and t.p. to no. 1 wanting. Vol. I: Provenance: Missouri School of Mines Library (bookplate); Stillman Drake (bookplate and letter from University of Missouri, School of Mines and Metallurgy).

1896. SCILLA, AGOSTINO, 1639-1700. *La vana speculazione disingannata dal senso: lettera risponsiva circa i corpi marini, che petrificati si trouano in varij luoghi terrestri / di Agostino Scilla....*
In Napoli: Appresso Andrea Colicchia, 1670. [8], 168 p., 28 [i.e. 29] leaves of plates: ill.; 22 cm. A Latin translation was published in 1759. Added engraved t. p. Two plates are numbered 11.

1897. SCOTT, DAVID WARDLAW. *Terra firma: the earth not a planet, proved from scripture, reason and fact / by David Wardlaw Scott.*
London: Simpkin, Marshall, Hamilton, Kent, 1901. xvi, 288 p., [1] folded leaf of plates: ill., map; 20 cm. Includes bibliographical references and index.
Provenance: Charles Atwood Kofoid (bookplate).

1898. SCOTT, ORAL E., 1882- . *Stars in myth and fact, by Oral E. Scott.*
Caldwell, Id.: The Caxton Printers, Ltd., 1942. 374 p. front., illus., plates, diagrs. (1 fold.) charts (1 fold.) 24 cm.

1899. *Scriptores logarithmici; or, A collection of several curious tracts on the nature and construction of logarithms, mentioned in Dr. Hutton's historical introduction to his new edition of Sherwin's Mathematical tables: together with some tracts on the binomial theorem and other subjects connected with the doctrine of logarithms....*
London: Printed by J. Davis, and sold by B. White and Son, 1791-1807. 6 v. illus., port., diagrs. (part fold.) 27 x 22 cm. Prefaces signed: Francis Maseres. Vol. 4 has imprint: London, Printed by Davis, Wilks and Taylor, and sold by J. White; v. 5-6: London, Printed by R. Wilks, and sold by J.White.
Provenance: presentation copy by the editor to Francis Wollaston (inscription), Sion College Library (inkstamp).

1900. SCROPE, GEORGE POULETT, 1797-1876. *Considerations on volcanos; the probable causes of their phenomena, the laws which determine their march, the disposition of their products and their connexion with the present state and past history of the globe; leading to the establishment of a new theory of the earth.*
London: W. Phillips; sold by W. & C. Tait, Edinburgh, 1825. xxxi, 270 p. illus., fold. col. map. 24 cm. Subsequently pub. under title: *Volcanos.*

1901. SCROPE, GEORGE POULETT, 1797-1876. *The geology and extinct volcanoes of central France. By G. Poulett Scrope ... 2d ed., enl. and improved....*
London: J. Murray, 1858. xvii, 258 p. front., illus., xvii [i.e. 15] pl. (partly fold., partly col., incl. front.) fold. maps. 24 cm. Includes bibliographical references and index.
Two folded maps in pockets. Advertisements: pub-

lisher's catalogue [16 p.] dated November 1857 at end. Binder: Edmonds & Remnants (ticket). Provenance: presentation inscription from T. Ruprt. Jones to John Morris; inscription from J. M. to S. N. Pattison; Herbert McLean Evans (bookplate).

1902. SECCHI, ANGELO, 1818-1878. *Catalogo delle stelle di cui si è determinato lo spettro luminoso all'Osservatorio del Collegio romano, dal P. A. Secchi, direttore del medesimo osservatorio....*

Parigi: Per Gauthier-Villars, 1867. 32 p. fold. pl. 23 cm. "Estratto delle *Memorie della Società Italiana* de' XL, 3a serie, vol. 1, 1867."

Bound with the author's *Sugli spettri prismatici delle stelle fisse.* Roma, Tipografia delle belle arti, 1868.

1903. SECCHI, ANGELO, 1818-1878. *Fisica solare: sulle ultime scoperte spettroscopiche fatte nel sole: lettura all' Accademia tiberina / del P. A. Secchi ...; nella tornata del 19 aprile 1869.*

Roma: Tipografia delle Belle Arti, 1869. 32 p.; 23 cm. "Estratto dal Giornale arcadico. Tomo LIX della nuova serie" – p. [24]. "Lettera del P. A. Secchi, al signor Cav. Salvatore Betti uno de' compilatori del Giornale arcadico": p. 25-32.

With: *Sugli spettri prismatici delle stelle fisse* / del P. A. Secchi. Roma: Tipografia delle belle arti, 1868.

1904. SECCHI, ANGELO, 1818-1878. *Le recenti scoperte astronomiche; lettura fatta alla Pontificia accademia tiberina nella tornata del giorno 27 gennais 1868. Dal. P. A. Secchi....*

Roma: Tipografia delle Belle Arti, 1868. 31, [1] p. 23 cm. "Estratta dal *Giornale arcadico.* t. LIV della nuova ser." Stelle cadenti. – Spettri stellari. – Sole e sistema solare. – Teorie astronomiche. – Questioni storiche agitate.

Bound with the author's *Sugli spettri prismatici delle stelle fisse.* Roma, Tipografia delle belle arti, 1868.

1905. SECCHI, ANGELO, 1818-1878. *Le soleil, par le P. A. Secchi ... 2. éd., rev. et augmentée....*

Paris: Gauthier Villars, 1875-1877. 2 v. fronts. [v. 2], illus., plates (part col.), diagrs. 26 cm. And atlas. 2 p. l., vi double plates. 26 cm.

Provenance: Académie de Paris (prize binding). Imperfect: lacks atlas.

1906. SECCHI, ANGELO, 1818-1878. *Sugli spettri prismatici delle stelle fisse: memoria / del P. A. Secchi....*

Roma: Tipografia delle Belle Arti, 1868. 48, 68 p., [1] folded leaf of plates: ill.; 22 cm. "Estratta dagli *Atti della Società Italiana* dei XL, Serie III-Tomo I-Parte I." "Memoria seconda" has caption title only.

With: *Catalogo delle stelle di cui si è determinato lo spettro luminoso all'Osservatorio del Collegio romano* / dal P. A. Secchi. Parigi: Per Gauthier-Villars ..., 1867 – *Le recenti scoperte astronomiche* / dal P. A. Secchi. Roma: Tipografia delle belle arti, 1868 – *Fisica solare* / del P. A. Secchi. Roma: Tipografia delle belle arti, 1869.

1907. SEE, T. J. J. (THOMAS JEFFERSON JACKSON), b. 1866. *Researches on the evolution of the stellar systems ... by T. J. J. See....*

Lynn, Mass.: T. P. Nichols; [etc., etc.]. 2 v. front. [v. 2] illus., plates, tables, diagrs. (1 fold.) 31 x 24 cm. (v. 2: 33 x 27 cm). v. 1. On the universality of the law of gravitation and on the orbits and general characteristics of binary stars. – v. 2. The capture theory of cosmical evolution, founded on dynamical principles and illustrated by phenomena observed in the spiral nebulae, the planetary system, the double and multiple stars and clusters and the star-clouds of the Milky Way.

1908. SELLER, JOHN, fl. 1658-1698. *Atlas cælestis: containing the systems and theoryes of the planets, the constellations of the starrs, and other phenomina's of the heavens, with nessesary tables relateing thereto / collected by John Seller.*

[London: J. Seller, 1680?]. [2], 72 p., 56 folded leaves of plates: ill., charts, diagrams, maps; 15 cm. Engraved illustrated t. p., by S. Moore. Caption title: A brief description of the several systems, theories, schemes, and tables contained in this book. Also, a discourse of the celestial bodies ... Signatures: engr. t.p., A-I4. With 56 double plates including both illustrative matter and tables. Warner, D. J. *The sky explored*, p. 236.

Provenance: Strickland Freeman (armorial bookplate), Jirimy Sambrook (signature).

1909. SELLER, JOHN, fl. 1658-1698. *Atlas cælestis: containing the systems and theoryes of the planets, the constellations of the starrs, and other phenomina's of the heavens.*

London: Sold by Ier. Seller & Cha. Price ... & Phil. Lea ... , [169-?] .2, 72 p., [53] leaves of plates (49 folded): ill., maps, ports.; 15 cm. Added engraved t. p. by S. Moore.

1910. SELYE, HANS, 1907- . *The chemical prevention of cardiac necroses.*

New York: Ronald Press Co., 1958. 235 p., [17] p. of plates illus. 24 cm. Includes index. Bibliography: p. 172-194.

Provenance: presented by H. M. Evans by the author (inscription).

1911. SEMENOVSKII, P. *Conquering the atom; a story about soviet atomic engineering and the uses of atomic energy for peaceful purposes. (Translated from the Russian by V. Shneerson)*

Moscow: Foreign Languages Pub. House, 1956. 94 p. illus. 20 cm. Translation of *Mirnyi atom.*

1912. SEMMELWEIS, IGNÁC FÜLÖP, 1818-1865. *Die Aetiologie, der Begriff und die Prophylaxis des Kindbettfiebers / von Ignaz Philipp Semmelweis.*

Pest: C. A. Hartleben's Verlags-Expedition, 1861. vi, 543, [1] p.; 23 cm. Druckfehler: last p. Includes bibliographical references.

Provenance: Rud. Ferber (bookplate); Herbert McLean Evans (bookplate). In slipcase. Several newspaper cuttings pasted and bound in at end. With the author's: *Zwei offene Briefe an Hofrath Dr. Edward Casp. Jac. v. Siebold* ... Pest: Gustav Emich, 1861 – *Offener Brief an sämmtliche Professoren der Geburtshilfe.* Ofen: aus der königl. ungar. Universitäts-Buchdruckerei, 1862 – *Zwei offene Briefe an Dr. J. Spaeth.* Pest: Emich, 1861 (Loose in slipcase).

1913. SEMMELWEIS, IGNÁC FÜLÖP, 1818-1865. *Offener Brief an sämmtliche Professoren der Geburtshilfe / von Ignaz Philipp Semmelweis.*

Ofen, [Hungary]: Aus der königl. ungar. Universitäts-Buchdruckerei, 1862. viii, 92 p.; 19 cm.

Provenance: Rud. Ferber (bookplate and signature); Herbert McLean Evans (bookplate). With the author's: *Die Aetiologie, der Begriff und die Prophylaxis des Kindbettfiebers.* Pest: C. A. Hartleben, 1861. Bound to 23 cm. and in slipcase.

1914. SEMMELWEIS, IGNÁC FÜLÖP, 1818-1865. *Zwei offene Briefe an Dr. J. Spaeth, Professor der Geburtshilfe an der K. K. Josefs Akademie in Wien, und an Hofrath Dr. F. W. Scanzoni, Professor der Geburtshilfe zu Würzburg.*

Pest, Emich: 1861. 21 p.; 21 cm.

With the author's: *Die Aetiologie, der Begriff und die Prophylaxis des Kindbettfiebers.* Pest: C. A. Hartleben's, 1861 (loose in slipcase).

1915. SEMMELWEIS, IGNÁC FÜLÖP, 1818-1865. *Zwei offene Briefe an Hofrath Dr. Eduard Casp. Jac. v. Siebold, Professor der Geburtshilfe zu Göttingen und an Hofrath Dr. F. W. Scanzoni, Professor der Geburtshilfe zu Würzburg.*

Pest, Emich: 1861. 40 p.; 19 cm.

Provenance: Rud. Ferber (bookplate and signature); Herbert McLean Evans (bookplate). With the author's: *Die Aetiologie, der Begriff und die Prophylaxis des Kindbettfiebers.* Pest : C.A. Hartleben's, 1861. Bound to 23 cm. and in slipcase.

1916. SENECA, LUCIUS ANNAEUS, ca. 4 B.C.-65 A.D. *1620. The workes of Lvcivs Annævs Seneca, newly inlarged and corrected byThomas Lodge....*

London: Printed by Willi: Stansby, 1620. 19 p.l., 921 p., 11 l. 32 cm. Title pages engraved. Head-pieces; initials. The "Epistles" and "The memorable and famous tracts, both morall and natvrall" have special t.-p. "The life of Lvcivs Annaevs Seneca, described by Ivstvs Lipsivs": prelim. leaves 7-19. Imprint date from colophon. Includes index. *STC* 22214.

1917. SERVISS, GARRETT PUTMAN, 1851-1929. *Astronomy in a nutshell, the chief facts and principles explained in popular language for the general reader and for schools, by Garrett P. Serviss; with 47 illustrations.*

New York, London: G. P. Putnam's Sons, 1912. xi, 261 p. front., illus., plates, diagrs. 19 cm.

With [4] p. of advertisements at end.

1918. SERVISS, GARRETT PUTMAN, 1851-1929. *Astronomy with an opera-glass: a popular introduction to the study of the starry heavens with the simplest of optical instruments ... / by Garrett P. Serviss. Seventh edition, with appendix.*

New York: D. Appleton and Company, 1893. vi, 158 p.: ill., maps; 23 cm. Advertisements: [4] p. following text. Includes index.

1919. SERVISS, GARRETT PUTMAN, 1851-1929. *Curiosities of the sky, a popular presentation of the great riddles and mysteries of astronomy, by Garrett P. Serviss ... With many illustrations from photographs and drawings.*
New York, London: Harper & Brothers, 1909. xvi p., 2 l., 267, [1] p. incl. front., plates, charts. 21 cm.
Provenance: L. A. Thompson (signature).

1920. SERVISS, GARRETT PUTMAN, 1851-1929. *The moon; a popular treatise, by Garrett P. Serviss.*
New York: D. Appleton and Company, 1907. xii, 248 p. front., illus., 26 pl. 20 cm.
With [2] p. of advertisements at end.

1921. SERVISS, GARRETT PUTMAN, 1851-1929. *Other worlds; their nature, possibilities and habitability in the light of the latest discoveries, by Garret P. Serviss ... With charts and illustrations.*
New York: D. Appleton and Company, 1901. xv, 282 p. front. (chart) illus., plates. 20 cm.
With advertisements on verso of half title and [6] p. at end. Provenance: L. A. Thompson (signature).

1922. SERVISS, GARRETT PUTMAN, 1851-1929. *Pleasures of the telescope; an illustrated guide for amateur astronomers and a popular description of the chief wonders of the heavens for general readers, by Garett P. Serviss.*
New York: D. Appleton, 1901. viii, 200 p. illus. (incl. maps). 23 cm. "Various chapters ... were, in their original form, with the exception of chapter IX, published in *Appletons' Popular Science monthly.*"
Provenance: J. C. Deagan (signature); Mars Baumgardt (signature).

1923. SERVISS, GARRETT PUTMAN, 1851-1929. *Round the year with the stars, the chief beauties of the starry heavens as seen with the naked eye, by Garrett P. Serviss ... with maps showing the aspect of the sky in each of the four seasons and charts revealing the outlines of the constellations....*
New York, London: Harper and Brothers, 1910. 19, [1] p., 1 l., 21-146, [1] p. incl. charts. 21 cm.

1924. SEVERINO, MARCO AURELIO, 1580-1656. *Zootomia democritæa: id est, Anatome generalis totius animantium opificii, libris quinque distincta, quorum seriem sequens facies delineabit.*
Noribergæ: Literis Endterianis, 1645. [24], 408, [34] p. illus., ports. 20 cm. Added engr. t.-p. Port. signed by P. Troschel. Ed. by J. G. Volkamer. Errata: on p. [33]-[34]. Includes bibliopgraphical reference and index.
With: *Georgii Hieronymi Velschii Dissertatio Medico-philosophica de ægagropilis.* Augustæ Vindelicorum: Impensis Jo.Wehe ... typis Jacobj Kopmajerj et heredum Jo. Prætorij, 1668. Provenance: Herbert McLean Evans.

1925. SHAPLEY, HARLOW, 1885-1972. *Star clusters, by Harlow Shapley.*
New York [etc.]: Pub. for the Observatory by the McGraw-Hill Book Company, Inc., 1930. xi, 276 p. incl. front., tables, diagrs. plates. 23 cm. Harvard Observatory Monographs; no. 2. Bibliography: p. 235-267.

1926. SHAPLEY, HARLOW, 1885-1972. *Starlight, by Harlow Shapley.*
New York: George H. Doran Company, [c1926]. xiii p., 1 l., 17-143 p. illus., diagrs. 18 cm. Humanizing of knowledge series.

1927. SHAPLEY, HARLOW, 1885-1972. *The stars, by Harlow Shapley.*
Chicago: American Library Association, 1927. 28 p., 1 l. 18 cm. Reading with a purpose; 30. "Books recommended in the course": 1 leaf at end.

1928. SHERRINGTON, CHARLES SCOTT, SIR, 1857-1952. *The integrative action of the nervous system, by Charles S. Sherrington.*
New York: C. Scribner's Sons, 1906. xvi, 411 p. illus., diagrs. 23 cm. Yale University. Mrs. Hepsa Ely Silliman Memorial Lectures. Includes index. "Bibliographical references": p. [395]-402.

1929. SHERRINGTON, CHARLES SCOTT, SIR, 1857-1952. *Man on his nature, by Sir Charles Sherrington, O. M. The Gifford Lectures, Edinburgh, 1937-8.*
Cambridge, [Eng.]: The University Press, 1940. 5 p.l.,

413, [1] p. illus., VII pl. 23 cm. Gifford lectures. "At numerous places, especially in its opening chapters, my text turns to the writings of a sixteenth-century physician, Jean Fernel." – Pref. Bibliographical footnotes. Includes index.

1930. SIEMENS, CHARLES WILLIAM, SIR, 1823-1883. *On the conservation of solar energy; a collection of papers and discussions, by C. William Siemens....*
London: Macmillan and Co., 1883. xx, 111 p. illus., pl. 23 cm.
Jas. B[ruceless?] (signature).

1931. SILBERSTEIN, LUDWIK, b. 1872. *The theory of relativity, by L. Silberstein....*
London: Macmillan and Co., Limited, 1914. viii, 295 p. diagrs. 22 cm. Leaf of Corrigenda inserted after p. viii. Includes index.
Provenance: George B. Jeffery (signature).

1932. SIMMS, FREDERICK WALTER, 1803-1865. *A treatise on the principal mathematical instruments employed in surveying, levelling, and astronomy: explaining their construction, adjustments, and use ... / by Frederick W. Simms ... Third edition.*
London: Sold, for the author, by Messrs. Troughton and Simms ... and J. Weale, Architectural Library ..., 1837. xi, [1] (blank), 188, [8], 7, [1] p.: ill.; 23 cm. Catalogue of instruments made by Troughton and Simms: 7 p. at the end. Advertisements: p. [1] at the end.

1933. SIMON, JOHN, SIR, 1816-1904. *English sanitary institutions, reviewed in their course of development and in some of their political and social relations.*
London, New York: Cassell, 1890. xv, 496, [16] p. 22 cm. Includes index. Advertisements: [16] p. following text. Errata: on p. xv.

1934. SIMPLICIUS, OF CILICIA. *Simplikiou Hypomnemata eis tessara biblia Aristotelous peri ouranou, meta tou hypokeimenou tou autou = Simplicii Commentarii in quatuor Aristotelis libros De coelo, cum textu eiusdem.*
Venetiis: in Aedibus Aldi Romani, & Andreæ Asulani Soceri, [1526], mense Ianuario. [4], 84, 89-134, 137-178 leaves; 33 cm. Imprint from colophon, with date in roman numerals. At foot of title page: Ne quis alius impune, aut Venetiis, aut usquam locor[um] hos Simplicii Commentarios imprimat, & Clementis VII ... & Senatus Veneti decreto cautu[s?] est. Large Aldine device on title page and verso of leaf 178. Initial spaces with printed guide letters. Text in Greek. Signatures: $*^4$ ($*4$ blank) A-K^8 L^4 M-Q^8 R^6 S-X^8. Considered by some authorities not to be the true Simplicius text but a Greek translation from the Latin of Guilelmus of Moerbeke. Cf. Grässe. Houzeau & Lancaster. *Astronomie* (1964 ed.), 936. Adams, A1785.
Ms. marginalia in Latin.

1935. SINGLETON, ESTHER, d. 1930. *The story of the universe, told by great scientists and popular authors; collected and ed. by Esther Singleton....*
New York: P. F. Collier and Son, [c1905]. 4 v. col. fronts., plates, charts. 21 cm. Paged continuously. I. The starry skies. – II. The earth: land and sea. – III. The earth's garment: flora. – IV. The earth's creatures: fauna.

1936. SLOSSON, EDWIN EMERY, 1865-1929. *Chats on science, by Edwin E. Slosson.*
New York & London: The Century Co., [c1924]. ix, 273 p. illus. 19 cm.
Provenance: Mars F. Baumgardt (signature).

1937. SMALL, ROBERT, 1732-1808. *An account of the astronomical discoveries of Kepler: including an historical review of the systems which had successively prevailed before his time....*
London: Printed for J. Mawman by T. Gillet, 1804. viii, 367 p. diagrs. on 11 fold. plates. 22 cm. Illustrated by Lowry.
Provenance: J. A. Edmonston (inkstamp).

1938. SMART, W. M. (WILLIAM MARSHALL), 1889- . *Astronomy, by W. M. Smart....*
London: Oxford University Press, H. Milford, 1937. 158 p. front., illus., plates (1 col.) diagrs. 23 cm. Pageant of Progress.

1939. SMART, W. M. (WILLIAM MARSHALL), 1889- . *Foundations of astronomy, by W. M. Smart.*

London, New York [etc.]: Longmans, Green and Co., 1942. vi p., 1 l., 268 p. diagrs. 22 cm. "First published in 1942. Second impression 1944."

1940. SMART, W. M. (WILLIAM MARSHALL), 1889- . *The sun, the stars and the universe, by W. M. Smart.*

London, New York: Longmans, Green and Co., 1928. xii, 291 p. illus., xx pl. (incl. front.) diagrs. 23 cm.

1941. SMITH, ASA. *Smith's Illustrated astronomy: designed for the use of the public or common schools in the United States: illustrated with numerous original diagrams / by Asa Smith ... Ninth edition.*

New York: Cady & Burgess ..., 1852. 71, [1] p.: ill., charts; 30 cm. Advertisements: [1] p. at end.

1942. SMITH, DAVID EUGENE, 1860-1944. *Rara arithmetica: a catalogue of the arithmetics written before the year MDCI, with a description of those in the library of George Arthur Plimpton of New York, by David Eugene Smith.*

Boston and London: Ginn and Company, 1908. 3 p. l., ix-xiii, [2], 507 p. illus., IX facsim. (incl. front.) 25 cm. Includes indexes.

"Addenda" ([4] p.) inserted after p. 494.

1943. SMITH, HOMER WILLIAM, 1895-1962. *Studies in the physiology of the kidney, by Homer W. Smith....*

Lawrence: University Extension Division, University of Kansas, 1939. 5 p. l., [3]-106 p. ill., plate. 23 cm. Porter lectures; series IX. "Delivered at the University of Kansas School of Medicine, Lawrence, Kansas City." Bibliography at end of each lecture. Renal function in man. – The evolution of the kidney. – The renal blood flow in normal and hypertensive subjects.

1944. SMITH, WILLIAM, 1769-1839. *A delineation of the strata of England and Wales, with part of Scotland; exhibiting the collieries and mines, the marshes and fen lands originally overflowed by the sea, and the varieties of soil according to the variations in the substrata, illustrated by the most descriptive names. By W. Smith....*

London, J. Cary, 1815. 2 maps on 4 sheets, mounted. fold. to 32 x 28 cm. + 1 book (ix, [3], 51, [1] p., [2] folded leaves. 21 cm.). Scale [ca. 1:316,800]. Hand colored. Accompanied by: *A memoir to the map and delineation of the strata of England and Wales, with part of Scotland,* by William Smith. London, John Cary, 1815. References: Horblit, H. D. *Grolier 100 science books,* 94.

Library has: 2 maps (on 16 sheets), 1 v. Variant mounting as described by Horblit: 15 sheets in 12 sections each, mounted on linen, 56 x 63 cm. folded to 14 x 21 cm., plus general map, 56 x 42 cm., also folded. Maps and memoir in solander case, with unidentified French armorial bookplate and spine title: Carte minéralogique de l'Angleterre.

1945. SMITH, WILLIAM, 1769-1839 *Observations on the utility, form and management of water meadows, and the draining and irrigating of peat bogs: with an account of Prisley Bogand other extraordinary improvements, conducted for His Grace the Duke of Bedford, Thomas William Coke ... and others / by William Smith....*

Norwich: Printed for John Harding ... London, 1806. [4], xviii, [19]-121, [1] p. (last page blank), 2 folded leaves of plates: plans; 23 cm. Spine title: Smith on water meadows, & c.. "Printed by Bacon ... Norwich" – T. p. verso.

Advertisements: 3, [1], 4 p. at end. Provenance: Josiah Wedgwood (booklabel); Herbert McLean Evans (bookplate).

1946. SMYTH, CHARLES PIAZZI, 1819-1900. *Madeira spectroscopic: being a revision of 21 places in the red half of the solar visible spectrum with a Rutherfurd diffraction grating, at Madeira ... during the summer of 1881. By C. Piazzi Smyth .... .*

Edinburgh: W. & A. K. Johnston, 1882. x, 32 p. front., 18 pl. (1 col.) 28 cm. Title vignette (phot.)

1947. SMYTH, CHARLES PIAZZI, 1819-1900. *Teneriffe, an astronomer's experiment, or, Specialties of a residence above the clouds / by C. Piazzi Smyth ...; illustrated with photo-stereographs.*

London: L. Reeve, 1858. xvi, 451, [1] p., [21] leaves of plates: ill., map; 19 cm. Twenty stereoscopic photographs printed by A. J. Melhuish. Errata: p. (xii). Includes index.

Advertisements: [2], 23, [1], 15, [4] p. at end. Binder: Westleys & Co., London (ticket).

1948. Smyth, Henry De Wolf, 1898- . *A general account of the development of methods of using atomic energy for military purposes under the auspices of the United States government, 1940-1945, by H. D. Smyth....*

London: Reprinted by H. M. Stationary Office, 1945. iv, 143, [1] p. diagrs. 25 cm. On cover: Atomic energy. "Written at the request of Major General L. R. Groves, United States Army. Publication authorized August 1945." "Sample list of reports": p. [144]. Published in the United States of America by the Government Printing Office.

Advertisements on lower wrapper. Colophon reads: London: Printed and published by His Majesty's Stationary Office..., 1945 (reprinted 1946).

1949. Smyth, W. H. (William Henry), 1788-1865. *A cycle of celestial objects, for the use of naval, military, and private astronomers. Observed, reduced, and discussed by Captain William Henry Smyth....*

London: J. W. Parker, 1844. 2 v. illus., tables. 23 cm. List of astronomers, mathematicians, navigators, opticians, engineers, and mechanicians, arranged chronologically by the year of death from 1729 to 1840 inclusive, with a note on the principal works of each: v. 1, p. 68-73. Includes bibliographical references and indexes. v. 1. Prolegomena. – v. 2. The Bedford catalogue.

Provenance: Morris Valentine (signature); W. LeRoy Brown (inscription).

1950. Smyth, W. H. (William Henry), 1788-1865. *The cycle of celestial objects continued at the Hartwell Observatory to 1859. With a notice of recent discoveries, including details from the Aedes hartwellianae, by Vice-Admiral W. H. Smyth....*

London: Printed for private circulation by J. B. Nichols, 1860. ix, 480 p. illus., 6 plates. 31 cm. Publisher's lettering: Speculum Hartwellianum. "Recent cultivators of science": p. 18-24. Includes index. Plates engraved by Js. Basire.

Binder: Leighton, Son and Hodge (ticket). Provenance: Admiral W. H. Smyth (armorial bookplate); armorial bookplate with motto: Verum atque decens; presentation inscription from Smyth and Dr. Lee to William Lassell.

1951. Société d'Arcueil. *Mémoires de physique et de chimie de la Société d'Arcueil. t. 1-3.*

Paris, J. J. Bernard, 1807-17. 3 v. tables (part fold.) fold. diagrs. 20 cm. The society was founded by C. L. Berthollet. No more published.

Library has: t.1-3; t.3, p. 497-512 misbound.

1952. Soddy, Frederick, 1877-1956. *The chemistry of the radio-elements, by Frederick Soddy.*

London; New York: Longmans, Green and Co., 1911. v, 92 p. diagrs. 22 cm. Monographs on inorganic and physical chemistry. Includes index. Pt. ii. has subtitle: Pt. ii. The radio-elements and the periodic law. "References": p. 89-90.

Erratum slip inserted between p. 64-65.

1953. Soddy, Frederick, 1877-1956. *Radio-activity: an elementary treatise, from the standpoint of the disintegration theory / by Fredk. Soddy.*

London: "The Electrician" Printing & Publishing Co., Ltd., 1904. xi, 214 p.: ill., diagrs.; 22 cm. "The Electrician" series. Includes index. Advertisements: [5], 12 p. at end.

Provenance: author's presentation copy to G. Beilby (inscription).

1954. Soemmerring, Samuel Thomas von, 1755-1830. *Vom Baue des menschlichen Körpers / Samuel Thomas von Sömmerring. Neue umgearb. und vervollständigte Original-Ausg. / besorgt von W. Th. (i.e. Th. L. W.) Bischoff ... [et al.]*

Leipzig: L. Voss, (1839-1845). 8 v. in 9.: ill.; 22 cm. No more published. 1. Bd. Samuel Thomas von Sömmerring's Leben und Verkehr mit seinen Zeitgenossen / von Rudolf Wagner (2 v. in 1) – 2. Bd. Lehre von den Knochen und Bändern des menschlichen Körpers. Nach der zweiten Aufl. und nach den Handexemplaren des Verfassers mit den nöthigen Ergänzungen und Zusätzen, auch dem Katalog der von Sömmerring hinterlassenen Sammlung von anatomischen Präparaten herausgegeben / von Rudolf Wagner – 3. Bd. Lehre von den Muskeln und Gefässen des menschlichen Körpers /umgearb. von Friedrich Wilhelm Theile (2 v.) – 4. Bd. Hirn- und Nervenlehre / umgearb. von G. Valentin – 5. Bd. Lehre von den Eingeweiden und Sinnesorganen des menschlichen Körpers / umgearb. und beendigt von

G. Huschke – 6. Bd. Allgemeine Anatomie. Lehre von den Mischungs- und Formbestandhteilen des menschlichen Körpers / von J. Henle – 7. Bd. Entwicklungsgeschichte der Säuge thiere und des Menschen / von Th. L. W. Bischoff – 8. Bd., 1. Abt. (Allgemeiner T.) Pathologische Anatomie des menschlichen Körpers / von Julius Vogel.

1955. *Some thoughts on the reasonableness of a general naturalization: addressed to those of all denominations who act upon Whig-principles.*
London: Printed for H. Shute Cox ..., 1753. 8 p.; 31 cm.
With: *Experiments and observations on electricity*, by Benjamin Franklin. London: printed and sold by E. Cave, 1751-1753. Provenance: L'Ab. Boyer (bookplate); Domus Massiliensis (bookplate); bound to 26 cm.

1956. SOMERVILLE, MARY, 1780-1872. *The connexion of the physical sciences / by Mary Somerville. Tenth edition / corrected and revised by Arabella B. Buckley....*
London: John Murray ..., 1877. xix, [1] (blank), 447 p.: ill., port.; 18 cm. Port. by J. Cooper. Includes bibliographical references and index.
Provenance: Highbury Park School (lettering); Charles Atwood Kofoid (bookplate).

1957. SOMERVILLE, MARY, 1780-1872. *Mechanism of the heavens. By Mrs. Somerville.*
London: J. Murray, 1831. lxx, 621, [3] p. diagrs. 24 cm. Includes index.
8 p. of advertisements bound in following text.

1958. SOMERVILLE, MARY, 1780-1872. *On the connexion of the physical sciences / by Mary Somerville. Sixth edition.*
New York: John Murray ..., 1842. xv, [1] (blank), 499, [1], 16 p., 5 leaves of plates: ill.; 18 cm. Advertisements: 16 p. at the end. Includes index.
Provenance: George Henry Saunders (signature). Binder: Homecrafters (label).

1959. SOMERVILLE, MARY, 1780-1872. *Personal recollections, from early life to old age, of Mary Somerville: with selections from her correspondence / by her daughter, Martha Somerville.*
London: John Murray ..., 1873. vi, 377 p., [1] leaf of plates: 1 ill.; 21 cm.
Advertisements: 16 p. at end.

1960. SOMMER, JOHANNES, 1559-1622. *Centuria herbarum mirabilium, das ist, Hundert Wunderkräuter: so da theils in der Newen Welt, theil in Teutschland wachsen .... : auss vielen beglaubten Autoribus mit grosser Mühe und Fleiss zusammen getragen / durch Johannem Olorinum....*
Magdeburgk: Bey Levin Braunss ..., Im Jahr 1616. [18], 139, [3] (last 3 p. blank) p. ; 16 cm.

1961. SOMMERFELD, ARNOLD, 1868-1951. *Atombau und Spektrallinien / von Arnold Sommerfeld.*
Braunschweig: Friedr Vieweg & Sohn, 1919. x, 550 p.: ill.; 22 cm. Includes bibliographical references and index.

1962. SOMMERFELD, ARNOLD, 1868-1951. *Atombau und Spektrallinien / von Arnold Sommerfeld. 3. umgearb. Aufl.*
Braunschweig: F. Vieweg & Sohn, 1922. xi, 764 p.: ill., tables; 23 cm. Includes bibliographical references and index.
Provenance: C. A. Crommelin (inkstamp).

1963. SOMMERFELD, ARNOLD, 1868-1951. *Atombau und Spektrallinien. Wellenmechanischer Ergänzungsband. Mit 30 abbildungen.*
Braunschweig: F. Vieweg & Sohn Akt. Ges., 1929. x, 351 p. illus., diagrs. 23 cm. Includes index. "Ich habe diesen Ergänzungsband als 'wellenmechanisch' bezeichnet, weil die Schröderingerschen Methoden in der praktischen Handhabung offensichtlich den spezifischen 'quantenmechanischen' Methoden überlegen sind." – Vorwort.
Provenance: C. A. Crommelin (inscription).

1964. SOMMERFELD, ARNOLD, 1868-1951. *Zur Quantentheorie der Spektrallinien / von A. Sommerfeld.*
Leipzig: J. A. Barth, 1916. 167 p.; 23 cm. Cover title. "Separat-Abdruck aus den *Annalen der Physik*. Vierte Folge. Band 51.1916."
Advertisements: [3] p. on covers. Provenance: Herbert McLean Evans (bookplate).

1965. SOONAWALA, MINOCHEHAR IRAMJI. *Maharaja Sawai Jai Singh II of Jaipur and his observatories / by M. F. Soonawala; with a*

foreword by ... Maharaja Sawai Mansinghji of Jaipur.
Jaipur: Jaipur Astronomical Society, 1952. 43 p.: ill., port.; 24 cm.

1966. SPALLANZANI, LAZZARO, 1729-1799. *De' fenomeni della circolazione osservata nel giro universale de' vasi; de' fenomeni della circolazione languente; de' moti del sangue independenti dall' azione del cuore; e del pulsar delle arterie. Dissertazioni quattro dell' abbate Spallanzani....*
Modena: Società tipografica, MDCCLXXIII. viii, 343, [1] p. [1] leaf of plates, 24 cm. Errata: p. [1] at the end.

1967. SPALLANZANI, LAZZARO, 1729-1799. *Dissertazioni di fisica animale, e vegetabile.*
Modena: Presso la Società Tipografica, 1780. 2 v. in 1.: ill.; 20 cm. Errata: last leaf. Plates signed: Cagnoni sculp.

1968. SPALLANZANI, LAZZARO, 1729-1799. *Dissertazioni due / dell' Abate Spallanzani....*
Modena: Pergh eredi di Bartolomeo Soliani ..., 1765. [4], 87, [5], 44 p., [2] folded leaves of plates: ill.; 23 cm. Pt. 1: Saggio di osservazioni microscopiche concernenti il sistema della generazione de' signori di Needham e Buffon; pt. 2: De lapidibus ab aqua resilientibus.

1969. SPALLANZANI, LAZZARO, 1729-1799. *Opuscoli di fisica animale, e vegetabile / dell' Abate Spallanzani ...; aggiuntevi alcune lettere relative ad essi opuscoli dal celebre Signor Bonnet di Ginevra, e da altri scritti all'autore. Volume primo [-secondo].*
In Modena: Presso la Società Tipografica., MDCCLXXVI, [1776]. 2 v.: ill. (engravings); 22 cm. Vol. 1: xvi, 304 , [2] p.; v.2: [4], 277, [1] p., VI folding leaves of plates. Errata: p. [305], v. 1; final page, v. 2. Includes bibliographical references. Plates engraved by Cagnoni. Garrison-Morton (4th ed.), 102. V. I. Opuscolo I: Osservazioni e sperienze intorno agli animalucci delle infusioni in occasione che si esaminano alcuni articoli della nuova opera del sig. di Needham. Lettere due dissertatorie scritte dall'illustre Sig. Bonnet di Ginevra all'autore relative al suggetto degli animali infusorj – V.II. Opuscolo II: Osservazioni, e sperienze intorno ai vermicelli spermatici dell'uomo, e degli animali ... Opuscolo III: Osservazioni esperienze intorno agli animali, e ai vegetabili chiusi nell'aria. Opuscolo IV: Osservazioni e sperienze intorno ad alcuni prodigiosi animali, che è in balia dell' osservatore il farli tornare da morte a vita. Opuscolo V: Osservazioni e sperienze intorno all'origine delle piantine delle muffe.

1970. SPALLANZANI, LAZZARO, 1729-1799. *Prodromo di un' opera da imprimersi sopra le riproduzioni animali / dato in luce dall' Abate Spallanzani....*
In Modena: Nella Stamperia di Giovanni Montanari, 1768. 102 p.; 22 cm.

1971. SPALLANZANI, LAZZARO, 1729-1799. *Viaggi alle Due Sicilie e in alcune parti dell' Appennino dell' abbate Lazzaro Spallanzani....*
Pavia: Stamperia di B. Comini, 1792-97. 6 v. xi fold. pl. 20 cm. Vol. 6 has title: Opuscoli sopra diversi animali, che servono di appendice ai Viaggi alle Due Sicilie ... Illustrated by Ios. Lanfranchi and F. Anderloni.

1972. *Sphæra vetus, Græca, quam Latinis senarijs recentauit & recensuit Q. Sept. Fl. Christianus.*
Lutetiæ: Apud Federicum Morellum ..., 1587. 8 p.; 20 cm. Variously attributed to Empedocles and to Demetrius Triclinius. cf. *BLC*, v. 310, p. 24. Adams S1578. Houzeau & Lancaster. *Astronomie.* (1964 ed.), 798.

1973. SPINOZA, BENEDICTUS DE, 1632-1677. *B.d.S. opera posthuma: quorum series post praefationem exhibetur.*
[Amsterdam: Jan Rieuwertsz], 1677. [40], 614, [34], 112, [8] p.: ill.; 22 cm. Edited by Jarig Jelles, with a Latin translation of his pref., originally written in Dutch. Imprint from: Kingma, J. *Bib. of Spinoza's works up to 1800.* Errata printed on p. [6]-[8] (last group). Includes indexes. I. Ethica: more geometrico demonstrata – II. Politica – III. De emendatione intellectûs – IV. Epistolæ, & ad eas responsiones – V. Compendium grammatices linguæ Hebrææ. Kingma & Offenberg. Spinoza, 24. Spinoza, B. de Opera (1925 ed.), II, p. 311-319.
With: *Tractatus theologico-politicus* / [B. de Spinoza]. Hamburgi: Apud Henricum Künrath, 1670 [i.e. Amsterdam: Jan Rieuwertsz, not before 1678]. Provenance: E. P. Goldschmidt & Co. (booklabel); Unitarian College (embossed stamp).

1974. SPINOZA, BENEDICTUS DE, 1632-1677. *Tractatus theologico-politicus: continens dissertationes aliquot, quibus ostenditur libertatem philosophandi non tantum salva pietate & reipublicæ pace posse concedi: sed eandem nisi cum pace reipublicæ ipsaque pietate tolli non posse.*

Hamburgi: Apud Henricum Künrath, 1670 [i.e. Amsterdam: Jan Rieuwertsz, not before 1678]. (12), 233, [1] p.; 21 cm. Signatures: *4 **2 A-Z4 Aa-Ff4 Gg2 (Gg2 blank). Published anonymously. Actual imprint from: Bamberger. The 4th quarto ed., printed by Christoffel Conrad for Rieuwertsz. Cf. Bamberger. Errata: p. [234]. Page 130 misnumbered 830. Kingma & Offenberg. *Spinoza,* 6. Bamberger, F. "Early eds. of Spinoza's *Tractatus*" (in: *Studies in bib. and booklore,* v. 5, p. 9-33), T4.

With: Spinoza, Benedictus de. B.d.S. *Opera posthuma.* (Amsterdam: Jan Rieuwertsz), 1677. Provenance: E. P. Goldschmidt & Co. (booklabel); Unitarian College (embossed stamp).

1975. Erratum. Original citation duplicates citation 1974.

1976. *Splendour of the heavens; a popular authoritative astronomy, edited by Rev. T. E. R. Phillips ... and Dr. W. H. Steavenson.*

New York: R. M. McBride & Company, 1925. 2 v. col. front., illus. (incl. ports.) col. plates, diagrs. 28 x 22 cm. London edition published in 1923, has title: Hutchinson's *Splendour of the heavens.* Includes index.

Provenance: William Andrews Clark Jr. (bookplate).

1977. SPOTTISWOODE, WILLIAM, 1825-1883. *Die Mathematik in ihren Beziehungen zu den anderen Wissenschaften / von William Spottiswoode.*

Leipzig: Verlag von Quandt & Händel, 1879. [4], 43, [1] p.; 23 cm. "Aus dem Englischen".

No. 11 in a v. of 11 items with binder's title: Geometrie. Provenance: Ernst Mach (inkstamp).

1978. SPRAT, THOMAS, 1635-1713. *The history of the Royal Society of London, for the improving of natural knowledge. By Tho. Sprat.*

London: Printed by T. R. for J. Martyn ... and J. Allestry ..., 1667. 8 p.l., 438, [1] p. illus. (arms), fold. front., 2 fold. plates. 22 cm. Errata: final page. Wing S-5032.

Provenance: Warcop Hall (inkstamp); Will. Preston (signature). Imperfect: lacks frontispiece.

1979. SPRAT, THOMAS, 1635-1713. *The history of the Royal Society of London, for the improving of natural knowledge. By Tho. Sprat, D.D. late lord bishop of Rochester. 2d ed. cor.*

London: Printed for Rob. Scot. [etc.], 1702. 8 p. l., 438 p. incl. front., 2 fold. pl. 23 cm. The dedication is followed by verses to the Royal Society by A. Cowley. [6] p.

Provenance: Wm. Stevenson (signature); Anastasia Fletcher (inscription).

1980. SPRENGEL, CHRISTIAN KONRAD, 1750-1816. *Das entdeckte Geheimniss der Natur im Bau und in der Befruchtung der Blumen / von Christian Konrad Sprengel....*

Berlin: Bei Friedrich Vieweg dem aeltern, 1793. [6], 444 columns, [4] p., XXV leaves of plates: ill.; 27 cm. Nissen 1883. Pritzel 8856. Illustrations signed by the author, Capieux and Wohlgemuth. Includes index.

Provenance: R. Krull (inscription).

1981. STACKHOUSE, THOMAS, 1756-1836. *The rationale of the globes, or a development of the principles on which the operations of these useful instruments are founded ... / by Thomas Stackhouse.*

London: Printed for the author by T. Plummer ..., 1805. ix, 10-100 p., [1] leaf of plates with volvelle: ill.; 50 cm. Plate signed by T. Stackhouse and J. Noble.

1982. *Stars at a glance.*

London: George Philip & Son, 1944. 48, [2] p.: chiefly ill.; 19 cm. Advertisements: [1] p. at end.

1983. *Statements relating to the atomic bomb.*

London: H. M. Stationery Office, 1945. 23 [1] p. 25 cm. At head of title: H. M. Treasury. Statements by the prime minister and Mr. Churchill issued on Monday, August 6th, 1945. – Statement issued by the Directorate of Tube Alloys (Department of Scientific and Industrial Research) on Sunday, August 12th, 1945.

1984. STAUDT, KARL GEORG CHRISTIAN VON, 1798-1867. *Beiträge zur Geometrie der Lage / von Dr. Karl Georg Christian v. Staudt....*

Nürnberg: Verlag von Bauer und Raspe (Julius Merz), (1856-1860). 3 v. in 1; 22 cm. Each vol. has special t. p. Paged continuously. Vol.1: VI, 129, [1] (blank) p.; v. 2: IV, [131]-283, [1] p.; v. 3: [2], IV, [2], [285]-396 p.

Provenance: K. K. Technische Hochschule, Graz (inkstamp)

1985. Staudt, Karl Georg Christian von, 1798-1867. *Geometrie der Lage, von Dr. Georg Karl Christian von Staudt....*

Nürnberg: F. Korn, 1847. VI, 216 p. 23 cm.

Provenance: K. K. Technische Hochschule, Graz (inkstamp).

1986. Steavenson, William Herbert, 1894-. *Suns & worlds; an introduction to astronomy, by W. H. Steavenson....*

London: A. & C. Black Ltd., 1933. 104 p. front., illus., plates, diagrs. 19 cm. How-&-why series / edited by Gerald Bullet; no. 16.

1987. Steele, Joel Dorman, 1836-1886. *Fourteen weeks in descriptive astronomy / by J. Dorman Steele....*

New York and Chicago: A. S. Barnes & Company, 1874. 336 p., [1] folded leaf of plates: ill., 1 col. map; 19 cm. Bibliography: p. 7. Earlier ed. published in 1868 as *A fourteen weeks course in descriptive astronomy*.

With [1] p. of advertisements preceding t. p. and [1] p. at end. Provenance: [Sade?] Grassman (signature). Binder: Homecrafters.

1988. Steele, Joel Dorman, 1836-1886. *Popular astronomy: being the New descriptive astronomy by Joel Dorman Steele, PH. D., revised and brought down to date by Mabel Loomis Todd....*

New York, Cincinnati [etc.]: American Book Company, 1899. 349 p. incl. front., illus. 2 col. pl., fold. chart. 19 cm. Steele's Science series. "Reading references": p. 8. Revision of Steele's *Descriptive astronomy* – cf. Pref. Advertisements: [3] p. at end.

1989. Steele, Joel Dorman, 1836-1886. *The story of the stars: new descriptive astronomy / by Joel Dorman Steele....*

New York, Chicago: A. S. Barnes & Company, 1884. xii, 326 p., [4] leaves of plates (1 folded): ill. (some col.), 1chart; 19 cm. Steele's Sciences. Bibliography: p. [viii]. Includes index. A new edition of the author's *Fourteen weeks course in descriptive astronomy*. Spine title: Steele's new astronomy.

1990. Steele, Joel Dorman, 1836-1886. *The story of the stars: new descriptive astronomy / by Joel Dorman Steele....*

New York, Cincinnati, Chicago: American Book Company, 1884. xii, 326, [6] p., [4] leaves of plates (1 folded): ill. (2 col.), 1 chart; 19 cm. Steele's Sciences. Bibliography: p. [viii]. Includes index. A new edition of the author's *Fourteen weeks course in descriptive astronomy*. Advertisements: [6] p. at end. Spine title: Steele's New astronomy.

1991. Stefan, J. (Josef). [Bemerkungen / Stefan].

[1857-1873]. 1 v. (various pagings); 23 cm. Binder's title. Collection of 22 articles by Stefan detached from the *Sitzungsberichte* of the Kaiserliche Akademie der Wissenschaften in Wien; from the Ernst Mach Library. Includes bibliographical references. Bemerkungen über die Absorption der Gase – Über die Transversalschwingungen eines elastischen Stabes – Über das Dulong-Petit'sche Gesetz – Über die Bewegung flüssiger Körper – Über die Bewegung flüssiger Körper (zweite Abhandlung) – Über Interferenz des weissen Lichtes bei grossen Gangunterschieden – Theorie der doppelten Brechung – Über Longitudinalschwingungen elastischer Stäbe – Über Schwingungen von Saiten, welche aus ungleichen Stücken bestehen – Anwendung der Schwingungen zusammengesetzter Stäbe zur Bestimmung der Schallgeschwindigkeit – Über die Grundformeln der Elektrodynamik – Über die Erregung longitudinaler Schwingungen ... – Über das Gleichgewicht und die Bewegung, insbesondere die Diffusion von Gasgemengen – Über den Einfluss der Wärme auf die Brechung des Lichtes in festen Körpern – Über die Gesetze der elektrodynamischen Induction. Untersuchungen über die Wärmeleitung in Gasen: erste Abhandlungen – Über die dynamische Theorie der Diffusion der Gase – Über die Eigenschaften der Schwingungen eines Systems von Punkten – Über die mit dem Soleil'schen Doppelquarz aus geführten Interferenzversuche – Zur Theorie der magnetischen Kräfte – Versuche über die scheinbare Adhäsion – Versuche über die Verdampfung.

1992. Stengel, Johann Peterson. *Gnomonica universalis, oder ausführliche Beschreibung der Sonnen-Uhren: darinnen allerhand Gattungen derselben in Figuren vorgestellet ... / durch Johann Peterson Stengel....*

Augspurg: Bey Johann Weh, in Verlegung des Authors, 1675. [12], 360, [8] p., [102] leaves of plates: ill.; 16 cm. Errata: last p.

1993. Steno, Nicolaus, 1638-1686. *De solido intra solidum naturaliter contento dissertationis prodromus. Nicolai Stenonis De solido intra solidum naturaliter contento dissertationis prodromus.*

Florentiæ: Ex typographia sub signo stellae, (1669). 1 p.l., 78 p., 1 l. fold. illus. 25 cm. The plate is preceded by a folded leaf with descriptive letter-press. Title in red and black; engr. title vignette; head- and tailpieces; initial. Horblit, H. D. *Grolier 100 science books,* 96.

Provenance: Herbert McLean Evans (bookplate).

1994. Steno, Nicolaus, 1638-1686. *Nicolai Stenonis Elementorum myologiæ specimen, seu musculi descriptio geometria. Cui accedunt Canis carchariae dissectum caput, et Dissectus piscis ex canum genere.*

Florentiæ: Ex typographia sub signo stellæ., MDCLXVII, [1667]. [8], 123 p., VII folding leaves of plates: ill.; 23 cm. Errata: on p. 123. Garrison, F. H. *Medical bibl.* 676. Osler, W. *Bib Osleriana,* 4021. Waller 9223. Includes index.

1995. Stetson, Harlan True, 1885-1964. *Earth, radio and the stars, by Harlan True Stetson.*

New York: Whittlesey House, McGraw-Hill Book Company, Inc., 1934. xvii, 336 p. col. front., illus., plates, map, diagrs. 21 cm. "First edition." Bibliography: p. 311-321.

Provenance: A. W. Smith (signature).

1996. Stevin, Simon, 1548-1620. *De beghinselen der weeghconst, beschreven dver Simon Stevin van Brugghe.*

Tot Leyden: Inde druckerye van Christoffel Plantijn, by Françoys van Raphelinghen, 1586. 9, [25], 95 p. diagrs. 21 x 17 cm. Title vignette (Stevin's device) with legend: Wonder en is gheen wonder. Only p. 9 of the first group is paginated. "Simon Stevins vytspraeck vande weerdicheyt der dvytsche tael": p. 9, [1-23]. With this were issued and are bound the author's *De weeghdaet,* and his *De beghinselen des waterwichts.* The three works were republished together in 1605 as pt. 4 of his *Wisconstighe ghedachtenissen.*

Provenance: Harrison D. Horblit (bookplate).

1997. Stevin, Simon, 1548-1620. *De beghinselen des waterwichts, Elementa. Beschreven dver Simon Stevin van Brugghe.*

Tot Leyden: Inde druckerye van Christoffel Plantijn, by Françoys van Raphelinghen, 1586. 81 [i.e.71] p. diagrs. 21 x 17 cm. Page 10 wrongly numbered 38; pages 70-71 wrongly numbered 80-81. Title vignette (Stevin's device) with legend: Wonder en is gheen wonder. Issued and bound with the author's *De beghinselen der weeghconst,* and his *De weeghdaet.* The three works were republished together in 1605 as pt. 4 of his *Wisconstighe ghedachtenissen.*

Provenance: Harrison D. Horblit (bookplate).

1998. Stevin, Simon, 1548-1620. *De weeghdaet, Praxis artis ponderaria. Beschreven dver Simon Stevin van Brugghe.*

Tot Leyden: Inde druckerye van Christoffel Plantijn, by Françoys van Raphelinghen, 1586. 43 p. illus., diagrs. 21 x 17 cm. Title vignette (Stevin's device) with legend: Wonder en is gheen wonder. Issued and bound with the author's *De beghinselen der weeghconst,* and his *De beghinselen des waterwichts.* The three works were republished together in 1605 as pt. 4 of his *Wisconstighe ghedachtenissen.*

Provenance: Harrison D. Horblit (bookplate).

1999. Stewart, Matthew, 1717-1785. *The distance of the sun from the earth determined by the theory of gravity ... By Dr. Matthew Stewart ... Being a supplement to Tracts physical and mathematical....*

Edinburgh: Printed for A. Millar [etc.], 1763. viii, 103 p. 2 fold. diagrs. 22 cm.

2000. Stillwell, Margaret Bingham, 1887- . *The awakening interest in science during the first century of printing, 1450-1550; an annotated checklist of first editions viewed from the angle of their subject content.*

New York: Bibliographical Society of America, 1970. xxix, 399 p. 26 cm. Includes bibliographical references.

Extensive ms. marginalia.

2001. Stokes, George Gabriel, Sir, 1819-1903. *Mathematical and physical papers / by George Gabriel Stokes.*

Cambridge: University Press, 1880-1905. 5 v.: ill., ports.; 23 cm. Vol. 4-5: By the late Sir George Gabriel Stokes ... Reprinted from the original journals and transactions, with brief historical notes and references. Vol. 4-5 edited by J. Larmor. Mathematical tripos problems, 1846-1848: v. 5, p. 296-309. Smith's prize examination papers, 1850-1882: v. 5, p. 309-368. Reprinted from the original journals and transactions, with additional notes by the author.

2002. STOUGHTON, JOHN, 1807-1897. *Worthies of science. By John Stoughton....*

London: The Religious Tract Society, [1879?]. vi p., 1 l., 342 p. 19 cm. Roger Bacon, 1214-1292. – Nicholas Copernicus, 1472-1543. – Francis Bacon, 1561-1626. – René Descartes, 1596-1650. – Blaise Pascal, 1623-1662. – Isaac Barrow, 1630?-1677. – Robert Boyle, 1626-1691. – John Locke, 1632-1704. – John Ray, 1628-1705. – Gottfried W. Leibnitz, 1646-1716. – Isaac Newton, 1642-1727. – Georges Cuvier, 1769-1832. – John Dalton, 1766-1844. – Michael Faraday, 1791-1867. – David Brewster,1781-1869. – John F. W. Herschel, 1792-1871. – Adam Sedgwick, 1787-1873.

Advertisements: [2] p. at end. Provenance: Eliot Curwen (signature).

2003. STRASBURGER, EDUARD, 1844-1912. *Ueber Befruchtung und Zelltheilung / von Dr. Eduard Strasburger....*

Jena: Verlag von Hermann Dabis, 1878. 108 p., IX folded leaves of plates: ill.; 25 cm. Plates signed: Ed. Strasburger ad. nat. del. Advertisements on lower wrapper. Includes bibliographical references. Original imprint: Verlag von Hermann Dufft, 1877 is covered by label.

Provenance: Herbert McLean Evans (bookplate).

2004. STRAUCH, AEGIDIUS, 1632-1682. *D. Ægidii Strauchii professoris quondam Witteberg. Magnitudinum doctrina: in brevissimos aphorismos ... contracta. Editio secunda.*

Wittebergæ: Sumptibus hæred D. Tobiæ Mevii, & Elendi Schumacheri, typis Matthæi Henckelii ..., 1678. [14], 116, [4] (2 blanks), 111 p., [4] leaves of plates: ill.; 14 cm. Errors of pagination: p. 48 (2nd group) misnumbered as 84. Pars specialis has special t. p.

Some leaves repaired with loss of text. Ms.notes. With: *Ægidii Strauchii ... Doctrina astrorum mathematica.* [Wittenberg?]: Sumptibus autoris & auditorum ejus, Literis Michaelis Wendt, 1663.

2005. STRAUCH, AEGIDIUS, 1632-1682. *Ægidii Strauchii prof. Ante hac Witt. Astrognosia: synoptice et methodice in usum gymnasiorum et academiarum adornata ... Editio tertia, prima multo auctior.*

Wittebergæ: Sumptibus hæred. D. Tobiæ Mevii, & Elerti Schumacheri, typis Matthæi Henckelii ..., 1678. [8], 208 p., [1], XXXV leaves of plates: ill.; 14 cm. Plate XXXV signed by Joh. Dürr.

With: *Ægidii Strauchii ... Doctrina astrorum mathematica.* [Wittenberg?]: Sumptibus autoris & auditorum ejus. Literis Michaelis Wendt, 1663.

2006. STRAUCH, AEGIDIUS, 1632-1682. *Ægidii Strauchii professoris quondam Wittebergensis Aphorismi astrologici: methodice in usum docentium et discentium collecti. Accessit Cypriani Leovitii De judiciis nativitatum doctrina ... Editio secunda.*

Wittebergæ: Sumptibus hæred D. Tobiæ Mevii, & Elendi Schumacheri, literis Johannis Haken, 1675. [2], 281, [1] p., [1] folded leaves of plates; 14 cm. Errata: p. [1] at the end. p. 186 & 187 wrongly imposed.

With: *Ægidii Strauchii ... Doctrina astrorum mathematica.* [Wittenberg?]: Sumptibus autoris & auditorum ejus. Literis Michaelis Wendt, 1663.

2007. STRAUCH, AEGIDIUS, 1632-1682. *Ægidii Strauchii professoris Wittebergensis Doctrina astrorum mathematica: in brevissimos aphorismos methodice contracta.*

[Wittenberg?]: Sumptibus autoris & auditorum ejus. Literis Michaelis Wendt, 1663. 276 p.; 14 cm. Includes bibliographical references.

With: *Ægidii Strauchii ... Aphorismi astrologici.* Editio secunda. Wittebergæ: Sumptibus hæred D. Tobiæ Mevii & Elerdi Schumacheri, literis Johannis Haken, 1675 – *Ægidii Strauchii ... Astrognosia.* Editio tertia. Wittebergæ: Sumptibus hæred D. Tobiæ Mevii & Elerti Schumacheri, typis Matthæi Henckelii, 1678 – *D. Ægidii Strauchii ... Magnitudinum doctrina.* Editio secunda. Wittebergæ: Sumptibus hæred D. Tobiæ Mevii & Elerdi Schumacheri, typis Matthæi Henkelli, 1678 – *Ægidii Strauchii ... De numerorum doctrina.* Wittebergæ: Sumptibus hæred D. Tobiæ Mevii & Elerdi Schumacheri, literis Matthæi Henkelii, 1675.

2008. STRAUCH, AEGIDIUS, 1632-1682. *Ægidii Strauchii quondam professoris Wittebergensis De numerorum doctrina aphorismi CCCXLIV ... Editio secunda priori correctior.*

Wittebergæ: Sumptibus hæred. D. Tobiæ Mevii & Elerdi Schumacheri Literis Matthæi Hen Kelii [sic] ..., 1675. [6], 166, [1] p., [1] leaf of plates; 14 cm. Errata: last p. Errors in pagination: p. 18 misnumbered as 8, p. 27 as 2, p. 46 as 49.

With: *Ægidii Strauchii ... Doctrina astrorum mathematica.* [Wittenberg?]: Sumptibus autoris & auditorum ejus. Literis Michaelis Wendt, 1663.

2009. STRICKLAND, H. E. (HUGH EDWIN), 1811-1853. *The dodo and its kindred; or, The history, affinities, and osteology of the dodo, solitaire, and other extinct birds of the islands Mauritius, Rodriguez, and Bourbon. By H. E. Strickland ... and A. G. Melville....*

London: Reeve, Benham, and Reeve, 1848. 141 p. col. front., illus., facsim. plates (part col., part fold.) map. 33 cm. Includes index. Bibliography: p. [127]-134. Variously illustrated by Jos. Dinkel, Roelant Savery, Tuffen West, and Werner.

Advertisements: 16 p. at end. Provenance: Herbert McLean Evans (bookplate), William Thorn (signature). Binder: Westleys & Co. (ticket).

2010. STØRMER, CARL, 1874- . *Aus den Tiefen des Weltenraums bis ins Innere der Atome. Mit 65 Abbildungen. Deutsche ausg. von J. Weber....*

Leipzig : F. A. Brockhaus, 1925. 195, [1] p. illus., diagrs. 19 cm. Bibliography: p. 193-195.

Provenance: Rauletzel (signature)

2011. STRUVE, F. G. W. (FRIEDRICH GEORG WILHELM), 1793-1864. *Études d'astronomie stellaire. Sur la voie lactée et sur la distance des étoiles fixes. Rapport ... par F. G. W. Struve....*

St.-Pétersbourg: Impr. de l'Académie Impériale des Sciences, 1847. iv, 108, 57 p., 1 l. 24 cm. On verso of t.-p.: Publié avec autorisation de l'Académie.

Provenance: Freiherr von Lindenau (presentation inscription).

2012. STURM, JOHANN CHRISTOPHORUS, 1635-1703. *Physicæ modernæ sanioris compendium erotematicum: in Tironum gratiam pro lectionibus publicis dictari & explicari cœptum sub ipsum initium anni MDCXCIV. Nunc autem ad limam noviter revocatum publicoque usui destinatum anno MDCCIII. / à Joh. Christophoro Sturmio....*

Prostat Norimbergæ: Apud B. Joh. Hoffmanni viduam & Englebertum Streckium; literis Henrici Meyeri ..., 1704. [4], 699, [1] p. (last page blank): ill.; 17 cm.

2013. SUESS, EDUARD, 1831-1914. *Das Antlitz der Erde / von Eduard Suess....*

Prag: F. Tempsky, 1883-1909. Imprint varies. Band 3., 2. Hälfte, "Schluss des Gesamtwerkes ... Sach- und Namensregister in Beilage", by Dr. Lukas Waagen; issued with special t.-p. Includes bibliographical references and index.

Provenance: Charles Atwood Kofoid (bookplate).

2014. *The Sun and moon: their physical character, appearance, and phenomena.*

London: T. Nelson and Sons ..., [1885?]. vi, 7-120 p.: ill. (some col.) 17 cm. Wonders of the heavens. Includes bibliographical references.

Provenance: First Presbyterian Sunday School Library, Portland, Oregon.

2015. SUTHERLAND, LOUIS. *The book of the stars, by Louis Sutherland. With twenty-five illustrations in halftone and drawings by Olga Gnos.*

New York: B. Ackerman Incorporated, 1944. xii p., 1 l., 15-230 p. illus., 24 col. pl. (incl. charts) on 12 l., diagrs. 24 cm.

2016. SWAMMERDAM, JAN, 1637-1680. *Bybel der natuure, door Jan Swammerdam, Amsteldammer. Of, Historie der insecten, tot zeekere zoorten gebracht: door voorbeelden, ontleedkundige onderzoekingen van veerlerhande kleine gediertens, als ook door kunstigekopere plaaten opgeheldert. Verrykt met ontelbaare waarnemingen van nooit ontdekte zeldaamheden in de natuur. Alles in de Hollandsche, des auteurs moedertaale, beschreven. Hier by komt een voorreeden, waar in het leven van den avtevr beschreven is door Herman Boerhaave ... de Latynsche overzetting heeft bezorgt Hieronimus David Gaubius....*

Leyden: I. Severinus [etc.], 1737-38. 2 v. LIII fold. pl. 40 cm. Title vignettes. Paged continuously. Added t.-p. in Latin. Dutch and Latin in parallel columns. Includes indexes. Illustrated by J.v.d. Spyck.

Provenance: Hartogh Heijs van de Lier [?] Bibl. Entom. Delft (inkstamp).

2017. Swammerdam, Jan, 1637-1680. *Ephemeri vita, of, Afbeeldingh van 's menschen leven: vertoont in de wonderbaarelijcke en nooyt gehoorde historie van het vliegent ende een-dagh-levent haft of oever-aas: een dierken, ten aansien van sijn naam, over al in Neerlandt bekent, maar het welck binnen de tijt van vijf uuren groeyt, geboren wordt, jongh is, tweemaal vervelt, teelt, eyeren leght, zaat schiet, out wordt, ende sterft: waar in, als oock ontrent, verscheyde andere dierkens, veele ongehoorde, ende tot noch toe verborgene wonderen, tot kennisse Godts, ende onses selfs, uyt de natuur ondeckt worden: alles deur den autheur met figuren na het leeven afgebeelt: hier is achter bygevoeght, een grondige en noyt gehoorde verhandeling van den waaren stant des menschen, soo voor als na sijn val / door Johannes Swammerdam....*

t'Amsterdam: By Abraham Wolfgang ..., 1675. [32], 422, (8) p., VIII leaves of plates (2 folded): ill. (engravings); 17 cm. Device on t. p. Initials. Includes index. Engraved by D. Bosboom after J. Swammerdam. BM, v. 233, col. 34. BN, v. 180, col. 979.

Provenance: Herbert McLean Evans (bookplate).

2018. Swammerdam, Jan, 1637-1680. *Historia insectorum generalis; ofte, Algemeene verhandeling de bloedeloose dierkens ... 1. deel ... / Johannis Swammerdam Amsterdammer... .*

t'Utrecht: Merinardus van Dreunen, (1669). [28], 168 p.; 48 p.: table, plates.; 20 cm. Added half title. Part [2] has half title (p. 11): Verclaringe, ofte uitlegginge, van de vier orderen der veranderingen, deur middel van afbeeldingen. Mis-stellingen: p. [28]. Statement of responsibility transposed.

2019. Swan, John, d. 1671. *Speculum mundi, or, A glasse representing the face of the world: shewing both that it did begin, and must also end, the manner how, and time when being largely examined: whereunto is joyned an hexameron, or a serious discourse of the causes, continuance, and qualities of things in nature, occasioned as matter pertinent to the work done in the six dayes of the worlds creation.*

[Cambridge]: Printed by the printers to the Universitie of Cambridge, 1635. [16], 504, [26] p.: ill. (woodcut); 19 cm. Added engraved t. p. with title: Speculum mundi or A glasse representing the face of the world: Whereunto is added a discourse of the creation, together wth [sic] a consideration of such things as are pertinent to each dayes worke. / Written by John Swan ... Pri. in Cambridge: By T. Buckand R. Daniel, 1635. *STC* 23516.

Provenance: Sir Henry Mainwaring (armorial bookplate); Ph. Mainwaring (signature); A. Beresford (signature).

2020. Symposium on Atomic Energy and its Implications (1945: Philadelphia, Pa.). *Symposium on Atomic Energy and its Implications. Papers read at the joint meeting of the American Philosophical Society and the National Academy of Sciences, November 16 and 17, 1945.*

Philadelphia: The American Philosophical Society, 1946. iii, 79 p. illus. (diagrs.) 27 cm. *Proceedings of the American Philosophical Society;* v. 90, no. 1. Includes bibliographical references. Fifty years of atomic physics, by H. D. Smyth. – Atomic weapons, by J. R. Oppenheimer. – Health protection activities of the plutonium project, by R. S. Stone. – The development of the first chain reacting pile, by Enrico Fermi. – Resonance reactions, by E. P. Wigner. – Methods and objectives in the separation of isotopes, by H. C. Urey. – Problems and prospects in elementary particle research, by J. A. Wheeler. – Social adjustments to atomic energy, by J. H. Willits. – The implications of the atomic bomb for international relations, by Jacob Viner. – The control of atomic energy under the charter, by J. T. Shotwell. – World control of atomic energy, by Irving Langmuir. – Atomic energy as a human asset, by A. H. Compton.

2021. Tartaglia, Niccolò, d. 1557. *Noua scientia / inuenta da Nicolo Tartalea. B.*

In Vinegia: Per Stephano da Sabio, ad instantia di Nicolo Tartalea brisciano il qual habita a san Saluador, 1537. [95] p., [1] folded leaf of plates: ill.; 22 cm. Imprint from colophon. Signatures: *4 A-L4 (A4 and L4b blank). Adams T-189.

With: *Quesiti, et inuentioni diuerse* / de Nicolo Tartalea Brisciano. Stampata in Venetia: Per Venturino Ruffinelli..., 1546. Plate bound at the back.

2022. Tartaglia, Niccolò, d. 1557. *Quesiti, et inuentioni diuerse / de Nicolo Tartalea Brisciano.*

NOVA SCIENTIA INVENTA DA NICOLO TARTALEA.B.

Disciplinæ Mathematicæ loquuntur.
Qui cupitis Rerum uarias cognoscere causas
Discite nos: Cunctis hac patet una uia.

Tartaglia, *Nova scientia*, 1537

Stampata in Venetia: Per Venturino Ruffinelli ad instantia et requisitione, & à proprie spese de Nicolo Tartalea brisciano autore, nel. mese di luio, 1546. [2], 132 leaves: ill., port.; 22 cm. Imprint from colophon. Errors in foliation. Adams T-183. Stillwell, M. B. *Science*, 796.

With: *Noua scientia* / inuenta da Nicolo Tartalea. B. In Vinegia: Per Stephano da Sabio ..., 1537.

2023. TAWARA, SUNAO, b. 1873. *Das Reizleitungssystem des Säugetierherzens. Eine anatomisch-histologische Studie über das Atrioventrikularbündel und die Purkinjeschen Fäden. Mit einem Vorwort von L. Aschoff.*

Jena: Fischer, 1906. ix, 200 p. illus., x pl. (partly col., 5 fold.) 25 cm. Illustrated by the author. "Aus dem pathologischen Institut der Universität zu Marburg."

Provenance: Herbert McLean Evans (bookplate).

2024. TAYLOR, LUCY. *Astronomers and their observations / by Lucy Taylor ...; with a preface by W. Thynne Lynn....*

London: S. W. Partridge & Co. ..., 1895. 160 p.: ill.; 19 cm. World's Wonders series. Date of publication from *BLC*, v. 321, p. 467.

Advertisements: publisher's catalog, 24 p. at end. Provenance: prize bookplate from St. John's Boys' National School, Penzance awarded to Wilfred Richards.

2025. TEICHMANN, LUDWIG, 1823-1895. *Das Saugadersystem vom anatomischen Standpunkte.*

Leipzig: Engelmann, 1861. 124 p. 18 pl. 29 cm. Illustrated by Peters, Wagenschieber, Roth, Loedel. Includes bibliographical references.

Provenence: Herbert McLean Evans (bookplate).

2026 *Telescope making: with numerous engravings and diagrams / edited by Paul N. Hasluck....*

London ; New York : Cassell, 1905. 160 p.: ill.; 18 cm. "Work" handbooks. "The matter here presented forms the gist of a series of articles contributed to 'Work' by Mr. P. B. Stark" – P. [5]. Includes index.

Advertisements: [6] p., on paste-down endpapers and fly-leaves.

2027. TENNANT, J. F. (JAMES FRANCIS), 1829-1915. *Report of the total eclipse of the sun, August 17-18, 1868: as observed at Guntoor, under instructions from the Right Honourable the Secretary of State for India / by Major J. F. Tennant....*

London: Printed by Strangeways and Walden ..., [not before 1868]. [2], 53 p., [10] leaves of plates: ill., 1 plan; 29 cm. "Forming part of Vol. XXXVII of the *Memoirs of the Royal Astronomical Society*." Some engravings by D. J. Pound.

2028. THABIT IBN QURRAH AL-HARRANI, d. 901. *The astronomical works of Thabit b. Qurra, by Francis J. Carmody.*

Berkeley: University of California Press, 1960. 262 p. diagrs. 26 cm. Bibliography: p. [11]-12. Thâbit's life and works. Thâbit's translations and revisions. – The minor Arabic tracts. – De anno solis. Latin text. – The four Latin tracts: De motu octaue spere. Versio M. Versio N. – The three other tracts. Latin texts. – De figura sectore. – De imaginibus. Latin texts. – Appendices: Critical method. Linguistic analysis. Specimens. Manuscripts not reported. – Glossaries.

2029. THEON, of Smyrna. *Theonos Smyrnaiou Platonikou ton kata mathematiken chresimon eisten tou Platonos anagnosin = Theonis Smyrnaei Platonici, eorum, quae in mathemticis ad Platonis lectionem vtilia sunt, expositio. E bibliotheca Thvana. Opus nunc primum editum, latina versione, ac notis illustratum ab Ismaele Bvllialdo, Iuliodunensi.*

Lvtetiae Parisiorvm: Apud Lvdovicvm de Hevqveville, (1644). 10 p., 1 l., 308 p. illus. (diagrs.) 22 cm. Known by Latin title: *Expositio rerum mathematicarum ad legendum Platonem utilium.* Text in Latin and Greek in parallel columns. Includes index. Title vignette (printer's devices); head-pieces. Cancels for p. 133-134, 141-142, 7-8, 79-80 inserted after p. 132; cancel for p. 71-72 follows p. [190].

Inserts in the correct place. Provenance: William Goes (inscription).

2030. THOMAS, AQUINAS, SAINT, 1225?-1274. *Diui Thome Aquinatis sacri predicato[rum] ordinis in libros Aristotelis de celo [et] mu[n]do preclarissima co[m]mentaria: cum additionibus Petride de Aluernia eiusdem ordinis.*

[Venice]: Impressum Venetijs ac studiosissime elabor atum per Gregoriu[m] [et] Ioannem de Gregorijs fratres, 1495 die v[er]o vltimo Octobris [31 Oct.]. 72

leaves: ill.; 29 cm. Includes Latin version of *De caelo.* Leaf 72 verso: Hic finit co[m]me[n]tu[m] diui Thome de Aquino ...sup[er] duos libros De celo [et] mu[n]do cu[m] aliqua parte tertij. Qui morte preue[n]tus residuu[m] complere non potuit. Quod aut[em] sequit[ur] vsq[ue] ad finem quarti libri est ... Petri de Aluernia ... correctu[m] per ... Herma[n]nu[m] de Virsen ... Imprint from colophon. Signatures: a-m^6. Printed in double columns. Woodcuts: illustrations, diagrams, initials. Errors in foliation. BM *15th cent.*, V, p. 347 (IB.21105). Goff (rev.) A-979. *GW* 2356. Hain 1532. *ISTC*, ia00979000. Klebs 964.3.

Binder: Cav. Dante Gozzi e figlio, Modena (stamp on lower cover). Binding: tooled brown morocco. Binder's title: Aqcuino. Aristotelis Celo et mundo. Provenance: Honeyman sale.

2031. THOMAS, CORBINIANUS, 1694-1767. *Mercurii philosophici firmamentum firmianum: descriptionem et usum globi artificialis coelestis, ac asterismos ejusdem ad ineuntem annum 1730. reductos LXXXVI iconismis æri incisis exhibens / authore P. Corbiniano Thomas....*

Prostat Franckofurti & Lipsiæ: [s.n.], 1730. [6], 212 p., [83] leaves of plates (12 folded): ill., maps; 17 x 21 cm. Illustrated by: Aug. Cris. Fleischmann, I. C. Bernd and Hering.

2032. THOMAS, OSWALD, b. 1882. *Heaven and earth, a modern astronomy, by Oswald Thomas ... translated by Bernard Miall. 1st ed.*

New York: W. W. Norton & Company, [c1930]. 7 p.l., 3-231 p. illus., diagrs. 22 cm.

2033. THOMPSON, SILVANUS PHILLIPS, 1851-1916. *Elementary lessons in electricity & magnetism / by Silvanus P. Thompson....*

London; and New York: Macmillan and Co., 1893. xiv, 456 p.: ill., maps; 17 cm. Macmillan's School Class books. Cover title: Electricity & magnetism. Series statement from cover. Includes bibliographical references and index.

Provenance: E. R. Hedrick (signature and inkstamp); ms. marginalia.

2034. THOMSON, J. J. (JOSEPH JOHN), SIR, 1856-1940. *Applications of dynamics to physics and chemistry, by J. J. Thomson.*

London, New York: Macmillan and Co., 1888. viii, 312 p. tab., diagr. 19 cm. The substance of a course of lectures delivered at the Cavendish Laboratory (Cambridge) in the Michaelmas term of 1886. "Some of the results have already been published in the *Philosophical transactions* of the Royal Society for 1886 and 1887." – Pref. Includes index. Advertisements: (2) p. at end.

Provenance: R. E. Baynes (inscription).

2035. THOMSON, J. J. (JOSEPH JOHN), SIR, 1856-1940. *Conduction of electricity through gases, by J. J. Thomson....*

Cambridge: University Press, 1903. vi p., 1 l., 566 p. illus., diagrs. 23 cm. Cambridge Physical series. "Contains the subject-matter of lectures given at the Cavendish Laboratory." – Pref.

Provenance: Herbert McLean Evans (bookplate).

2036. THOMSON, J. J. (JOSEPH JOHN), SIR, 1856-1940. *Conduction of electricity through gases, by J. J. Thomson. 2d ed.*

Cambridge: University Press, (1906). vi, [2], 678 p. illus., diagrs. 23 cm. Cambridge Physical series. Includes bibliographical references and index.

Provenance: H. Bateman (inscription).

2037. THOMSON, J. J. (JOSEPH JOHN), SIR, 1856-1940. *The corpuscular theory of matter / by J. J. Thomson.*

New York: C. Scribner, 1907. vi, 172 p.: ill.; 22 cm. "An expansion of a course of lectures given at the Royal Institution in... 1906" – Pref. Includes index.

2038. THOMSON, J. J. (JOSEPH JOHN), SIR, 1856-1940. *Electricity and matter, by J. J. Thomson.*

New York: C. Scribner's Sons, 1905. 5 p. l., 162 p. diagrs. 21 cm. Yale University. Mrs. Hepsa Ely Silliman Memorial lectures.

[4] p. of advertisements following text. Provenance: Edw. A. Partridge (signature); Herbert McLean Evans (bookplate).

2039. THOMSON, J. J. (JOSEPH JOHN), SIR, 1856-1940. *Notes on recent researches in electricity and magnetism, intended as a sequel to Professor Clerk-Maxwell's 'Treatise on Electricity and Magnetism'; by J. J. Thomson.*

Oxford: The Clarendon Press, 1893. xvi, 578 p. illus. diagrs. 23 cm. Clarendon Press series. Includes index. Advertisements: 8 p. at end.

Spine title: Recent researches in electrictity and magnetism. Provenance: C. E. Ashford.

2040. THOMSON, J. J. (JOSEPH JOHN), SIR, 1856-1940. *Rays of positive electricity and their application to chemical analyses, by Sir J. J. Thomson ...*
London, New York [etc.]: Longmans, Green and Co., 1913. vii, 132 p. illus., diagrs. 23 cm. Monographs on Physics. Includes index.

2041. THOMSON, J. J. (JOSEPH JOHN), SIR, 1856-1940. *Tendencies of recent investigations in the field of physics / by Sir J. J. Thomson ... delivered on 27 January 1930.*
London: BBC, 1930. 27 p.; 19 cm. Broadcast National lectures; 4th.

2042. THOMSON, J. J. (JOSEPH JOHN), SIR, 1856-1940. *A treatise on the motion of vortex rings. An essay to which the Adams prize was adjudged in 1882, in the University of Cambridge. By J. J. Thomson.*
London: Macmillan and Co., Ltd. 1883. xix, 124 p. diagrs., 23 cm.

2043. THORPE, T. E. (THOMAS EDWARD), SIR, 1845-1925. *Essays in historical chemistry.*
London, New York: Macmillan, 1894. xi, 381 p. 21 cm. Mainly lectures and addresses which have already appeared in print but are here altered and corrected where necessary.
Advertisements: [2] p. at end. Provenance: David S. Jerdan (booklabel).

2044. THURET, GUSTAVE ADOLPHE, 1817-1875. *Recherches sur la fécondation des fucacées, suivies d'observations sur les anthéridies des algues, par M. G. Thuret.*
Paris: V. Masson, 1855. 46 p. 7 plates 25 cm. "Extrait des *Annales des sciences naturelles,* 4e ser,. t. II-III." – Cover. Includes bibliographical references.
Provenance: Herbert McLean Evans (bookplate).

2045. TIMBS, JOHN, 1801-1875. *Stories of inventors and discoverers in science and the useful arts. A book for old and young. By John Timbs.*
New York: Harper & Brothers, 1860. [v]-xiv, [15]-473 p. front., illus., plates, ports. 20 cm. Includes index.
Advertisements: 6 p. at end. Provenance: E. S. Foley (inscription & inkstamp).

2046. TISCHNER, AUGUST, b. 1819. *Sta, sol, ne moveare ... Von August Tischner....*
Leipzig: Zu haben bei G. Fock und bei dem Verfasser, 1882. 5 v. in 1 diagrs. 20 cm. In five parts, each with separate t. p. and paging. Includes bibliographical references.
Provenance: Charles Atwood Kofoid (bookplate); J. H. Wilterdink, Leiden (inkstamp).

2047. TODD, DAVID P. (DAVID PECK), 1855-1939. *Stars and telescopes; a hand-book of popular astronomy, founded on the 9th edition of Lynn's Celestial motions. By David P. Todd....*
Boston: Little, Brown, [1901, c1899]. xvi, 419 p. illus. 20 cm. Includes bibliographical references and index.
Advertisements: [4] p. at end. Provenance: Oliver J. Gustafson (signature).

2048. TODD, DAVID P. (DAVID PECK), 1855-1939. *Stars and telescopes; a hand-book of popular astronomy, founded on the 9th edition of Lynn's Celestial motions, by David P. Todd....*
Boston: Little, Brown and Company, 1899. 1 p. ., xvi, 419 p. col. front., illus. (incl. ports.) plates. 20 cm. With extensive bibliographical references. Includes index.

2049. TORRICELLI, EVANGELISTA, 1608-1647. *Lezioni accademiche d'Evangelista Torricelli, mattematico e filosofo del Sereniss. Ferdinando II, granduca di Toscana, lettore delle mattematiche nello Studio di Firenze e accademico della Crusca.*
Firenze: Nella stamp. di S. A. R. per J. Guiducci, e S. Franchi, 1715. xlix, [1] p., 1 l., 96 p. front (port.) illus. 24 cm. Title vignette. Preface with life of the author by Tommaso Bonaventura. I. Ringraziamento agli accademici della Crusca quando da essi fu ammesso nella loro accademia. – II-IV. Della forza della percossa. – V-VI. Della leggerezza. – VII. Del vento. – VIII. Del fama. – IX. In lode delle mattematiche. X-XI. Dell'architettura militare. – XII. Economia del secol d'oro.
28 cm. Provenance: Herbert McLean Evans (bookplate).

2050. *Transactions of the American Philosophical Society.*
Philadelphia [etc.], The Society, 1771-. v. ill. 30 cm. v.

1-6, 1769-1809 ; new ser. v.1- 1818-. Issued irregularly in parts. Indexes: Vols. 1-4, 1769-99. 1 v. Vols.1-6, n.s., v.1-50, 1769-1960. iv. Register of papers published in v.1-6 and new ser. v.1-15, 1769-1881, is included in "Register of papers published in the transactions and proceedings. Comp. by Henry Philips, jr.,1881"; subject register of papers published in v.1-6 and new ser. v.1-16, 1769-1888 in "Subject register of papers published in the transactions and proceedings... Comp. by Henry Philips, jr., 1889."

Library has: 1, 1771. Vol. I: Provenance: Garbutt's Improved File. (armorial bookplate)

2051. TREMBLEY, ABRAHAM, 1710-1784. *Mémoires pour servir à l'histoire d'un genre de polypes d'eau douce, à bras en forme de cornes. Par A. Trembley....*

Leide: Chez J. & H. Verbreek, 1744. xv, [1], 324, [1] p. illus., 13 fold. plates. 26 cm. Illustrated by C. Pronk, J.v. Schley and P. Lyonet. 1. mém. Où l'on décrit les polypes, leur forme, leur mouvemens, & une partie de ce qu'on a pu découvrir sur leur structure. – 2. mém. De la nourriture des polypes ... Du tems & des moïens les plus propres, pour trouver des polypes. – 3. mém. De la génération des polypes. – 4. mém. Operations faites sur les polypes, & les succès qu'elles ont eus.

2052. TREW, ABDIAS, 1597-1669. *M. Abdiae Trevven in Universitate Aldorffinâ math. & phys. pr. p. & h.t. rect. Observationes des jüngst erschienenen Cometen: sambt Muthmassung von dessen Würckung und Bedeutung, mit zweyen nothwendigen Kupffern versehen.*

Gedruckt zu Nürnberg: Michael Endter, 1653. [4], 11, [1] p., [1] folded leaf of plates: ill.; 20 cm. Signatures: A-B4.

2053. TURNER, R. (RICHARD), 1723 or 4-1791. *A view of the heavens: being a short, but comprehensive system of modern astronomy ... to which is added, the use of the cælestial globe .../ by the Rev. Mr. Turner....*

London: Printed for S. Crowder ... and S. Gamidge ..., 1765. [6], 59, [1] p., [1] leaf of plates: ill., volvelle; 32 cm. Advertisements: last page.

Hand coloured.

2054. *Two monographs on malaria and the parasites of malarial fevers: I. Marchiafava and Bignami. II. Mannaberg.*

London: The New Sydenham Society, 1894. xxvi, 428 p., II, 3, IV leaves of plates (3 folded): ill. (some col.); 25 cm. New Sydenham Society. Translation of *Sulle febbri malariche estivo-autumnali* done by J. Harry Thompson. Translation of *Die malaria-parasiten* done by R. W. Felkin. Bibliography: p. 417-428.

Provenance: Charles Atwood Kofoid (bookplate).

2055. TYNDALL, JOHN, 1820-1893. *Essays on the floating-matter of the air in relation to putrefaction and infection / by John Tyndall....*

London: Longmans, Green, and Co., 1881. xix, [1], 338, [2] p.: ill.; 20 cm. Half-title: Putrefaction and infection. Advertisements on p. [1]-[2] of last group. Garrison, F. H. *Medical bibl.* 2495. Includes bibliographical references.

Provenance: R. Stephenson (signature).

2056. TYNDALL, JOHN, 1820-1893. *Essays on the use and limit of the imagination in science, by John Tyndall....*

London: Longmans, Green, and Co., 1870. 4 p. l., 72 p. 23 cm.Cover title: Use and limit of the imagination in science. 24 p. advertisements follow text.

Provenance: R. S. Oldham (signature).

2057. TYNDALL, JOHN, 1820-1893. *Fragments of science; a series of detached essays, addresses, and reviews / by John Tyndall.*

New York: D. Appleton, 1897. 2 v.: ill.; 21 cm.

Provenance: R. P. Brady (inscription).

2058. TYNDALL, JOHN, 1820-1893. *Fragments of science; a series of detached essays, addresses, and reviews, by JohnTyndall....*

New York: D. Appleton and Company, 1900. 2 v. illus., maps, diagrs. 21 cm. Authorized edition; the 1st edition was published in 1871. Thirty-eight papers, including the Belfast address.

Advertisements: [6] p. at end, v. 2. Provenance: James Henderson (bookplate and signature).

2059. TYNDALL, JOHN, 1820-1893. *Fragments of science for unscientific people: a series of detached essays, lectures and reviews / by John Tyndall.*

New York: D. Appleton, 1873. xix, [1], [5]-422 p.; 20 cm. Other editions of this work appeared as: *Fragments of science: a series of detached essays, lectures and reviews.*

Advertisements: 3, [3] p. at end.

2060. Tyndall, John, 1820-1893. *New fragments, by John Tyndall....*

New York: D. Appleton and Company, 1897. 3 p.l., 500 p. 21 cm. "Authorized edition" – T. p. verso. The Sabbath. – Goethe's 'Farbenlehre'. – Atoms, molecules, and etherwaves. – Count Rumford. – Louis Pasteur, his life and labours. – The rainbow and its congeners. – Address delivered at the Birkbeck institution on October 22, 1884. – Thomas Young. – Life in the Alps. – About common water. – Personal recollections of Thomas Carlyle. – On unveiling the statue of Thomas Carlyle. – On the origin, propagation, and prevention of phthisis. – Old Alpine jottings. – A morning on Alp Lusgen (in verse).

2061. Tyndall, John, 1820-1893. *Researches on diamagnetism and magne-crystallic action, including the question of diamagnetic polarity. By John Tyndall....*

London: Longmans, Green, and Co., 1870. xix, 361 p. front., illus., plates (part fold.) diagrs. 23 cm. Advertisements: 24 p. following text. Includes index. Illustrated by: C. Becker, J. Basire, J. B. Jordan, H. Adlard.

2062. Tyndall, John, 1820-1893. *Six lectures on light, delivered in America in 1872-1873 by John Tyndall....*

London: Longmans, Green, 1873. xiii, 277 p. illus., 20 cm. Includes index. Advertisements following text: [2], 32 p.

2063. Tyndall, John, 1820-1893. *Six lectures on light: delivered in the United States in 1872-1873 / by John Tyndall ... Fifth edition.*

London: Longmans, Green and Co., 1895. [2], ix, [1], 244 p., [1] leaf of plates: port., ill.; 20 cm. Also titled: *Lectures on light.* Includes bibliographical references.

Provenance: I. C. M. Institute from F. O. Crump (dedicatory inscription).

2064. Ulugh Beg, 1394-1449. *Jadavil-i mavazi'-i savabit dar tul va 'arz ... sive Tabvlæ long. ac lat. stellarum fixarvm, ex observatione Ulugh Beighi. Ex tribus invicèm collatis mss. Persicis jam primùm luce ac Latio donavit, & commentariis illustravit, Thomas Hyde. In calce libri accesserunt Mohammedis Tizini tabulae declinationum & rectarum ascensionum. Additur demum elenchus nominum stellarum.*

Typis H. Hall., sumptibus authoris, 1665. 151, 88 p. 25 cm. Title partially romanized. Includes index. Wing U23.

Ms. notes.

2065. United States. Congress. Joint Committee on Atomic Energy. *Biological and environmental effects of nuclear war. Hearings before the Special Subcommittee on Radiation of the Joint Committee on Atomic Energy, Congress of the United States, Eighty-sixth Congress, first session....*

Washington: U.S. Govt. Print. Off., 1959. vi, 966 p. illus., maps (part fold.) 24 cm. Hearings held June 22-26, 1959. "Part 1 appears in error on title page." – U.S. monthly cat., Jan. 1960, p. 23. Includes bibliographies.

2066. United States. Department of State. Office of Public Affairs. *The international control of atomic energy: policy at the crossroads: an informal summary record of the policy developments concerning the international control of atomic energy, October 15, 1946 to May 17, 1948.*

Washington, D.C.: U.S. Govt. Print. Off., 1948. x, 251 p. 24 cm. General foreign policy series, 3. Publication / Department of State; 3161. Includes bibliographical references.

2067. United States Naval Observatory. *Explanation of the seal of the U.S. Naval Observatory.*

[Washington: s.n., not before 1864]. 3 p., [1] leaf of plates: 1 fascim. n; 29 cm. Cover title. Bibliographic citation on p. [1] mentions a title published in 1864.

Addenda: 3 additional copies of p. [1]-[3] of text within original wrapper.

2068. United States Naval Observatory. *Instruments and publications of the United States Naval Observatory ... Pub. by authority of the Hon. secretary of the Navy. Rear-admiral C. H. Davis, superintendant. Washington, 1845-1876.*

[Washington: s.n., 1876?]. 1 p. l., 45 p. front., 6 pl. 30 cm.

2069. UNITED STATES NAVAL OBSERVATORY. *Reports on observations of the total eclipse of the sun, August 7, 1869. Conducted under the direction of Commodore B. F. Sands, U.S.N., superintendent....*

Washington: Govt. Print. Off., 1869. v, [1] p., 1 l., 214 p.: illus., XII pl. (part col.) 30 cm. Washington observations, 1867; Appendix II. Report of B. F. Sands, U.S.N. – Report of Simon Newcomb, U.S.N., on observations of the eclipse, &c., made at Des Moines, Iowa and other places. – Reports of William Harkness, U.S.N., J. R. Eastman, U.S.N., and J. Homer Lane on observations of the eclipse, &c. made at Des Moines, Iowa. – Report of Edward Curtis, assistant surgeon, U.S.A., on photographic observations of the eclipse made at Des Moines, Iowa. – Report of W. S. Gilman, Jr., on observations of the eclipse made at St. Paul Junction, Plymouth County, Iowa. – Report of F. W. Bardwell on observations of the eclipse made at Bristol, Tennessee. – Report of Albert J. Myer, chief signal officer, U.S.A., on observations of the eclipse made at White Top Mountain, near Abingdon, Virginia. – Report of Asaph Hall, U.S.N., on observations of the eclipse made near Plover Bay, Siberia.

"Photographs of the total eclipse of the sun, August 7, 1869" issued by the Surgeon General's Office, [2] p. inserted between leaf and p. [1]; duplicate of plate X inserted between plates IX and X; colored plate inserted between p. 176 and 177; a.l.s. from B. F. Sands to William Crookes tipped in. Addenda: 3 duplicate photographs mounted for sale by James Cremer, Philadelphia, bearing Crookes' name in ms. loosely inserted. Provenance: Sir William Crookes (armorial bookplate) and a.l.s. from B. F. Sands.

2070. UNITED STATES NAVAL OBSERVATORY. NAUTICAL ALMANAC OFFICE. *Total eclipse of the sun, January 24, 1925. Pub. by the Nautical Almanac Office, U.S. Naval Observatory, under the authority of the secretary of the navy.*

Washington: Govt. Print. Off., 1923. 31 p. incl. tables. fold. diagr., 2 fold. charts (1 in pocket) 24 cm. Supplement to the American ephemeris, 1925.

Imperfect: lacks 1 chart in pocket.

2071. UNITED STATES STRATEGIC BOMBING SURVEY. *The effects of atomic bombs on Hiroshima and Nagasaki. Chairman's office, 30 June 1946.*

Washington: U. S. Govt. Print. Off., 1946. v, 46 p. illus., maps (part fold.) 26 x 20 cm. Reports. Pacific war; 3.

2072. UNIVERSITY OF WISCONSIN. LIBRARY. *Chemical, medical, and pharmaceutical books printed before 1800, in the collections of the University of Wisconsin Libraries. Edited by John Neu. Compiled by Samuel Ives, Reese Jenkins, and John Neu.*

Madison: University of Wisconsin Press, 1965. viii, 280 p. 25 cm. Includes titles in the Denis I. Duveen Collection in Chemistry and Alchemy, which the university acquired in 1951.

Provenance: editor's signed presentation copy to Sam and Cecile Barchas.

2073. UPTON, WINSLOW, 1853-1914. *Star atlas containing stars visible to the naked eye and clusters, nebulæ and double stars visible in small telescopes, together with variable stars, red stars, characteristic star groups, ancient constellation figures and an explanatory text. By Winslow Upton....*

Boston, London: Ginn & Company, 1896. iv, 34 p. incl. maps, tables. VI double maps. 36 cm.

2074. VALENTINER, WILHELM, 1845-1931. *Handwörterbuch der Astronomie. Unter Mitwirkung von Prof. dr. E. Becker ... E. Gerland ... (u.a.) hrsg. von Prof. dr. W. Valentiner....*

Breslau: E. Trewendt, 1897-1902. 4 v. in 5. illus., 11 pl., tables, diagrs. 25 cm. Encyklopaedie der Naturwissenschaften; 3. Abth., 2. Th. Vol. 3 is in two parts. Includes indexes. Bibliographies and references scattered through the text.

Provenance: Frank L. Grant (bookplate).

2075. VALIER, MAX, 1895-1930. *Der Sterne Bahn und Wesen; gemeinverständliche Einführung in die Himmelskunde, von Max Valier; mit 90 Abbildungen im Text und 13 Bildern auf 6 Tafeln.*

Leipzig: R. Voigtländer, 1924. viii, 500 p. front., illus., 6 pl. 21 cm. Welteis-Bücherei. Includes indexes.

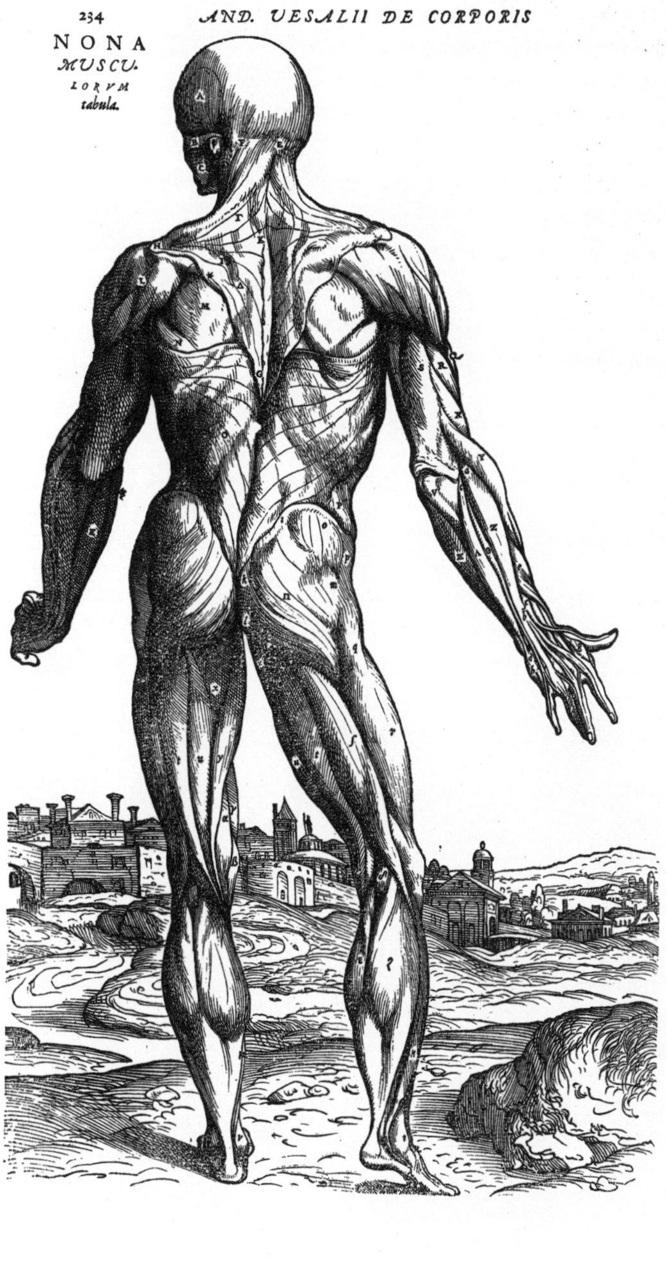

Vesalius, *De humani corporis fabrica*, 1555

2076. VARENIUS, BERNHARDUS, 1622-1650. *A compleat system of general geography: explaining the nature and properties of the earth ... Originally written in Latin. By Bernhard Varenius, M.D. Since improved and illustrated by Sir Isaac Newton and Dr. Jurin; and now translated into English; with additional notes, copper-plates, an alphabetical index, and other improvements. Particularly useful to students in the universities; travellers, sailors, and all those who desire to be acquainted with mixed mathematics, geography, astronomy, and navigation. By Mr. Dugdale. The whole revised and corrected by Peter Shaw. 2d ed., with large additions.*

London: S. Austen, 1734. 2 v. (xxiv, 898 p.) illus. 21 cm. Translation of the 1712 ed. of *Geographia generalis.* Frontispiece signed: J. Devoto inv., G. Van der Gucht sc.

Provenance: Haldane (inscription).

2077. VARIGNON, PIERRE, 1654-1722. *Nouvelle mécanique ou statique, dont le projet fut donné en M.DC.LXXXVII. Ouvrage posthume de m. Varignon....*

Paris: Chez C. Jombert, 1725. 2 v. fold. plates. 26 cm. Title vignettes; initials; head and tail pieces. "M. de Beaufort de l'Académie Royale des Sciences ... s'est chargé du soin de l'edition avec m. l'abbé Camus" – Avertissement.

2078. VAUCHER, JEAN PIERRE ETIENNE, 1763-1841. *Histoire des conferves d'eau douce, contenant leurs différens modes de reproduction, et la description de leurs principales espèces, suivie del'histoire des trémelles et des ulves d'eau douce. Par Jean-Pierre Vaucher....*

Genève: J. J. Paschoud, an XI-1803. 2 p. l., xv, 285, [3] p. XVII pl. 26 cm. Errata: p. [1-2] at end. Advertisements on p. [3] at end.

Provenance: Mauri (signature); Bibliotheca Domus Prob. Prov. Rom. (inkstamp).

2079. VAUCOULEURS, GÉRARD HENRI DE, 1918- . *The planet Mars / by Gérard de Vaucouleurs; translated from the French by Patrick A. Moore. 2nd ed., rev. and enl.*

London: Faber and Faber, 1951. 90 p., [5] p. of plates: ill., maps; 23 cm. Translation of: *Le problème martien.* 2nd impression, 1952. Includes index.

2080. VENABLE, F. P. (FRANCIS PRESTON), 1856-1934. *A short history of chemistry / by F. P. Venable....*

Boston: Published by D. C. Heath & Co., [1896, c1894]. viii, 163 p.; 19 cm. Science text-books. Cover title: History of chemistry. Series title from cover. Includes index.

Advertisements: [4] p. at end. Provenance: Charles Atwood Kofoid (bookplate).

2081. VESALIUS, ANDREAS, 1514-1564. *Andreae Vesalii Bruxellensis, scholae medicorum Patauinæ professoris, De humani corporis fabrica libri septem.*

Basileae: [Ex Officina Ioannis Oporini, 1543, mense Iunio]. [12], 659 [i.e. 663], [37] p.: ill. (woodcuts), 1 port. (woodcut); 39 cm. Name of publisher and date of publication from colophon on p. [36] of last group. Signatures: *[6] A-Z[6] a-l[6] m[8] n-z[6]2A-2L[6] 2M[8]. A second leaf m3 is sometimes found in copies of work. Cf. Cushing, H. *Vesalius.* Errors in pagination include the sequence 213-391 instead of the correct 313-491. Pages 313-[314] and 353-354 as numbered in the text are each printed on two folded leaves. Pages 662-63 misnumbered 658-59. Cf. detailed description of the work in: Cushing, H. *Vesalius.* Illustrated t. p., also serving as frontispiece. Illustrations by Jan Stephan van Calcar. Cf. Cushing, H. *Vesalius,* VI.A.-1. Osler, W. *Bib. Osleriana,* 567. Burndy. *Science,* 122. NLM *16th cent.* 4577. Waller, E. *Bib. Walleriana,* 9899. Adams V603. Grässe, v. 6, pt. 2, p. 289. Horblit, H. D. *Grolier 100 science books,* 98. Includes index. Errata: p. [660, i.e. 664].

Includes inserted half-sheet, second m3, as described by Cushing. Provenance: Herbert McLean Evans, William Bradley Coley, Bradley Lancaster Coley (bookplates).

2082. VESALIUS, ANDREAS, 1514-1564. *Andreae Vesalii Bruxellensis, inuictissimi Caroli V. Imperatoris medici, De humani corporis fabrica libri septem.*

Basileae: Per Ioannem Oporinum, [1555. mense Augusto]. [12], 505, [3] (1st & 3rd blank), 507-824, [48] p.: ill., port.; 44 cm. Date of imprint from colophon. Errata: p. [825]. p. 505-[506] on a folded leaf, p. 553-554 on the recto of a folded leaf, verso blank. Includes index. Cushing, H. *Vesalius,* VIA.-3. Waller, E. *Bib. Walleriana,* 9901.

Provenance: Bradley Lancaster Coley (bookplate).

2083. Vesalius, Andreas, 1514-1564. *Andreae Vesalii... Opera omnia anatomica & chirurgica, cura Hermanni Boerhaave & Bernhardi Siegfried Albini.*

Lugduni Batavorum, Apud Joannem du Vivie, et Joan. & Herm. Verbeek, 1725. 2 v. illus., 79 [i.e. 82] pl. (part fold.) port. 43 cm. Title vignettes; title in red and black; initials. Paged continuously. "Nomina dominorum inseriptorum hujus libri": v. 1, preliminary leaf 16. Includes index. Plates signed by J. Wandelaar. *Bib. Walleriana*, 9917. Cushing, H. *Vesalius*, VI.D-8. Osler, W. *Bib. Osleriana*, 579.

Provenance: Herbert McLean Evans (bookplate): R. F. Forester (signature).

2084. Vesalius, Andreas, 1514-1564. *Vesalius on the human brain [being a translation of a section of his Fabrica of 1543] Introd., translation of text, translation of descriptions of figures, notes to the translations, figures [by] Charles Singer.*

London, New York: Published for the Wellcome Historical Medical Museum by Oxford University Press, (1952). xxvi, 151 p. illus. 22 cm. Publications of the Wellcome Historical Medical Museum. New ser.; no. 4.

2085. *La Vie de maistre Iean Baptiste Morin: natif de Ville-Franche en Bauiolois, docteur en médecine et professeur royal aux mathématiques á Paris....*

À Paris: Chez Iean Henault ..., 1660. [8], 153, [7] p.; 15 cm. Includes index.

With: *Le ciel reformée* [G. Bruno]. [S.l.: s.n.], 1750.

2086. Viète, François, 1540-1603. *Canon mathematicus seu Ad triangula: cum adpendicibus.*

Lutetiæ: Apud Ioannem Mettayer, in mathematicis typographum regium, sub signo D. Ioannis, è regione Collegij Laodicensis., 1579. 2 v.: ill. (woodcuts); 42 cm. Vol. 2 has title: Francisci Vietæi Vniuersalium inspectionum ad Canonem mathematicum liber singularis. Vol. 1: (96), 45, (19) p.; v. 2: (8), 75, (5) p. (last p. blank). Signatures: $[pi]^2$ $A\text{-}K^4$ L^6 $[alpha]\text{-}[zeta]^4$ $*\text{-}4^{*2}$; v. [2]:$[\ ]^4$ $A\text{-}G^4$ H^6 I^4 $[chi]^2$. Title and much of text in red and black. Adams V717 and V724; Grässe, VI, pt. 2, p. 312; BN, v. 208, column 967 and 972; BM *STC French*, 1470-1600, p. 439; Burndy. *Science*, 105. Errata: v. [2], p, 74-75.

Bound in 1 v. Provenance: Nicolas Xaver Souciet (inscription), Hurtald (inscription), Robert Honeyman (dealer's information).

2087. Vieussens, Raymond, 1641?-1715. *Raymundi Vieussens doctoris medici Monspeliensis Neurographia universalis: hoc est omnium corporis humani nervorum ... descriptio anatomica ... Editio nova.*

Lugduni: Apud Joannem Certe ..., 1684. [20], 252, [2] p., XXX [i.e. 22] leaves of plates (13 folded): ill., port.; 35 cm. Errata: last [2] p. Port. signed: math. Boulanger fe. Plates signed: Beaudeau sculpsit Monsp.

Provenance: William Stirling Maxwell (armorial bookplate).

2088. Vince, Samuel, 1749-1821. *A complete system of astronomy / by the Rev. S. Vince. 2d ed., with additions and corrections.*

London: G. Woodfall, 1814. 3 v.: XIX plates, tables, diagrs.; 28 cm. Vol. 3 has imprint: London: Printed for J. Mawman, [and 4 others], 1823. "Dr. Bradley's catalogue of 389 fixed stars": v. 2, p. 462-473. "M. de la Caille's catalogue of 515 zodiacal stars": v. 2, p. 478-492. "M. de la Caille's catalogue of principal stars": v. 2, p. 493-501. "Zach's catalogue of 381 principal stars": v. 2, pg. 503-513. "Zach's catalogue of the declination of 162 principal stars": v. 2, p. 514-519. "Mayer's catalogue of 992 principal fixed stars": v. 2, p. 520-548. Includes index.

2089. Vince, Samuel, 1749-1821. *The elements of astronomy: designed for the use of students in the university / by the Rev. S. Vince. The first American edition, corrected and enlarged.*

Philadelphia: Kimber and Conrad, 1811. ([United States]: T. & G. Palmer). [4], 242 p., [1] folded leaf of plates: ill.; 22 cm. Signatures: $pi^2A\text{-}2G^42H^2$. Shaw & Shoemaker 24348.

Binder: Homecrafters (ticket).

2090. Virchow, Rudolf Ludwig Karl, 1821-1902. *Die Cellularpathologie in ihrer Begründung auf physiologische und pathologische Gewebelehre: zwanzig Vorlesungen, gehalten während der Monate Februar, März und April 1858 im Pathologischen Institute zu Berlin/ von Rudolf Virchow....*

Berlin: Verlag von August Hirschwald ..., 1858. xvi, 440 p.: ill.; 23 cm. Includes bibliographical references. Garrison-Morton (4th ed.), no. 2299. Horblit, H. D. *Grolier 100 science books,* 99.

Provenance: Ritter v. Braun-Fernwald (inkstamp); J. G. Strobl (inkstamp).

2091. VITRUVIUS POLLIO. *M. Vitruuii Pollionis, viri suae professionis peritissimi, De architectura libri X ... / adiunctis nunc primum Gulielmi Philandri Castilionii Galli ... castigationibus atque annotationibus in eosdem ...; vna cum lib. II. Sex. Iulii Frontini De aquaeductibus vrbis Romae, & Nicolai Cusani Dialogo de staticis experimentis....*

Argenterati: Ex Officina Knoblochiana, per Georgium Machaeropieum, mense Augusto 1550. [60], 493, [57] p.: ill.; 20 cm. Imprint from colophon. Includes indexes in Latin and Greek.

Provenance: John Flamsteed (inscription); armorial bookplate purported to be that of John, 3rd Earl of Bute. Some marginalia.

2092. VOLTA, ALESSANDRO, 1745-1827. *On the electricity excited by the mere contact of conducting substances of different kinds: in a letter from Mr. Alexander Volta ... to the Rt. Hon. Sir Joseph Banks ... : read June 26, 1800.*

London : Printed by W. Bulmer and Co. ... and sold by Peter Elmsly ..., 1800. p. 403-431, [1] leaf of plates : ill. ; 23 cm. In: *Philosophical transactions* / Royal Society of London, v. 90. Caption title. Text in French. Horblit, H. D. *Grolier 100 science books,* 37b. Burndy. *Science* 60. *PMM* 255.

2093. VOLTAIRE, 1694-1778. *Elémens de la philosophie de Neuton, mis à la portée de tout le monde. Par Mr. de Voltaire.*

À Amsterdam: Chez E. Ledet & Compagnie, 1738. 1 p. l., 399, [1] p. front., illus., port., fold. table, diagrs. 21 cm. Errata: p. [400]. Engraved title vignette, head and tail-pieces. Illustrated by L. F. Dubourg, J. Folkema, B. Picart, J. v. Schley. "A Madame la marquise du Ch.**": p. [3]-13. Wallis & Wallis. *Newton,* 155. *Babson Newton Coll.* 120.

2094. VOLTAIRE, 1694-1778. *Letters concerning the English nation.*

London: Printed for C. Davis and A. Lyon, 1733. 8 p. l., 253, [18] p. 21 cm. First edition, translated by John Lockman. The Letters were first published in French in the following year, 1734. cf. Bengesco, *Voltaire, bibliographie de ses oeuvres,* v. 2, p. 9-14. Includes "A letter concerning the burning of Altena, as related in the History of Charles XII., king of Sweden": p. [245]-253. Advertisements: p. [15-16] first group.

Provenance: Alex. Cosby Jackson (armorial bookplate).

2095. *Vorträge über die kinetische Theorie der Materie und der Elektrizität, gehalten in Göttingen auf Einladung der Kommission der Wolfskehlstiftung, von M. Planck. P. Debye, W. Nernst, M. v. Smoluchowski, A. Sommerfeld und H. A. Lorentz, mit Beiträgen von H. Kamerlingh-Onnes und W. H. Keesom, einem Vorwort von D. Hilbert und 7 in der Text gedruckten Figuren.*

Leipzig, Berlin, B. G. Teubner, 1914. iv, 196 p. 1 illus., diagrs. 23 cm. Mathematische Vorlesungen an der Universität Göttingen: VI. Die gegenwärtige Bedeutung der Quantenhypothese für die kinetische Gastheorie von Max Planck. – Zustandsgleichung und Quantenhypothese mit einem Anhang über Wärmeleitung von P. Debye. – Kinetische Theorie fester Körper von W. Nernst. – Gültigkeitsgrenzen des zweiten Hauptsatzes der Wärmetheorie von M. v. Smoluchowski. – Probleme der freien Weglänge von A. Sommerfeld. – Anwendung der kinetischen Theorien auf Elektronenbewegung von H. A. Lorenz.

Advertisements: [4] p., at end. Provenance: Karl Horovitz (inscription).

2096. VOSSIUS, GERARDUS JOANNES, 1577-1649. *Gerardi Ioannis Vossii De quatuor artibus popularibus, de philologia, et scientiis mathematicis: cui operi subjungitur chronologia mathematicorum libri tres.*

Amstelædami: Ex typographeio Ioannis Blaeu, 1650. [16], 94, [22], 83, [29], 467, [35] p.; 20 cm.

Special t. p.: Gerardi Ioannis Vossii De philologia liber. Amstelædami: Ex typographeio Ioannis Blaue, 1650 – Gerardi Ioannis Vossii De vniuersæ mathesios natura & constitutione liber ... Amstelædami: Ex typographeio Ioannis Blaeu, 1650. Errata: following each v. Includes bibliographical references and indexes.

Provenance: Joannes Ross (bookplate).

2097. VRIES, HUGO DE, 1848-1935. *Die Mutationstheorie: Versuche und Beobachtungen über die Entstehung von Arten im Pflanzenreich / von Hugo de Vries.*

Leipzig: Veit, (1901-1903). 2 v., [12] leaves of col. plates: ill.; 25 cm. Includes index. "Literatur": v. 2, p. [715]-717. 1. Bd. Die Entstehung der Arten durch Mutation – 2. Bd. Elementare Bastardlehre. Horblit, H. D. *Grolier 100 science books*, 73b.

Provenance: J. Moll (signature).

2098. WALDEYER-HARTZ, WILHELM VON, 1836-1921. *Eierstock und Ei. Ein Beitrag zur Anatomie und Entwickelungsgeschichte der Sexualorgane. Von Wilhelm Waldeyer. Mit 6 Tafeln Abbildungen.*

Leipzig: W. Engelmann, 1870. viii, 174 p. VI fold. pl. 24 cm. Advertisements on lower wrapper. "Literatur," p. [161]-169. Illustrated by: Assmann, Waldeyer, and Wagenschieber.

Provenance: Lees Museum, Amsterdam (inkstamp), Charles Atwood Kofoid (bookplate).

2099. WALKER, WILLIAM, 1623-1684. *Idiomatologia anglo-latina, sive Dictionarium idiomaticum anglo-latinum: in quo phrases tam latinæ quam anglicanæ linguæ sibi mutuò respondentes ... collocantur. In usum tam peregrinorum, qui sermonen nostrum anglicanum, quàm nostratium, qui latinum idioma callere student. 5. ed. Cui accessit istiusmodi phrasium & idiomatum additio in utraque lingua ad minus trium millium. Operâ, studio, & industriâ Gvlielmi Walker, S. T. B.*

Londini: Typis W. Horton, impensis T. Sawbridg, 1690. 6 p.l., 538 p. 17 cm. Added t.-p., engr., in English. Advertisements: p. 538-[540].

Provenance: John Tweedie (inscription); William Saunders (bookplate).

2100. WALLACE, ALFRED RUSSEL, 1823-1913. *Darwinism; an exposition of the theory of natural selection, with some of its applications, by Alfred Russel Wallace....*

London and New York: Macmillan and Co., 1889. xvi, 494 p. front. (port.), illus., fold. map, diagrs. 20 cm. Includes bibliographical references and index. Advertisements: [2] p. at end. Ms. marginalia.

2101. WALLACE, ALFRED RUSSEL, 1823-1913. *Island life, or, The phenomena and causes of insular faunas and floras: including a revision and attempted solution of the problem of geological climates. / By Alfred Russel Wallace.*

London: Macmillan, 1880. xvii, 526 p., [3] leaves of plates: ill., 20 maps (some col.); 24 cm. "The present volume is the result of ... research on the lines laid down in [the author's] *Geographical Distribution of Animals*, and may be considered as a popular supplement to and completion of that work." – Pref. Colophon reads: London: R. Clay, Sons, and Taylor, printers. Advertisements: [2] p. following text. Includes index.

Provenance: Charles Singer (signature).

2102. WALLACE, ALFRED RUSSEL, 1823-1913. *The Malay Archipelago: the land of the orang-utan, and the bird of paradise: a narrative of travel, with studies of man and nature / by Alfred Russel Wallace....*

London: Macmillan and Co., 1869. 2 v.: ill., plates (some folded), maps; 20 cm. Includes index.

Advertisements. [2], 53, [2] p. at end, v. 1. Provenance: John C. Eckel (bookplate); Talygarn (armorial bookplate).

2103. WALLACE, ALFRED RUSSEL, 1823-1913. *Man's place in the universe: a study of the results of scientific research in relation to the unity or plurality of worlds / by Alfred R. Wallace. 4th ed.*

London: Chapman and Hall, 1904. vii, 341 p., [1] folded leaf of plates: ill., maps; 21 cm. "With new chapter entitled 'An additional argument dependent on the theory of evolution'." Includes bibliographical references and index.

Provenance: Charles Atwood Kofoid (bookplate).

2104. WALLACE, ALFRED RUSSEL, 1823-1913. *Studies scientific & social, by Alfred Russel Wallace....*

London: Macmillan and Co., Limited; The Macmillan Company, 1900. 2 v. illus., fold. map. 20 cm. Mainly reprints of articles contributed to reviews and

Wallis, *A Treatise of Algebra*, 1685

periodicals from 1865 to 1899. Includes indexes. 1. Earth studies. Descriptive zoology. Plant distribution. Animal distribution. Theory of evolution. Anthropology. Special problems. – 2.Education. Political. The land problem. Ethical. Sociological.

2105. Wallis, John, 1616-1703. *Mechanica: sive, De motu, tractatus geometricus. / Authore Johanne Wallis ... Pars prima [-tertia].*

Londini: Typis Gulielmi Godbid; impensis Mosis Pitt ..., 1670-1671. 3 pts.: ill., port.; 21 cm. Pt. 1: [6] 109, [1] p., [2] folding leaves of plates; pt. 2: [2],109-569 [i.e. 567], [1] p. (blank), [9] folding leaves of plates; pt. 3 : [2], 571-771, [1] p., [6] folding leaves of plates. Pages 337-338 omitted in numbering. Advertisements on last page of pt. 1. "Errata": pt. 1: p. [110]; pt. 2: p. 569; "Emendanda": pt. 3, p.771-[772]. Wing W593 (pts. 1 and 2). (From t. p.): 1. De motu generalia – De gravium descensu, & motuum declivitate – De libra – 2. De centro gravitatis – Ejusque calculo – 3. De vecte – De axe in peritrochio – De trochleâ, seu polyspasto – De cochleâ – De motibus compositis, acceleratis, retardatis, & projectorum – De percussione – De cuneo – De elatere – De hydrostaticis, & aeris æquipondio – Variisque quæstionibus mechanicis.

Bound in 1 v. Imperfect: port. missing. Provenance: Ignatius Dominicus S.R.J. Gomes de Chorinsky (bookplate); Robert Honeyman IV (bookplate). Binder: James Macdonald Co. (stamp in slipcase).

2106. Wallis, John, 1616-1703. *A treatise of algebra, both historical and practical: shewing the original, progress, and advancement thereof, from time to time, and by what steps it hath attained to the heighth at which now it is: with some additional treatises, I. Of the Conocuneus ...: II. Of angular sections,and other things relating thereunto, and to trigonometry: III. Of the angle of contact ...: IV. Of combinations, alternations, and aliquot parts / by John Wallis....*

London: Printed by John Playford, for Richard Davis ..., 1685. [20], 374 [i.e. 372], [4], 17, [1] (blank), [2], 76 [i.e. 176] p., [11] leaves of plates (10 folded): ill., port.; 31 cm. The additional treatises have each a special t.-p.; I.-III. dated 1864. Pagination: nos. 34-35 omitted (2nd group); 76 for 176 (final p.); other errors in pagination. Wing W613. With, as issued: *A brief (but full) account of the doctrine of trigonometry, both plain and spherical* / by John Caswell. London: Printed by John Playford, for Richard Davis ..., 1685.

Pages 333-336 (2nd group) duplicated. The second treatise has 2 variant t. p.'s, with identical imprints, the 1st with title: Of angular sections: with the accomodation of algebra to geometry and other subjects; the 2nd with title: A treatise of angular sections. Provenance: Lord Gerard (bookseller's label); Robert Honeyman (Honeyman sale).

2107. Ward, Mary. *The telescope: a familiar sketch ... / by the Hon. Mrs. Ward. Fourth edition.*

London: Groombridge and Sons ..., 1876. viii, 150, [2] p., 12 leaves of plates: ill. (some col.), maps; 19 cm. Advertisements: [2] p. following text. Includes bibliographical references and index.

Provenance: G. L. Newth (inscription).

2108. Ward, Seth, 1617-1689. *Astronomia geometrica: ubi methodus proponitur qua primariorum planetarum astronomia sive elliptica, circularis possit geometricè absolvi. Opus, astronomis hactenus desideratum. Authore Setho Wardo, S. T. D.....*

Londini: Typis Jacobi Flesher, 1656. 3 v. in 1, fold. pl., diagrs. 19 cm. Vol. 2 has title: Astronomiae geometricae liber secundus, De astronomia coelesti seu reliquorum planetarum primariorum; v. 3: Astronomiae geometricae liber tertius, Astronomia circularis geometrice proposita. Vols. 2 & 3 have imprint: Londini, Typis Jacobi Flesher, Prostant apud Cornelium Bee, 1656. Errata: [1] l. at end. Wing, W-816. Houzeau & Lancaster. *Astronomie* (1964 ed.), 11840.

With: *Nicolai Mercatoris ... Institutionum astronomicarum libri duo.* Londini: Typis Gulielmi Godbid, sumtibus Samuelis Simpson ..., 1676. Provenance: Michael Chasles (bookplate).

2109. Warren, Henry White, 1831-1912. *Recreations in astronomy: with directions for practical experiments and telescopic work / by Henry White Warren.*

New York: Chautauqua Press, 1886. xiii, 284 p., [4] leaves of plates: ill., maps; 20 cm. Includes index.

Advertisements: 3 p. preceding frontispiece.

2110. Washburne, Carleton Wolsey, b. 1889. *The story of earth and sky by Carleton and Heluiz Washburne; in collaboration with Frederick Reed; illustrated with line drawings by Margery Stocking. Student's ed.*

New York: Appleton-Century-Crofts, [c1935]. vi, 376 p., [30] leaves of plates: ill.; 21 cm. Also published same year by D. Appleton-Century Co. Includes index.

2111. Watson, James D., 1928- . *Genetical implications of the structure of deoxyribonucleic acid / by J. D. Watson and F. H. C. Crick.*
London: Macmillan; New York: St. Martin's, 1953. p. 964-967: ill.; 26 cm. *Nature;* v. 171, no. 4361. Caption title. Includes bibliographical references.

2112. Watson, James D., 1928- . *Molecular structure of nucleic acids: a structure for deoxyribosenucleic acid.*
London: Macmillan; New York: St. Martin's, 1953. p. 737-738: 1 ill.; 26 cm. *Nature;* v. 171, no. 4356. Caption title. Signed at end: J. D. Watson, F. H. C. Crick. Includes bibliographical references.

2113. Watts, Isaac, 1674-1748. *The knowledge of the heavens and the earth made easy, or, The first principles of astronomy and geography: explained by the use of globes and maps ... / by I. Watts ... The fourth edition, corrected.*
London: Printed for T. Longman and T. Shewell ... and J. Brackstone, 1745. xiii, [1], 222, [12] p., [6] folded leaves of plates: ill., map; 21 cm.
Provenance: Library of the Northern Academy of Arts and Sciences (bookplate); Dartmouth College Library (inkstamp).

2114. Webb, T. W. (Thomas William), 1807-1885. *Celestial objects for common telescopes, by the Rev. T. W. Webb. 5th ed., rev. and greatly enlarged by Rev. T. E. Espin.*
London, New York, [etc.]: Longmans, Green & Co., 1893-1894. 2 v. fronts. (v. 1, port.) illus., plates, fold. map. 19 cm. Includes bibliographical references and index.
Advertisements: publisher's catalog, 32 p. at end, v. 2.

2115. Webb, T. W. (Thomas William), 1807-1885. *Celestial objects for common telescopes / by the Rev. T. W. Webb ... Sixth edition, being a reprint of the fifth edition, revised and greatly enlarged (in 1893) / by Rev. T. E. Espin....*
London, New York, and Bombay: Longmans, Green, & Co., 1896-1899. 2 v.: ill., maps, port; 20 cm. Includes bibliographical references.
Advertisements: 24 p. at end.

2116. Webb, T. W. (Thomas William), 1807-1885. *Celestial objects for common telescopes, by the Rev. T. W. Webb ... 6th ed., throughly revised by Rev. T. E. Espin.*
London and New York: Longmans, Green and Co., 1917. 2 v.: fronts. (v. 1, port.) illus., plates (part fold.), fold. map. 19 cm. Includes bibliographical references and index. Folded maps in pocket at end of volume 1.
Advertisements: [1] p. at end of v. 2. Imperfect copy: lacks map in pocket at end of v. 2.

2117. Weber, Ernst Heinrich, 1795-1878. *Wellenlehre auf Experimente gegründet, oder, Über die Wellen tropfbarer Flüssigkeiten: mit Anwendung auf die Schall- und Lichtwellen/ von den Brüdern Ernst Heinrich Weber ... und Wilhelm Weber....*
Leipzig: Bey Gerhard Fleischer, 1825. xxviii, 574, [1] p., xviii, [2] folded leaves of plates: ill.; 21 cm. Errata: p. [575]. Includes tables on [2] folded leaves. Includes bibliographical references.

2118. Weber, Nicolaus. *Cometas sublunares sive aereos non prorsus negandos: dissertatione inaugurali philosophica sub praesidio viri nobilissimi ... Dn. Jo. Henrici Mulleri in inclyta Altorfina physices et mathematum professoris ... / D. xxv. Iunii 1722 publice defendenda asserit Nicolaus Weber....*
Altorfi: Literis Magni Danielis Meyeri, 1722. 24 p.; 19 cm. Inaugural dissertation – Altdorf, 1725. At head of title: Q.D.B.V. Date in statement of responsibility transcribed into Arabic numerals.
Disbound.

2119. †Webster, Noah, 1758-1843. *An American dictionary of the English language: intended to exhibit, I. The origin, affinities and primary signification of English words, as far as they have been ascertained. II. The genuine orthography and pronunciation of words, according to general usage, or to just principles of analogy. III. Accurate and discriminating definitions, with numerous authorities and illustrations. To which are prefixed, an introductory dissertation on the origin, history and connection of the languages of Western Asia and of Europe, and a concise grammar of the English language. By Noah Webster, LL.D. In two volumes.*

New York: Published by S. Converse, 1828. 2 v. port. 30 cm. On t. p.: Printed by Hezekiah Howe – New Haven. Additions and corrections: [2] p. at end, v. 2.

"Advertisement" to subscribers dated Nov. 28, 1828: [2] p. following t. p., v. 1. Imperfect? v. 2 lacks frontispiece.

2120. WEBSTER, THOMAS, 1773-1844. *On the freshwater formations in the Isle of Wight, with some observations on the strata over the chalk in the south-east part of England / by Thomas Webster....*

London: Geological Society of London, 1814. p. [161]-254, [4] leaves of plates (3 folded): 1 col. ill., 3 maps; 29 cm. Caption title. Detached from the *Transactions of the Geological Society of London*, vol. 2 (1814). Plates numbered 9, 10, 10*, 11 are dated 1814.

Provenance: Herbert McLean Evans (bookplate).

2121. WEDEL, CHRISTIAN, 1678-1714. *Epistola anatomica, problematica, tertia & decima ... Ad ...Fredericum Ruyschium ... De oculorum tunicis.*

Amstelædami: Apud Joannem Wolters, 1700. 40 p.; plate. 22 cm. "Frederici Ruyschii responsio ...": p. [9]-34. Plate numbered: XVI. Signed: C. Huyberts ad vivum sculp.

With: *Frederici Ruyschii ... Observationum anatomico-chirurgicarum centuria.* Amstelodami: Apud Henricum & Viduam Theodori Boom, 1691.

2122. WEIDLER, JOHANN FRIEDRICH, 1691-1755. *Io. Friderici Weidleri Historia astronomiae sive ortu et progressu astronomiae liber singularis.*

Vitembergae: Sumtibus G. H. Schwartzii, Bibliopolae, 1741. 12 p. l., 624, [40] p. 22 cm. Includes index. Corrigenda: on p. 624.

Provenance: Herman S. Davis (bookplate); Herbert McLean Evans (bookplate). 4 p. with title: "Historical and descriptive astronomy: illustrated lectures by Herman S. Davis, Ph.D." inserted.

2123. WEIGEL, ERHARD, 1625-1699. *Speculum Uranicum aquilæ Romanæ sacrum das ist, Him[m]els Spiegel: darinnen ausser denen ordentlichen, auch die ungewöhnlichen Erscheinungen des Himmels ... vornehmlich aber der im Gestirne des Adlers jüngsthin entstandene Comet ... / von Erhardo VVeigelio....*

Frankfurt: In Verlegung Thomas Matthias Götzen ...; Gedruckt zu Jehna bey Samuel Krebsen, 1661. [128] p., [6] leaves of plates: ill.; 21 cm. Added engraved t. p. by Johann Dürr. Engraved plate signed: Ioh. Reinh. Schildtknecht fec.

2124. WEIL, ERNST, 1891-1965. *Albert Einstein, 14th March 1879 (Ulm)–18th April 1955 (Princeton, N.J.): a bibliography of his scientific papers, 1901-1954 / compiled by E. Weil.*

London : [s.n.], c1960. 41 p. ; 23 cm.

2125. WEINEK, LADISLAUS, 1848-1913. [Collection of ten photographs of the surface of the moon / assembled by L. Weinek].

[1891-1894]. 10 photoprints : sepia toned ; 18 x 13 cm. and 39 x 33 cm. in portfolio 42 x 47 cm. Includes 10 photoprints, of which 6 are mounted, from negatives taken at the Lick Observatory, and by Puiseux and Loewy at the Paris Observatory. All have ms. annotations of subject, observatory, and date of negative. Mounted photos bear collector's stamp and that of the K. K. Sternwarte, Prag.

2126. WEISMANN, AUGUST, 1834-1914. *Vorträge über Descendenztheorie, gehalten an der Universität zu Freiburg im Breisgau, von August Weismann. Mit 3 farbigen Tafeln und 131 Textfiguren.*

Jena: G. Fischer, 1902. 2 v. 3 col. pl., diagrs. (part col.) 24 cm.

Bound 1 v. Provenance: Oscar Fröhlich (inkstamp).

2127. WELLCOME HISTORICAL MEDICAL LIBRARY. *A catalogue of printed books in the Wellcome Historical Medical Library; with a foreword by Sir Henry Hallett Dale.*

London: Wellcome Institute for the History of Medicine, (1962-). v.; 30 cm. Its Publications. Catalogue series, PB, 1-3. Includes indexes. v. 1. Books printed before 1641. – v. 2. Books printed from 1641-1850. A-E. – v. 3. Books printed from 1641-1850. F-L.

2128. Wells, Edward, 1667-1727. *The young gentleman's astronomy, chronology, and dialling, containing such elements of the said arts or sciences, as are most useful and easy to be known. By Edward Wells. 3d ed., rev. and corr., with additions.*
London: J. & J. Knapton, 1725. 3 v. in 1. plates (part fold.) tables. 20 cm. Each vol. has also special t.-p.

2129. Wells, William Charles, 1757-1817. *An essay on dew: and several appearances connected with it / by William Charles Wells....*
London: Printed for Taylor and Hessey ..., 1814. [4], 146, [2] p.; 23 cm. Advertisements: last [2] p.
Provenance: W. F. Harrison (signature).

2130. Welsch, Georg Hieronymus, 1624-1677. *Georgii Hieronymi Welschii Dissertatio medico-philosophica de ægagropilis. Cui secunda hac editione emendatiori, auctarii vice altera accedit.*
Augustæ Vindelicorum: Impensis Jo. Wehe ... Typis Jacobj Kopmajerj et heredum Jo. Prætorij, 1668. [8], 70, [9], [2], 101, [23] p., [7] leaves of plates (some folded): ill.; 20 cm. (Pt.) II has special t. p. with imprint: Typis Jacobi Kopmair hæred.Joannis Prætorii, 1668. Includes stanzas 133-169 of a poem by A. Gatti in Italian and in Latin translation. Includes bibliographical references and indexes.
With: *Zootomia democritæa* / Marci Aurelii Severini. Noribergæ: Literis Endterianis, 1645. Provenance: Herbert McLean Evans.

2131. Wendelin, Marcus Friedrich, 1584-1652. *Contemplationum physicarum sectio III: de corporibus cœlestibus, continens vranologiam & astrologiam ... / autore Marco Friderico Wendelino....*
Hanouiæ: Sumtibus Clementis Schleichii, & Viduæ Danielis Aubrii, 1628. [40], 788 p.; 18 cm.

2132. Werner, Abraham Gottlob, 1749-1817. *Herrn Bergrath Werner's letztes Mineral-System / nun nach den neuesten und letzen Entdeckungen herausgegeben und mit neuen Beobachtungen und Zusätzen vermehrt von Christoph Mayr ...; nebst einem Anhang die Beschreibung der nothwendigsten Theile eines Apparates enthaltend, um die Mineralien auf die zweckmässigste Weise zu sammeln und zu untersuchen.*
Wien: Im Verlage bey Leopold Grund, 1819. xii, 238, [2] p.; 21 cm. Advertisements: [2] p.

2133. Werner, Abraham Gottlob, 1749-1817. *Neue Theorie von der Entstehung der Gänge: mit Anwendung auf den Bergbau besonders den freibergischen / von Abraham Gottlob Werner.*
Freiberg: Gedrukt und verlegt in der Gerlachischen Buchdrukkerei, 1791. XXXX, 256 p.; 18 cm. (8vo). Includes bibliographical references.
Provenance: J. Knett (inkstamp); Ms. annotations.

2134. Werner, Abraham Gottlob, 1749-1817. *New theory of the formation of veins; with its application to the art of working mines. By Abraham Gottlob Werner ... Tr. from the German. To which is added, an appendix, containing notes illustrative of the subject; by Charles Anderson....*
Edinburgh: A. Constable and Company; [etc., etc.], 1809. xxxvi, 259, [1] p. incl. front. (port.) 22 cm. Translation of: *Neue Theorie von der Entstehung der Gänge.* Errata: final page.

2135. Werner, Abraham Gottlob, 1749-1817. *Nouvelle théorie de la formation des filons: application de cette théorie à l'exploitation des mines particulièrement de celles de Freiberg / par A. G. Werner ...; ouvrage traduit de l'allemand et augmenté d'un grand nombre de notes, dont plusieurs ont été fournies par l'auteur même.*
À Freiberg: Chez Craz ..., 1802. XXII, 311, [8] p., [1] leaf of plates: port.; 18 cm. Translaton of: *Neue Theorie von der Entstehung der Gänge* by J. F. Daubuisson. Port. by Vogel and C. F. Hoelzel. Errata: p. [8]. Includes bibliographical references.

2136. Werner, Abraham Gottlob, 1749-1817. *Von den äusserlichen Kennzeichen der Fossilien, / abgefasst von Abraham Gottlob Werner....*
Leipzig: Bey Siegfried Lebrecht Crusius, 1774. 302, [2] p. 8 folded leaves of plates; 19 cm. Decorations on

p. [5] and 12. Druckfehler: p. [304]. Burndy. *Science* 91. California. *Epochal Achievements* 64. Adams, F. D. *Birth and development of geological sci.*, p. 212.

2137. WEYL, HERMANN, 1885-1955. *Mind and nature, by Hermann Weyl....*

Philadelphia, University of Pennsylvania Press, 1934. vi p., 1 l., 100 p. 1 illus., pl., diagrs. 21 cm. The William J. Cooper foundation lectures, 1933, Swarthmore College. References to related literature are included in the first lecture (p.2).

2138. WEYL, HERMANN, 1885-1955. *Raum. Zeit. Materie: Vorlesungen über allgemeine Relativitätstheorie/ von Hermann Weyl.*

Berlin: J. Springer, 1918. viii, 234 p.: ill.; 25 cm. Bibliography: p. 228-230. Includes index.

Provenance: Karl Horovitz (inscription).

2139. WHEWELL, WILLIAM, 1794-1866. *Astronomy and general physics considered with reference to natural theology, by the Rev. William Whewell ... Fifth edition?*

London: W. Pickering, 1836. 1 p. l., [v]-xv, [1], 381, [1] p.; 23 cm. The Bridgewater treatises on the power, wisdom and goodness of God as manifested in the creation. Treatise III. Colophon: C. Whittingham. Preface from 5th ed. Includes bibliographical references.

Binder: Homecrafters, Tuscon, Ariz.

2140. WHEWELL, WILLIAM, 1794-1866. *History of the inductive sciences, from the earliest to the present time. By William Whewell ... A new ed., rev. and continued....*

London: J. W. Parker, 1847. 3 v. 23 cm. Includes indexes. v. 1. I. The Greek school philosophy, with reference to physical science. II. The physical sciences in ancient Greece. III. Greek astronomy. IV. Physical science in the middle ages. V. Formal astronomy after the stationary period. – v. 2. VI. Mechanics, including fluid mechanics. VII. Physical astronomy. VIII. Acoustics. IX. Optics, formal and physical. X. Thermotics and atmology. – v. 3. XI. Electricity. XII. Magnetism. XIII. Galvanism or Voltaic electricity. XIV. Chemistry. XV. Mineralogy. XVI. Systematic botany and zoology. XVII. Physiology and comparative anatomy. XVIII. Geology.

Binder: Hayday (stamp). Binding: full calf. Provenance: T. Bosworth (inkstamp).

2141. WHEWELL, WILLIAM, 1794-1866. *The plurality of worlds ... With an introduction, by Edward Hitchcock....*

Boston: Gould and Lincoln, 1854. xvi, [17]-307 p. front. 20 cm.

Advertisements: [4] p. at end.

2142. WHIPPLE, FRED LAWRENCE, 1906-. *Orbital data and preliminary analyses of satellites 1957 Alpha and 1957 Beta, compiled by F. L. Whipple [and others].*

Washington, Smithsonian Institution, 1958. vii, 189-347 p. illus., diagrs., tables. 26 cm. *Smithsonian contributions to astrophysics* ; v.2, no.10. Includes bibliography.

2143. WHISTON, WILLIAM, 1667-1752. *An account of a surprizing meteor, seen in the air March 19, 1718/19. Containing, I. A description of this meteor, from original letters of those who saw it in different places. II. Some historical accounts of the like metoeors before. III. A demonstration that such meteors are not comets. IV. That such meteors are not a concourse of vapours above our atmosphere. V. That they are prodigious blasts of thunder and lightnings in the upper regions of our air. VI. Observations from the whole. By William Whiston, M.A. The 2d ed. To which is added, A vindication of his account of the late meteor, from the different account given of it by Dr. Halley, in the Philosophical transactions, numb. 360.*

London: Printed for W. Taylor. 1719. 56 p. fold. front. (map) 20 cm. "Books writ by W. Whiston, M.A.": p. [38-9].

Provenance: Herbert McLean Evans; ms.marginalia. Imperfect: Last leaf damaged with some loss of text; map missing.

2144. WHISTON, WILLIAM, 1667-1752. *Astronomical principles of religion, natural and reveal'd ... / by William Whiston....*

London: Printed for J. Senex ... and W. Taylor ..., 1717. [4], xxxij, 304, [3]-16 p., [7] leaves of plates: ill., map; 20 cm. "The cause of the Deluge demonstrated": p. [3]-16 at end. Illustrated by I. Senex.

Provenance: George Baillie (armorial bookplate).

2145. WHISTON, WILLIAM, 1667-1752. *A new theory of the earth, from its original, to the consummation of all things. Wherein the creation of the world in six days, the universal Deluge, and the general conflagration, as laid down in the Holy Scriptures are shewn to be perfectly agreeable to reason and philosophy. With a large introductory discourse concerning the genuine nature, stile, and extent of the Mosaick history of the creation. By William Whiston....*

London: Printed by R. Roberts, for B. Tooke, 1696. 2 p. l., 95, 388, [2] p., 1 l. front., illus., diagrs. on 7 pl. (1 fold.) 20 cm. *Babson Newton Coll.* 231.

Provenance: John Wentworth (armorial bookplate).

2146. WHITE, ANDREW DICKSON, 1832-1918. *A history of the warfare of science with theology in Christendom / by Andrew Dickson White.*

New York: D. Appleton, [1907, c1896]. 2 v.; 23 cm. "Sixteenth printing." Includes bibliographical references and index.

Advertisements: 4, [2] p. at end, v. 2. Provenance: Viola Lasalle (signature).

2147. WHITE, CHARLES J. (CHARLES JOYCE), 1839-1917. *The elements of theoretical and descriptive astronomy: for the use of colleges and academies / by Charles J. White ... Fifth edition, revised.*

New York: John Weley & Sons ..., 1884. ix, [1], 11-274 p., VI leaves of plates: ill.; 20 cm. Includes bibliographical references and index.

Provenance: Arthur R. Crathorne (bookplate); A. R. Crathorne (signature).

2148. WHITE, W. B. *Seeing stars, by W. B. White; illustrated by Ruth C. Williams.*

Cleveland: The Harter Publishing Company, [c1935]. [3]-61, [1] p. illus. (incl. charts) 17 cm. On cover: H166. Text on lining-papers. Includes index.

2149. WHITEHEAD, ALFRED NORTH, 1861-1947. *Adventures of ideas, by Alfred North Whitehead.*

New York: The Macmillan Company, [1933]. xii, 392 p. 22 cm. "The three books – Science and the modern world, Process and reality, Adventure of ideas – ... supplement each other's omissions or compressions." – Pref. Includes indexes. Bibliography included in the preface. pt. I. Sociological. – pt. II. Cosmological. – pt. III. Philosophical. – pt. IV. Civilization.

2150. WHITEHEAD, ALFRED NORTH, 1861-1947. *The concept of nature: Tarner lectures delivered in Trinity College, November, 1919 / by Alfred North Whitehead.*

Cambridge: University Press, 1926. viii, 202 p.; 22 cm. "First edition 1920; reprinted 1926" – T. p. verso. "This volume on '*The concept of nature*' forms a companion book to my previous work '*An enquiry concerning the principles of natural knowledge*'" – P. [vi]. Includes bibliographical references and index.

2151. WHITEHEAD, ALFRED NORTH, 1861-1947. *The concept of nature, Tarner lectures delivered in Trinity College, November, 1919 by A. N. Whitehead....*

Cambridge: The University Press, 1920. viii p., 1 l., 202 p. 22 cm. A companion volume to the author's *An enquiry concerning the principles of natural knowledge.* cf. Pref.

Provenance: A. W. Richards (signature).

2152. WHITEHEAD, ALFRED NORTH, 1861-1947. *The principle of relativity with applications to physical science, by A. N. Whitehead.*

Cambridge: The University Press, [1922]. xii, 190 p. diagrs. 22 cm.

Provenance: E. C. Goldsworthy (signature).

2153. WHITEHEAD, ALFRED NORTH, 1861-1947. *Science and the modern world / by Alfred North Whitehead.*

New York: Macmillan, 1926. xii, 304 p.; 20 cm. Lowell lectures; 1925. Includes index.

Provenance: Wroe Alderson (bookplate); Herbert McLean Evans (bookplate).

2154. WHITEHEAD, ALFRED NORTH, 1861-1947. *Science and the modern world / by Alfred North Whitehead.*

Cambridge: University Press, 1926. xi, 296 p.; 23 cm. Lowell lectures; 1925. Includes bibliographical references and index.

Provenance: Presentation inscription to F. S. Lewis from A. F. S.

2155. Whitehurst, John, 1713-1788. *An inquiry into the original state and formation of the earth: deduced from facts and the laws of nature to which is added an appendix, containing some general observations on the strata in Derbyshire. With sections of them representing their arrangement, affinities, and the mutations they have suffered at different periods of time, intended to illustrate the preceding inquiries and as a specimen of subterraneous geography.*
London: Printed for the author and W. Bent by J. Cooper; sold at G. Robinson's, 1778. [20], 195 p. illus. 27 cm. A list of subscribers: p. [5-15]. Errata: p. [16].
Provenance: J. A. Bayly (signature).

2156. Whitehurst, John, 1713-1788. *An inquiry into the original state and formation of the earth; deduced from facts and the laws of nature. The 2d ed., considerably enl. ... By John Whitehurst....*
London: Printed for W. Bent, 1786. 6 p.l., 283 p. front. (port.) VII pl. (part fold.) 29 cm. Port. signed: Jos. Wright pinx., J. Hall sculp., plates drawn by the author.

2157. Whyte, Charles. *The constellations and their history, by Rev. Charles Whyte ... With plates of stellar spectra and star maps.*
London: C. Griffin & Company, Ltd., 1928. 5. p. l., 284 p. illus., IV pl. (part fold.) 23 cm. Advertisements half-title verso. Bibliography: p. [274]. Includes index.

2158. Whyte, Charles. *Our solar system and the stellar universe: ten popular lectures / by Charles Whyte.*
London: Charles Griffen; J. B. Lippincott, 1923. xi, 234 p., [19] leaves of plates: ill.; 23 cm. Advertisements: half-title verso. Includes index.

2159. Whyte, Charles. *Stellar wonders, by Charles Whyte....*
London: The Sheldon Press, 1933. v, 196 p. front., illus., plates. 19 cm. "First published 1933" – T. p. verso. "Most of the talks contained in this volume were given several years ago, at the British Broadcasting Station, Aberdeen." – P. v. Bibliography: p. 5-6. Includes index.
Provenance: Miriam Gzibeck (signature).

2160. Wicks, Mark. *To Mars via the moon; an astronomical story, by Mark Wicks ... with illustrations.*
Philadelphia: J. B. Lippincott Company; Seeley and Co., Limited, 1911. xxiii, 25-327, [1] p. front., 15 pl. 21 cm.
Provenance: William Andrews Clark, Jr. (booklabel).

2161. Wiedersheim, Robert, 1848-1923. *Der Bau des Menschen als Zeugniss für seine Vergangenheit, von Dr. R. Wiedersheim....*
Freiburg: Mohr, 1887. [4], 114, [2] p. 25 cm. "Besonderer Abdruck aus den *Berichten der Naturforschenden Gesellschaft zu Freiburg i.B.*, Band II, Heft 4." Advertisements: [2] final p. and lower wrapper.
Provenance: Herbert McLean Evans (bookplate); Bibliotheck, Leesmuseum, Amsterdam (booklabel).

2162. Wiener, Norbert, 1894-1964. *Ex-prodigy: my childhood and youth.*
New York: Simon and Schuster, 1953. 309 p. illus., ports., 22 cm. Includes index.

2163. Wilder, Alexander, 1823-1908. *History of medicine: a brief outline of medical history and sects of physicians, from the earliest historic period ... / by Alexander Wilder.*
New Sharon, Me.: New England Eclectic Publishing Co., [1901, c1899]. xxix, 946 p., [1] leaf of plates: port.; 20 cm. "Fifth thousand." Bibliography: p. 838-871. Includes index.
Binder: Smith & Reid (inkstamp).

2164. Wilhelm, Wolf. *Rektorwechsel an der Friedrich-Wilhelms-Universität zu Berlin am 15. Oktober 1913: I. Bericht des abtretenden Rektors D. Dr. Wolf Wilhelm Grafen Baudissin über das Amtsjahr 1919/1913: II. Rede des antretenden Rektors Dr. Max Planck: Neue Bahnen der physikalischen Erkenntnis.*
Berlin: Druck der Norddeutschen Buchdruckerei, 1913. 45 p.; 26 cm.

2165. Wilkins, John, 1614-1672. *A discovery of a new world, or, a discourse: tending to prove, that 'tis probable there may be another habitable world in the moon. With a discourse concerning the probability of a passage thither.*

Unto which is added, a discourse concerning a new planet ... / by John Wilkins, late Lord Bishop of Chester. The fourth edition corrected and amended.

London: Printed by T. M. & J. A. for John Gillibrand ..., 1684. 2 v.: ill.; 18 cm. Added engraved t. p.: A discourse concerning a new world & another planet ... London: Printed for Iohn Gellibrand ..., 1683. Includes bibliographical references. Vol. 1: [16], 187 p.; v. 2: [8], 184 p. Advertisements: v. 1, p. 16; v. 2, p. 184. Wing W2186.

Bound in 1 v. Provenance: Wm. Oliver (armorial bookplate).

2166. Willey, Arthur, b. 1867. *Amphioxus and the ancestry of the vertebrates, by Arthur Willey. With a preface by Henry Fairfield Osborn.*

New York and London: Macmillan, 1894. xiv, 316 p. front., illus. 23 cm. Columbia University Biological series; v. 2. Includes index. "References": p. 295-309.

Provenance: Radcliffe Library, Oxford (inkstamp).

2167. Williams, W. Mattieu (William Mattieu), 1820-1892. *The fuel of the sun / by W. Mattieu Williams....*

London: Simpkin, Marshall & Co. ..., 1870. xx, 222 p.: ill.; 23 cm. Includes bibliographical references.

Advertisements: [1] p. at end. Binder: Hanbury & Simpson (ticket). Provenance: Author's signed inscription to T. Sterry Hunt; James Douglas (bookplate).

2168. Willis, Robert, 1799-1878. *William Harvey; a history of the discovery of the circulation of the blood, by R. Willis ... With a portrait of Harvey, after Faithorne.*

London: C. K. Paul & Co., 1878. xvi, 350 p. front. (port.) 23 cm. Osler, W. *Bib. Osleriana*, 758. Yale. *Cushing Coll.* W210.

Advertisements: [1] p. at end; publisher's catalog, 32 p. at end. Imperfect: lacks port.

2169. Wilson, Benjamin, 1721-1788. *A series of experiments relating to phosphori and the prismatic colours they are found to exhibit in the dark / by B. Wilson ...; together with a translation of two memoirs, from the Bologna Acts, upon the same subject by J. B. Beccari....*

London: Printed for J. Dodsley [and 4 others], 1775. [4], 92, 96 p.: ill.; 23 cm. Includes: *An account of a great number of phosphori discovered by J. B. Beccarii ...* published in the *Bologna Acts*, 1744 – *A further account of a great number of phosphori, lately discovered by J. B. Beccarii* ...published in the *Bologna Acts*, 1747 vol. II and third part. Errata: p. 96.

With: *New experiments and observations on electricity. Part II* / by Benjamin Franklin. -The second edition. London: printed and sold by D. Henry and R. Cave ..., 1754. Provenance: Dr. Darwin (signature).

2170. Wing, John, 1643-1726. *Scientia stellarum, or, the starry science: exposed in the calculation of the planets places, both in longitude and latitude, for any time, past, present, or to come ... being added, as a supplement to the preceding book of surveying / by John Wing, Math.*

London: Printed, for Awnsham and John Churchill ..., 1699. 134, [1] p.; 31 cm. Errors in pagination: p. 122 misnumbered as 126, p. 127 as 131. Wing W2985. "Preceeding book" was *Geodaetes practicus redivivus: the art of surveying formerly published by Vincent Wing, math.*

2171. Wing, Vincent, 1619-1668. *Harmonicon coeleste: or, The cœlestiall harmony of the visible world: conteining, an absolute and entire piece of astronomie. Wherein is succinctly handled the trigonometricall part, generally propounded, and particularly applyed in all questions tending to the diurnall motion. Especially respecting, and truly subservient to the main doctrine of the second motions of the luminaries and the other planets: together with their affections as eclipses &c. Grounded upon the most rationall hypothesis yet constituted, and compared with the best observations that are extant, especially those of Tycho Brahe, and other more modern observators ... By Vincent Wing, philomathemat.....*

London: Printed by R. Leybourn, for the Company of Stationers, 1651. 12 p. l., 309 p. tables, diagrs. 29 cm. The second, third, and fourth books of *Harmonicon coeleste*, "Tables of the middle motions and æquations of Sol, Luna, Saturn, Jupiter, Mars, Venus, and Mercury," "Canon triangulorum logarithmicus," and "Chiliades decem logarithmorum" each have special

t.-p. included in pagination. Wing W2993.
Provenance: David Joans (inscription).

2172. WINTERHALTER, ALBERT G. (ALBERT GUSTAVUS), b. 1856. *The International Astrophotographic Congress and a visit to certain European observatories and other institutions: report to the superintendent [of the U.S. Naval Observatory] By Albert G. Winterhalter.*
Washington: Govt. Print. Off., 1889. 1 p. l., XV, 354 p. illus., pl. 30 cm. *Washington observations for 1885; Appendix I.* "Transactions of the International Astrophotographic Congress, held at Paris, April, 1887": p. 5-71. "Notes of a visit to certain European observatories ..." and "Sundry astronomical and nautical constructions and processes": p. 73-319. Advance edition. Reissued, with half-title, in "Observations made during the year 1885 at the United States Naval Observatory." 1891.
Provenance: A. M. W. Downing (inkstamp).

2173. WITELO, 13th cent. *Vitellionis ... Peri optikes, id est de natura, ratione, & proiectione radiorum uisus, luminum, colorum atq[ue] formarum, quam uulgo perspectiuam vocant, libri X ... Nunc primum opera ... Georgij Tanstetter & Petri Apiani in lucem ædita.*
Norimbergæ: Apud Io. Petreium, 1535. [4], 297 l. ill. 33 cm. Title partially romanized; Known as: *Perspectiva.* Adams V898. Stillwell, M. B. *Science,* 254.

2174. WITHAM, HENRY THORNTON MAIRE, 1779-1844. *The internal structure of fossil vegetables found in the carboniferous and oolitie deposits of Great Britain, described and illustrated. By Henry T. M. Witham,*
Edinburgh: A. & C. Black, 1833. 2 p. 1., 84 p. XVI pl. (part col.) incl. front. 28 x 22 cm. Illustrated by W. MacGillivray and W. H. Lizars.
Provenance: author's presentation inscription. Minster Acres Library (bookplate).

2175. WITHERING, WILLIAM, 1741-1799. *An account of the foxglove, and some of its medical uses: with practical remarks on dropsy, and other diseases / by William Withering....*
Birmingham [England]: Printed by M. Swinney; for G. G. J. and J. Robinson ... London., 1785. xx, [2], 207, [1] p., [1] folded leaf of plates: col. ill.; 21 cm. The plate, possibly by James Sowerby or William Kilburn, appears in one of two states in this edition. This is the original unsigned state described in the *Hunt botanical cat.,* 676. Osler, W. *Bib. Osleriana,* 4261. Yale. *Cushing Coll.,* W254. Advertisement on the last page.
Provenance: Walter Reginald Bett, Herbert McLean Evans (bookplates). Binder: Sangorski & Sutcliffe, London (stamp). Maltby, Oxford (stamp on slipcase).

2176. WITTE, GILLES DE, 1648-1721. *Histoire de l'Inquisition: suivie de documents sur l'inquisition de Goa établie par les Jésuites / par Gilles de Witte....*
Paris: Chez Carpentier et Compagnie ...; Chez Faverio ..., 1826. 80 p.; 12 cm.
With: *Astronomie des dames* / par Jérome de Lalande. Nouvelle édition. Paris: Chez Salmon, 1824.

2177. WOLF, JOHANN CHRISTIAN, 1673-1723. *Epistola anatomica, problematica, undecima ... ad ... Fredericum Ruyschium ... de intestinorum tunicis, glandulis, &c. / authore Joh. Christian. Wolf....*
Amstelædami: Apud Joannem Wolters, 1698. 13, [2] p.: plate.; 22 cm. "Frederici Ruyschii responsio ...": p. 7-13. Statement of responsiblity transposed. Plate numbered: 12.
With: *Observationum anatomico-chirurgicarum centuria* / Frederici Ruyschii. Amstelodami: Apud Henricum & Viduam Theodori Boom, 1691.

2178. WOLF, RUDOLF, 1816-1893. *Handbuch der Astronomie, ihrer Geschichte und Litteratur.*
Zürich: F. Schulthess, 1890-93. 2 v. illus. 24 cm. Issued in 4 pts. Includes bibliographies.
In 4 v.

2179. WOLF, RUDOLF, 1816-1893. *Taschenbuch für Mathematik, Physik, Geodäsie und Astronomie / von Dr. Rudolf Wolf ... Zweite, ganz umgearbeitete und sehr erweiterte, mit zahlreichen Tabellen und fünf Figurentafeln ausgestattete Auflage.*
Bern: Druck und Verlag von Fr. Haller: (Für Deutschland in Commission bei J. Dalp), 1856. XVI, 200, [36] p., V leaves of plates: ill.; 16 cm. Tables: [36] p. (3rd sequence). Includes index.
Provenance: Steiner (signature); ms. marginalia. Interleaved with blanks.

2180. WOLFF, CASPAR FRIEDRICH, 1733-1794. *Caspar Friedrich Wolff über die Bildung des Darmkanals im bebrüteten Hühnchen. Uebers. und mit einer einleitenden Abhandlung und Anmerkungen versehen von Johann Friedrich Meckel; mit zwei Kupfertafeln.*
Halle: Renger, 1812. 263, [1] p. 2 fold. pl. facsim. 22 cm. Errata: p. [264]. First published 1768.
Provenance: Charles Atwood Kofoid (bookplate); Herbert McLean Evans (bookplate).

2181. WOLLASTON, FRANCIS, 1731-1815. *Fasciculus astronomicus, containing observations of the northern circumpolar region; together with some account of the instrument with which they were made and a new set of tables by which they were reduced to the mean position for the beginning of January 1800....*
London: Printed by L. Hansard and sold by G. Wilkie, 1800. 256, 87 p. 28 cm.
Provenance: S. P. Rigaud (inscription); Radcliffe Observatory, Oxford (inkstamp).

2182. WOOD, J. G. (JOHN GEORGE), 1827-1889. *Common objects of the microscope. By the Rev. J. G. Wood ... With upwards of four hundred illustrations by Tuffen West.*
London, New York: G. Routledge & Sons, 1861. iv, 132 p. illus., XII col. pl. (incl. front.) 17 cm.
Advertisements: t. p. verso; 6 p. on endpapers. Provenance: J. S. Leonhardt (booklabel); J. H. Chambers (bookseller's label).

2183. WOODHOUSE, ROBERT, 1773-1827. *A treatise on astronomy, theoretical and practical. By Robert Woodhouse... Vol. 1 ... A new ed.*
Cambridge: Printed for J. Deighton & Sons; [etc., etc.], 1821-1823. 1 v. in 2 diagrs. 21 cm. Paged continuously. No more published. Includes bibliographical references. Errata: [2] p. at end, pt. 2.

2184. WOODWARD, JOHN, 1665-1728. *Johannis Woodwardi ... Naturalis historia telluris, illustrata & aucta. Una cum ejusdem defensione; preæsertim contra nuperas objectiones d. El. Camerarii ... Accedit Methodica, & ad ipsam naturæ normam instituta, fossilium in classes distributio.*
Londini: Typis J. M., impensis R. Wilkin; [etc., etc.], 1714. [151] p. 20 cm. Various pagings. Includes *Syllabus rerum corrigendarum in Geographiæ physicæ Woodwardianæ versione Scheuchzerianâ nunc demum recognitâ.*
Provenance: Stanislas Meunier (inkstamp).

2185. WOTTON, EDWARD, 1492-1555. *Edoardi VVottoni Oxoniensis De differentiis animalium libri decem.....*
Lutetiae Parisiorum: Apud Vascosanum., M.D.LII, 1552. [12], 220, [14] leaves (versos of leaves 1 of 1st group and 220 of 2nd group; and the last leaf blank): ill.; 33 cm. Colophon: Imprimebat Michael Vascosanus, Lutetiæ Parisiorum, Ann, M. D.LI, [1551]. Decorated initials throughout text. Includes indexes. Errata on verso of leaf [13] of 3rd group. Osler, W. *Bib. Osleriana*, 4282. Wood, C. A. *Lit. of vertebrate zoology*, p. 637.
Provenance: Herbert McLean Evans (bookplate).

2186. WRIGHT, JULIA MCNAIR, 1840-1903. *Astronomy: the sun and his family: how to know the stars: the reason for the seasons, for nights, for tides, and for eclipses / by Julia MacNair Wright.*
Philadelphia: Penn Publishing Co., [1911, c1898]. 203, [9] leaves of plates: ill.; 15 cm.
Advertisements: 4 p. at end.

2187. WRIGHT, THOMAS, 1711-1786. *An original theory or new hyposthesis of the universe,: founded upon the laws of nature, and solving by mathematical principles the general phænomena of the visible creation; and particularly the Via Lactea. / Compris'd in nine familiar letters from the author to his friend. And illustrated with upwards of thirty graven and mezzatinto plates, by the best masters. By Thomas Wright, of Durham.*
London: Printed for the author, and sold by H. Chapelle ..., MDCCL, [1750]. viii, [4], 84 p., 32 leaves of plates (2 folded): ill.; 29 cm. Some decorated borders, initials, and tail pieces.
Provenance: Herschel Library Collingwood (inkstamp), Herbert McLean Evans (bookplate). Ms. note supposed to be by William Herschel.

2188. WRIGHT, WILBUR, 1867-1912. *Some aeronautical experiments / Wilbur Wright.*

p. 133-148, [1] leaf of plates: ill.; 23 cm. Caption title. "Presented to the Western Society of Engineers September 18, 1901. Reprinted ..., after revision by the author, from *Journal of the Western Society of Engineers*, December, 1901" – P. 133.

In: Smithsonian Institution. Board of Regents. *Annual Report of the Board of Regents of the Smithsonian Institution*, 1902.

2189. Wundt, Wilhelm Max, 1832-1920. *Beiträge zur Theorie der Sinneswahrnehmung. Von Dr. Wilhelm Wundt....*

Leipzig und Heidelberg: C. F. Winter'sche Verlagshandlung, 1862. xxxii, 451, [1] p. 21 cm. Includes bibliographical references. 1. Über den Gefühlssinn, mit besonderer Rücksicht auf dessen räumliche Wahrnehmungen. – 2. Zur Geschichte der Theorie des Sehens. -3. Über das Sehen mit einem Auge. – 4. Über das Sehen mit zwei Augen. – 5. Über einige besondere Erscheinungen des Sehens mit zwei Augen. – 6. Über den psychischen Prozess der Wahrnehmung.

Advertisements on p. [2-4] of wrappers. Provenance: Herbert McLean Evans (bookplate).

2190. Wundt, Wilhelm Max, 1832-1920. *Grundzüge der physiologischen Psychologie / von Wilhelm Wundt.*

Leipzig: W. Engelmann, 1874. xii, 870, [2] p.: ill.; 24 cm. Spine title: Physiologische Psychologie. Errata: p. [871]. Includes bibliographical references and index. Horblit, H. D. *Grolier 100 science books*, 100a.

Provenance: S. A. Arendsen Hein (inkstamp).

2191. Wurfbain, Johann Paul, 1655-1711. *Salamandrologia, h.e. Descriptio historico-philologico-philosophico-medica salamandræ quæ vulgò in igne vivere creditur, S.R.J. Academiæ Naturæ Curiosis exhibita, atâq[ue] novis aliquot capitibus, experimentis, figurisq[ue] æri eleganter incisis, nec non rerum & verborum indice adaucta, studio & opera Joh. Pauli Wurffbainii....*

Norimbergæ: Sumtibus G. Scheureri, typis Johannis M. Spörlin, 1683. 3 p.l., 133, [14] p. front., V pl. 21 x 16 cm. Added t.-p., engr. includes index. Errata: p. [14] (3rd sequence).

2192. Yahya ibn Serabi, d. ca. 930. *Iani Damasceni Decapolitani summæ inter Arabes autoritatis medici, therapeutice methodi: hoc est, curandi artis libri VII / partim Albano Torino Vitodurano paraphraste; partim Gerardo iatro Cremonensi metaphraste.*

Apud inclytam Basilaeam: per Henrichum Petrum: 1543. [464] p.; 26 cm. Includes index. Signatures: a-b^6 A-O^6 P^4 Q-2S^6. Adams I14. NLM *16th cent.* 4778. *Wellcome cat. of printed books*, 4272.

Leaves a1 and a6 missing, supplied in photocopy; R-S 6 missing. Title and imprint taken from supplied t. p. Gatherings a & b are bound at the end. With: *Onomasikon* / Othonis Brunfelsii. Argentorati: Ionannes Schottus, 1543 [i.e. 1544]. Provenance: Edwin S. Clarke (signature).

2193. Youmans, Edward Livingston, 1821-1887. *Chemical atlas, or, The chemistry of familiar objects: exhibiting the general principles of the science in a series of beautifully colored diagrams and accompanied by explanatory essays ... / by Edward L. Youmans.*

New York: D. Appleton & Co., 1857, [c1854]. 106 p.: col. ill.; 31 cm. Cover title: Youman's Atlas of Chemistry.

Provenance: Alfred J. Hill (signature); Minnesota Historical Society (bookplate; withdrawal stamp).

2194. Young, Alexander. *Mysteries of the sun: solar electric distribution and sun habitation / by Alexander Young. [2nd ed.]*

Buffalo, NY: Carnation, 1904. [2], v-xi, [1], 13-87 p., [6] leaves of plates: ill., port.; 21 cm. Published in 1903 under title: *Solar electric distribution and sun habitation.*

2195. Young, Charles A. (Charles Augustus), 1834-1908. *Lessons in astronomy, including uranography; a brief introductory course without mathematics, by Charles A. Young ... Rev. ed.*

Boston and London: Ginn & Company, 1903. ix, 420 p., front., illus., maps, diagrs.; 19 cm. Includes index.

With newspaper clipping tipped in. Provenance: P. E. Graber (signature).

2196. Young, Charles A. (Charles Augustus), 1834-1908. *Le soleil / par C. A. Young....*

Paris: Librairie Germer Baillière et Cie ..., 1883. VIII, 268 p.: ill.; 23 cm. Bibliothèque scientifique internationale; 44. Translation of: *The sun.* Includes index.

Advertisements: publisher's catalog dated septembre 1882, 32 p. at end. Binder: Ch. Magnier (stamp).

2197. YOUNG, CHARLES A. (CHARLES AUGUSTUS), 1834-1908. *Die Sonne / von C. A. Young ... Autorisirte Ausgabe.*

Leipzig: F. A. Brockhaus, 1883. VIII, 318, [2] p., [2] leaves of plates: ill.; 19 cm. Internationale wissenschaftliche Bibliothek; 58. Bd. Translation of: *The sun*. Includes index. Advertisements on [2] p. at end.

2198. YOUNG, CHARLES A. (CHARLES AUGUSTUS), 1834-1908. *The sun, by C. A. Young ... New and rev. ed.*

New York: D. Appleton and Company, 1896. 1 p.l., v-xii, 363 p. front., illus., pl., diagrs. 20 cm. Includes index.

2199. YOUNG, J. R. (JOHN RADFORD), 1799-1885. *Navigation and nautical astronomy: in theory and practice: with attempts to facilitate the finding of the time and the longitude at sea / by J. R. Young....*

London: John Weale ..., 1858. vii, [1], 280 p.: ill.; 18 cm. Rudimentary series; 99. Includes bibliographical references. "The Navigation tables to accompany this work will shortly be published ..." – P. [viii].

Advertisements: 12 p. at end.

2200. YOUNG, THOMAS, 1773-1829. *The Bakerian lecture: experiments and calculations relative to physical optics / by Thomas Young....*

London: Royal Society of London, 1804. 16 p.; 30 cm. Caption title. "Read November 24, 1803." Detached from the *Philosophical transactions* of the Royal Society, 1804.

Provenance: Yale Medical Library, Historical Library (bookplate); John Farquhar Fulton (bookplate); Harvey Cushing (bookplate). Blank leaves bound in at end.

2201. YOUNG, THOMAS, 1773-1829. *A course of lectures on natural philosophy and the mechanical arts. By Thomas Young....*

London: Printed for Joseph Johnson ... by William Savage ..., 1807. 2 v. 58 pl. (2 col.) incl. maps, tables, diagrs. 28 cm. "A catalogue of works relating to natural philosophy, and the mechanical arts. With references to particular passages and occasional abstracts and remarks": v. 2, p. [87]-520. BM, v. 262, col. 550. 1. pt. I. Mechanics. pt. II. Hydrodynamics. pt. III. Physics. – II. Mathematical elements of natural philosophy: pt. I. Pure mathematics. pt. II. Mechanics: Of the motions of solid bodies. pt. III. Hydrodynamics: Of the motions of fluids. A systematic catalogue of works relating to natural philosophy and the mechanical arts; with references to particular passages, and occasional abstracts and remarks. Miscellaneous papers. Account of the *Proceedings of the Royal Society*, from November 1801, to July 1802.

2202. YOUNG, THOMAS, 1773-1829. *On the theory of light and colours / by Thomas Young....*

London : Printed by W. Bulmer & Co. ... and sold by G. and W. Nicol ..., 1802. p. 12-48, [1] leaf of plates : ill.; 23 cm. The Bakerian lecture. In: *Philosophical transactions* / Royal Society of London, v. 92. Caption title. "Read November 12, 1801." *PMM*, 259. Burndy. *Science*, 152.

2203. YOUNG, THOMAS, 1773-1829. *A syllabus of a course of lectures on natural and experimental philosophy.*

London: From the Press of the Royal Institution, 1802. 161, [1], 32 p. diagrs. 22 cm. Each part has special t.-p., pt. 1-3, paged continuously. pt. 1. Mechanics. – pt. 2. Hydrodynamics. – pt. 3. Physics. – pt. 4. Mathematical elements.

Provenance: Societas Medica Edinensis (inscription).

2204. ZAGREB (Croatia). GEOFIZICKI ZAVOD. *Godisnje izvjesce Zagrebackog meteoroloskog opservatorija. Jahrbuch des meteorologischen observatoriums in Zagreb (Agram).*

Beograd, Stampa Drzavne stamparije kraljevine Jugoslavije; [etc., etc.] 1902-. v. 24-45 cm. god. 1-1901-.

Library has: [9, 1909]. Godina IX: Provenance: Herbert McLean Evans (bookplate).

2205. ZAHN, JOHANN, 1641-1707. *Specula physico-mathematico-historica notabilium ac mirabilium sciendorum, in qua mundi mirabilis œconomia, nec non ... thesaurus curiosis omnibus cosmosophis inspectandus proponitur. Opus omnigena eruditione quo universae naturae majestas in triplici mundo, coelesti, aereo, & terrestri, ob miros ex optimorum in diversis saeculis illustrium scriptorum monumentis depromptos eventus ... ostenditur....*

Norimbergae: Sumptibus J. C. Lochner, 1696. 3 v. plates (part fold.) maps, ports. 42 cm. Includes indexes. Ports. by G. C. Eimmart.

Provenance: Charles Atwood Kofoid (bookplate); Kantonsbibliothek Solothurn (inkstamp).

2206. ZANOTTI BIANCO, OTTAVIO, b. 1852. *Storia popolare dell'astronomia, libretto di coltura generale, con introduzione del senatore prof. Giovanni Celoria....*

Torino: Società Tipografico-Editrice Nazionale, 1913. xxiii, 322 p. 19 cm. Storia delle scienze; 2. "Elenco dei homi di alcuni autori": p. xvi-xvii.

Imprint partially covered by bookdealer's label.

2207. ZEEMAN, PIETER, 1865-1943. *Magnetooptische Untersuchungen: mit besonderer Berücksichtigung der magnetischen Zerlegung der Spektrallinien / von P. Zeeman; Deutsch von Max Iklè.*

Leipzig: J. A. Barth, 1914. xi, 242 p., viii leaves of plates: ill.; 25 cm. Translation of: *Researches in magneto-optics*. Advertisements: [2] p. following text, and lower wrapper. Bibliography: p. 205-236. Includes index.

2208. ZEHNDER, LUDWIG, b. 1854. *Der ewige Kreislauf des Weltalls, nach Vorlesungen über physikalische Weltanschauungen an der K. Technischen Hochschule, Berlin, von Prof. Dr. Ludwig Zehnder. Mit 214 Abbildungen und einer Tafel.*

Braunschweig: F. Vieweg & Sohn, 1914. viii p., 1 l., 408 p. illus., fold pl., diagrs. 24 cm. Includes bibliographical references and index.

2209. *Zhurnal obshchei khimii. Khimicheskii zhurnal. Seriia A. Zhurnal 1869-1930*

Leningrad. v. ill., ports., maps. 23-27 cm. t. 1- 1869-. At head of title, 1931-37: Khimicheskii zhurnal. Seriia A. Frequency varies. Separately paged supplements accompany some numbers. In v. 6-38 (1874-1906) each number as issued contained papers on physics and chemistry separately paged to be assembled in separate sections upon the completion of the volume; in v. 39-62 (1907-30) the sections were issued in separate covers, each forming a volume annually. Issued by Russkoe khimicheskoe obshchestvo 1869-78 (with Russkoe fizicheskoe obshchestvo 1873-78); by Russkoe fiziko-khimicheskoe obshchestvo 1879-1930. Indexes: Chemical section. 1909-1918. v. 41-50. 1 v.; Physics section. 1873-1930. v. 5-62. 1 v. Physics section superseded by *Zhurnal eksperimentalnoi i teoreticheskoi fiziki*. Separately paged supplements accompany some numbers. Horblit, H. D. *Grolier 100 science books*, 74.

Library has: 1, 1869. Vol. I: Provenance: Osnovnaia biblioteka moskovsk. gornoi akademii (inkstamp); Gosudarstvennaia biblioteka SSSR im. V. I. Lenina (inkstamp).

2210. ZINDLER, KONRAD, 1866-1934. *Ueber räumliche Abbildungen des Continuums der Farbenempfindungen und seine mathematische Behandlung / von Konrad Zindler.*

Leipzig: 1899. [225]-293 p.; 23 cm. Sonderabdruck aus *Zeitschrift für Psychologie und Physiologie der Sinnesorgane*, Bd 20, p. [225]-293.

No. 1 in a v. of 11 items with binder's title: Geometrie.

2211. ZIRKEL, FERDINAND, 1838-1912. *Die mikroskopische Beschaffenheit der Mineralien und Gesteine von dr. Ferdinand Zirkel. Mit 20 Holzschnitten.*

Leipzig: W. Engelmann, 1873. viii, 502 p., 1 l. illus. 24 cm. Includes bibliographical references and index.

2212. ZÖLLNER, JOHANN KARL FRIEDRICH, 1834-1882. *Über die Natur der Cometen: Beiträge zur Geschichte und Theorie der Erkenntniss / von Johann Carl Friedrich Zöllner ... Dritte Auflage.*

Leipzig: In Commission bei L. Staackmann, 1883. [2], XCIV, 443, [1] p., [25] p. of plates (some folded): ill., facsims.; 23 cm. Includes bibliographical references. "Zur Abwehr": p. (355)-443.

2213. ZURCHER, FRÉDÉRIC, 1816-1890. *Meteors: aerolites, storms, and atmospheric phenomena / from the French of Zürcher and Margollé; [translated] by William Lackland; illustrated with twenty-three fine woodcuts, by Lebreton.*

New York: Scribner, Armstrong, & Co., 1874. 324 p., [17] leaves of plates: ill.; 20 cm. Illustrated Library of Wonders. "Marvels of nature, science & art" – Cover. Translation of: *Les metéores*. Includes bibliographical references.

Name Index

C

D

E

F

G

H

I

M

R

S

T

U

V

W

X

Y

Z

Title Index

A

B

C

D

E

F

G

H

I

J

K

L

M

N

O

S

U

V

W

THE BARCHAS COLLECTION AT STANFORD UNIVERSITY
is set in Scala, a Renaissance-inspired text face, designed by Martin Majoor. Typesetting by Richard Seibert. Printed in an edition of 1060 copies by Publishers Press.
Cover and endsheets printed by Peter Koch, *Printer*.

Designed by Peter Rutledge Koch.